WORDS CANNOT BE FOUND

SOURCES FOR AFRICAN HISTORY

Volume 1

WORDS CANNOT BE FOUND

German Colonial Rule in Namibia:
An Annotated Reprint of the 1918 Blue Book

BY

JEREMY SILVESTER AND JAN-BART GEWALD

BRILL
LEIDEN · BOSTON
2003

This co-publication with the National Archives of Namibia in the Republic of Namibia was made possible by the African Studies Centre in Leiden, The Netherlands.

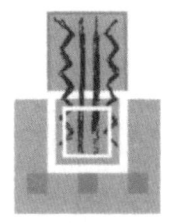

African Studies Centre

National Archives of Namibia

This book is printed on acid-free paper.

Text design by *Vocking in Vorm* (Utrecht); cover photography by Ivo Romein (Gouda).

Library of Congress Cataloging-in-Publication Data

South-West Africa. Administrator's Office.
 [Report on the natives of South-West Africa and their treatment by Germany]
 Words cannot be found : German colonial rule in Namibia : an annotated reprint of the 1918 Blue Book / by Jeremy Silvester and Jan-Bart Gewald.
   p. cm. – (Sources for African history, ISSN 1570-8721 ; v. 1)
 Includes bibliographical references (p.) and index.
 ISBN 90-04-12981-2 (pbk.)
 1. Indigenous peoples–Namibia–Government relations. 2. Namibia–History–1884-1915. I. Silvester, Jeremy. II. Gewald, Jan-Bart. III. Title IV. Series.

DT1603.S68 2003
323.1'6881'09034–dc21

2003044435

ISSN 1570–8721
ISBN 90 04 12981 2

© *Copyright 2003 by Koninklijke Brill NV, Leiden, The Netherlands*

All rights reserved. No part of this publication may be reproduced, translated, stored in a retrieval system, or transmitted in any form or by any means, electronic, mechanical, photocopying, recording or otherwise, without prior written permission from the publisher.

Authorization to photocopy items for internal or personal use is granted by Brill provided that the appropriate fees are paid directly to The Copyright Clearance Center, 222 Rosewood Drive, Suite 910 Danvers MA 01923, USA. Fees are subject to change.

PRINTED IN THE NETHERLANDS

CONTENTS

Preface	vii
Acknowledgements	ix
List of Illustrations	xi
Footsteps and tears: an Introduction to the Construction and Context of the 1918 'Blue Book'	xiii

REPORT ON THE NATIVES OF SOUTH-WEST AFRICA AND THEIR TREATMENT BY GERMANY

Preface	7
Part One: Natives and German Administration	19
Part Two: Natives and the Criminal Law	247
Appendices	321
Bibliography	357
Index	361

PREFACE

On Sunday 6 April 2003, after conducting a church service in the informal settlement of Babilon, on the outskirts of Windhoek, I went to see a "house" of a council member of the congregation, which had just burned to the ground. As we were observing the ashes and ruins of what had once been their home, the wife said something striking which is still in my mind: *Where does one start now?* she asked. I just looked at her without knowing what to say. This is my reaction now, after reading the Blue Book, especially the statements under oath that reveal one long nightmare of suffering, bloodshed, tears, humiliation and death. In one of the statements under oath, Hosea Mungunda states: "…it was one continuous ill-treatment…" Yes, it certainly was! I read this book with tears and anger but also with a strengthened determination that we should make sure that these things do not happen again in Namibia and that we should commit ourselves to justice, peace and reconciliation for our country and beyond. This we do for our own sake and for the sake of generations yet unborn.

The re-publication of the Blue Book of 1918 is an invaluable gift from a period in which we have mostly one-sided or vague accounts of what really happened during that time. This book offers a better and more comprehensive understanding of the liberation struggle and the suffering of the Namibian people. What it clearly shows is that the brave struggle for liberation started in 1904 against a very brutal, imperial, and savage power. It is the continuation of this very same struggle, which erupted at different times during the course of the last century, that resumed in 1959 and culminated in independence in 1990. It is important that when this very important aspect in the history of our country is recounted and taught, that we start from the very beginning.

For the sake of the present and the future it is important to know where we are coming from. The foundation of our independence lies in the tears and blood, the determination, bravery and vision of our forbearers. The railway on which we today comfortably travel in our trains was literally built with and on the blood, suffering and death of our mothers and fathers. People who know this will jealously protect what they have today. Racism, corruption, crime and violence cannot be tolerated with such an invaluable heritage for which we paid so dearly. The vision for justice, peace and a harmonious society is not only ours but also that of the many thousands who were brutally wiped out by the colonial powers. I firmly believe that, in honour of these brave women and men whose blood waters our freedom, we should completely reject racism, tribalism, corruption, crime and any form of violence, and stand up together in a concerted effort to remove all of these evils from the face of Namibia, as we did with colonialism.

In the name of the many people in Namibia and elsewhere who will appreciate the re-publication of the Blue Book and also on behalf of our children and the coming generations, I wholeheartedly thank Dr. Jan-Bart Gewald (University of Leiden) and Dr. Jeremy Silvester (University of Namibia) for the work they did to uncover "the footprints and tears, blown over by the sand." The Introduction to the Construction and context of the 1918 "Blue Book", and their extensive research in this regard is very helpful to the understanding and support of this remarkable book. In the same vein I also pay homage and respect to the spirit of Major T.L. O'Reilly, the Military Magistrate based in Omaruru at that time, for his commitment to justice and for his tireless efforts to provide humane treatment for the devastated people of Namibia during that period.

It is indeed for my family and I, on behalf of my grandparents and great-grandparents who were part of this ordeal, a great honour to be part of the re-publication of the Blue Book and with it the resurrection of the voices of our forefathers. I am looking forward to the day of the launch of this book. For me that day will be holy, as was the day of independence. Yes, on that day in 1990 we shed tears of joy that, at last, the dark night of humiliation and death was over and that the sun was rising in all its beauty and splendour. But we also cried when we remembered the thousands of sons and daughters of Namibia who had suffered and died while resisting this brutal force of humiliation, slavery and injustice.

May God bless Namibia and her children.

Rt. Rev. Dr. Z. Kameeta
Windhoek, April 2003

ACKNOWLEDGEMENTS

The re-publication of the Blue Book has taken far more time than we ever anticipated, and it would have taken even more time if a number of people had not provided the selfless help and assistance which they did.

Werner Hillebrecht, of the National Archives of Namibia, provided us with ongoing general assistance ranging from the scanning of photographs through to discovering the original glass plate negatives of the photographs that graced the Blue Book. Casper Erichsen, as a fellow historian and friend, supported us in all manner of means, from acting as chaffeur through to being prepared to engage with the past. Mandhavela Khasera provided us with invaluable assistance with initial proof-reading of the scanned text, whilst Lovisa Ndaoya and Lovisa Nampala scanned the text.

On a personal level we would like to thank a few people for providing emotional support and hope for the future, in contrast to the depressing and damaging material which we were dealing with. We would like to explicitly express thanks to Gertie and Kasai, and to our children Meta, Shelley, and Sieme in whom we see our shared futures.

We have noted in the introduction that we see this re-publication as a memorial to those Namibians who died and suffered as a result of the Namibian War. At times our work on this re-publication has been brought to a temporary halt on account of the sheer immensity of what was being said. Yet, these very same intensely unsettling words ensured that we did not break off from our work. To have done so would have been to insult the past. It is thus with deep respect for those who have come before us and whose suffering is described in such graphic detail in this book that we give thanks.

We would also like to thank the Publications Committee of the African Studies Centre for generously providing a guaranteed subsidy which allowed for the co-publication at a reasonable price of this re-publication in the Republic of Namibia.

Time and again the students that we have taught, in Germany, Namibia, and the Netherlands, have urged us to carry on, to bring to the fore the past. A past which had become obscured and all but lost. Thus, in conclusion we would wish to dedicate this re-publication to the young historians of Namibia. They hold within their hands the key to a better future.

Jeremy Silvester and Jan-Bart Gewald

ILLUSTRATIONS*

TO TEXT

1	Execution of natives by hanging, showing primitive arrangement of gallows and drop	5
2.	Execution of natives by hanging from a tree	118
3.	Condition of Herero on surrender after having been driven into the desert	176
4.	Showing condition of back of native woman Maria after flogging	282
5.	Showing condition of back of native woman Auma	283

TO APPENDIX I

A.	Neck chains for native prisoners	325
A1.	Native convicts in neck chains and prison clothing	326
A2.	Collar of neck chain perforated by bullet. (Enlargement of Fig. 1, Plate A)	326
B.	Combined leg and arm fetters	328
C1.	Native convicts in prison clothing with leg and arm fetters	329
C2.	Native convicts in prison clothing with leg and arm fetters	330
C.	Other varieties of leg and arm fetters	331
D.	Sjambok used by Germans for corporal punishment	333
E1.	Natives hanged by Germans	334
E2.	Closer view of two of these	334

* This is the *original* list of illustrations and captions, as used in the *original* Blue Book

FOOTSTEPS AND TEARS:
AN INTRODUCTION TO THE CONSTRUCTION AND CONTEXT OF THE 1918 'BLUE BOOK'[1]

Jan Kubas was an eyewitness of the events that took place following the defeat of Herero combatants at the battle of Hamakari in 1904 and the German pursuit of the Herero community into the parched Omaheke and Kalahari Desert. When interviewed thirteen years later he struggled to articulate his memories complaining that "Words cannot be found to relate what happened; it was too terrible".[2] A Herero woman who survived the thirst and hardship refused to describe her experience to a concerned missionary in 1907 arguing that 'the wind has blown sand over the footprints and tears'.[3] Whilst the Herero and Nama communities have a strong legacy of oral history and tradition, these stress historical victories and praise wealthy and successful leaders.[4] An oral heritage that describes the horror that Herero and other communities experienced during the war can, it seems, no longer be found.[5]

Yet the words of Jan Kubas and forty-six other eye-witnesses of events which have been described as 'war atrocities' (and even 'genocide') that took place during the German colonial period in Namibia were recorded and published in an official British 'Blue Book' in 1918. These statements form a rare documentation of African voices describing the encounter of African communities with a colonial power. However, in 1926, only a few years after its publication, the Blue Book, was withdrawn from the public domain and orders given for its destruction. An active attempt was made to ensure that the words which relate what happened from an African perspective would also no longer be found and preserved in a written form. The Blue Book was removed from circulation as an official act to consciously remove a critical account of the German colonial period of Namibian history. Copies of the report were

---

[1] The Report is known colloquially as the 'Blue Book'. A Blue Book was a published British Government report.

[2] Great Britain, *Report on the Natives of South West Africa and their Treatment by Germany*, HMSO, London, August, 1918: p. 65

[3] Neitz, J. Die Herero betreffend. Reise zu Samuel Maharero, Makapaanspoort on 8 November, 1907, ELCIN II.5.14. quoted in Nils Ole Oermann *Mission, Church and State Relations in South West Africa under German Rule (1884-1915)*, Franz Steiner Verlag, Stuttgart, 1999.

[4] Sundermeier, Theo; H. Tjituka; H. Hengari; A. Kajovi; H. Kavari; P. Katjivikua & E. Ketjipota, *The Mbanderu*, MSORP, Windhoek, 1985.

[5] Kirsten Alnaes, an anthropologist who worked among the descendents of Herero refugees in the Republic of Botswana in the 1970s, noted that few examples of the war and flight could be found in Herero orature. Alnaes, K. Oral Tradition and Identity; the Herero in Botswana, in *The Societies of Southern Africa in the 19th and 20th Centuries*, vol. 11 (1981), pp. 15 – 23 & Living with the past: The songs of the Herero in Botswana, in *Africa*, 59.3. (1989), pp. 267 – 299.

destroyed with the aim of achieving reconciliation within the white settler community between the remaining German community and a new wave of, mainly Afrikaner, settlers. African voices were forgotten and their written statements actively erased.

It has recently been argued that this silencing of African accounts of the events which took place in Namibia during this period extends to Germany itself as a "... new permanent exhibit of German history in Berlin passes over the near genocide without a word.[6]" This brief introduction will attempt to contextualise this republication of the 1918 Blue Book within the broader context of 'colonial amnesia'. It will discuss the motivation behind the compilation of such an unusual document by imperial authorities and the reasons why it was subsequently suppressed. It will also seek to make an initial assessment of the criticisms that were made of the Blue Book and suggest some of the larger issues that are raised by the text and which the current editors hope can be addressed in greater detail in the future.

It has been argued that in Southern Africa there is a particularly strong case of 'dissonant heritage', where the legacy of monuments that celebrate a particular perspective of the colonial past are in conflict with the 'values of post-colonial majority rule'.[7] In Namibia it is certainly true that at independence all national monuments that related to the conflicts of the German colonial period celebrated the sacrifice and victories of the German *Schutztruppe* (colonial army).[8] In addition the processes of documentary production that created colonial archives also tended to exclude indigenous accounts of events.[9] The papers of Hendrik Witbooi are the only archival documents to have been published that present an African perspective on the German colonial period.[10]

In Namibia the post-colonial state has recently taken major initiatives to address the perceived visual and archival gaps in an attempt to weave a nationalist narrative that is inclusive of different voices. Whilst monuments that celebrate German colonial heroes, such as the statue of Colonel Curt von Francoise that stands outside the offices of Windhoek Municipality, have been allowed to remain, a massive 'Heroes Acre' has recently been opened that embodies a visual counter-narrative celebrating leaders of anti-colonial resistance. Six of the first nine heroes celebrated at the site played leading roles in resisting German colonial rule.[11] In addition a large-scale project has been

---

[6] Smith, Helmut 'The Talk of Genocide, the Rhetoric of Miscegenation: Notes on Debates in the German Reichstag concerning South West Africa, 1904-1914' in Sara Friedrichsmeyer, Sara Lennox and Susane Zantop (eds), Ann Arbor, University of Michigan, 2000: p. 109.

[7] Tunbridge, J.E. and Ashworth, G.J., *Dissonant Heritage: The Management of the Past as a Resource in Conflict*, John Wiley & Sons, 1996.

[8] Jeremy Silvester 'Monumental Questions: The Rider', *The Namibian* 18th July, 1997; 'Monumental Questions: The Old Location Graveyard Part 2', *The Namibian* 25th July, 1997; 'Monumental Questions: Part 3', *The Namibian* 31st August, 1997.

[9] For a more extensive discussion of the shaping of the archives of southern Africa see Hamilton, Conolyn (ed.), *Refiguring the Archive*, London 2002 and Christof Maletsky '9 heroes honoured', *The Namibian*, 23rd August, 2002, pp. 1-2.

[10] *The Hendrik Witbooi Papers*, National Archives of Namibia, Windhoek, 1989.

[11] *The Namibian*, "Heroes Day Supplement: August 26 2002", 23 August 2002, pp. 2 – 3.

undertaken to facilitate the collection of an 'Archive of Anti-colonial Resistance and the Liberation Struggle'. In this context the statements recorded and reproduced in the Blue Book provide an invaluable collection of post-war narratives by Namibians describing their experience of German colonial rule. Whilst these narratives should be read within the context within which they were produced, they form a strong counter narrative to the countless written autobiographical accounts produced and widely republished by German soldiers who served in the *Schutztruppe* campaigns in Namibia.[12]

The Construction of the Blue Book

At the outbreak of the First World War South African forces, under British command invaded 'German South West Africa' (as Namibia was known at the time) and successfully defeated the German army. Between 1915 and 1920 Namibia therefore fell under the control of a military administration run by the Union of South Africa. As the war continued, the United States of America entered the war, and it became increasingly likely that Imperial Germany would be defeated, and serious consideration began to be given to the fate of the captured German colonies.

Lord Buxton, the Governor-General of South Africa, openly claimed that the participation of the Union of South Africa in the invasion of Namibia was welcomed by the Union Government which sought to remove 'the German menace from its borders.[13]' By the end of April 1917 the Imperial War Cabinet, within which General Smuts played a prominent role, had already determined that "The restoration to Germany of South West Africa is incompatible with the security and peaceful development of the Union of South Africa, and should in no circumstances be contemplated.[14]" It is clear that senior South African politicians were aware of the importance of building a strong case to avoid the possibility that German control over its colonies would be restored as part of the peace settlement. John X Merriman, the last Prime Minister in the Cape Colony prior to Union in 1910, wrote to his close friend Jan Smuts on 6th September, 1915 advocating the collection of evidence to support the Union's case: "We must have the case of the Natives presented with the utmost care and fullness – *ab ovo* – with all written evidence that you can get hold of. This is our strong point, our sheet anchor in any diplomatic storm. Above all let it be accurate."[15] The suggestion therefore emphasised the importance of 'written

---

[12] For details see Jeremy Silvester 'The Politics of Reconciliation: Destroying the Blue Book', Paper presented at the 'Public History, Forgotten History' Conference, University of Namibia, August, 2000.

[13] The Times, 5th August, 1915 quoted in Swanson, Maynard 'South West Africa in Trust, 1915-1939', Ch. 21 in Prosser Gifford and Roger Louis, *Britain and Germany in Africa: Imperial Rivalry and Colonial Rule*, YUP, New Haven/London, 1967 p. 635.

[14] 'Report of Committee on Territorial Desiderata', Imperial War Cabinet, 28th April, 1917 quoted in Louis, Roger, 'Great Britain & German Expansion in Africa, 1884-1919' in Gifford and Louis.

[15] Cited in Hancock, W.K. and Jean van der Poel (eds), *Selections from the Smuts Papers*, Vol. III, June 1910-November, 1918, CUP, Cambridge, 1966: pp. 311-312.

evidence' and accuracy, rather than fanciful propaganda with Merriman urging the gathering of any 'authentic documents bearing on this subject'.[16]

Yet even before Merriman had written his letter, officials in Namibia had done substantial work on the translation of key German documents. For example, within a month of the German surrender on 9th July, 1915 two Native Affairs officials had produced a 108 page document containing an English translation of the German laws in force in the Protectorate and other relevant reports.[17] In 1917 Captain Gage and Crown Prosecutor Waters published an English translation of the Imperial German Criminal Code.[18] English translations were also made of important documents such as the 'Protection Treaties' made between the 'German Empire' and various local traditional leaders and the proceedings of German criminal cases, such as the notorious case of Ludwig Cramer.[19]

Whilst it seems that the initiative for the collection of evidence in Namibia came from the Union, it also seems likely that General Smuts, in his capacity as a leading member of the Imperial Cabinet, encouraged a broader investigation into German policies and practices throughout its former colonies.

On 4th January, 1918 a confidential telegram was dispatched to the authorities in Australia, New Zealand and South Africa, stating that:

> It is the firm conviction of His Majesty's Government that, for security of Empire after the War, it is necessary to retain possession of German Colonies, but it has not been possible to secure general acceptance of this view owing to divergence of opinion among Allies. Great stress was laid by Russians during recent negotiations with Germans on right of population of country to determine its future, and proposal was made to apply this to German Colonies. There are indications in French newspapers, for instance, that this line of argument will be pressed in other quarters. I should, therefore, be glad if could be furnished with a statement suitable for publication, if necessary, containing evidence of anxiety of natives of (German New Guinea) (Samoa) (South-West Africa) to live under British rule ...[20]"

A fortnight after this telegram was received the Administrator for South West Africa, E.H.L. Gorges, was writing a preface to a substantial report which initially consisted of around 400 double-spaced typed foolscap pages. The explanation for the efficiency and speed with which the report was submitted was that a collection of translated German documents was already available, whilst an initiative had also already been taken to gather further information in the territory. The Minister of Public Works and the Interior, J. Watts had suggested to Gorges in August, 1917 that 'a full historical account should be

---

[16] Ibid.

[17] Pretoria Archives NTS 266 4349/1910/7 639 'The Laws of the Protectorate ... translated and compiled by J.J.R. Coetzee & R. Dickman', Native Affairs Dept, August, 1915.

[18] Gage, R.H and A.J. Waters *Imperial German Criminal Code Translated into English*, W.E. Horton & Co. Ltd, Johannesburg, 1917. NAN, ADM 147 contains the translations of the protection treaties.

[19] Contained in NAN A312 1/2 'Preparation of Imperial Blue Book cd. 9146'.

[20] PRO CO 537/1-17 Telegram from Mr Long to Australia, New Zealand and South Africa, 4th January, 1918 quoted in 'Memo. For War Cabinet', 15th October, 1918.

prepared shewing the treatment received by the native races in the Protectorate'. Within a few days the Administrator and the Secretary for South West Africa, the top two civil servants in the territory, had rung Major T.L. O'Reilly, the Military Magistrate based in the small town of Omaruru to ask him whether he was interested in taking on the task. O'Reilly's response was enthusiastic:

> I am as keen as mustard on it – I have been doing quite a lot of graft locally in that direction and even if they change their minds, I intend going into the matter privately ... [It] ... is quite enough to make ones hair stiffen and it would give old Theo Schreiner & his Exeter Hall conferees epilepsy & hysterics to hear of it.[21]

The official letter authorising Major O'Reilly to start work on the Report was sent on 17th September, 1917. It is clear that O'Reilly drew heavily on the library of Major Herbst which contained a number of key texts, such as the autobiography of the former German Governor, Theodor Leutwein. The German colonial regime had also left behind an extremely well organised and detailed administrative archive. Apart from files dealing in detail with the incarceration of 'rebel' communities in 'concentration camps', the archives also contained a series of files dealing with the concerns raised in Berlin about the excessive flogging that was taking place in the territory.[22] Similarly glass plate negatives, of hangings and displaying the torn and rotting backs of victims of excessive 'paternal correction', were found by the incoming South African forces.

Major Thomas Leslie O'Reilly was to be the prime compiler of the Blue Book and author of the entire first section (150 pages of the original 212 page published report). Originally section one had twenty-six chapters with the final chapter consisting of statements concerning the wishes of Africans in Namibia as to the future form of government for the territory. Statements from a total of seventy-five witnesses were featured in the chapter which was later withdrawn and included in another Blue Book which was published in November, 1918.[23] The second section was the responsibility of Mr A.J. Waters who had served as the Crown Prosecutor for Namibia since October, 1915.[24] The final pages of the

---

[21] Senator Theo L. Schreiner brother of the famous South African author Olive Schreiner. Speaking in the South African senate in Cape Town, shortly after the South African invasion, Schreiner noted that merely because Germany had defeated the Herero and taken their land, this did not mean that they, as the new victors need do the same. NAN, ADM 156, Native Reserves, Speech of Senator Theo L. Schreiner in the senate in the debate on the question of the second reading of the treaty of peace and South West Africa mandate bill, 17 September 1919. Exeter Hall was a hall in London where the anti-slavery society held meetings.

[22] NAN, A 41, *Translation of German Records re: Infliction of Corporal punishment on Natives.*.

[23] Great Britain, *Correspondence relating to the Wishes of the Natives of the German Colonies as to their Future Government*, HMSO, London, 1918, Cd. 9210. Thanks are due to Reinhart Koessler for pointing out the existence of a 'missing chapter' to the Blue Book.

[24] Waters was already familiar with the laws of the territory. See Gage, Capt. R.H. and A.J. Waters *Imperial German Criminal Code: Translated into English*, W.E. Hortor & Co. Ltd., Johannesburg, 1917.

report reproduce as an appendix three more sets of documents. The first is a short 'medical report on German methods of punishment', the second a letter sent by the German Governor to his District Officers demanding a reduction in the use of corporal punishment and the third letters from the District Officer in Luderitz complaining of widespread abuse of the local black population. German sources therefore played a significant role as sources for the evidence used in the Blue Book.

The pressure of producing the report within a tight timeframe led O'Reilly to make the maximum use of conveniently available material.[25] O'Reilly served from 1916 as a member of the 'Special Criminal Court' which acted as the highest court in the territory during the period of martial law (1915-1920). Fifty-seven of the cases referred to in the second part of the Blue Book relate to cases brought against German employers for the maltreatment of their employees.[26] A number of other court cases that were described in the second setion had already been described in a previous Blue Book that had already been published in October, 1916.[27]

The most powerful evidence in the Blue Book are the statements made by eye-witnesses and the report was unusual in the prominence that it gave to African voices. The central role played by O'Reilly in gathering the evidence contained in the report can be seen in the fact that eight of the forty-seven witnesses quoted in the report were specifically described as living in the Omaruru District. In his role as Military Magistrate, O'Reilly had developed a close (indeed some might argue sympathetic) relationship with local Herero leaders, such as Daniel Kariko. The relationship had resulted in a successful application to the administration for the establishment of a 'reserve' at Otjohorongo where the local Herero community, largely scattered over the farms of the District as labourers, might gather and collect their livestock.[28] However, O'Reilly was also described as having spend a 'couple of months' travelling around the country conducting interviews and archival documents includes correspondence with local military magistrates to set up meetings with key informants.[29]

The Blue Book does not contain all the conclusions that O'Reilly reached during his research. His concern about the continuing excessive use of corporal punishment by local policemen apparently led to the ending of his civil service career shortly after the completion of the Blue Book. The use of flogging and chains as forms of punishment had been quickly abolished under martial law, but O'Reilly expressed concern that, despite this reform, unjustified beatings

---

[25] The Administrator's 'Preface' is dated 19th January, 1918 and the report was presented to Parliament in August, 1918.
[26] See National Archives of Namibia, Finding Aid, Special Criminal Court SCC1-SCC11.
[27] South Africa, Union of. *Papers relating to Certain Trials in German South West Africa*, HMSO, London, October, 1916.
[28] Gewald, Jan-Bart, *Herero Heroes*, James Currey, Oxford, 1999, pp. 305-308.
[29] See NAN ADM 39 351/5 'Investigations conducted by Major O'Reilly' and NAN ADM 157 'Gorges to Botha', 23rd November, 1917.

were still common practice. He warned the Administrator that the people that he had interviewed had expressed concern about "... the treatment meted out by the Constabulary who were by some natives described as 'just the same as the German police'. At the very time that the Blue Book was being finalised O'Reilly was complaining that his local police chief, Lt. Col. Fourie was 'unfit for police work' as he had repeatedly expressed the view that corporal punishment was 'what the natives require'.[30] When an internal inquiry failed to take action against Fourie, O'Reilly resigned on 26th November, 1918 and travelled to Cape Town.[31] Within a year Major O'Reilly was dead (possibly as a late victim of the Spanish Influenza which had decimated communities throughout the world during 1918).[32]

Shortly before his resignation he had been working on a report involving concessions that had been made to the *Otavi Minen und Eisenbahn Gesellschaft*. After his death, Major O'Reilly's brother, J.A. O'Reilly, a solicitor, quoted from confidential documents which had been in Major O'Reilly's possession for the purposes of writing the report. The Crown Prosecutor (Mr Waters, the co-author of the Blue Book) and the Secretary of the Concessions Commission both made visits to O'Reilly's brother to reclaim the documents. During the search an 'iron box' containing the handwritten notes and statements that had been gathered to produce the 1918 Blue Book was searched. Unfortunately the papers were returned to Major O'Reilly's brother and were never deposited in the National Archives of Namibia.[33]

It is beyond doubt that the events and issues presented so clearly in the Blue Book served to scuttle any attempt by Germany to retain control over Namibia. In the event Namibia was classified as a 'C' Class Mandate of the League of Nations and placed under the administrative jurisdiction of the Union of South Africa.[34] In the aftermath of the humiliations of Versailles, and in direct response to the Blue Book, the Germans published a White Book that dwelt largely on atrocities committed by Britain in its colonies.[35]

One of the criticisms expressed in the German White Book of 1919 with regard to the Blue Book was that it did not refer to contemporary German sources commenting on the atrocities allegedly being perpetrated in Namibia. In this manner the White Book sought to suggest that, in the absence of contemporary German accounts, the atrocities did not take place. Thus the compilers of the White Book noted:

---

[30] Gorges, Windhoek to Botha, Cape Town, 23rd November, 1917. ADM 157 – W41.

[31] O'Reilly to Sec. Prot., 26th November, 1918; 14th February, 1919 NAN LOM 3/1/1 – 1K/1916.

[32] Spanish Influenza struck Omaruru 'like a thunderbolt' on 12th November 1918, 'Annual Report, Omaruru', 25th January, 1919 ADM 108 3370/3; O'Reilly was dead by the middle of 1919 'Estate of the late T. O'Reilly' ADM 144 202

[33] ' Statement of Ernest David Richardson', 12th July, 1920; 'Statement of Alfred John Waters, 12th July, 1920, ADM 144 – C202.

[34] Du Pisani, Andre, *South West Africa/Namibia*, Windhoek, 1982: p. 76.

[35] German Colonial Office, *The Treatment of Native and other Populations in the Colonial Possessions of Germany and England*, Engelman, Berlin, 1919

The authors of the Blue Book rely for the greater part on "sworn" utterances of the Natives... It is remarkable that apparently only a few *White* witnesses were examined in the matter of the Herero rising.[36]

Furthermore the German compilers of the White Book argued that the authors of the Blue Book should have "recognised the plain fact that the natives were lying" [37]

In response to the criticisms levelled by the compilers of the White Book, it must be noted that, though it is true that Major O'Reilly, as the prime author of the Blue Book, did not directly interview German officers or missionaries, O'Reilly depended to a large extent on published German accounts, most notably those of Schwabe and Leutwein, as well as the documents from the local German archives. It must be borne in mind that in 1917, the writings, letters, chronicles, and so forth, (which would later come to form the core of the archives of the Evangelical Lutheran Church in the Republic of Namibia) were scattered amongst the numerous Rhenish Mission stations in the territory, and as yet not collected into a single and accessible archive. Indeed, if O'Reilly had had access to these papers and been able to make use of the German missionary archives he would have found much to substantiate the statements of his African respondents. Recent historical research has shown, that there were numerous contemporary German observers who commented explicitly on what they saw happening at first hand.[38] Most notable amongst these observers were the missionaries of the Rhenish missionary society, although there were also German officers who made explicit mention of the abuses being committed. For example, one such missionary was the young Heinrich Vedder, later to become the doyen of settler history in Namibia, who recorded the fact that initially there were few Herero prisoners in the harbour town of Swakopmund when he arrived to start his mission work, but:

> Shortly thereafter vast transports of prisoners of war arrived. They were placed behind double rows of barbed wire fencing, which surrounded all the buildings of the harbour department quarters [*Hafenamtswerft*], and housed in pathetic [*jammerlichen*], structures constructed out of simple sacking and planks, in such a manner that in one structure 30 - 50 people were forced to stay without distinction as to age and sex. From early morning until late at night, on weekdays as well as on Sundays and holidays, they had to work under the clubs of raw overseers [*Knutteln roher Aufseher*], until they broke down [*zusammenbrachen*]. Added to this the food was extremely scarce: Rice without any necessary additions was not enough to support their bodies, already weakened by life in the field [as refugees] and used to the hot sun of the interior, from the cold and restless exertion of all their powers in the prison conditions of Swakopmund. Like cattle hundreds were driven to death and like cattle they were buried. This opinion may appear hard or exaggerated, lots changed and became milder during the

---

[36] Ibid, p. 70

[37] Ibid, p. 71

[38] In this regard see in particular the detailed work conducted by Nils Ole Oermann, *Mission, church and state relations in South West Africa under German rule (1884-1915)*, D.Phil. University of Oxford 1998, chp. 5.

course of the imprisonment (...) but the chronicles are not permitted to suppress that such a remorseless rawness [*rucksichtslose Roheit*], randy sensuality [*geile Sinnlichkeit*], brutish overlordship [*brutales Herrentum*] was to be found amongst the troops and civilians here that a full description is hardly possible.[39]

In 1904, following the battles at Hamakari, Major Ludwig von Estorff, an officer with substantial experience in Namibia, was ordered to pursue the Herero ever further into the *Omaheke*. In later years Estorff noted of this pursuit that:

> It was a policy which was equally gruesome as senseless, to hammer the people so much, we could have still saved many of them and their rich herds, if we had pardoned and taken them up again, they had been punished enough. I suggested this to General von Trotha but he wanted their total extermination.[40]

In April 1907, when von Estorff was in command of German forces in the southern Namibian port town of Lüderitz, he ordered that prisoners be taken off Shark Island and reported:

> Since September 1906, 1,032 out of 1,795 natives have died on Shark Island. I am not prepared to assume responsibility for the killing nor can I expect my officers to do so...[41]

In the event Oskar Hintrager, the Deputy Governor, reprimanded von Estorff for his action.

It has also been alleged by the late Brigitte Lau that, due to the wartime context in which the Blue Book was written (when Allied leaders were already debating the terms of the post-war settlement) that it should be dismissed as "an English piece of war propaganda with no credibility whatsoever".[42] The suggestion that the contents of the Blue Book had been fabricated as a propaganda exercise echoed the original German response to its publication which had argued, in 1919, that "The text and illustrations of this specious document have no other purpose in view than to make propaganda for the idea that South-West Africa should be incorporated in the colonial empire of Great Britain".[43] It is evident that Britain and its imperial subject, the Union of South Africa, did

---

[39] Evangelical Lutheran Church in the Republic of Namibia (ELCRN), V. Ortschroniken Swakopmund. Translation by J-B Gewald. The author of the text, Dr. Heinrich Vedder, would later become an acclaimed national socialist, anthropologist and historian of Namibian affairs. After World War II Vedder was appointed to the South African senate as representative of the black population of Namibia

[40] Ludwig von Estorff, *Wanderungen und Kämpfe in Südwestafrika, Ostafrika und Südafrika. 1894 - 1910*, (Windhoek 1979) p. 117. Translation by J-B Gewald.

[41] Cited in, Horst Drechsler, *"Let us Die Fighting": The struggle of the Herero and Nama against German Imperialism (1884 - 1915)*, London: Zed Press 1980, p. 212.

[42] Lau, Brigitte, 'Uncertain Certainties: The Herero-German war of 1904', *Mibagus*, no. 2, April, 1989, p. 5. For a critical response to Lau see Tilmann Dedering, 'The German-Herero War of 1904: Revisionism of Genocide or Imaginary Historiography?', *Journal of Southern African Studies*, Vol. 19, no 1, 1993.

[43] German Colonial Office, *The Treatment of Native and Other Populations in the Colonial Possessions of Germany and England: An Answer to the English Blue Book of August, 1918 'Report on the Natives of South-West Africa and their Treatment by Germany*, Hans Robert Engelmann, Berlin, 1919, p. 17.

have a clear ulterior motivation for presenting evidence that showed German colonial rule in a bad light, their shared desire to persuade the international community that the German colonies should not be returned to Germany as part of the peace settlement. However the editors of this volume would argue that whilst this context obviously determined the particular selection of evidence and timing of the compilation of a highly critical evaluation of German colonial rule in Namibia, this does not mean nor suggest that the evidence presented in the Blue Book should be judged to be false. The evidence should, instead, be judged on its own merits.

It has further been alleged that the Blue Book was compiled by a man directly involved in the nascent British Ministry of Information (Propaganda) with the implication that it was therefore a work of fiction. Gail-Maryse Cockram has claimed that the Blue Book was subsequently "compiled under the editorship of John Buchan, whose literary inventiveness was given full rein".[44] John Buchan was a popular contemporary novelist, most famous for his novel *The Thirty-nine Steps* which was set against a backdrop of German espionage. The British Government did establish official mechanisms for the production of propaganda during the First World War, mainly through the War Propaganda Bureau. On 9th February, 1917 a new Department of Information was established under the auspices of the Foreign Office. Its first Director was the author, John Buchan.[45] However, strangely, Cockram cites no reference that shows the source of her claim that Buchan was involved in the writing of the Blue Book, despite the fact that her book is, otherwise, well referenced throughout. Indeed the list of publications produced by Wellington House, the Bureau's headquarters, does not include the 1918 Blue Book and only lists two publications attributed directly to Buchan whose main energy went into the production of the 24 volume 'Nelson's History of the War'.[46] Currently available evidence indicates that the Blue Book was based largely on existing materials available in Namibia and compiled by local officials with access to those materials. An original carbon copy of the typed manuscript was held by the National Archives of Namibia and showed no substantial differences to the report that was later published strongly suggesting that the report was not rewritten in London.[47]

It is interesting to note that one of the most disputed publications of the War Propaganda Bureau, the *Report of the Committee on Alleged German Outrages* of 1915 which claimed that human rights abuses were committed by German troops in Belgium in 1914 has been substantially supported by recent research

---

[44] Cockram, Gail-Maryse, *South West African Mandate,* Juta and Co., Cape Town/Wynberg/Johannesburg, 1976, p. 11.

[45] Sanders, Michael and Philip Taylor *British Propaganda during the First World War, 1914-18,* Macmillan, London and Basingstoke, 1982, p. 63.

[46] Grieves, Keith '*Nelson's History of the War*: John Buchan as a Contemporary Military Historian, 1915-22', *Journal of Contemporary History,* Vol. 28, 1993, p. 550.

[47] See NAN ADM 255.

by historians of the First World War.[48] The British approach to propaganda was to present 'a generally cautious and academic [text], seeking to present a mass of evidently factual material without recourse to emotional overstatement".[49] This Report was produced by Viscount James Bryce who was a worker at Wellington House. Viscount James Bryce was also responsible, as the co-compiler, for a Blue Book that dealt with the Armenian genocide perpetrated during 1915 by Germany's wartime ally, Turkey.[50] The evidence in this Blue Book has been used to provide further evidence on the genocide perpetrated by the Ottoman Empire on its Armenian subjects.

To be sure, there are those who have sought to discredit the work of James Bryce, most notably the Turkish authorities. Interestingly, the dispute parallels the debate that has surrounded allegations of German genocidal intent in Namibia. As with the White Book of 1919, which sought to dispute the genocide in Namibia, the Turkish authorities criticise the evidence presented in the Blue Book on two grounds. Firstly the credibility of the witnesses quoted, alleging that as there were no Turks quoted, the evidence presented was bound to be biased. Secondly that the Armenians were also guilty of human rights abuses and that these were ignored in the report.[51] The lengthy German response to the Blue Book also sought to accuse Britain of hypocrisy and to raise doubts about the credibility of the witnesses – apparently because they were African, rather than European![52]

One of the other original criticisms of the Blue Book made by the German Government when it was first published was that the British had not been critical of German colonialism at the time that the atrocities were, allegedly, actually taking place and, it was suggested, this cast doubt on statements made by witnesses years after the events had taken place:

---

[48] See Trevor Wilson 'Lord Bryce's Investigation into Alleged German Atrocities in Belgium, 1914-1915', *Journal of Contemporary History,* Vol. 14, 1979. For recent substantiating research see John Horne and Allan Kramer, *German Atrocities, 1914: A History of Denial,* Yale University Press, Yale, 2001.

[49] Description of a 'typical' pamphlet given in Michael Sanders and Philip Taylor, *British Propaganda during the First World War, 1914-18*', Macmillan, London and Basingstoke, 1982. p. 142.

[50] Bryce, James and Arnold Toynbee, *The Treatment of Armenians in the Ottoman Empire, 1915-1916* (original, HMSO, London, 1916; new edition edited by Ara Sarafian, Gomidas Institute, Princeton, 2000)

[51] Bryce, James and Arnold Toynbee *The Treatment of Armenians in the Ottoman Empire, 1915-1916* (Uncensored Edition), Reprint, Gomidal Institute, Princeton, 2000 (Original, HMSO, London, 1916). See 'Introduction' by Ara Sarafian for a discussion of the politics of the debate surrounding the authenticity of the material. For a response to the republication of this Blue Book see the notes on a lecture given by Prof. Justin McCarthy on 21st January, 2001 on the web site of the Turkish Embassy in London, 'Armenian Allegations', http://www.turkishembassy_london.com/new_page_62.htm

[52] Silvester, Jeremy 'The Politics of Reconciliation: Destroying the Blue Book', Paper presented at the 'Public History, Forgotten History' Conference, University of Namibia, August, 2000.

> The English "Blue Book" upon South-West Africa is in remarkable contradiction to the fact that during the years preceding the World War and immediately before its outbreak, many eminent English colonial authorities had paid splendid tributes to the methods of German colonization.[53]

Many of the additional annotations included in our new edition of the Blue Book contain contemporary evidence from the German colonial period which support statements made in the report. It is clear that concerns about German actions in 'German South West Africa' were raised at the time in both the media and through official channels. A few examples will briefly be presented in this introduction to support this point.

In September, 1905 the Cape Argus ran three substantial articles based on statements taken from transport riders who had been hired to help carry German military supplies from the coastal ports to the interior (copies of these letters and the response to them are provided in an additional appendix to this volume). A Mr F. Wepener had reportedly been hired in Johannesburg on 13 September 1904, and had told the paper that "At Okanjiso about February 12, I saw a number of women and children executed. There were eight women and six children. They were all strung up to trees by the neck and then shot." He went on to argue that the execution of non-combatants was common. "All the women and children we captured while I was on the march were treated in the same way. I have seen at least twenty-five of them with my own eyes hanged and shot.[54]" Several letters were published in response to such allegations, denying that 'ill-treatment' of prisoners had taken place, although one, by Karl Brehmer, stated that he believed that captured women prisoners had been shot, but justified this on the basis of the German belief that Herero women often mutilated and 'roasted' flesh from the corpses of German soldiers. Therefore, according to Brehmer, "one will hardly wonder that the soldiers can sometimes not be constrained from killing such bestial creatures". In disputing the allegation Brehmer therefore actually seems to support it.

Another important theme in the statements made by African witnesses in the Blue Book are the conditions in the military-run concentration camps [*Konzentrationslagern*].[55] The most deadly camps described in the Blue Book were those at Lüderitzbucht and Swakopmund. Yet once again such allegations were not new, but were similar to those made by the transport-riders at the time. It was reported that:

> The women who are captured and not executed are set to work for the military as prisoners. They saw numbers of them at Angra Pequena [Luderitzbucht] put to the hardest work, and so starved that they were nothing but skin and bones.
> "You will see them," said one, "carrying very heavy loads on their heads along

---

[53] *An answer to the Blue Book*, p. 9.

[54] 'The German Operations: British Subjects as Combatants: Further Evidence: Women and Children Hanged and Shot: Sensational Allegations', 25th September, 1905, *Cape Argus*

[55] The German authorities used the term *Konzentrationslager*. NAN, ZBU 454 DIV 1.3. Band 1, Telegramm des Reichskanzlers an das Gouvernement, eingegangen am 14 Januar 1905.

the shore in connection with the harbour works, and they are made to work until they fall down. While I was there, there were five or six deaths every day. The other women have to bury them. They are made to work till they die. All they have on is a blanket. If one falls down of sheer exhaustion as they constantly do, they are sjambokked.[56]

The allegations were repeated by another transport rider named as Mr Percival Griffith who worked in the two coastal towns containing camps and also supported by an earlier letter by nine other transport riders who supplied their names and addresses. The paper stated that all its informants were "... prepared, if called upon, to make affidavits in support of all their allegations."[57] It is clear that not just rumours, but substantial and detailed allegations, of wartime atrocities and maltreatment of prisoners were circulating before and during the 1904-1908 war in the Cape Colony and in imperial journals such as *Nineteenth Century*.[58] Modern readers might therefore ask, as did the German White Book of 1919, why no official British investigation took place into the allegations made at the time. In order to answer this question it is necessary to consider the reports being sent to London by British officials in direct contact with events taking place in Namibia and to consider the response of the British Government to these reports.

The British Government had two significant official contemporary sources of information. The first was the Magistrate based at the port of Walvis Bay, which, whilst lying on the coastline of 'German South West Africa' had been annexed by Great Britain in 1878, six years before Germany secured its colonial interests over the surrounding territory and another official with the rank of 'Consul' who was, intermittently, based at Luderitz. The second source were the interviews and reports from officers involved in gathering military intelligence during the 1904-1908 war. Information clearly filtered through these official channels on three of the key issues discussed in the Blue Book – the attack on Hornkranz in 1893, the treatment of prisoners during the 1904-1908 war and the post-war use of flogging within the German colonial judicial system.

The Magistrate at Walvis Bay described the surprise attack by German troops on the community at Hornkranz of 12th April, 1893 as "... an indiscriminate slaughter ... in which a most undue proportion of women and children were slain in circumstances of great brutality.[59]" Survivors of the

---

[56] 'In German S.W. Africa: Further Startling Allegations: Horrible Cruelty: British Subjects as Combatants, 28th September, 1905 *Cape Argus*.

[57] 'The German Operations: British Subjects as Combatants: Further Evidence: Women and Children Hanged and Shot: Sensational Allegations', 25th September, 1905, *Cape Argus* The names given were C. Hughes, T. Petzer, A.J. Hammond, F.H. Windle, M.J. Pretorius, P. Griffith, F.H. Smith, F.S. Cooke and O. McLeod, Letter, 28th September, 1905, *Cape Argus*

[58] Mackenzie, Kenneth, 'Some British Reactions to German Colonial Methods, 1885 – 1907', *The Historical Journal*, Vol. 17, no. 1 (1974).

[59] Magistrate, Walvis Bay to Rose-Innes, London, 9th May, 1893 quoted in Ronald Dreyer *The Mind of Official Imperialism: Britain and Cape Government Perceptions of German rule in Namibia from the Heligoland-Zanzibar Treaty to the Kruger Telegarm (1890-1896)*, Reimar Hobbing Verlag, Essen, 1987: p. 173

attack, travelled to Walvis Bay and made sworn statements to the Magistrate there. Ronald Dreyer has argued that the Cape Colony Government expressed concern about German actions, but that this reflected their unease about the proximity to South Africa of a rival colonial power. However the failure of the British Government to intervene (through their ability to control the flow of arms and ammunition to the two sides) was a result of the Foreign Office's policy of seeking co-operation, rather than confict, with Germany in the imperial sphere. This attitude was best summed up by the comment made by foreign minister Lord Rosebery, later to become prime minister, that "It won't be easy to tell a great military power that its troops wage war like barbarians."[60]

In reports concerning the actions of the German military during the 1904-1908 war officials also expressed particular concern about the treatment of women. The Magistrate at Walvis Bay stated that "I have heard myself, Germans who were in action describing boastfully how their troopers bayoneted Herero women.[61]" A report from a Colonel Neylan of the Cape Police, who had spent time gathering information in southern Namibia in 1905, focussed on detailed descriptions of troop deployment, but mentioned, in passing, that 'The Germans have shot a great many women.[62]' Another intelligence report described women who were 'weak' and 'badly fed' being forced to do heavy labour unloading ships in Luderitz and breaking stones for the construction of the railway line.[63] A British Military Attaché, Colonel Trench, travelled extensively in Namibia during the war and produced a series of detailed reports on German troop movements. Comments on the treatment of prisoners were also incidental to the main focus of his reports, but, for this very reason telling. Trench referred to the particularly harsh conditions in the prison camp on Shark Island at Luderitz. The survivors of Hendrik Witbooi's guerrilla unit had been sent there and Trench argued that the nature of the camp indicated that "... if they still exist, it is not easy to avoid the impression that the extinction of the tribe would be welcomed by the authorities.[64]" An official Foreign Office report dating from 1909 clearly states that "The war against the Hereros, conducted

---

[60] Letter from Rosebery to Ripon, 7th June, 1897 quoted in Ronald Dreyer, *The Mind of Official Imperialism: Britain and Cape Government Perceptions of German rule in Namibia from the Heligoland-Zanzibar Treaty to the Kruger Telegram (1890-1896)*, PhD Thesis, University of Geneva, p. 197.

[61] Magistrate, Walvis Bay to Secretary of Native Affairs, Cape Town, 18th May, 1904 in Colonial Office, *South Africa. Further Correspondence [1903-1904] relating to the Affairs of Walfisch Bay and the German South-West African Protectorate*, No. 723, HMSO, London, June, 1908, p. 107

[62] 'Memo on interview with Col. Neylan, Cape Police to Mr Lyttelton,' 21 June, 1905 in Colonial Office, *South Africa. Further Correspondence [1905] relating to the Affairs of Walfisch Bay and the German South-West African Protectorate,*' No. 766, HMSO, London, September, 1906, p. 79

[63] Major Berrange, Upington to Commissioner, Cape Mounted Police, Cape Town, 18 November, 1905 in Colonial Office, *South Africa. Further Correspondence [1905] relating to the Affairs of Walfisch Bay and the German South-West African Protectorate,*' No. 766, HMSO, London, September, 1906, pp. 217-218.

[64] PMO 227 – 35/07 British Military Attaché, Col. F. Trench to British Embassy, Berlin, 21 November, 1906.

by General Trotha, was one of extermination; hundreds – men, women and children – were driven into desert country, where death from thirst was their end.[65] Whilst it is clear that the primary British concern was the increase in German troop concentrations in a territory bordering the British Empire and not the welfare of the indigenous inhabitants, it is also clear that officials expressed concern about German practices which, they felt, contravened the acceptable 'rules of war'.[66]

A file was constructed by the British Consul at Luderitz on the 'status of natives' in Namibia, which expressed concern about the high rate of flogging in the territory. An official scribbled on the cover of the file that "Ample discretion to be brutal appears to be allowed to those who administer the law".[67] The 1909 report referred to above was also critical of the post-war labour conditions stating of the released prisoners that "... labour is forced upon them and naturally is unwillingly performed." A Foreign Office minute from 1912 stated "These Hereros were butchered by thousands during the war & have been ruthlessly flogged into subservience since.[68]"

The complexity of imperial rivalry in Southern Africa has been explored in greater depth elsewhere.[69] Whilst officials in Cape Town showed concern about German military activity in Namibia and viewed the territory within a clearly sub-imperial agenda, the perspective from London cast events taking place in Namibia within a wider imperial context. As early as 1892 the Secretary of State for Colonial Affairs, the Earl of Ripon, advised the Magistrate at Walvis Bay as to how to respond to complaints from Hendrik Witbooi, a powerful local leader, about German colonial practices. The Earl of Ripon argued that "The chief should be informed in kindly terms that the British Government has promised that of Germany not to interfere in certain parts of West Africa, among which is his own district and that it is impossible for Great Britain now to retract that promise. The British Government has no knowledge of what is done in those countries, over which German protection is exercised and are in no way responsible for anything that may be done.[70]" The demands of imperial diplomacy and international relations were considered to outweigh the concerns of local colonial officials about possible human rights abuses.

---

[65] 'Report on German SWA', Capt. H.S.P. Simon, 6 April, 1909 quoted in Louis. p. 34.

[66] The Hague Conventions of 1899, and 1907 marked an effort by the major European powers to draw up mutually acceptable rules for 'civilised' warfare. During the 1899 Conference it was actually the British delegation who were amongst the strongest opponents of the clause banning the use of 'dum dum' bullets as 'nothing less would stop "savages"', Mark Levine 'Introduction' in Mark Levine and Penny Roberts (eds), *The Massacre in History*, Berghahn Books, New York/Oxford, 1999.

[67] Pretoria Archives GG276 'Status of natives in German South West Africa: Report by HM Consul on.', 13 July, 1911.

[68] 'Minute', F.E.F. Adam, Foreign Office, 20 August, 1912 quoted in Louis. p. 38.

[69] See Dreyer, Ronald *The Mind of Official Imperialism: Britain and Cape Government Perceptions of German rule in Namibia from the Heligoland-Zanzibar Treaty to the Kruger Telegarm (1890-1896)*, Reimar Hobbing Verlag, Essen, 1987.

[70] Pretoria Archives NTS 266 4349/1910/F639 Sec of State Ripon to High Commissioner, Sir H.B. Loch, 14th December, 1892.

All this shows that officials in the Cape and in London were cognisant of the evidence of human rights abuses in German, but unwilling to take action within the context of international economic rivalry and the chessboard politics of imperial consolidation. In 1907 Great Britain had been party to the Second Hague Conference which had revised the 1899 'Convention concerning the Laws and Custom of War on Land'. Article 23c of the convention stated that "It is particularly forbidden ... To kill or wound an enemy who, having laid down his arms, or no longer having means of defence, has surrendered.[71]" Yet, despite this noble rhetoric, one might surmise that the recent heated international criticism of the high death rates in the 'concentration camps' run by Britain from September, 1900 during the South African War (1899-1902) made the British Government sensitive about raising concerns about high death rates in 'concentration camps' or other human rights abuses in a neighbouring colony.[72] The reluctance of Great Britain to criticise its colonial rivals at this time was, perhaps, most neatly summarised in a minute prepared by the Head of the Africa Desk at the Foreign Office who in 1906 argued that "France and Germany are boys too big to interfere with.[73]" The extent to which Britain was prepared to publicly criticise other colonial powers was clearly largely determined by the Foreign Office.

In 1904, the very year in which German forces were pursuing genocidal policies in Namibia, the British Government did publish a highly critical report on human rights abuses in the Congo Free State. The report of a British Consul, Roger Casement, on alleged atrocities in the Congo Free State fuelled a human rights campaign that led in 1908 to international intervention to end King Leopold's control of the territory.[74] The Report was circulated to a number of imperial powers who were challenged to investigate the alleged atrocities as being in conflict with the 1885 Berlin Act that they had signed. Instrumental in the campaign to end the abuses taking place in the Congo Free States was the work of E. D. Morel, who, following the transfer of the Congo as the personal possession of Leopold to Belgium as a colony, remained a dedicated anti-colonial campaigner for the rest of his life.

---

[71] The convention was repeatedly cited during the propaganda war over the conduct of the competing armies during operations in the European field during World War One. For example, see Great Britain, *Evidence and Documents laid before the Committee on Alleged German Outrages*, HMSO, London, 1915.

[72] It is calculated that 27,927 people (10% of the Afrikaner population) died in the camps and a further 18,003 'verifiable deaths' occurred in the separate 'black and coloured concentration camps' See Albert Grundlingh 'The Anglo-Boer War in 20th century Afrikaner consciousness', p. 244 and Stowell Kessler 'The black and coloured concentration camps', p. 148, both in Fransjohan Pretorius (ed.), *Scorched Earth*, Cape Town: Human & Rousseau 1999.

[73] Minute by E.A.W. Clarke, 21 December, 1906 FO 367/5 in Louis. p 38.

[74] Casement, Roger 'Report on the Administration of the Congo Free State', *British Parliamentary* Papers, 1904, LXII, Cd. 1933. Hochschild, Adam *King Leopold's Ghost*, Papermac, London, 2000: pp. 200-206.

In the aftermath of World War I, Morel published, *The Black Man's Burden*,[75] which discusses critically the activities of European colonial powers in Africa. In his book, Morel devoted a full chapter to the role of Imperial Germany in Namibia, and referred directly to the 1918 Blue Book. At the outset Morel noted that the Blue Book needed to be read with a 'sense of perspective', as it was, he stated 'more in the nature of a 'War Aims' publication'. However, as Morel cautioned his readers:

> Without minimising in the slightest degree the action of the Germans in South West Africa, we should do well to have at the back of our minds the sort of indictment which would have been drawn up by a succesful enemy in occupation of Rhodesia and Bechuanaland, desirous of demonstrating our iniquities to the world in order to make out a case for retaining those territories for himself.

Dealing with events that took place in the so-called Bechuanaland rebellion of 1895, Morel in no way sought to play down atrocities committed by British authorities. Indeed, Morel refered to the 'wholesale confication of native lands... and the fate which overtook the 3,000 odd 'rebels' who surrendered' and noted that these events would also have made 'other than excellent reading for a world audience sitting in judgment upon our sins'. Morel concluded by noting that:

> Between the decrees of a von Lindequist or a Leutwein, the brayings of a Schlettwein *et hoc genus omne*, and the pompous pronouncements of certain leading South African statesmen there is fundamentally little difference.

Colonialism and colonial rule, be it that of Germany, Great Britain, The Netherlands, or any other colonising power, was fundamentally cruel, unjust, and disrespective of fundamental human rights. British forces, as the German White Book of 1919 points out, committed atrocities in India and elsewhere in its far-flung empire. Similarly, representatives of the Kingdom of the Netherlands committed wholesale massacres in southern Africa and the Indonesian archipelago. Most notably and contemporaneously with events in Namibia was the infamous fourth Atjeh War 1898 - 1910, where Dutch forces were led by J.B. van Heutsz.

To be sure, accounts of atrocities committed by an earlier generation make for troubling reading. Similarly, the statements and accounts included in the Blue Book make for extremely troubling reading, nevertheless, this is not to deny that they took place, nor that the validity of the statements presented is in dispute.

---

[75] E.D. Morel, *The Black Man's Burden: The White Man in Africa from the Fifteenth Century to World War I* (Manchester: National Labour Press, 1920).

The Destruction of the Blue Book

The formal German response to the Blue Book had dismissed it as 'a bulky bit of propaganda' and argued that "No efforts are being spared in the attempt to lull the world into the belief that England is actuated not by selfish ends, but by lofty moral motives".[76] It is certainly true that, whilst a number of prosecutions took place in a 'Special Criminal Court' in the four and a half years of South African military rule that immediately followed the defeat of the German forces in 1915 there were no detailed investigations into specific allegations contained in the Blue Book (such as the alleged massacre at Ombakaha or the extraordinarily death rates at the coastal prisoner-of-war camps) and certainly no attempt to put German officers on trial for war crimes. Such inaction might be contrasted with the official investigations that followed public concern regarding for instance civilian death rates in British concentration camps in South Africa and the massacre of civilians in Amritsar.[77] Once the mandate for Namibia was awarded to the Union of South Africa in 1920 it became clear that a new agenda was becoming important, the building of a unified white settler community. General Smuts himself visited Namibia in September, 1920 and stated very clearly that "… in my opinion the future of South-West lies in co-operation between the old German community and the new Union community that was settling her.[78]" Despite the heavy criticism that had been contained in the Blue Book the emphasis was now placed on reconciliation, rather than retribution.

The publication of the Blue Book and proposals to produce an Afrikaans edition provoked early opposition to its contents in South Africa. Mr Malan, of the National Party, argued that the 'statements on oath' should not be published at all, but only a short summary of the Blue Book.[79] When a 'German delegation' from Namibia travelled to Cape Town for talks with the South African Prime Minister, General Smuts, on 24th January, 1924 they noted with 'particular satisfaction' the assurance they were given that there would be 'no further official reference to the Blue Book'.[80] A few months later, General Hertzog (the leader of the National Party) became the new leader of the country at the head of the Pact Government.[81] On 10th November, 1924 during a visit to

---

[76] German Colonial Office *The Treatment of Native and Other Populations in the Colonial Possessions of Germany and England: An Answer to the English Blue Book of August, 1918* 'Report on the Natives of South-West Africa and their Treatment by Germany, Hans Robert Engelmann, Berlin, 1919, p. 1

[77] Great Britain, *Report on the Concentration Camps in South Africa by the Committee of bodies appointed by the Secretary of State for War, containing reports on the camps in Natal, the Orange River Colony and the Transvaal,* HMSO, Cd. 893, London, 1902. Great Britain *Report of the Committee Appointed by the Government of India to Investigate the Disturbances in the Punjab, etc,* HMSO, Parliamentary Papers, 1920, vol. 14;

[78] Quoted in Steer, G.L. *Judgement on German Africa,* Hodder and Stoughton, London, 1939: p. 340

[79] 'Memo.' P. Horsfall to Governor-General, 13th December, 1918. Pretoria Archives, GG 728.

[80] Steer, G.L. *Judgement on German Africa,* Hodder and Stoughton, London, 1939: p. 340

[81] Walker, Eric *A History of South Africa,* Longman, Green & Co., London, New York, Toronto, 1947 p. 600.

Namibia the newly elected South African Prime Minister, expressed his view that "... as to the historical Blue Book, he doubted whether anyone believed its contents. It was considered a war pamphlet – one among many that had gone into oblivion or soon would do so".[82] The leaders of the mandatory power had clearly stated their view that the accusations supported by the statements contained in the Blue Book would no longer be pursued and the Report itself would be forgotten. The lid had been taken off the dustbin and it only remained for the mechanisms of limited settler self-government to be put in place and the demands of the local white community to be articulated before the Blue Book would be literally consigned to the dustbin of history.

The year 1926 saw the first election campaign in Namibia since the South African conquest of the territory – under a franchise that was limited to white males. In a campaign speech made at Keetmanshoop, Mr Jooste, the local Chairperson of the National Party, argued strongly for: "The co-operation of all sections of the community – the farmers must work together whether they were German, Dutch or English.[83]" The editorial of the local English-language newspaper argued that "South Africans should not engage in a racial quarrel with a people who are bowed down by a recent defeat" and advocated 'reconciliation' that could deal with the "race hatred ... [that] ... has eaten like a cancer into the nation.[84] " The 'racial hatred' that was causing so much concern was not associated with any of the allegations that had been printed in the Blue Book or German accounts of the 1904-1908 war, but rather that which it was claimed existed between German-speaking white residents of the territory and the influx of new white immigrants from the Union.

In 1926 the first all-white legislative assembly for 'South West Africa' assembled and one of the first motions to be tabled, by Mr August Stauch, concerned the destruction of the Blue Book. Stauch stated that the Blue Book:

> ... only has the meaning of a war-instrument and that the time has come, to put this instrument out of operation and to impound and destroy all copies of this Bluebook, which may be found in the official records and in public libraries of this Territory.
>
> That the administration be requested to make representations to the Union Government and to the British Government to have this Bluebook [sic] expunged from the official records of those Governments.
>
> That the Administration be requested to take into consideration the advisability of making representations to the Union Government and the British Government to impound and destroy all copies of the Bluebook, which may be found in the public libraries in the respective Countries and with the official booksellers mentioned on the title-sheet of the Bluebook ...[85]"

---

[82] Cockram, Gail-Maryse, *South West African Mandate,* Juta and Co., Cape Town/Wynberg/Johannesburg, 1976, p. 32

[83] 'Nationalists at Keetmanshoop', *Windhoek Advertiser,* 6th March, 1926, p5.

[84] 'Mr Ballot and the Mandate', *Windhoek Advertiser,* 20th March, 1926, p2.

[85] NAN, ADM 255 'Memorandum on the Blue Book, Annexure A'.

Copies of the Blue Book were systematically removed from public libraries throughout South Africa and Namibia and destroyed. In Windhoek in 1935, Mr. Ballot, member of the executive committee, Advisory Council and the Legislative Assembly since 1921, reported that, "all known copies of the Blue Book" had been destroyed.[86] In the rest of the British Empire copies were transferred to the Foreign Office and, as late as 1941, it was noted that 'no copy may be issued without authority of the librarian'.[87]

Stauch had motivated his motion with the claim that it "would ... remove one of the most serious obstacles to mutual trust and cooperation in this country." In his view "the honour of Germany had been attacked in the most public manner and it was right that the attack should be repudiated in an equally public fashion ... The defence of the honour of one's country was a solemn duty imposed upon all sons of that country." The validity of Stauch's claim was not questioned by any member of the assembly, instead the prospect of nurturing political and social unity proved paramount.[88] Stauch's claim that "the Germans were ready and anxious to cooperate in the building up of South West but they could not do so fully until the stigma imposed by the publication of the Bluebook ... had been removed from their name", was considered to be more important that historical veracity or any sort of investigation into the charges made by Namibia's African inhabitants. The dead of the Herero genocide and other atrocities were dismissed and forgotten in the interests of white settler reconciliation.

Conclusion: Reviewing the Blue Book

The aim of this publication is to make the 1918 Blue Book available to a wider public. In republishing the 1918 Blue Book as a historical source we are well aware of the historical context in which the report will once again circulate. Its republication is bound to stimulate comments, criticisms and debate that go way beyond the scope of this short introduction. Nevertheless, in republishing the 1918 Blue Book we believe that the text is likely to provoke debate in relation to three specific areas of academic and popular interest as it raises questions about genocide, comparative colonialism and the relationship between violence and memory.

It is our belief that the Namibian genocide can only be fully understood in the context of the phenomena of genocide as a whole and that the genocides committed in the course of the twentieth century, after 1904, need to be dealt with in the context of preceeding genocides, including the Namibian genocide. Furthermore, we would contend that genocides do not take place in a vaccum.

---

[86] NAN, KSW 2, Evidence to SWA Committe, Windhoek, 24 July 1935, p. 76.

[87] PRO FO 371/26574 'Minute', Foreign Office, 20th June, 1940.

[88] Twenty years later a South African MP would suggest that the motivation behind the destruction of the Blue Book had been 'political', Steenkamp,W.P. *Is the South-West African Herero Committing Race Suicide?*, 1944.

Genocides take place within a historical context, with a definite trajectory. Thus the intent to commit genocide is predicated upon a belief in the attainability of such a goal. A goal which becomes evident in the light of previous examples. In the context of the twentieth century, it is important to bear in mind that genocides, as phenomena, are not unique events. Genocides can be, and indeed need to be compared, in order for us to attain a fuller and more detailed understanding of these events.

Until now, within the field of genocide studies, the Namibian genocide of 1904 has received little or no attention. Those accounts which do refer to Namibian events, have tended, on the whole, to rely on the secondary literature primarily the early works of Bley and Drechsler.[89] The Blue Book, as a prime source material presenting an early African perspective on the particular features of colonial genocide is here presented for the first time in an easily accessible manner. Henceforth the views of both observers and survivors of the Namibian Genocide will be accessible to a broader audience.

The Blue Book may also be read as a key text in the production of colonial discourse. For example, the ways in which the treatment of crime and punishment in the German period is represented in the Blue Book might be used by those wishing to engage with debates about the construction of comparative colonialisms. The text can be read as an example of colonial discourse that seeks to construct contrasting identies for 'German' and 'British'. The report explicitly states that the evidence can also be read as a contribution to 'a study of German mentality' that can be juxtaposed with 'British ideas of the administration of justice' and 'the well-ordered control of British government', whilst the 'rigidity' of the German legal system is contrasted favourably with the 'elasticity' of the system used by the British. Emphasis is placed on the contrast between practices in German colonial territories and the Cape with regard to the use of corporal punishment (flogging) and other aspects of crime and punishment.[90] The Blue Book therefore constructs contrasting images of the 'German' and 'British' settler that invites a more extensive study of the debates within settler society around this issue. This would examine the tensions within the colonial state following the conquest of 1915 and between the racially distinguished factions within the white settler community.[91]

As noted above, the events described in the Blue Book are related in part by both observers and survivors of the Namibian Genocide. Recent work in the southern African region has begun to deal with the issue of 'Violence and

---

[89] Mark Cocker, *Rivers of Blood Rivers of Gold: Europe's conflict with tribal peoples*, London: Pimlico, 1999; Alison Palmer, *Colonial Genocide*, London: Seahurst, 2000.

[90] *Report on the Natives*, pp. XXXX

[91] Ann Stoler has argued about the dangers of assuming 'a shared European mentality' and failing to analyse the complexity of 'the colonial state' in 'Rethinking colonial categories: European commmunities and the boundaries of rule', *Comparative Studies in Society and* History, Vol. 31, 1989, p. 135. For a range of perspectives on the role of law in defining models of colonial rule see Mann, Kristin and Richard Roberts (eds), *Law in Colonial Africa*, James Currey, Oxford, 1991.

Memory' in a concerted manner.[92] This invites further discussion and research about the ways in which the incidents of extreme violence described in the Blue Book have been processed in the accounts that it contains and by subsequent generations.

The horrifically graphic images of violence contained in the Blue Book have been a powerful tool in support of Franz Fanon's argument that the inate violence of the colonial state provided the justification for a violent anti-colonial response. The argument that "Armed struggle has been justified by demonstrating sustained imperial and settler violence in conquest and dispossession" can certainly be applied to in Namibia.[93] The Blue Book was quoted by Michael Scott, one of the earliest petitioners to the United Nations in the 1950s, is drawn on in SWAPO publications during the liberation struggle and was cited by President Sam Nujoma in an interview prior to the opening of the new Heroes Acre on 26th August, 2002.[94] Study of the Blue Book can therefore also inform debate about the discourse of the liberation struggle and the later use of a nationalist reading of history as a tool in nation-building.

The republication of the images contained in the Blue Book today in an independent Namibia may draw criticism on two grounds – that it replicates humiliating images of violence and that remembrance may challenge the policy of national reconciliation. A photograph of a group of naked Herero women, probably taken in the context of the camps established by the Germans in the aftermath of the defeat of the Herero in 1904, provoked a heated correspondence about the ethics of reproducing images of abuse and whether this reproduced and even invited the further perpetuation of colonial voyeurism and visual violence.[95] Similar arguments could be made with regard to the language that we reproduce in the republishing the Blue Book. The Blue Book uses the derogatory terms, 'Hottentots', 'Bushmen' and so forth. It is certainly not our intention to reproduce racism, neither do we condone the language of the Blue Book. However, we have retained the language as it stands, as it illustrates the colonial discourse of the time that should now be rejected and condemned just as much as some of the events that the report describes. Some might argue that the reproduction of text, images and vivid descriptions of physical humiliation and death are unjustified. Nevertheless, as countless encounters with the descendents of survivors, as students, informants and friends, has shown people want to know about their past and do not wish it to be hidden away in the whitewashed landscape of Namibian history.

---

[92] William Beinart 'Political and Collective Violence in Southern African Historiography', *Journal of Southern African Studies*, Vol. 18, no. 3, 1992; Jocelyn Alexander, JoAnn McGregor and Terence Ranger, *Violence & Memory: One Hundred Years in the 'Dark Forests' of Matabeleland*, James Currey, Oxford, 2000; Inge Brinkman, 'Ways of Death: Accounts of Terror from Angolan Refugees in Namibia', *Africa*, Vol. 70, no. 1, 2000.

[93] Beinart, p. 459.

[94] NBC News (English), 23rd August, 2002. J.B. Gewald, "Presenting the past to fight the present: an overview of the manner in which the Herero Genocide has been used for political purposes in the course of the 20th Century", presented to the African Studies Centre Conference, Revolt and Resistance in African History, 11 and 12 October 2001, Leiden.

[95] John Grobler, Still no redress for Hereros, Mail & Guardian March 13-19, 1998, and letters published subsequently to the article.

The stunning natural landscape of Namibia, coupled to a well developed tourist infrastructure, ensures that thousands of tourists annually visit Namibia to marvel at its sights. The majority of tourists will be impressed with the legacy of German imperialism. Though Namibia was only colonised by Imperial Germany for thirty years, Namibia is unmistakably a former German colony. Almost everything, from clothing styles to architecture, from food to drink, from religious expression to sport, and much much more reflects the German influence. Most tourists and visitors to the country will have a particular understanding of this colonial legacy. Tourist guide books emphasise and reflect on the German past and presence in the country. Indeed the German colonial legacy of Namibia is marketted as a major attraction for tourists travelling in the country.[96] Visitors can take guided tours in period style motor-vehicles that focus on the historical buildings of the German period in Windhoek or exclusive German-speaking tours to sites firmly associated with the German colonial moment, such as Luderitz.[97] A person interested in the German colonial history of Namibia would appear to be well catered for.

Namibia is crowded with monuments to the wars that ravaged the country in the late nineteenth and early twentieth century. Visitors to the country marvel at statues, forts, churches, cenotaphs and graveyards constructed in the memory of soldiers who died a century ago. Yet these monuments only honour the dead who fought with the German colonial forces. There is not a single monument in Namibia that has been raised to the memory of the thousands who died on account of the enforcement of Germany's colonial will on the territory. Instead of memorials, beach resorts, camping areas and game resorts cover the sites of concentration camps and battle grounds.

In the coastal resort of Swakopmund, tourists gamble money in a converted railway station built by slave labour, drink coffee overlooking the site of a concentration camp, and ride dune buggies over the mass graves of Herero P.O.W.s.[98] In Lüderitz campers set up their trekking tents on the municipal camping ground at Shark Island; an island where between 1905 - 1907 thousands of Nama prisoners were starved and beaten to death.[99] At the Waterberg Nature Reserve hikers and nature lovers camp on part of the battleground that saw the defeat of the Herero and eat and drink in a converted German police station where in the past colonial justice in the form of 'parental chastisement' was meted out.[100] Indeed one might argue that the absence of

---

[96] In a sense this is no different from a country like Kenya which gains substantial tourist revenues through emphasising its 'great white hunter' and 'happy valley' past.

[97] In 1991 one of the co-editors participated in a journey by steam train to Luderitz which was heavy with nostalgia for the German colonial period and included a visit to the ruins of the camp at Aus where thousands of Germans were interned during the First World War.

[98] Jeremy Silvester 'A Living Cemetery in Swakopmund', *The Namibian Weekender*, 21st November, 1997, p. 9.

[99] Jeremy Silvester 'Death on the Rocks', *The Namibian Weekender*, 22nd August, 1997, p. 9; Casper Erichsen and Jeremy Silvester 'Luderitz's Forgotten Concentration Camp', *The Namibian Weekender*, 16th February, 2001, pp. 1-3.

[100] Jeremy Silvester 'Layers of History at the Place of the Calabashes', *The Namibian Weekender* 23rd June, 2000, p. 4

marked heritage sites really leaves the past 'a foreign country' and transforms Namibians into tourists in their own historical landscape.[101] Indeed, Namibians currently walk through a colonial German reading of their own history.

Stanley Cohen has argued that "Whole societies have an astonishing ability to deny the past – not really forgetting, but maintaining a public culture that seems to have forgotten".[102] In Namibia after independence there was, in contrast to South Africa, a policy of 'national reconciliation' which initially sought to avoid reopening the 'wounds of the past', rather than confront them. However recent years have seen a number of major initiatives in the heritage sector which show an active willingness by the state to engage with the past, although, as in South Africa, this has been firmly linked to efforts to strengthen a nationalist historical narrative.[103] It is within this context that we must return to the theme of 'violence and memory'.

The year 2004 will mark the centenary of the outbreak of the Namibian war against German rule. It is our intention that this republication of the Blue Book will, in some measure, be a memorial to those that died. Through its republication voices hidden and obscured for too long will, once again be heard. In the run-up to the centenary of the war there will be other forms of commemoration, planned both in Germany and Namibia. It is to be hoped that this republished Blue Book will contribute and inform the manner in which they choose to commemorate the war. The challenge to both Namibians and Germans is whether they choose a national or a sectional commemoration.[104]

Does Germany, as it clearly did with the Berlin exhibition, choose to see the Namibian war as a colonial aberration, or as an integral part of twentieth century German history? Does Namibia, as many Namibians have done in the past, seek to emphasise ethnically based claims for redress, or will Namibians seek to acknowledge and commemorate the national character of the war? That is, that the Namibian War affected and determined the course of Namibian history as a whole, and not just sectors of Namibian society. We would contend that the war and its consequences had a fundamental impact on the subsequent history of Namibia. Access to land, population distribution, economic power,

---

[101] D. Lowenthal, *The Past is a Foreign Country*, Cambridge University Press, Cambridge, 1985.

[102] Stanley Cohen, *States of Denial: Knowing About Atrocities and Suffering*, Polity, Cambridge, 2001, p 138.

[103] For a discussion of the role of heritage projects in the effort to promote new forms of national identity in South Africa see Ciraj Rassool, 'The Rise of Heritage and the Reconstitution of History in South Africa', *Kronos*, August, 2000.

[104] The difficulties created through a revision of heritage sites that attempts to incorporate 'missing' perspectives in the context of the centenary of the 'Anglo-Boer War' of 1899-1902 are explored in Leslie Witz, Gary Minkley and Ciraj Rassool, 'No End of a [History] Lesson: Preparations for the Anglo-Boer War Centenary Commemorations', *South African Historical Journal*, Vol. 41, November, 1991. For an attempt 'to provide guidelines for the commemoration of controversial events' in the same context see Graham Dominy and Luli Callinicos, '"Is There Anything to Celebrate?" Paradoxes of Policy: An Examination of the State's Approach to Commemorating South Africa's Most Ambiguous Struggle', *South African Historical Journal*, Vol. 41, November, 1991.

urbanisation and political power, have all been shaped, and are only understandable, in terms of the Namibian War.[105]

As historians we believe that the evaluation of stories/histories about the past are an important way of engaging with contemporary debates about the legacy of the colonial state and the actions of the post-colonial state. The accounts contained in the Blue Book should be read. Readers may accept them or wish to challenge them, but they should no longer be ignored or silenced. Though words can never be found to describe the full horror of genocide, the Blue Book does provide us with African voices that will enable us to come some way to a shared realisation and understanding of the horrors of colonial rule.

---

[105] For further arguments on this theme see Henning Melber, 'Namibia: The German roots of Apartheid', *Race and Class*, Vol. 27, no. 1, 1985.

UNION OF SOUTH AFRICA.

REPORT

ON THE

NATIVES OF SOUTH-WEST AFRICA

AND

THEIR TREATMENT BY GERMANY.

Prepared in the Administrator's Office, Windhuk,
South-West Africa, January 1918.

Presented to both Houses of Parliament by Command of His Majesty.
August, 1918.

LONDON:
PUBLISHED BY HIS MAJESTY'S STATIONERY OFFICE.

To be purchased through any Bookseller or directly from
H.M. STATIONERY OFFICE at the following addresses:
IMPERIAL HOUSE, KINGSWAY, LONDON, W.C. 2, and 28, ABINGDON STREET, LONDON, S.W. 1;
37, PETER STREET, MANCHESTER; 1, ST. ANDREW'S CRESCENT, CARDIFF;
23, FORTH STREET, EDINBURGH;
or from E. PONSONBY, LTD., 116, GRAFTON STREET, DUBLIN.

1918.

[Cd. 9146.]   *Price* 2s. 6d. *Net.*

CONTENTS

PART ONE

NATIVES AND GERMAN ADMINISTRATION

I	How German influence was introduced into South-West Africa	21
II	First acquisitions of land	27
III	Germany's declared policy in regard to the native races	33
IV	First steps after annexation	35
V	The massacre at Hornkrantz	41
VI	Leutwein and the Protection Agreements	49
VII	Native population statistics	59
VIII	The Hereros of South-West Africa	63
IX	Confiscation of Herero cattle by the German Government	75
X	The German traders and how they traded	83
XI	Gradual appropriation of Hereroland and violation of Herero customs	89
XII	The value set on native life by the Germans	93
XIII	The outbreak of the Herero rising and the humanity of the Herero	99
XIV	Preliminary steps and treachery of the Germans	105
XV	How the Hereros were exterminated	111
XVI	The Hottentots of South-West Africa	123
XVII	Laws and customs of the Hottentots	131
XVIII	The Hottentots under German protection	139
XIX	The Bondelswartz rising of 1903 and the general Hottentot Rising of 1904-7	159
XX	The treatment of the Hottentots in war and of the Hereros and Hottentots after surrender	169
XXI	The Berg-Damaras of South-West Africa	181
XXII	The policy of Germany after the great rising of the natives up to the British conquest of South-West Africa in 1915	191
XXIII	The Bastards of Rehoboth	207
XXIV	The Ovambos of South West-Africa	223
XV	The Bushmen of South West-Africa	235

PART TWO

NATIVES AND THE CRIMINAL LAW

I	The native as an accused person	249
II	The position of a native when complainant	267
III	The relations between Germans and natives as evinced in Criminal proceedings after our occupation	297

Method of executing a number of natives. Note the boxes. The victims were made to stand on these while the ropes were adjusted. They were then kicked or pulled away.

PREFACE

In preparing a statement dealing with the native races of South-West Africa, and having special reference to their history and treatment while under German domination, it is desirable to give a brief outline of the ways and means by which German influence was introduced, and of the events which led up to the consolidation of such influence by subsequent annexation.

It is furthermore necessary, in order to establish a basis from which to examine the matter and to obtain a correct perspective, that the avowed native policy of Germany, as given utterance to by her statesmen and other representative Germans, should be indicated.

Of particular value and significance would be the official declarations of policy made about, or prior to, the year 1890, when the Anglo-German Agreement was entered into.[1] Such statements must at that time at least have carried much weight with British statesmen, and must, without doubt, have influenced them in deciding on behalf of Great Britain, officially to sanction the formal annexation according to agreed boundaries of South-West Africa to the German Crown. More especially must Germany's aims have been of interest in view of the fact that British statemen knew then that the Hereros and other native races in this area desired British protection in preference to that of Germany, and it must presumably have been expected that they would be as well off under German control as under the Union Jack.

Having ascertained what those declarations of policy were, it will not be a difficult tas to discover, on theincontrovertible evidence of proved historical facts, whether Germany ever at any time put her defined policy into practice. It will be easy to judge whether, in terms of this publicly declared policy, the native races of South-West Africa were humanely, honestly, and justly treated, or whether, owing to alterations in or departure from that policy or an express refusal to apply it in actual practice, the reverse was the case.

In Part I a rapid survey of the history of this country from the time Europeans first penetrated into it is given, the methods by which Germany proceeded to establish her dominion are shortly shown, and an account of the atrocities committed on the natives is furnished. Part II is devoted to an analysis of the position of the natives under the criminal law. The time available for the collection of material for incorporation into this report and for the careful collation of that material has been brief; but, notwithstanding, a large amount

---

[1] Agreement between Great Britain and Germany respecting, Heligoland, and the spheres of influence of the two countries in Africa. United Nations Institute for Namibia, *Independent Namibia: Succession to Treaty Rights and Obligations: Incorporating Namibian Treaty Calendar*, (Lusaka 1989) p. 63

of evidence is presented which contains irrefutable proofs of the gross ineptitude with which Germany entered upon her scheme of colonizing this territory, of the callous indifference with which she treated the guaranteed rights of the native peoples established here, and of the cruelties to which she subjected those peoples when the burden became too heavy and they attempted to assert their rights.

To publish all the information that has been obtained would form too bulky a volume. The object of this report is to present the essential features only in an easily assimilable form. Enough is, I think, contained herein to leave no doubts as to the terrible courses pursued both by the German Colonial Administration, acting either under the orders or with the acquiescence of the Berlin Government, and by individual Germans settled or stationed in the country, or as to the deplorable plight the natives fell into under the brutalities and robberies to which they were systematically subjected.

It will be found that for the native there was, in effect, during the first 17 years after the formal annexation of the country by Germany, no law, and that such protection as the law eventually provided was granted not out of motives of humanity, but because it was at length recognized that the native was a useful asset in the country, and that, without his labour, cattle-ranching, for which large areas of the country are well suited, and diamond and copper mining, were impossible. In Chapter XV it is pointed out how the German writer Rohrbach condemned the extermination of the Herero tribe in 1905 *because the cattle and sheep of the Hereros shared the fate of their native masters.* There was then not a word of sympathy for the unfortunate Herero people or recognition of their value in the economic scheme of things in the colony. That came later when the mischief had been done. The only regret expressed at the time was that the flocks and herds of the natives, on which the settlers had set greedy eyes, were sent, in the blind fury of von Trotha, to the same fate as their owners.

One can, however, fairly believe that the colonists, or a proportion of them, became at length so satiated with the sight of the human blod that was shed in 1904 and 1905, and so alarmed for their future labour supply and at the destruction of the native livestock that went on *parri passu*[2] with the extermination of the Hereros, that they used such influence as they possessed to call a halt to the insensate slaughter that was taking place. The surviving natives, then reduced to serfdom and distributed as farm labourers, were thereby freed from the terror of organized destruction and became instead, as individuals, subject only to the cruel punishments awarded by the courts and police sergeants and to the parental chastisement which, under the German *régime,* every farmer exercised over his native servants. The limits to which "parental chastisement" were sometimes carried are aptly illustrated in Part II., Chapter II., by the records of a case (one of the very few tried by the German courts), and by the photographs

---

[2] At equal pace

appearing in that chapter. The presiding judge of the German Appeal Court characterized the acts of the offending farmer as being reminiscent of the blackest deeds of the slave days, and then reduced the sentence of 21 months' imprisonment which had been imposed in the lower court on seven separate counts of cruelty of the most terrible nature to a sentence of four months' imprisonment altogether and a fine of 2,700 marks. Two of the victims – they were both women – in this case died shortly afterwards. If the photographs are examined it will be wondered how it was they did not expire under the lash.

It was a matter of constant remark amongst the British element now here how little was known outside this territory – at all events in South Africa – of the dreadful occurrences that were taking place herein. Germany, however, always kept the country, as far as she was able, a close preserve, and persons of alien nationality were neither assisted nor encouraged to settle here.[3] When the worst of these deeds – the massacre of the Hereros – was taking place, the diamond fileds of Luderitzbucht had not yet been discovered, and the somewhat considerable foreign population, which on the opening of those fields was attracted to that coast, whether the Germans willed it or not, was not yet present. Residents of the Union at the time will recall that in those days but little, if any, interest was evinced in affairs here. The rights of the case between the opposing parties were not understood, and no opportunity was lost by Germans either here or in the neighbouring colonies of showing the natives in the worse light. It is reasonable to surmise that, had the facts been known as we have now, by careful examination of documentary evidence and by interrogation of the survivors, ascertained them, a protest would have been addressed to Germany by the Powers who subscribed to the Resolutions of 1885 and 1890.[4]

It is known that the facts commenced to leak out in Germany after 1905, with the result that laws dealing with natives, their rights, obligations, and treatment were promulgated. There is no doubt that, viewed from the standards to which we are accustomed in South Africa, portions of these laws, on paper at least, are satisfactory; but it is generally conceded that in very few instances was proper effect given to their provisions. The occasions where the natives obtained the rights to which they were entitled under those laws are found to have been few in number. The authority delegated to minor officials to flog or

---

[3] The distribution of land was primarily intended to consolidate the territory as a German settler colony. German citizens were charged roughly half the price of others wishing to buy farms. The consistency of black resistence to German rule and the high cost of transporting expeditionary forces from Germany meant that preferential conditions for farm purchase were offered to those liable to military service. Farms of up to 5,000 hectare were made available to this special category of German settler for just 30 pfennig per hectare. Many of the German soldiers who traveled to Namibia to fight in the 1904 - 1907 war took the opportunity to obtain land.

[4] The discussions of the Berlin Conference of 1884 were embodied in the General Act with was signed in February 1885 and ratified by all except for the United States. Article VI of the Act referred to the *Preservation and Improvement of Native Tribes*, and stated inter alia "All the powers... bind themselves to watch over the preservation of the native tribes". Bruce Fetter, editor, *Colonial Rule in Africa: Readings from Primary Sources*, (University of Wisconsin, Madison 1979) pp. 34 - 38.

chain natives for certain offences was indulged in to the extreme by practically every member of the police force in the most trivial cases of complaint by masters, and it is known that numerous assaults were committed on native women, and, for the most part, went unnoticed or unpunished. The natives were thus kept in a state of abject fear, and no opportunity of redress was open to them, as they dared not go to the police with their complaints. They had been dispossessed of such cattle as survived the rebellion of 1904, and of their lands. The law forbade them possessing great stock; and deprived of their accustomed form of sustenance, they were forced to accept work at a wage which was ridiculously inadequate and which was often never paid. They were subjected to forced labour of the worst kind, and the masters regarded their native servants as slaves without rights and amenable only to the lash. The servants regarded their German masters as their inveterate enemies from whom there was no escape.

This was the position as I found it when, in July 1915, I was entrusted with the task of putting the affairs of this Protectorate in order. The endeavour to secure the establishment of better relations between white and black has been uphill work indeed. All the obnoxious provisions in the German native code have been repealed by me and others more in keeping with the practice in force in the Union of South Africa have been substituted. The love of inflicting severe corporal punishment on their native servants is, however, strongly retained by the German farmers, and though clearly diminishing as the result of numerous convictions obtained in our courts, cases still occur with far too much frequency. I am satisfied that, owing to the wide extent of the country, the scattered situation of the farms, and the fact that here and there natives are still terrorized, and therefore reluctant to lodge complaints, many cases never reach the courts.

The natives, freed from the oppression under which they had suffered for 25 years before our advent into this country, and in their simple way of thinking unable to understand why after having conquered the Germans here we did not utterly despoil them of their property, have also since the Occupation provided a considerable amount of difficulty for the Administration. The terms under which the German forces of South-West Africa capitulated in July 1915 provided that the civil population and the reservists then under arms would be allowed to resume their normal avocations, and at once there arose throughout the Protectorate a strong demand for native labour.[5] The natives, after the ill-treatment to which they had been subjected by their former employers, were in a very large number of cases most reluctant to accept service, and much patience has been required to teach them that it is necessary to work to live and that the liberties they now enjoy also carry obligations, and that while our officials afford protection to all and assist every labourer to secure fair

---

[5] For more detail see Gerald L'Ange, *Urgent Imperial Service: South African Forces in German South West Africa: 1914 - 1915*, (Ashanti Publishing: Rivonia 1991) pp. 322 - 329.

treatment and a fair wage, it is incumbent on them to perform their labour in a proper manner.

The native policy now in force here has been based largely on the practice of the Transvaal, and under it it is our endeavour, in order to reduce vagrancy and crime amongst the native population, to see that every able-bodied native who has no visible means of support is in some kind of employment. At first there were constant representations from the farming community that no labourers were forthcoming. Natives had deserted right and left from the farms on which they had been located before our troops occupied the country. There was a strong disinclination in many cases to re-engage with former masters, and when engagements were entered into refusals to remain were frequent. The knowledge, however, that we do not tolerate the ill-treatment of natives and that our curts make no distinction, where an offence has been committed, between white and black, has gradually spread, and that knowledge, coupled with the fact that heavy sentences have from time to time been imposed on Europeans for offences against natives when such have come to light, has done much to reassure the native mind, and the situation has become easier of late, though there still is an undoubted shortage of labour, which seemingly cannot be made good out of the existing native population. A case of "chickens coming home to roost!" And we have seen the spectacle of the Luderitzbucht Diamond Mining Companies from 1908 to 1914 importing thousands of coloured labourers from the Cape of Good Hope at great expense and at a high rate of wages, because the Protectorate could not supply sufficient labour from within its own borders, where but a few years before over 90,000 native lives had been ruthlessly sacrificed.

It goes without saying that the present native policy is strongly disapproved of by the German inhabitants of this country. It has been frequently and openly stated by German farmers that our permanent stay in this country might prove tolerable were our native policy altered to suit their views. They bitterly resent any curtailment of the rights they formerly exercised to punish how and when they pleased. For some months after the close of the campaign constant applications were received from Germans for the return to them of the firearms they had surrendered "in order to afford them protection from the natives." About November 1915 alarming rumours were set in circulation by Germans that a rising by the natives was imminent and that no European's life would be safe.[6] We were besought on all sides to provide protection. Confidential inquiries which were set on foot shewed not a shadow of substance for these reports, and I declined to move, as I was certain that these stories were deliberately spread for the purpose of coercing me into allowing the farming population to have firearms with which again to menace their native servants.

In Part II., Chapter III., will be found a statement of the number (35 in all),

---

[6] Following the German surrender there were consistent rumours amongst the settler population that the Herero and Nama were planning an insurrection. J.B. Gewald, *Herero Heroes* (James Currey: Oxford 1999) pp. 237.

and description of serious cases (*i.e.*, cases necessitating trial before the chief tribunal of the Protectorate, the Special Criminal Court) of murders of, and assaults on, natives by Europeans since our Occupation. On the other hand, there have been but two cases of a similar kind where natives were involved with Europeans, and in one of those cases there was a suggestion that the Europeans ahd been tampering with the natives' womenfolk.

In the lower courts no fewer than 310 cases of ill-treatment of native servants by their masters have been heard and penalties imposed since the establishment of those courts on 20th September, 1915.

A letter full of interest on this question of native treatment in the event of the return of Germany to power in South-West Africa came into my hands some time ago. It was addressed to the late Governor of this country, who is a present on parole, by one of the principal ex-officials (also on parole) of the late Administration, and it contained a number of speculations as to the future of the Protectorate and the measures to be adopted "on resumption of control by the German Government." A considerable portion of it was devoted to the discussion of future native policy. The writer urged the need for the organization as soon as peace is declared of a strong force of police to cope with the natives, and ventured the opinion "that it is an open question what impression will be made on the natives by the re-transfer of power to the German authorities." He strongly blamed the present German inhabitants for frightening the natives *with constant threats of thrashings and hangings as soon as German rule is restored.*

It is common knowledge to the officials of the Administration that such threats are often made, as they have formed the subject of frequent complaints by natives and numerous convictions in our courts.

He went on to advocate the limitation to the utmost of the movement of natives from farm to farm or district to district, and, in order to improve the native labour supply, that Ovamboland should be effectively occupied.

To that country the Germans had never really penetrated. The climate is malarious, and between Outjo, Tsumeb, and Grootfontein lies a wide stretch of waterless country difficult to pass.

He added that if Germany failed to do this her prestige amongst those tribes (which it should be noted are still intact) in the north and north-east would cease. He concluded by stating —

> It is a well-known fact that some of our countrymen have not always acted in manner free from objection. Unreliable men of this kind in an out-of-the-way colony of the German Empire are not merely insufferable but they are a danger. Such persons must be removed without any consideration. If no criminal proceedings can be instituted against them banishment should be the punishment ... The Government should refuse them assistance, and it is precisely in the rendering of assistance in procuring native labour, to which a blunt refusal must be given and may be given, that a weapon is available to make them tired of the country.

He had been learning the lesson of the past; but I fear that however heartily the German colonists would endorse his views on the subject of the control of the natives and the anticipated spoliation of Ovamboland, but few supporters would rally to his cry for the ejection of farmers who ill-treat their servants. Their sole idea is complete domination over every one who has a dusky skin.

In the suggestion that farmers who are guilty of constant ill-treatment of their native servants should be denied native labour he is, apparently unconsciously, merely repeating what His Excellency the German Governor had already, so long ago as 1912, threatened to do. This threat was contained in a secret letter, now in my possession, from the Governor to all the District Heads, and a translation is reproduced in Chapter XXII. The words of the Governor in that letter contain what will probably be considered as the most damning piece of evidence of all that has been collected as to the point to which the ill-treatment of natives had been carried.

He admitted therein that the natives did not obtain justice in the courts, expressed his regret that he was powerless to influence the courts to improve matters, and threatened by administrative means to stop the native labour supply of persons who continually ill-treat their servants.

His Excellency was then new to the country, and as the threatened rising of the natives of which he had fears did not take place he seems to a certain extent to have accommodated himself to local conditions, for on 20th April 1914 we find that he presided over a meeting of the District Heads and other principal officials of the colony at Windhuk, whereat *inter alia* the following exchange of views took place. These are taken from the confidential minutes of the meeting:–

The Governor: By virtue of the von Lindequist Ordinances we have at present a kind of compulsory labour. An extension of this compulsion as desired by the Landesrat[7] would hardly have any prospects of fulfilment at home ... The question arises whether any alteration of the von Lindequist Ordinances is necessary and if such alteration would serve any purpose. In my opinion an improvement in the present conditions is not possible.

Bezirksamtmannen[8] *Schultze* and *Boehmer* and *Court Assessor Weber* declare the Ordinance to be sufficient.

Bezirksamtmann Wasserfall: ... In the district the continuous increase in the number of native stock has proved very detrimental. (*Note*. He obviously means that through the increase in the sheep and goats which the natives were allowed in special cases to own, the natives are becoming independent again).

The Governor: It will become necessary to force the natives to sell small stock which they possess beyond a certain number ...

The Governor: It is far more necessary to enforce strict adherence to the existing provisions of the Ordinances than to issue new provisions. I declare it to be the general opinion of this meeting that nothing should be altered, but strict adherence should be enforced; especially in the case of natives

---

[7] Legislative Council.
[8] 'Magistrates' They are also referred to in the text as District Heads

who appear at any police station it must at once be ascertained exactly from whence they have come (? So that they may be placed out to labour).

At a certain stage in the proceedings *Bezirksamtmann Boehmer* of Ludertizbucht ventured the opinion that fines and imprisonment might be admitted in cases of disciplinary punishments instead of the lash and manacles, but this received no endorsement from anyone else.

Bezirksamtmann Schultze represented that it was very necessary to take energetic steps against the Bushmen, and urged that the only efficient measure would be to transport them

The Governor (evidently thinking of public opinion in Germany) retorted that this would be impossible.

Bezirksamtmann von Zastrow, of Grootfontein: It might serve the purpose if a portion of this people was transported. The rest would very soon become aware of this and would behave themselves accordingly as they fear removal from their native country more than death.

Bezirksamtmann Wellmann, of Swakopmund: An understanding should be arrived at with the Walfish Bay[9] authorities in respect of the return of natives (? who have sought refuge there) who have committed a breach of their labour contracts.

The Governor: I am afraid that any such discussions would be unsuccessful.

Bezirksamtmann Wellmann then referred to the practicability of extending the contracts of service of Ovambos who had come south to seek work, and he also urged that corporal punishment should be introduced for native women who loaf about the locations without employment.

The Governor: The extension of the service contracts system to the Ovambo would be risky. The whole labour question in East Africa came about through an attempt of that kind. The utmost care must be exercised with regard to the banishment of the Bushmen to Swakopmund as a lot of them have already died in consequence of their removal there.[10] The main reason for this is that they are entirely unaccustomed to the food. (*Note.* – He should have added, "and climate which is damp and foggy and totally unlike the hot and dry area in the interior which is inhabited by the Bushmen.") It is necessary that the Bushmen be first made accustomed to the new food somewhere inland before they are removed to Swakopmund.

These extracts from the discussion do not betoken much desire to improve the lot of the natives of the country, though there is a note of alarm at the suggestion to bring the Ovambos under the labour contract system and an indication of some solicitude for the unfortunate Bushmen who were being sent to their deaths on the cold and bleak sand wastes of Swakopmund.

Of almost equal interst and value to Governor Seitz's secret letter are the letters reproduced in Part II., Chapter II,. From *Bezirksamtmann* Boehmer, of Luderitzbucht, and Acting *Bezirksamtmann* Heilingbrunnner, the first written

---

[9] From 1878 Walfish Bay was administered by the Cape Colony and from 1910 the South African Union, as such it provided a safe haven for refugees fleeing German rule. Gewald, *Herero Heroes*, pp. 177 - 8, 181, 190.

[10] For more details see: Robert Gordon, *The Bushman Myth: The Making of a Namibian Underclass*, (Westview Press: Boulder 1992) pp. 49 - 98, particularly pp. 70 - 72 & 82.

on 31st January, 1908, the second on 14th June 1911, and the third on the 21st April 1913. These are contained with a number of other letters in a dossier in the German records, marked *Misshandlungen von Eingeborenen durch Weise (Specialia)*.[11] ("Ill-treatment of natives by white men – Particulars) Matters had evidently reached a climax when in 1913 Herr Boehmer was forced to write to the Imperial Governor that "the law courts are utterly useless".

Another extremely objectionable feature in the social fabric of the Protectorate moulded by the Germans has been the licentiousness in the relations between the European male population – soldiers, police, and others – and native women, regardless of objections to such intercourse on the part of the women themselves and their male relatives. With the destruction of the tribal system which followed the events of 1904-1905, and the distribution of the surviving population as labourers amongst the European settlers, native women in large numbers were forced into concubinage with Europeans, with the inevitable result that the natives speedily acquired a contempt for their masters, who in turn have endeavoured to maintain their positions by a policy of severity often amounting, as a perusal of the report will show, to the grossest brutality.

As a colonist, the German in South-West Africa, speaking generally, has been a failure. He has never shown the slightest disposition to learn the natives' point of view, to adapt his ideas to the long-established customs and habits of the people, or to fall in with the ways of the country. When he arrived here he found the natives both rich and comparatively numerous. His sole object seemed, as soon as he felt strong enough, to take the fullest advantage possible of the simplicity of these people and despoil them utterly. When the process did not, by means of the system of trading that sprang up, k which in itself was often but a thinly disguised form of chicanery and knavery, go quickly enough, rapine, murder, and lust were given full play with the disastrous results of which we see evidences every day around us.

This is all the more strange, as in the Cape of Good Hope and Natal German settlers have proved themselves, at all events in years past, adaptable and successful colonists. Possibly the reason may be found in the fact that in those British possessions the German emigrant found a clean-cut line and well-defined understanding between the European element and the aborigines. As a pioneer on his own account in savage lands, and as a colonist left to his own devices without the influence and advice of persons of other nationality who have had longer colonial experience than he has had, he has proved himself, at all events in South-West Africa, to be utterly incapable and unsuitable.

The land here, when colonizing was decided on in earnest in Berlin, and after the missions, companies, and traders had been allotted their selected portions, was at first given out, for the most part, to soldiers who had taken their

---

[11] The three files under this title are still held in the National Archives of Namibia and contain details of investigations covered 1908-1914 (NAN ZBU 2054).

discharges in this country and had expressed a desire to settle her; rough men who, when released from the military organization under which they had been trained, carried with them to their new possessions the militarist methods and aggressive ideas towards the natives with which they had become imbued during their term of active service here. In their view the native was an out-and-out barbarian, little better than the baboons, which frequent the kopjes, and to be treated and disposed of at the sweet will of the master. The police, too, brought up in the same environment and drawn from the same organization, were no different. If anything they were worse, as they were principally selected from the non-commissioned ranks of an army in which the severity of the sergeant is proverbial.

Later, when the rough work was deemed to have been completed, officialdom in Berlin bethought itself of a German colonial aristocracy. It is said locally that the Kaiser took a deep personal interest in the matter, and that to his influence we owe the presence of the large number of persons of rank who are settled in the better portions of the Protectorate. If one can believe the tales that are circulated by the less favoured portion of the Germancommunity about their more distinguished brethren, amongst the latter were included no inconsiderable proportion of persons who were no ornament to the caste to which they belonged.

It is interestingto read what Leutwein, who was Governor of this territory for 11 years, has to say on the attempts of Germany to establish colonies. In Chapter XV., pages 542, 543 and 544 of the book he published after his recall to Germany, he remarks, referring the earlier avowed policy of Germany, which was one of attempting to "reconcilethe original inhabitants to their fate":–

> I have personally assisted in conducting this policy in perfect unanimity with the original population, all the more for the reason that the war with Witbooi had openedmy eyes at the very beginning of my colonial activity concerning the difficulties experienced in suppressing native risings in South-West Africa. Since that time I have used my best endeavour to make thenative tribes serve our cause and to play them off one against the other. Even an adversary of this poicy must concede to me that it was more difficult, but also more serviceable, to influence the natives to kill each other for us than to expect streams of blood and streams of money from the Old Fatherland for their suppression. That this policy has proved itself impossible of being carried through uninterruptedly for reasons which will be found in my forgoing expositions is, however, no proof that it should not have been tried at all.
>
> In this connection it will be interesting to review for a moment the British world-wide Empire. A census of the population in the same which was ordered in 1901, and the results which have been published a short while ago, has elicited the fact that of approximately 400 million subjects of the King of England, only 54 millions or 13½ per cent. Are whites, *i.e.,* that the latter are even less in numbers than the white subjects of the German Empire. In truth, it would certainly be worth while studying in what manner these 54 million whites within the British Empire succeed in dominating over the 350 millions natives. It appears impossible that this should be done on the whole by a policy of force and

suppression, as such a policy could not be carried through. There consequently only remainsthe supposition that the British understand better than ourselves how to interest the natives in their cause and to make them subservient to the same.

They seem to apply completely different systems, according to the character of their colonial territories and their inhabitants. We know, for instance, that in the Cape Colony, a country in which the suppression of native risings would present just as many difficulties as in our South-West Africa, they have simply made full citizens of the natives.[i]

Only when a native tribe would not accommodate itself to law and order, as, for instance, the robber-like Korannas, they have destroyed such tribe by armed force, but not without the assistance of the other native tribes.[12] Of course, they got rid of a portion of their restless Hottentot tribes by the immigration of the same into our present Protectorate, as we have seen in Chapter I., pages 1-3 (the Orlams).[13] However, in Basutoland, where a warlike tribe resides in a rather un-inviting and mountainous country, the English have been satisfied with nominal rule, and in order to prevent any disturbance have not permitted a white immigration into that country.[14]

In fact, it requires a special understanding of the usages and customs of the natives if a white race is to remain master in its own house under the numerical conditions as they exist in the British Empire. And unless a nation understands that art it should rather leave colonizing alone; for it will hardly experience joy therefrom.

I must in fairness say that there are notable exceptions to the general rule as we have found it here, men who take a keen and intelligent interest in their pursuits and in the welfare of the natives and who treat their natives reasonably; but their numbers, according to the information at my disposal, are relatively few. It is difficult to eradicate the pernicious influence of the adventurers who seem to have dominated the policy of this country in the earlier days of the establishment of German influence.

Enough should be found in this report to convince the most confirmed sceptic of the unsuitability of the Germans to control natives, and also to show

---

[i] He reproduces in a footnote a letter, dated Banksdrift (Transvaal), 25th January 1904, from a Herero, who had been recruited for the mines at Johannesburg, containing the following sentences, which he says proves that the writer has very quickly recognized the difference between English and German treatment of natives:

"I inform you that the country of the Englishman is really a good country; there is no ill-treatment; whites and blacks stand on the same level, and if he strikes you (unreadable) everywhere you like. And there is plenty of work and plenty of money, and even if your Baas is there, he does not hit you, but in case he hits you and has contravened the Law, he is punished accordingly.

---

[12] For more on the Koranna see: T. Strauss, *War Along the Orange*, (Cape Town 1979); Robert Ross, *Adam Kok's Griqua*, (Cambridge 1976) & M. Legassick, 'The Northern Frontier to c. 1840: The Rise and Decline of the Griqua People,' in R. Elphick and H.B. Giliomee, eds, *The Shaping of South African Society, 1652 - 1840*, 2nd ed., Cape Town, 1989)

[13] Page numbers as in original report.

[14] Basutoland is the present day Republic of Lesotho which is geographically situated within the Republic of South Africa. In 1868 the territory was annexed to the British Crown, in 1966 Basutoland ceased to exist and the independent Republic of Lesotho came into being. Richard P. Stevens, *Lesotho, Botswana, & Swaziland: The former High Commission Territories in southern Africa*, (Pall Mall Press: London 1967)

him what can be expected if the unfortunate natives of this part of Africa are ever again handed back to the former *régime*. For their pains in making the statements and for their share in furnishing the information that has been brought together herein, those whose names are mentioned and their associates would become – if, indeed, they have not already become – marked men, and their "removal" would only be matter of time. A campaign of smelling-out, the police sergeant as the witch-doctor, with all its attendant evils and horrors would most assuredly be inaugurated.

Native opinion here is unanimously against any idea of ever being handed back to the tender mercies of Germany, and any suggestion of the possibility of an act of that kind on the part of Great Britain produces the utmost consternation.

Before closing these introductory remarks, I desire to express my obligations to the compilers of the accompanying chapters for the assistance they have rendered. The framer of Part I. is Major T.L. O'Reilly (Attorney of the Supreme Court of South Africa, Transvaal Provincial Division), Military Magistrate of Omaruru in this Protectorate, to whom, owing to the extent of the ground to be covered, has fallen the larger share. Major O'Reilly has been here in an official capacity for nearly three years past and is well acquainted with the country and its inhabitants. Part II. Has been prepared by Mr. A.J. Waters, B.A., Crown Prosecutor for the Protectorate, who has been stationed here since October 1915. Both have attacked the tasks assigned to them with much assiduity, and beyond indicating to them the lines on which I wished them to proceed and exercising a general supervision over the work, the credit for any value this report may possess will be theirs.

E.H.M. Gorges[15]
Administrator
Government House,
Windhoek
South-West Africa
19th January, 1918

---

[15] Served as the first South African civilian Administrator of South West Africa from 1st November, 1915 to 30th September, 1920 (Taylor 1985: 4)

PART ONE

NATIVES AND GERMAN ADMINISTRATION

CHAPTER ONE

HOW GERMAN INFLUENCE WAS INTRODUCED INTO S.W. AFRICA

In her colonies the missionary has always been Germany's advance agent, and the pioneer of her trade. Later on, the missionary and the merchant have, hand in hand, paved the way for German influence, ascendancy, annexation, and government. It was a favourite saying of Prince Bismarck's that "the missionary and the trader must precede the soldier." Of this system South-West Africa is a striking example.

So long ago as the year 1814, the British Government (of the Cape of Good Hope) sent one Von Schmelen, a German missionary, to carry on mission work among the Hottentots[16], living across the Orange River, in Great Namaqualand. Von Schemelen settled at Bethany and, later on, having attached himself to the then rising clan of Afrikaner Hottentots, under Jager Afrikaner, he moved north with them. Jager Afrikaner made his headquarters in Southern Damaraland; his village was named Schemelen's Hope, in honour of this most adaptable of missionaries, who, having taken a Hottentot girl to wife, became an influential member of the tribe. The present town of Okahandja, near Windhuk, is said to be on the site of Schmelen's Hope.

Once he was firmly established, Von Schmelen appears to have forgotten all about the Cape Government. He placed himself in direct communication with Berlin. His reports on the country and its inhabitants, which, from time to time, reached Germany, had the result of attracting other German missionaries to South-West Africa.

Eventually, about 1840, the Rhenish Mission Society of Berlin began to take official notice of this new field for missionary labour and enterprise.[17] By the year 1867 thriving mission stations had been established at nearly every important centre in Great Namaqualand and Damaraland.

These good missionaries had to support and maintain themselves and families. They could only do so by combining religion with business. Accordingly,

---

[16] This term was used by early European travellers 'to refer to the indigenous people at the Cape of Good Hope'. The term is now seen as extremely offensive and the name 'Khoikhoi' is more commonly used. In the Namibian context the term 'Hottentot' was commonly used in historical texts to refer to people from various 'Nama' communities (Boonzaier, Emile, Candy Malherbe, Penny Berens and Andy Smith, *The Cape Herders: A History of the Khoikhoi of Southern Africa*, David Phillip/Ohio University Press, Cape Town & Johannesburg, Athens, 1996, pp. 1-2).

[17] The Rhenish Mission Society was established in 1828. Its first three missionaries to Namibia arrived at Jonker Afrikaner's capital at /Ai//Gams in December, 1842 (Dedering, Tilman 'Southern Namibia c. 1780-c.1840: Khoikhoi, missionaries and the advancing frontier'. PhD, University of Cape Town, 1989, p. 135; Hellberg, Carl-J. *Mission Colonialism and Liberation: The Lutheran Church in Namibia, 1840-1966*, New Namibia Books, Windhoek, 1997, p. 49.

it was found necessary to establish a general store, in conjunction with each mission station, from the profits of which the missionary could live. There the natives could obtain goods, clothing, arms and ammunition, and groceries in exchange for cattle and sheep and the products of the chase.

Whether this combination of shop-keeper and evangelist was calculated to have the best of spiritual results, in so far as concerns the simple savages, it is difficult to say. That progress was slow there can be no doubt, as it took 30 years of preaching and trading before the first Herero convert, a pious old lady of Otjimbingwe, forsook the worship of her ancestors and allowed herself to be baptized.[18] Report has it that her example was soon followed by many others.

As the field of missionary labour was extended, by the founding of new mission stations, it followed, under the circumstances, as a natural result, that the field for mercantile achievement expanded in proportion. In fact, the volume of mundane business by far exceeded the harvest from religious work.

In the early fifties of the last century, that is, about 10 to 12 years after the Rhenish Mission had commenced its labours, the monopoly was rudely broken by the intrusion of Cape Colonial cattle traders from the south. These new comers had no fixed stores. They "trekked" or "smoused"[19] about among the natives, selling or exchanging goods from their heavily laden ox-wagons and receiving cattle, sheep, and produce in exchange. Having disposed of their goods, they returned to the south and sold their cattle and sheep, at good profits, in the Cape markets. The missionaries felt this competition very keenly. Not only was it keenly felt, it was also deeply resented. The more so, because the majority of the rivals was composed of English traders (*grossenteils englische Händler*).[20] Moreover, these rivals were certainly not brother missionaries, as they are reported to have sold dop[21] brandy to the natives!

In 1860, or thereabouts, competition grew so keen that the missionaries decided on a determined effort to oust their adversaries. The trader from the Cape had the advantage of wagon transport, but this advantage was, to a certain extent neutralized by his great distance from his markets and the impossibility of replacing broken-down vehicles in those desert wilds. If the missions could only build and maintain in good repair on the spot a sufficiency of wagons and supply the necessary number of tradesmen to carry this out, half the fight was

---

[18] The first European missionaries, from the London Missionary Society settled in southern Namibia as early as 1806. The work of the Rhenish mission amongst the Herero is usuallly dated from 1844. By 1871 the mission claimed to have baptised 69 Herero converts (Dedering 'Southern Namibia', p. 149; Lau, Brigitte '"Thank God the Germans Came": Vedder and Namibian Historiography' in Brigitte Lau, *History and Historiography* (Discourse/MSORP, Windhoek, 1995, p. 54).

[19] To trek means to move around, especially by ox-wagon. To 'smouse' was to travel around trading. The word originally derived from Yiddish. In Afrikaans the word *smouse* means 'trader'.

[20] 'largely English traders'.

[21] The production of brandy in the Cape Colony doubled between 1865 and 1871 when a million gallons of brandy were being produced every year. Pamela Scully, 'Liquor and Labor in the Western Cape, 1870-1900', Ch. 2 in Jonathan Cruch and Charles Ambler (eds) *Liquor and Labor in Southern Africa*, Ohio University Press/University of Natal Press, Athens, Pietermaritzburg, 1992, p. 76

won. In this way it was hoped that the "thieving and lawless dealings"[ii] of the English traders would be effectively checked.

It was at this juncture that an inspired missionary suggested that, in addition to converting the natives, they should be taught "useful trades and handicrafts."[iii] The sympathetic Society thereupon arranged for certain competent artisans to migrate from Germany with their families and to settle at Otjimbingwe, the headquarters of the Mission.

The wagon-maker Tamm from Thuringen and the blacksmith Hälbich from Schlesien are worthy of a niche in history. They were the first real colonists of South-West Africa. Not as missionaries to convert, not as profit-seeking traders to exploit the native, but as honest workmen did they come with hammer and saw in hand, prepared to earn their daily bread by the sweat of the brow, to teach the dusky savage the dignity of labour, the usefulness of honest work, that *laborare est orare*.[22] Tamm and Halbich were followed shortly afterwards by two other tradesmen, whose names are not obtainable, and also by the merchant Redecker. The latter took over the general management of the Mission's stores. In due course wagons were built. Then it was found necessary to allow the colonists (Tamm, Hälbich and the unnamed two) to travel with loaded wagons among the natives and open up an opposition trade, under the auspices and with the blessing of the Rhenish Mission Society. They sold, so the records of the Mission inform us, "all things which the English traders sold except liquor." Yet, notwithstanding this, they could make little headway. The Cape traders more than held their own, and large droves of cattle found a yearly market in Cape Town and elsewhere.

The irritated missionaries ascribed their failure to the reason that their motto was "genuine goods and no humbug and cheating."

In 1864 war broke out between the Hereros and the Hottentots. The Hereros, led in battle by the English traders Frederick Green and Haybittel and the traveler Andersson, signally defeated the dominant Afrikaner Hottentots, under Jonker Afrikaner, and freed Hereroland (Damaraland) from Hottentot oppression.[23] As a result of this war the Hereros regained their territory and the independence which they had partially lost to the Hottentots over 25 years previously.

The war dragged on, however, and peace was not restored before 1870. In the

---

[ii] P. Rohrbach and German Mission Records.
[iii] P. Rohrbach and German Mission Records.

---

[22] 'To work is to be revered'.
[23] Jonker Afrikaner actually died on 18th August, 1861. His son and successor, Christian Afrikaner, died in an attack on Otjimbingwe on 15th July, 1863. Jan Jonker Afrikaner, another son, became the new leader. According to Brigitte Lau it was Andersson who gathered Herero at Otjimbingwe, insisted on the election of a Herero 'Paramount Chief' and even designed a flag for the 'Herero Nation' (Lau, Brigitte *Namibia in Jonker Afrikaner's Time*, Archea 8, Windhoek 1987, pp. 127, 129, 131, 133). An interesting insight into Andersson's perspectives on events during this period can be found in his diaries published as *Trade and Politics in Central Namibia, 1860-1864*, National Archives of Namibia, Windhoek, 1989.

meantime the missionaries, like their secular opponents from the Cape, specialized in the sale of arms and ammunition, and there is reason to believe that a very brisk trade was carried on.

The active intervention of Green and other traders on the side of the Hereros was resented by the Hottentots. In 1868 a Hottentot raiding party plundered Andersson's store at Otjimbingwe, and also that of the Rhenish Mission. This sent the Mission's representatives post haste to Berlin, and in 1869 the Society petitioned the King of Prussia for protection. They asked for the establishment of a Prussian Naval Station at Walfish Bay. The King assured the missionaries of his warmest interst; but the outbreak of the Franco-Prussina war distracted further attention for the time being.

In 1870 peace between the Hottentots and Hereros was once more restored, and this stimulated the Mission to fresh interest in its trading ventures.[24]

It was then recommended by the missionary in charge that a special merchant should be appointed to trade "as a branch of the Rhenish Mission." This, however, did not look nice, and a Limited Liability Company (ostensibly a separate and entirely independent concern) was floated in Germany in 1873 for the purpose of trading "in the Mission fields of the Rhenish Mission Society." The Society undertook to give this company all the assistance and support possible, and in return therefore was to receive fifty per cent. (50%) of the net profits. A special proviso was also made to the effect that only devout persons (*Christlich gesinnte*) were to be sent out for work as managers and traders.

The Rev. Hugo Hahn, one of the prominent missionaries who had controlled the Otjimbingwe Station for some years, resigned on the establishment of this company. He also disbanded the labour colony and closed down the Industrial School. Mr. Hahn's contention was that the Mission could more strongly influence the natives by keeping trade under direct control.

The main object of the newly formed company was to develop the cattle business and open up an export trade to Europe. Owing, however, to the inevitable transport difficulties, the incapacity and, sad to relate, the dishonesty of the "Christianly minded" folk, who had come out to manage the business, very heavy losses were sustained. In six years these totaled over 200,000 marks (10,000*l*.), and the outbreak in 1880 of another Herero-Hottentot war ruined all hopes of recovery.[25] The company was hopelessly insolvent and went into liquidation.

---

[24] Lau argues that the Treaty is significant because it embodied the absolute decline of the earlier Afrikaner hegemony. It clearly stated "... that Kaptain Jan Jonker Afrikaner has obtained no right whatsoever to interfere or meddle with the affairs of the Herero people or their land, nor with foreigners living in or travelling among them" (Lau, *Namibia in*: pp. 140-141)

[25] In her introduction to *The Hendrik Witbooi Papers*, Brigitte Lau makes the point that the 1880 war is under-researched, but that to reduce the war to 'ethnicity' ie. 'another Herero-Hottentot war' is too simplistic. She argues that the period was actually marked by 'a very complex pattern of shifting, cross-ethnic alliances' (Lau, Brigitte 'Introduction' in Annemarie Heywood and Ebeb Maasdorp (trans), *The Hendrik Witbooi Papers*, Archeia 13, Windhoek, 1989).

In the interim an event of great importance had taken place. In the year 1876, a British commissioner, Mr. W.C. Palgrave, visited the country with a view to ascertaining the wishes of the native chiefs in regard to control by Great Britain, and also for the purpose of reporting to the Cape Government on the desirability or otherwise of "the extension of the limits of this Colony, on the West Coast of this continent, so as to include Walfish Bay and such tract of country inland as may be found expedient and approved of by Her Majesty" (*vide* Commission by Sir Henry Barkly, Governor of the Cape of Good Hope, to William Coates Palgrave, Esq., dated 16th March 1876).[26]

Palgrave was well received by the Herero people, who, on 9th September 1876, handed him a petition to Sir Henry Barkly, signed by 58 chiefs,[27] under chiefs, and headmen, in the course of which they say:–

> We want to live at peace with each other, and with our neighbours, and we want to have our country kept for us. We wish to see our children grow up more civilized than we have had any chance of being, and so, after many meetings amongst ourselves, we have agreed most humbly to ask Your Excellency to send someone to rule us, and be the head of our country ... We also most humbly ask that Your Excellency will everywhere make it known that the sea boundary to our country is in your possession, and that we have given you the right to such ground as may be required for its protection, as well as for the building of towns and villages in the vicinity of all landing places.

The Bastards of Rehoboth and several Hottentot tribes also asked for British protection and control.

In his report to the Cape Governor, Mr. Palgrave recommended the annexation, as British territory, of the whole coastline of Great Namaqualand and Damaraland, and the appointment of a British Resident in each of these areas. Instead of following this advice the British Government annexed, in 1878, only Walfish Bay, and a few square miles of desert sand in the immediate vicinity thereof.

Of this fact, German enterprise was not slow to take advantage. The next important step towards the extension of German influence and the acquisition of what Great Britain had apparently definitely discarded as worthless, is represented by the activites of Adolf Luderitz, a merchant, of Bremen, who arrived in the country in 1882.

From 1882 to 1890 the merchant missionaries were gradually reinforced by the professional merchants, and the work of building up German trade and influence, to the exclusion of Britain and the British, was recommenced with

---

[26] The report was published in 1877 (G50-'77). It has been reprinted as Palgrave, W.C. *Report of W.C. Palgrave, Esq., on his mission to Damaraland and Great Namaqualand in 1876*, State Library, Pretoria, 1869.

[27] At the same meeting, the English trader, Lewis presented the boundaries of Herero territory. He claimed that the southern boundary of 'Hereroland' at that time lay along a line from Rehoboth to the coast. A copy of the petition can be found in Palgrave's report (Stals, E.L. P. *The Commissions of W.C. Palgrave, Special Emissary to South West Africa, 1876-1885*, Van Riebeeck Society, Cape Town, 1990; Palgrave, *Report*; pp.41-42)

renewed vigour. This period is aptly described by Governor Leutwein as the days of the "Merchants' Administration" (*Kaufmannischer Verwaltung*), and deserves to be dealt with in some detail.

CHAPTER TWO

FIRST ACQUISITIONS OF LAND

It did not take Luderitz very long to discover that, after Walfish Bay, the bay at Angra Pequena (now known as Luderitzbucht) was the best port on the coastline between the Orange and the Kunene rivers.

By deeds of sale, dated 1st May and 25th August 1883, the chief of the Aman[28] Hottentots of Bethany, Joseph Fredericks[29], sold to Luderitz that territory which is situated between the 26th degree of Southern Latitude and the Orange River, bounded on the west by the sea and on the east by a line running 20 miles inland from north to south.

Early in 1884 a party of German scientists and prospectors visited Damaraland and Great Namaqualand, and inquired into the mineral and agricultural possibilities.

On the 24th April in the same year, Prince Bismarck, by telegram, formally sanctioned the hoisting of the German flag at Angra Pequena and placed Luderitz and his acquisition under the protection of the German Empire.

Greatly encouraged by these special marks of Imperial recognition, Luderitz went further afield, and on the 19th August 1884 he entered into another deed of purchase with the captain of the Topnaar Hottentots[30], who lived near Walfish Bay, whereby he acquired from that half-starved and improvident chieftain the proprietary rights in the remained of the coast belt from Degree 26 South to Cape Frio (hundreds of miles to the north), near the Kunene mouth. To avoid complications the area already annexed by the British at Walfish Bay was specially excluded. It is interesting to observe that the agent for Luderitz

---

[28] The agreement between Lüderitz and Josef Frederiks led to the sale of a coastal strip of 20 miles wide. Where Lüderitz took the mile to be a geographical or 'German' mile which is 7.4 kilometres in length, Frederiks took the mile to be 1.5 kilometres in length. Horst Drechsler, *Let Us Die Fighting*, (Akademie-Verlag: Berlin 1966) p. 23.

[29] Joseph Fredericks did on 20th October, 1890. His father (also named Joseph) had married a woman from the Witbooi community at Gibeon. When he had died, she married David Christian Fredericks who served as the leader at Bethanie whilst the young Joseph Fredericks was still young. David Christian Fredericks led a delegation from Bethanie on a year long visit to Britain and met Queen Victoria. An ongoing leadership dispute seems to have taken place between the descendents of Joseph Fredericks and the descendents of David Christian Fredericks. The second son of Joseph Fredericks, Paul Fredericks, was elected as 'Headman' following the death of his father in 1890 and remained 'loyal' to the German Administration during the 1904-1908 War. In contrast, Cornelius Fredericks, the grandson of David Christian Fredericks, led a guerilla unit that fought against the Germans [ADM 71 - 1341/2 'Acting Magistrate Bethanie to Secreatary for South West Africa, 28th August, 1922]

[30] Piet Haibib, sold a strip of land 20 geographical miles wide between 26 and 22 degrees. Drechsler, *Let Us Die Fighting*, p. 24.

on this occasion was one, J. Boehm, described as "the missionary of the Rhenish Mission at Walfish Bay," and that probably no one was better aware than was the said Boehm of the fact that the Topnaar chief might, with equal validity and right, have sold Australia to Luderitz.[iv]

Nevertheless, the agreements served their object. They were required for the purpose of inducing the German investor to participate in the schemes of Luderitz. Armed with these documents, Luderitz proceeded to Germany, where, in 1885, he succeeded in floating a company called the "German Colonial Company for South-West Africa," with a capital of 300,000 marks (15,000*l.*). (This company is not to be confused with the wealthy and entirely distinct German Colonial Company: *Deutsche Kolonialgesellschaft*).[31]

It was publicly stated in Germany at the time that the shareholders of the company had taken over his desert acquisition from Luderitz out of motives of pure patriotism in order that the country which might in the future prove valuable would not pass into the hands of a foreign Power.

Of the actual colonizing and constructive work done by this company with its 15,000*l.* capital, much need not be said, for the simple reason that nothing much was done.

Dr. Paul Rohrbach in his book[v] (page 223), says:–

> The mere idea of doing something substantial towards the opening up of a country like South-West Africa, with such ridiculously small working capital, is about as absurd as the idea of a man who would try to cut a tunnel through the Alps with a pickaxe. In fact, all that the company has done from the time it was founded up to the present time (1907) has been to sit on its land and mining rights and to wait until some one came along who was prepared to pay for them.

However true Rohrbach's statement may be, the fact remains that Luderitz received all the help he required from the German Government. On the 21st October 1885 the Government Controller of the newly formed company, Dr. Goering, arrived with the Secretary Nels, and the Police Superintendent Goldammer. Goering was a kind of commercial agent, with certain limited powers and jurisdiction over German settlers in the country, but with not the slightest authority to promise the protection of Germany to the natives. Aided by the missionary, Carl Büttner, Dr. Goering immediately proceeded, however, to make "Protection Agreements" with such native chiefs as he had persuaded to ask for the protection and good will of the Emperor. In return for such protection the chierfs were required to give Germans favoured-nation treatment, and they undertook to give no facilities or rights to others than Germans, without the Emperor's consent. Amongst these, Kamaherero, the chief of the Okahandja Hereros, styled "Chief Captain of the Hereros in Damaraland,"

[iv] The Hereros, hearing of this, on 29th December 1884 made a Deed of Cession of Hereroland to the British Crown (*See* Cape Blue Book, A.5-85).

[v] *Deutsche Kolonial-Wirtschaft*

---

[31] For more details see: Drechsler, *Let Us Die Fighting*, pp. 30 - 39.

entered into such an agreement on the 21st October 1885.[32] Writing of these agreements (which, owing to their importance, will be more fully dealt with later on) Governor Leutwein remarks, "those persons who promised this protection in the name of the German Emperor had not the slightest authority to do so." (*Elf Jahre Gouverneur*, page 13.)

It is of more than passing interest to South Africans to note that, in the very same year when the German flag was hoisted at Angra Pequena, a party of Transvaalers and Cape colonists, under the leadership of Willem Jordaan, purchased the whole of the vast area in the north which is now known as Grootfontein District, from the Paramount Chief of Ovamboland. At Grootfontein, Jordaan, in 1884, founded the Republic of Upingtonia, distributed farms to his burghers, drew up a constitution, had a Volksraad election, and became the first President.[33] In addition to the land rights, Jordaan had, with the approval of his people, acquired personal rights to all minerals in the rich area where the Tsumeb Copper Mine now is. In olden days the Bushmen had worked these mines on tribute to the Ovambo ruler, and their existence was well known. It is hardly necessary to state that this move greatly upset the ambitions of Luderitz and his associates, and that Jordaan's achievements were viewed with grave apprehension and distrust. The problem was solved in 1886 by the murder of Jordaan while on a journey through Ovamboland to Mossamedes. The Ovambo chief Nechale was responsible for this murder, but it was done, so Germans allege, at the instigation of Kamaherero, the Herero Chief of Okahandja, who nursed a grudge against Jordaan for having, some years before, helped the Hottentots against the Hereros. This may or may not be so. It is difficult to prove who was the instigator; but others had even greater interst than Kamaherero in the removal of Jordaan. The ever candid Dr. Rohrbach says, referring to Jordaan's death and the break up of the Republic, "Jordaan's settlement failed not for natural but for political reasons … the political situation was unfavourable."

As soon as Jordaan's death (1886) became known, Dr. Goering took steps to advise his followers at Grootfontein that the German Emperor could not for one moment tolerate the idea of a Boer Republic in "his territory." The awed and embarrassed Republicans packed up their goods and chattels and trekked off in all directions: some went back to the Transvaal and the Cape, while others joined the Boer colony at Humpata in Angola.[34] This was the end of Upingtonia.

It is not to be imagined that the British traders in the country viewed the work of Goering and his *Gesellschaft* with equanimity and indifference. On the contrary, every obstacle was placed in their way; but persons situated as the British traders were could not fight the new-comers on equal terms. Never-

---

[32] For further details see Gewald, *Herero Heroes*, pp. 31-32

[33] On the short-lived Republic see Gordon, *Bushman Myth*, pp. 40 - 42.

[34] On the subsequent fortunes of the settlers in Angola see: Gervase Clarence-Smith, *Slaves, Peasants and Capitalists in Southern Angola, 1840 - 1926,* Cambridge 1979

theless every effort was made, both by the Cape Government and the traders, to secure and retain British influence in the hope that the country would eventually be placed under British rule, thereby ensuring the destruction of German designs and ambitions not only on South-West Africa, but also on the whole of the sub-continent. The men on the spot saw the danger clearly, but it was neither understood nor appreciated in London.

In 1888 matters came to ahead and well nigh ended disastrously for the German agents. Teutonic writers appear to be unanimous in describing the event as "almost a political catastrophe." The prime cause of all the trouble was an English trader and prospector named Robert Lewis.[35] Germans confidently assert that Lewis was the paid agent and emissary of the late C.J. Rhodes.[36] In any event, Lewis, who had traded extensively throughout Damaraland and Great Namaqualand, was very popular with the natives and exercised considerable influence over the chiefs. In fact, when Mr. Palgrave visited the Hereros in 1876-1877 and received their request for British protection, Mr. Lewis and the missionary Brincker acted as interpreters for him at all the principal discussions. The one aim and object in the life of Lewis was to get the Germans out of the country.

On a certainday in 1888, at a meeting at the Herero headquarters, Okahandja, the old Chief Kamaherero, in the presence of his councillors' informed Dr. Goering that he recognized no German claims to control his country and his people. He gave Goering and his staff to understand that "if they did not wish to see their heads lying at their feet they should be out of Okahanda and well on their way to Germany before sunset."

Goering and company did not stand on the order of their going; they retired in haste and made for Otjimbingwe. There they hurriedly disposed of or packed all the copany's goods and fled in terror to Walfish Bay to the protection of the British Residency.

From Walfish Bay the fugitives proceeded to Berlin and appealed to the German Government for protection against the machinations of Lewis, who has been described as:–

> The agent in the country of Cecil Rhodes, who in all mannerof shameless ways and with matchless impudence carried on activities dangerous to the Commonwealth (Dove; Deutsch S.W. Afrika, page 14)

---

[35] Trader who worked particularly with Herero communities and was, reportedly, a fluent speaker of OtjiHerero. He was a close adviser of the Herero leader, Maharero, and even served as a member of his Council for a period of time. He actively discouraged Maharero from signing protection agreements with the Germans and instead urged links with the Cape Colony and the British Empire. He died in 1894 at the age of fifty after being mortally wounded by a leopard (Tabler 1973: 68-70)

[36] Much has been written on the imperial aspirations of Cecil John Rhodes, for example see: Ronald Robinson and John Gallagher with Alice Denny, *Africa and the Victorians: The Official Mind of Imperialism,* Second Edition, (Macmillan Education: London 1992, Chapter VII

Dr. Paul Rohrbach refers to Lewis as:–

> An English trader who had long lived among the Hereros and had from the very beginning been a most bitter enemy to the Germans. Lewis (continues Rohrbach) had so long practiced on Kamaherero and his peole with schnapps, promises, and all sorts of lies that the Hereros repudiated their agreement made three years previously with Dr. Goering.

It has already been pointed out on the evidence of Governor Leutwein that Dr. Goering had no authority to bind the German Crown to any agreements, and that therefore Lewis as a private individual had quite as much right as Goering to influence or deal with the Hereros.

If there were any question on this point, the reply of the Imperial German Chancellor to the further appeals for protection removes all possible doubt. The company and its fugitive representatives appealed for the "practical protection of the German Empire" to enable the company "to carry out and make effective their rights and interests in Damaraland." (At that time they had neither rights nor interests in Damaraland.)

To this the Chancellor replied (*see* C. von François, D.S.W.A., page 31):–

> That it could not be the function of the Empire, and that it lay outside the adopted programme of German colonial policy to intervene for the purpose of restoring, on behalf of the State, organizations among uncivilized peoples; and, by the use of military power to fight the opposition of native chiefs towards the not yet established business undertakings of German subjects in oversesea countries. He could therefore give no promise, on behalf of the Empire, that the peaceful pursuit of mining and suchlike undertakings in South-West Africa would be ensured by the military force of the Empire.

This declaration was hotly assailed in the German mercantile press, and the various companies and missionary societies created a great uproar.

In March 1889 the missionary Brincker of Okahandja (the gentleman who, with Lewis, had acted as interpreter for Commissioner Palgrave) wrote a strong letter of protest to the Chancellor, in the course of which he remarked:–

> To make agreements with Kamaherero is useless. It is like making agreements with a baby. Here the rights granted are of value only in proportion to the power behind the recipient. If a share of the treasure is to be assured a European Power must be established here, so that each case of arrogance on the part of the natives and each case of damage to vested interests may be punished. Under such protection the cattle-farming of the natives will develop, every European undertaking will be secured and the labour of the missionaries will prosper.[vi]

In conclusion, the enthusiastic Mr. Brincker ventured the opinion that 400 soldiers and two batteries of artillery would be required to achieve his ideals.

It will be interesting to observe how the cattle-farming of the natives actually did develop under "such protection." At the time Brincker wrote, the

---

[vi] Bundesarchiv Berlin, RKA 2105, H. Brincker, 13/3/'89, Reichskanzler Bismarck

Herero people possessed cattle which could be estimated in tens and, probably, in hundreds of thousands. Within 12 years after the furnishing of "such protection," the surviving Hereros did not possess an ox, a heifer, or a calf between them. They were forbidden by German laws to own large stock.

In view of the agitation in Germany following on his reply to the petitioners, the Chancellor somewhat modified his attitude, and later on in the year 1889 the first German soldiers, 21 in number under command of the brothers C. and H. von François, arrived in South-West Africa and marched to Otjimbingwe.[37] Captain C. von François left portion of his command at Otjimbingwe and hastened in person to Okahandja to pay his respects to Kamaherero. From Okahandja he proceeded on a similar mission to Omaruru to greet the Herero chief Manasse. He was, however, so icily received by both potentates that he returned in haste to Otjimbingwe, evacuated the place and fell back on Tsaobis on the main transport road to the coast, where he build a fort and awaited developments.

---

[37] Horst Drechsler points out that as there was no regular German shipping service to Namibia in 1889 the German troops had to travel on English ships and land at the British-controlled port of Walvis Bay. For this reason they had to pretend they were a 'group of explorers', rather than the vanguard of a colonial army. Drechsler, *Let Us Die*, p. 42

CHAPTER THREE

GERMANY'S DECLARED POLICY IN REGARD TO THE NATIVE RACES

In the year 1884, shortly after Prince Bismarck had cabled the Emperor's blessing and the protection of Germany to the merchant Luderitz at Angra Pequena[38], another event of great importance took place. In November of that year Prince Bismarck convened the famousBerlin-Congo Conference, which sat at Berlin until February 1885. Under Bismarck's guidance the Conference declared all equatorial Africa to be a kind of free trade area, grated France a large slice of the lower Congo, and, in addition to other decisions, made it the duty of all Colonial Powers to come to an agreement with one another on the occasion of fresh aggrandizements. "English colonial monopoly," states a German writer, "was thereby broken and a juster distribution of colonial possessions was at all events inaugurated."

The Conference went further, and before breaking up the conferring Powers solemnly and emphatically pledged themselves and placed on record their recognition of the sacred duty:–

Of preserving the aboriginal races of Africa.
Of watching over their interests.
Of cultivating their moral and material advancement and development

In July 1890, Germany was again very prominent at the Anti-Slavery Conference in Brussels, when it was placed on record by solemn pledge and resolution that it was the emphatic desire of the conferring Powers effectively to protect the native races of Africa from oppression and slavery.[39]

It is not to be wondered at, therefore, knowing what Germany's declared and avowed native policy was, that the statesmen and people of Great Britain had no hesitation in welcoming that Power into the arena of world colonisation as a co-partner in the great work of civilizing and uplifting the heathen races of the earth. It was apparently in this spirt and on those pledged assurances at

---

[38] The Portuguese name for a 'Small Bay'. The bay was apparently originally known in Khoekhoegowab as Nûi-doms. The small European settlement that grew up on the site was later renamed Lüderitzbucht (Lau, Brigitte *Carl Hugo Hahn: A missionary in Nama- and Damaraland, Part V: Register and Indexes*, Archeia 5, Windhoek, 1985, p 1243

[39] The Conference involving all the major colonial powers took place over an eight month period from July 1889 and was particularly concerned with efforts to stop the 'Arab' slave trade. Slavery had only been abolished in Brazil (the destination of many of the slaves exported from the Angolan coast) in 1888. Hochschild, Adam, *King Leopold's Ghost*, Papermac, Basingstoke and Oxford, 2000, pp.92-94

Berlin and Brussels that Great Britain allowed Germany to annex the 322,450 square miles of territory in South-West Africa, and by a stroke of the pen placed the Ovambos, Hereros, Damaras, Hottentots, Bastards, and Bushmen of that vast land under the guardianship and control of the German Emperor.

Referring to this event a German historian writes:–

> In consideration of the increasing expansion of German dominion, the first thing needful seemed to be a more definite determination of the German and English spheres of influence, so as to secure a firmer foundation for the civilizing labours of the two nations. With this object, the much-discussed Anglo-German Agreement was concluded, which extended to Africa and also brought the island of Heligoland, off the German coast, into the possession of Germany. The great value of this acquisition to the German Fleet and to the defence of the mouths of the Elbe, Weser, and Jade in now universally recognized (Historians' History of the World: Vol. XV., page 556)

After annexation had become an accomplished fact and German statesmen had done their work, true German opinion began to reveal itself and, not many years after annexation, the real German policy was made horribly manifest to the unfortunate natives of South-West Africa.

Commenting on this policy, the effects of which had never been so strongly evidenced as just after the second and last Herero rebellion in 1904, Dr. Paul Rohrbach, the accepted and candid oracle of German colonial policy (who in 1890 was a highly placed official in the German Colonial Office), writes as follows:–

The decision to colonise in South-West Africa could after all mean nothing else but this, namely, that the native tribes would have to give up their lands on which they had previously grazed their stock in order that the white man might have the land for the grazing of his stock.

When this attitude is questioned from the moral law standpoint, the answer is that for nations of the "Kultur-position"[40] of the South African natives, the loss of their free national barbarism and their development into a class of labourers in service of and dependent on the white people is primarily a "law of existence" in the highest degree.

It is applicable to a nation in the same way as to the individual, that the right of existence is justified primarily in the degree that such existence is useful for progress and general development.

By no arguments whatsoever can it be shown that the preservation of any degree of national independence, national property, and political organization by the races of South-West Africa, would be of a greater or even of an equal advantage for the development of manking in general or or the German people in particular, than the making of such races serviceable in the enjoyment of their former possessions by the white races. (Deutsche Kolonialwirtshaft, page 286.)[41]

---

[40] The 'law of existence'. A specific example of the way such thinking could be applied to particular ethnic groups in Namibia was recently cited by Robert Gordon. A Prof. Schultze writing about Namibia in *Die Deutsche Kolonialreich* in 1910 argued that "If we consider the natives according to their value as cultural factors in the protectorate, than one race is immediately eliminated right of: "The Bushmen" (Gordon, Robert, 'The stat(u)s of Namibian anthropology: a review', *Cimbebasia* Vol. 16, 2000, p. 4)

[41] Rohrbach, Paul, *Deutsche Kolonialwirtschaft*, Buchverlag der 'Hilfe', Berlin-Schöneberg, 1907.

CHAPTER FOUR

FIRST STEPS AFTER ANNEXATION

When, in 1890, Captain C. von François was formally appointed to act as Administrator of the newly annexed territory, he found matters in a very chaotic state. The *Kaufmännische Verwaltung* (Merchant Administration) of the fugitive Dr. Goering, who had now returned, had been wrecked by Robert Lewis. Von François had first to dispose of Lewis, and then by judicious application of honeyed words and the eating of more humble pie than was exactly desirable, if the prestige of the Fatherland were to be upheld, to mollify the ruffled natives and re-secure their adherence to the Protection Agreements.[42]

Lewis gave no further trouble. The annexation by Germany disposed of him, and it is reported that he left the country shortly afterwards.

Von François' position was extremely precarious, as he had only 21 soldiers. Moreover, contemporaneously with his arrival, war had broken out afresh between the Hereros under Kamaherero and the Hottentots, led by that wonderful character and fine soldier, Hendrik Witbooi,[43] the chief of the Kowese (Queen Bee) Hottentots.

Hendrik Witbooi and his father, the chief Moses Witbooi, refused from the outset to make any Protection Agreements with Goering or in any way to encourage a German influx. In fact, when in 1886 the missionary Rust, on behalf of Goering, presented a drafted and prepared agreement to Moses Witbooi merely for favour of signature, the old chieftain was so enraged that he closed the Mission church and forbade Rust to hold any further religious services there. He dispensed with the missionary and became High Priest of his own people, a practice which his son therefore, to try and negotiate with Witbooi, so Goering and von François turned their attention to Kamaherero. BY promising that the German Emperor would send soldiers to help the Hereros against Hendrik Witbooi, they eventually prevailed on Kamaherero to re-affirm the agreement of 1885 which he made with Goering and which on Lewis's advice he had repudiated in 1888.

---

[42] Lewis engaged in lengthy litigation in an attempt to get his investments back again. Unfortunately *real-politik* was such that Lewis never regained his investments. For further details see Gewald *Herero Heroes*, pp. 34-5

[43] Charismatic, extremely intelligent and talented Nama leader. Opposed to the coming of Imperial Germany. Attacked in 1893 by German forces. Cooperated with German forces between 1894 and 1904. He was killed in action in 1905. *The Hendrik Witbooi Papers*, Translated by Annemarie Heywood and Eben Maasdorp, annotated by Brigitte Lau, Second, revised edition, (National Archives: Windhoek 1995).

Goering immediately after this wrote to Hendrik Witbooi on 20th May 1890, from Okahandja, as follows:–

> To the Chief Hendrik Witbooi.
>
> I am informed from Namaqualand that it is yur intention to carry on the War against the Hereros and that you intend, as you have hitherto done, to destroy villages and steal cattle.
> The GermanGovernment cannot however tolerate your constant disturbance of the peace of a land and people which are under German protection, and whereby work, trade, and travel suffer.
> You will therefore be compelled by all means to restore Peace, which is necessary in the entire land.
> I request you to cease your interminable wars, make peace with the Hereros and return to Gibeon. I, or a Representative who will later succeed me, am prepared to intervene in order to restore Friendship. That the English Government is supporting us in our efforts to secure peace has been made plain to you, to your disadvantage, as they have stopped import of your munitions through British Bechuanaland.
> That the German Government possesses quite other powers to damage you, will be made plain.
> Therefore, I again earnestly request you to make Peace if you wish to preserve yourself, your land, and your people.

The concluding paragraph is worthy of note in view of what occurred shortly afterwards at Hornkranz.

Hendrik Witbooi received the letter and ignored it. The threats and the information therein conveyed did not fail, however, to make a deep impression. Accordingly, on the 30th May, Hendrik Witbooi wrote the following characteristic letter to his hereditary enemy, Kamaherero, at Okahandja[44]:–

> To dear Captain Maherero Tjamuaha.
>
> To-day I write to you in your capacity as the Paramount Chief of Damaraland, because I have received a letter from Dr. Goering which tells me great things and which has shown me the necessity of addressing you.
> From the contents of Dr. Goering's letter I hear and understand that you have placed yourself under German protection, and that thereby Dr. Goering has acquired full influence and power to order and arrange things and to interfere in the affairs of our land, even to intervene in this war which of old existed between us. You astonish me and I greatly blame you because you call yourself the Paramount Chief of Damaraland and that it true. Because our arid country has only two names "Damaraland" and "Namaland" that is to say Damaraland belonging to the Herero nation and is an independent nation and is an independent kingdom, and Namaland belongs only to all the red coloured nations in independent kingdoms, just as the same is said of the lands of the white people, Germany, England, and so on.
> They are independent kingdoms and all the different nations have their own heads

---

[44] The original is in the archives of the Evangelical Lutheran Church in the Republic of Namibia, V. *Politischen Briefe etc., 1879-1892.* 'Hendrik Witbooi at Hornkraans, 30/5/90 to '*Wel geliefde Kapitein Maharero Tsamaua*'. Gewald *Herero Heroes* pp. 39-40

and each head has his own land and people, over which he alone can rule, so that no other person or chief can order or compel him ... For in this world each Head of a nation is merely the representative of our Almight God and stands responsible alone to that God, the King of all Kings, the Lord of Lords, before whom we all, who live under the Heavens, must bend the knee ...

But, dear Captain, you have now accepted another Government; you have surrendered to that Government in order to be protected by another human Government from all dangers, chiefly and foremost to be protected from me in this war... You are to br protected and helped by the German Government, but dear Captain do you appreciate what you have done? ... You have looked upon me as a hindrance and a stumbling block (steen des aanstoots) and so you have accepted this great Government ir order to destroy me by its might ... but it appears to me that yu have not sufficiently considered the matter, having in view your land and people, your descendants who will come after you and your Chieftain's rights. Do you imaging that you will retain all the rights of your independent chieftainship after your shall have destroyed me (if you succeed)? [sic] That is your idea, but dear Captain in the end you will have bitter remorse, you will have eternal remorse, for this handing of your land and sovereignty over to the hands of white people.

Moreover, our war is not so desperate that you should have taken this great step (here Witbooi recapitulates the reasons for the war and the steps which will bring about peace and points out that he and Maherero are competent to make Peace, in the same way as they are competent to make war, without "outside interference"), but notwithstanding all this, I do hope that our war will end and will be succeeded by Peace? But this thing which you have done, this giving of yourself into the hands of white people for government, thinking that you have acted wisely, that will become to you a burden as if you were carrying the sun on your back. I cannot say whether you have sufficiently pondored over and whether you actually understand what you have done by giving yourself into German Protection.

I do not know whether you and your Herero nation understand the customs and laws and policy of this Government, and will long remain in peace and content thereunder. You will not understand and will be dissatisfied with Dr. Goering's doings, because he will not consult your wishes or act in accordance with your laws and customs. This you will discover too late however as you have already given him full powers.

Continuing, the old Hottentot statesman adds that the Hereros and Germans were never friends, and that this agreement between them is made merely "to destroy me as Herod and Pilate of old banished their differences and enmities and combined in order to remove the Lord Jesus." In conclusion, Witbooi hopes that he will never descend to such "unbelief and little faith" as to rush for protection for himself and his people to any other than the "Lord of Heaven ... the best Protector." (This letter is quoted by several German writers, and is copied into H. Witbooi's journal, which is in the writer's possession. There is no doubt as to its authenticity.)[45]

---

[45] Witbooi's notebook containing copies of his correspondence was captured at Hornkranz in 1891 by the Germans. Most recently republished, in an English translation, as *The Hendrik Witbooi Papers*. Translated by Annemarie Heywood and Eben Maasdorp, annotated by Brigitte Lau (Windhoek, 2nd edition, 1995).

Lengthy extracts from a lengthy letter are quoted, because the words of the chief explain the Hottentots' instinctive mistrust of the Germans and indicate the only reason why the Hereros accepted German protection.

The independent and liberty-loving Hottentots wished to remain entirely free and unrestricted by foreign Governments. The proud and peacefully disposed Hereros, on the other hand, regarded the Hottentots on their suouthern flank as a standing menace to the security of their large droves of cattle. The Herero lived for, and practically worshipped, his lowing herds. His traditions, religious ceremonies, and national rites necessitated that he should own cattle, the more the better. Cattle spelt power to him in this world and felicity in the next. It was to preserve his cattle, therefore, tht the Herero accepted German protection; for was he not told that the mighty German Emperor would send troops to annihilate the Hottentots and give him peace? This promise, like all German promises made to the natives, was never kept. It was not seriously made; it was merely a trick. When, in after years, the German Emperor did send his armeid to Hereroland, they came for quite another purpose.

Having unburdened his views on the Germans to Kamaherero, Hendrik Witbooi showed what he though of Dr. Goering's demands by prosecuting his war[vii] against the Hereros with renewed vigour and invincible determination. The harassed Hereros looked in vain to von François for the promised German military assistance. What could von François do? He only had sufficient troops to form a personal bodyguard, and there was no immediate prospect of reinforcements for offensive purposes; in fact, he could not venture to ask for any, as his definite instructions from Berlin, when he landed, were "to take no sides but to remain strictly on the defensive."

Eventually von François, driven nearly to desperation by the taunts and recriminations of his Herero allies, decided to pay a personal visit to Hendrik Witbooi at the latter's village at Hornkranz. The old chief, who in all his wars regarded the persons and property of the white people as sacred, received von François coolly but courteously. With his usual thoroughness, Hendrik Witbooi caused the minutes of their interview to be carefully entered in his journal by his secretary. A few extracts from this delightful exchange of views will not be out of place here.

The meeting took place on 9th June 1892.

(1) Address of the German Captain Commissioner (his words) to Captain Witbooi:–

> I have heard many things about you from white people and also from Bastards. I hear that you always restore any property of white people or Bastards which may fall into your hands, as they take no part in this war ... This pleases me greatly and I approve of your friendliness, your just acts and your wisdom, in that yu injure or prejudice no one who takes no part in this war ... but here are very many

---

[vii] It appears that this war originated owing to the murder of certain Hottentot horse-dealers by the Okahandja Hereros, and that Witbooi was not on this occasion the aggressor.

complaints concerning the Hereros on account of their stupid and unlawful acts ...The Government has asked me what should be done, so I replied and said that first of all I will go to Hendrik Witbooi and speak to him. Therefore have I come to you, in order to speak. I have come as a friend to give you good advice, and to ask you if you will not as all[viii] the other chiefs of this land have done, namely, to put yourself under German protection ... In the next ship Europeans will arrive and these people must be protected, and the German Government is pledged to protect all who come under its protection ...

(2) The Chief (Hendrik Witbooi) answers:–

Yes, I have heard of your coming and of your intentions... In the first place are your people sent here by the German Emperor?

(3) Von François replies:–

Yes, we gave have been sent by the German Government. Dr Goering was sent and I am now his successor and have my official capacity.

(4) Chief Hendrik Witbooi says:–

In the second place allow me to ask you what is protection? And from what are we to be protected? From what danger and difficulty and trouble is one chief protected by another?

(5) Von François answers:–

From the Boers and the other strong nations who wish to force their way into this land. They wish to come and live here and work and do as they please, without asking permission from the chiefs of the land. Even now on my journey I met with Boers who have already arrived and wish to approach on the side where Willem Christian is. But because they know that his land is already under Germany's Protection they have neither power nor right to enter: and, chief, you must clearly understand that the chiefs will not be deprived of their rights and laws. The chief (Witbooi) will have jurisdiction over his own people as is the case with the chief at Rehoboth.

The Chief (Witbooi) says:–

So, I understand it. To me it is a matter of wonder and impossibility, and I cannot conceive that a chief, being an independent chief and ruler over his own land and people (for every chief is this), able to defend his people against all danger or threats... can, if he accepts protection from another, still be regarded as a chief, as an independent chief...Everyone under protection is a subject to the one who protects him...Moreover, this Africa is the land of the Red chiefs (i.e. Hottentots) and when danger threatens a chief, and he feels he is unable alone to oppose such danger, then he may call upon his brother chief or chiefs of the Red people, and say. "Come brother or brothers and let us stand together and fight for our land Africa and avert this danger which threatens our land" for we are the same in colour and manner of life, and although divided under various chiefs, the land is ours in common.

[viii] This is a deliberate misrepresentation.

CHAPTER FOUR

(7) Von François replies:–

> Yes, what the captain has just said is right and true; I myself could never do that, I mean agree to stand under another chief; but the captain must well understand that he is not being forced to submit to protection; it is left to his own free will and choice and the captain should consider and ponder over it…
>
> (At this juncture von François points out that only people under German protection will be allowed rifles and ammunition, and that it would be pathetic to see Witbooi's "brave and efficient" men fighting their enemies with the butt ends of their guns owing to lack of powder and shot. He also volunteered the information that Witbooi's wars with the Hereros had so riveted the attention of all the nations of that world that the "Germans, English, Russian, Spanish, and Italian nations" have unanimously decided to prohibit further export of munitions to the country.)

(8) This news intensely annoyed Hendrik Witbooi, who remarked that he was quite unable to "praise" such a decision, and a long discussion followed as to the justice of such a step.

(9) After a time the German Commissioner got a chance to speak again, and said:–

> I think the chief can now, after all is aid and done, make peace with the Hereros. In the last battle he gave them a severe knock on the head, a fact which greatly delighted and pleased me, because the war hinders everything… and if, after the chief makes peace with the Hereros, they again try to do anything wrong to your people, the German Government will take care to prevent it and it will not take so long to do that as the chiefs' war has taken – but it will all be over in 14 days.

In reply to this feeler the chief deftly evaded further discussions by reverting to the question of arms and ammunition; he resolutely refused to discuss peace.

Shortly afterwards the German Commissioner left, his errand having been fruitless, he thought. Yet Hendrick Witbooi had received a great shook. For the first time it dawned upon him that his country had been annexed by Germany with the consent of England, and that he, the Paramount Chief of Great Namaqualand, was a German subject.

He was not slow to decide what steps to take in his own interests and those of his people.

Goering had stated in his letter of May 1890: "I again earnestly request you to make peace if you wish to preserve yourself, your land and your people." And the hint of Von François about the Europeans who would arrive in the next ship did not fall on deaf ears. Witboot decided to open peace negotiations with the Hereros through the mediation of Bastard chief at Rehoboth, and by August1892, a formal treaty of peace had been signed.[46] He also decided to send a protest to the British Government, through the Magistrate at Walvis Bay.

---

[46] See Gewald, *Herero Heroes*, pp. 52-54.

CHAPTER FIVE

THE MASSACRE AT HORNKRANZ

For the first 12 months after the annexation the German Government had left von François practically to his own resources, and nothing definite was decided on in regard to the occupation and settlement of South-west Africa. In the beginning of 1891 the great *Kolonialgesellschaft*,[47] or Colonial Company, began to move, and inquiries were instituted through the German missionaries on the spot as to whether it would pay to retain and develop the country.

To this the Mission Inspector, Dr. Buttner, replied ...

> (Von François, D.S.W.A.)
> "Damaraland[48] is a key (gate) to South Africa which we should not let pass out of our hands." He also went on to advise that "the troops should intervene," that "the best the to beat Hendrik Witbooi would be to attack him when, after one of his usual defeats by the Hereros, he is retreating to the south." Dr. Hopfner reported (referring presumably to the Hereros) that "if the German Empire would not or could not give the guaranteed protection to the natives, and if the troops had to tolerate the reflections cast upon them (as would appear from reports in the press), it would be better to surrender the land at once."

The German Colonial Company decided to follow Buttner's views, and in May 1891 the following resolution was passed at a meeting held in Berlin:–

> That this meeting regards the Colony of South-west Africa as one of the most valuable German dependencies. Owing to its situation that colony is destined to secure to German influence its decisive position in South Africa. The favourable climate and the available uninhabited areas make settlement by German farmers and agriculturists possible on a large scale. In order to promote the development of the colony in the right direction and to utilise for the benefit of the Mother-country all the advantages there to be derived, the Imperial Colonial Administration should come to the help of the spirit of German enterprise by securing peace there and the establishment of an organised administration. This meeting gives utterance to the conviction that the costs of an established Government on the lines followed by the English in Bechuanaland[49] will very soon be covered by the revenues of the colony.

---

[47] A shortened name for the German South West Africa Company – *Deutsche Kolonial Gesellschaft für Südwestafrika*

[48] Name previously applied to Hereroland; 'Dama' being the Khoekhoegowab word used to refer to 'black' people irrespective of ethnicity

[49] The territory of Bechuanaland became a British protectorate in 1885, and in 1966 it became the independent Republic of Botswana. Stevens, *Lesotho, Botswana, & Swaziland*, pp. 112 - 172

CHAPTER FIVE

To this the Chancellor, Count von Caprivi (who had succeeded Prince Bismarck) replied to the effect that the present position was very unfavourable, but that, in view of the fact that it was hoped, shortly to form a new and strongly financed company, and also that the financial resources of the Colonial Company of South-West Africa would probably be increased before long, he would hold out a possibility, if the contingencies mentioned came to pass, of compliance with the wishes of the *Kolonialgesellschaft*, as expressed in the resolution.

Early in 1892, in view of the continued war between Witbooi and the Hereros, the German garrison in the country was increased to 200 troops. Again the Hereros expected active help in terms of promises made, but none was forthcoming. Von François preferred to make the personal visit to Witbooi of which details were given in the preceding chapter to congratulate Witbooi on his victories and to endeavour to persuade him, like his Herero enemies, to accept German protection. While resolutely refusing to entertain any German offers of protection or peace mediation, Hendrik Witbooi and his people were careful to maintain personal friendship with the new-comers. German traders came and went; their cattle and goods were never touched; and on official matters Witbooi invariably sent prompt and civil replies to any communications from the German Administrator, who by this time was established in the new headquarters at Windhuk.

While maintaining this correct and amicable attitude, the old chief, in addition to cherishing his powers as chief, jealously guarded the rights of his people in their land. He would sanction no German farmers in his country. Early in 1892, Goering's rejuvenated colonial company decided to start an experimental wool farm. Merino sheep were imported and a German farmer named Hermann placed in charge of the stock. Without in any way consulting the chief, Hermann established himself at Nomtsas[50], in Witbooi's territory, and commenced farming operations.

The Herero war did not occupy all Hendrik's time, so he decided to write to Hermann. The letter is of interest because it shows the courtly temperament and dignity of the old warrior

It is as follows:–

Hornkranz, 20th May 1892.

My dear friend Hermann,

I SEND these few lines to you. We have never yet seen one another, but I now hear something about you, through reports received from people – namely, that it

---

[50] A farming area situated North of Maltahöhe, occupied against the wishes of Hendrik Witbooi by Ernst Hermann a trained agriculturalist employed by the *Kolonial-Gesellschaft*. Hermann sought the support of German forces to assist him in retaining control of Nomtsas

[51] A fortified village in the mountains to the southwest of Windhoek. Occupied by the Witbooi's in 1889 until it was destroyed during the German attack in 1893. The remains now lie within the boundaries of a commercial farm.

is your intention to go to Nomtsas, and to live there. I don't know, however, whether this is true. I can hardly believe that you would do such a thing. It has been told to me for truth though, so I feel compelled to let your honour know, in good the, that I cannot approve of this. I do not give you permission to go and live at Nomtsas and to start big works there. So will you please be so good not to remain on the place, but to return. I cannot agree because, very shortly, the land will be required for some of my own people.

I entreat you, my dear friend, to understand me rightly and correctly; do not take offence, because I mean well towards you, and that is why I am sending this letter to you, in good the, to advise you – so that you may be saved the trouble and expense of starting extensive work on the ground.

> With hearty greetings – I am –
> Your friend
> the Captain Hendrik Witbooi.

In August 1892, when peace with the Hereros was certain and the treaty was being considered at Rehoboth by the delegated representatives of Witbooi and Maharero, Hendrik decided to bring his apprehensions to the notice of the British Government.

Writing from Hornkranz on 4th August 1892[52] to the "English Magistrate" of Walvis Bay, he states:–

I feel obliged and compelled to advise you of the position and circumstances under which I now live, I mean of the position of the Germans who have come into our land ... for I hear things and I see things which to me are impossible-things which are neither just, nor good – and therefore I write to you, the English Magistrate, in the hope and encouragement which is based on the old friendship which my late grandfather[53] had with the English Government ... which ancient friendship I acknowledge to this day ... We have seen and have learnt from experience that we can agree with the English in business and in ordinary life and if it can be thought or said that any nation should have a preference over this Africa that can be said of the English because they were the first to come into this land and we have become acquainted with them in business and personal friendship that friendship is quite sufficient for us. I require no other sort of friendship or treaty with a white nation ... that is my view of the English Government and of the old friendship of my grandfather towards you English and I in my day still rely on that old friendship. But now I see another man who is an entire stranger to me. His laws and deeds are to me entirely impossible and unintelligible and untenable. Therefore I write this letter to Your Honour in the hope that you will, in reply, advise me of the full truth in regard to my questions concerning the coming of the Germans; because the works of the Germans are encroaching on my land and now even my life is threatened they come to destroy

---

[52] A file containing correspondence from the British Magistrate for the period 1891-1893 was ordered sent from Pretoria and contained the original copy of this letter. The original with an English translation is still held in the National Archives in Pretoria ('Sec of Interior, Pretoria to Sec. Native Affairs 15th January, 1918, Hendrik Witbooi, Hornkranz to Magistrate, Walvis Bay, 4th August, 1892. NTS 266 4349/1910/F639).

[53] David Moses Witbooi (Kido, Kwido, Cupido). *c. 1783, + Gibeon 31 December 1875. Became leader of the Witboois in 1805 in Pela in the northern Cape of South Africa. Led his followers into Namaland in the first half of the nineteenth century. Forged links with missionaries of the Rhenish Mission Society. *Hendrik Witbooi Papers*, pp. 251 - 2.

CHAPTER FIVE

me by War without my knowing what my guilt is ... I have been told that it is their intention to shoot me and ask Your Honour. Perhaps you can tell me why? Perhaps you will know because you are parties to a treaty and of you English and Germans the other nation can do nothing without the knowledge of the other; because as I have heard (and ask Your Honour) that the English Government and the German Government held a big meeting and discussed to whom this land Africa should be assigned – for the purpose of concluding Protection Agreements with the Chiefs of the land; and thereupon you English surrendered the land to the Germans. But you also said at the meeting that no Chief should be compelled by force; you said that if a Chief were willing and understood to accept the Protection he could accept it ... That was your decision in your meeting and you unanimously agreed. So also has it come to pass that some Chiefs have accepted German protection. Those Chiefs to-day bitterly regret it, however, and are full of remorse, for they have seen no result from the nice words (*lekkere woorden*) which the Germans spoke to them. The Germans told those Chiefs that they wished to protect them from other strong nations, which intended to come into the land with armies and deprive the Chiefs, by force, of their lands and farms; and that therefore it was their (the Germans) desire to protect the Chiefs from such stupid and unjust people ... but so far as I have seen and heard, it appears to me wholly and entirely the reverse. The German himself is that person of whom he spoke, he is just what he described those other nations as. He is doing those things because he rules and is now independent, with his Government's laws; he makes no requests according to truth and justice and asks no permission of a chief. He introduces laws into the land according to his own opinions and those laws are impossible untenable unbearable unacceptable unmerciful and unfeeling (*ongevoelig*)... He personally punishes our people at Windhuk and has already beaten people to death for debt... It is not just and worthy to beat people to death for that. They were five people in all.[54] Four Bergdamaras and one of my red-men. He flogs people in a scandalous and cruel manner. We stupid and unintelligent people, for so he regards us, we have never yet punished a human being in such a cruel and improper way. He stretches persons on their backs and flogs them on the stomach and even between the legs, be they male or female, so Your Honour can imagine that no one can survive such a punishment

Secondly when some Damaras fled to my farm they went to sleep there, being tired; then there came four white men, who are under the (German) Captain, accompanied by a Bastard and there on my farm they murdered six of the Damaras.

So already eleven persons have without reason been murdered by the Germans ... therefore I write and ask Your Honour whether you know of these things and of the deeds and intentions of the Germans.

The chief then goes on (his letter covers 14 foolscap pages and is too long to insert in full)[55] to assert that his land was conquered by his grandfather from the Chief Oasib, and that he again, years later, defeated Manasse, the Red Chief, who disputed his title.

So Namaqualand was purchased by us in blood, twice over, from our grandfather's days even to mine, and it is clear therefore and unquestionable that Oasib's territory is mine according to all well-known laws of War and thus,

---

[54] Relates to cases in which men who were alleged to have owed money were beaten to death. Referring to the executions Witbooi stated that the owing of money was: "not a sufficient and worthy crime for capital punishment". *Hendrik Witbooi papers*, p. 98

[55] The full letter can be found in *Hendrik Witbooi papers*, p. 97 - 102.

because I am an independent Chief, I have not submitted myself, my land, and my people to German protection.

Growing more and more eloquent as he proceeds, he points out how all trading rights and concessions in his area have invariably been given by him to Englishmen, and he asks in spite of all this and of their ancient friendship, "Have you English delivered me into the hands of the Germans?"

After alleging that the English must have been misled by the Germans at that meeting (he has probably in mind the Anglo-German Conference of 1890), the Hottentot chief continues:–

> Therefore, my dear Magistrate, I write to you as a true friend, that you may know the depth of my feelings, for I complain to you of the inmost heavy feelings of my heart and it hurts and pains me much and brings remorse when I consider that your people have allowed such persons into our country. I send you this letter and I request you to give it to the Cape Government – let all the great men of England know of it so that they may have another meeting and consider this position of the Germans and if possible call these people back. Because they are not following the Agreements and Resolutions on the strength of which you let them enter this land ...

The quotations are from a copy of the letter in Witbooi's handwriting recorded in his journal. Whether or not the Magistrate of Walvis Bay ever received this letter which was sent by hand by one of my own men – or whether any notice was taken of it when received cannot[ix] be said, but there is ample food for reflection and possibly for self-reproach.

Having unburdened his very soul to the Magistrate of Walvis Bay, Hendrik Witbooi remained at his chief village, Hornkranz, and awaited results. His conscience was clear; he was at peace with the Hereros and with everyone else. He ruled his people, settled disputes, conducted Church services, preached and prayed and wrote letters.

This tranquillity was not to last very long.

In the beginning of 1893 the German garrison had been increased to about 250 soldiers with two batteries of artillery.

The Peace of Rehoboth[56] between the Hereros and the Hottentots had rendered German military intervention unnecessary. Notwithstanding this, the garrison was reinforced and Captain von François received (says Leutwein):–

> The simple instruction to uphold German domination under all circumstances. It was left to him to do so either by means of attack or defence. The Commissioner decided, after weighing all the circumstances, for the purpose of intimidating the others, to give one of the native races an impression of our power. He considered that the Witboois would be suitable for this purpose... The humiliation of Hendrik Witbooi would exercise the greatest influence on the others.

[ix] (Page 26 in original) Since writing the above it has been ascertained that the letter was duly received and sent to the Cape Government, and was by them transmitted to the Imperial Government in October 1892.

---

[56] For details see: Gewald, *Herero Heroes*, pp. 53-55.

CHAPTER FIVE

The German ex-Governor may be allowed to continue in his own words his brief description of this treacherous and most disgraceful piece of business:–

> Under preservation of the greatest secrecy, the troops on the morning of 12th April 1893 attacked Hornkranz, the location of Witbooi. The chief apparently reckoned on a formal declaration of war, and was completely taken by surprise; he was peacefully drinking his morning coffee.[57] Yet he succeeded, by judicious flight, in saving himself[*] and nearly all his fighting men. Only wives and children fell into the hands of the troops ... The troops were, probably owing to over-estimation of the achieved results, returned to Windhuk.

Leutwein is careful and brief, so we have to go elsewhere for further information.

Captain K. Schwabe, of the German Army, who was senior Lieutenant with the forces under von François, writes, describing incidents of the fight:–

> Suddenly a Hottentot warrior stepped from behind a rock and aimed at a distance of at most 20 paces at an advancing soldier. Instantaneously the soldier took aim as well. The finger of the Hottentot pressed the trigger, but, wonderful to relate, his rifle missed fire; the soldier's shot took effect, and the brave Witbooi, wounded through the chest, wallowed in his blood. On all sides terrible scenes were disclosed to us. Under an overhanging rock lay the corpses of seven Witboois, who, in their death agony, had crawled into the hollow, and their bodies lay pressed tightly together. In another place the body of a Berg-Damara woman obstructed the footpath, while two three-to-four year old children sat quietly playing beside their mother's corpse... English papers laid the charge against us that at Hornkranz we killed women and children, and in hateful and lying manner alleged that our soldiers spared neither wife nor child.[58] They had done us a bitter injustice; because if, at the range we fired, it had been possible to distinguish men from women, certainly no women would have been shot (he forgets to add, however, that the Germans opened fire, at early dawn, on the huts in which the men, women, and children were quietly sleeping, and that they knew full well that women and children would be killed).
>
> The Stad itself was a fearful sight (continues Schwabe); burning huts, human bodies and the remains of animals, scattered furniture, destroyed and useless rifles, that was the picture which presented itself to the eyes. From the burning pontoks (huts) came now and then the reports of exploding cartridges which had been left or buried there by the Witboois. Among the prisoners brought forward were the wife and daughter of the chief Hendrik Witbooi. The latter, named Margaret, was an exceedingly sell-possessed girl of between 17 to 19 years of age. Without the slightest sing of fear she stood before us and answered all our questions freely and with a proud air. Then, through the Interpreter, she made the following statement:–"I have heard that you have come from over the sea, in ship, in order to make war on my father. To-day the victory is on your side, but luck is changeable, and if you will take my advice you will return to your own homes;

---

[*] But they captured his journal and took it to the Archives at Windhuk, and it is now at the writer's disposal.

---

[57] A week after the attack Witbooi wrote "Is it a straightforward, or usual way of making war: that the Germans stop ammunition and then kill me. Without ammunition I am like a beast without horns. It looks to me like murder." (Official translation, Hendrik Witbooi, Hornkranz to Magistrate, Walvis Bay, 20th April, 1893, NTS 26 4349/1910/F639).

[58] See Hendrik Witbooi's own references and letters regarding this attack. *Hendrik Witbooi Papers*, pp. 126 - 130

because, before long, my father will come down on you like a lion and take his revenge."

I estimate the losses of the enemy (continues Schwabe) at about 150 persons, of which 60 were soldiers, that is, men of the Hottentot race. Unfortunately, there must be included women and children who had been in the pontoks during the fight; then, also, there were 50 prisoners, and a number of severely wounded, which were taken to Windhuk and treated there.[59] The booty, a number of rifles,

---

[59] The complete statement made by Hendrik Witbooi's son is still in the South African Archives in Pretoria and reads as follows: "After the new German troops arrived at Windhoek our under Captain Samuel Isaac who was at the time staying there, was told by Captain von François that he Samuel, must go to his people and tell the Headmen of Witboois' natin to talk with Captain H. WItbooi about making a treaty with the Germans.

Captain von François also said that a letter to H. Witbooi would follow on the subject.

When H. Witbooi heard the message he said that the great man must cine together and consult with him and with each other as to the answer to be given to the letter when it came.

They said 'let us first wait and see what the letter says, so that we may make an answer when it comes'. The Captain said 'Yes, that is best'.

Instead of the letter coming the soldiers followed Samuel and early in the morning before sunrise the firing woke us. Hendrik Witbooi said to the people round him 'Who can it be firing on us, I have made peace with the Damaras [Herero - eds], what is it?' We did not know who it was, but Captain Witbooi told all his men to leave the werft as soon as possible. After all the men had left the German soldiers stormed into the werft. Then we saw it was the Germans. The women and children were left in the werft, and the soldiers began to shoot at them, they shot little children, children at the breast, children on their mother's backs were shot through by the same bullet that killed the mothers."

The women saw that the attacking party were white men and sat still as they thought their lives were safe and that though they might be taken away for servants they would not be killed. So we all thought. We thought the men would be killed, but not women. Some of the women ran away with the men, but most remained when they saw that white people came in thinking they would be safe.

The women and children that they shot in the houses, the wounded as well as the dead they did not bring out, but burnt the houses over them. We know for certain that at least 3 women, a mother and two daughters, all wounded were burnt alive in the houses. This was seen by some old women who were not killed and were too crippled to be taken away prisoners with the other survivors.

The Germans stayed in the place till the next midday. On the day of attack the Germans caputed an old man, a church elder, who was too old and infirm to run away, and who had hidden himself in the rocks. They tied him up and took him to their wagons and shot him the next morning with 3 bullets.

Some of the women and children, part of whom were wounded the Germans left behind, the reset a large number they took away to Windhoek. They took more than they left. Two of the women left behind died of their wounds. Our total loss on the place was 8 old men, 2 young boys and 78 women and children. Of the two young boys one was Capt. Hendrik Witbooi's youngest son about 12 years old, who was paralised on one side. The other Keister Keister's nephew was about 10 years old.

When the Germans stormed into the palce, there of our men ran into the church and fired on the troops, a solder called to them to surrender and our magistrate who was one of the three said 'no' and shot the soldier dead. The three then escaped after firing several shots. We did not fire first. The Germans fired before they came into the place. Our men did not fire till the Germans were inside. Those three men were the only Hottentots who fired at all. The women told us that two Germans were buried on the place and 3 taken away wounded in their wagons.

We lost one buck wagon of the Captains, two horses, several foals, cows & calves that were shot down and some cows they took away & also some sheep & goats. We lost also our saddles about 50 or 60 destroyed and taken away, one good gun & some old ones and some loose powder and a few cartridges. We had no idea of war and so our cartridges were in our boxes and our bandoliers were empty. We only got away with our guns.

(Statement by Klein Hendrik Witbooi (son of Captain Hendrik Witbooi) and Keister Keister (under-Captain) given in presence of Magistrate, Walvis Bay, enclosure with Magistrate, Walfish Bay to Under-Sec for Native Affairs, 9th May, 1893 NTS 26 4349/1910/F639). The statement and another by Petrus Jafta have been published in Heywood, *Witbooi Papers*, p208

munitions, saddlery, harness, a herd of cattle, a flock of small stock, and about 20 horses, was not of much value to us; the loss of these was, however, a considerable blow to the Witboois. The most remarkable piece of loot was an ox-wagon on which had been fixed a harmonium used by the Witboois at divine service; unfortunately it was badly damaged by rifle fire.

Hendrik Witbooi might well have cause to return "like a lion"; but the surprise had deprived him of practically all food and munitions, and he and his following, living on wild fruits, field mice, lizards, and the larva of ants, took refuge in the mountain fastnesses of the Naauwkloof.[60]

Before closing the subject it may be recorded, however, that according to information given by the chief's son, and namesake, who now lives at Gibeon and who accompanied his father from Hornkranz, the surprise was so complete that many of the fugitives escaped only in their shirts. A certain percentage grabbed rifles and bandoliers; but many had not time even to do that. Hendrik Witbooi, junior, relates that a few days after the Germans had left on their return to Windhuk, he and a party of his father's men came down from the mountains to see if anything had been spared to them. At the village they found that the Germans had set a huge land mine, which, if it had exploded, would have brought further disaster on the visitors. The quick eye of the Hottentot detected the trap; the spring gun which was to fire the mine was detached and a sufficient supply of powder was unearthed to enable Witbooi to continue an obstinate resistance for nearly 18 months longer.

Von François had succeeded in giving the natives "an impression of our power"; but he had also succeeded in doing more: he had given the natives an impression of the true German character and of the real worth of German pretensions. To this massacre at Hornkranz is to be ascribed the fact that the Ovambos never came under German influence. The news spread like wildfire and shocked and horrified the natives throughout the country. The Ovambos, in anticipation of a visit from the Germans, prepared for war; the Hereros grew sullen and suspicious.

When Major Leutwein took over from von François the next year, he pretended to feel astonishment at the "aloof and openly hostile bearing of the natives"; but he was more than astonished when, having written to the Ovambo chief, Kambonde[61], expressing his intention "soon of having the pleasure of paying you a visit," that potentate replied. "Personally, I don't care whether I ever see you as long as I live."

All respect for the white man had disappeared. After Hornkranz, Germany's prospects of ruling the natives by kindly sympathy and mutual co-operation (had she ever intended so to do) vanished for ever; her only way to gain ascendancy was by pitiless severity and brute force. The "mailed fist" had to be applied. This she proceeded to do without compunction or hesitation.

---

[60] 'Narrow cleft', currently known today as the Naukluft. Situated to the south east of Windhoek

[61] After the death of Iitana in 1884 there was a succession dispute in the kingdom on Ondonga. Kambonde controlled the western part of the kingdom known as Ontananga and established his palace at Okaloko. He died in 1909. (Williams 1991: 145-146, 189)

CHAPTER SIX

LEUTWEIN AND THE PROTECTION AGREEMENTS

The Berlin Government fully approved the steps taken by von François against Witbooi at Hornkranz, and that gentleman was promoted to the rank of Major.

Towards the end of 1893, namely, on 20th November, Count Caprivi, the Imperial Chancellor, with the approval of His Majesty the Emperor and King, wrote a letter of instruction to Major Theodor Leutwein, directing him to proceed to South-west Africa and to send a report on the situation there as the result of his own observations. The Chancellor went on to say that, owing to the difficulty of obtaining regular and frequent communications from the Acting Commissioner, Major von François, he was unable to get such details as would enable him, satisfactorily, to control from Berlin military and administrative work there. Leutwein was specially asked not to interfere in the military control or administration; but –

> His Majesty the Emperor has decided that should Major von François be prevented during your presence in the territory from carrying out his duties by death or other permanent causes you are authorised to take over his work in an acting capacity.
>
> Your task will be to inquire into the relations between the Europeans and the natives in the central portions of the territory, and particularly into the offensive measures already taken and to be taken. In this connection you will keep this point of view before you, namely, that our power over the natives must be maintained under all circumstances and must be more and more consolidated. You must inquire whether the troops are strong enough to accomplish this task.

Armed with this letter of instructions, Major Leutwein arrived in South-west Africa in January 1894. His impressions of the state of affairs in the country are recorded in the interesting work *Elf Jahre Gouverneur*[62] (Eleven Years Governor), which he wrote after his return to Germany in 1905.

He writes (page 17):–

> The position in the territory on my arrival was certainly not rosy. And in certain respects resembles the position to-day (1905)... The natives were openly our enemies or at best preserved a very doubtful neutrality. Only the Bastards of Rehoboth openly took sides with us. It is far from my intention by a candid mention of actual facts to impute blame to anyone. Circumstances had quite logically evolved in this way. Quite too long had the Empire procrastinated in showing its power to the natives. It is, indeed, a good axiom, once spoken by

---

[62] Leutwein, Theodor *Elf Jahre Gouverneur in Duetsch-Südwestafrika*, (Reprint), Namibia Scientific Society, Windhoek, 1997.]

CHAPTER SIX

> Prince Bismarck, that "In the colonies the merchant must go on ahead and the soldier and the Administration must follow him; but, nevertheless, especially with regard to the warlike natives which we found in South-west Africa, people should not have to wait too long for the soldier ... Notwithstanding our lack of power, we had promulgated Ordinances which the natives treated with contempt. One of the Ordinances concerning arms and ammunition could be enforced because these articles were imported mainly by sea ... Furthermore, we issued and ratified concessions over rights and territories which did not belong to us. For example, in 1892 we established a syndicate for land settlement which was to dispose of settlements from Windhuk in the direction of Hoachanas and Gobabis. Yet there sat at Gobabis the robber Khauas Hottentots... Hoachanas was claimed by Chief Hendrik Witbooi and these claimed that the boundaries of their spheres of influence were close by the tower of Windhuk.
>
> All this gave rise to the impression at home that we were masters in the Protectorate. In actual fact up to 1894 the exercise of any governmental powers outside of the capital, Windhuk, was out of the question... The reinforced troops were not strong enough to exercise powers in the remainder of the Protectorate and at the same the to carry on the war against Witbooi.
>
> In the same way little influence or impression of power was created over the natives by the first white influx.
>
> For 60 years past the whites had come to them (the natives) not as proud conquerors, but as missionaries, traders, and hunters.
>
> The agreements concluded with the natives were merely trading agreements... The fact that the so-called protection given to the natives in recompense, was merely on paper (*lediglich auf dem Papier stand*) indicates that they gave and we took.
>
> The growing "respect" for the troops, occasioned by the capture of Hornkranz, had, in the natives, sunk to zero, on account of the long struggle put up by Witbooi thereafter. The fact that, in addition to this, we had before our attack made an agreement with the Hereros would not influence them to understand that this attack had been made to benefit them. Therefore we could not reckon them as friend, and Witbooi, on the other hand, had become our embittered enemy, and thus we had sat between two stools.

As a study of German mentality, apart from their significance on the native question, these extracts are of interest:–

> Already (continues Leutwein), on my journey to Windhuk, I had an opportunity of coming into contact with the Hereros and to ascertain, with astonishment, their dark mistrust (*finsteres mistrauen*) of the German Government, which constituted a grave danger at the rear of the troops fighting Witbooi.

Before continuing to quote Leutwein's illuminating views, it is now necessary to place on record the exact position, based entirely on agreements ("mere trading agreements," as Leutwein correctly called them) between the Germans and those chiefs who had accepted German protection, and also it is necessary to indicate the position in regard to native races who had up to January 1894 refused to enter into such agreements.

The races of natives in South-west Africa at the time of the annexation by Germany may be classified under the following tribal heads:–

CHAPTER SIX

(1) The Ovambos (various tribes).
(2) The Hereros (various tribes).
(3) The Hottentots (various tribes).
(4) The Berg-Damaras.
(5) The Bushmen.
(6) The Bastards (or cross-breeds).

The total population at that time, according to the various estimates, may reasonably be fixed at approximately 250,000 to 275,000 souls.

The Ovambos, who lived in the extreme north, had made no Protection Agreements, and can at no time be said to have come under German control.[63] These tribes under their despotic and powerful chiefs –

Nechale of Omandonga
Negumbo of Olukonda[64];
Kambonde of Omalonga; and
Uejulu of Onipa;

were numerically the strongest race in the Protectorate, their total population being between 100,000 and 150,000.

The Hereros occupied the whole area marked on most maps as Damaraland, and were from 80,000 to 90,000 strong. Palgrave in 1876 estimated the total Herero population at 85,000. In 1890 the chief tribes or clans were located at

Okahandja under Chief Kamaherero;
Omaruru under Chief Manasse[65];
Otjimbingwe under Chief Zacharias;
Okandjose under Chief Tjetjoo;
Gobabis (Nossob) under Chief Nikodemus;
Otjizasu (Ovambandjera) under Chief Kahimena; and
Waterberg under Chief Kambazembi.

---

[63] When Captain Victor Franke visited northern Namibia in 1908 he made a number of agreements which he described as *Gehorsamserklärung* (declarations of obedience), rather than Protection Treaties. King Iita yaNalitoke of Uukwaluudhi signed a declaration on 26th may, 1908. King Tshaanika tsaNatshilongo signed on 27th May, 1908. King iipumbu ya Shilongo signed on 28th May, 1908. King Nande ya Hedimbi of Oukwanyama signed on 2nd June, 1908. King Kambonde kaMpingane of Ondonga signed on 22nd June, 1908. The declarations stated that each ruler recognised 'the supremacy of the German Emperor over my territory' and gave the rulers agreement 'to the recruitment of workers by the German Government in my tribe'. However it might be argued that the real independence of the Ovambo kingdoms only really came to an end with the death of the defiant Kwanyama ruler, Mandume ya Ndemufayo in 1917. (Eirola, Martti, *The Ovamogefahr: The Ovamboland Reservation in the Making*, Historical Association of Northern Finland, Jyväskylä, 1992, pp. 234-238, 299-300).

[64] The Blue Book seems to be incorrect here as there was no known ruler of Oukwanyama with the name of Negumbo. However, during the 1904-1908 war there was a King with this name ruling over Uukwambi. Negumbo had spent much of his early life in Ombalantu and Ongandjera before coming to power in 1875. He was reported to be hostile to German approaches up to his death in 1907 (Williams 1991: 159-161, 191

[65] Manasse Tjiseseta was the Chief of the Herero at Omaruru (1884-1898). He was succeeded by his oldest son, Michael Tjiseseta (de Vries 1999)

Of these tribes, several of which were again subdivided into groups under wealthy, powerful, and practically independent minor chiefs, only two, namely, the tribes of Okahandja and Omaruru, had through their respective chiefs entered into protection agreements.

The others were not bound, and never considered themselves bound, by any agreement, until compelled to submit by the power of the German arms. In this connection the German authorities made a most extraordinary blunder. They constituted the chief of the Okahandja Hereros as Paramount Chief of all Herero tribes, and held that all other chiefs were bound by his agreements and decisions. That this was contrary to all Herero laws and customs, an endeavour will be made to show later on. But German craft went even further. When Kamaherero of Okahandja died, his heir was ignored, and the Germans compelled the Herero people to accept the weak and inefficient younger son, Samuel Maharero, as Chief of Okahandja and Paramount Chief of Hereroland.[66] Samuel, when in his cups, would agree to anything, and sign anything; and as a keg of rum was to him more than his kingdom the Germans saw to it that he got his rum, and, eventually, lost his kingdom; and not only his kingdom, but also 80 per cent of the fine race which he and his German masters had so villainously exploited and misruled.[67]

The Hottentots occupied the whole of Great Namaqualand, and were scattered in more or less disjointed groups or clans under chiefs who had waxed powerful in their perpetual wars with the Hereros in the north.[68] Their population was estimated at about 20,000 souls. Notwithstanding their lack of numbers, they were always formidable opponents, owing to their ability as horsemen and riflemen.

The Hottentot chiefs who had entered into the so-called protection agreements only did so out of fear that, as the Germans took care to tell them, the *Boeren* or Dutch farmers of South Africa were trekking up to take their country

---

[66] For more detail on the succession dispute see: Pool, Gerhard, *Samuel Maharero*, Gamsberg Macmillan, Windhoek, 1990, pp. 77-82; Gewald, *Herero Heroes*, pp. 29-60.

[67] Allegations that Samuel Maharero drunk excessively were widespread amongst contemporary missionary records with Rev. Viehe, for example, describing him as 'completely given over to drink'. Gerhard Pool provides a list of the massive quantities of liquor purchased on Samuel Maharero's account at Wecke & Voigts over a three year period, 1896-1898. However, there is no evidence that this alchohol was all for personal consumption (Pool, *Samuel*, p. 168)

[68] Brigitte Lau argued strongly against the reduction of Nineteenth Century conflict to the simple consequence of 'ethnic or racial difference'. She described 'the picture of central Namibia as a war-ridden zone of ruthless intertribal bloodshed' as 'inaccurate' and 'improbable' and largely blames the work of this image on the work and 'colonial fantasy' of the influential local historian, Heinrich Vedder. The plaque at the entrance to *Die Alte Feste* (the old fort) in Windhoek (now the National Museum of Namibia) still reflects this view of the pre-colonial past. It reads "the Alte Feste was built in 1890 by the Schutztruppe under Captain C. von Francois as a stronghold to preserve peace and order between the rivalling Namas and Hereros". The same text is also written in German and Afrikaans. On the other side of the entrance is a second plaque erected by the *Alte Kameraden* (a German war veterans association) in memory of the German soldiers who died during the military campaign of 1914-1915 when South African forces invaded and conquered the German colony during World War One. At this date there is still no monument to the Namibians who died fighting against the German Schutztruppe during their colonial operations.

away from them. Attention has already been directed to Jordaan and his Upingtonia Republic of 1884. This trek of the Boers into the south-west was made the fullest use of by Goering and Buttner, for the attainment of their own ends.

Of the *Berg-Damara* and *Bushmen* – subordinate races – and the *Bastard*s of Rehoboth, more will be recorded in the separate chapters dealing with those tribes.

The German pretensions to control were based on eight protection agreements, namely:–

(1) The Agreement of 28th October 1884, between Dr. Nachtigal (for Luderitz) and the chief Joseph Fredericks, of Bethany, agreeing to German protection, granting trade rights, and confirming the acquisitions by Luderitz in 1883.

(2) The Agreement of 23rd November 1884, between Dr. Nachtigal and chief Piet Heibib, of the Topenaar Hottentots, whereby the cession of certain territorial rights (excluding the Walvis Bay area) to Luderitz was confirmed, and the protection of the German Empire was accepted by the chief.

(3) The Agreement, at Hoachanas, of 2nd September 1885, between the missionary Carl Buttner, described as "the Plenipotentiary of His Majesty the German Emperor," and Manasse, "the independent Chief Captain of the Red Nation of Great Namaqualand," whereby Manasse is represented as asking the Emperor for "his All-Highest protection," which protection Buttner extends and the German flag will be hoisted as an outward sign of this protection.

Note. – A few years after this "All-Highest protection" was accorded, chief Hendrik Witbooi came along with a punitive expedition against Manasse, whom he regarded as one of his subjects. Having suitably dealt with Manasse, Witbooi seized the German flag and took it with him to Hornkranz. Arrived at Hornkranz, Hendrik sat down and wrote a letter to the Commissioner, Dr. Goering, in which the following characteristic passage appears:–

Further I wish to inform you that I have obtained possession of the flag which you gave to Manasse is now in my hands at Hornkranz. I should like to know what you wish me to do with this flag, as to me it is a strange thing (vremdeding). All Manasse's possessions belong to me.

(4) The "Treaty of Protection and Amity" between the Bastards of Rehoboth and the missionary Carl Buttner ("for the German Emperor"), dated 15th September 1885.

(5) The Agreement, dated at Okahandja the 21st October 1885 (repudiated in 1888 and revived in 1890 under circumstances already stated), between Maharero Katjimuaha, "Chief Captain of the Hereros in

Damaraland", and Dr. Goering and Missionary Buttner, "both duly empowered and authorized by the German Emperor."

(6) The confirmation by the Herero chief Manasse of Omaruru of the terms of the agreement No. 5 with Maharero as per certificate signed at Omaruru on 2nd November 1885.

This document is worthy of reproduction; it reads:–

Completed at Omaruru on the 2nd November 1885

There appeared to-day before the undersigned Imperial Commissioner for the South-West African Protectorate, Dr. jur. Heinrich Ernst Goering, assisted by the Secretary Louis Nels, the Captain of Omaruru, Manasse Tysiseta, and the undersigned members of the Council. The Treaty of Protection and Friendship, entered into with Maharero, was verbally translated to them by the Missionary Diehl, who acted as interpreter, and explained.

After consultation had taken place amongst themselves they made the following declaration:–

We herewith join the treaty of protection and friendship entered into between His Majesty the German Emperor, King of Prussia, etc., Wilhelm I., and Maharero Katjimuaha, Chief Captain of the Hereros, dated Okahandja, 31st October 1885, in all points.

Read out and translated:–
:– G. Diehl, Missionary.
:– The Imperial German Commissioner for the South-west African Protectorate, Dr. Heinrich Ernst Goering.
(X) Manasse Tysiseta, Captain of Omaruru.
(X) Mutate.
(X) Hairsa.
(X) Barnaba.
(X) Kanide.
(X) Katyatuma.
(X) Asa.

As Witnesses:–
:–Andreas Purainen
Agent of the Rhenish Mission.
:–Traugott Kanapirura.
:– Nels, Secretary.

(7) The Agreement, dated at Warmbad 21st August 1890, between Dr. Goering and chief Jan Hendricks, of the Veldschoendrager Hottentots.

(8) The Agreement, dated at Warmbad 21st August 1890, between Dr. Goering and Willem Christian, the chief of the Bondelswartz Hottentots.

The last two agreements were made after the annexation of the territory by Germany.

The Witbooi, Tseib (Keetmanshoop), Berseba, Khauas (Gobabis), Swartbooi, and Afrikaner chiefs had not made agreements.

Referring to these agreements, Governor Leutwein remarks (page 13):–

> Our supremacy (*herrschaft*) in South-west Africa was obtained by concluding agreements whereby the chiefs ceded to us a portion of their rights, and received, in return, the promise of our protection. But those persons who promised this protection in the name of the German Emperor had not the slightest authority to do so.

However that may be, the German Government, when it suited its policy and designs, did not hesitate to hold their part of the agreements binding on the natives, while thus absolving itself from the liability to give protection as promised by Buttner and Goering.[69]

It is unnecessary to reproduce the agreements, but it is perhaps desirable to give the main heads (which were practically all similar) indicating what was promised to or given by the contracting parties.

The Native Chiefs undertook –

(1) To give German subjects right and freedom to carry on unrestricted trade in their territories.

(2) To protect their lives and property.

(3) To recognise the German Emperor's jurisdiction over Europeans, and to refer all disputes between natives and Europeans to the German authorities.

(4) To grant no concessions, enter into no treaties and to dispose of no land, or the interests therein, to any other nation or the subjects thereof without the prior consent of the German Government.

(5) To assist in the preservation of peace and, in the event of disputes with other chiefs, to call in the German authorities as mediators.

The German Emperor, on the other hand through his agents aforementioned – pledged himself –

(a) To give his All-Highest protection to the chief and his people.

(b) To recognise and support the chief's jurisdiction and control over his own people.

(c) To take care that the Europeans respected the laws, customs, and usages of the natives and paid the usual taxes.

Is it necessary, at this stage, to state that these pledges were observed only in the breach thereof, and that protests and appeals from the chiefs fell on deaf ears. These pledges were *lediglich auf dem papier* merely on paper!

---

[69] For more detail on the structure of the German colonial state in Namibia see Bley, Helmut, *South-West Africa under German Rule, 1894-1914*, Heinemann/Evanston, London, 1971 pp.46-49]

Governor Leutwein grows very discursive when dealing with these agreements. He writes:–

> It is not necessary to believe, however, that the chiefs sat like German law students over their *corpus juris* perusing the contents of the agreements with a view to getting a full knowledge of their contents ...

(He knew only too well that this was so, for the reason that the chiefs did not receive copies, and even if they had could not have read them, as they were in German.)

> The specific provisions of the agreements did not matter (*kamen daher nicht an*), the fact of their conclusion was sufficient. The manner of the carrying out of those agreements thus depended entirely on the power which stood behind the German makers of the agreements. So long as the German Government in the Protectorate had no means of enforcing its power (*macht-mittel*) the agreements were of small significance. After this state of affairs had been changed the agreements were, in practice, dealt with uniformly without regard to their stipulated details... So the native tribes were all in the same way, and as a whole, whether this was arranged for in the agreements or not, made subject to German laws and German jurisdiction, and received German garrisons ...
>
> Taxes and duties due on the part of the Europeans to the natives were, on the contrary, except in the Rehoboth territory, never collected. (See *Elf Jahre Gouverneur*, page 240.)

Leutwein continues:–

> Even although the native chiefs could form little idea of the contents of the protection agreements, they were clearly aware of the actual existence thereof. That means they knew that the Governor, as Deputy of the German Emperor, had to exercise a sort of dominion over them as the result of agreements for the most part voluntarily made (*auf grund von meist freiwillig eingegangenen verträgen*).

Leutwein has already affirmed that Dr. Goering and Buttner had not the slightest authority to bind the German Crown. In regard to the subsequent agreements which he himself made with the chiefs Hendrik Witbooi, Lambert, Simon Kooper, and others it will be seen to what extent they may be regarded as having been "voluntarily" entered into.

> And this voluntariness (continues Leutwein) was the rock on which the power of the Governor might be shattered... There were two ways in which the danger might be met. Either the protection agreements had to be repudiated and in place of the system of protection-control an actual dominion, based on the force of arms, substituted; or, alternatively, the representative of the German Government had to play up to the chiefs, to conciliate them and thus by degrees accustom them to German control. If, notwithstanding this, there was opposition, the one tribe could be played off against the other. The adoption by me of the first alternative was impossible. This the old Fatherland neither understood nor approved of, until the impracticability of the second course was clearly established, not by mere conviction, but by actual proved facts. This proof came only in 1904. and then we had to pay costly blood-money for our tuition.

CHAPTER SIX

Leutwein goes on to relate how, in following his second alternative, he recognized the protection agreements, brought in troops, and used the loyal natives to co-operate as soldiers with the Germans in operation against rebel tribes. This system –

> gave rise (he writes) to the hope that the natives would gradually become accustomed to the existing state of affairs. Of their ancient independence nothing but a memory would remain. In conjunction with such a peace-policy, a gradual disarming of natives, in cases of insubordination, could go hand in hand with a severing of tribal ties; and this, in part, actually did take place. This course required patience, however, not only on the part of the Government, but also on the part of the white immigrants, and here it was, to a certain extent, not forthcoming.

Leutwein complains that "people" not only were lacking in patience, but that some actually worked at cross-purposes and made his conciliation policy – as above outlined – quite impossible and unworkable.

As an example he quotes the following specific case:–

> For example, shortly before the Bondelswartz rebellion[70] the German Colonial Confederation (*Deutsche Kolonialbund*) imposed the following demands on the Bondelswartz tribe:–
>
> (1) Every coloured person must regard a white man as a superior being (*Höheres wesen*)
> (2) In court the evidence of one white man can only be outweighed by the statements of seven coloured persons.
>
> These demands were nowhere contested in Germany, and in the Protectorate they were hailed with satisfaction. I will express no opinion as to their utility; but, in practice, one can apply them only to subjected races (*unterworfenen völkerschaften*).

The Hottentot rebellion of 1903 and the Herero rebellion of 1904 gave Germany her chance of converting the survivors into *unterworfenen völkerschaften*.

The fact, however, that the German Colonial Confederation could, in this manner, intervene and override the Governor, the law and the pledges and the agreements, is one of the unexplained mysteries of the German system.

---

[70] The reference here is obviously to the Bondelswarts rising that started on 25th October, 1903 and not the later, better known, 'rebellion' of 1922.

CHAPTER SEVEN

NATIVE POPULATION STATISTICS

The actual Government control by Germany commenced, therefore, only in 1894, when Major Theodor Leutwein took over the command from von François, and was appointed first Governor of German South-west Africa.

The attached sketch will indicate:–

(1) the boundaries of the new colony;
(2) the location and spheres of influence of the various native tribes in 1894.

It will now be advisable to deal with each native race separately, showing briefly:–

(a) their origin and characteristics;
(b) their laws and customs;
(c) their relations with the Germans, and their treatment;
(d) the causes which led to the various rebellions.

Having done this it will be necessary to indicate what treatment was meted out to the natives during and after these rebellions. It will be necessary, moreover, to deal with the German judicial system as applied to the natives, and in conclusion to voice the views of the native population of South-west Africa in regard to the future destiny and government of this country.

These views are reflected in voluntary statements made on oath by surviving chiefs, headmen, and prominent leaders of the aboriginal tribes, and they represent the unanimous views of the peoples concerned.

At this stage, however, it is necessary to quote certain figures the details of which should be burnt into the memory, as they are in themselves the best indicators of the black deeds which, were it possible to record them all, would require more space than the scope of this report allows.

While there is little difficulty in fixing the areas in which the native tribes lived and exercised influence, it is not so easy to arrive at an accurate idea of the total numbers of the population.[71]

The only guides we have are the considered estimates given by the men, who after years of residence in the country, extended travel, observation, and inquiry, were able confidently to place on record certain definite figures.

The British Commissioner, W. C. Palgrave, in his report of 1877, estimated the native population in 1876 as under:–

(1) *Ovamboland*:–
Various Ovambo tribes	98,000

(2) *Hereroland (or Damaraland)*:–
Hereros	85,000
Berg-Damaras	30,000
Hottentots	1,500
Bastards	1,500
Bushmen	3,000
	121,000

Great Namaqualand:–
Various Hottentot tribes	16,850
Making a total for all races of	235,850

---

[71] The demographic history of Namibia has yet to be systematically researched. However, the debate over the size of pre-1904 population figures of the Herero, Nama and Damara communities was one of the central areas of dispute in Brigitte Lau's attack on the claims by Horst Dreschler that the German forces carried out a policy of genocide against the indigenous population. Dreschler supported the figures provided by the Blue Book to support his claim that 80% of the Herero population and 50% of the Nama population were killed by the Germans during the war. Dreschler accepts the criticism of the statistics given here for the Damara population as stated in the German response to the Blue Book, but asserts that 'one-third' of all Damara were also killed by the Germans during the conflict. The substance of Lau's criticism was that the size of the pre-war and post-war Herero population are 'not known' and that all the statistics and percentages provided were based purely on estimates. It might be argued that the focus on the quantification of death during the conflict has detracted from the more central question of whether there was racially inspired genocidal intent. The key contrasting positions in the demographic debate can be found in Dreschler, Horst *Let Us Die Fighting: The Stuggle of the Herero and Nama against German Imperialism (1884-1915)*, Akademi-Verlag, Berlin, 1966, pp. 211-214, 229; Lau, Brigitte 'Uncertain Certainties: The Herero-German War of 1904' in Brigitte Lau, *History and Historiography*, Discoures/MSORP, Windhoek, 1995, pp. 42-46, German Colonial Office, *The Treatment of Native and other Populations in the Colonial Possessions of Germany and England*, Engelman, Berlin, 1919. pp. 43-45. For some preliminary comments on the human cost of the war for the Damara population of Namibia see Gaseb, Ivan 'A historical hangover':The absence of Damara from accounts of the 1904-08 war', paper presented at the 'Public History: Forgotten History' Conference, University of Namibia, August, 2000.

In his book, Governor Leutwein gives the following estimate of the native population at the the of his arrival (1894):–

Ovambos	100,000
Hereros	80,000
Hottentots	20,000
Bastards	4,000
Bushmen and Berg-Damaras	40,000
Total	244,000

In the second edition of *Mit Schwert und Pflug* (published in 1904), Captain K. Schwabe, of the German Army, while remarking that a correct estimate of the Berg-Damara and Bushman population is difficult, gives the following figures in regard to the other tribes, as at 1st January 1903[72]:–

Ovambos	100,000 to 150,000
Hereros	80,000
Hottentots	20,000
Bastards	4,000

It will be seen that, in regard to the Hereros and Hottentots these authorities entirely independently, and dealing with the years 1876, 1894, and 1903 respectively, give practically the same estimate.

If Palgrave and Leutwein were at all accurate the later estimate by Schwabe of

80,000 Hereros and
20,000 Hottentots

may reasonably be regarded as a minimum figure for the adult native population, no allowances having been made from 1876-1894, and 1894-1903 for natural increases.

The consensus of opinion and evidence goes to show that, if anything, the population of those races was in 1904 nearer 100,000 and 25,000 respectively.

Palgrave's estimate of 30,000 Berg-Damaras in 1876 was probably too low, but it is practically confirmed by Leutwein, and as it is nowhere called into question by German writers who were conversant with and quoted from his report, there is no reason why Palgrave's estimate should not be accepted and, again discarding natural increases, fixed at the same figure for the adult population in 1904, *i.e.*, 30,000.

---

[72] Schwabe comments on population estimates in '*Mit Schwert und Pflug in Deutsch-Südwestafrika. Vier Kriegs- und Wanderjahre* Mittler und Sohn, Berlin, 1904' (2nd ed), 1904, p. 454.]

The minimum estimate of the adult population of the three races in 1904 is therefore fixed at –

80,000 for Hereros,
20,000 for Hottentots,
30,000 for Berg-Damaras.

In 1911, after tranquillity had been restored and all rebellions suppressed, the German Government of South-west Africa had a census taken. A comparison of the figures speaks for itself.

	Estimate 1904	Official Census 1911	Decrease
Hereros	80,000	15,130	64,870
Hottentots	20,000	9,781	10,219
Berg Damaras	30,000	12,831	17,169
	130,000	37,742	92,258

In other words, 80 per cent. of the Herero people had disappeared, and more than half of the Hottentot and Berg-Damara races had shared the same fate.

Dr. Paul Rohrbach's dictum:– "It is applicable to a nation in the same way as to the individual that the right of existence is primarily justified in the degree that such existence is useful for progress and general development" comes forcibly to mind

These natives of South-west Africa had been weighed in the German balance and had been found wanting. Their "right of existence" was apparently not justified.

CHAPTER EIGHT

THE HEREROS OF SOUTH-WEST AFRICA[73]

The Herero tribe is probably a branch of the Great Bantu family, which at one time occupied approximately one-third of the African Continent from 5° North to 20° South.

Unlike their black neighbours, the Berg-Damaras, the colour of the Hereros varies from light brown to a darker hue of chocolate brown. Tall and muscular, with proud and dignified bearing and a supreme contempt for other people, the Herero more closely resembles the Zulu than any other of the South-African races. It is a singular fact, however, that their physical likeness to the Zulu is confined to the men only. The women are generally undersized, and when tall are lanky and angular. They compare very unfavourably with the women of the other Bantu tribes. This may be due to the fact that, unlike the Kaffir and Zulu woman, the Herero woman, beyond milking the cows and attending to her children, did little or no manual labour. Instead of being the drudge and slave of her husband, as is the case with most Bantu tribes, the Herero woman was his pampered pet. The position and influence of their women and the general deference and respect shown towards them by the Hereros place this tribe quite in a class by itself among the Bantu peoples. Their religious beliefs, their sacred rites, and their laws of inheritance through the mother's side, combined with their mythical conceptions of their original descent from female ancestors, all united to raise the Herero woman far above her other Bantu cousins. In their courts, the Hereros, before giving evidence, took an oath "by my mother's tears" to tell the truth:– this was the usual oath; others were "by my mother's hood" and "by the bones of my ancestors."

In his annual memorandum for 1904, the Imperial German Chancellor asserted that Mashonaland was the place of origin of the Herero tribe. The language of several tribes in Angola and Central Africa is said to be similar to that of the Hereros, but, beyond marking the probable route followed by the people in their migration southwards from the interior, and giving rise to the supposition that they were centuries back located in Upper Angola and Northern Rhodesia, this information does not warrant assertion of any definite place of origin.[74]

---

[73] For more on the history and tradition of Herero communities in the region see: Michael Bollig and Jan-Bart Gewald editors, *People, Cattle and Land*, (Rüdiger Köppe Verlag: Cologne 2001).

[74] Debates relating to Herero origins and society have changed substantially since 1918. For a more contemporary view on developments see, Bollig & Gewald, *People, Cattle and Land.* 2001

Pastor Meinhof, a German ethnologist, holds that it is not improbable that before becoming part of the Bantu group of nomads, the Hereros came from the Nile areas in the far north, and that they were then a mixture of Negro and Hamite.[75]

This writer indicates certain philological similarities which would imply derivation from some common Hamite stem.

"Tobacco pipe" – (1) Hamitic Galla (East Africa) = *Gaya*.
(2) Herero = *Amakaya*.
"Town" (1) = *ganda*.
(2) = *onganda*.

He quotes many similar instances.

It is also alleged by close students of the native languages that on investigation the speech of the Herero is not so genuine a Bantu language as had at first been thought. In addition thereto the position of their women already referred, to and certain customs, such as the extraction of the lower front teeth and the V-shaped filing of the upper front teeth (known also among certain Nile tribes) seem to indicate influences other than Bantu. Moreover, the holy fire which Dr. Felix Meyer[76] describes as their concrete conception of religious observance, burning perpetually in the *Okurua* or holy place, and tended solely by the principal wife of the Chief, or his eldest daughter, is reminiscent of the Temple of Vesta at Rome, and its holy fires tended by the patrician ladies. Space does not permit an exhaustive inquiry into a subject, which to ethnologists cannot but be attractive and fascinating. It is sufficient to say that, no matter what the various theories may be, and no matter how dissimilar -especially to the European ear – the Herero and Bantu languages of South Africa may sound, the fact remains that members of the South African Bantu tribes, coming from the Union to South-west Africa, are able with an almost incredibly short period of the to speak and understand the Herero language.

---

[75] In the nineteenth century a myth developed in academia and later popular discourse that had it that the Hamites, of the Hamitic races, allegedly the descendents of Ham, had been the prime instigators for development and change in African societies. Hamites were held to have entered Africa and travelled towards the south, establishing civilizations as they went. Thus Great Zimbabwe, the Kingdom of Buganda, and so forth were said to have been established on account of the Hamitic influence. In the course of the twentieth century, particularly in the aftermath of World War II, racial theories came to be disproved and the Hamitic hypothesis was shown to be what it was, a myth. Saul Dubow, *Illicit Union: Scientific Racism in Modern South Africa*, (Cambridge 1995) pp. 82 - 90 & E. R. Sanders, 'The Hamitic Hypothesis: Its Origin and Functions in Time Perspective', *Journal of African History*, 10/4 (1969), 528.

[76] Dr Felix Meyer (1851-1925) served as the editor of the *Blätter für vergleichende Rechtswissenschaft und Volkswirtschaftslehre* during the period 1905-1908. He later wrote a dissertation entitled 'Skorbuterkrankungen unter den kriegsgefangenen Eingeborenen in Südwestafrika in den Jahren 1905-07' (Berlin, 1920). Unfortunately the National Archives of Namibia has been unable to locate a copy of this work.

CHAPTER EIGHT

At the time of the annexation by Germany the Hereros occupied the heart of South-west Africa. Their sphere of influence extended from Swakopmund in the west to the Kalahari border in the east, and from the mountains of Outjo in the north to Windhuk and Gobabis in the south.

It is certain that, except during the period of their partial and temporary subjugation by the Afrikaner Hottentots, under Jonker Afrikaner (circa 1830-64), they had been supreme masters of this area for over 100 years, and that the Kaokoveld in the north-west of the Protectorate had for two centuries or more been inhabited by portions of the tribe.

Crossing the Kunene River from Angola about the beginning of the 18th century and followed at no great distance by their Ovambo neighbours, their first place of settlement undoubtedly was the Kaokoveld. They remained there for a generation or two before the steady influx of Ovambos on their eastern flanks gradually pressed the Hereros and their countless herds of cattle further westward towards the sand dunes of the arid coast belt. Soon there was insufficient grazing and not enough elbow room, and after defeating the nearest Ovambo tribe in battle and incidentally annexing more cattle, the squeezed Herero clans began their gradual movement south and south-east into what are now known as the Outjo and Grootfontein districts.

This migration from the Kaokoveld appears to have taken place in a leisurely manner, and the last organised clans to leave the area moved towards the end of the first quarter of the last century. Grootfontein was then evacuated, and that area and the belt extending westwards past the Etosha pan became an unoccupied zone (save for wild Bushmen and fugitive Berg-Damaras) and a neutral belt between the Ovambos and the Hereros.

It is true that a degenerate and impoverished remnant of the tribe remains in the Kaokoveld to this day. These people speak the language and retain the ancient heathen rites and customs of the Herero. But they possess few cattle, and are little better than the Bushmen. The Hereros gave to their degraded kinsmen the name of *Ovatjimba* (the "veld beggars"), and by that name they are known today.[77]

The name "Herero" itself has been variously derived and explained. Palgrave asserts that it comes from HERA = the assegai swingers, and Dr. Hans Schinz and other inquirers seem to accept this view. The Missionary Dannert, on the other hand, states that Hereros themselves informed him that it meant "the joyful people" – the people who take delight in their cattle, thus indicating their temperament (HERERA = to rejoice). This explanation seems more probable than Palgrave's. There is a third contention, however, that the word Herero is a derivative of ERERO = the past, yesterday – "the ancient people."

---

[77] For a more complex reading of the history of OtjiHerero-speaking communities in the Kaoko see, G. Miescher & D. Henrichsen, *New Notes on the Kaoko*, (Basel 2000) & Michael Bollig 'Power & Trade in Precolonial & Early Colonial Northern Kaokoland, 1860s-1940s' in Patricia Hayes *et al. Namibia under South African Rule: Mobility and Containment, 1915-46*, James Currey, Oxford, 1998

Thus the old Chief Kamaherero of Okahandja, when asked the meaning of his name, proudly replied, "ma-ha-erero" = one who is not of yesterday (*i.e.*, one of ancient lineage).

Several writers agree in reporting that a favourite remark of the irate Herero, when smarting under oppression or injustice, was *Oami Omuherero ka Omutua* = "I am a Herero no barbarian no stranger."[78] This reminds one of the *Civis Romanus sum* of the ancient Roman;[79] and it would indicate that the name Herero has more to do with ancient origin than with "joyfulness" or the "waging of war." The Hereros of today can throw no light on the subject. In religion the Herero paid deference to, and revered, a mystic spirit whom he called the "Great Magician."[80] The "good spirit," who had made the world and peopled it, and who sent good luck and bad luck. Personally he could not hope to approach this potent being, so he relied on the intercessory prayers and powerful influence of the spirits of his deceased ancestors. It was the ancestors who were really worshipped, the holy fire, ever burning on the holy place, the blessed water, the symbolic wands of *Ovampuvu*[81] and "wild plum tree" (representing the male and female ancestors). and the sacred gourds filled daily with milk from the holy cattle were all dedicated to the service of the mighty dead. This cult of ancestor worship exercised a powerful influence over the life and family relations of the Herero. It bound the family together in a sacred and inseparable tie of past, present and future relationship. The Hereros firmly believed in continued existence of the soul after death. Belief in and terror of ghosts was universal. Probably here, as elsewhere, ancestor worship had its real origin in fear of the ghosts of the departed, and was the chief motive, until eventually deeper religious feeling and real affection for deceased relatives became the accepted reason.

In addition to being ancestor worshippers, the Hereros were totemists, but had no totem badges or signs.

The Herero story of the Creation is interesting and must be mentioned, because the division of the tribe into totemistic groups or families arises therefrom.

At the behest of the "Great Magician" there emerged one day from the trunk of an *Omborombonga* tree[82], men and women in pairs, and also all living

---

[78] The proto-Bantu word *Twa, which is found in the Herero word -*tua*, is generally glossed as slave or pygmy

[79] The dictum that the rule of law/civilisation is what identified a Roman.

[80] This appears to be a rendition of the Herero word *Ndjambi Karunga*. For a discussion on Herero terms for God, ancestral spirits and related subjects see: Gewald, *We Thought We Would be Free* (Cologne 2001) Chp. 6.

[81] A series of articles by W.A. Norton writing in the South African Journal of Science in 1919 clearly drew on information contained in the Blue Book. Writing of the Herero he claims "They worshipped two little sticks called ancestors, the male a wand of Ovampuvu and the female of wild plum" Norton explicitly thanks the 'late Magistrate of Omaruru' ie. Major O'Reilly for providing this and other information. Norton, W.A. 'The South-West Protectorate and its Native Population', *South African Journal of Science*, Vol. 16, 1919 p. 458.

[82] Van Wyk, Ben-Erik & Nigel Gericke, *People's Plants: A Guide to Useful Plants of Southern Africa*, Briza, Pretoria,2000: 288.

animals, all likewise in pairs. The first parents of the Hereros were there too, and all other races were represented. Light had not yet been created. All the world was in darkness, and the people and animals crowded round the parent tree and pressed against one another in sheer terror; no one knew where to go to. The stupid Berg-Damara "Adam" lit a fire, whereupon the lion, the tiger, and all the wild animals of today, and all the wild game, took fright and ran away. To this day they have remained wild. Then the "Great Magician" sent the light, and the people saw that the horses, cattle, goats, and other domestic animals had not taken fright but had stayed. The people then decided to divide the animals. The Herero ancestors immediately took the bull and cow. The others violently disputed their right to these animals; but Herero Adam held on and persisted. He eventually got his own way. The acute differences of opinion which had arisen and the anger and excitement of all the people, speaking and shouting at the same the, resulted in so much confusion of tongues that the different languages were immediately evolved. And thus it came that, owing to this original fight over the first cattle, the various "Adams and Eves," no longer understanding the others, separated in all directions. Away also went the Herero pair taking their chosen cattle with them in triumph.

Their descendants ever since have loved cattle, and regard the herding, tending, and accumulation of large herds of cattle as their sole destiny.

The legend goes on to state how the first parents begot only female children. These virgin daughters were, in due course, mystically influenced by coming into contact with things of the outside world and bore male and female children, from whom the Herero race descended.

It is said that, in this way, the various maternal clans or *Eanda* originated, claiming descent, always on the mother's side, from the traditional progenitress of the clan.[83]

The animal or object supposed to have influenced the progenitress was the totem, and the Hereros called themselves the "marriage relations" of the totem. Thus, there were the "sun's brothers," belonging to the *Ejuva Eanda* or sun clan, the family of the "running spring," the "chameleon," the "limestone," while the silver jackhal, totem of another clan, was called "little brother." It will therefore be understood that Herero communities, independently of their local distribution into tribes, bands, or villages, were composed of several, probably eight or nine, maternal clans, and these again, in some cases, were divided into subgroups. At first, as was the case with the totemistic North American Indians,

---

[83] Regarding the the dual descent and inheritance system practised by Herero in the past see, Eduard Dannert, *Zum Rechte der Herero insbesondere über ihr Familien- und Erbrecht*, (Berlin 1906); Gordon D. Gibson, *The Social Organization of the Southwestern Bantu*, Unpublished D.Phil thesis, University of Chicago (Chicago 1952); Josaphat Hahn, 'Die Ovaherero', in *Zeitschrift der Gesellschaft für Erdkunde zu Berlin*, Verlag von Dietrich Reimer (Berlin 1869); J. Irle, *Die Herero. Ein Beitrag zur Landes-, Volks- und Missionskunde* (Gütersloh 1906); Hendrik Gerhardus Luttig, *The religious system and social organisation of the Herero*, Published Ph.D. thesis University of Leiden (Utrecht 1933); I. Schapera, *Notes on some Herero Genealogies*, (Johannesburg 1979); Heinrich Vedder, "The Herero", in *The Native Tribes of South West Africa*, compiled by C. Hahn, H. Vedder and L. Fourie (Cape Town 1928).]

the members of a clan never intermarried. The result was that they intermingled with other clans. Yet, despite marriage, they retained their *Eanda* membership and based their descent and rights to *Eanda* inheritance, always on the mother's side. (The object of this will be clear when the *Eanda* property is dealt with).

Each clan, or "mother group" (as it is preferable to call the *Eanda*), had a senior member or head who exercised certain powers over the members, and in whom were vested fiduciary functions in regard to the administration, control, and distribution of the property of the group. He alone could dispose of or alienate the cattle of the group, and he only did so in the interests of the group to pay debts or acquire other assets; he generally consulted the tribal council before acting. There is a kind of Socialism about this system of *Eanda* property. It was of great benefit to the poorer members, who could always rely on receiving cows and oxen, on loan, from their *Eanda*, to support and maintain themselves therewith. They lived almost solely on milk. This head was not necessarily the chief. On occasions when the inheritance devolved on the same person through the mother as *Eanda* head and the father as tribal head, this was so, but not often. He was, however, invariably, from the very importance of his position, a sub-chief or Chief Councillor.

Co-existent and contemporary, but of unknown origin, there was, side by side the "Mother-group" or *Eanda*, another division of the tribe into Orders (Herero = *Oruzo*), purely paternal and also totemistic in origin. There were about 16 known orders. Thus a Herero belonged to his *Eanda* by descent through his mother and to his *Oruzo* through his father.

The totems of mother groups and orders were sacred to the members thereof, and in the case of animals their flesh was "taboo" (Herero *Zera* = forbidden). A severe and strict sacrifice-and-diet-law bound the members of the various groups together.

To the *Oruzo* belonged certain inalienable assets. It was essentially a religious order. The head of the order was *ex-officio* chief or head of the clan and high priest of his people. The ritualistic articles, such as the emblematic wands, the holy gourds, the holy place (*okurua*) were in the chief"s keeping. There the holy fire burned perpetually under the devoted care of his chief wife or eldest daughter. To the *Oruzo* also belonged the sacred stock, consisting of specially selected cattle. These animals were the best formed and most beautiful, and were carefully picked out from the herds. The milk of the sacred cows was placed daily in the gourds of the ancestors at the holy place, and never touched. True, indeed, the dogs lapped it up; but, apparently, the ancestors did not mind that, as the dogs lived on. No Herero would, however, dare to touch it. On religious occasions some of the sacred cattle would be sacrificed, but their meat was burnt; it was likewise *zera*.

Having given this very brief outline of their religious and totemistic conceptions, the curious division of the cattle into three distinct classes will be more readily understood.

They were –

(1) the sacred specially selected cattle, which were *res sacrae*[84] and inalienable even by the chief.

(2) the *Eanda* or mother-group trust cattle, owned by no particular individual, but the common property of the family group, and administered by a fiduciary head, who was the eldest son or eldest male descendant of the senior mother.

(3) the privately-owned cattle, the property of the individual. These he could dispose of, during life, at will, and after death his expressed desires were always given effect to, for fear that his spirit might return and wreak vengeance. The individual Herero always reserved a number of his stock, also specially selected, the number being in proportion to his wealth, for sacrifice at his funeral. The skin of his favourite ox was his shroud, and at his graveside the selected cows and oxen were slaughtered so that their master's spirit might not go unaccompanied into the land of shades.

When this division of stock is borne in mind, the atrocious treatment of the Herero people by German traders and the German Government and its effect on the Herero mind will be more fully understood.

It has already been stated that the chief of the clan derived his rights through the *Oruzo* or paternal order to which he belonged. The eldest son of the chief by his principal wife was his heir; failing this his eldest surviving brother became chief, and failing him the eldest surviving son of the brother, always, be it noted, by the chief wife of such brother the idea being that the senior male member of the *Oruzo* in the nearest line from the paternal ancestor should be chief. A younger son by a second or third wife (as Samuel Maharero was) had, elder heirs being alive, no legal claim to the chieftainship.

The chief of the most powerful clan embodied in his person the functions of governor and high priest. Under him, and in a lesser degree vested likewise with powers of government and priestly dignity, were the sub-chiefs or captains, the heads of non-ruling orders, the heads of the mother-groups, and the heads even of the individual families.

The Hereros, like all natives, had no conception of the impersonal nature of government as understood by Europeans. They regarded the person of their chief as the *fons et origo*[85] of all government. Like the king, he could do no wrong; he could not be deposed, nor could he be brought to trial before the council. His person was sacred during lifetime, and after death, when his spirit had gone to join those of his great ancestors, the burial-place of his body was a hallowed and consecrated spot. [*Note.* – The Germans, before the Herero rebellion, desecrated the sacred burial-place of the great chiefs Tjamuaha and Kamaharero at Okahandja by turning it into a vegetable garden, despite all

---

[84] 'Sacred objects'
[85] 'The source and the origin'

protests.[86] This will be referred to again later on.] The chief invariably upheld the laws and usages of his tribe and preserved inviolate their ancient rites and customs. Herein, like the meanest and poorest of his subjects, he was stimulated and preserved by a wholesome fear of the spirits of his ancestors and. the power of the Great Magician. It was only when German intrigue and German policy thrust the ineligible Samuel Maharero into power, merely to use him as their willing tool, as Paramount Chief of all the Hereros, that the customs of the people were violated, their tenderest feelings outraged, and their laws and traditions trodden under foot. And yet the Germans had *pledged* themselves to uphold and respect these "laws and traditions."

In regard to temperament and character, the Hereros of to-day may be described as an intelligent, honest, and proud people, who have had nearly all the good crushed out of them by the German oppressor.

Missionary Brincker described them as candid and sincere. Dr. Hahn says their chief characteristics are self-will, and proneness to fits of depression. Dr. Goering testifies to their frugality and industry; von François (as may well be expected) describes them as crafty knaves. Pechual Losche says they are sincere, reliable, and trustworthy. Mr. Christopher James, the Mining Engineer, in his report of 1903 to the Otavi Mines, Ltd., says they are willing, good hearted, diligent, and quick of perception. When the Herero rebellion broke out, the Hereros under special orders from their chiefs spared the lives of all German women and children and all missionaries.[87] Dr. Felix Meyer says, they were a proud, liberty-loving race, jealously guarding their independence, and with very strong family ties. In their favour may also be mentioned the custom whereby the dying father, his descendants in a circle around him and his favourite child on his bosom, bestows his last blessing on his loved ones (*okusere ondaja ombua*). This proves without doubt the strong affection existing between parents and children. So also the Herero proverb, "the love of the parent is blind." The birth of twins was a great event. The proud father immediately set out on a tour and called on all his and his wife's relations bringing the glad news. It was worth his while because, according to traditional custom, he was not allowed to depart without a present for the twins.

These are the people who were mercilessly slaughtered by the German, Von Trotha, and his Prussian soldiers in 1904-6. These are the human beings of whom von Trotha said, "let not man, woman, or child be spared – kill them all." And 80 per cent. of them were actually so killed or died of thirst in the desert wastes whither they were driven by the merciless German soldiers.

---

[86] The Voigts trading family, which was engaged in horticulture in Okahandja, established vegetable and tobacco gardens on land purchased by them in the immediate vicinity of the graves.

[87] Some of the missionaries who worked with the Herero (such as Eich from Waterberg and Kuhlmann from Okazeva) were strongly critical of German war-time abuses, on the other hand Samuel Kutako claimed after the war that missionaries had "... acted as informers against prominent Hereros, and were the cause of their being hanged by the Germans." Nils Ole Oermann, *Mission, Church and State Relations in South West Africa under German Rule (1884-1915)*, Franz Steiner Verlag, Stuttgart, 1999: pp. 108-109, "Great Britain, 'Correspondence relating to the Wishes of the Natives of the German Colonies as to their Future Government', HMSO, London, 1918: p. 13.

From the moment when the new-born babe was named and touched the head of a calf, presented as a birthday gift, until the death hour when the skin of the favourite ox (*ongombe ohivirikua*) served as his shroud, and the skull of the beloved animal bleached (as a grave memorial) on a neighbouring tree, the Herero's ever-present companions were his cattle. At the graveside, when the holy cattle were being slaughtered so that they might follow their master, the remainder of his herd was collected around the spot in order that the spirit of the deceased might derive pleasure from hearing the lowing and bellowing of his cherished animals. For the sake of his cattle no labour was too great. For long hours beneath a scorching tropical sun, the Herero would draw water, bucket by bucket, from the water-holes or wells for his animals to drink. They dug their water-holes at cost of infinite labour, the sharp horn of the gemsbuck being the substitute for a spade, and a gourd serving for a bucket. And for days and weeks he would persevere, despite terrible hardships and privations, in search of some lost or strayed animal. His whole object in life was the increase and preservation of his herds, which, in the favourable environment and climate of Damaraland, thrived wonderfully. The killing of cattle, except on religious and festive occasions, or when an ox by its strange or peculiar behavior presaged evil, was regarded as a criminal waste bordering on sacrilege. Cows were never killed for food. For nourishment, in addition to wild onions and other roots and herbs and veld berries, the Herero drank sweet milk (*Omaihi*) in the mornings and at night sour milk (*Omaere*) prepared and preserved in stoppered bottle-gourds. The oxen were used for transport and riding and for barter and exchange.

When there was scarcity of provisions, the Herero tightened his belt and held out as long as he could. Hence the belt was called the "hunger killer" (*Etizandjara*). He would have to be very hungry before he killed an ox, and probably a cow would only be sacrificed when death by starvation seemed imminent. "Gluttony," said a Herero proverb, "is the great leveller that is why people become poor".

In this respect the Hereros were the antithesis of the easy-going and improvident Hottentot, who would, if necessary, slaughter one animal after another, until he had none left for breeding purposes.

The earliest available information goes to show that the Hereros were always very rich in horned cattle. As far back as 1760 the South African hunter, Jacob Coetzee (probably the first white man to traverse Great Namaqualand) crossed the Orange River and traveled far north to the vicinity of Rehoboth or Gibeon.[88] He returned to the Cape with reports of Damaras[xi] living in the north who possessed great herds of horned cattle.

[xi] All early British travelers, such as Alexander, Galton, Green, Andersson and others refer to the natives as "Damaras." This accounts for the name Damaraland, which correctly should be "Hereroland" The word Damara is a corruption of the Hottentot word "Daman." They called the Hereros "Buri-Daman" or Cattle Damaras; while the Ovambos and Berg-Damara were called respectively "Corn-Damaras" and "Dirty-Damaras." Captain J.E. Alexander, "An Expedition of Discovery into the Interior of Africa" (1837), was the first writer to refer to "Damaraland" and the "Damaras."

---

[88] Coetzee's account has been republished several times. See, for example, E.C. Godeé Molsbergen, *Reizen in Zuid Afrika in de Hollandse Tijd*, (Gravenhage 1916)

Coetzee's report led to the abortive expedition from the Cape in 1761 under Captain Hope, the object of which was to open a cattle trade with the Hereros. The expedition, after undergoing great hardships, turned back somewhere in the vicinity of the present town of Keetmanshoop.

In 1792, Willem van Renen and Piet Brandt, also South African hunters from the Cape, traveled right up to Hereroland and returned in a state of great enthusiasm regarding the countless herds of horned cattle they had seen. Nothing further appears to have happened until about 1835, when Captain J.E. Alexander visited the country.[89] He confirmed previous reports, and tried to open up a cattle export trade through Walvis Bay and St. Helena. This venture likewise failed, owing to transport difficulties.

In 1876 Palgrave wrote (page 54 of Report):–

> It is impossible to estimate the Damaras wealth, (Palgrave, like other English writers, will persist in calling the Hereros "Damaras"), even approximately, although there is evidence enough to indicate that it is considerable. The poorest families in a tribe possess something, three or four cows, a few oxen, 20 or 30 sheep.

It has already been mentioned that the Herero socialistic system of *Eanda* trust property rendered it impossible for even the poorest Herero to be without sustenance. If he possessed no stock of his own through disease or misfortune, he could always call on the head of his *Eanda* for an issue of stock on loan. Palgrave mentions one under – chief of Kambazembi's named Kavingava, who possessed over 10,000 head of cattle. Kambazembi himself, at his death in 1903, was reported to have possessed no less than 25,000 head of cattle; but included in this number was probably the *Eanda* stock, held by him as trustee for his people. M'Buanjo, an under-chief of Omaruru, possessed in 1903 over 4,000 head of cattle, while the Okahandja and Omaruru chiefs were equally wealthy. Tjetjoo, the chief of the Eastern Hereros, was reputed to be nearly as wealthy as his neighbour Kambazembi. A German soldier, now a settler in the country, who came to the Protectorate with von François in 1890, informed the writer that, at that time, the Omaruru and Waterberg districts were teeming with cattle. He relates that at the sound of a rifle shot the vast herds would stampede in all directions like wild springbok, and that the very earth seemed to quiver and vibrate as they thundered across the veld.

When Germany annexed the country in 1890 the Herero people must have possessed well over 150,000 head of cattle. The Rinderpest scourge in 1897, which destroyed probably half, left, notwithstanding export and slaughter,

---

[89] See Molsbergen (1916) for the accounts by Willem van Reenen (note normal spelling) and Piet Brandt. See also James Alexander *Expedition of Discovery into the Interior of Africa*, Vols 1 & 2, 1838

something like 90,000 head.[90] By 1902, i.e., in less than 10 years after the arrival of the first German settlers, the Hereros retained 45,898 head of cattle, while the 1,051 German traders and farmers then in the country owned 44,487 between them. In 1903 the total value of the live stock exported from the whole territory was 23,337,682 M., equal to over 1,000,000 stg.

By the end of 1905 the surviving Hereros had been reduced to pauperism and possessed nothing at all.

In 1907 the Imperial German Government by Ordinance prohibited the natives of South-west Africa from possessing large stock.

The story of the German traders and how they, with the direct connivance, sanction, and approval of the German Government, deliberately robbed the Hereros of their cattle is one of the darkest of the very black pages of German history in South-west Africa, and will be dealt with in a separate chapter.

---

[90] This devastating disease swept the African continent in the period 1889-1897 and killed hooved animals within days. The social, cultural and economic impact of the rinderpest, which was alleged to have killed up to 90% of the cattle belonging to some Herero communities, has yet to be researched in detail, although it is clear that the disease seriously disrupted the colonial transport network which relied on ox-wagons and thus encouraged the building of railway lines in Namibia. However, added tension came from the perception that the inoculation of German herds meant that there losses were considerably less than Herero losses. Thomas Ofcansky, 'The 1889-97 Rinderpest Epidemic and the Rise of British and German Colonialism in Eastern and Southern Africa', *Journal of African Studies*, Vol. 8, no. 1 (1981).

CHAPTER NINE

CONFISCATION OF HERERO CATTLE BY THE GERMAN GOVERNMENT

The wholesale and unblushing theft by the Germans of the cattle of the Hereros was one of the primary causes which led to the Herero rebellion of 1904. There were other causes, however, all arising out of German oppression and misrule. It is necessary, therefore, that, before dealing specially with what must for ever be one of the most shameful incidents in the history of German colonisation, the other contributory causes should be outlined in brief. In order to do this, it is necessary to go back to May 1890, when, owing to the death of Kamaharero, chief of the Okahandja Hereros, the question of his successor arose. In terms of the agreement of 1885 the Germans had pledged themselves "to respect the customs and usages existing in the country of Maharero." Kamaharero was the leader (under Frederick Green, the English hunter) of the Hereros in their war of emancipation against the Hottentots in 1864, when the latter were overthrown and large herds of cattle captured. As a result of this, Kamaharero styled himself the great and powerful leader. He was however never acknowledged, even by his own people, as paramount chief of all the Hereros. As Dr. Felix Meyer puts it (*Wirtschaft und Recht der Herero*:– 1905):–

> An ordained leader of all the Herero tribes was not known in Herero law at the the of the German occupation. Only the knowledge of their national community of origin held the various tribes together.

The German agreement of 1885 was made with Kamaharero, whom the Germans, to suit their own purposes, were pleased to regard as the paramount chief over Hereroland; but even they had qualms on the subject, as they went to Omaruru and got Manasse, as powerful a chief as Kamaharero, to sign a ratification. The other chiefs were ignored. Nevertheless, as Dr. Meyer clearly points out, the chiefs Kambazembi, Muretti, Tjetjoo, Zacharias, and others not mentioned by Meyer, such as Kahimema, Nikodemus, and M'Buanjo, in no way recognised his (Kamaharero's) pretensions to paramountcy, and held that they were not bound by his agreements.

Of this fact the Germans were, in 1890, well aware; but they ignored it on the plea that it was more convenient to deal with one authority than with the lot (*Es ist bequemer, mit einer Autorität, als mit einer masse zu verhandeln*). So when Kamaherero died, his younger son, Samuel Maharero, described by von François as a vain, selfish drunkard, and referred to by Leutwein as devoid of character (he was, states Leutwein, "selfish, had a weakness for alcohol, and last, but not least, a fondness for women"), was pitchforked into the chieftainship and declared paramount chief of the Hereros. He was alleged to be a Christian – 90 per cent. of his people were heathens.[91] "As a Christian," says Leutwein, "the Mission got little joy out of him, he none out of the Mission." Hereros say that the missionaries supported the Government, and told the Hereros that Samuel was the rightful heir according to the Christian laws, whatever they may be.

Samuel preferred the cases of rum with which the bounty of the *Kaiser und König* kept him liberally supplied; it being well-known that, to such an individual, the signing of treaties or agreements was not surrounded with much difficulty as long as rum was plentiful.

This foisting of Samuel on to them as chief immediately to the great joy of the Germans, split the Hereros into two sections. Here we have the first example of the policy of playing off one section against another, or, as Leutwein later styled it, my *divide et impera* policy.

The lawful heir to Kamaherero was a sub-chief of the Eastern Hereros named Nikodemus. He was the eldest son of a predeceased brother to Kamaherero, and the recognised head of his *Oruzo*.[92] Kamaharero had no sons by his principal wife, and Samuel, a younger son by another, was not even heir to his father's stock; his poverty was also a great recommendation from the German point of view, as will be seen. Dr. Felix Meyer has no doubts as to the illegality of the German procedure. Meyer was a *Kammergerichtsrat*, a kind of judicial Privy Councilor, so his opinion is worth quoting. In his *Wirtschaft und Recht der Herero*, already frequently quoted from herein, he says (at page 24), referring to this incident –

> Thereby the Colonial Administration created not only a new authority (which probably was in the interests of a simple and centralised system of government); but it also, as will be indicated, broke into the laws of succession and inheritance of the Hereros.

Later on (see page 38), referring again to the appointment of Samuel Maharero as chief in preference to the rightful heir Nikodemus,[93] in regard to whom Samuel was, according to Herero law, only in the position of a younger brother, Meyer adds:–

> It can easily be understood how deeply this illegal interference with their laws must have aroused the feelings of the Hereros; more particularly when, at the same the, a hitherto non-existent de jure ruler over the whole nation (i.e., paramount chief) was forced upon them. One can appreciate how bitterly disillu-

---

[91] On the development of Christianity in Herero society in the nineteenth century see, Dag Henrichsen, *Herrschaft und Identifikation im vorkolonialen Zentralnamibia: Das Herero- und Damaraland im 19. Jahrhundert*, PhD thesis University of Cologne 1997. On Christianity during the 1904 - 1908 war see, Gewald, *Herero Heroes*, chp. 6

[92] Patrilineal descent line

[93] For a discussion on the succession dispute that accompanied Samuel Maharero's rise to power see, Gewald, *Herero Heroes*, Chp. 2

sioned Nikodemus and his supporters were, when not only the dignity to which he aspired, but also the Oruzo assets (i.e., the holy cattle, &c., of the religious order) of his late uncle, were taken from him and bestowed on a younger and less worthy person.

(*Note.* Samuel, being a declared Christian could not exercise the office of high priest, and to place the holy assets under his charge was, to heathen Herero thinking, an insult to the ancestors and a sacrilege.)

> For the same reason the other chiefs refused to recognise Samuel, whom they despised as a mere child, as the actual paramount chief of their land. Nikodemus, in his anger (continues Meyer, whose candid words give much food for reflection), was at the bottom of the intrigue which resulted in the rebellion of his sub-clan of Ovambandjera, under his under-chief Kahimema, assisted by the Khauas Hottentots of Gobabis. It was only the rapid victory at Otyunda, 1896, which enabled German arms to nip the rebellion in the bud. Of course Nikodemus and Kahimema were, after sentence by Military Court, shot as rebels at Okahandja on 12th June 1896. The tribe of Khauas Hottentots was practically exterminated (*zo gut wie vernichtet*) and their territory declared Crown land. The fire was however still glowing under the ashes and it was fed by Asa Riarua, the half brother of Nikodemus. An undying hatred inspired him and his party against Samuel and his protectors and it eventually became one of the main causes of the great rebellion.

Yet Governor Leutwein was astonished at the "dark mistrust" of the Hereros! Having created a "paramount chief," it was essential that he should be used to German advantage. The opportunity came in 1894, when Leutwein was Governor. As already stated, the Germans had formed a land settlement syndicate and immigrants were coming into the country to settle on the land. The land however was claimed by the natives, and they declined to give it up. Thereupon the syndicate (under the auspices of the German Colonial Co.) formally applied to the Government for grant of 50,000 square kilometres (approximately 4,500,000 acres), east of Windhuk and stretching towards Gobabis and Hoachanas. This application was made on the recommendation of Professor Dr. Karl Dove, of Jena, who had inspected the area. In reply to the application, the Government informed the syndicate that the land was claimed by Bastards, Hereros, and Hottentots, and that as the troops in occupation were not strong enough to occupy and protect the area, the request would have to be deferred till later. This was in 1892. The more practicable and more honest way of acquiring land would have been to purchase from the chiefs. The soldiers were coming however and this idea did not find favour apparently.

In April 1893, von François noticed that the agents of the syndicate were, to quote his words, "acting recklessly," giving out land "to which they were not entitled and making promises which they were unable to fulfil," so he wrote to Berlin suggesting that the syndicate's work should be suspended and that the Government should control all questions of immigration and land settlement. The then *Kolonial-Direktor* at Berlin (Dr. Kayser) refused to accept the recommendations of Von François, and said that the syndicate should continue its work, confining itself, for the present, to the neighbourhood of Windhuk. Immigrants continued to arrive and were given, or rather sold, farms which existed only in the imagination of the directors of this precious syndicate.

Rohrbach, to whom we are indebted for most of this information, describes these farms as *luftschwebenden i.e* floating in the air,

In 1894, Leutwein decided to solve the problem once and for all. He went to Okahandja and on the 6th December 1894 drew up an agreement for "Chief-Captain Samuel Maharero" to sign, whereby the whole southern boundary of Hereroland from Swakopmund to Gobabis was defined. The astute Leutwein had described the boundaries in such a way as to secure to the land settlement syndicate the town and grazing lands of Gobabis (belonging to the Khauas Hottentots) and some of the finest cattle grazing veld on the White Nosob River. The Chief-Captain was promised an annual salary of 2,000 marks (100*l*.), payable half-yearly, provided that the "Southern boundary line as determined upon ... is respected by the Hereros and that their cattle posts are withdrawn from the territory now falling with the area of the German Government." (Original agreement filed at Windhuk; Records A.1.a.2.Vol.I.).

This boundary line extended over 400 miles. Samuel Maharero was not recognised by his fellow chiefs. In any event the southern boundary of his own district, Okahandja, was probably less than a sixth of the whole line. Yet, at a stroke of Maharero's pen, chiefs like Zacharias, Tjetjoo, Nikodemus and Kahimema were, without having so much as even been consulted, deprived of rights which they had held, through their ancestors, for generations past.

Leutwein writes (page 64): "This difficult agreement for them to assent to was signed by Samuel, as was always his way, light heartedly and with pleasure; but his headmen pondered earnestly over it" ... Having fixed this boundary line, it was the easiest thing in the world, for the Germans at any rate, to decide on measures against trespassers.

This unbeaconed and unfenced boundary line, to the simple Hereros grazing their cattle along its edges, was not unlike the farms Rohrbach described as floating in the air.

Nothing could be risked however until more troops arrived, and this necessitated a wait of nearly 12 months. Towards the end of 1895, Leutwein was able to make his next move. He entered into an agreement (which must have been secret and private, as it cannot be found in the records at Windhuk) with Samuel Maharero whereby the German Government would impound "all the herds of Herero cattle found trespassing over the boundaries." There was no question of fining or warning the owners and then returning their cattle. No. The settlers and the syndicate were badly in need of cattle, and the "trading business" had not yet fully developed. "The impounded cattle," says Leutwein (page 92), "would then be sold and the proceeds divided between the German Government and the paramount chief."

"Whereas, formerly, the confiscation of their cattle in this manner, would undoubtedly have caused war," says the self-complacent Leutwein, "we had, by means of the above-mentioned agreement, obtained the legitimate right thereto."

In other words, he meant to imply that from then on any other Herero chief taking up arms to protect his cattle from confiscation had no legitimate *casus belli*[94] and no standing. He could therefore be shot as a rebel and this is exactly what happened to the chiefs Nikodemus and Kahimema. "Of this right," continues Leutwein:–

> advantage was taken in the beginning of 1896, when a force under Major Mueller took away several thousands of cattle belonging to Hereros at Heusis and Aris. Only then did the significance of the agreement become clear to the Hereros. Excitement and war fever extended throughout the entire Protectorate. The white traders in the interior were threatened and had to take hurried flight. As characteristic (proceeds Leutwein) I here wish to mention that the son and nephew of the paramount chief, who, at the time were doing voluntary service with the troops at Windhuk, burst into tears on hearing of the confiscation of these cattle and begged for immediate release from military duty. The war fever slacked down at Okahandja when, some days later, the half share of the proceeds of sale, in terms of the agreement, was paid to the chief as indication that the German Government merely acted in the exercise of its rights under the agreement. Outside Okahandja however the desire for war increased, and eventually even the Europeans were infected, not only private persons, but also members of the Government. Especially among a section of the Officers, the war fever, combined with under-estimation of their opponents, was very noticeable.

On the 20th January 1896, Leutwein addressed a meeting of white inhabitants at Windhuk, and succeeded in persuading them to preserve peace. On the same day he proceeded to Okahandja. There the alleged paramount chief and about thirty headmen and also chiefs from outside, among whom appeared Nikodemus and Kahimema, were awaiting the arrival of the German Governor. The Herero "opposition," says Leutwein, "was led by the old Riarua ... who tried to pass himself off as leader of all Hereros." After severely snubbing Riarua, Leutwein put the following two questions to the meeting:–

(1) What boundaries do you desire?
(2) What punishment is to be imposed on trespassers?

He told them that "both questions were fraught with the alternative danger of threatening war" (*i.e.*, if not satisfactorily answered). That such a war would result "only in the extermination of the one party thereto, and that party could only be the Hereros."[95] "Even to this day" (1905), says Leutwein, "I can dis-

---

[94] 'Cause for war' - An act regarding as justifying war
[95] Meeting held by Leutwein in Okahandja on 21rst January 1896, Theodor Leutwein, *Elf Jahre Gouverneur in Deutsch-Südwestafrika*, (Berlin 1906) p. 95. Original text, *Ein solcher könnte nur mit Vernichtung der einen Partei endigen, und diese Partei könnten nur die Hereros sein.* ("Such a [war] could only end in the extermination of one party, and this party could only be that of the Herero.")

tinctly remember the ominous silence which followed on my remarks, of which one could say it would have been possible to hear a pin drop."

After several days of discussion the Hereros of Okahandja demanded –

> (I) That the Seeis River, the water in which was indispensable for their herds, should be retained by them.
> (II) That the paramount chief and the Governor should decide on punishment for trespass.

"This first demand," says Leutwein, meant a shifting forward of the boundaries some 8 kilometres. As the advantages of this change of boundary would have been of benefit only to the Western Hereros, *i.e.*, those of Okahandja, Nikodemus, on behalf of the Eastern Hereros, immediately came forward and on behalf of his people, asked for the return of the Gobabis area to them. This gave me the most beautiful opportunity (*die schonste gelegenheit*) to put into force my *divide et impera* policy.

Therefore I granted the wish of the Okahandja Hereros and definitely refused the request of Nikodemus. As a result of this the latter went into rebellion three months later, while the Okahandja Hereros remained on our side."

Later on in the same year it was decided to disarm the Eastern Hereros, their kinsmen the Ovambandjeru and the Khauas Hottentots of Gobabis. They were called upon to hand in all firearms, and they refused to do so.

The reason for this will now be perfectly clear. The native chiefs disputed Samuel Maharero's right to fix their boundary lines, and they were legally correct in this attitude. The Germans ignored their protests and confiscated all cattle found over the borders. Fearing that this would lead to reprisals, the Germans, who were keen not only on the cattle, but also on the land of these people (it was the area asked for by the land settlement syndicate) decided to render the people innocuous by depriving them of their arms.

Chiefs Nikodemus and Kahimema of the Hereros and Andreas Lambert[96] of the Khauas Hottentots of Gobabis refused to hand in their arms. An expedition was sent out from Windhuk and fighting resulted. The chief of the Hottentots was killed, his land and stock confiscated and his tribe, as Felix Meyer puts it, practically exterminated (*so gut wie vernichtet*).

After the first fight, Nikodemus and Kahimema went in to Okahandja voluntarily and openly to protest against the action of the German forces. There they were both arrested, tried by court-martial and shot as rebels.

The chief crime against Nikodemus was that he was the lawful heir to the chieftainship and his continued existence was a nuisance to the Germans. Leutwein deliberately treated him in such a way as to goad him into doing something which would give a pretext, even the flimsiest pretext, for removing

---

[96] The Gei-/Khauen were often referred to as the 'Amraal Oorlam' after their original leader Amraal Lambert who had led them from Bethanie in 1820 to settle in the area to the south of Gobabis. Andries was executed at //Nao-sanabes (Köhler 1959a: 19)

him altogether. *Divide et irnpera.* The brave Kahimema died with his chief, whose legitimate cause he had espoused from the very outset.

Before leaving the subject a description of the closing scene in the life of Nikodemus, as it flowed from the pen of Schwabe, Captain of Infantry of the German Army (*mit Schwert und Pflug*, page 304), may be added:–

> "12th June ... At 10 a.m. the First Field Company under Estorf arrived to fetch the condemned men (Nikodemus and Kahimema), to whom, at their request, I gave some wine. Then they were bound and lifted on to an ox-cart and the procession started. Mounted police led the way, then followed Estorff and myself on horseback, a half-company under Kageneck on foot, the cart surrounded by horsemen and in the rear Ziethen, on foot, with the remaining hall-company.
>
> We had to travel through the entire village. There was no male Herero to be seen; but the women were rolling about on the ground, and covering their heads with sand and earth. From every house, every hut, every garden, the long drawn blood-curdling lamentations accompanied the distinguished chiefs on their last journey. In silence, and drawn up in a great square, the guns unlimbered at the sides, the troops received us. Then we went on through the deep sand of the river bed to the place of execution. Commandos of Hendrik Witbooi's and Simon Cooper's Hottentots guarded the place. Halt! The condemned men were lifted from the cart. Proudly, and with head erect, Kahimema walked to the tree to which he was bound; Nikodemus, half dead with fear, had to be carried. The eyes of the two were then bound, and the firing sections under Lieutenants von Ziethen and Count Kageneck marched into their places. Captain von Estorff gave the signal:– Short commands:– Present Fire! The volleys rolled like thunder through the neighbouring mountains and two traitors had ceased to live."

This bombastic description of a pitiful tragedy helps us to understand the feelings of the Hereros, even those living in Okahandja, towards their real chief, Nikodemus. The presence, as guards, of the Hottentot Commandos of Witbooi and Simon Cooper recalls to mind the fact that "protection" from these Hottentots was the promise on which the Hereros had relied when making the original agreements with the Germans.

This was only in June 1896. Nearly eight years had yet to elapse before, January 1904, the crowning catastrophe occurred, and by that the even Samuel Maharero, conscience stricken and goaded to desperation by German oppression and injustice, had turned and was foremost in leading a once more united nation, companions in utter misery, against the unbearable tyranny and brutality of Germany.

CHAPTER TEN

THE GERMAN TRADERS AND HOW THEY TRADED

In addition to the shooting of Nikodemus and Kahimema, large numbers of cattle and sheep belonging to them and to their people were seized and confiscated by the German Government as a punishment for their rebellion.

After these happenings, and after witnessing the unhappy fate of the Khauas Hottentots of Gobabis, the terrified natives withdrew their flocks and herds as far north of the so-called southern boundary line as possible. This was the only means by which they could reasonably hope to preserve their property.

This move embarrassed the German Administration and placed the "Land Settlement Syndicate" in a quandary.

Rohrbach describes the position very accurately.

> "The chief necessity in the establishment of the new settlers was the supply of stock, and the difficulties in this direction increased in proportion with the growth of the newly opened up farming propositions. Every newly founded farming venture required, above all things, a supply of breeding stock. The White ranchers and farmers who had breeding stock, held on to them as far as possible and only sold in cases of extreme necessity; moreover no farm had at that the been so far developed that the number of stock acquired by breeding was in excess of the available grazing ground. So for the newly arrived farmer no other course remained but, before starting business as a farmer, to enter into trading work with the Hereros, and there to acquire the cows he needed by barter...
> In addition to breeding stock the future farmer required transport oxen. The Hereros were also the chief producers of these ... the trade with the Hereros constituted for the commencing farmer the normal channel through which in the first instance he could get possession of the required breeding stock ... it is, therefore, an error to take it for granted that before the rebellion (1904) the farmer and trader were distinct and separate occupations. In any case, there were very few persons who had not found it necessary to be traders first of all before they could become farmers. When public opinion in Germany, on the outbreak of the 1904 rebellion, sharply criticised the excesses of the traders, no one in the country wanted to admit ever having been a trader and everyone had always been a farmer only."

Thus it came about that, when the Hereros no longer trespassed and gave cause for confiscation, it was found necessary for the German to go out and trade with him for his cattle and sheep.

In the earlier part of this report mention is made of the views of the German missionaries and others in regard to the British traders who in the early days had been their competitors. It is needless to remark that, shortly after German annexation, the British trader was made to leave and a clear field opened for his German successor. Here is an instance of how the German traders carried on:–

(Schwabe's *Mit Schwert und Pflug*.)

> As an example (writes Captain Schwabe) of the ignorance of the veld-living Herero as to the value of money I may quote the following. A trader camps near a Herero village. To him are driven oxen which the Herero wishes to sell. "How much do you want for the oxen?" says the trader. "Fifty pounds sterling," replies the Herero. "Good," says the trader, "here you have a coat valued at 20*l*., trousers worth 10*l*., and coffee and tobacco worth 20*l*., that is in all 50*l*." The Herero is satisfied; he knows that according to the custom of the traders, he cannot expect more for his cattle. He may probably exchange the coat for a blanket and get some sugar in lieu of tobacco, and he will also (as is customary) by begging get a little extra; if, however, he does not succeed the transaction is closed. It will be admitted that this sort of trading is exceptional and quite original; it requires to be learned and the newcomer will have to pay for his experience, before he is able to emulate the dodges and tricks of the old traders.

It will be of interest to learn from the Hereros themselves how these traders behaved. The following quotations are taken from sworn affidavits made in the course of the past three or four months:–

Under-Chief Daniel Kariko[97] *of Omaruru* states (dealing with the reasons why they rebelled in 1904):–

> Our people were being robbed and deceived right and left by German traders, their cattle were taken by force; they were flogged and ill-treated and got no redress. In fact the German police assisted the traders instead of protecting us. Traders would come along and offer goods. When we said that we had no cattle to spare, as the rinderpest had killed so many, they said they would give us credit. Often, when we refused to buy goods, even on credit, the trader would simply off-load goods and leave them, saying that we could pay when we liked, but in a few weeks he would come back and demand his money or cattle in lieu thereof. He would then go and pick out our very best cows he could find. Very often one man's cattle were taken to pay other people's debts. If we objected and tried to resist the police would be sent for and, what with the floggings and the threats of shooting, it was useless for our poor people to resist. If the traders had been fair and reasonable like the old English traders of the early days we would never have complained, but this was not trading at all, it was only theft and robbery. They fixed their own prices for the goods, but would never let us place our own valuation on the cattle. They said a cow was worth 20 marks only. For a bag of meal they took eight cows, which to us were equivalent to 16 oxen, as the Hereros would always give two oxen for the cow, as she is a breeder, and we loved to increase our herds. For a pair of boots a cow was taken. Most traders took only cows, as they were farmers also and wanted to increase their herds. Often when credit had been given, they came back and claimed what they called interest on the debt. Once I got a bag of meal on credit, and later on the trader came and took

---

[97] Leader of a Herero force sent in 1880 by Chief Willem Zeraua to defend Okombahe. By 1891 Kariko was reported to be in conflict with the Damara community at Okombahe led by Cornelius Goreseb. Kariko and his followers left Okombahe shortly after a German garrison was established there in 1892 and settled at Eharni (!Kawab), but followed a raid moved again to Otujap near Omikana and!Gorixas. Kariko was reportedly removed from his position as sub-chief by Manasse of Omaruru. When the Herero rose against the Germans in January, 1904, Kariko wrote several letters to Cornelius Goreseb unsuccessfully urging him and the Damara community at Okombahe to join the rising. (Wagner 1957: 33-36)

CHAPTER TEN

eight cows for the debt and two more cows for what he called credit; thus it cost me 10 cows altogether. Just before the rebellion, in 1903, things got worse than ever. All traders came round and started to collect debts.
(*Note.* This arose out of an Ordinance enacted in Berlin whereby outstanding trading debts were declared prescribed after a lapse of 12 months.)[98]

Some debts they claimed had never existed; often their claims were quite false, and they were deliberately stealing our cattle. We complained to the German police, but were told that we were all liars and that, as a German could never lie, his word would always be taken even if half a dozen of us had the impudence to contradict him. This made us feel as if it were just as well not to be alive. Our people cried and lamented the loss of their stock; our poorer people no longer had enough milk to drink; all our cows were going and every month saw our property dwindle away. We saw our chiefs, who complained and complained till they were tired. No heed was taken of them, and we had no courts of law to which to appeal for justice.
(N.B. This is actually true. There were no courts before July 1903.)

Headman Moses M Buanjo of Omaruru, whose father M'Buanjo, an under-chief, was one of the wealthiest Hereros and owned several thousand cattle (he to-day owns 20 or 30 goats), states:–

Although we all protested and were dissatisfied, Germans came into our country, soldiers and traders. They soon began to do just what they pleased. They took our cattle, ill-treated our people, flogged them and we had no protection. It takes too long for me to tell all that they did. Their traders charged extortionate prices for goods and undervalued our stock. Our chiefs were powerless; our old laws and customs were no longer recognised; even the sacred cattle and the cattle of the tribe which no one could sell (the *Eanda* stock) were taken by force for real and bogus claims. Heavy interest was charged. If a debtor disputed the claim, the police came and assisted the trader.

Hosea Mungunda, headman of the Hereros of Windhuk, in giving a sworn statement as to the reasons for the great rebellion in 1904, places this taking of cattle first among their reasons. This man, one of the finest types of Bantu humanity, is a first cousin of the late chief Kamaherero.

The reasons for rebellion were:–

(a) The extortion of German traders who robbed us of our cattle. Which had been greatly diminished owing to rinderpest. Our cattle were appropriated at such a rate that we felt it was intended to reduce us to pauperism. The Germans took sacred cattle and private cattle, quite regardless of our customs and organisation. We protested and complained bitterly, but the Germans took no notice. Sometimes we persuaded them to return our holy cattle, but then we had to give them three or four ordinary cattle in exchange.[99] This we often did, but it greatly diminished our stock.

---

[98] Helmut Bley argues that the new credit regulations and the reaction of German traders to them were blamed by Governor Leutwein for increasing friction between Herero and German communities. However he points out that four male German traders were also explicitly protected by Samuel Maharero at the outbreak of the war. Bley, *South-West*, pp. 135-138.

[99] On account of colouring or horn shapes specific cattle were considered to be ritually important to individual Herero. This meant that certain cattle could not be traded, sold or slaughtered, as to do so would be to transgress specific taboos and incur the wrath of ancestors.

This affidavit by Hosea was made in the presence of the following leading Hereros, who agreed with Hosea's statement and signed the affidavit in corroboration:–

(1) Barmenias Zerua, son of the late chief of the Otjimbingwe Hereros.
(2) Nickanor Kanungatji, nephew of the late chief Kahimema,
(3) Leonard Gautheta, nephew of the late chief Nikodemus,
(4) Hugo Tjetjoo, nephew of the late chief Tjetjoo,
(5) Elias Gorambuka, nephew of the late chief Kamaherero
and several others.

Samuel Kutako, a well-educated man, says:–

> The German traders forced our people to buy goods and took our cattle in payment. They robbed our people by charging a certain price when giving credit, and later increasing the price when asking for payment. They used to select the cattle they wanted from the Hereros' herds and drive them away. It was useless to object. They simply took cattle by force. The police did not help us; we were black and got no justice. I have personally had to give a cow for a pair of cord trousers or a pair of boots. We had no idea of the value of goods in those days… Nowadays I pay 10s. to 15s. for trousers. That is why I say the German traders robbed us. A cow is worth much more… We used to beg and pray of the traders not to take our holy cattle … but as our holy cattle were the best we had, the traders would reply "that is a matter of indifference. You owe me money and I will take the cattle I select."

Christof Katsimune, an assistant headman of Hereros at Omaruru, states:–

> I knew a Herero named Kamukowa. who lived at Okakenge in the Okahandja district. He had many cattle and small stock. The traders came and took every head of stock that he had, and he had to go into the veld and look for herbs and roots as food and to beg from his friends. The trader who took all his stock was afterwards a lieutenant in the German forces. It was useless to go to the German authorities and police to complain. They took no notice of us and helped the traders.

These instances could be multiplied *ad nauseam* but there is no space in this report for more.

To the reader of these extracts there may arise doubts as to whether it can be believed that the prices given by the traders for cattle were so low as 20s. To people used to the well-ordered control of British government the question will also arise: Surely these Hereros are exaggerating: surely no man could take the law into his own hands and deprive simple savages of their property in this way. There must have been courts of law, and some police protection? To such queries, the reply is that the Hereros are telling the plain truth. There were no courts of law to which they might appeal; there was no police protection for them; and the valuation of 20s. alleged by them, as the traders price for a cow, is substantially correct.

Let us see what the Germans themselves have to say on the subject. Professor Pr. Karl Dove, of Jena, sometime Director of Land Settlement at Windhuk, in his book *Deutsche Südwest Afrika*[100] (at page 10) says:–

> The normal price of a good Herero ox was 40 marks. As the traders were in a position however to regulate prices and place their own valuation on the goods given by them in exchange for such cattle to the natives, I am of opinion, after careful inquiry, that one cannot go far wrong in assuming that in actual fact the value of an ox would not work out at more than 20 marks.

The rebellion broke out in January 1904. Up till about July 1903 (*i.e.*, from 1890), no provision had been made in regard to the administration of civil law.

> "It was not necessary to do so" (says Leutwein) "so long as the territory was inhabited by a small white population. The parties to a dispute endeavoured to come to a settlement through the mediation of the nearest official or officer. With the increase of white population and the extension of trade and travel, matters however assumed a different aspect."

It will be observed therefore that the unfortunate natives could only rely on the mediation of the nearest officer or official. They have already stated with what results.

Did they get common justice? No German will deny that they did not; for, as Professor Dr. Karl Dove (in his above quoted book) characteristically puts it, "leniency towards the natives is cruelty to the whites" (*milde gegen die Eingeborenen ist grausamkeit gegen die Weisze*). As for justice, the learned Professor waves it aside, and says:–

> As to the ideas of their sense of justice, these are based on false premises. It is incorrect to view justice, in regard to the natives, as if they were of the same kultur-position as ourselves. They have no conception of what ownership of ground means.

It will now be understood how by 1903 more than half of the cattle in Hereroland had passed into German hands. Even after 1903, when their courts were established, natives were not allowed to give evidence on oath.

One is here reminded of the demand already referred to, that in court the evidence of one white man can only be outweighed by the corroborated statements of seven coloured persons.

---

[100] Karl Dove, *Deutsche-SüdWest Afrika*, Wilhelm Süsserott, Berlin, 1913.

CHAPTER ELEVEN

GRADUAL APPROPRIATION OF HERERO LAND AND VIOLATION OF HERERO CUSTOMS

Notwithstanding what has been written in the foregoing chapter, it will be said by some people that after all this unblushing system of stock theft, which Germans were pleased to call trading, must have been carried on unknown to the heads of the German Government and that it could not possibly have been sanctioned in Berlin.

But what do we find? Not only that it was known and approved, but also that it was regarded as a desirable and cheap means of attaining an end, i.e., the displacement of the native in favour of the white immigrant. The white man was able to acquire stock without financial aid from the State, and having acquired stock. he could graze it on the land on which the despoiled natives had formerly grazed it. The natives, reduced to penury and being no longer independent, would be compelled to enter into the service of the white man and act as the herds of the stock which they formerly called their own. Thus Germany had in mind the solution of the land settlement, stock supply, and native labour questions. and she considered that the end justified the means.

As early as 19th January 1893, von Lindequist, Government Assessor and acting Governor, in the absence of Leutwein, wrote to the Imperial Chancellor in Berlin, reporting on the steps taken by him to preserve the southern boundary line, as fixed between Samuel Maharero and Leutwein. Referring to the large Herero population on the Nosob River and remarking on the size of their herds of cattle, this gentleman (who afterwards became Governor and later Under-Secretary of State for the Colonies) says:–

> Only a continued blood-letting by the German traders. as was done annually by Witbooi up to three years ago, will again reduce the quantity of their cattle to the right proportions and enable the Germans to make use of the right bank of the Nosob.(German Records, Windhuk. Vol. Al., A2, Vol. 1.)

This is a report by the acting Governor to the Imperial Chancellor. Here we find the Germans emulating the Hottentot chief Hendrik Witbooi, who at any rate formally declared war before raiding Herero cattle.

To his credit be it said that Governor Leutwein, when the scandal grew to such great proportions as to forebode war, took steps with a view to suppressing the giving of credit by unscrupulous traders which, as has been indicated, was generally the preliminary to the robberies. In 1899 he submitted a draft Ordinance to Berlin, by which he proposed to create courts of law, in which claims against natives by traders and others could be adjudicated on. The native chiefs were to be co-assessors with Germans on the courts and claims based on credit would after a certain period be illegal and not actionable. Leutwein points out how he wished to abolish the credit system altogether, and he bitterly complains of how his proposals were described as "unheard" of and "monstrous," and how he was described as lacking in knowledge of the legal position. The white settlers raised a howl of indignation and "holy-wrath," and for five years the struggle continued between Leutwein on the one side and on the other the Berlin Government, plus the Directors of the Land and Trading Syndicates (living in Germany, of course), plus the traders – and settlers in South-west Africa.

In the meantime the blood-letting, after the style of Witbooi, was going on merrily, and the Herero people were groaning under the weight of the accumulated injustices perpetrated on them. In 1903 Leutwein succeeded in getting something definite from Berlin. The famous Credit Ordinance was promulgated in the middle of that year. Traders were (against Leutwein's direct advice) given one year in which to collect outstandings, which would be prescribed thereafter, and they fell upon the Herero cattle like a pack of ravenous wolves.

The authorities in Germany probably suspected that this would be the last straw, and that the Hereros would now give them the chance for which they were ready waiting. Rohrbach says: "For the results of this measure, decided upon in Berlin, Leutwein rightly repudiated responsibility." Referring to the direct results of the 1903 Ordinance, Rohrbach says, "the traders hastened to notify their outstanding claims against the Hereros, and, where possible, to collect them personally." No fewer than 106,000 claims against the Hereros were filed in terms of the Ordinance.

Apart from the taking of their cattle, there was the gradual appropriation of their land, a process which went on concurrently with the cattle-lifting and grew in proportion as the number of cattle acquired by the white "traders" increased.

On 19th August 1901 the Herero headmen on the White Nosob River addressed the following letter to the German Governor from Otjinene through the missionary Lang:–

Most Honoured Governor,

The undersigned Herero headmen have just come to me and have requested me to convey the following to your Honour: "Kayata of Okatumba declares that in Easter 1900, a settler, Mr. Westphal, camee to Okatumba, where he built a house of poles and opened a small store therein. Five weeks ago he has started to build a house of limestone. Kavata and Muambo forbade him to do this, aṣ he had no ownership; but Mr. Westphal took no notice of them. They cannot give Mr. Westphal a settlement at Okatumba. as the place will remain theirs and their childrens. This treatment has caused them to call the other headmen together for a council... Last week Mr. Stopke came here, and he told us that he had purchased the place, between the farm of Mr. Conrad on Orumbo and the farm of Mr. Schmerenbeck in Onunaudjereke, from the Government at Windhuk, and he demanded therefore that Mbaratjo and his people who live there should leave the place. In Otjivero lives Mr. Heldt. He has been there three years and has made Herero endeavour to buy the place. In Okamaraere, opposite Orumbo, lives Mr. Wosillo; in Omitara Mr. Gilers, and in Okahua Mr. von Falkenhausen has settled lately ... Otjipaue has been acquired by Mr. Schmerenbeck and Otjisaesu by Mr. Voigts.

But now, Honoured Governor, where are we to live when our entire river and all our land is taken away from us? We annex a sketch showing all werfts (Herero villages) in the area of Otjitsaesu up to Omitara. These all water their cattle on the White Nosob, so we again ask, where are all these people to go to?

We see with dismay how one place after another is going into the hands of the white people and therefore, Honoured Governor, we pray you most respectfully not to sanction any further sales here in the area of the White Nosob."

This letter, of which as usual no notice was taken, is, says Rohrbach, "an example of how the land settlement syndicate managed its settlement work."

"Every one of these farms," says he, "as enumerated by the Hereros, were situated in Herero territory on the White Nosob or near the river, along the northern boundary of the concession territory of the syndicate."

Here we see that the Germans, after severely punishing the Hereros for trespassing over their boundaries, as fixed by agreement, did not hesitate for a moment to break that agreement, cross the Herero boundaries, and take land there as soon as it suited their purpose; and again the Hereros got no protection.

Having so appropriated a piece of land in Herero territory, the German fixed his own boundaries and immediately, in imitation of the example set by the Government, started to confiscate any suitable Herero cattle found trespassing. Samuel Kutako in his affidavit, after referring to the cattle thefts, says:–

> The next reason for our rebellion was the appropriation of Herero lands by the traders, who took the ground for their farms and claimed it as their private property. They used to shoot our dogs if they trespassed on these lands, and they confiscated any of our cattle which might stray there. If holy cattle trespassed we were allowed to get them back, if we paid three to four ordinary cattle in exchange for one holy one. Under the Herero law the ground belonged to the tribe in common and not even the chief could sell or dispose of it. He could give people permission to live on the land, but no sales were valid and no chief ever attempted to sell his people s land. Even the missionaries who settled amongst us, only got permission to live there. (*Note.-* This is borne out by the records of the Rhenish Mission Society). Land was never sold to Germans or anyone else. We did not have any idea of such a thing.

Despite this statement, it is true that Samuel Maharero, the so-called paramount chief, did sell land, but this land was nearly all in the territory of Nikodemus and other chiefs who did not recognise such sales. Samuel had often, as a result of these dealings, to take refuge in Windhuk and ask for German protection. Trading on his poverty and his passion for alcoholic liquors, the German authorities got Samuel to sign deeds of sale of land: but the deponent, Samuel Kutako, is perfectly correct when he says that "no chief ever attempted to sell his people s land." Samuel Maharero was not a lawful chief, and in any event had no influence or jurisdiction at all outside Okahandja, his own district, and even there his position was never safe. In consequence he lived most of his time at Osona.

In this connection an old friend of Samuel Maharero s has stated:–

> I knew Samuel well ... he was very fond of liquor and the Germans kept him well supplied. He used to get cases of rum and brandy... Samuel was afraid of his life... He told me that the Germans made him drunk and got him to sign papers he knew nothing of and for which he was sorry afterwards ... Samuel, in his better moments, bitterly complained of how the Germans had taken advantage of his weakness ...

So we cannot place all the blame on Samuel Maharero.

Apart from the taking of their cattle and their land, there are other instances of injustice and misrule which may be briefly mentioned. In a previous chapter of this report reference has already been made to the great respect and reverence shown by the Hereros towards their dead. It is now desirable to record a happening which proves, perhaps more than anything else hitherto mentioned, how long-suffering and patient the Hereros were, and how callously indifferent the Germans and the Government proved themselves to be.

Hosea Mungunda, in corroborated affidavit (mentioned in a previous chapter), states:–

> Our burial places or graveyards were set aside as sacred and holy ground. We selected groves of green trees (evergreen trees if possible) for our burial places and then all trees there were holy and consecrated. No Herero would dare to damage or cut the trees in a burial place. Our two greatest leaders, Kamaherero and his father Katjamuaha, were buried together near Okahandja in a specially selected burial ground under beautiful green trees on the river bank. It was the most sacred place in the whole country to all Hereros. The place was fenced off and constantly attended to by the people. The Germans came; they cut down all the beautiful trees and they turned the sacred burial place into a vegetable garden. They appropriated the place as private property and no Herero could go there as he would be prosecuted for trespass. We were terribly upset at this and protested against what we regarded as sacrilege. Our chiefs complained to the authorities, but no notice was taken.

At page 67 of his work, Dr. Felix Meyer, dealing with the land laws of the Hereros, says:–

> Each Herero was free to select the spot where he wished to settle. He could build, graze, hunt and dig wherever he pleased. Only the burial places of the ancestors, in the locality of the sacred trees, were prohibited land as at one time the *res diis manibus relictoe*. It was *zera* (forbidden).Notwithstanding this (according to information given me by the missionary Irle), the holy grove of trees at Okahandja, which Maharero had allowed to grow around the graves, was cut down by the Germans, ... so that as a result the graves lay bare and exposed and were eventually taken in by the gardens of the white people.

CHAPTER TWELVE

THE VALUE SET ON NATIVE LIFE BY THE GERMANS

From the point of view of the, at that time, comparatively few German settlers in the country there were far too many Hereros. Once robbed of their land and their cattle, they could not possibly all be employed as farm labourers, and no one seemed to look to the future.

Dr. Karl Dove's "leniency towards the natives is cruelty to the whites" became generally known as proverbial, and it formed the rule of conduct not only of the white settler, soldier, trader, and policeman, but it also actually represented the settled and accepted policy of the Government. Considerations of justice, honesty, and common humanity never arose, or if they did arise were brushed aside by the more brutal demands of convenience and utility. It will be remembered that Leutwein, when referring to the claim that the evidence of seven coloured persons was necessary to outbalance the statement of one white man, said: in regard to the utility of this I will express no opinion.

Having settled the point of view, it is easy to understand what Dr. Karl Dove is hinting at when he writes:–

> While however the single Herero cannot be regarded as a very brave person, he must not be looked upon as harmless. On the contrary the chief danger from them is their numbers and these numbers are a standing menace to our safety.

Therefore the settler who helped to reduce the number of Hereros was performing a public service. There can be no doubt that during the period 1890 1904 very many Hereros were done to death in one way or another or died as the result of brutal floggings and ill-treatment. Despite this, such murders were treated lightly; where possible they were hushed up entirely, and at worst the murderer in his own interests was advised, for fear of reprisals, to leave the country or go to another district. In only four cases during the period 1890-1904 was a German murderer brought to trial, and then the imposition of anything like an adequate or commensurate penalty was unheard of. It was generally endeavoured by the German authorities to compound the offence by allowing the murderer to pay compensation in the shape of a few dozen goats to the relatives of the deceased.

When Leutwein was relieved of the Governorship, one of the charges leveled against him was that he had precipitated the rebellion of 1904 owing to his excessive leniency towards the natives. To show his difference of treatment as between natives and white people, Leutwein (page 431) quotes the following details of murder trials:–

A. Europeans murdered by Natives

Name   *Sentences*

(a) 1894, Christie (Englishman)   – 1 death and 1 penal servitude.
(b) 1895, German soldier   – 6 death sentences.
(c) 1895, Smith (Boer)   – 2 death sentences.
(d) 1896, Feyton (Englishman)   – 1 death sentence.
(e) 1899, Claasen Durr   – 2 death sentences.
(f) 1900, German policeman   – 3 death sentences.

B. Natives murdered by Europeans

(a) 1896, Hottentots Jantje and Kurieb – On trial: 5,5 years confinement. On appeal: reduced to 3 months imprisonment.
(b) 1901, Herero Leonard   – 1 year imprisonment.
(c) 1902, Herero Kamawu   – 2 years imprisonment.
(d) 1903, The daughter of Zacharias, Chief of Otjimbingwe. – On trial: acquitted. On appeal (by prosecutor): 3 years imprisonment.

It will be seen therefore that native murderers were invariably sentenced to death, while in the four cases actually tried the highest penalty imposed on a white man was three years imprisonment. Moreover these white criminals never served their full term, as will be shown later on. "Surely," says Leutwein, "this goes to prove that a higher value was placed on the life of a white man than on that of a native."

The death of a native as the result of a severe thrashing was not regarded by the German courts as murder. Leutwein says the natives could not understand such "subtle distinctions, to them murder and beating to death were one and the same thing." Germans who thrashed natives to such an extent as to render it necessary "to send them to hospital" were always allowed to escape with a fine. "On the other hand," says Leutwein, "natives who assaulted white men were always punished by lashes and imprisonment in chains (*kettenhaft*)."

Ordinary flogging of natives by their masters (euphemistically termed "paternal chastisement") was permitted unrestrictedly, and, provided the native had not to go "to hospital" as a result thereof, nothing was said about it.

Dealing with murders by Germans, Hosea Mungunda states on oath:–

> Under Herero law our chief punished people who committed willful murder with death. Under the Germans no German was ever sentenced to death for murdering a Herero. Some Germans were sent away to Germany (so we are told); but others who murdered our people are in the country up to the present day. I know of the men Kamahuru, Leonard, a woman Kamahuru and another man Willie Kain[101] ...

---

[101] The killing of Willy Kain is described in great detail in Drechsler, *Let Us Die Fighting*, pp. 133 - 135.

also Kasambouwe, a Herero of Otjimbingwe, who was killed by a policeman at Okahandja, because he did not take off his hat and greet the policeman. The last-named, Kasambouwe, was an under-chief of Kamaharero's family. It was the general rule to shield German murderers from justice. The reply to our complaint was "the man has been sent to Germany." None of us believed that these people were ever punished. We see the murderers here to-day ...

Samuel Kariko (son of Under-Chief Daniel Kariko, formerly secretary to the Chief at Omaruru, now schoolmaster at Kalkfeld), states on oath:–

> Our people were shot and murdered; our women were ill-treated; and those who did this were not punished. Our chiefs consulted and we decided that war could not be worse than what we were undergoing.. We all knew what risks we ran ... yet we decided on war, as the chiefs said we would be better off even if we were all dead.

Under-Chief Daniel Kariko states on oath:–

> Our people were compelled to work on farms, and the farmers had them chained up by the police and flogged without mercy for the slightest little thing... Then the wife of Barmenias Zerua (the daughter-in-law of Chief Zacharias Zerua of Otjimbingwe) was cruelly murdered in cold blood near Omaruru by a German named Dietrich. She was shot by him 14 days after her baby was born because she refused to be false to Herero law and to her own husband. This broke our hearts, because the family of Zerua is a great old Herero family from which many big chiefs had come in past years, and nearly all the reigning chiefs in 1903 were related to the Zerua family. We were more than astonished too when the German murderer was declared not guilty and liberated. This decided us for war. Later on we heard that the murderer had been re-arrested and on a new trial given three years. Three years for a chief's daughter s life when we ourselves would have sentenced a Herero murderer to death. We could see then that there was no justice for us and no protection. Dietrich was released from gaol after a short time and made an Under-Officer of the German troops who shot down our men, women, and children in the rebellion.

A full statement has been obtained from Barmenias Zerua, relative to the murder of his wife above referred to. He states that it took place not 14 days but a few months after her child was born, and that he was asleep when the shot was fired and is unable personally to impute a reason for the murder. This is what Barmenias says:–

> In 1899 I married Louisa Kamana, daughter of Kamana, an under-chief of the Hereros of chief Manasse of Omaruru. My wife was also a Christian and we were married in the church at Otjimbingwe by the Missionary Meyer. In 1903 my wife was expecting her first baby, so in accordance with the universal custom of the Hereros I sent her, by ox-wagon, to her mother's home at Otjimbingwe for her confinement. In due course she gave birth to a baby boy. When the news reached me I rode on horseback from Otjimbingwe to Otjimpaue to bring my wife and baby back to my home...
> We started on our return.journey by ox-wagon. We had to pass through Omaruru and there rested a few hours. Before leaving Omaruru we met a German named Dietrich, who asked me whether he would be allowed by me to travel with us my

wagon to Karibib. I said I had no objection, so Dietrich came along with us ... I agreed, because I thought I would help the white man. He travelled with us on the wagon, and chatted in a friendly way with me and my wife. That evening we outspanned about 12 miles from Omaruru on the main road. We killed a sheep and had our evening meal which Dietrich shared with us. We gave him the fried sheep liver to eat. Then two boys went to attend to the cattle and my wife went into the hood of the wagon with her baby to sleep.

After relating how the chief of Omaruru then rode up on his way from Karibib to Omaruru and how at Dietrich's invitation they had a drink together, Barmenias continues:–

Then the chief greeted us and rode away. I said "Good-night" to Dietrich and went to sleep ... suddenly I was awakened from my sleep by the report of a revolver. I jumped out of the tent of the wagon and saw Dietrich running away on the road to Omaruru... I went back to the wagon the baby was crying and I shook my wife to wake her.
As I touched her I felt something wet. I struck a match and saw that she was covered with blood and quite dead... I took up my baby and found that the bullet which killed my wife had gone through the fleshy part of its left leg just above the knee... We were never told what punishment Dietrich received. The chiefs were not informed and to this day I don t know what the court did. Later on I saw Dietrich in Karibib. Where he still lives ... None of the Hereros really believed that Dietrich had ever been punished. This murder was one of the chief reasons which influenced my father Zacharias and Samuel Maharero and Michael Tjaherani (the chiefs of Okahandja and Omaruru) to go into rebellion the next year.

They had many other reasons for rising against the Germans, but this event decided their policy ...[112]

Mentioning this murder, Leutwein (page 222), says:–

In the early part of 1903 an intoxicated white man shot a Herero woman, who was sleeping peacefully in a wagon, for the reason that he imagined, he was being attacked by Hereros and fired blindly in all directions. The court rejected the entirely unfounded story of attack by the Hereros as alleged by the white man. The case turned entirely on the point of the hallucinations of a no longer sober person. Notwithstanding this, the judges in the first instance found the white man not guilty, because they accepted as a fact the defence that he had acted in good faith (*er habe in gutem glauben gehandelt*)! This acquittal aroused extraordinary excitement in Hereroland, especially as the murdered person was the daughter of a chief. Everywhere the question was asked: Have the white people then got the right to shoot native women. I thereupon travelled personally to Hereroland to pacify the people so far as I could, and also to make clear to them that I did not agree with the judgment of the court, but had no influence thereover. Luckily the prosecutor had correctly appealed. The accused was then brought before the Supreme Court at Windhuk and sentenced to three years' imprisonment. This event had however contributed its share towards the unrest among the Hereros which resulted half a year later in the outbreak of the rebellion.

---

[102] The Dietrich case is discussed further in Drechsler, *Let Us Die Fighting*, pp. 135 - 136

CHAPTER TWELVE

In October 1903 the Hottentot chief of the Bondelswartz Hottentots, Willem Christian, was murdered by German soldiers at Warmbad. This resulted in the Bondelswartz rising. The spark once applied, it took little time for the conflagration to spread, and by January 1904 the entire Herero tribe had risen against their German masters and was in the course of the year joined by the majority of the Hottentot races in the south.

CHAPTER THIRTEEN

THE OUTBREAK OF THE HERERO RISING AND THE HUMANITY OF THE HERERO

Governor Leutwein was in the south dealing with the Hottentots when the news of the Herero rising reached him. He was pained and astonished to learn that Samuel Maharero (the "Paramount Chief") had forsaken Germany and her unlimited supplies of rum for the purpose of going into rebellion, and that not only was Samuel a rebel, but he was the leader, the life and soul of the movement.

Leutwein immediately wrote an upbraiding letter to "my dear Samuel," asking for his reasons for this rash step. The letter was duly delivered by a missionary, and throughthe same channel Leutwein received the following reply (printed by Rohrbach at page 333):–

To the Great Ambassador of the Kaiser:
Otjisonjati,

Governor Leutwein: 6th March 1904
I have received your letter, and what you have written to me and my headmen is well understood. I and my headmen reply to you as follows I did not commence the war this year; it has been started by the white people; for as you know how many Hereros have been killed by white people, particularly traders, with rifles and in the prisons. And always when I brought these cases to Windhuk the blood of the people was valued at no more than a few head of small stock, namely, from fifty to fifteen. The traders increased the troubles also in this way that they voluntarily gave credit to my people. After having done so they robbed us; they went so far as to pay themselves by, for instance, taking away by force two or three head of cattle to cover a debt of one pound stg. It is these things which have caused war in the land. And in these times the white people said to us you (*i.e.*, Leutwein) who were peacefully disposed and liked us, were no longer here. They said to us the Governor who loves you has gone to a difficult war; he is dead and as he is dead you also (the Hereros) must die. They went so far as to kill two Hereros of Chief Tjetjoo: even Lieutenant N. began to kill my people in the gaol. Ten of them died, and it is said they died of illness; but they died by the hands of the labour overseer and by the lash. Eventually Lieut. N. began to treat me badly and to see a reason for killing me.[103] He said, "The people of Kambazembi and

---

[103] The claim that the Germans attempted to assassinate Samuel Maharero is also found in Herero oral tradition. One oral account claimed that a plot to capture Samuel Maharero was revealed by a Damara worker. He overheard Hauptmann Franke discuss a plan to invite Samuel for a drink at the German fort at Okahandja and then capture him. On receiving this intelligence, he refused to enter the fort. The Germans then tried, unsuccessfully, to assassinate Samuel. For details see Sundermeier, Theo *Die Mbanderu*, Anthropos-Institut, St Augustin, 1977 pp. 66-69

Uanja are making war." He called me to question me. I answered him truthfully "No," but he did not believe. At last he hid soldiers in boxes at the fort and sent for me so that he might shoot me. I did not go, I saw his intentions and I fled. Thereupon Lieut. R. sent soldiers with rifles after me to shoot me. For these reasons I became angry and said "No, I must kill the whitemen, they themselves have said that I must die." This – that I must die – was told me by a white man named X. (Note. The names are suppressed by the German printers..

I am the Chief,
Samuel Maharero

It seems quite true that German settlers did take advantage of Leutwein's absence in the south to spread the report that he was dead and also to renew with vigour their outrages and robberies. They had never forgiven Leutwein for his open antagonism on the trading and credit question, and appear to have taken every opportunity of belittling him in the eyes of the natives and of undermining his authority. It was the desire of the Germans to precipitate a general rebellion. The extermination of the Hereros and the confiscation of the cattle and sheep they still possessed was their main objective. Of Governor Leutwein, whatever his faults may have been, let it be said that he personally was no party to this miserable plot.

The settlers had achieved their object. The Hereros were in open rebellion and it remained only to secure the spoils.

Before actually opening hostilities the principal Herero chiefs met and drew up a strict instruction to all their selected military leaders: It read as follows:–

I am the Chief leader of the Hereros, Samuel Maharero. I have proclaimed a law and a lawful order and it ordains for all my people that they shall not lay hands on the following: namely, Englishmen, Boers, Bastards, Berg-Damaras, Namas (i.e., Hottentots). We must not lay hands on any of these people. I have taken an oath that their property will not be regarded as enemy property, neither that of the missionaries. Enough!

In his affidavit, Under-Chief Daniel Kariko (a bitter life-long enemy of the Germans) says:–

We decided that we should wage war in a humane manner and would kill only the German men who were soldiers, or who would become soldiers. We met at secret councils and there our chiefs decided that we should spare the lives of all German women and children. The missionaries, too, were to be spared, and they, their wives and families and possessions were to be protected by our people from all harm. We also decided to protect all British and Dutch farmers and settlers and their wives and children and property as they had always been good to us. Only German males were regarded as our enemies, and then not young boys who could not fight these also we spared: We gave the Germans and all others notice that we had declared war.

A Dutch housewife resident in Omaruru has informed the writer that when the rising broke out she was living in the village while her husband was on his farm some 30 miles away. The Germans hastily fled into the fort taking their wives and children with them. My informant says she hesitated about going to the fort for fear that the Hereros might consider her action hostile and take revenge on her husband. While pondering over what she should do to protect herself and her small children, the Herero chief, Michael Tysesita called on her. He said:–

> I have come to assure you that you and your children will be quite safe in your own home. You are under my protection. Do not go into the German fort. The Germans are foolish to take their women and children there as they may be killed by our bullets, and we are not making war on women and children. Keep calm and stay indoors when there is fighting, I assure you my people will do you no harm.
>
> Yes, Chief (replied my informant), but my poor husband is alone on the farm, surely he has been murdered by this.
>
> The Chief smiled and replied: We are not barbarians. Your husband is our friend; he is not a German. I have already sent a special messenger to him, to tell him he is under my protection as long as he remains quietly on his farm. His cattle and sheep are safe also. In order not to inconvenience your husband, I have specially ordered my people who are working for him to remain there and do their work loyally until I send further instructions.

This humane and chivalrous attitude is confirmed by Leutwein (page 467). He says:–

> It seems to have been the definite intention of the Herero leaders to protect all women and children.[104] When, in spite of this, some were murdered, this is to be ascribed to the fact that everywhere inhuman people are to be found who do not confine themselves to such limits.

---

[104] The most photographed monument in Namibia today is undoubtably *Der Reiter* statue that was unveiled on the birthday of Kaiser Wilhelm II (27th January) in 1914. The statue is a monument to the 1,633 Germans who died during the war. A plaque at the foot of the statue states "Zum ehrende angedenken an die tapferen deutschen krieger. Welche für Kaiser und Reich zur erretung und erhaltung dieses landes waehrent des Herero – und Hottentotten Aufstandes 1903-1907 und waehrend der Kalahari-Expedition 1908 ihr leben liessen.

Zum Ehrenden angedenken auch an die Deutsche buerger welche den eingeborenen im aufstande zum opfer fielen.

Gefallen, verscholen, verlungluecckt, ihren wunden erlegen und an krankheiten gestorben.

Von der schutztruppe:

Offiziere	100
Unteroffiziere	254
Reiter	1180

Von der Marine

Offiziere	7
Unteroffiziere	13
Mannschaften	72

Im aufstande erschlagen

Maenner	119
Frauen	4
Kinder	1

It has probably never occurred before in native wars that a definite line was drawn between combatants and non-combatants, enemies and friends. It speaks volumes for the humane temperament and mildness of the Hereros.

It cannot possibly have been on account of their barbarity that Germany exterminated the majority of this fine race.

Having decided on how they should wage the war, the Herero chiefs decided to notify their neighbours, the Hottentots and the Bastards, and the following letters are of interest:–

> To Chief Hendrik Witbooi,   11.1.1904
>
> I make known to you that the white people have broken their peace with me. Hold on well as we have heard (you are doing?) And if God so wills it don t let the work in Namaqualand go backward. It now remains for you to go to Swakopmund and see what they are doing there. I am without ammunition.[105] When you have acquired ammunition help me and give me two English and two German rifles as I have none. That is all. Greetings.
>
> To the Bastard-Chief,   11th January 1904
>
> I make known to you that our treaty between us and the Germans is broken. We are now become enemies. I make this known to you as the Bastards (like the Hereros), the Namaquas and the Englishmen must know. A Berg-Damara is the servant of these races. These are all on our side and that is a fact; accept it and hold on to it. Complete this business; that is all. Let us go to Swakopmund and remain there. Send the enclosed letter (to Witbooi) on, and keep your man there as he has no work. Do not interfere with any Boers or Englishmen.

A little while later the following undated letter was sent by Samuel Maharero to Witbooi:–

> To Witbooi
>
> Rather let us die together and not die as the result of ill-treatment, prisons, or all the other ways. Furthermore let all the other chiefs down there know so that they may rise and work. I close my letter with hearty greetings and the confidence that the chief will comply with my wishes. Send me four of your men that we may discuss matters. Also obstruct the operations of the Governor so that he will be unable to pass. And make haste that we may storm Windhuk then we shall have ammunition. Furthermore I am not fighting alone, we are all fighting together.

The letters to Witbooi never reached him. The Bastard chief through whose hands they passed, handed them over to Leutwein!

Basing the total strength of their force of effective fighting men at 10 to 15 per cent. of the population, Leutwein estimates that the total available military strength of the Hereros was 7,000 to 8,000 men, of whom only 2,500 were armed with rifles (page 436). These rifles were a varied collection of all sorts

---

[105] The shortage of ammunition can be directly linked to concerted efforts by the colonial powers to control the arms trade and restrict the access of African leaders to modern military technology. Sue Miers, 'Notes on the Arms Trade and Government Policy in Southern Africa between 1870 and 1890', *Journal of African History Vol 12, no. 4 (1971).*

and included muzzle-loaders and ancient flintlocks. As will be seen however from the letters, the Hereros had little or no ammunition.

Barmenias Zerua, son of Chief Zacharias Zerua of Otjimbingwe, states (in his affidavit to the writer):–

> He (*i.e.*, the chief) knew that if we rose we would be crushed in battle, as our people were nearly all unarmed and without ammunition. We were driven to desperation by the cruelty and injustice of the Germans, and our chiefs and people felt that death would be less terrible than the conditions under which we lived.

Heinrich Tjaherani of Omaruru, younger son of the Chief Willem Tjaherani of Omaruru (predecessor of the Chief Manasse), states on oath:–

> When the Hereros rose I took the field with my people. We were badly armed. Only about one man in ten had a rifle and most of the rifles were very old. Very few men had 15 to 20 cartridges. Some had ten, and I know of many who only had three or five ...

There is something deeply pathetic in this picture of the desperate Herero warrior with his ancient rifle and half-a-dozen cartridges deciding to rise and defend his liberties against the might of the German Empire, and despite his worries and anxieties and the terrible future which faced him passing resolutions and giving orders to ensure the safety of the women and children of his oppressors.

Can anyone allege that these poor mild-mannered creatures who had borne the German yoke for over 14 years had no justification for the step they took? Is there anyone in the civilised world who can assert that Germany was justified when she allowed von Trotha and his soldiers mercilessly to butcher and drive to their death 60,000 or more of these unfortunate people and to destroy every asset in the way of cattle, sheep, goats, and other possessions?

CHAPTER FOURTEEN

PRELIMINARY STEPS AND TREACHERY OF THE GERMANS

It is now necessary, distasteful as the task may be, to disclose some of the ways and means by which von Trotha carried out his "extermination policy."[106]

As might have been expected, the Hereros, encumbered in their movements in the field by the presence of their women and children and their cattle and sheep, and poorly armed and organised, were, from the very outset, no match for the trained and disciplined soldiers of Germany who were poured into the country.

What could the Hereros do when faced with the modern rifle, the Maxim and the quick-firing Krupp gun? By August 1904 the German troops had defeated the Hereros with great losses and had captured several thousands of prisoners. The rising was virtually over. Samuel Maharero and several leading chiefs gathered their cattle and sheep and made a wild dash through the Kalahari Desert with a view to seeking British protection and that peace and fair government which had been denied them in their own land.

The bulk of the Herero nation however clinging to their remaining cattle and small stock, had withdrawn into the mountains of the Waterberg and the bushveld north of Gobabis. It was about this time that Leutwein, having been

---

[106] In the run up to Namibian independence there was a flurry of activity relating to the term *Vernichten*, exterminate. See, Brigitte Lau's, 'Uncertain Certainties: The Herero-German war of 1904', in *Mibagus*, Nr. 2, April 1989, pp. 4-8; a slightly reworked copy of this article was published in B. Lau, *History and Historiography*, edited by A. Heywood, (Windhoek 1995) pp. 39 - 52. Lau's article elicited responses from Randolph Vigne and Henning Melber in *The South African Review of Books*, Feb/March 1990, June/July 1990, Aug./Oct. 1990; Tilman Dedering, 'The German-Herero-War of 1904: Revisionism of Genocide or Imaginary Historiography? in: *The Journal of Southern African Studies*, Vol. 19, No. 1, 1993, pp. 80 - 88 and J.B. Gewald, 'The Great General of the Kaiser' in: *Botswana Notes and Records*, Vol. 26 1994, pp. 67 - 76. Lau's article followed on in a series of articles and books which have sought to deny the genocide, or, at the very least, called for a revision of histories dealing with the war. See in this regard: Horst Kühne, 'Die Ausrottungsfeldzüge der'Kaiserlichen Schutztruppen in Afrika' und die sozialdemokratische Reichstagsfraktion.', in *Militärgeschichte*, Band 18, 1979; Walter Nuhn, *Sturm über Südwest: Der Hereroaufstande von 1904 - Ein düsteres Kapitel der deutschen kolonialen Vergangenheit Namibias*, (Koblenz 1989); Karla Poewe, *The Namibian Herero: A History of their Psychosocial Disintegration and Survival*, (Lewiston 1986); Gunter Spraul 'Der "Völkermord" an den Herero: Untersuchungen zu einer neuen Kontinuitätsthese' in *Geschichte in Wissenschaft und Unterricht*, 1988/12, pp. 713-739; Gert Sudholt, *Die deutsche Eingeborenenpolitik in Südwestafrika. Von den Anfängen bis 1904*, Georg (Hildesheim, 1975).

declared too lenient, was superseded by von Trotha.[107] This new commander was noted in Berlin for his merciless severity in dealing with natives. In the Chinese Boxer rebellion he had carried out his Imperial master's instructions to the letter; and no more worthy son of Attila could have been selected for the work in hand. He had just suppressed the Arab rebellion in German East Africa by bathing that country in the blood of thousands and thousands of its inhabitants, men, women and children; and his butchery there ended, he was ordered by Wilhelm II. To proceed to German South-West Africa and deal with the rebel natives. Von Trotha was indifferent as to the means by which his objects should be attained. Treachery and breaches of faith were to him admissible. No doubt the reason and excuse advanced was as usual the inferior kultur-position of the natives. Shortly after he took command the Hereros were given to understand that reasonable terms of peace might be granted if their leaders came in and treated. The subtle German felt that it would be easier to dispose of the masses, once their best leaders were gone. In the meantime von Trotha was drawing his cordon of troops into position and preparing for the final massacre. Let us read in the words of two Herero eye-witnesses the manner in which von Trotha initiated his campaign.

Gottlob Karnatoto (who was a servant to one of the officers in the field) states on oath:–

> I accompanied the troops to Ombakaha above Gobabis and near Epikiro in the Sandveld. At a farm called Otjihaenena the Germans sent out messages to the Hereros that the war was now over and they were to come in and make peace. As a result of this message seven Herero leaders came into the German camp to discuss peace terms. As soon as they came in they were asked where Samuel Maherero the chief was. They said he had gone towards the desert on his way to British Bechuanaland. That evening at sunset the seven peace envoys were caught and tied with ropes. They were led aside and shot. Before being shot they protested bitterly; but seeing that they were doomed they accepted their fate.

Relating another instance, the well-known story of German treachery at Ombakaha, Gerard Kamaheke (at present Herero headman at Windhuk and a leader of the Hereros in the rising) states on oath:–

> The chiefs Saul, Joel[108] and I with a number of our followers were camped in the veld at Ombuyonungondo, about 30 kilos. from Ombakaha. This was in September. A messenger, a German soldier, came to our camp on horse-back. He

---

[107] General Adrian Dietrich Lothar von Trotha, born in 1848 entered the Prussian army at an early age, involved in combat in 1866 in the Seven Weeks War against Austria. In 1894 shipped to German East Africa, where as the German military commander he was involved in the defeat of the Wahehe. Commanded German forces in the defeat of the Chinese Boxer uprising in 1900. Personally selected by Kaiser Wilhelm II of Germany to command German forces in South West Africa. Drafted the infamous 'extermination order'. Memorable for noting that, "I shall annihilate the revolting tribes with rivers of blood and rivers of gold. Only after a complete uprooting will something emerge" Mark Cocker, *Rivers of Blood Rivers of Gold: Europe's Conflict with Tribal Peoples*, (London 1998) p. 328.

[108] Joel Kavizeri. A letter found on his body claimed that 300 people in his group had died of thirst. Gerhard Pool *Samuel Maharero*, Gamsberg Macmillan, Windhoek, 1991: 271.

said he had come from the German commander at Ombakaha, who had sent him to tell us to come to Ombakaha and make peace. Joel then sent the schoolmaster Traugott Tjongarero personally to Ombakaha to confirm the truth of the soldier's message and to inquire if peace were intended whether the Herero leaders would be given safe conduct and protection if they went into Ombakaha. Traugott came back a few days later and said he had seen the German commander, who had confirmed the message brought by the soldier. Traugott said that the German commander had invited us all to come in and make peace; that our lives would all be spared; that we would be allowed to retain our cattle and other possessions; and that we would be allowed to go to Okahandja to live. I fell in with the wishes of the majority and we left for Ombakaha in the evening, and arrived at the German camp at noon the next day. With me were the chiefs Saul and Joel, and the under-chiefs Traugott, Elephas, Albanus, Johannes Munqunda, Elephas Mumpurua and two others whose names I now forget. We had with us 70 Herero soldiers. The wives and children we had left at our camp. On arrival at Ombakaha the 70 men who were under my command were halted near the German camp under some trees, as the sun was hot and we were very tired. Joel and the other leaders went on to the German commander's quarters about 100 yards away; they left their arms with us. The Germans then came to me and said we were to hand over our arms. I said, "I cannot do so until I know that Joel and the other leaders who are now in the camp have made peace." I sat there waiting, when suddenly the Germans opened fire on us. We were nearly surrounded, and my people tried to make their escape. I tried to fight my way through, but was shot in the right shoulder and fell to the ground (I show the wound), and I lay quite still and pretended to be dead. I was covered with blood. The German soldiers came along bayoneting the wounded; and as I did not move they thought I was dead already and left me. The chiefs Saul and Joel and all the other headmen were killed. I got up in the night and fled back to our camp, where I found our women and children still safe and also some survivors of my 70 men. We then fled away further towards the Sandveld and scattered in all directions.

After the departure of von Trotha, the German Governor von Lindequist made every effort to get the few thousand starving Hereros who survived and were dying of sheer hunger and thirst in the mountains and bush to come in and surrender. He had the greatest difficulty in getting them to do so. Dr. Paul Rohrbach (page 361), in dealing with this strong distrust of the Hereros, ascribes it mainly to this horrible piece of treachery (worthy of a Dingaan[109]) which has just been described. Says Rohrbach:–

It happened during the war that a number of Herero leaders, among them the chief Saul of Otjonga, were shot down after (in the confidence that negotiations concerning their surrender were to be opened) they had placed themselves within reach of German rifles. This incident, which took place at Ombakaha in the district of Gobabis, had the most unfortunate and difficult consequences, because all later attempts to open up peace negotiations even in Namaqualand, were rejected by the distrustful natives, who said, Yes, but Ombakaha?

---

[109] In the early twentieth century in the Union of South Africa, the epitomy of cold-blooded treachery was held to be the killing of unarmed Voortrekker leader, Piet Retief, and his followers by the soldiers of the Zulu king Dingane. Reader Digest, *Illustrated History of South Africa - The Real Story*, Third edition, Second Printing (Cape Town 1995), p. 121.

CHAPTER FOURTEEN

Having completed his plans, von Trotha issued his notorious *Vernichtungs Befehl* (or extermination order) in terms of which no Herero man, woman, child or suckling babe was to receive mercy or quarter.[110] "Kill every one of them," said von Trotha, "and take no prisoners." "I wished," says von Trotha, "to ensure that never again would there be a Herero rebellion.[111]"

This order, be it remembered, was made against an already defeated people, ready to come in and surrender on any terms and entirely without ammunition or other means of waging war. In his report to Berlin, von Trotha said (see page 359, Rohrbach):–

---

[110] Some debate has taken place about the 'meaning' of this order. Karla Poewe for example claimed that the German word 'vernichten' should not be translated as 'exterminate', but rather as 'in the usage of the times, breaking ... military, national, or economic resistance' (*The Namibian Herero* 1985). One of the original copies of the *Vernichtungsbefehl*, 'extermination' order translated into OtjiHerero is still held at the National Archives of Botswana. Jan-Bart Gewald writes that "The *Vernichtungsbefehl*, in Otjherero, is printed on the reverse side of stationery which bears the letterhead, *"Kommando der Kaiserlichen Schutztruppe in Windhoek"* (headquarters of the Imperial protection troops in Windhoek). The printed document, which would appear to have been roneoed, is a little smaller than an A4 and was folded four times. The script on the document is cursive. The text, which is in Otjiherero, is not punctuated and contains a number of spelling and grammatical mistakes." Kovihende Kaotozu translated the OtjiHerero text as follows "I am the great General of the Germans. I am sending a word to you Hereros, you who are Hereros are no longer under the Germans. You have stolen, killed and owe white people. You have cut ears and noses, but now out of cowardice say you will not fight. I am saying to you Herero, you who are great, anyone who catches and brings a chief will be paid 50 pounds, especially chief Samuel Maharero shall get 250 pounds. You Hereros must now leave this land it belongs to the Germans. If you do not do this I shall remove you with the big gun. A person in German land shall be killed by the gun. I shall not catch women and the sick but I will chase them after their chiefs or I will kill them with the gun. These are my words to the Herero nation. The Great General of the Kaiser.Trotha.

The original text – as written in OtjiHerero read as follows:

"Ouami Omuhona omunene ongenerala jo vadeutschi. Metumuembo indi kovaherero ene mbumuri ovaherero kamutjiri mo vandeotji muavaka nu muazepa nu muazepa ozondja nezovavapa mua konda omatui no majuru nu nambano muato umumandu nu Kamunokurua Ami mutja kuene ko vaherero kuene kovahona ngua kambura omuhona umue na eta masninu ovi pona 50 vindano nutjinene ingui ngua eta vimiuhona Samuel Maharero mapeva ovi pondo omasere jevari nomi rongo 250 ene vaherero nambano ehi etheje orovandoitji nu tjimuhino kuvanga okutjita otji otji naihi ami meverura kizjatjinene nondjembo onene omundu mehi ro vandoitji matu no ndjembo hino ku kambura ovakazendu no vavere korukuao meve rambere kovahona vao poo meve zepa nondjembo. Ono mambo vandje komuhoko uovaherero. Omuhona omunene ongenerala jomukesere. Trotha." (Gewald, "The Great General of the Kaiser", in *Botswana Notes and Records*, Vol. 26, 1994, p.72

[111] A contemporary account of the context within which the OtjiHerero version of this order was distributed can be found in a Cape Town newsletter, *The Owl*, of 18th November, 1904. "At Osombo-Windimbe, on the morning of 3 October, H.E. General von Trotha consoled himself for his futile pursuit of the Herero by ordering a number of natives, who had been picked up by patrols to be hanged ... The women were forced to watch every detail of the executions and then chased away to tell their compatriots about this demonstration of German might." Quoted in Drechsler, *Let us die*, p. 174.

CHAPTER FOURTEEN

> That the making of terms with the Hereros was impossible, seeing that their chiefs had nearly all fled, or through their misdeeds during the rebellion had rendered themselves so liable that the German Government could not treat with them. In addition to this he regarded the acceptance of a more or less voluntary surrender as a possible means of building up the old tribal organisations again and, as such, it would be a great political mistake, which earlier or later would again cause bloodshed.

It is perfectly clear from this that von Trotha definitely decided not to allow the Hereros to surrender, even though nearly all their chiefs had fled and he in cold blood decided to butcher this now disorganised, leaderless, and harmless tribe in order to ensure that there would be no trouble from the Hereros in the future.

When the spirit in which this order was conceived and given and carried out is understood, and when the real purport and object of the preliminary acts of treachery, whereby the chiefs and leaders were murdered, are borne in mind, it will be easier to understand that the following sad and terrible details as to how the extermination order was carried out are not figments of the imagination, but the sworn descriptions of eye-witnesses, and that the ghastly slaughter which took place was approved of by von Trotha and the master whom he served.

CHAPTER FIFTEEN

HOW THE HEREROS WERE EXTERMINATED

In "Peter Moor s Journey to South-West Africa"[xii] (Gustav Frenssen), a disjointed narrative of happenings during the Herero rising, as related by returned soldiers, little of the actual horrors and butcheries which took place is conveyed.[112]

A German author writing for a German public would naturally take care to conceal the entirely barbaric side of the affair, lest it should shock those simple-minded people who really believed in the superior *kultur* of their race. There are, however, here and there little sidelights, little slips of the pen apparently, which, when read in conjunction with the evidence which follows, help to create a picture of merciless inhumanity and calculated ferocity which is well-nigh unbelievable.

On their way to the battle-front the newly arrived soldiers of von Trotha are discussing the causes of the rising with the old settlers (page 77).. and one of the older men, who had been long in the country, said:–

> Children, how should it be otherwise. They were ranchmen and proprietors and we were there to make them landless working men, and they rose up in revolt ... this is their struggle for independence ... They (the Hereros) discussed, too, what the Germans really wanted here. They thought we ought to make that point clear. The matter stood this way: there were missionaries here who said you are our dear brothers in the Lord and we want to bring you these benefits namely, faith, love and hope: and there were soldiers, farmers and traders, and they said we want to take your cattle and your land gradually away from you and make you slaves without legal rights. These two things didn t go side by side. It is a ridiculous and crazy project. Either it is right to colonise, that is to deprive others of their rights, to rob and make slaves, or it is just and right to christianise, that is to proclaim and live up to brotherly love.

[xii] Mrs May Ward's Translation.

---

[112] The novel was translated into English by Margaret Ward and published in 1908. Dreschler describes this novel as 'fiction... [but] ... based on reports of persons with first-hand experience of the war'. Dorian Haarhoff argues that the novel should be read as 'ambivalent' and not simply a glorification of German colonialism. He argues that it reveals '... a set of disturbing questions about colonisation itself'. Frenssen never visited Namibia himself, but claimed to have interviewed German veterans of the campaign extensively. Frenssen, Gustav *Peter Moor's fahrt nach Südwest: ein Feldzugsbericht*, G. Grote'sche, Verlagsbuchhandlung, 1906; Dreschler, *Let us die*, p. 173; Haarhoff, Dorian, 'A Soldier in Namibia: Gustav Frenssen's Peter Moor's Journey to Southwest Africa', *Logos*, Vol. 8 (2), 1988, pp. 81-83. See also John Noyes 'National Identity, Nomadism, and Narration in Gustav Frenssen's *Peter Moor's Journey to Southwest Africa*' in Sara Friedrichsmeyer, Sara Lennox, and Susanne Zantop, *The Imperialist Imagination*, Ann Arbor, University of Michegan Press, 1998

CHAPTER FIFTEEN

The narrator relates how, on a night-scouting journey, he located a large Herero encampment (page 158):–

> Setting down on my knees and creeping for a little way, I saw tracks of innumerable children s feet, and among them those of full-grown feet. Great troops of children, led by their mothers, had passed over the road here to the north-west. I stood up, and going to a low tree by the road climbed up a few yards in my heavy boots. Thence I could see a broad moonlit slope, rising not a hundred yards distant, and on it hundreds of rough huts constructed of branches, from the low entrance of which the fire light shone out and I heard children's crying and the yelping of a dog. Thousands of women and children were lying there under the roofs of leaves around the dying fires... The barking of dogs and the lowing of cattle reached my ears. I gazed at the great night scene with sharp spying eyes, and I observed minutely the site and the camp at the base of the mountains. Still the thought went through my head: There lies a people with all its children and all its possessions, hard pressed on all sides by the horrible deadly lead and condemned to death, and it sent cold shudders down my back.

(Page 186):–

> Through the quiet night we heard in the distance the lowing of enormous herds of thirsty cattle and a dull, confused sound like the movement of a whole people. To the east there was a gigantic glow of fire. The enemy had fled to the east with their whole enormous mass – women, children and herds. The next morning we ventured to pursue the enemy... The ground was trodden down into a floor for a width of about a hundred yards, for in such a broad, thickly crowded horde had the enemy and their herds of cattle stormed along. In the path of their flight lay blankets, skins, ostrich feathers, household utensils, women's ornaments, cattle and men, dead and dying and staring blankly... How deeply the wild, proud, sorrowful people had humbled themselves in the terror of death! wherever I turned my eyes lay their goods in quantities, oxen and horses, goats and dogs, blankets and skins. A number of babies lay helplessly languishing by mothers whose breasts hung down long and flabby. Others were lying alone, still living, with eyes and nose full of flies. somebody sent out our black drivers and I think they helped them to die. All this life lay scattered there, both man and beast, broken in the knees, helpless, still in agony or already motionless, it looked as if it had all been thrown down out of the air.
>
> At noon we halted by water-holes which were filled to the very brim with corpses. We pulled them out by means of the ox teams from the field pieces, but there was only a little stinking bloody water in the depths At some distance crouched a crowd of old women, who stared in apathy in front of them... In the last frenzy of despair man and beast will plunge madly into the bush somewhere, anywhere, to find water, and in the bush they will die of thirst.

(Page 192):–

> We chanced to see a Cape wagon behind some bushes, and we heard human voices. Dismounting, we sneaked up and discovered six of the enemy sitting in animated conversation around a little campfire. I indicated by signs at which one of them each of us was to shoot. Four lay still immediately; one escaped; the sixth stood half erect, severely wounded. I sprang forward swinging my club; he looked at. me indifferently. I wiped my club clean in the sand and threw the weapon on its trap over my shoulder hut, I did not like to touch it all that day ...

(*Note.* These "clubs " were, with bayonets and rifle butts, the weapons with which the German soldiers and not the black drivers "helped" the women and children to die.)

(Page 204):–

> One fire was burning not far from us in the thick bush... Before dawn we got up, discovered the exact place in the bush, and stealthily surrounded it. Five men and eight or ten women and children, all in rags, were squatting benumbed about their dismal little fire. Telling them with threats not to move, we looked through the bundles which were lying near them and found two guns and some underclothing, probably stolen from our dead. One of the men was wearing a German tunic which bore the name of one of our officers who had been killed. We then led the men away to one side and shot them. The women and children, who looked pitiably starved, we hunted into the bush ...

(Page 230):–

> The guardsman got up with difficulty and went with bent back down the slope to one side where there were bushes. I said "What does he want? I believe he is out of his senses and wants to search for water."
> At that moment there came from the bushes into which he had vanished a noise of cursing and leaping. Immediately he reappeared holding by the hip a tall thin negro dressed in European clothing. He tore the negro's gun from his hand and swearing at him in a strange language dragged him up to us and said, "The wretch has a German gun, but no more cartridges." The guardsman had now become quite lively and began to talk to his captive, threatening him and kicking him in the knees. The negro crouched and answered every question with a great flow of words and with quick, very agile and remarkable gestures of the arms and hands... Apparently the guardsman at last learned enough, for he said: "The missionary said to me beloved, don t forget that the blacks are our brothers. Now I will give my brother his reward." He pushed the black man off and said, "Run away." The man sprang up and tried to get down across the clearing in long, zigzag jumps, but he had not taken five leaps before the ball hit him and he pitched forward at full length and lay still ... the lieutenant thought I meant it was not right for the guardsman to shoot the negro, and said in his thoughtful, scholarly way, "Safe is safe. He can't raise a gun against us any more nor beget any children to fight against us. The struggle for South Africa will be a hard one, whether it is to belong to the Germans or to the blacks."

The last clause gives von Trotha's reasons for this no-quarter policy far better than the writer could describe them.

The following are statements by Hereros as to their treatment during the rising. *Daniel Kariko* (Under-Chief of Omaruru):–

> The result of this war is known to everyone. Our people, men, women and children were shot like dogs and wild animals. Our people have disappeared now. I see only a few left; their cattle and sheep are gone too, and all our land is owned

by the Germans ... after the fight at Waterberg[113] we asked for peace; but von Trotha said there would only be peace when we were all dead, as he intended to exterminate us. I fled to the desert with a few remnants of my stock and managed more dead than alive to get away far north.[114] I turned to the west and placed myself under the protection of the Ovambo chief Uejulu, who knew that I was a big man among the Hereros ... in 1915 they told me that the British were in Hereroland, and I hurried down to meet them... I was allowed to return to Hereroland after 10 years of exile.

Hosea Mungunda (Headman of the Hereros at Windhuk):–

We were crushed and well-nigh exterminated by the Germans in the rising. With the exception of Samuel Maharero, Mutati, Traugott, Tjetjoo, Hosea and Kaijata (who fled to British territory) all our big chiefs and leaders died or were killed in the rising, and also the great majority of our people.[115] All our cattle were lost and all other possessions such as wagons and sheep. At first the Germans took prisoners, but when General von Trotha took command no prisoners were taken. General von Trotha said, "No one is to live; men, women and children must all die." We can't say how many were killed.

Samuel Kariko (son of Daniel Kariko, formerly Secretary to time Omaruru Chief):–

A new General named von Trotha came, and he ordered that all Hereros were to be exterminated, regardless of age or sex. It was then that the wholesale slaughter of our people began. That was towards the end of 1904. Our people had already been defeated in battle, and we had no more ammunition ... we saw we were beaten and asked for peace, but the German General refused peace and said all should die. We then fled towards the Sandfeld of the Kalahari Desert. Those of our people who escaped the bullets and bayonets died miserably of hunger and thirst in the desert. A few thousand managed to turn back and sneak through the German lines to where there were water and roots and berries to live on.

---

[113] The Waterberg is now a tourist resort run by Namibia Wildlife Resorts. The mountain was known as *Omuverumue* in OtjiHerero ('The Pass') whilst the natural springs at its base were known as *Otjozondjupa* ('The Place of the Calabashes'). The latter name is now used for the whole region. At present whilst visitors standing on top of the mountain can look across the battlefield of *Ohamakari*, the resort does not contain any public display about the events that took place there. Silvester, Jeremy 'Layers of History at the Place of the Calabashes', *Namibian*, 23rd June, 2000.

[114] A significant number of Herero refugees apparently sought shelter with King Tshaanika in Ongandjera, King Negumbo in Uukwambi and King Kambonde in West Ondonga.. By early 1905 it was estimated by one visiting trader that 400 Herero refugees were also with King Nehale in East Ondonga.. Herero refugees were also reported in Kaokoland and some travelled as far as southern Angola, the most famous of these exiles being Harunga, who was often known as 'Oorlog' (War). Eirola, *The Ovambogefahr*, 181-185; Bollig, Michael and Tjakazapi Mbunguha (trans.) *"When War Came the Cattle Slept ..." Himba Oral Traditions*, Rüdiger Köppe Verlag, Köln, 1997, pp. 176-177.

[115] A translation of an article from the National-Zeitung for 26th August, 1904 claimed that "The leader of the Ovambandjeru, Tjetjo with his son Traugott and Kajata, the most capable of the Herero leaders, were already negotiating with the English frontier authorities some weeks ago when Samuel called them back to Waterberg with the false news of the arrival of quantities of ammunition from Amboland." (FO 64/1645).

CHAPTER FIFTEEN

A few examples of how the Germans "helped the Hereros to die" now follow.

Manuel Timbu (Cape Bastard), at present Court Interpreter in native languages at Omaruru, states under oath:–

> I was sent to Okahandja and appointed groom to the German commander, General von Trotha. I had to look after his horses and to do odd jobs at his headquarters. We followed the retreating Hereros from Okahandja to Waterberg, and from there to the borders of the Kalahari Desert. When leaving Okahandja, General von Trotha issued orders to his troops that no quarter was to be given to the enemy. No prisoners were to be taken, but all, regardless of age or sex, were to be killed. General von Trotha said, "We must exterminate them, so that we won't be bothered with rebellions in the future." As a result of this order the soldiers shot all natives we came across. It did not matter who they were. Some were peaceful people who had not gone into rebellion; others, such as old men and old women, had never left their homes; yet these were all shot.[xiii] I often saw this done. Once while on the march near Hamakari beyond the Waterberg, we came to some water-holes. It was winter time and very cold. We came on two very old Herero women They had made a small fire and were warming themselves. They had dropped back from the main body of Hereros owing to exhaustion. Von Trotha and his staff were present. A German soldier dismounted, walked up to the old women and shot them both as they lay there. Riding along we got to a vlei, where we camped. While we were there a Herero woman came walking up to us from the bush I was the Herero interpreter. I was told to take the woman to the General to see if she could give information as to the whereabouts of the enemy. I took her to General von Trotha; she was quite a young woman and looked tired and hungry. Von Trotha asked her several questions, but she did not seem inclined to give information. She said her people had all gone towards the east, but as she was a weak woman she could not keep up with them. Von Trotha then ordered that she should be taken aside and bayoneted. I took the woman away and a soldier came up with his bayonet in his hand. He offered it to me and said I had better stab the woman. I said I would never dream of doing such a thing and asked why the poor woman could not be allowed to live. The soldier laughed, and said. "If you won t do it, I will show you what a German soldier can do." He took the woman aside a few paces and drove the bayonet, through her body. He then withdrew the bayonet and brought it. all dripping with blood and poked it under my nose in a jeering way, saying, "You see,I have done it." Officers and soldiers were standing around looking on, but no one interfered to save the woman. Her body was not buried, but, like all others they killed. Simply allowed to lie and rot and be eaten by wild animals.
>
> A little further ahead we came to a place where the Hereros had abandoned some goats which were too weak to go further. There was no water to be had for miles around. There we found a young Herero, a boy of about 10 years of age. He had apparently lost his people. As we passed he called out to us that he was hungry and very thirsty. I would have given him something. but was forbidden to do so. The Germans discussed the advisability of killing him, and someone said that he would die of thirst in a day or so and it was not worth while bothering, so they passed on and left him there. On our return journey we again halted at Hamakari. There, near a hut, we saw an old Herero woman of about 50 or 60 years digging

---

[xiii] In this way thousands of harmless and peaceful Berg-Damaras met the same fate as the Hereros.

in the ground for wild onions. Von Trotha and his staff were present. A soldier named Konig jumped off his horse and shot the woman through the forehead at point blank range. Before he shot her, he said, "I am going to kill you." She simply looked up and said, "I thank you." That night we slept at Hamakari. The next day we moved off again and came across another woman of about 30. She was also busy digging for wild onions and took no notice of us. A soldier named Schilling walked up behind her and shot her through the back. I was an eye-witness of everything I have related. In addition I saw the bleeding bodies of hundreds of men, women and children, old and young, lying along the roads as we passed. They had all been killed by our advance guards. I was for nearly two years with the German troops and always with General von Trotha. I know of no instance in which prisoners were spared.

Jan Cloete (Bastard[116]), of Omaruru, states under oath:–

I was in Omaruru in 1904. I was commandeered by the Germans to act as a guide for them to the Waterberg district, as I knew the country well. I was with the 4th Field Company under Hauptmann Richardt. The commander of the troops was General von Trotha. I was present at Hamakari, near Waterberg when the Hereros were defeated in a battle. After the battle, all men, women and children, wounded and unwounded, who fell into the hands of the Germans were killed without mercy. The Germans then pursued the others, and all stragglers on the roadside and in the veld were shot down and bayoneted. The great majority of the Herero men were unarmed and could make no fight. They were merely trying to get away with their cattle. Some distance beyond Hamakari we camped at a water-hole. While there, a German soldier found a little Herero baby boy about nine months old lying in the bush. The child was crying. He brought it into the camp where I was. The soldiers formed a ring and started throwing the child to one another and catching it as if it were a ball. The child was terrified and hurt and was crying very much. After a time they got tired of this and one of the soldiers fixed his bayonet on his rifle and said he would catch the baby. The child was tossed into the air towards him and as it fell he caught it and transfixed the body with the bayonet. The child died in a few minutes and the incident was greeted with roars of laughter by the Germans, who seemed to think it was a great joke. I felt quite ill and turned away in disgust because, although I knew they had orders to kill all, I thought they would have pity on the child. I decided to go no further, as the horrible things I saw upset me, so I pretended that I was ill, and as the Captain got ill too and had to return, I was ordered to go back with him as guide. After I got home I flatly refused to go out with the soldiers again.

---

[116] This originally derogatory word was used at the time to refer particularly to a community descended largely from white men and Khoisan women who trekked into Namibia and settled at Rehoboth in 1870. The route taken by the trek and the geneologies of some of the families are on display in the town's museum. Today the community proudly refer to themselves as Rehoboth Basters. See also Rudolf Britz, Hartmut Lang and Cornelia Limpricht, *A Concise History of the Rehoboth Basters until 1990*, Klaus Hess Publishers/Verlag, Windhoek/Göttingen (1999).

Johannes Kruger[117] (appointed by Leutwein as chief of the Bushmen and Berg-Damaras of Grootfontein area), a Bastard of Ghaub, near Grootfontein, states under oath:–

> I went with the German troops right through the Herero rebellion. The Afrikaner Hottentots of my werft were with me. We refused to kill Herero women and children, but the Germans spared none. They killed thousands and thousands. I saw this bloody work for days and days and every day. Often, and especially at Waterberg, the young Herero women and girls were violated by the German soldiers before being killed. Two of my Hottentots, Jan Wint and David Swartbooi (who is now dead) were invited by the German soldiers to join them in violating Herero girls. The two Hottentots refused to do so.

Jan Kubas (a Griqua living at Grootfontein), states under oath:–

> I went with the German troops to Hamakari and beyond... The Germans took no prisoners. They killed thousands and thousands of women and children along the roadsides. They bayoneted them and hit them to (death with the butt ends of their guns. Words cannot be found to relate what happened; it was too terrible. They were lying exhausted and harmless along the roads, and as the soldiers passed they simply slaughtered them in cold blood. Mothers holding babies at their breasts, little boys and little girls; old people too old to fight and old grandmothers, none received mercy; they were killed, all of them, and left to lie and rot on the veld for the vultures and wild animals to eat.[118] They slaughtered until there were no more Hereros left to kill. I saw this every day; I was with them. A few Hereros managed to escape in the bush and wandered about, living on roots and wild fruits. Von Trotha was the German General in charge.

Hendrik Campbell (War Commandant of the Bastard tribe of Rehoboth. who commanded the Bastard Contingent called out by the Germans to help them against the Hereros in 1904), states on oath:–

> At Katjura we had a fight with the Hereros, and drove them from their position. After the fight was over, we discovered eight or nine sick Herero women who had been left behind. Some of them were blind. Water and food had been left with them. The German soldiers burnt them alive in the hut in which they were lying. The Bastard soldiers intervened and tried to prevent this, but when they failed, Hendrik van Wyk reported the matter to me. I immediately went to the German commander and complained. He said to me "that does not matter, they might have infected us with some disease." ... Afterwards at Otjimbende[119] we (the Bastards)

---

[117] Three Krueger brothers are believed to have been hunter-traders who operated in the Waterberg area during the 1850s from a base at Karakobis (Karakuwisa). Krueger fled to the north after an attack by an Oorlam raiding group, but returned with his allies and defeated them. One of the brothers married a local woman and they had at least two sons, John and Adam. On 31st August, 1895 the German Government recognised J. Kruger of //Ghaub as 'Chief' of various communities living within the Concession Area that had been granted to the South West Africa Company Ltd in 1892 (Köhler 1959b: 16-19)

[118] Burial rituals were particularly important in Herero tradition and the failure to bury the bodies was seen as particularly offensive. For details of traditional funeral customs see Irle, Jakob, *Die Herero. Ein Beitrag zur Landes-, Volks- und Missionskunds*, Bertelsmann, Gütersloh, 1906, pp. 126-130

[119] German missionary sources refer to an incident at Ombakaha that took place on 2nd November, 1904 when around 70 surrendering Herero led by Joel Kaviziri of Okahandja and 'Saul' of Otjenga were killed. Gewald, *Herero Heroes*, p. 182; Dreschler, *Let Us Die*, pp. 159-160; Pool, *Opstand*, p. 256.

Plate 2: Execution of natives by hanging from a tree.

captured 70 Hereros. I handed them over to Ober-Leutenants Volkmann and Zelow. I then went on patrol, and returned two days hater, to find the Hereros all lying dead in a kraal. My men reported to me that they had all been shot and bayoneted by the German soldiers. Shortly afterwards, General von Trotha and his staff accompanied by two missionaries, visited the camp. He said to me. "You look dissatisfied. Do you already wish to go home?"

"No," I replied, "the German Government has an agreement with us and I want to have no misunderstandings on the part of the Bastard Government, otherwise the same may happen to us weak people as has happened to those lying in the kraal yonder."

Lieut. Zelow gave answer: "The Hereros also do so." I said, "but, Lieutenant, as a civilised people you should give us a better example." To this von Trotha remarked, "The entire Herero people must be exterminated."

Petrus Diergaard, an under-officer of the Bastard Contingent, who was present, corroborates on oath the foregoing statement of the Commandant Hendrik Campbell.

Evidence of other eye-witnesses:–

Daniel Esma Dixon (of Omaruru, European, who was a transport driver the Germans during the rebellion) states under oath:–

I was present at the fight at Gross Barmen, near Okahandja, in 1904. After the fight the soldiers (marines from the warship *Habicht*[120]) were searching the bush. I went with them out of curiosity. We came across a wounded Herero lying in the shade of a tree. He was a very tall, powerful. man and looked like one of their headmen. He had his Bible next to his head and his hat over his face. I walked up to him and saw that he was wounded high up in the left hip. I took the hat off his face and asked him if he felt bad. He replied to me in Herero, "Yes, I feel I am going to die." The German marines, whose bayonets were fixed, were looking on. One of them said to me, "What does he reply?" I told him. "Well." Remarked the soldier, "if he is keen on dying he had better have this also." With that he stooped down and drove his bayonet into the body of the prostrate Herero, ripping up his stomach and chest and exposing the intestines. I was so horrified that I returned to my wagons at once.

In August 1904, I was taking a convoy of provisions to the troops at the front line. At a place called Ouparakane, in the Waterberg district, we were outspanned for breakfast when two Hereros, a man and his wife, came walking to us out of the bush. Under-officer Wolff and a few German soldiers were escort to the wagons and were with me. The Herero man was a cripple, and walked with difficulty, leaning on a stick and on his wife s arm. He had a bullet wound through the leg. They came to my wagon. and I spoke to them in Herero. The man said he had decided to return to Omaruru and surrender to the authorities, as he could not possibly keep up with his people who were retreating to the desert, and that his wife had decided to accompany him. He was quite unarmed and famished. I gave

---

[120] The first German reinforcements to arrive in Namibia after the outbreak of the war consisted of the sailors of this German warship which landed at Swakopmund on 18th January, 1904. The marine units that fought in the war are commemmorated by a monument that can still be seen near the seafront at Swakopmund. Pool, Gerhard *Die Herero-Opstand, 1904-1907*, Hollandsch Afrikaansche Uitgevers Maatschappij, Pretoria, 1979, p. 130.

them some food and coffee and they sat there for over an hour telling me of their hardships and privations. The German soldiers looked on, but did not interfere. I then gave the two natives a little food for their journey. They thanked me and then started to walk along the road slowly to Omaruru. When they had gone about 60 yards away from us I saw Wolff, the under-officer, and a soldier taking aim at them. I called out, but it was too late. They shot both of them. I said to Wolff, "How on earth did you have the heart to do such a thing? It is nothing but cruel murder." He merely laughed, and said, "Oh! these swine must all be killed; we are not going to spare a single one."

I spent a great part of my time during the rebellion at Okahandja, loading stores at the depot. There the hanging of natives was a common occurrence. A German officer had the right to order a native to be hanged. No trial or court was necessary. Many were hanged merely on suspicion. One day alone I saw seven Hereros hanged in a row, and on other days twos and threes. The Germans did not worry about rope. They used ordinary fencing wire, and the unfortunate native was hoisted up by the neck and allowed to die of slow strangulation. This was all done in public, and the bodies were always allowed to hang for a day or so as an example to the other natives.[121] Natives who were placed in gaol at that time never came out alive. Many died of sheer starvation and brutal treatment ... The Hereros were far more humane in the field than the Germans. They were once a fine race. Now we have only a miserable remnant left.

Hendrik Fraser (Bastard), of Keetmanshoop, states under oath:–

In March 1905 I was sent from Karibib and accompanied the troops of Hauptmann Kuhne to the Waterberg. I then saw that the Germans no longer took any prisoners. They killed all men, women and children whom they came across. Hereros who were exhausted and were unable to go any further were captured and killed. At one place near Waterberg, in the direction of Gobabis, after the fight at Okokadi, a large number (I should say about 50) men, women and children and little babies fell into the hands of the Germans. They killed all the prisoners, bayoneted them.

On one occasion I saw about 25 prisoners placed in a small enclosure of thorn bushes. They were confined in a very small space, and the soldiers cut dry branches and piled dry logs all round them men, women and childrenand little girls were there when dry branches had been thickly piled up all round them the soldiers threw branches also on the top of them. The prisoners were all alive and unwounded. but half starved. Having piled up the branches, lamp oil was sprinkled on the heap and it was set on fire. The prisoners were burnt to a cinder. I saw this personally. The Germans said, we should burn all these dogs and baboons in this fashion. The officers saw this and made no attempt to prevent it. From that time.to the end of the rising the killing and hanging of Hereros was practically a daily occurrence. There was no more fighting. The Hereros were merely fugitives in the bush. All the water-holes on the desert border were

---

[121] Evidence suggests that the bodies may not even have been buried. A German officer in the Schutztruppe wrote in 1907 that "A crate with Herero skulls was recently packed by the troops in German South West Africa and sent to the Pathological Institute in Berlin, where they are going to be used for scientific measurements. The skulls, whose flesh had been removed by Herero women with pieces of broken glass before they were put in the mail, belong to Herero who were hanged or killed in action." Quoted in Tilman Dedering 'A Certain Rigourous Treatment of all parts of the Nation': The Annihilation of the Herero in German South West Africa, 1904, Ch. 10 in Mark Levine and Penny Roberts (eds) *The Massacre in History*, Berghahn Books, New York/Oxford, 1999.

poisoned by the Germans before they returned. The result was that fugitives who came to drink the water either died of poisoning or, if they did not taste the water, they died of thirst.

This gruesome story by eye-witnesses could be continued until the report would probably require several thick volumes. Enough has been placed on record to prove how the Germans waged their war, and how von Trotha's extermination order was given effect to. Many more statements have been collected, but these as samples are sufficient. Further instances will be quoted when dealing further on with the Hottentot wars. Evidence of violation of women and girls is overwhelming, but so full of filthy and atrocious details as to render publication undesirable.

When viewed from the point of view of civilisation and common humanity, what a comparison there is between this German barbarism and the attitude of the Herero chiefs, who before a shot was fired ordered their people to spare the lives of all German women and children and non-combatants.

Rohrbach (page 323) says that at the time of the rebellion the Hereros still possessed approximately 50,000 head of cattle and at least 100,000 small stock. He says that a valuation of Herero assets at 500,000*l*. (10,000.000 marks) before their rising is probably much too low (*wohl zu gearing*). and the practical and quite unsentimental Rohrbach bitterly rebukes von Trotha because, owing to the latter's senseless extermination policy (*Vernichtungs Principe*) the cattle and sheep of the Hereros shared the fate of their masters. All, with the exception of 3,000 head captured before von Trotha's time, had perished in the desert. Viewing matters from the economical point of view, Rohrbach cannot find words strong enough to condemn von Trotha.

Writing in 1906, Leutwein (at page 542) says:–

> At a cost of several hundred millions of marks and several thousand German soldiers, we have, of the three business assets of the Protectorate – mining, farming, and native labour – destroyed the second entirely and two-thirds of the last. What is however more blameworthy is the fact that with all our sacrifices we have up to to-day (March 1906) not been able fully to restore peace again.

Referring to the peace overtures made in August 1904 by the Hereros.[122] Rohrbach (at page 358) says:–

> In this manner it would have been possible to have saved considerable quantities of stock and above all things to have ended the Herero war in the year 1904.

---

[122] In fact correspondence between Governor Leutwein and Samuel Maharero had taken place as early as March, 1904. Gewald, *Herero Heroes*, pp. 167-170.

Out of between 80,000 and 90,000 souls only about 15,000 starving and fugitive Hereros were alive at the end of 1905, when von Trotha relinquished his task.[123] What happened to the survivors will be told in the concluding parts of this report.

---

[123] Gerhard Pool has calculated a higher 'survival rate' arguing that up to 11th January, 1905 8,889 Herero had been taken prisoner, that 12,500 more came to the camps run by the missionaries in the period up to 31st March, 1907, that up to 1,000 refugees found refuge in Walvis Bay and that 1,175 successfully crossed the desert to Botwana. However these calculations do not take account of the high mortality rates amongst prisoners. *Samuel Maharero*, Gamsberg Macmillan, Windhoek (1991): p. 280.

CHAPTER SIXTEEN

THE HOTTENTOTS OF SOUTH-WEST AFRICA

It is now necessary to leave the Hereros for a time and to give a brief outline of the Hottentots and their history under German rule.

At the time of the German annexation in 1890, the habitable parts of the vast arid country known as Great Namaqualand were, with the exception of the Bastard territory of Rehoboth, occupied almost exclusively by various Hottentot tribes. It is probable that this area had been in their unchallenged possession for upwards of five centuries.

When Johann van Riebeck and the first Dutch settlers landed at Table Bay in 1652 the surrounding country was occupied by two distinct races of natives. By the name "Bushmen"[124] the white settlers called the wild and primitive men who avoided intercourse with the new-comers and lived only in the densest bush and in the most remote and inaccessible mountain fastnesses. These brown-skinned pigmies, armed with bows and arrows tipped with a mysterious and deadly poison, lived only from the products of the chase. They possessed neither flocks nor herds, they built no villages, cultivated no lands, and regarded all who ventured into their chosen hunting grounds as intruders and enemies. The other race, less savage and more intelligent, less primitive and more amicably disposed, came down to stare, in simple curiosity, at the first white settlers. From the point of view of physical beauty, nature had been unkind to them. Small, but well built and wiry, with ashen-brown and yellow skins, little beady eyes (which peered through narrow almond-shaped slits), high and prominent cheek-bones, flat bridgeless noses, low foreheads, thick lips and receding chins, their appearance was anything but attractive. As if to crown this embodiment of ugliness, nature had distributed little tufted knots of dark frizzy wool here and there, in lieu of hair, On the hardest of heads. These weird looking people called themselves *Khoi-khoi* (or men of men) and their race *Nama*. Living in the open, in scattered villages, where water and grazing were most plentiful, they sheltered under rude huts or "pontoks" made of grass mats, portable and easily removable from place to place.

From the trading point of view, their large herds of sheep, goats, and horned cattle were an asset to be cultivated by the new-comers. Their friendliness was

---

[124] In the course of the twentieth century a small battle has been raging within academic circles regarding the correct terms to be used and applied to people. In southern Africa this debate has raged particularly stridently around the issue of what to call the first inhabitants of southern Africa. For an introduction to the terms used see, Emil Boonzaier et al., *The Cape Herders: A History of the Khoikhoi of Southern Africa*, (Cape Town 1996) pp. 1 - 3.

heartily reciprocated – for a time at any rate – and the Dutch East India Company soon built up a thriving trade.

Van Riebeck's Hollanders gave them the name"Hottentot." It is said that their curious clicking language, sounding so uncanny and strange to European ears, gave the impression that they all stuttered. According to Dr. Leonard Schultze (*Aus Namaland und Kalihari*), the word "Hottentot" was used by Hollanders, in those days, as a nick-name for a stuttering person. The Rev. Hugo Hahn's theory was that the word was a corruption of the low German *Huttentut* (= a stupid, muddle-headed person, a fool). That the name was not intended as a compliment seems clear. Even to this day the more educated and intelligent Hottentots secretly resent being called what Chief Christian Goliath of Berseba describes as a *spot en veracht naam* (i.e., a name of derision and contempt). However that may be, Europeans in South and South-West Africa have, ever since the days of Johan Van Riebeck, called these people *Hottentot* or *Hotnots*, and the name is likely to stick to them.

The problem of the origin of this race of dusky yellow-skimmed nomads (or "red-people," as they, with delightful disregard for colour, love to call themselves) is still unsolved and will probably always remain so. Some ethnologists fix their place of origin so far north as Upper Egypt; others, like Hahn, allege that the Hottentots are really the aborigines of South Africa; some claim that they are the product of an intermingling of some now extinct and unknown light yellow-skinned nomad race with the aboriginal Bushmen; some argue that the Hottentot is an evolved and more progressive type of Bushman (but they cannot get over the difficulty presented by the fact that the Hottentot retains not the slightest suspicion of knowledge of the primitive arts of rude painting and sculpture possessed, to this day, by the Bushmen); there are others who go so far as to claim that they have discovered certain similarities of idiom and speech, especially in the characteristic clicks, which would indicate origin in Indo-China. There is no doubt about it that some Hottentots are in appearance not unlike Chinamen. The same may however be said of some Bushmen. The writer has seen Bushmen from the Grootfontein district who only required a pigtail in lieu of "peppercorns" to enable them to pass off as Chinese. These were probably half-breed Bushman and Hottentot. It is related by German writers that, when German troops who had participated in the suppression of the Boxer rising in China, arrived in South-West Africa in 1904 and saw the Hottentots for the first time, the usual remark was, "Why, here are the Chinese again!" After all is said and done, these arguments as to origin are based merely on conjecture. The fact remains that South-West Africa is, to-day, the only part of the sub-continent where pure remnants of the once numerous and powerful Hottentot race are still to be found. A few dying clans still live with some semblance of racialcohesion, respecting their hereditary chiefs and speaking the wonderful language of their forbears; but of their mysterious past, their ancestors, their heathen beliefs and customs they know nothing. They are now all Christianised.

It is generally believed that the Hottentots are not an aboriginal South African race. They appear to have migrated long centuries back from the far interior of north-east Africa, well in advance of the southward moving Bantu hordes.[125] According to Stow ("The Native Races of S.A."), they moved south-west to the Atlantic coast near the Equator. Then they turned southwards and, traveling always in a defined zone, parallel to the western seaboard, they traversed Angola, South-West Africa, and crossed the Orange River into the present Cape Province. Stow is of opinion that the southward movement must have commenced about the year 1300 A.D., and that several centuries had elapsed before the slow moving tribes, encumbered by their flocks and herds, sheltered in the shadows of Table Mountain.[126] He argues, rather unconvincingly, that:–

> The relative conditions of the Hottentots and Bushmen in 1652 (*i.e.*, when van Riebeck landed) may be received as confirmatory evidence of the fact that the Hottentots had not long settled in those parts of the country. The Bushmen were still living in the mountains and wooded parts – even Table Mountain was occupied by them.

As against this, there is historical evidence that 150 years prior to the date mentioned by Stow, the Hottentots were already settled at the Cape. Vasco da Gama saw them there in 1497, and so did da Saldanha in 1503. In the year 1510 the first Portuguese Viceroy of India, Francisco D'Almeida, landed at Table Bay on his way home for water and provisions. His party picked a quarrel with the Hottentots, and a fight resulted in which the Viceroy and 65 of his followers were slain. The others only saved their lives by a precipitate retreat to the boats.

On their way from the north a large proportion of the Nama travellers settled down permanently on the high and healthy plateaux of Damaraland and Great Namaqualand. These people did not at any time cross the Orange River to the south and never came into contact with the Dutch settlers at the Cape. The fact that Damaraland and Great Namaqualand were apparently too small to support all the immigrants with their flocks and herds would indicate that they numbered in all probability hundreds of thousands and that they were rich in cattle and sheep. Before they could settle in Damaraland and Great Namaqualand, the Hottentots had to deal with the aboriginal Bushmen and a strange ebony-skinned negro race – known to-day as the Berg-Damaras. The Bushmen were driven to the arid marches of the Namib and the Kalihari deserts, while the Berg-Damaras, heavier and more sluggish of temperament than their Bush-

---

[125] The use of the term 'Bantu Hordes' in the text is little in keeping with what probably happened. It is more likely that small groups of Bantu-speaking people, and aspects of their material culture slowly trickled down into the southern African region, where over time they came to be taken over or incorporated within groups already living in the area. Jan Vansina 'Equatorial Africa and Angola: Migrations and the emergence of the first states', Ch. 22 in D. Niane (ed) *Africa from the Twelfth to the Sixteenth Century, Vol. IV, General History of Africa*, Heinemann/California/UNESCO, 1984: 552-555.

[126] Archeaological evidence suggests that people have been living in the Cape for at least the past 30.000 years. John Parkington, "Changing views of the Late Stone Age of South Africa" in F. Wendorf and A.E. Close (eds), *Advances in World Archaeology*, 3, pp. 89 - 142.

men neighbours, were gradually overpowered and enslaved. This accounts for the fact that the Berg-Damaras of to-day, though an entirely distinct and separate race, speak what is considered the purest Nama language, although they are said even now to find some difficulty in mastering the clicks. Of their own language, whatever that may have been, they retain neither memory nor the slightest trace. They called themselves *Hau-Khoin* (= real men); but this Nama name, obviously of later origin, gives no clue to their identity. It appears to have arisen out of a patriotic desire to be uncomplimentary and sarcastic towards their small and lightly built conquerors the *Khoi-Khoi* or "men of men."

Judging from the recorded happenings at the Cape, it is not unreasonable to presume that the Hottentots of South-West Africa had long been settled there when Vasco da Gama first saw their compatriots a thousand miles further south in 1497. It is probable also that when van Riebeck landed in 1652 the whole of Damaraland, Great Namaqualand, and the western and north western districts of the Cape Province were occupied by these people.

With the landing of the white settler at Table Bay and the gradual spreading Out of the settlements to the north and north-east, the southern extremities of the Hottentot zone were slowly absorbed and taken in. Just about this time, too, the right flank pioneers of the great Bantu hordes, moving south and south-west from the Equator, began to push the Hottentots in the far north. It was then that the squeezing and exterminating process started, and it continued for upwards of two centuries. By the year 1825 the last remnants of the former Hottentot tribes of the Cape Province had re-crossed the Orange River to the north and had placed themselves under the protection of the "red chiefs" of Great Namaqualand. The latter under pressure from the advancing Hereros, had by that time practically evacuated Damaraland. Under the leadership of the brigand Jonker Afrikaner, the Afrikaners for a time regained possession of the southern portion, but by 1867 the Hereros had once more secured the mastery, and only Great Namaqualand remained in the hands of the Hottentots. There they were when Germany annexed the area in 1890.

The Hottentots of Great Namaqualand may be classified under two headings or groups:–

> (1) The pure Nama group, consisting of tribes which, having remained in Great Namaqualand from the time of their arrival, were in no way influenced by contact and intermixture with Europeans and Bastards at the Cape. Speaking only their own language, they until quite recently retained their ancient customs, religious beliefs and traditions. They waged war in the primitive style of their ancestors, and relied mainly on the bow and arrow.
>
> (2) The bi-lingual "Orlams"[xiv] Hottentot group, consisting of those tribes which had returned to Great Namaqualand from the Cape areas. Through generations of contact with Europeans and "coloured people" (as the Bastards at the Cape are

---

[xiv] (Page 70 in original) The word *Orlams* is of doubtful origin. It is not Dutch. Some allege that it is of Cape-Malay extraction. However that may be, the accepted meanings are "intelligent," "old-fashioned" or in a bad sense "cunning."

CHAPTER SIXTEEN

termed) they no longer retained the pure Nama strain.[127] The majority of them spoke Cape Dutch as well as Nama, and had acquired proficiency in the use of the rifle and as horsemen. They were nearly all Christians and had in addition got an elementary idea of the European systems of government, and unfortunately a more than elementary idea of European weaknesses and failings, which some of them were not slow to emulate. The Orlams group found that their brethren in the north would tolerate their presence only on certain conditions, namely, that they should recognise the jurisdiction of the chiefs in whose territories they settled and that as an outward sign of submission an annual tribute of cattle or horses should be paid to these chiefs in return for the right to live and to graze their stock in Great Namaqualand.

The effect of this restriction may easily be imagined. No sooner had the newcomers settled down and become accustomed to their surroundings than they refused to pay any more tribute. In the inevitable wars which followed the Namas were no match for their better armed and more experienced adversaries. Before very many years had passed the order of things was reversed and the Orlams were the ruling clans, while the Nama tribes were (with the exception of the Bondelswartz) either absorbed or retained their lands on the same terms of tribute and vassalage which they had formerly exacted. The dreaded Afrikaner Hottentots under Jager Afrikaner and his son Jonker were for many years the ruling clan. The chief claimed paramount over the whole of Great Namaqualand, and from 1840 to 1867 their influence was felt throughout Damaraland, where the Hereros were partially subjugated and paid tribute, and even to the far north where at one time raiding parties under Samuel Afrikaner, brother of Jan Jonker, were the terror of Southern and Central Ovamboland.[128] The Hereros, aided by the Nama-Swartboois and led by Frederick Green, eventually defeated the Afrikaners and their allies in 1864, and from that day their power began to wane.[129] Christian Afrikaner, who succeeded his father Jonker, was killed in action at Otjimbingwe in 1864, and his brother Jan Jonker proved too weak to uphold the martial reputation of their father, the redoubtable Jonker. In the eighties, after years of conflict, the Kowese or Witbooi Hottentots under Hendrik Witbooi had practically subjugated and absorbed the Afrikaners, and Hendrik Witbooi claimed that he was Paramount Chief or King of Great Namaqualand. The Swartboois, owing to their participation with the Hereros in the sixties against the other Hottentots, were practically outlawed by their own race. They disposed of their area, Rehoboth, about 1869 to the Cape Bastards, who had migrated from De Tuin and other places in the Cape Colony. With the permission of the Herero chiefs, the

---

[127] Oorlam communities emerged on the north-western Cape colonial frontier in the late eighteenth century around the institution of the Commando, and consisted of an amalgam of Khoi community remnants, runaway slaves, Basters, Cape Outlaws and others.

[128] For an introduction to this period of the history of Cental and Southern Namibia see, Lau, *Nambia*

[129] For contemporary accounts by two of the European traders directly involved in the conflict see: Charles John Andersson, *The Matchless Copper Mine in 1857*, edited by Brigitte Lau (Windhoek 1987) & *Trade and Politics in Central Namibia 1860 - 1864*, edited by Brigitte Lau (Windhoek 1989)

Swartboois moved northwards to Ameib, near the Erongo Mountains (also known as the Bokberg), and not far from the site of the present town of Karibib. Eventually, owing to disputes with the Hereros, about 1885 they moved further north over the Ugab River, and settled permanently at Franzfontein and Otjitambi, near Outjo.

Of the Topnaars, near Walvis Bay, a miserable and dilapidated remnant of humanity, without stock, living on fish, dead seabirds and the *nara* fruits of the Namib Desert, whose impotent chief had "sold" to Luderitz the coast area from near Conception Bay to Cape Frio in the far north, the bulk had fled for fear of the Hereros to the Kaokoveld and settled at Zesfontein. The remainder sheltered under the protection of Britain in the arid sandy wastes near Walvis Bay.

The names and locations of the various Hottentot tribes at the time of annexation by Germany were as follows

Orlams Hottentots

Name of Tribe	*Chief*	*Location*
(1) Koweses or Witboois.	Hendrik Witbooi.	Hornkranz and Gibeon.
(2) Gei- Khanas or Gobabis.	Andreas Lambert.	Gobabis and Nossanbis.
(3) Hei-'Khauas or Berseba.	Jacobus Izaak Khachab	Berseba.
(4) 'Amas or Bethany. 'Aman,	Joseph Frederiks Khorebeb	Bethany.
(5) Eicha-ais or Afrikaner.	Kootje Afrikaner.	North Bank Orange River in Warmbad District.

Pure Namas

(6) Gaminus or Bondelswartz.	Willem Christian. Naochab	Warmbad (old name, Nesbit's Bath)
(7) Khora-gei-Khois or Franzmann.	Simon Kooper Gomchab	Gochas
(8) Geikons or Red Nation.	Manasse Noreseb	Hoachanas.
(9) Khau-Goas or Young Red Nation (Swartboois).	Abraham Swartbooi	Otjitambi and Franzfontein.
(10) Kharo-oas or Tseib Tribe.	Piet Tseib[xv]	Keetmanshoop (old name, Zwart-Modder)
(11) Habobes or Veldschoendragers.	Jan Hendricks	Daberas Hasuur
(12) Topnaars.	Piet Heibib.	Zesfontein and portion of Walvis Bay.

[xv] (Page 71 in original) Piet Tseib was really an under-chief to Willem Christian of the Bondelswartz, the Tseib tribe having been subjugated and their territory declared under jurisdiction of the Bondelswartz chief

The total Hottentot population of South-West Africa in 1890 has been fixed by various authorities at between 20,000 and 25,000. The strongest and most influential chiefs were, in order:–

Hendrik Witbooi,
Willem Christian,
Joseph Frederiks, and
Simon Kooper.

Approximately three-quarters of the Hottentots were at that time under their tribal jurisdiction or control.

Mr. W. C. Palgrave, in his report (1877), mentions three other tribes:–

(1) The Khogeis (a small remnant, only 100 strong).
(2) The Ogeis, or Groot Doode (Great Deaths).
(3) The Gunugu or Lowlanders.

By 1890 those tribes had ceased to exist as separate organisations and had been absorbed by the stronger chiefs. The same fate befell the once all-powerful Afrikaner tribe of Eik-hams (Windhuk). After their defeat, first by the Hereros and later by Hendrik Witbooi, the survivors of the tribe scattered and mingled with other friendly tribes, whose chiefs gave them food and protection in return for their support.

By 1906, that is sixteen years after formal annexation, the only tribes of the 12 enumerated who still retained their chiefs and their territory were:–

(1) The Hei-Khauas of Berseba, who did not participate in the general rising.
(2) The Topnaars of Zesfontein in the extreme north, who were too inaccessible to German bayonets and too poor to be worth killing.

Of the others not a vestige of tribal or communal life remained; the chiefs were all either dead or fugitives in British territory, and the population had been reduced by more than half. The miserable survivors could beidentified by name only with their former tribal chiefs; they owned not a square inch of land and not so much as a scabby goat. They were dumped into "reserves," and every person over the age of seven years was compelled to seek work under penalty of the lash and manacles for vagrancy.

There are no figures available for reference just after the rising, but the census taken in 1910, that is 20 years after annexation, gives the total number of adult Hottentots in the whole Protectorate as 9,781. This figure is less than half of the general minimum estimate for 1890.

It will be seen that, so far as concerns their land and possessions, the Hottentot had fared no better than the Hereros, and that while the latter race was all but exterminated, the Hottentots managed to escape total destruction. This was due, not to German clemency and humanity, but to the superior skill, mobility and experience of the Hottentot as an elusive and hardy guerrilla fighter.

It will be necessary to defer details as to the relations between the Germans and the Hottentots and their wars, pending a short reference to some of the characteristic laws and customs of these "red" people.

CHAPTER SEVENTEEN

LAWS AND CUSTOMS OF THE HOTTENTOTS

The Hottentots had no written laws. Their laws were oral and traditional. Dr. Theo Hahn divides their laws into two classes:–

(1) Laws based on decided cases. Such laws took their origin from decisions of the Chief Council duly ratified by the chief.
(2) Customs and superstitions developing in time into accepted rules of life and conduct and binding as such on the tribe.

The Hottentots were very much attached to their traditional and inherited customs and manners.

The people were divided into tribes or clans, each under its hereditary chief. When the chief died, his eldest son was, under normal conditions, the heir to the chieftainship, and as such he was accepted without question by his subjects. Failing a son, the chief s eldest surviving brother became his successor. A chief had the right during his lifetime owing to advancing old age, ill-health, or any other good reason, to abdicate in favour of his heir. This was, however, an entirely personal right which he could not be compelled to exercise against his will. "Our chiefs," say the Hottentots, "are not made, they are given by God." The system of government by the chief was on democratic lines, even if it were not always in strict accordance with popular views. The chief, though hereditary and as such commanding great respect and influence, was bound to act in terms of the advice and resolutions of his councillors.

The councillors were elected by the "men" of the tribe. As "men" were reckoned only those who were *married.*

Formerly this way of acquiring the vote was not so easy as it may appear. Some tribes had strict laws by which young men were absolutely prohibited from marrying until they had reached a certain age. Among the Hei-Khauas of Berseba the age limit was as high as 30. Chief Christian Goliath explains that the reason for this was to keep the young people "in their proper place" and to prevent the elders of the tribe from being outvoted. It appears also that a young Hottentot who too young married a rich heiress and got, say, 50 ewe goats with her, soon became an unbearable and indolent "snob." Moreover, the fixing of the age limit gave elderly widowers the chance of selecting a young heiress for the second, and the monopoly of youth was broken. Needless to say there was no age limit for the woman.

In the council the vote of the chief was of no greater weight or value than that of anyone of his councillors, though his expressed opinion bore great influence and probably ensured a majority for him in most cases.

The council made wars and treaties, rules and regulations, and dealt with the internal and economic affairs of the tribe and all inter-tribal disputes. Generally it was composed of the chief and his under-chiefs *ex-officio* and by the elected councillors. Senior officials, such as the tribal magistrate, war commandant, and later (as Christians) the elders of the church, were generally members of the council.

This council was also the supreme court and the final court of appeal to whichcivil litigants and criminals, who were usually dealt with by the magistrate or the Under-chiefs acting as the chief s deputies, could appeal.

Cases of serious import or serious charges involving possibly, a sentence of capital punishment were generally dealt with by the full tribal council as a court of first instance. In such cases the appeal lay to the chief in person, and he, in common with most sovereigns, had the right to exercise his prerogative of mercy.

No sentence of capital punishment could legally be executed without the prior express sanction of the chief personally.

To some of the Orlams chiefs, whose military powers had made them feared and respected throughout the country, the temptation to become autocrats was very strong. Few could survive it. They generally contrived therefore either to act quite independently of the council, which was treated as a mere advisory body, or as was the case with Hendrik Witbooi they dispensed with elections altogether and nominated their own council and officials. Thereby they ensured that only their own trusty friends and supporters were placed in power.

Democratic government was very irksome and distasteful to a warrior-chief like Hendrik Witbooi. At the height of his power he styled himself the "Lord of the Water and the Head Chief of Great Namaqualand." Letters addressed to him as "King of Namaqualand" received immediate and gracious attention and tohis death he was a firm believer in the "Divine Right of Kings," claiming that he owed responsibility to no one except to "God the Father in Heaven."

The following "Proclamation" by Hendrik Witbooi, dated, 3rd January 1891, is of interest, because it gives an idea of the system existing at the time of the annexation among all the Hottentots tribes. The only difference was that while Witbooi was an autocrat to a certain extent, the other chiefs, like Willem Christian and Simon Kooper, relied more on popular approval and the support of the councilors than on their royal prerogatives.

Hornkranz, 3rd January 1891

Beloved Community of Hornkranz,

To-day I make public fresh appointments for the New Year. I have caused certain alterations to be made in the Civil and Church laws. (*Note*. Hendrik was spiritual head as well as chief). I have also appointed new officials according to the times and the prompting of the Lord. Therefore have I appointed younger men, like children who are being trained and, when the time is accomplished, they will be taken into full membership. For this reason I have relieved some of the older officials and have substituted young men in full authority of the laws, in order that they may publicly perform their authorised duties. I have however re-appointed some of the old officials as well, so that they may train and teach the younger team (*jongespan*). I have also appointed two additional Elders. The names of those appointed will be read to the community, and are as follows:–

Then follows a list of the names and of the offices to which they have been appointed. These posts were all honorary, and carried no salaries or emoluments. The seven chief appointments are those of Under-Chief, Magistrate, War Commandant, Chief Field Cornet, and three senior Councillors. The remainder (there are 30 in all) include "the Overseer of the whole village," a "Second Magistrate," Second, Third, and Fourth Field Cornets, Elders, Junior Councillors, Messengers of the Council and of the Elders, and a "Corporal" and a "Second Corporal." It must not be imagined that the Corporal was so humble a personage as his designation might imply. He was really the Quartermaster-General in the field!

This is the "beloved Community," with its Church Elders and Corporals, which at early dawn on an April day in 1893 was cruelly attacked and lost 150 men, women and children, not because any crimes had been committed, not because there was war, but because Germany had selected this chief and his people as a fit object on make "an impression of our power."

It is clear that, by 1891, the influence of the Orlams Hottentots had spread throughout Great Namaqualand, and that, although all ancient customs were still retained and ruled personal conduct, their system of tribal control had gradually undergone a change, and the old simple ideas of rule and government were being slowly exchanged for a crude imitation of the European system which their fore-fathers had seen at the Cape. In addition to this Orlams influence on the pure Namas, missionary influence on both cannot be overlooked. By 1890 the Hottentots were nearly all professing Christians. and there is no denying the fact that the missionaries, some of them at any rate, had done excellent work towards uplifting and developing the race. The pity of it is that, after annexation and in the ten years prior thereto, the Rhenish missionaries, actuated by a deadly hatred for England and all things English, regarded political propaganda as far more important apparently than church duties, and prostituted their noble work in order to serve the base ends of a callous Government, whose soldiers were not patterns of morality and virtue by any means. In this way the missionaries became merely the tools and agents of Germany, and the inevitable result was that they lost all prestige and all control over the natives, besides forfeiting their affection and respect.[130] The natives grew suspicious and distrustful of their missionaries. Hendrik Witbooi dispensed with his altogether and conducted his own church services.

---

[130] The Rhenish Mission prepared a pastoral letter to all Christian Herero that was issued on 9th May, 1904 which warned them that they had 'raised the sword against the Government which God has placed over you' Hellberg, *Mission*, p. 118.

Better proof of how the missionaries lost caste and influence cannot be given than the fact that the Herero rising of 1904 and the great Hottentot rising came like a bolt from the blue and without a word of warning. The missionaries, living among the natives, preaching and talking and understanding their ways and customs thoroughly, were not aware of their intentions.

Against these missionaries must it also be recorded that, knowing the native mind and character so well as they must have known them, and knowing their cherished customs and laws, they were indifferent onlookers at the violation and trampling under foot thereof by German soldiers and settlers. They had neither the courage nor the inclination to stand up boldly and defend the helpless creatures who looked up to them for guidance and protection. On the contrary, like the missionary Brisker, they applied for soldiers and guns in order that the work of the Missions might prosper.

Despite this, the natives, grateful for the mere fact that these people had brought the Christian religion to them, in Hereroland and Great Namaqualand, throughout their wars invariably spared the lives of all missionaries and their families. Their possessions were never touched, and the Mission Station was regarded as a sanctuary.

A simple nomadic people never burdens its criminal law with a huge category of crimes. Apart from offences against morality, their chief crimes were murder and theft.

For wilful murder the penalty was death.

To prevent the possible shielding of rich and influential murderers there grew up in the Hottentot system a law of vendetta (*Kharas* – to pay back or retaliate).

If through favouritism, fear, or for political reasons, a murderer were acquitted by the council, the next relation in blood of the murdered person had the right to take the law into his own hands and to kill the murderer. This killing would in such event be no crime, and neither the chief nor the council had the right or power to intervene and punish the relative for his act.

There is the case of the well-known traveller Andersson, who about 1861 shot an Afrikaner Hottentot in self-defence, so he alleged, near Windhuk. Andersson reported the matter to the chief Jonker Afrikaner, and as a result he was brough before the chief and tribal council for trial. The council, after hearing the evidence, was, rightly or wrongly, satisfied that Andersson had exceeded his rights and had gone too far. But, in view of the fact that he was a European and a British subject, the chief was reluctant to punish him. So Jonker said: "I release you; but according to our law, the brother of Hartebeest will kill you and must kill you, so flee for your life."

Theft was regarded very seriously and was punished by severe fines and ostracism, and even by flogging. Theo Hahn writes: "There is a deep sense of justice innate in the Hottentots. To a Hottentot stealing is a disgrace, and amongst the aborigines of Great Namaqualand a thief is cut by everyone and becomes almost an outcast."

In wartime to take from the enemy Hereros or hostile clans was not theft. If it could be safely managed even in peace time it was not theft either. In this theHottentots were not exceptional, however.

To take the goat of a friend for food, even in his absence and without permission. is not, and never was, regarded by the. Hottentots as unlawful. This is a general custom arising out of the conditions of the country, where for long distances food is practically unobtainable. The rule is based on reciprocity, and no Hottentot need leave a stranger s hut or pontok hungry, especially if they are of the same tribe; he is welcome, even in the owner's absence, to help himself to whatever there is.

Speaking of punishments which would be efficacious under European rule, Hahn recommends –

> Hard labour and spare diet. To people of rank the application of the lash makes a deep impression. There is nothing more degrading to a Bantu nobleman than to receive a blow... A Hottentot feels punishment as keenly as a white man. I did not flog my Hottentot servants if I could help it. Often a private earnest talking to had a most beneficial effect.

And yet to-day there is in South-West Africa not one adult male in ten, Herero, Berg-Damara or Hottentot, who does not bear on his body the scars and indelible marks of the German sjambok. "Flogging," recently said a Herero headman, "came to our people more regularly than their meals;" and this view is endorsed by the Hottentots.

In their court the Hottentots followed strict rules of procedure. No hearsay evidence was allowed. The circumstances determined what weight should be given to the evidence of informers or accomplices.

> The Hottentots (says Hahn) avoid as far as possible the drawing of a woman in into court to give evidence. The reason for this is the respect they have for women. (The word for "woman" in Hottentot is *taras* = ruler, mistress).[131] If the evidence of a woman, especially one of rank, must be heard, generally two or three councillors see her privately, cross-examine her, and communicate the results to the council.
>
> False testimony (says Hahn) is abhorred, lying is disgraceful, and a person guilty of having given false testimony is punished according to the mischief done by his false testimony.

It is well to remember that in 1904 the Deutsche Kolonial Bund demanded that the evidence of one white man should only be upset by the corroborated

---

[131] In an article originally published in 1925 Winifred Hoernlé, a lecturer in Ethnology at the University of Witwatersrand, argued that traditionally the sister of an individual's father was given particular respect in Nama culture and the title *Gei Tàras* and that this could also be applied to a man's eldest sister. The word *Tàras* would be used by a man speaking about his sister and was '... a person to be respected, not to be spoken to or of lightly'. A word *Tarás* (with a different inflection) was used for a wife or by a man to his brother's wife and her sisters. Hoernlé, Winifred, *The Social Organization of the Nama and other Essays*, edited by Peter Carstens, Witwatersrand University Press, Johannesburg, 1985, pp. 52-55

statements of seven coloured persons, apparently because the Hottentots were ignorant of truth and the white man was a "superior being" (*Höheres Wesen*).

The Hottentots were, even in their heathen state, nearly all monogamists. The only case in which in later times polygamy was recognised or sanctioned in their heathen state was where there were no children of the first marriage. The man was then allowed to take a concubine (*aris* the younger one) after the fashion of Abraham. Jonker Afrikaner had two wives, although he professed to be a Christian. No one would however hold Jonker up as a model Hottentot. Their marriages were always based on mutual consent. The system of lobola, or purchase, of the Bantu tribes was never known to the Hottentots.

The wife is among Hottentots the equal of her husband. She has her separate property, and the husband would not venture to sell or slaughter an animal belonging to her without her consent or in her absence. If he intends to barter his own stock or buy anything even with his own money he first consults his wife.

In the Hottentot home the wife is the ruler (*taras*). The husband, though looked upon as the food provider, has nothing to say. As a result he will not take a mouthful of milk without first asking his wife for it.

Last wills or testaments were not known to the Hottentot. During his lifetime a man might bestow his possessions as he pleased, but after death his remaining property was distributed according to the traditional laws. Their laws of succession were very fair and just. The nearest male relative of minor orphans was their guardian during minority and the trustee of their stock. No chief or council could interfere with the guardian s rights; but as he was always very closely watched by the other relatives, he could not easily appropriate anything in an illegal manner.

Land Rights. – Among the Hottentots, as with the Hereros, land was the communal property of the tribe. It was regarded as inalienable. The fact that the chiefs Joseph Frederiks and Piet Heibib did sell land to Luderitz in 1883-84 merely goes to show either that the waterless desert wastes of the Namib coast belt were not of any use to the tribe or, as was the case with Piet Heibib, that the territory (particularly that from Walvis Bay north to Cape Frio) did not belong to him. Piet Heibib was merely a dummy created to suit German plans, and Luderitz knew this. Every member of the tribe had a personal right to the use of land, water and grazing for himself, his family and his stock. No chief could interfere or deprive a subject of such rights.

The first comer had prior rights. If a man dug a well and opened a spring, it was his property and he had the sole right to it. Every passer-by and new-comer must have the owner s permission before using the well or spring to draw water for himself or his cattle. The Herero custom was identical. This reminds one of the Roman-Dutch Law maxim *qui prior est in tempore potior est in jure.*[132]

---

[132] 'What is first in time, has better rights' – an early version of the principle 'First come first served'

> These laws and rights of the natives (says Hahn, writing in 1882) have been constantly overlooked by traders, who, considering themselves a superior race of men, disregard altogether the rights and claims of natives. I know of instances where traders coolly allowed people to tear away the fence of Hakkies thorn (*Acacia Detinens*) and allowed their oxen to rush into the water and make a mud pool of it.

Originally the Hottentots were not an agricultural people. Since they came into contact with Europeans they have at mission stations and other suitable spots cultivated gardens. Here the first comer retained the rights to the soil cultivated, which he generally fenced in. Tobacco, mealies, pumpkins, and corn are the chief crops cultivated; but, owing to the scanty rainfall and lack of irrigation facilities, no family may be said to have grown enough even for its own consumption.

Tribal boundaries were always carefully fixed between the "brother" chiefs and encroachments were not allowed but deeply resented. If a tribe wished to move into the territory of another, application had first to be made to the chief of the neighbouring tribe. If they were on friendly terms the permission might be given without charge; but if relations were not too good a tribute of heifers or horses was generally demanded as an acknowledgement of the resident tribe s ownership and supremacy over the area.

As an example of their jealous regard for boundary and territorial rights the following may be mentioned. In 1889 Hendrik Witbooi, the Kowese chief, while travelling from Keetmanshoop to Gibeon, rather went out of his way, and with his men passed over a corner of the territory of the Bondelswartz of Warmbad. In November of that year the chief of the Bondelswartz, Willem Christian, wrote to Hendrik Witbooi strongly protesting against this. He says, such circumstances are likely to cause dissatisfaction, and that if the "dear Captain" required anything in his area, it was only right that he should first apply for permission to enter and await the reply before doing anything. This, writes Willem Christian, would have avoided "misunderstandings"; because it is above my comprehension (*boven mij verstand*) that one chief should enter another chief s area without notifying him and making a request.

In large tribes each sub-village or kraal was governed by an under-chief, appointed by the Chief-in-Council as deputy of the chief of the whole tribe. This under-chief had his own local councillors, court, and officials. From the under-chief"s courts there was always an appeal to the Chief-in-Council. The chief, however, never dealt with such an appeal without first referring it back to the under-chief for report.

In all instances the people implicitly obeyed the orders of their chief. For instance, he could order certain grazing grounds to be vacated in order that they might be rested; he had also the right to use the labour of his people for public purposes, such as mending roads, building schools or churches, opening up water and furrows, and so on. All adult males were liable to be called out for military duty at any time. The people never paid any taxes. Certain court fees were paid, and the fines levied went to the chief as a rule. He could also accept a share of damages awarded in a civil dispute, but there was no obligation on the successful litigant to pay. It was regarded merely as a voluntary gift for the trouble taken.

If a Hottentot could not pay his debts a system of *cessio bonorum*[133] was known. A trustee took over and divided his assets among the creditors; but he was allowed to keep a few cows and goats in trust for his creditors merely for the maintenance of himself and his family. He could not slaughter these animals, but used their milk. This arrangement with creditors was called *ma-ams* (a gift for the mouth).

The total Hottentot population was approximately one quarter that of the Hereros, and their possessions in cattle, sheep, and goats, proportionately even less.

The Hottentot never viewed life too seriously. His was more of the "eat, drink, and be merry" temperament than his Bantu neighbours. No Hottentot would dream of drawing his belt tighter, as did the Hereros, while fat heifers and goat ewes were grazing around. The result was that, while the Herero waxed rich and sat with an empty stomach watching his beloved cattle grazing, finding therein one of the sweetest pleasures of life, the Hottentot was never so happy as when, having had a good square meal, he could doze away in the shade of his pontok, consoled by the fact that the ewe goat just killed and eaten was one less to tend and therefore more worry off his hands. It would be wrong to regard the Hottentot as entirely blameless sort of person or as the Rhenish records described their first trader colonists (the immortal Halbich, Tamm, and Redecker), to refer to him as a paragon of virtue – (*Muster von Sittlichkeit*).

Even old Hendrik Witbooi, when in holy wrath he sent a declaration of war to Maharero informing him that "I am the rod of correction sent by God to punish you for your sins," never lost sight of the prospect of capturing a thousand or two of the sinful Maharero s best cattle and thereby, incidentally, setting a bad example to the Germans who came after him. They were, according to von Lindequist only too glad to emulate and carry on "the bloodletting of Herero cattle by German traders" as it was done "annually by Witbooi up to three years ago."

---

[133] 'A surrender of goods'

CHAPTER EIGHTEEN

THE HOTTENTOTS UNDER GERMAN PROTECTION

In 1890, when annexation took place, only three of the twelve Hottentot tribes had by the so-called agreements accepted the protection of Germany. They were –

(1) The Orlams tribe of Aman or Bethany Hottentots under Paul Fredericks (1884).
(2) The Nama tribe of Topnaars under Piet Heibib (1884).
(3) The Nama tribe of Geikous (Red Nation) under Manasse Noreseb (1885).

Of these (1) and (2) were the people who had sold the coast belt to Luderitz. The Topnaars and Geikous were miserable and powerless remnants of no weight, influence, or standing. In fact, the former fled shortly afterwards (or rather the majority fled) to Zesfontein in the extreme north of the Kaokofeld, while the remainder took refuge under British protection at Walfish Bay. The latter were a remnant of the once ruling clan under their old Chief Oasib, but they had been subjugated in turn by the Afrikaners and then by the Witboois.

It will be remembered that when in 1885 Dr. Goering made the agreement with Chief Manasse he hoisted a German flag as a sign of protection. Hendrik Witbooi later came along, punished Manasse, removed the flag, and then wrote to Goering asking what he wished should be done with the flag, as to me it is a strange thing (*een Vreemde ding*).

It was on the strength only of these three agreements, the 1885 agreement with Kamaherero, which had been definitely repudiated by the latter in 1888, and the agreement with the Bastards of Rehoboth that Germany in 1890 gave the impression that her sphere of influence had been extended from the Kunene to the Orange, and from the Western Coast line to the 20th degree of longitude East, along the borders of the Kalihari. It was under this impression that annexation was agreed to by Great Britain.

It is outside the scope of this report to detail the protests and humble remonstrances which the Cape Government in 1884 and 1885 made to Great Britain, and how, in spite thereof, the declaration of a partial protectorate in 1884 and a final Annexation in 1890 of the whole area of South-West Africa was not only approved of, but was facilitated by the then Imperial British Government. The matter need only be mentioned in order to point out that the late Sir Thomas Upington and the late Sir Gordon Sprigg, the responsible Cape statesmen, strained every nerve to protect South Africa from foreign encroachment, but they did so in vain, as their representations were taken no notice of. It is due to their memory that the unjust criticism which is occasionally heard to the effect that the Cape Government should never have let South-West Africa pass into German hands – a criticism based on erroneous and superficial information and on ignorance of the true facts p should be controverted. The Chief of the powerful Bondelswartz tribe, Willem Christian, had, since 1870, been under treaty obligations to the Cape Government. He had co-operated in every way with the Magistrates of Little Namaqualand (south of Orange) and had loyally preserved law and order in his territory on the north bank of the river. He, in common with the majority of the Hottentot Chiefs and the Hereros had long desired and repeatedly asked for the placing of his territory under a British Protectorate, but for some reason or other this was withheld.[134]

Relations between the Bondelswartz and the Cape Government were definitely broken off in 1885, and all the native races of Great Namaqualand and Damaraland were, against their own wishes and notwithstanding protests from Cape Town, definitely abandoned to German influence.

The Cape Government did not act voluntarily, but on definite instructions from Downing Street.

On 28th April 1885, under Minute 150 to the High Commissioner at Cape Town Lord Derby stated that the German Ambassador to Great Britain had expressed the hope

> that no endeavour will be made to obtain influence in the country north of the Orange River and west of the 20th parallel of longitude. This hope continues Lord Derby, is in conformity with the policy which your Ministers are aware Her Majesty s Government have adopted iii regard to the portion of South Africa in question.

That policy was adopted against
(1) The express representations of Sir Thomas Upington who had pointed out that – "If the Cape Colony be shut in upon the north a serious blow will be dealt at British trade and British influence in South Africa." (17.9.1884).
(2) The desires of the Hereros, who, as a last resort on 29.12.84, voluntarily ceded their whole country to H.M. Government ... in order that we may receive that protection which we have for so long a the asked for in vain.
(3) The pressing representations by Sir Gordon Sprigg on behalf of the Cape Government urging the annexation of Damaraland (3.3.1885.)*

---

[134] For a detailed discussion as to the intricacies and the diplomatic wrangling surrounding the acquisition of Namibia by German see, Brian Wood (editor), *Namibia 1884 - 1984: Readings on Namibia's history and society* (London 1988) chps. 7 - 9.

* (Page 78 in original) See Parliamentary Blue Book. Cape of Good Hope, A5- 85, entitled Papers, Minutes, and Correspondence relating to the Territories of Great Namaqualand and Damaraland.

This withdrawal by the Cape Government left Germany a clear field for operations, but the first five years were barren of results. It has already been indicated that by 1890 only three agreements had been secured, and the vast majority of the natives looked within suspicion on the newcomers and refused to treat with them. They still hoped that England would annex the country, but the final annexation by Germany in 1890 astonished and disappointed them. Hendrik Witbooi was voicing the feelings of his brother Chiefs when in 1891 he wrote to the Magistrate of Walfish Bay and asked. "Have the English delivered us over to the Germans?"

German agents were not slow to take advantage of what the Hottentots regarded as abandonment. They held up the Boers as a bogey, and the Hottentot Chiefs were told in effect:–

> Now that the English have left you, the Boers and other nations will come and take your land from you. We, the philanthropists, are here to protect you from such very wicked people. (See Interview between Captain von François and Hendrik Witbooi referred to in this report.)

Notwithstanding this, only three Hottentot tribes swallowed the bait. In 1890 Goering was able by the above-mentioned methods to induce the Bondelswartz of Warmbad, the Tseibs of Keetmanshoop and the Veldschoendragers to sign agreements. The others remained obstinate and, as related earlier in this report, notwithstanding the fact that the whole country was wrapped in peace, Germany decided in 1893 to give one tribe an impression of her power as an object lesson to the others. The terrible murder and massacre of the unoffending Witboois at Hornkranz in April 1893 was the result, but it did not have the desired effect.

When Leutwein took over the Governorship in 1894 no new agreements had been made. Hendrik Witbooi in his stronghold at Naauwkloof still defied all efforts to crush him, while the other native races were "openly hostile or, at best, preserved a doubtful neutrality," and the "dark mistrust of the Hereros quite astonished" him (Leutwein). Moreover, says Leutwein, "Respect for German arms had fallen to zero."

Governor Leutwein decided to give Hendrik Witbooi a rest pending the arrival of more troops from Germany. In the meantime he thought it advisable to deal with the other obstinate Chiefs, prominent among whom were Andreas Lambert of the Gei-Khauas tribe, and Simon Kooper of the Franzmann Hottentots.

The Khauas or Gei-Khauas Hottentots

This Orlams tribe, formerly under the well-known Chief Amiraal, had lived at Gobabis and in the vicinity thereof for upwards of 50 years. Originally they had moved up from the Cape districts early in the 19th century, and after residing for a generation or so in the south they parted company with their kinsmen the

Hei-Khauas, now living at Berseba, and trekked northwards to Gobabis.

When the British Commissioner, Mr. Palgrave, visited Damaraland in 1876, the successor to Amiraal, Chief Andreas Lambert and his councillors sent a petition to Palgrave for delivery to Sir Henry Barkly. They described themselves as "living in Gobabis and the district around, up nearly to the lake N'gami" and after detailing the conditions under which they were living and asking for a missionary to be sent to them, went on to state that the petitioners:–

> pray humbly that it may please Your Excellency to extend your protection, under which so many nations of South Africa, and in other countries, happily and peaceably live, also to this country, that we may be allowed to live in peace.

This petition, like all the others, was taken no notice of. The tribe had suffered severe ravages from small-pox some years previously, and at that the Palgrave estimated its total strength at 600 souls.

In March 1894 Leutwein proceeded to arrange for German protection, for which they had not asked, to be accepted by the Khauas people.[135]

His *modus operandi* was typical of German methods and is worthy of record only for that reason. He left Windhuk with a strong commando of men and artillery, and by means of forced night marches he succeeded before dawn on 7th March 1894 in taking the Khauas Chief quite unawares. The village of Nossanabis, where the Chief lived, was surrounded and the Chief and his principal men captured before they were even aware of the Germans approach. The captives were brought before Leutwein, who immediately expatiated on the advantages of German protection from other people, a theme which, under the circumstances, seems rather out of place, and suggested to the Chief and his councilors that they should in their own best interests sign an agreement. It does not take much imagination to believe that the Chief and councillors were not only enthusiastic, but quite unanimous. Incidentally, Leutwein held an inquiry into the alleged murder of a German trader named Krebs, which had taken place near Nossanabis about six months previously. Leutwein relates that he understood as a result of the conference that Andreas Lambert and his councillors were quite agreeable to sign a protection agreement and, in regard to the murder, he was prepared to believe that the Chief was not guilty of the murder of the white trader, and that he could not deliver the murderer on account of the latter s flight.

If Andreas Lambert had (as he apparently had said he would) signed the agreement it is perfectly clear from Leutwein s own statement that nothing more would have been heard or said about the murder of Krebs.

The conference over, it was arranged that the agreement would be drawn up and signed the next day. The Chief and his councillors were then released and allowed to return to their village for the night, and Leutwein retained the brother of the Chief and another councillor as hostages. That evening (according to Leutwein s account):–

---

[135] Leutwein, *Elf Jahre,* pp. 23-27. Leutwein was well aware of the dubious nature of his activities, yet as he also noted, this was, in his view necessary were he to retain control over the territory assigned to him.

Spies reported that the Chief was taking steps which pointed either to attack or to flight. In haste the village was again surrounded and searched; the rifles found there were confiscated; the horses, already saddled, were taken away, and the Chief again captured.

Thereupon the "former charges," says Leutwein, "were again gone into," and it was found (he does not say by whom) that the Chief had actually

> instigated the murder of Krebs in order thereby to escape paying certain debts. As a result his condemnation to death followed, and the sentence was carried out a day later.

The shooting of Andreas Lambert was not a judicial proceeding; it. was merely another impression of German power: it was murder.

Leutwein s statement is suspiciously vague as to Krebs and his murder, and it is necessary to go elsewhere for the details. Schawabe, in his book *Mit Schwert und Pflug* (page 71), writes:–

> A German trader named Krebs, who, in spite of the warnings of his friends in Windhuk, had travelled into the territory of the Khauas Hottentots on the white Nossob to collect debts, was murdered there.
>
> It is unquestionable (continues Schwabe, who writes *after* the shooting of Lambert but, like Leutwein, gives not one tittle of evidence to support what he alleges) that this treacherous and cowardly deed was carried out at the instigation of the Chief of the Khauas, Andreas Lambert. who wished to free himself of a troublesome creditor.
>
> The fatal shot at the peacefully slumbering Krebs was fired by a Witbooi Hottentot, then of Nossanabis, named Baksteen. The effects of the unfortunate trader were sent by Lambert, merely to clear himself from suspicion, to Windhuk, where they were sold by auction.

Krebs was murdered in October 1893. In the previous April the treacherous attack on the Witboois at Hornkranz had taken place. If the shooting of the peacefully slumbering Krebs by the Witbooi Baksteen was a treacherous and cowardly deed, how is one to describe the shooting by von François and his Germans of 150 peacefully slumbering kinsmen (men, women and children) of Baksteen at Hornkranz?

Baksteen, a Witbooi, was probably an escaped survivor of the Hornkranz affair. He came across a German asleep and shot him. The motive was clearly not robbery, as the "effects" of the trader were not touched. After the deed Baksteen disappears; the murder comes to the notice of the Chief, Andreas Lambert, and he at once reports it to Windhuk and sends in the dead man's effects. Baksteen is not available to give evidence as to whether or not he was instigated by Lambert. Is it likely that he, the member of another and not too friendly tribe, would do any such work for any but his own Chief: is it reasonable that Andreas Lambert would have gone to a stranger when, had he wished Krebs murdered, he had dozens of trusty retainers of his own to do his bidding? According to Schwabe the facts of the murder were well-known in Windhuk long before Leutwein marched to Nossanabis. Leutwein knew all the facts. If it were unquestionable that Andreas Lambert had instigated the murder and Leutwein knew it, as he must have done, is one to believe that the latter was prepared to compound the crime on condition that the murderer of a German made (as Chief) a protection agreement with the German Emperor? No matter what Leutwein knew or what his suspicious were, he was, on his own showing, prepared to believe that the Chief had no connection with the murder, so long as the Chief was willing to sign the agreement. The moment the Chief changed his mind and tried to escape (he, the murderer, who could avoid death by merely fixing his name to a beneficial agreement), *new facts* miraculously come to light, the murder case is reopened on the spot, and with most indecent haste and without even the semblance of a trial the Chief is condemned to death and shot. Naturally a murder of this description had to be explained away if possible, but the explanation is very feeble, and there appears to be not the slightest doubt that the Chief Andreas Lambert was one of the many victims who paid the penalty for refusing to accept German rule. This at any rate was the feeling of the Khauas Hottentots on the subject.

Living at Windhuk there are three men, the sole elderly survivors of the tribe. Their names are Jacobus Ghoudab, an elder and nephew of the late Chief, Cornelius Reiter, and David Beukes. In their joint statement under oath they say:–

> We were at Nossanabis, living at the Chief's werft, when the Germans under Major Leutwein came there. Our Chief lived there at the time, Gobabis being under our Magistrate, Jonathan Fledermuis. The Germans wanted Chief Andreas to sign an agreement accepting German rule. He refused to do so. Thereupon the Germans shot him. They trumped up a charge of murder. They said Andreas was responsible for the murder of Krebs, a German trader. Andreas protested his innocence. The trader was murdered by a Hottentot (Witbooi) named Baksteen. The Germans said Andreas should have arrested Baksteen. Andreas said he had reported the murder to Windhuk and had sent the wagon and goods of Krebs intact to Windhuk; he could do no more. He could not arrest Baksteen, as lie had run away to the bush and mountains. The Germans then said that because Andreas had not arrested Baksteen he was also guilty of the murder. They shot him ...
> The Germans shot Andreas, not because of the murder of which he was innocent, but because he refused to sign the agreement.

The defiant and independent attitude of Andreas Lambert in refusing eventually to sign the agreement, which would necessarily have placed him on good terms with the Germans. was not the attitude of a criminal who knew that he the displeasure of the authorities would result in his punishment sooner or later.

The tragedy over and Andreas in his grave, a farce was enacted by the representative of the Kaiser. Now that he had shot the chief, there was no tribal head available with whom to make the protection agreement. For some reason or other Leutwein considered the making of these agreement a *sine qua non*[136]; moreover he desired that they should be voluntarily made (*Freiwillig*), although he has also said that the terms did not matter, the fact of the signing was

---

[136] 'Without Which Not' an essential condition, a necessity

sufficient, and that in actual practice the Government's policy was carried out on general lines, quite regardless of the details in the various agreements.

The new Chief, according to Hottentot laws of succession, was the eldest son of the Chief's predeceased elder brother. Andreas Lambert had no son. This young man, Manasse Lambert, was however some hundreds of miles away at Berseba. He was living there with his kinsmen. the Hei-Khauas, for the purpose of attending school. Such a triviality as the absence of the new Chief was not going to interfere with the plans of the resourceful Leutwein. He sent for the the murdered Chief's brother, Eduard Lambert, appointed him Acting Chief, and demanded that he should sign the agreement forthwith. To Eduard Lambert this was verily a case of having greatness thrust upon him.

He explained to Leutwein that, according to Hottentot views, "one has to be a Chief even before you are born," which was another way of stating the Hottentot rule: "Our Chiefs are not made, but are given by God."

Therefore Eduard at first politely declined to be Chief or to sign the agreement. Eventually however he did sign it, and the incident was closed. Leutwein is significantly silent as to how he induced Eduard to change his mind.

It was now possible for His Imperial Majesty the King and Emperor to contract with Eduard Lambert, "Acting Chief of the Khauas Hottentots."

In the contract

> the German Emperor promises to afford the Khauas Hottentots all and every protection within the boundaries of the territory, which will be left to them after the definition of the boundaries.

(The boundaries were to be fixed in a later agreement, which, needless to say, was never made.)

> It is necessary to remember that a year or so previously the German Land Settlement Syndicate (the people who sold *luft schwebenden farmen* – farms floating in the air. – Rohrbach) had applied for a Crown grant of two million morgen (over four million acres), the major portion of which fell in the territory of the Khauas Hottentots. The syndicate was requested by Berlin to have a little patience and to defer the application for a while. The reason for not wishing to define any boundaries in the agreement is therefore quite clear.

Within two years the Khauas had been goaded into rebellion, Eduard Lambert had fallen in battle, and all the territory, livestock and other possessions of the people had been confiscated to the German Crown, while the tribe itself was practically exterminated.[137] In this way the Emperor's promise of protection within the boundaries was automatically cancelled.

The Khauas Hottentots were the owners of their land. Leutwein admits that it was "their unquestioned property," but, despite the agreement and the Emperor's promise, it was never from the very outset intended that the rights

---

[137] An attack on Gobabis took place on 6th April, 1896 and it was during this attack that the local Magistrate, Lt. Lampe, was killed. Eduard was killed by a retaliatory force led by von Estorff at Spitskop, about 7km to the east of Gobabis (Köhler 1959a: 19).

of these natives should be recognised. Gobabis and the excellent farming areas on the White Nosob River were intended for the syndicate. Moreover, says Leutwein, "Gobabis ... *was the indispensable key to the East (der unentbehrliche Schlussel-punkt des Ostens)*. The "key to the East"!" but the East was British territory? Regardless of the unquestioned title of the Khauas Hottentots it will also be remembered that in the following year (1895) Leutwein entered into the boundary agreement with Samuel Maharero of Oka handja, whereby Gobabis and the rich grazing land on the White Nosob became Crown land. This annoyed and irritated the Khauas Hottentots and their northern neighbours, the eastern Hereros (Nikodemus) and the Ovambandjeru Hereros (Kahimema). They refused to recognise imaginary boundaries which they disputed, and their trespassing cattle and sheep were summarily confiscated. This made them restive and inclined for war, whereupon it was decided to disarm them by force. They resisted and were declared rebels. On 6th May 1896 the Hereros and Hottentots (ancient enemies now united in misery) were defeated at Otjunda, and the rebellion crushed. Eduard Lambert had already fallen in action at Gobabis. Let the Khauas people relate in their own words what happened (statement of Johannes Ghoudab and two others)

> The Germans wanted to disarm us by force. The Germans came and fought us. We were defeated and our Chief killed in battle at Gobabis. The Germans took us prisoners and confiscated our land, our cattle and sheep, and all our possessions. The survivors of the tribe were sent to Windhuk as captives and made to work. We were never allowed to return to our old places.
>
> The Germans treated us with great brutality; many of our people were flogged. Our people are now nearly all dead, only a few remain. We were not allowed to have a Chief again. The women and girls were made to work for the German soldiers, who used them as concubines. The majority of the young girls, even those who had not vet reached puberty. were violated by the German soldiers. Some died as a result of this ill-treatment.

The Franzmann Hottentots

After Eduard Lambert had signed the agreement in March 1894, Leutwein left Nossanibis and marched on Gochas, near Gibeon. There lived Chief Simon Kooper and the Franzmann tribe. Simon was on friendly terms with Hendrik Witbooi, and the massacre at Hornkranz had created in his mind, as it did in the minds of all the natives, a profound hatred and disrespect for all Germans. He likewise had obstinately refused to believe in the disinterested philanthropy of the German Emperor. Leutwein made a night march on Simon's village, and at dawn on 17th March 1894 the troops had surrounded the place and the artillery was unlimbered and ready for action. So were the Hottentots. They were in their rude forts, but had received definite orders from the Chief not to fire the first shot.

Leutwein writes (page 28):–

CHAPTER EIGHTEEN

> The shooting of Andreas Lambert had made Simon Kooper with his guilty conscience very nervous, and had created the greatest excitement in him and his people.

Six hundred armed and desperate Hottentots were however not to be despised, and Leutwein decided to avoid a collision if possible.

Accordingly, with a few attendants and unarmed, he boldly rode into the village. There he found the Chief and his staff posted on a knoll overlooking the positions. "I bade him a friendly 'Good-morning' and offered my hand." A short discussion followed, during which the Chief explained that he was determined not to fire the first shot, as he had no desire for war. The energetic Leutwein thereupon broached the subject of protection, and after inviting the Chief to meet him at 10 a.m. at the Mission House, he returned to his troops.

Punctually at 10 a.m. Leutwein was waiting at the Mission House, but Simon Kooper did not appear. Shortly afterwards a messenger arrived from the Chief and stated that he would not attend as *he had nothing to communicate to Leutwein (er hatte mir nichts mitzuteilen)*.

The Governor pocketed his pride and again rode down to see the Chief. For three days he came and went, but always with the same negative results. Eventually Leuitwein got wrathful; he trained his artillery on the Chief s headquarters and delivered an ultimatum. Simon signed the document with unconcealed reluctance and then asked, "For how long is this to hold good?" "For ever," said Leutwein. "This," observes the latter, "he did not like."

In the agreement

> the German Emperor assures the Chief of the Franzmann Hottentots of his *All-Highest protection* for his whole country against all enemies amid within the following boundaries (but no boundaries are even so much as mentioned).

For over ten years Simon Kooper remained loyal to his new masters. In 1905 he joined in the general rising with his old friend and colleague, Hendrik Witbooi. After Hendrik Witbooi's death in action, Simon Kooper, with the remnants of his tribe, crossed over the border into British territory in the Kalihari. For several years he was the terror of the German settlers and patrols on the eastern frontier until Captain Surmon, of the Bechuanaland Protectorate Police, and Mr. Herbst[138] (now Major Herbst) the present Secretary for the South-West Protectorate, then Magistrate of Rietfontein, met the old warrior at Lehututu in the Kalihari and after a prolonged conference persuaded Simon to promise to molest no more Germans and to settle down peacefully under

---

[138] Served as Secretary for South West Africa (the senior civil servant in the Administration below the Administrator) from 13th December, 1916 to April, 1923 (Taylor 1985: 4)

British protection.[139] He died a few years later, but his tribe still lives in British territory and has never given the authorities any trouble.

The news of what happened to Andreas Lambert spread throughout Great Namaqualand, and when Simon Kooper capitulated there was no difficulty in getting the Berseba, Keetmanshoop, and other Chiefs to sign agreements. In fact, Chief David Swartbooi came down voluntarily to Windhuk, all the way from Otjitambi beyond Outjo, and offered to sign. This voluntariness on his part did not, as will be related further on, save his tribe or preserve his rights. In connection with the other agreements, Leutwein gratefully places on record his obligations to the Rhenish missionaries for their patriotic assistance and co-operation.

The subjugation and submission of Hendrik Witbooi

It now remained to deal with the old septuagenarian who, in his rock-bound stronghold of Naauwkloof, had since April 1893 defied all the efforts of the mailed fist to crush him.

In the beginning of May 1894 Leutwein moved against Witbooi with all his available guns and troops. Leutwein had asked for strong reinforcements from Germany, and pending their arrival he was not too keen on testing the military prowess of the most famous Hottentot soldier. Accordingly he wrote to Witbooi demanding to know whether he desired peace or war. The exchange of letters which followed discloses such illuminating and interesting views that the temptation to reproduce extracts therefrom is too great to be resisted. The letters are all published by Leutwein in his book, page 32, *et seq.*

The Chief replies (Naauwkloof, 4th May 1894):–

> Your Honour inquires whether I desire peace or war. To this I reply: von François knows full well and so does Your Honour, although you were not here at the the, that I have of old always kept peace with you, within von François and with all white people.

Leutwein adds this footnote:–

> (It is quite true that during his wars with the Hereros, Witbooi always protected the lives and property of white people).
> ... von François did not open fire on me for the sake of Peace; but because I was at peace with him... (Witbooi is referring to the Hornkranz affair). I was

---

[139] Reports relating to the surrender of Simon Kooper in Bechuanaland are to be found in the Botswana National Archives, RC. 12/12, Sub-Inspector Hodson: second visit to Kalahari. (Patrols to Lehututu to intercept and disarm Damara refugees from South West Africa and investigate alleged violations of the Protectorate border by Hottentot rebels under Witbooi and Simon Kooper.) RC.13/6 Sub-Inspector H.V. Eason: patrol to Lehututu (to preserve German South West Africa border from violation by belligerents in Hottentot rebellion). (Interception of armed Koranas and of Hottentots under Simon Kooper.) S.36/11, S.37/1 Steps to be taken against Simon Kooper (and agreement with Protectorate Government for his settlement with his followers from German South West Africa near Lehututu).

CHAPTER EIGHTEEN

> quietly sleeping in my house when von François came and tried to shoot me, not because of any misdeed, whether by word or act, of which I may have been guilty, but only because I refused to surrender that which is mine alone, to which I have right, I would not surrender my independence ... I am unable to understand and I am astonished and wonder much that I should suffer such sad and terrible treatment at the hands of a big man like von François ...
>
> Your Honour now says in your letter that von François has returned to Germany. That you have been sent here by the German Emperor with instructions to exterminate me if I do not agree to peace. To this I reply that if you have now come to speak to me in a friendly and honest way about peace (which von François deprived me of) and if you have come prepared to adjust and repair all the wrong and injustice done to me von François (when he opened fire on us) ... if you have come solely to make peace, I will in that event not oppose Peace ...

To this letter Leutwein replied as follows (The deliberate misstatements and misrepresentations in this letter are, on the facts already revealed in this report too glaringly apparent to require special attention to be drawn to them.):–

> At the wish of the majority of the Nama as well as of the Herero Chiefs His Majesty the German Emperor has extended his protection over both allowing those Chiefs who will not accept protection to remain uninterferedwith, provided they keep peace with the other Chiefs.
>
> This latter von have however not done ... but you have attacked various Chiefs in Namaland and you eventually settled yourself at Hornkranz from which place you conducted looting raids into Hereroland ... You have broken peace and order in the territory which is under the protection of the German Emperor. His Majesty viewed your doings for a long time in patience; but then, as you would not desist, he ordered that you should be attacked. Had you remained quietly in Gibeon, and ruled your people in peace, you would not have been attacked. (*Note.* Witbooi had moved from Gibeon and was settled at Hornkranz years before the German annexation.)
>
> That you have never before done anything to us, the white people, I know full well. But you have not been attacked for our benefit (*nicht unseres Vorteils willen*), but, as I have above said, solely for the sake of rest and peace in Namaland.

Witbooi replied asking for time to consult with his councillors and people as to whether or nor they should submit themselves to the will of His Majesty, and he requested that in the meantime the German troops should withdraw to Windhuk Witbooi. of course, only wanted to gain time.

On 7th May 1894, Leutwein answered as follows:–

> An out-and-out war is better than a worthless peace. And if I leave this place merely with your assurances of peace and without at the same the your submission to the will of His Majesty, the German Emperor, it will be a worthless peace. Although I have not been long in the land, I know nevertheless that since 1884, that is for ten years, you have lived only from robbery and bloodshed, although in the meantime you did make peace.
>
> Therefore I will not depart from you until you are defeated and captured or destroyed, even though it should take months and years to do so. If you personally find it so hard, and if you yet desire peace for your people, place your son in your position and he can then conclude the agreement. In such a case I will guarantee to you your life and the right to reside outside of German territory.

> I again repeat that peace without submission to the German Protectorate is now out of the question.
> This is my last word on the subject...

But it was not his last word. On 22nd May 1894 Leutwein received news that the expected reinforcements were being sent and would land in July. He accordingly decided, as he says, "to put water in my wine" and he wrote to Witbooi granting an armistice of two months.

The Chief, unaware of the reasons for this change of front and hoping apparently against hope, replied:-

> I thank the Lord of hearts that He has Himself stood in between us and has worked as mediator in this great matter, so that the shedding of blood, which we had in mind, has not taken place, but that we have parted in peace. May the Lord help us further so that no bloodshed may take place between us.

This letter encouraged Leutwein to ride over to Witbooi s camp (probably to spy out the position) in order "to make his acquaintance."

The old Chief was, as was his wont, reserved but courteous. After a conversation Leutwein returned and with his troops marched back to Windhuk.

The reinforcements arrived from Germany and in the beginning of August the operations were resumed. Captain Schwabe with an advance column, including two guns, marched up and took possession of the first line of defences held by the Witboois. The Hottentots were under strict instructions not to fire first, and as the Germans boldly walked up into their positions they decided to fall back. This move greatly annoyed Witbooi, who regarded it as a deliberate breach of the armistice. He wrote a protesting letter to Schwabe in which he stated, "I do not understand this peace and armistice, seeing that Your Honour has driven my people out of their fortifications."

In conclusion, he adds, "I am, with hearty greetings, your friend, the Lord of the Water and King of Great Namaqualand, Hendrik Witbooi." This lofty style did not forebode any intention of submitting to the will of the Emperor.

When Leutwein arrived on 4th August 1894, he found perfect tranquility reigning between the opposing forces. He relates how the women from Witbooi's laager "came down daily and were busy washing the clothes of our soldiers on the river bank in return for coffee or tobacco." They did this for the last the on 26th August. The general assault on the position commenced at daybreak on the 27th.

In the interim, while the women were washing clothes, Leutwein and Witbooi returned to their pens and paper. Leutwein initiated the correspondence on 15th August, when he wrote to Witbooi:-

> You have so utilised the two months of consideration given to you that you still refuse to recognise German supremacy... The thes of the independent Chiefs of Namaqualand are gone for ever. Those Chiefs who rightly and openly recognised and attached themselves to the German Government were more clever than you are; because they have gained only advantages thereby and have suffered no loss. I take you also for a clever man, but in this matter your cleverness has left you

because your personal ambition has overclouded your understanding. You fail to understand present-day circumstances. In comparison the German Emperor you are but a small Chief. To submit yourself to him would not be a disgrace but an honour.

These Teutonic blandishments were quite wasted on the astute old patriot, who, on 18th August, replied:–

You say that it grieves you to see that I will not accept the protection of the German Emperor, and you say that this is a crime for which you intend to punish me by force of arms. To this I reply as follows: I have never in my whole life seen the German Emperor: therefore I have never angered him by words or by deeds. God, the Lord, has established various kingdoms on the earth, and therefore I know and I believe that it is no sin and no misdeed for me to wish to remain the independent Chief of my land and my people. If you desire to kill me on account of my land and without guilt on my part, that is to me no disgrace and no damage, for then I die honourably for my property... But you say that, "Might is Right," and in terms of these words you deal with me, because you are strong in weapons and all conveniences. I agree that you are indeed strong, and that in comparison to you I am nothing. But, my dear friend, you have come to me with armed power and declare that you intend to shoot me. So I think I will shoot back, not in my name, not in my strength, but in the name of the Lord and under His power. With His help will I defend myself... So the responsibility for the innocent blood of my people and of your people which will be shed does not rest upon me, as I have not started this war ...

Leutwein, who was no match for the Chief in a verbal argument and had repeatedly to change ground, replied (21.8.94):–

The fact that you refuse to submit yourself to the German Empire is no sin and no crime, but it is dangerous to the existence of the German Protectorate. Therefore, my dear Chief, all further letters in which you do not offer me your submission are useless

To this Witbooi did not reply, and on 28th August the Witbooi stronghold was shelled and stormed by the German troops. Desperate fighting ensued in which German losses were considerable. Soon however artillery, more modern rifles, and abundance of ammunition and food began to weigh in the balance. After three further weeks of stubborn resistance in which they tried in vain to break through the German cordon, their ammunition ran out and their food was exhausted. For days they had been living on wild roots, gum, field mice, lizards, and the larvae of ants. "They were famished," says Leutwein, "and their condition was pitiful." Some of their bravest warriors had fallen.

Under the circumstances the old Chief had no alternative but to agree to Leutwein's terms. He signed the "Protection Agreement" on 15th September 1894, and remained true to his pledged word for over eleven years. He actively aided the Germans in their wars against the Hereros and other tribes, and it was only in 1905 that, goaded by German injustice, ingratitude and tyranny, the old warrior, then 80 years of age, rose and with him rose the majority of the

Hottentot tribes of Great Namaqualand. He died, probably as he would have wished to die, leading his men in battle near Tses in October 1906. His faithful followers with desperate valour held back the onward rushing Germans, while the body of their Great Chief was being hurriedly buried on the battle field to prevent its falling into German hands. (Von Trotha had offered a reward of 1,000*l*. for Witbooi, dead or alive.)[140]

The agreement with the Swartboois and their subsequent destruction

At the the of annexation the Swartboois or "young red nation," as they called themselves, were living in the north at Otjitambi and Franzfontein, near Outjo.[141] In 1895, the Chief David Swartbooi visited Windhuk, and in the absence of Leutwein on military duties he made a "Protection Agreement" with Acting-Governor von Lindequist. In terms of this agreement the Swartboois were taken under the protection of Germany, "pending All-Highest sanction." In this agreement also the exact delineation of the tribal boundaries of the territory was reserved for a future agreement.

The old Chief, David Swartbooi, still lives at Windhuk (whither the Germans banished him as a captive 21 years ago), with a few survivors of his tribe. When asked how it was that he was the only Chief who voluntarily came forward and accepted German protection, he replied:–

> The missionary Reichmann told us that it would be good to accept German rule, as Germany was the Head of the whole world and more powerful than England. Dr. Hartmann, the Manager of the South-West Africa Company, of Grootfontein, also said it would be in our best interests to accept German rule. The Germans promised to respect the laws and customs of my tribe, but that they never did.

Towards the end of 1896 Leutwein visited the Swartbooi tribe at Franzfontein and there met the Chief. There was at the time a dispute between the Swartboois and Omaruru Hereros relative to tribal boundaries. The Swartbooi Chief, relying on his Protection Agreement, approached Leutwein and asked him to adjust their difference. This Leutwein avoided. He explains (page 121) that there was no reason why "we, by our intervention, should remove what would probably be for us a useful rivalry" (*fur uns veilleicht noch nützliche Rivalität*). And this is the same man who attacked Witbooi "for the sake of peace and rest." Leutwein was also aware that the Chief's cousin, Lazarus Swartbooi, was intriguing and plotting to depose David and to secure the Chieftainship. In this

---

[140] The Witbooi survivors were shipped off to Cameroon and Togo where more than half of them succumbed to intestinal diseases and malaria. Drechsler, *Fighting*, pp. 184 - 186

[141] Very little research has been done, let alone written on the history of Zwartbooi community that eventually settled at Fransfontein in the Kaokoland in the 1880s. Kuno Budack, *Die Traditionalle Politische Struktur der Khoe Khoen in Südwestafrika*, PhD thesis University of Pretoria 1972, pp. 43, 61, 166, & 247 - 249. N.J. van Warmelo, though terribly dated, did provide some notes regarding the Zwartbooi community in the Kaokoveld, see, *Notes on the Kaokoveld (South West Africa) and its people*, (Pretoria 1962).

matter he also did not interfere. David Swartbooi also asked for rifles and ammunition, and "was consoled with hopes for the future."

Referring to the agreement with the Swartboois, Leutwein remarks (page 238):–

> At the close of the Witbooi war this tribe voluntarily offered to enter into an agreement in the hope that they would get protection from the surrounding Hereros, if only by supply to them of arms and ammunition. When they were disappointed in these hopes, they commenced their agitation, which eventually resulted in the Swartbooi rebellion.

In May 1897, the pretender, Lazarus Swartbooi, caused rumours to be spread to the effect that the Chief David Swartbooi contemplated giving trouble. The Magistrate of Outjo, Captain von Estorff, thereupon made a night march with 20 soldiers and surprised and arrested the Chief at his house in Otjitambi. After an inquiry had been held and the "correctness of the allegations established" ("although,"says Leutwein, "only words and not deeds were proved"), Chief David was deposed and sent to Windhuk as a captive, and the pretender Lazarus, who had no title at all to the Chieftainship, was made Chief in David s stead.

> Thereby (says Leutwein) Lazarus succeeded in gaining his object. The supporters of David were not satisfied, however, and the agitation against the German Government and the new Chief, Lazarus Witbooi, continued on an increasing scale.

In 1897 the adherents of the two factious came to blows, purely between themselves. The old Chief s followers represented probably 90 per cent, of the tribe, and they resented Lazarus s assumption of authority. Headed by Samuel Swartbooi, the deposed Chief s brother, they took possession of the Chief s stock, grazing near Franzfontein, which the Germans had illegally and in breach of all law and custom vested in their "created" Chief, Lazarus. Incidentally some German military horses and mules were grazing with this stock at the time, and were removed as well. This, remarks Leutwein with astonishing equanimity, though he makes mention only of German Government stock, was "rightly regarded" by Captain von Estorff as "an act of war." Without further ado, the German troops marched against "the rebels." The Hottentots retired to the Grootberg and prepared to defend themselves. In February 1898 their position was bombarded by troops under Major Mueller. The position was a very strong one however, and before wasting more German lives an attempt was made to achieve by treachery and bad faith what was not too attractive for achievement by force of arms. The German missionary Reichmann aforementioned, he who had told Swartbooi that "Germany was Head of the world and more powerful than England," was sent in to the Hottentot camp with a message to the effect that if the rebels surrendered, their lives and property would be spared and they would be allowed to return to their former homes.

Reichmann returned bearing a letter from Samuel Swartbooi, which Leutwein prints (page 150), but he is carefully silent as to the inducements held out.

The letter reads as follows:–

Grootberg, 13th March '98

> The undersigned sends this letter and thereby gives notice that it is the heartfelt wish of us all to make peace. We thank the Lord that what appeared an impossibility has now become possible, as a result of the prayers of the many Christians here in the mountain. And I hope this will be a real peace, which God wishes to bring about in all of us, and I pray the Lord that it will be realised. Also do I ask Your Honour for a real peace; and as a token I send you two men, Sem Swartbooi and Paul Hendriks in advance with Boab Davids. I will leave here on Monday afternoon, and Mr. Reichmann may go from your side on Tuesday, so that we may meet at the fort in the forenoon and discuss matters.
>
> (Signed) Samuel Swartbooi

The missionary Reichmann met the rebels, and as a result of his communications the whole Swartbooi tribe (the few adherents of Lazarus were negligible) Surrendered to the German Commander.

Josephat Jaeger, an Afrikaner Hottentot, now gaol warder at Grootfontein, who was a soldier in the German native forces at the time, states on oath:–

> The war was caused through the Germans having deposed the lawful Chief, David Swartbooi. They sent David as a prisoner, and appointed Lazarus as Chief in his stead. The people, with a few exceptions, stood by David and refused to recognise the new Chief. The result was war. After some fighting the Hottentots were surrounded in the Grootberg. It was a difficult place to attack. The Germans bombarded it. Then they sent the missionary Reichmann out to the Hottentots to ask them to surrender. The missionary was told to inform them that if they surrendered they would get the following terms:–
>
> (a) they would be allowed to return to Franzfontein and Otjitambi to live.
>
> (b) they would retain all their stock and possessions, including their arms The Hottentots thereupon came in voluntarily and surrendered. No sooner had they done this when the Germans disarmed them all, confiscated their stock, and sent them all (men, women and children) as prisoners to Windhuk
>
> This was a great breach of faith by the Germans. They had broken their promises, but the Hottentots were powerless. Along the road they were very badly treated, and many died. The others were never allowed to return from Windhuk
>
> ...

Every Swartbooi Hottentot who has been interrogated is clear on the point that the war was caused because the Germans had deposed the lawful Chief, David Swartbooi, and appointed Larazus, whom the majority of the tribe would not recognise.

Abraham Swartbooi sworn, states –

> My brother Lucas was killed, and I was shot through the leg. I show the bullet wound now. The Germans made this war simply for nothing at all. We gave them no reason. We only had quarrelled over the taking away of our lawful Chief. The Germans took all the people s cattle and sheep. The survivors were all sent to Windhuk to work, and were not allowed to return. Only the few Hottentots who adhered to the party of Lazarus Swartbooi were allowed to stay at Franzfontein.

CHAPTER EIGHTEEN

> I went to work for a German and was sent to Karibib. I was brutally thrashed by this German, but had to stay with him. I was there for four years, living all the time like a dog... Before I was sent to this German, I was ordered to receive 75 lashes for having taken part in the objections to Lazarus Witbooi. I got 25 lashes each month for three months. I will show you the scars on my buttocks (shows huge scars on buttocks and thighs) – my flesh was cut to ribbons by the sjambok. That I suffered for standing by my lawful Chief.

Jonathan Booyse (a Veldschoendrager Hottentot, living at Franzfontein, who was employed with the German troops) sworn, states:–

> While we were on the march back from the Grootberg (this is after the surrender), we were camped on the veld, when two Hottentot men came walking along the road from Outjo towards Franzfontein. They were unarmed and not a bit afraid. They must have seen our camp a long way off, they just walked up. When they got to the camp, I recognised them as old residents of Franzfontein. Their names were Petrus and Gawieb. The Germans asked them what they meant by walking about like that. They said they meant no harm, they had heard of the war, and were anxious about their old mother, who lived at Franzfontein. They were on their way, they said, to see if she were alive, and if so, they intended to take her back with them to live at Outjo. They were told by Von Estorff, the German officer, that they were liars, and that he was going to hang them as an example to others who wandered about to do mischief.
> On hearing this, Willem Swartbooi, one of the Franzfontein Hottentots, who like me had been working for the German troops, went up and pleaded for their lives. He said to the officer, I know these men and I know they are innocent, I have worked for you, but if you hang them, then take me and hang me with them. The officer only laughed. Willem then said, If you kill them I refuse to work for you any more, as they are guilty of nocrime." The officer said, "Well, we won't hang them, we'll shoot them instead."
> The soldiers had already placed ropes round the necks of Petrus and Gawieb and were waiting for the order to pull them to the tree. They were then led aside, crying for mercy and protesting their innocence. They were both shot and their bodies left there for the wild animals. We moved on, but that same night Willem ran away. I afterwards heard that he had gone to Walfish Bay to live with the British people.

The Swartbooi tribe thus, for the reasons given, shared the fate of the Khauas Hottentots. The survivors, men, women and children, were employed as labourers on what Leutwein calls public works at Windhuk.

The old Chief, David Swartbooi, referring to his deposition from the Chieftainship and the subsequent happenings, made the following statement under oath:–

> I was sent to Windhuk and placed in gaol for three months. They made me do hard labour with the convicts. I was never tried by any court of law, and to this day I don t know why they did this. After releasing me from gaol they took me, as a prisoner still, with their troops to the campaign against my people who had rebelled owing to my removal and the placing by the Germans of Lazarus as Chief in my stead. When I got there the people had already been beaten and had surrendered. The Germans tied me to a wagon wheel, and as my people came in after their surrender they saw me there. My people complained bitterly when the

Germans ordered us all to march on the road to Windhuk. They all told me that the missionaryReichmann had come from the Germans and had persuaded them to surrender on condition that they retained all their stock and that they would be allowed to return to their old homes at Franzfontein and Otjitambi. As soon as the people were in their power the Germans broke this promise, took all their stock and forced us to march to Windhuk.

They drove us before them. Some people died on the journey. We were located at Windhuk, on the hill where the Government buildings now stand. We were paupers and got food, that is the old people who could not work. The others had to work for the Germans and got good pay, 10s a month after a time. At first they only gave us 3s. a month. They eventually gave me a few goats for my people, about 50, but they all died of scab and the Germans gave us no more. We have lived in Windhuk ever since. We have been slaves to the Germans all these years. I was often thrashed with a sjambok while in gaol in the early days, because I said I was an innocent man. The rest of my people were treated very cruelly and harshly. We were helpless and were captives, we could not defend ourselves. Our women were violated and made to act as concubines. Our daughters were not safe. The mother and father could protest, but it was in vain. One of my men, Timotheus Richter, had a daughter Sarah, a young girl. A German lieutenant, whose name I forget, came to Timotheus and demanded the girl as a concubine. The lieutenant was told by Timotheus that he would not allow this, whereupon the lieutenant knocked him down and kicked him in the ribs. He died from his injuries and the lieutenant forced Sarah to go with him. I complained to another German officer, who said for peace and quiet s sake I should say nothing more, but let the girl go. I was afraid and let the matter drop as the other lieutenant also threatened to thrash me for interfering. The soldiers also took our women in this way, and we could do nothing for fear of the sjambok and worse things.

Before leaving the Swartboois it may be added that the German-made Chief, Lazarus Swartbooi who had remained with his remnant of followers at Franzfontein, got very little thanks in the end.[142] When the general rebellion broke out in 1905 Lazarus was arrested as a precautionary measure and sent in chains with his school-master and the senior councillor to the Okahandja Gaol. They died in captivity.

Daniel Esma Dixon at that time in German employ at Okahandja, states on Oath:–

Natives who were placed in gaol at that time never came out alive. Many died of sheer starvation and brutal treatment. I remember seeing Lazarus Swartbooi, the Hottentot Chief of the Swartboois at Franzfontein, brought into Okahandja Gaol. He was manacled and chained by the neck to another Hottentot. At the same time, Willem Cloete, a Bastard (the brother of Jan Cloete of Omaruru), was taken to the gaol and with him was Johannes Honk, an educated Hottentot a schoolmaster. It was alleged that Lazarus had tried to foment rebellion in the north. They were, the four of them, so badly treated in the gaol that they all died within a few weeks. I was present when they were buried.

---

[142] For detailed information regarding German-Swartbooi relations see, Evangelical Lutheran Church in the Republic of Namibia (ECRN) VII 27.3 Gemeinde Glieder Franzfontein Anfang 1905; VII 27.2 Franzfontein (Alte Akten) Fragmente Ca. 1895 - 1904; & VII 27.1 Alte Akten aus der Franzfontein Gemeinde 1895 - 1904 Missionar Reichmann.

The Afrikaner Hottentots

A remnant of this once all-powerful Orlams tribe was living at the time of annexation on the north bank of the Orange River, close to the eastern boundary line below Nakob. In 1897, owing to allegations of stock-theft against certain individuals, the German lieutenant in charge at Warmbad deemed it advisable to punish the whole tribe, and he accordingly led a small party against them. He paid for his temerity by a severe set-back, blood was shed and, as German honour had now to be vindicated, a strong punitive force was sent against the rebels. The tribe was not numerically strong, probably not more than three or four hundred and they could only muster about 60 to 70 rifles. The German troops inflicted very heavy losses and captured all their stock and possessions.[143] The unfortunate survivors fled through the Orange River to British territory and surrendered to the Cape Police: who were on posts along the frontier. The Germans demanded their extradition. This was agreed to by the Cape Government and the Afrikaners were taken across and handed back to their German masters. No sooner had this been done when every one of the poor wretches was shot without mercy (as Leutwein puts it *Samtlich er-erschossen*).[144]

Thus disappeared the last surviving remnant of a tribe which at one time had dominated South-West Africa from Ovamboland to the Orange River.

It is now necessary to pass on to the Bondelswartz rising of 1903 and the general Hottentot rising of 1904.

---

[143] A newspaper alleged that "... the whole tribe was practically annihilated. As an instance of the way in which the Germans treated rebellion, there were at the close of the war twenty odd prisoners in the hands of the Germans. These were marched to Keetmanshoep [sic] for trial. On the way any falling out, unable to walk, were shot on the spot, and the remained on arrival at Keetmanshoep were tried and shot ... It was noted not a single native of the district attended the execution". 'German Rule in South-West Africa. Some Interesting Facts', *Cape Times*, 18th November, 1903.

[144] "On that occasion fifteen Hottentots, including their Chief Cupido Afrikander fled into this district when pursued by German troops. After being imprisoned in the local gaol for stock theft committed in this district, they were extradited in two parties to German South Wet Africa on the 28th March, 1898 and the 16th of June, 1898, respectively, and were all shot at Keetmanshoop with the exception of one boy, aged about sixteen years." 'Acting Resident Magistrate, Gordonia to the Sec. Law Dept., Cape Town, 17th November, 1903 in Colonial Office, 'South Africa. Further Correspondence (1903-1904) relating to the Affairs of Walfisch Bay and the German South-West African Protectorate', No. 723, June, 1908.

CHAPTER NINETEEN

THE BONDELSWARTZ RISING OF 1903
AND THE GENERAL HOTTENTOT RISING, 1904-7

Towards the end of 1903 the continued exploitation and robbery of the Hereros in the north, which had been greatly intensified and increased by the promulgation through Berlin of the Credit Ordinance, had brought about a state of affairs in Damaraland which Leutwein rightly describes as something similar to a powder magazine, which only required the application of a match to bring about a terrific upheaval. The robberies, floggings, murders and general injustices had reduced the Herero people to a state of sullen desperation. They only wanted a lead.

Unexpectedly, and without a word of warning, this lead came from the Hottentots in the south. The typically high-handed and overbearing conduct of a young German officer at Warmbad, followed by the murder of the Bondelswartz Chief, was the last straw.

The manner in which the Hereros had been treated is known. It is now necessary, before dealing with the actual rising of the Hottentots, to detail some of their experiences. It will be of interest to hear the views of those Hottentots who, as one of them has stated, by the grace and mercy of Almighty God have survived German rule and are alive to tell the tale.

Abraham Kaffer (a venerable old man of over seventy, who was for many years "Chief Magistrate" of the Bondelswartz tribe and one of the tribal councillors) states on oath:–

> We in our tribal laws were used to the control of our Chief; he was our "Government" and could decide disputes, punish evil-doers, and settle differences... We have never been able to understand the German Government. It was so different to our ideas of a Government; because every German officer, sergeant, and soldier, every German policeman and every German farmer seemed to be the "Government." By this we mean that every German seemed to be able to do towards us just what he pleased, and to make his own laws, and he never got punished. The police and soldiers might flog us and ill-treat us, the farmers might do as they pleased towards us and our wives, the soldiers might molest and even rape our women and young girls, and no one was punished.
>
> If we did complain, we were called liars, and ran the risk of revenge or punishment. And thus it was that a Hottentot got to take such happenings as the German custom. It was "Government" to us, and we had to submit.

Joseph Schayer, of Warmbad (who, with Marengo and Morris, was one of the "Commandants" of the rebel Hottentots, 1903-7), states on oath:–

> Before the rebellion our people were very harshly treated, especially in the prisons... (*Note.*- From 1901-1903 Joseph was a native constable in the German police, and he speaks of his own knowledge). Many people died in prison owing to cruel treatment, insufficient food, floggings and hardships... The prisoners were practically allowed to starve, and while in this state of weakness they could not stand the repeated floggings they received. Prisoners were sent to Keetmanshoop in gangs. They were marched by road (140 miles). They had iron rings round their necks, connected by chains to one another. If one of them got exhausted, the gang was made to walk on and drag him. He was sjambokked and driven on. Eventually, if he became too weak and fell, he was dragged by the rest, who were urged on with sjamboks and was kept at a trot to keep pace with the horses. In this way men were choked to death. I know of many cases like this. On one of our treks from Warmbad to Keetmanshoop two prisoners were actually beaten to death with ox reims. This happened at Grundoorns. The officer in charge was present, and watched the floggings. These prisoners were on their way to gaol; and they were beaten because they were too weak to walk. I can show their graves at Grundoorns to this day... On another occasion four prisoners were sent from Warmbad to Keetmanshoop via Kalkfontein One prisoner got exhausted at Draaihoek, near Kalkfontein. The German soldiers then beat him to death with sjamboks. He is buried there. I was present at the time. The escort was composed of four German soldiers and myself; there was no officer there that day. One day at Warmbad a German soldier shot one of the prisoners for no reason at all. For these murders no one was ever punished.

Adam Pienaar (also known as Adam Christian, nephew of the old Chief, Willem Christian), states on oath:–

> The law gave us no protection; the German soldiers did just what they pleased. We were helpless and powerless. Our Chief complained, but all in vain. I was a German police-boy for seven years before the rebellion broke out. Many of our people died in prison through starvation, floggings, and general ill-treatment... Accused persons were never given a fair trial. They were never allowed to give evidence, or to open their mouths. The evidence of one white man, conveyed by means of a letter of complaint, was quite sufficient to secure a conviction for almost anything. Our people were literally flogged to death. Very many died. Matters came to a head in 1903, when the Germans murdered our Chief, Jan Abraham Christian, at Warmbad. We then all rebelled against German tyranny.
>
> The courts gave us no protection, as our word was not accepted and our complaints were never believed... Prisoners were sent in chains to the central gaols. They had to walk in gangs ahead of mounted soldiers. If a prisoner became exhausted on the way he was flogged and driven. His only release was death and many died. The march from Warmbad to Keetmanshoop was over 140 miles by road, with water only obtainable at great distances apart. The mounted police showed the prisoners no mercy. Prisoners were also made to walk in chains from Ukamas to Warmbad. The country is full of the graves of those who died of exhaustion or were beaten to death by the German police. I have buried very many myself. They were made to walk till the blood came through the soles of their feet. The hot sand burnt their feet, and walking was then impossible. Such people all died under the sjambok or fell down and died from sheer exhaustion.

Willem Christian (grandson of the Chief Willem Christian, and son of the late Chief Johannes Christian who died in 1910), states on oath:–

Before the rebellion many of our people died in gaol owing to insufficient food, ill-treatment and flogging.

A white man could do as he pleased to us. White men were not punished. Our word was never taken in a court. If we complained we were not believed. Any number of us could give the same evidence, but it carried no weight. We were not allowed to give evidence on oath. On the other hand, a white man was always believed and his evidence was always accepted. In this way injustice was done and many innocent people suffered ... If any one of our people was arrested on a farm by the German police, a rope was tied round his neck and it was held in the hand of the mounted policeman, alongside of whose horse the prisoner had to trot all the way. If he tired or lagged back, he was flogged and hit and made to go on... Our women and girls were constantly being molested by German soldiers, and even officers. We objected to this, but were powerless to prevent it. We were beaten if we intervened. This is why we lost all respect for the Germans.

The shooting of the chief Jan Abraham Christian

On the afternoon of the 25th October 1903, a party of German troops under Lieutenant Jobst went to the Bondelswartz village at Warmbad and attempted forcibly to remove the Chief, Jan Abraham Christian, under arrest. The Chief objected, and was shot dead. The Hottentots retaliated by shooting Lieutenant Jobst and several of his men. The following sworn statement as to what actually took place was supplied by an eye-witness:–

Jantje Izaak states on oath:–

I am a Bondelswartz Hottentot and live at Warmbad. I used to be the messenger of the old Chief, Wihlem Christian. This Chief died and was succeeded by his son, Jan Abraham Christian.

I remember in October 1903, I was living in the Hottentot werft at Warmbad. A child of the Chief s sister got very ill with inflammation, and the warm stomach of a goat was required as medicine.[145] Our own goats were all grazing outside some distance away. A goat was urgently required. The Chief asked some Hereros who were passing through with goats to let him have one. They refused, whereupon the Chief ordered his men to take a goat from the Hereros and slaughter it. This was done. The Hereros went to the German officer in charge (Lieutenant Jobst) and complained. He sent a message to the Chief, who in reply sent 18s in payment for the goat. (Leutwein says it was 20s.) This the Hereros were satisfied with, and they accepted the money.

Lieutenant Jobst was not satisfied and wanted to punish the Chief. He, ordered the Chief to come over and see him. The Chief sent six of his councillors to explain the matter and the lieutenant immediately bound them, and put them into prison. The next day the Chief sent over and asked for the release of his men. He said that he had already settled the matter of the goat, and as he was a Chief he could do such things in his own territory. He pointed out that the terms of his treaty with the Germans allowed him to govern in his own area. The lieutenant refused to listen to these messages and decided to arrest the Chief. So that

---

[145] For further details on traditional medicine in the Bondelswarts community see Hoernlé, Winifred 'Certain Rites of Transition and the Conception of!Nau among the Hottentots' (1918) in Winifred Hoernlé *The Social Organization of the Nama and other* Essays (edited by Peter Carstens), Witwatersrand University Press, Johannesburg, 1985: pp.69-71

> afternoon he set out armed and with his armed soldiers, about eight or ten men, towards the Chief's werft. When they got there the lieutenant ordered two men to go into the Chief's house and arrest him. They did so. We were watching them from our pontoks. Our people had arms. When the Chief was dragged out of his house by the two soldiers, he tried to wrench away from their grasp, whereupon the German sergeant drew his revolver and shot the Chief dead on the spot. Thereupon the rest of us opened fire on the Germans and killed the lieutenant, the sergeant, and one man. The others fled back to their fort.
>
> That is how the great rebellion started in 1903, and it lasted until the death of Marengo in 1907.[146]

Except as to the reasons for taking the goat and as to who fired the first shot, this narrative agrees in all essentials with the official German reports. Leutwein (page 440) agrees that the Chief s attitude was correct, in terms of clause 4 of the Protection Agreement, wherein he had reserved to himself (after excluding disputes between Europeans and natives) "the right of jurisdiction in all other cases. I expect from the European population that they will respect the laws, customs and usages of my country."

While agreeing that the Chief was right and the lieutenant was wrong, Leutwein goes on, however, to blame the Hottentots for the death of their Chief.

He writes:–

> While the two soldiers were dragging the struggling Chief behind them. between the two positions, the Hottentots opened the fire as a result of which the Chief, the two soldiers, and the District Commander (Lieutenant Jobst) were killed and two soldiers wounded.

Leutwein s statement is on the face of it open to grave doubt and his explanation may be dismissed as incorrect. It is absurd to imagine for one moment that the Hottentots would have jeopardised their own Chief s life by firing in the manner alleged. All the Bondelswartz leaders who have been questioned laugh the German version to scorn, and are unanimous in affirming that not a shot was fired from their side until after the Chief had fallen with a German bullet through his head. It has been repeatedly pointed out in this report that as an invariable rule the Hottentots never fired the first shot.

The question arises, why should the Germans conceal the truth then? The reason is not far to seek. and Leutwein unwittingly reveals it himself. He has

---

[146] It is interesting to note that Izaak cites 1903 as the date on which on which 'the great rebellion' broke out, and sees it as ending in 1907. Historians have, generally, followed the dates provided in the Official German history of the war which used the dates 1904-1907. Jan-Bart Gewald has recently argued that the official date given for the end of the war should be questionned. He argues that the final operation against one of the main guerilla leaders operating in southern Namibia, Simon Kooper, only took place in March, 1908, whilst the POW camps were only finally closed in April, 1908. Gewald, *Herero Heroes*, p. 141; Haacke, Wulf 'The Kalahari Expedition, March 1908: The Forgotten Story of the Final battle of the Nama War', *Botwana Notes and Records*, Vol. 24, 1992. *Kämpfe der deutschen Truppen in Südwestafrika, bearbeitet nach Angaben der Kriegsgeschichtlichen abteilung I des Großen Generalstabes*, Berlin, 1906-1908.]

published a letter, dated 21st November 1903, addressed to him by von Burgsdorff the Magistrate of Gibeon. in which the latter writes:–

> Incidents like that at Warmbad damage us in every respect, economically in Europe, in our prestige and with the natives. The old Witbooi remains loyal to us but happenings like that at Grootfontein[147] and the last have unsettled him. I sincerely hope that it can be definitely established that at Warmbad the first shot came from the side of the Bondels. That will create a possibility that he (i.e.. Hendrik Witbooi) may be convinced that all the blame rests with the Bondels.

The old Chief Hendrik Witbooi, despite his 80 years, was still active and the most powerful and influential leader in Namaqualand. Hitherto he had always loyally stood by his obligations which had been forced on him by the agreement signed after Hornkranz and the fights in the Naauwkloof. His prowess as a skilful and daring guerrilla fighter was held in the greatest respect by the Germans, and every effort was necessary, therefore, to keep him loyal and quiet.

This being so, it did not take German officialdom long to declare that the first shots at Warmbad had been fired by the Bondelswartz.

In view of the fact that the German Commander at Warmbad had deliberately broken German pledges and obligations under the agreement. and that the ill-fated Chief had been perfectly correct in his attitude; in view, moreover, of the actual circumstances, from which it appears clear that the Hottentots had not premeditated rebellion or attack and that the Germans were the aggressors, one would have imagined that the events called rather for an inquiry than for an armed punitive expedition.

What followed is indicative of German policy throughout, public and private. It seems to have been based on the rule that even where the German is the aggressor in the wrong, the native who objects to or opposes his conduct must be punished. Merely a variation of the "Might is Right" theory.

The Bondelswartz were accordingly declared to be in a state of rebellion, and all available German forces plus Hottentot and Bastard contingents, under Hendrik Witbooi and the Rehoboth Chief, were sent down to crush the rebels. During December 1903 and January 1904 a few petty engagements took place in the mountains near Warmbad and in the Karas range south of Keetmanshoop. It was then that the famous guerrilla leader, Jacob Marengo (half Hottentot, half Herero), came into prominence.

Before the German plans could be co-ordinated news of a general Herero rising in the north came like a thunderbolt.

Leutwein could not deal with both parties at once, and he decided on a peace at any price with the Bondelswartz in order that the greater menace in Damaraland be attacked with all available strength.

It would have been better under the circumstances and in view of the great

---

[147] The reference to Grootfontein is to a small settlement in southern Namibia, not the larger town in the north-east. In 1901 a German force supported by a group of soldiers provided by Hendrik Witbooi confiscated the land and property of the community who were deported to Windhoek as forced labour. Dreschler *Let Us Die*, pp. 104-105; Leutwein, *Elf Jahr*, pp. 166-169.

danger of a general rising throughout the south-west (a danger that Leutwein must have known of even if he did not appreciate it), to have made a peace simply by reverting to the *status quo ante*.[148]

This, however, German arrogance and fatuity were incapable of achieving. It was not even attempted, though in actual effect the results were the same, but with a far different aspect.

The new Bondelswartz Chief, Johannes Christian, was a weak-minded person who had no desire for armed conflicts, even in defence of sacred rights. Accordingly, when at the end of January 1904 Leutwein offered to make peace, the Chief readily opened negotiations.

The German authorities thereupon could no longer resist the temptation of disclosing and endeavouring to put into operation their long-cherished and definitely arranged schemes in regard to the native races. Governor Leutwein proposed the following terms:–

(1) Surrender of all arms and ammunition and restoration of all looted property.
(2) The delivery of all persons charged with murder.
(3) The cession to the German Crown of the entire territory of Keetmanshoop and the Karas Mountains and the confinement of the whole tribe to a relatively small reserve at Warmbad.

It was clause 3 which sent a thrill of apprehension through Great Namaqualand.

Hendrik Witbooi became restive and suspicious, and his feelings were shared by every Chief in the country.

Naturally, under the circumstances, the enforcement of this Condition was out of the question at the time and it was held over for later discussion.

Clause 2 was likewise inoperative, because the wanted persons refused to come in and surrender. A strong band still held positions in the Karas Mountain, while Marengo and his adjutant, Abraham Morris, had temporarily betaken themselves to the south bank of the Orange River, outside German jurisdiction.

In terms of clause 1 of the proposals Johannes Christian handed in 289 rifles at Kalkfontein and, pending further discussion of the other peace terms, a patched-up peace was made, and the Chief with those of his followers who had surrendered was allowed to return to his head village at Warmbad.

Leutwein moved north to attack the Hereros, and with him went the Bastard contingent and a picked commando of over 120 Witboois. The old Chief Hendrik, on the plea of ill-health, remained behind and returned to his headquarters near Gibeon.

By June 1904, thousands of fresh troops had arrived from Germany, and Leutwein was replaced in the field by Lieut.-General von Trotha fresh from

---

[148] 'the previously existing state of affairs'

his bloody solution of the native problem in German East Africa.[149]

Von Trotha issued the notorious and merciless "Extermination Order," whereby his troops were instructed to take no prisoners, to give no quarter, and to show no mercy to man, woman or child.

Then it was that the true German ideals, which had been an open secret since the negotiations at Kalkfontein South in the previous January, were blazoned forth from the house-tops. The German settlers and farmers and the directors of land syndicates and other speculative ventures began to open their mouths very widely. Now that von Trotha had arrived and Germany was at last able to show her military power the "great general" would effectively settle the native question throughout South-West Africa before he returned to the Fatherland.

The local newspapers took up the theme with zest and vigour. It was openly forecasted that

(a) All tribal bonds would be broken.
(b) The Chiefs would all be deposed.
(c) All natives would be forcibly disarmed and placed in reserves.

In other words, Germany was about to repudiate all pledges and promises made in the protection agreements, now that she felt strong enough to do so, and in the general breaking up of the old order the loyal Chieftains amid natives would suffer the same fate as those who had gone into rebellion.

Chiefs like Hendrik Witbooi, Christian Goliath, and Johannes Christian read the newspapers and received food for deep and serious thought.

Christian Goliath walked into the Magistrate s office at Keetmanshoop one day and said to the Magistrate: "The newspapers say that we Chiefs are to be deposed and our people disarmed. Is this correct?"

The matter was reported to Leutwein, who thereupon wrote a gentle lecture to the editor of the Windhuk "*Zeitung*" in which he remarked "You should at least deal cautiously with such matters in your paper, otherwise the rifles in Namaqualand will go off of their own accord.

As might have been expected, judging from their records. there were certain German missionaries too who could not resist the temptation to fulminate from their pulpits.

The missionary Holzapfel, of Rietmond (in Hendrik Witbooi s territory), declared from his pulpit that the German Government intended to disarm the Witbooi tribe as a punishment for their sins. (Page 294: Leutwein).

About the same the a report reached Hendrik Witbooi at Gibeon that the missionary Wandres had declared from his pulpit at Windhuk: "God will punish Izaak Witbooi (Chief Witbooi's son and heir) through the German

---

[149] General Lothar von Trotha arrived in Namibia on 11th June, 1904 to take over command of the German forces. Dreschler, *Let us die*, p. 153.

Government, even in the same way as He allowed Chief Abraham Christian of Warmbad to be punished."

Hendrik Witbooi reported what he heard to Windhuk whereupon Wandres denied having said so. The Chief thereupon produced statements from members of the congregation who were present and had personally heard Wandres use the words complained of. Leutwein promised to investigate, but in the meantime Hendrik Witbooi had decided to go into rebellion.

The figure of this 80-year-old warrior Chieftain, gathering his little band of faithful followers and deciding to make one last and desperate stand against German oppression and injustice, cannot be regarded without feelings of deep sympathy and admiration. He felt their oppression and injustice keenly, no doubt, but the gross ingratitude and bad faith displayed towards him (he who had risked his life for them times without number, and who during 11 long years had been true to his pledged word) must have hurt him even more, and it probably killed in Witbooi the last vestige of respect for and trust in the white race.

Coming on top of the newspaper articles and the pulpit utterances, quite apart from the daily talk of the braggart settlers Witbooi received news from the north which definitely settled his plans.

Von Trotha's "Extermination Order" against the Hereros was issued in August 1904. The Witbooi contingent, like the Bastards, definitely refused, as Christians, to kill women and children and captured prisoners. This resulted in friction and recriminations. The Witboois, loyal allies – and very useful allies they were – were harshly treated by von Trotha's officers. The result was that 19 men deserted and, despite all endeavours to intercept them, made their way safely from the Waterberg to Gibeon, where they reported to their revered Chieftain. They brought him news of the common camp talk among von Trotha's soldiers, that, when the Hereros were finished with, it would be the Hottentots turn next.

Hot on the tracks of these returned men came the news that their comrades (over 90 all told), who had loyally remained with von Trotha, had been arrested and disarmed and were on their way to Togo and the Cameroons, whither they were being deported, and where (as Leutwein says) the "climate" killed the majority of them. This was the treatment meted out to the loyal and faithful subjects of a loyal and faithful Chief who for over ten years had been a pillar of strength to Germany in South-West Africa.

Leutwein gives (page 300) the following list of campaigns in which Hendrik Witbooi and his people rendered sterling services[150]:–

---

[150] A heated debate took place in the Windhoek Observer at the end of 1997 and beginning of 1998 following the publication of an article by Emil Appolus that questioned the status of Hendrik Witbooi as a national hero of anti-colonial resistance in Namibia because of the fact that Witbooi supplied troops to assist German operations over a ten year period. Witbooi's profile is shown on many of the denominations of the Namibian dollar. See Appolus, Emil 'Hendrik Witbooi: Swapo's phoney hero', *Windhoek Observer*, 20th December, 1997. The debate continued for several weeks in the *Windhoek Observer*, see: 27th December, 10th January, 17th January, 31st January and 7th February.

1896, against Eastern Hereros and Khauas Hottentots.
1897, against Afrikaner Hottentots.
1898, against Swartbooi Hottentots.
1900, against Bastards of Grootfontein.
1903, against Bondelswartz.
1904, against Hereros.

In an appreciation written after the Chief s death in action, Leutwein says:–

> His life was forfeit. And therefore the German bullet which killed him was a release for him and for us. It brought to him the honourable death of a soldier and it saved us from a serious dilemma. The little Chief had, however, immortalised his name in the history of the South-West African Protectorate. First his obstinate resistance of the mighty power of the German Empire, at the head of a small band of warlike but nevertheless tired and impoverished people; then his loyal support of our cause for ten years; and, eventually, the change and the rebellion these have bound his name inseparably with the history of the country. To me he is still the little Chief who so loyally stood by my side for ten long years... He was the last national hero of a dying race.

The news of the deportation of his warriors to the Cameroons was more than Witbooi could bear. He decided to rally his tribe and to die fighting.

He issued a manifesto to his brother Chiefs, and by the end of 1904, Simon Kooper and the Chiefs of the Bethany, Veldschoendrager, Red People of Hoachanas, and, in fact, all the Hottentots in Great Namaqualand, except those of Berseba and the town of Keetmanshoop. had joined the veteran s forces. After some hesitation even the peace-loving Johannes Christian of Warmbad (despite the peace of Kalkfontein in the previous January) took the field, urged on by the fearless Marengo and "at all events" (says Leutwein) "not without contributory guilt on our side."

Leutwein wrote to Witbooi asking him why he had rebelled. The Chief replied:–

> The reasons go far back ... you have written in your letter, I have for ten years observed your laws ... I fear God the Father. The souls of those, who during those ten years (those of all nations and of all Chiefs) without guilt or cause and without actual war have fallen in peace the and under agreements of peace press heavily on me. The account which I have to render to God the Father in Heaven is great indeed. God in Heaven has cancelled this agreement. Therefore do I depend on Him and have recourse to Him that He may dry our tears and in His the liberate us ...
>
> And I pray you when you have read this letter sit down quietly and think it over and reckon out and reckon out the number of souls who, from that day from which you came into this land to this day for ten years have fallen ... Reckon out also the months of those ten years and the weeks, days, hours and minutes since those people have died ... furthermore I beg of Your Honour do not call me a Rebel.

After a year of desperate fighting, Hendrik Witbooi (then over 80 years of age) was killed in action near Tses. Von Trotha had offered a reward of 1,000*l*. for

Witbooi, alive or dead. To prevent his body falling into the hands of the enemy, his followers held back the advancing Germans while his son and a few others hastily dug a grave on the battlefield. His only requiem was the screeching of shells and the whistling of German bullets. After burial every effort was made to remove all indications of the presence of a grave, and then the broken-hearted band retired. Thus fell Hendrik Witbooi, a victim of Germany's ambition and a sacrifice to her blood-lust.

"A born leader and ruler," says Leutwein, "that Witbooi was; a man who probably might have become world-famous had it not been his fate to be born to a small African throne."

After Witbooi's death the heroic and chivalrous Jacob Marengo took his place at the head of the rebels, and for nearly two years longer the struggle continued. Eventually, through sheer exhaustion, the Hottentots began to give way. The concentrated power of German arms proved too much for them, and tribe after tribe surrendered (this was only after von Trotha had been recalled). Previously they had asked for peace on terms, but his blood-lust had not yet been satiated and the killing continued. Eventually the protraction of the campaign and the enormous cost created an uproar in Germany. Von Trotha went home. Marengo had fled into the Kalihari, and with him Simon Kooper and the survivors of his Franzmann tribe. Those who were left agreed to the Peace of Ukamas, the terms of which were identical with those settled at Kalkfontein South in January 1904.[151] By the end of 1907 the survivors of the Hottentot tribes, now reduced, like the Hereros, to penury and starvation, all their stock having been taken in the course of the campaign, were captives at the mercy of the conquering German. Early in 1908 Jacob Marengo. who had refused to return to South-West Africa to the certain death which awaited him, or to surrender to the British forces and by them be sent back captive to his German masters, was shot by the Cape Police near Rietfontein. The pity of it that even one British bullet should have aided in that horrible outpouring of human blood.

Simon Kooper moved northwards along the Kalihari frontier, and was for some the the scourge and the terror of the German froZ-Chantier posts. Eventually, through the mediation of the British Government, he was met at Lehututu, as already related and persuaded to settle down peacefully in British territory and to give up molesting his mortal enemies across the frontier. He died shortly after wards, but his people still live in exile in the arid Kalihari.

---

[151] The Treaty was signed on 23rd December, 1906 and defined the boundaries of Bondelswarts Territory. These same boundaries formed the basis for their 'reserve' during the South African period. Influential leaders like Jakob Marenga, Abraham Morris and Jacobus Christian remained in exile in the northern Cape. Jakob Marenga was shot by a South African patrol on 20th September, 1907 whilst, allegedly trying to return to Namibia to continue the struggle. Events surrounding the return of Abraham Morris from exile in 1922 led to the 'Bondelswarts Rising' of that same year that culminated in the aerial bombing of the Bondelwarts community and the death of Abraham Morris. Lewis, Gavin 'The Bondelswarts rebellion of 1922', MA Thesis, Rhodes University, Grahamstown, 1977.

CHAPTER TWENTY

THE TREATMENT OF THE HOTTENTOTS IN WAR AND OF THE HEREROS AND HOTTENTOTS AFTER SURRENDER.

It must not be supposed that as a body the Hottentots continued their resistance right up to the Peace of Ukamas in the end of 1906.

In the beginning of 1906, after von Trotha had left, the survivors of the Witbooi tribe, broken and depressed by the death of their leader, had surrendered on the terms originally fixed at Kalkfontein. Their submission was followed by the surrender of the remnant of the Bethany tribe under Cornelius Fredericks. Only Jacob Marengo with the Bondelswartz and Veldschoendragers, aided by Simon Kooper, continued the struggle until the end of 1906.

So early as April 1905, a general peace would have been possible but for the obstinate adherence of von Trotha to his extermination policy. It was then that Marengo signified his willingness to surrender on terms. All that he asked for was (a) that the lives of all should be spared, (b) that they should be allowed to retain their own livestock and their own bon fide possessions. (c) that the reserves into which they were to be put should be large enough for their stock to find sufficient grazing and water.

Then it was that von Trotha lost all chances of an early peace by replying that the surrender was to be unconditional, that they would receive no guarantee as to the sparing of their lives, and that they would have to hand over all their livestock.[152]

Little wonder, then, that Marengo decided to fight on to the bitter end.

Rohrbach is very clear on the subject of von Trotha s obstinacy and vindictiveness. He writes (page 351):–

> Not only with regard to the menaced destruction of the most valuable us labour-material for the carrying on of our farming pursuits or on grounds of humanity was the policy of General von Trotha loudly and adversely criticised, but also above all things (*vor allen Dingen*), because, on account of his so-called exter-

---

[152] Von Trotha's issued a proclamation on 19th May, 1905 to 'the war-waging Namaqua tribes' stating that "The great and powerful Emperor of Germany will be lenient with the Namaqua people and has ordered that the lives of those who give themselves up will be spared ... [But] ... If anyone thinks that after this notice there will be any leniency shown him he had better quit the country, because if he is agains seen in German territories he will be shot and thus all rebels will be eliminated". On 29th May this final line was amended to read " ... had better quit the country because wherever they are seen in German territory they will be shot at until all the outlaws have been exterminated." (Governor Sir Hely-Hutchinson to Mr Lyttelton, Telegram, 19th May, 1905 containing translation of Proclamation in Colonial Office, 'South Africa. Further Correspondence [1905] relating to the Affairs of Walfisch Bay and the German South-West African Protectorate, No. 766, September, 1906).

mination programme, the restoration of peace was further delayed and the war costs increased out of all proportion.

In the end of 1905 von Trotha was recalled, but it took a year to persuade all the Hereros and Hottentots who survived to surrender finally. The new Governor, von Lindequist. issued a special proclamation to the Hereros offering them work and promising to spare the lives of all who came in and surrendered voluntarily.[153] On these terms also the Witboois and the Bethany people eventually surrendered, and gradually opposition became weaker and weaker until the general Peace of Ukamas was agreed to in the end of 1905.

The following will show how far their surrender brought peace and happiness to the natives.

Joseph Schayer (Commandant under Marengo) states under oath:–

> I was never captured by the Germans, and remained in the field until peace was made in end of 1906 or beginning 1907... We were so ordered by our Chief to spare all women and children. The missionaries and the English and Dutch settlers were not molested by us if they remained on their farms. When we captured German soldiers we always released them after taking their arms and ammunition. We fought fairly, and only killed in battle. The Germans, on the other hand, killed all who fell into their hands. There was no mercy, even women and children were killed. When we eventually made peace we had lost everything. We had nothing to live on. We used to eat the dead horses and mules of Germans which we found on the veld.

Adam Pienaar (nephew of the old Chief Willem Christian) states on oath:–

> I took the field with my people and was a field cornet in the Commando of the leader Abraham Morris (under Marengo)... I was in the field for nearly three years. Just before the rebellion ended I was badly wounded in action, in the face and groin, and my people carried me into British territory. I returned to this country after everything was settled. Our Commandant ordered us not to molest women and children in any way. We were all Christians, and did not kill prisoners or non-combatants. The Germans, on the other hand, spared no one. They killed all prisoners, wounded and unwounded. Women, girls and little boys were not spared either. That is why we fought to the bitter end, as we knew that surrender meant death. It was only after three years of war that the Germans got tired and made peace with us on terms we could accept.

Owing to their superior mobility and knowledge of the country the Hottentot losses in actual battle were probably smaller than those of the Germans, and the people who survived in the field to the bitter end were better off than the Witboois and Bethany tribes which had surrendered earlier.

After von Trotha had left and surrenders were once more possible, the Germans decided to use their prisoners (men and women) as labourer on the

---

[153] Upon assuming office in late 1905, the new civilian governor of the territory, Friedrich von Lindequist, issued a proclamation to the Herero still hiding in the field. In it he urged the Herero to give themselves up. Gewald, *Herero Heroes*, p. 195.

harbour works[154] at Luderitzbucht and Swakopmund, and also on railway construction.[155]

It must be borne in mind that these poor wretches had been driven to surrender mainly owing to sheer starvation, and that their physical condition after the privations and hardships they had undergone did not warrant expectations of too much in the way of manual labour for some considerable period. But work they had to, well or unwell, willing or unwilling. Then it was that, to use Samuel Maharero's expression, many again died at the hands of the labour overseer and by the lash. Probably 60 per cent. of the natives who had surrendered after von Trotha left perished in this way. True indeed the cold and raw climate of the two coast ports contributed greatly to this huge death-roll. But for this the Germans who placed these naked remnants of starving humanity on the barren islets of Luderitzbucht and on the moisture-oozing shores of Swakopmund must take the fullest blame and submit to the condemnation of all persons with even an elementary feeling of humanity towards the native races.[156]

Statements as to treatment of the natives after capture and while in captivity at Luderitzbucht and elsewhere

The Hereros and Hottentots were treated alike and in some cases herded together. These statements refer (except where special mention is made to the contrary) therefore to the treatment of all captives.

Benjamin Burger (Dutch South African) states on oath:–

> In 1904 I was living on the farm Rietkuil, in the Gibeon district. I served as a guide to the German troops ... when the Germans were fighting the Witboois under Hendrik Witbooi. I accompanied the troops from Gibeon to Koses on the

---

[154] A contemporary intelligence report stated that at Luderitz "Native women break stones for railroad, work on jetty off-loading, and do other work about camp. They are badly fed and appear to be weak" (Major Berrange, Upington to Commissioner, Cape Mounted Police, Cape Town, 18th November, 1905 in Colonial Office, 'South Africa. Further Correspondence (1905) relating to the Affairs of Walfisch Bay and the German South-West African Protectorate, No. 766, September, 1906.

[155] The 94 mile Lüderitz-Aus railway line was reported to have been built between 27th December, 1905 and 1st November, 1906 and have employed "250 white engineers, gangers and workmen, 95 officers and men of No. 2 Railway Company, some **900 prisoners of war** (our emphasis), and a small number of Cape boys (Despatch, Colonel Trench, Military Attaché, British Embassy, Berlin to Ambassador, Sir F. Lascelles, 22nd April, 1907. Colonial Office, 'South Africa. Further Correspondence [1907] relating to the Affairs of Walfisch Bay and the German South-West African Protectorate', No. 868, June, 1908.

[156] The British Military Attaché in Namibia at the time reported on the 'exposure and lack of sanitation' at Shark Island and wrote of the prisoners ('if they still exist') that "it is not easy to avoid the impression that the extinction of the tribe would be welcomed by the authorities. The hardness of their fate (anglice, harshness of treatment) excited even the sympathy of two officers who had known them, and who reminded me that they [the Witbooi – eds] never murdered or ill-treated civilians or prisoners, but wager war without cruelty, and proved useful allies against the Hereros ... I have observed, however, that a quarter of a century of Colonial Empire has not sufficed to teach the fact that a black man is a human being ('British Military Attaché, Col. F. Trench to British Embassy, Berlin, 21st November, 1906).

> Norop River. We had a fight that morning and took the Hottentot camp. The Commanding Officer gave instructions to search for natives along the river-bed near the camp. We found thirteen women and old men in a cave ... As they came out of the cave each native was shot dead. This was done to avoid the trouble of escorting them to Gibeon... That same day a German soldier raped a young native girl about 16 to 18 years of age. I came upon him in the veld. After he had raped her he stuck his bayonet through her stomach and then shot her...
> I was in Gibeon when two Hottentots surrendered in terms of a Proclamation issued by the German Government to the effect that any natives surrendering would be protected. Ober-Lieutenant Zweinicke, who was in charge, said the two Hottentots had only come in for the purpose of spying, and without trial he ordered them to be hanged. I was present the next day when they were hanged by the soldiers.

Hendrik Campbell (Commandant of the Rehoboth Bastard contingent, who served through the Herero and Hottentot rising with the Germans) states on oath:–

> I was sent down to the south to participate in the war against Hendrik Witbooi. At Pakriver, in the district of Gibeon, we captured eight Hottentots of whom only one was armed. Seven were immediately shot dead. The eighth was promised that his life would be spared if he showed the locality of their camp at Korob. After he had pointed out the locality he was shot by Lieutenant von Trotha personally with a revolver; this I saw with my own eyes.

Petrus Diergaard (Field Cornet of the Bastards under Commandant Hendrik Campbell) states on oath:–

> I was present when the events (related above by the Commandant) took place. I personally tied up the seven prisoners before they were shot.

Edward Fredericks (son of the old Chief Joseph Fredericks and at present headman of the Bethany Hottentots) states on oath:–

> In 1906 the Germans took me a prisoner after we had made peace, and sent me with about a thousand other Hottentots to Aus, thence to Luderitzbucht, and finally to Shark Island.[157] We were placed on the island, men, women, and children. We were beaten daily by the Germans, who used sjamboks. They were most cruel to us. We lived in tents on the island; food, blankets, and lashes were given to us in plenty, and the young girls were violated at night by the guards. Six months later we went by boat to Swakopmund, and thence by train to Karibib. Lots of my people died on Shark Island. I put in a list of those who died. (*Note*. This list comprises 168 males, including the Chief, Cornelius Fredericks, 97 females, 66 children, and also 18 Bushwomen and children) ... but it is not complete. I gave up compiling it, as I was afraid we were all going to die. We remained at Karibib six months, and were returned to Shark Island for a further six months, when we were again removed by sea to Karibib and thence to Okawayo, where we remained till 1915, when the British sent us back by train to Bethany. We had to work for the troops and received wages and a good deal of

---

[157] No trace of the camp, nor monument to those that died on it can be found on the island today. Silvester, Jeremy & Erichsen, Casper 'The Angel of Death: Luderitz's Forgotten Concentration Camp' *The Namibian*, 16th February, 2001

lashes with sjamboks. I received 10s. per month, and later 20s. per month, and other men received 2s. per month for a year, but this only commenced in 1911. Lots of my people died in Damaraland ...

This statement will indicate what the German peace terms were really worth. In violation thereof these people were kept in captivity under such conditions that the majority died, and eventually they were permanently exiled in North Damaraland as forced labourers. It was only after the British conquest that the survivors returned to their old homes at Bethany.

Fritz Isaac (son of the Under-Chief to the Witboois, Samuel Isaac[158]) states on oath):–

After the war I was sent to Shark Island by the Germans. We remained on the island one year. 3,500 Hottentots and Kaffirs were sent to the island and 193 returned. 3,307 died of the island.

These figures are corroborated by other native witnesses.

Referring to the Witboois who were deported to the Cameroons by von Trotha, *Franz Lambert*, a Witbooi Hottentot, states on oath:–

At the time of the Herero rebellion, I was deputed by Chief Hendrik Witbooi to assist the Germans. After that rebellion we who had assisted the Germans (115 men) were captured by the Germans at Okahandja. They told us that Hendrik Witbooi had made war and that was why we were captured. We were all sent to the Cameroons. We were employed there on the railways... The climate was unhealthy and the work heavy. Many of us died, but I don t know how many.

Another Hottentot, also named Lambert, states on oath:–

On our return from the Herero rebellion, 115 of us were arrested and deported to the Cameroons ... there we were *inspanned* to wagons loaded with railway iron, and these we had to pull every day. The work was very hard and many of us collapsed. 77 Hottentots died in the Cameroons in consequence of having to pull heavy wagons. There were no horses or oxen there. 38 of us returned from the Cameroons.

The figures given and the treatment are corroborated by other Hottentots who survived this deportation.

In addition to the 115 men sent to the Cameroons, a further 93 were sent with young Hendrik Witbooi later on. Of these 51 died in exile, and of the survivors some were allowed to return to South-West Africa about 1910, while the remainder still in exile, were released by the British columns in 1916.

Thomas Alfred Hite (who has lived in South-West Africa since 1881), states on oath:–

About the the the railway to Aus was completed, I was at Aus waiting to transport goods. Close to the outspan was the Herero camp, where the Germans had a number of native prisoners taken in the native rising. I personally saw two German soldiers in broad daylight grab hold of two little females, about 13 to 15

---

[158] Also described as the 'scribe' and 'Secretary' to Hendrik Witbooi. The famous Hendrik Witbooi Diaries might therefore contain Samuel Isaac's handwriting (Gugelberger 1984: 95, 103)

years of age, and flog them until they were limp. They then dragged these children into their quarters and violated them. The screams were so pitiful that I left.

Johann Noothout[159] (a Hollander and a naturalised British subject) states on oath:–

I left Cape Town during the year 1906, and signed on with the Protectorate troops in South-West Africa. I arrived at Luderitzbucht, and after staying there a few minutes I perceived nearly 500 native women lying on the beach, all bearing indications of being slowly starved to death. Every morning and towards evening four women carried a stretcher containing about four or five corpses, and they had also to dig the graves and bury them. I then started to trek to Kubub and Aus, and on the road I discovered bodies of native women lying between stones and devoured by birds of prey. Some bore signs of having been beaten to death ... If a prisoner were found outside the Herero prisoners camp, he would be brought before the Lieutenant and flogged with a sjambok. Fifty lashes were generally imposed. The manner in which the flogging was carried out was the most cruel imaginable ... pieces of flesh would fly from the victim's body into the air.

My observations during my stay in the country (in the German time) gave me the opinion that the Germans are absolutely unfit to colonise, as their atrocious crimes and cold-bloodied murders were committed with one object to extinguish the native race.

Hendrik Fraser states on oath:–

When I got to Swakopmund I saw very many Herero prisoners of war who had been captured in the rebellion which was still going on in the country.[160] (*Note*. These were prisoners captured before von Trotha s arrival). There must have been about 600 men, women and children prisoners. They were in an enclosure on the beach, fenced in with barbed wire. The women were made to do hard labour just like the men. The sand is very deep and heavy there. The women had to load and unload carts and trolleys, and also to draw Scotch-cart loads of goods to Nonidas (9 10 kilos. away) where there was a depôt. The women were put in spans of eight

---

[159] The name 'J. Noothout' can be found on an official German list of those employed in the Luderitz district dated 15th March, 1907. NAN GLU 331 '*Listen der im dienste der Truppe befindlichen buren und kapboys*', Aus, 15th March, 1907. Thanks to Casper Erichsen for this reference.

[160] A series of disturbing photographs taken at the camp are displayed and discussed in '"Wie Vieh wurden hunderte zu Tode getrieben und wie Vieh begraben": Fotodokumente aus dem duetsche konzentrationslager in Swakopmund/Namibia, 1904-1908' in *Zeitschrift für Geschichtswissenschaft* Vol. 49 (3), 2001. Jeff Gaydish consulted local German records which showed that in the period 29th January, 1905 to 6th March, 1906 four-fifths of the 1,224 'native deaths' in Swakopmund consisted of residents of the prison camp. See Gaydish, Jeff, 'Fair Treatment is guaranteed to them': The Swakopmund Prisoner-of-War Camp, 1905-1908', paper presented at the 'Public History, Forgotten History' Conference, University of Namibia, August, 2000; Gewald, *Herero Heroes*, pp. 188 – 190

to each Scotch-cart and were made to pull like draught animals.[161] Many were half-starved and weak, and died of sheer exhaustion. Those who did not work well were brutally flogged with sjamboks. I even saw women knocked down with pick handles. The German soldiers did this. I personally saw six women (Herero girls) murdered by German soldiers. They were ripped open within bayonets. I saw the bodies. I was there for six months, and the Hereros died daily in large numbers as a result of exhaustion, ill-treatment and exposure.[162] They were poorly fed, and often begged me and other Cape boys for a little food... The soldiers used the young Herero girls to satisfy their passions. Prisoners continued to conic in while I was there; but I don t think half of them survived the treatment they received.

After six months at Swakopmund I was sent to Karibib towards the end of September 1904. (*Note.* Von Trotha's extermination order was issued about August 1904.)[163] There I also saw an enclosure with Hereros waiting for transport to Swakopmund. Many were dying of starvation and exhaustion. They were all very thin and worn out. They were not made to work so hard at Karibib, and appeared to be less harshly treated.

Samuel Kariko[164] (Herero schoolmaster and son of Under-Chief Daniel Kariko), states on oath:–

---

[161] A statement made by a South African, James Tolibadi, on 11th August, 1906 (after having spent seven months as a 'Foreman Labourer' in Swakopmund) seems to confirm this allegation. Tolibadi stated – "These unfortunate women are daily compelled to carry heavy iron for construction work, also big stacks of compressed fodder. I have often noticed cases where women have fallen under the load and have been made to go on by being thrashed and kicked by the soldiers and conductors. The rations supplied to the women are insufficient and they are made to cook the food themselves. They are always hungry, and we, labourers from the Cape Colony, have frequently thrown food into their camp.

The women in many cases are not properly clothed. It is a common thing to see women going about in public almost naked ... Old women are also made to work and are constantly kicked and thrashed by soldiers.

This treatment is meted out in the presence of the German officers, and I have never noticed any officers interfering. (Affidavit attached to 'Ministers to Governor, 22nd August, 1906 Cape Archives, GH 23/97, 1906).

[162] In 1916 a Doctor visiting Swakopmund noted that "Beyond the European cemetery is what is said to be the native burial-place. Rows and rows of little heaps of sand occupy about a thousand yards of desert. Some of these heaps have rude little crosses or sticks placed on them. It was very puzzling to explain why so many natives were buried near Swakopmund, in a place that was not even enclosed." The wind-swept mounds can still be made out today, but are gradually being eroded by the elements and local people riding 'dune buggies' over the site. It seems likely that this neglected barren memorial contains the graves of many of those who died in the Swakopmund camp. A student survey found one surviving gravestone on the site that dated from 1903. Walker, *A Doctor's Diary in Damaraland*, quoted in Silvester, Jeremy 'A Living Cemetery in Swakop', *The Namibian Weekender*, 21st November, 1999. Erichsen, Casper 'A Legacy of Neglect', *The Namibian Weekender*, 11th December, 1998.

[163] The order was actually not issued until 2nd October, 1904 and was officially replaced by an order from the Kaiser on 8th December, 1904, although new instructions had apparently already been issued by the new Governor, von Lindequist, at least a week earlier. Oermann, Nils Ole *Mission, Church and State Relations in South West Africa under German Rule, (1884-1915)*, Franz Steiner Verlag, Stuttgart, 1999: 99

[164] According to the Rhenish Mission archives Samuel Kariko was sent to Lüderitz by the mission to minister to prisoners there. Gewald, *Herero Heroes*, p. 199

Plate 3: Condition of Herero on surrender after having been driven into the desert.

When von Trotha left, we were advised of a circular which the new Governor, von Lindequist, had issued, in which he promised to spare the lives of our people if we came in from the bush and mountains where we lived like hunted game. We then began to come in. I went to Okambahe, near my old home, and surrendered. We then had no cattle left, and more than three-quarters of our people had perished, far more. There were only a few thousands of us left, and we were walking skeletons, with no flesh, only skin and bones. They collected us in groups and made us work for the little food we got. I was sent down with others to an island far in the south, at Luderitzbucht. There on that island were thousands of Herero and Hottentot prisoners. We had to live there. Men, women and children were all huddled together. We had no proper clothing, no blankets, and the night air on the sea was bitterly cold. The wet sea fogs drenched us and made our teeth chatter. The people died there like flies that had been poisoned. The great majority died there. The little children and the old people died first, and then the women and the weaker men. No day passed without many deaths. We begged and prayed and appealed for leave to go back to our own country, which is warmer, but the Germans refused. Those men who were fit had to work during the day in the harbour and railway depots. The younger women were selected by the soldiers and taken to their camps as concubines.[165]

Soon the greater majority of the prisoners had died, and then the Germans began to treat us better. A Captain von Zulow took charge. And he was more humane than the others. After being there over a year, those of us who had survived were allowed to return home. After all was over, the survivors of our race were merely slaves.

Hosea Mungunda (Herero Headman at Windhuk) states on oath:–

Those who were left after the rebellion were put into compounds and made to work for their food only. They were sent to farms, and also to the railways and elsewhere. Many were sent to Luderitzbucht and Swakopmund and died in captivity; and many were hanged and flogged nearly to death died as the result of ill-treatment. Many were mere skeletons when they came in and surrendered, and they could not stand bad food and ill-treatment.

---

[165] There are numerous references in the Blue Book to allegations of sexual abuse in the prison camps. Concerns about the low birth rate in the post-war Herero community led the South African administration to send Dr Simpson-Wells to Namibia in 1920 to investigate claims that what one might today call post-traumatic stress syndrome was leading to a high rate of abortion and 'race suicide' (ADM 76 1534/6). A South African MP later interviewed an unidentified 'group of the most intelligent and leading Herero' who blamed the low birth rate on the recent history of sexual abuse – "'At Windhoek a house of prostitution was opened for the German military. Our daughters were placed in it and when they returned from there and got married to Herero men, they were sterile. Our wives in this way also infected us and we too became sterile' ... they said that before their tribal life was destroyed ... even the name for gonorrhea was unknown in their language. The word for gonorrhea now is Xgams, a Damara word. Why such a term did not exist in their language is because the disease was unknown. Another word for it now with them is 'trepper', which they have adopted from the German word for it." Samuel Kutako in a statement to Major O'Reilly not included in the Blue Book complained that "The [Herero] girls are interfered with by Germans when they are quite young ... There is a great deal of sexual disease among the people and it spreads as a result of this immorality." Great Britain, 'Correspondence relating to the Wishes of the Natives of the German Colonies as to their Future Government', HMSO, London, 1918: p. 13, Steenkamp, W.P. *Is the South-West African Herero Committing Race Suicide?*, 1944: pp. 10, 18-19. For a more detailed discussion of this issue see Wallace, Marion Wallace 'Health & Society in Windhoek, Namibia, 1915-45' (PhD Thesis, University of London, 1997).

> ... The young girls were selected and taken as concubines for soldiers; but even the married women were assaulted and interfered with ... it was one continuous ill-treatment... When the railways were completed and the harbour works, we were sent out to towns and to farms to work. We were distributed and allocated to farmers, whether we liked them or not.

Traugott Tjienda (Headman of the Hereros at Tsumeb, who also surrendered under von Lindequist's Amnesty Proclamation), states on oath:—

> I was made to work on the Otavi line which was being built. We were not paid for our work, we were regarded as prisoners. I worked for two years without pay... As our people came in from the bush they were made to work at once, they were merely skin and bones, they were so thin that one could see through their bones they looked like broomsticks. (*Note.* See photograph on opposite page.) Bad as they were, they were made to work; and whether they worked or were lazy they were repeatedly sjambokked by the German overseers. The soldiers guarded us at night in big compounds made of thorn bushes. I was a kind of foreman over the labourers. I had 528 people, all Hereros, in my work party. Of these 148 died while working on the line. The Herero women were compounded with the men. They were made to do manual labour as well. They did not carry the heavy rails, but they had to load and unload wagons and trucks and to work with picks and shovels. The totals above given include women and children... When our women were prisoners on the railway work they were compelled to cohabit with soldiers and white railway labourers. The fact that a woman was married was no protection. Young girls were raped and very badly used. They were taken out of the compounds into the bush and there assaulted. I don t think any of them escaped this, except the older ones.

The following statements by two well-educated English residents of the territory in German times corroborate the reports of the natives.

Edward Lionel Pinches (of Keetmanshoop) states on oath:—

> At the time I entered the country then known as German South-West Africa in the year eighteen hundred and ninety-six the Hottentots and Damaras were divided into tribes and were living under the jurisdiction of their Chiefs. The natives were prosperous and the country was fairly well populated. Any estimation of the actual native population would be extremely difficult to give. At this the I was continuously travelling about the country, and I got a fairly accurate idea of the number of natives of the different tribes I came in contact with. On the outbreak of the Hottentot war the natives were about the same in number as when I entered the country, but on the conclusion of that war in my estimation the total native population was not more than one-fifth of its former number. The war was to all intents and purposes a war of extinction of the native races, and has been admitted to be so by Germans of high standing. This tremendous reduction of population was by no means owing to actual losses through the war, but is directly due to the treatment received by the natives during captivity. I have myself been several times in Luderitzbucht, where large numbers of Damaras were kept in confinement, and have seen them being buried by their fellows, who were little better than dead themselves, at the rate of twelve to fifteen per diem. Judging by the appearance of these natives, they were dying from sheer starvation.

CHAPTER TWENTY

Leslie Cruikshank Bartlet states on oath:–

> I came to German South-West Africa with the first transport during the Hottentot war in 1905. The prisoners, Hereros and Hottentots, mostly women, and all in a terribly emaciated condition, were imprisoned on an island adjoining Luderitzbucht. The mortality amongst the prisoners was excessive, funerals taking place at the rate of ten to fifteen daily. Many are said to have attempted escape by swimming, and I have seen corpses of women prisoners washed up on the beach between Luderitzbucht and the cemetery. One corpse, I remember, was that of a young woman with practically fleshless limbs whose breasts had been eaten by jackals. This I reported at the German Police Station, but on passing the same way three or four days later the body was still where I saw it first. The German soldiery spoke freely of atrocities committed by Hereros and Hottentots during the war, and seemed to take a pride in wreaking vengeance on those unfortunate women. When the railway from Luderitzbucht to Keetmanshoop was started gangs of prisoners, mostly women, scarcely able to walk from weakness and starvation, were employed as labourers. They were brutally treated. I personally saw a gang of these prisoners, all women, carrying a heavy double line of rails with iron sleepers attached on their shoulders, and unable to bear the weight they fell. One woman fell under the rails which broke her leg and held it fast. The Schachtmeister (ganger), without causing the rail to be lifted, dragged the woman from under and threw her on one side, where she, died untended. The general treatment was cruel, and many instances were told me, but that which I have stated I personally saw.

It will be interesting to reproduce the famous Amnesty Proclamation of von Lindequist. It is a document which speaks tellingly of what the treatment of Hereros had been prior to its publication.

When one considers the fate and treatment of these unfortunates who, "like broomsticks," and so thin that "one could see through their bones," came in and surrendered to German "mercy," it seems doubtful, in view of the foregoing statements, whether they would not have been as well off if they had remained to perish of starvation in the bush.

The Proclamation, dated 1st December 1905, reads as follows:–

> Hereros! His Majesty the Emperor of Germany, the high Lord Protector of this Land, has graciously nominated me Governor of this Land a few days after General von Trotha, who commanded the German troops against you, returned to Germany. His departure means that the war will now cease.
>
> Hereros! You know me! Formerly I was for five years in this land as Imperial Judge. and, as Assessor and Councillor, the representative of Governor Leutwein in the days when Manasse of Omaruru and Kambazembi of Waterberg, who were always loyal supporters of mine, still lived.
>
> It is my desire that the Rebellion which your Chiefs and Headmen (and the children who followed them) so wickedly began and which has desolated the land should now come to an end, so that Peace and Order may again rule. I therefore call upon the Hereros who still are wandering about the veld and in the mountains and who nourish themselves by eating wild roots and by theft. Come and lay down your arms, Hereros! Thousands of your fellow tribesmen have already surrendered and are being clothed and fed by the Government. I have taken every precaution to ensure that you will be justly treated. That I also personally guarantee to you. Further, it is ordained that from 20th December onwards, that is three

weeks from today, no Herero habitations will be searched after and taken, as I wish to give you time personally to come in peacefully to me and surrender yourselves. Come to Omburo and Otjihaenena! Your Missionaries will be sent there by me.[166] They will also take provisions with them, so that your first and great hunger may be appeased. Some small stock will also be left for provisional use of your wives and children in so far as you still possess such for their support. Those who are strong and can work will, when they work with exceptional diligence, receive a small wage. No European soldiers will be stationed at Omburo and Otjihaenena. so that you need not have fear and imagine that further shooting will take place. The sooner you come in and surrender your arms, the sooner can the question of amelioration of the present lot of your captive fellow tribesmen be considered and their freedom later again given to them. If Omburo and Otjihaenena are too far away, anyone may hand in the arms at any Military Post and surrender there. The solders at those stations will not shoot either. In addition, the soldiers escorting the transport and travelling through the land will not shoot at you as long as you attempt nothing hostile towards them. Therefore do not be afraid of them when you see them. So come quickly in Hereros, before it is too late. In Namaland also there will soon be quiet, as Hendrik Witbooi has been killed by a German bullet and Samuel Isaac has surrendered and is in our hands.

On this Proclammation the surviving Hereros surrendered, and thousands of them then met the fate already depicted at Luderitzbucht and Swakopmund and in the Railway Concentration Labour Camps.[167]

In conclusion, the words of a frank German thinker may suitably be recalled, suitably and appropriately, as he gives in a nutshell the reason for all this inhumanity.

Professor Bonn, in his lecture before the Royal Colonial Institute in January 1914, referring to South-West Africa, "where we solved the native problem by smashing tribal life and by creating a scarcity of labour" says: "We tried to assume to ourselves the functions of Providence, and we tried to exterminate a native race, whom our lack of wisdom had goaded into rebellion. We succeeded in breaking up the natives tribes, but we have not yet succeeded in creating a new Germany."

---

[166] These two collection points, were later increased to four: Otjihaenena, Omburo, Otjozongombe and Okomitombe. By the time the camps were finally closed on 31st March, 1907 mission records showed that 11,937 Herero had passed through the camps. Oermann, Nils Ole *Mission, Church and State Relations in South West Africa under German Rule (1884-1915)*, Franz Steiner Verlag, Stuttgart, 1999: 110

[167] The term 'concentration camp' was used at the time for any camp where people were gathered by the authorities. The Germans for example referred to the camps in Botswana where Herero survivors were 'concentrated' as 'concentration camps'. For a perspective that deals predominantly with Herero in the camps, Gewald, H*erero Heroes*. pp. 185-191 & 193 - 204. Very little work has been done to date on the experience of Nama prisoners in the camps, apart from Drechsler, *Fighting,* pp. 210 - 214. Casper Erichsen is currently working on an M.A thesis on the history of Shark Island in the History Department at the University of Namibia

CHAPTER TWENTY-ONE

THE BERG-DAMARAS OF SOUTH-WEST AFRICA

In addition to the Hottentots and Hereros, there live in scattered bands or groups throughout the countries known as Damaraland and Great Namaqualand survivors of the once numerous race of Berg-Damaras (called by the Hottentots "Klip-Kaffirs" and "Dirty Damaras").

According to various estimates the population of this tribe at the time of the German annexation in 1890 was probably not less than 30,000 to 40,000, and it may have been much higher. Estimates were based on the numbers in a state of slavery under the Hottentots or in a state of semi-independence under the, at times, rather doubtful "protection" of the Hereros.

No estimate could possibly be formed of the considerable number who, under force of circumstances and to avoid slavery and worse, had adopted the habits of the wild Bushmen and, under petty patriarchal chiefs, shared with them the shelter of the remote mountain caves and the most impenetrable bush.

So late as 1892 a German writer relates how, coming unexpectedly on a party of Berg-Damaras near Heusis in the Windhuk district, he called to them with a view to conversation. But the whole party at the sight of the white man sprang up and fled like deer up the mountain side, never stopping to look back once. Such terror of a white face must not have been without its sinister reasons.

The origin of this ebony-skinned race, which now speaks pure Nama (Hottentot) still remains, like their now dead language of which no trace is retained, a fascinating puzzle for the ethnologist.[168]

The Rev. Hugo Hahn, who had lived amongst them for over 30 years, wrote about 1876 as follows (extract from article in the "Cape Monthly Magazine"):–

> The Berg-Damaras are a nation whose language and past history remain an insoluble riddle. So much is certain, that they inhabited these parts (*i.e..* Damaraland) and those far southward towards the Garieb or Orange River long before the Namaquas (Hottentot) came from the south, and afterwards, when the invasion of the Hereros took place about one hundred and fifty or two hundred

---

[168] A popular and widely available anthropological guide to the population groups of Namibia still argues that the way in which the Damara people came to be in Namibia remains a 'mystery'. Malan, J.S. *Peoples of Namibia*, p. 128. Rhino Publishers, Wingate Park, 1999. It has been argued that linguistic evidence suggests that 'proto-Damara' groups migrated from 'northern Botswana' through 'northern Namibia' and that Damara communities have not 'lost' a language, but are ancient speakers of Khoekhoegowab. On this, as on many issues concerning pre-colonial Namibian history, there is a need for greater academic debate between the disciplines. Wilfrid Haacke 'Linguistic Evidence in the Study of Origins: the Case of the Namibian Khoekhoe-speakers', Inaugural Lecture, University of Namibia, 2001

years ago, they were still to a great extent the owners of the mountainous parts of North Great Namaqualand and the undisputed masters of Hereroland, living in large and powerful tribes. It can scarcely be doubted that they also, before they were enslaved, worked in their rude way the different copper places in Great Namaqualand and Hereroland. Numerous indications prove that such working was carried on in former centuries.

Hahn held that the Hottentots, as South African aborigines, had moved up from the south, but this theory is not generally accepted, and his contention that, at the the of the Herero influx, the Berg-Damaras were still masters of Hereroland does not find support from the facts. If this were so, a conquest by the Hereros of the large and powerful tribes would have been necessary, and in that event it would be quite impossible to explain how it is that the conquered people, having lost their own language, speak not Herero, but Nama.

The more tenable theory is that the Berg-Damaras had been entirely conquered centuries before the Herero influx by the southward-moving Hottentot hordes. After the stream had passed down to the south it is quite possible, in fact, it is certain that, here and there, scattered groups came together and settled down under their tribal chief with some semblance of racial cohesion, but then they were already speaking Nama, and their period of servitude under the "Khoi-Khoi" must have been, therefore, even then of considerable duration. Only thereafter did the resurrected tribe come under Herero influence. Whether these very black, thick set, but not over tall people are also a branch of the Bantu group is very doubtful. Their outward appearance presents all the characteristics of the pure negro.

Dr. Hans Schinz, following the views of the great majority of missionary students, holds that while the Bushman was the aborigine of South Africa and South-East Africa, the Berg-Damara was the South-West African aborigine, and that the great Bantu influx which drove a wedge across Central Africa right to the western coast line had the effect of isolating the Berg-Damaras in the south.

This view is probably the correct one. They are not Bantu people. Circumcision and other characteristic Bantu customs are not known to them. The writer has had long discussions with the present hereditary Chief and his older councillors, but beyond the fact that they are able to give the names of no less than fifteen Chiefs who at various thes ruled over them, and unhesitatingly assert that they were the very first people in this land, one can glean very little of their mysterious past.

In reply to questions, the Chief Judas Goresib[169] of Okambahe (the head

---

[169] When Cornelius Goreseb the leader at Okombahe died on 3rd April, 1910, his Council of five councillors continued to lead the community, but the arrangement was considered unsatisfactory. In July, 1915 the new South African administration, through the local 'Native Commissioner', Maj. Pearson, appointed Judas Goreseb, as 'Captain'. Judas Goreseb appointed a new Council of three to advise and support him. Opposition to the new system was reported to have continued up to the death of Judas on 26th April, 1923 (Köhler 1959c: 37)

village), in the Omaruru district, who is a fine dignified specimen of black humanity, said:–

> We are the original inhabitants of the country now known as Hereroland. My people were here long before the Hereros and Hottentots came. Our Chief's village used, many years ago, to be at the place now known as Okanjande near the Waterberg. It was known to us by the name of Kanubis. Later on the Ovambos (the Chief is certain that these were Ovambos. He says that the Hereros were in the Kaokoveld at that time) drove our people away and they trekked south, and had their chief town where Windhuk now stands, we called it Kaisabis (= the big place.) One of my ancestors, Nawabib, was Chief then. It was only later, by agreement with the Herero Chiefs (Willem Zerua and Kamaherero) that we shifted our chief town to Okambahe during the Chieftainship of my great uncle Abraham ...

It is clear that the head village at Okanjande or Kanubis (a Hottentot name) must only have been established after centuries of subjugation to the Hottentots. Probably the southward-moving stream had, when once the main body was settled in the Cape and Namaqualand areas, left gaps of uninhabited or thinly populated Hottentot areas and under some bold Berg-Damara leader a successful war of emancipation was fought with the now weakened Nama rearguard. By that time, however, the race had already lost its language to such an extent that even the surnames and tribal names were Nama.

Nawabib, who was the grandfather of Abraham, must have had to evacuate Kanubis and to move south to Windhuk about the beginning of the last century, and he could not have been very long there before the Berg-Damaras, and with them the Hereros. were once more brought under the ancient yoke of the Hottentot under the brigand leadership of Jonker Afrikaner.

The move of the remnants of the Berg-Damara tribe from Kaisabis (Windhuk) to Okambahe took place about 1866, when, as a result of the Herero war of emancipation in which the Berg-Damaras were phlegmatic and rather useless allies, the ascendency of the "Khoi-Khoi" in Damaraland vanished for ever.

The Chief goes on to say:–

> Our origin I cannot speak definitely of, but we remember a long line of Chiefs who lived in this country. I am descended from them. Their names have been handed down by tradition, but beyond their names we know very little.
>
> The first Chief our elders spoke of was Saub. He was followed by Ahhana, Knu-'Karib, Kari-'Karup (= the young tiger), Narira, Kong-'Kteb, Arusib, Karesib, Tsobasib, Nawabib, Kausib, Abraham, Cornelius. (The change from Hottentot to European names designates conversion to Christianity.)
>
> I am the eldest son of Cornelius. Of the last four Chiefs, Nawabib lived to a very old age, Kausib died young, Abraham got so old (he was Kausib's son) that he had to resign the Chieftainship to my father, Cornelius. Cornelius died at Okambahe in 1910, aged about 60, and I succeeded him. I am now about 46 years old.

The Berg-Damaras of today divide themselves into two classes, namely: (a) the Omene or settled people, and (b) the Chau-Damaras (Hottentot = Dirty Damaras) or wild people.

The Omene, or settled people, are those living in villages, possessing sheep and goats and later on even cattle. They have managed, apparently from the days of Saub, despite the oppression of the Nama and Bantu peoples, to retain some semblance of tribal unity and identity. They were a conquered people, but under Saub appear to have emerged from utter slavery and through the ensuing generation gradually to have rehabilitated themselves to a certain extent.

These people call themselves Berg-Damaras now, or Omene, and strongly resent the Nama appellation of Chau-Damara, which is a term of utter contempt, the real translation of which decency forbids. The translation already given is merely relative. What Palgrave wrote of them in 1877 may with perfect truth be repeated today.

He writes (referring to their life at Okambahe):–

> They make gardens in which they grow mealies, pumpkins and tobacco. In 1875 they had a mile of the river-bed under cultivation and harvested 300 muids of wheat, the greater part of which was sold for more than 40 shillings a muid. For people who have been so recently reclaimed from a perfectly savage state the progress they are making is astonishing. They are a provident people, and are fast becoming rich in cattle and goats... They have not that love for cattle which distinguishes the Hereros and Namaqua, and from the fact that so long as they have been known they have made gardens it is assumed as probable that they were originally a agricultural people, like the Ovambos ... They are industrious and make good servants.

With this most people who know them will agree, but they are as a rule not nearly so intelligent as the Hereros, nor are they personally so clean and proud. The Herero s pride keeps him from committing theft, while the Berg-Damara will occasionally fail to resist temptation in regard to his neighbour's or his master's goods. As a manual labourer the Berg-Damara far excels the Herero, who, not unlike some Europeans, is inclined to be too proud to work. It is as cattle herd and caretaker that the Herero excels. He is probably the finest native cattle master in the world, and an indispensable assistant to every cattle farmer in Hereroland.

The Berg-Damara is the hewer of wood and drawer of water, and he rather likes it! With him the fates have made it constitutional.

It is not necessary to deal with Berg-Damara customs and laws, as they were not a ruling people at the time of the German annexation, and made no protection agreement. They speak of having made an agreement with Leutwein, but he does not mention it and there is no record of it.

Before giving a few historical details it is necessary to mention that the second class of Berg-Damara, probably four-fifths of the tribe, known as Chau-Damaras, was scattered throughout the Protectorate. They either lived as neighbours of or with the Bushmen in the inaccessible bush or mountains, or as servants and slaves of Hereros and Hottentots; they were content to exist and to labour merely for their food and the rude protection afforded them. Some of them intermixed with Bushmen, and the tall Bushmen of the Kaokoveld and the Hei-Kom Bushmen of the Grootfontein area are probably to a certain extent the result of an ancient intermingling of these two wild and aboriginal races.

The Berg-Damaras under Herero rule

Chief Judas Goresib says:–

> I remember the time when my father lived at Okambahe before the Germans came. We were under the Hereros, but. governed in our own way according to our laws and customs. The Herero Chiefs at Omarurn, Tjaherani, and his successor Manasse, ruled the whole area, and we were under their protection. We paid the Hereros no tribute or taxation, but as they were very rich and had plenty of cattle our poor people worked for them as herds and got food for their labour. We were on friendly terms with the Herero Chiefs and, although there was trouble at thes, we were recognised by them as a separate tribe and could always bring grievances and complaints to the notice of the Chiefs... I will say that, taking everything into consideration, we were better off under the Hereros than under the Germans who came later ...

The Chief's uncle and head councillor, a brother of the late Chief Cornelius, corroborates these views. His name is Gottlieb Goresib. He says:–

> We hated the Hereros, but they treated us even better than the Germans. They were enemies and conquered us after battles, but then they let us live in peace under our own Chief, and they never interfered with our laws and customs. They were a savage people like us, but they were more lenient than the Germans, and their Chiefs, Kamaherero, Zerua, and others, were just. Only our poor people who worked for the Hereros had a hard the. The rest of us were free and could move about the Hereros land, graze our cattle; rand live in peace. In those days we used to help the Hereros in their wars against the Hottentots. They were not our tribe, so we often disagreed, but our Chief and the Herero Chiefs always settled matters. The Hereros were not a warlike people, they loved their cattle and did not interfere much with their neighbours. I have many good friends among the Hereros, but no German was ever our friend..

It speaks well for the Herero people that quite voluntarily, and many years before German soldiers came to South-West Africa, they set aside for the Berg-Damaras the large reserve at Okambahe, probably over 200,000 acres in size, for the use as residences and grazing grounds of their weaker neighbours. Here the Omene class of Berg-Damara have lived since about 1866, and had up to 1910 enjoyed their own government under the Chiefs Abraham and Cornelius. (After the death of Cornelius the German Government refused to allow his heir, Judas, to rule the tribe, for reasons explained later.)

After the Germans came there was a tendency to scatter again, and today Omene are to be found all over the country. The majority of the Chau-Damara, or unsettled class of Berg-Damara, has disappeared. They were either serfs in the employ of Hottentots and Hereros, or they lived as has already been stated in the wilds, chiefly round the Omatako and Waterberg areas. When the "iron-cordon" of von Trotha was stretched from Gobabis to Waterberg, and the squeezing process in terms of his extermination order began, thousands of these wild people met the fate intended for the Hereros. How was the newly arrived German soldier in the field to distinguish between a Berg-Damara and a Herero? He had orders to kill all men, women and children without mercy. Thousands and thousands of Berg-Damara servants went with their Herero masters towards the desert and died there on the way. The same fate was meted out to the majority of those who were servants and serfs to the Witboois and other Hottentot clans.

After all, what did it matter? German policy wished to exterminate the native races and create a "new Germany," as Professor Bonn puts it. This goes far to explain how a minimum estimate of 30,000 Berg-Damaras (probably far too low) had by 1911 sank to 12,831, according to the official German census.[170] The Hereros certainly did not massacre them, and the Germans must explain what became of these people. When the Hereros went into rebellion the orders of their Chiefs placed Berg-Damaras on the list of those who were to be spared. The Germans were not so delicately discriminative.

Palgrave, in his Report (1877), writing of the reserve at Okambahe, says

> I told the Damaras (i.e., *Hereros*) that any plan they might have to submit to Your Excellency for their own protection and the government of their country must recognise the independence of these Berg-Damaras and provide for their settlement or it would meet with no favour, and they readily agreed with me that it should be the first duty of any one Your Excellency sent to them to select Berg-Damara locations, even if there was no immediate prospect of their being occupied.

The idea, therefore, that the Berg-Damaras were all slaves of the Hereros is quite erroneous. The Chau-Damaras, more by reason of their poverty than from any other cause, were certainly servants and, as such, serfs of their wealthy masters. Even in regard to these, however, there is this singular and somewhat extraordinary fact, that they could by becoming Hereros emancipate themselves, become adopted members of the "Eanda" and "Oruzu," and immediately acquire the dignity and status of a full-blooded Herero. Very few followed this means of gaining liberty. For this the reasons are probably two. The first is that, no matter how depraved or subjected a native may become, there remains, smouldering in the ashes of his self-respect, a glimmer of national pride. He hates the very idea of losing his nationality. It is one of the characteristics of the South African native that he is always deeply hurt if by any chance he is designated as belonging to another tribe. To call a Zulu a Kaffir, or a Kaffir a

---

[170] The official German reply to the Blue Book was particularly critical of the statistics given for Damara losses during the war. It claimed that the Blue Book bases its post-war Damara population figures on the German census of 1911 and argues that it, incorrectly, quotes the Damara population as 12,831. In fact it is claimed that the figure given in the 1911 census should be 19,581 as the figure given by the British excludes 6,750 Damara children. Unfortunately, as Brigitte Lau points out, it has not been possible, to date, to locate the 1911 census figures. Some initial research on the impact of the war on the Damara community has recently been carried out by Ivan Gaseb. German Colonial Office, *Treatment*, p. 45; Lau, 'Uncertain', p. 44, Gaseb, Ivan 'A historical hangover':The absence of Damara from accounts of the 1904-08 war', paper presented at the 'Public History: Forgotten History' Conference, University of Namibia, August, 2000.

Fingo, and *vice versa*, is to these people a grave insult. The same applies to Hereros and Berg-Damaras.

Before the born-Herero male could claim full membership of his family group and religious order certain things had to happen, viz., circumcision and the knocking out of the three lower front teeth and the inverted V-shaped filing of the upper teeth. Hereros who have gone through the ordeal tell, that there was nothing pleasant about it. There were no dentists with cocaine or gas, and the instruments used to remove the lower teeth were a piece of iron (like a cold chisel) and a rock, serving the purpose of a hammer. The filing was also done with a jagged piece of iron.

To the pain and inconvenience attendant on these steps preliminary to admission to the Herero "citizenship and full franchise" must be ascribed the second reason why so many Berg-Damara serfs decided to remain serfs.

The Berg-Damaras under German rule

When the Germans annexed the country in 1890 they did not worry much about the Berg-Damaras. Shut away behind the Erongo mountains and bordering on the waterless Namib desert, Okambahe lay outside the main routes to the interior It so happened, however, that when Major Leutwein landed at Swakopmund in 1894 the Chief Cornelius happened to be there with a wagon to fetch provisions, and met the Kaiser's representative. The following account of what transpired and what resulted therefrom is related in the words of old Gottlieb Goresib, the brother of Cornelius, who says:–

> Cornelius happened to be at Swakopmund on business when Major Leutwein handed. He invited Cornelius to come to Windhuk and see him there. Cornelius did so, and ordered his councillors, Mattheus, Lucas, Jonas, Joshua and Solomon to meet him at Karibib. They all went to Windhuk. There Leutwein got Cornelius to sign an agreement placing the Berg-Damaras under the German protection. Cornelius came back and explained matters. He said he had pointed out that the land belonged to the Hereros, and that we were really under their protection by verbal agreement with their Chiefs, and that he, Cornelius, could not sign such an agreement as Leutwein suggested. Leutwein said that he would fix up all disputes with the Hereros, and that he would protect us from them. Then the agreement was made. Cornelius had to agree to German protection and the posting of German troops at Okambahe. He also undertook to supply the Germans with all Berg – Damaras they required for labour on public roads, & c. In return for this Cornelius received 25*l*. and then 75*l*. in gold and silver. Leutwein. also promised him (a) that the Berg-Damaras would be ruled as an independent nation by their Chief and his successors, (b) that our laws and usages would be respected, (c) that all the scattered Berg-Damaras living under the Hottentot and Herero Chiefs would be collected and one big nation formed at Okambahe, (d) that a big piece of land extending from Okambahe north up to the Ugab River and beyond would be allotted to the Berg-Damara nation.
>
> These were the inducements we had, not a single one of these promises was ever fulfilled. On the contrary, our customs and laws were over-ruled, and the soldiers at Okambahe became the real governors. Cornelius hardly had any power. Our people were flogged and beaten, and there were no courts to which

they could go for justice. When Cornelius died in 1910 the Germans said they did not recognise him, and they had decided to have no more Chiefs or allow them to rule their people. They said Judas was no Chief and only an ordinary Berg-Damara like any one else in the tribe. We were all very angry and upset at this, and refused to recognise the five men whom the Germans themselves appointed to rule over us.[171] We did not know these people. We only knew the heir of our Chief. We protested, but the Germans merely laughed at us. Once before his death Cornelius and his council went to see the German Governor at Windhuk to complain of the ill-treatment and injustice and to point out that no promises made had ever been kept. The German Governor refused to see Cornelius. Some of the Governor's men saw Cornelius and chased him back to Okambahe. He got no hearing and no redress. That was in 1909, and Cornelius died the next year. After that we had to apologise and ask forgiveness for having sent a deputation to Windhuk. Then the Germans said we were to have no more Chiefs at all.

In the Herero rebellion we remained loyal to the Germans because we were entirely unarmed. The Germans had taken all our rifles.

After he had made, the agreement, Leutwein, towards the end of 1895, when he had dealt with the Khauas, Franzmann and Witbooi Hottentots, visited Omaruru and had a palaver with the Herero Chief, Manasse Tjaherani. Leutwein writes:–

About a day's march below Omaruru, on the river of the same name, is the Berg-Damara settlement of Okambahe. I declared (to Manasse) that the German Government required this on account of the labour supply available there.

The Chief, astonished at first that I should have had any knowledge of this settlement ... made over the place to the German Government.

Up to the present day (1905) Okambahe has remained directly under the German Government, and has remained loyal during the present rebellion.[xvi]

It seems curious that Leutwein's account should differ so much from the Berg-Damara version. Leutwein is silent as to agreements and promises. He does not make any reference to any payments, and in fact, throughout the rest of his work beyond a few passing remarks, he is strangely reticent in regard to the Berg-Damaras.

What the Berg-Damaras thought of this emancipation from "the Herero yoke" and the change to German control has already been stated. Before concluding the chapter a few further opinions may be recorded.

[xvi] (Page 109 in original) Leutwein desired to pose as the emancipator of the Berg-Damaras. In a footnote he adds:- "This knowledge I acquired shortly beforehand, as the result of a confidential visit to me in Windhuk of the Berg-DamaraChief, Cornelius. He had come to me solely with the object of begging me to free them from the Herero yoke, and for this reason I more readily took "As against this, continues Leutwein, "Missionary Irle ascribes the emancipation of the Berg-Damaras of Okambahe to the Mission, and says that it had taken place in 1870.

"However that may be, Cornelius did not, in any event, feel that he was free from the Hereros in 1895. If he had, he would not have come to me to Windhuk with that request to take advantage of the opportunity afforded."

---

[171] Judas, eldest son of Cornelius, was appointed leader on the arrival of invading South African forces on 18th June, 1915. However the leadership at Okombahe continued to be contested. Köhler, Oswin *A Study of Omaruru District*, Govt. Printer, Pretoria, 1959: p. 37

Simon Tsobasib (an old councillor of the tribe, and a cousin of the Chief's) states on oath:–

> I was born at Windhuk before the Berg-Damaras came to Okambahe. Old Abraham was the Chief then. I came with old Abraham to this district. and have lived here ever since under the Berg-Damara Chief at his werft. I know all about the agreement with the Germans under Leutwein. It is as stated by Gottlieb. The Germans did not keep any of their promises. They broke their word. They promised to let us keep our rifles, but after the agreement was signed they disarmed us all. No one could trust them or place any reliance on their word. I would a hundred thes prefer to live under and be governed by the Hereros in preference to the Germans. The Hereros had some mercy, and always respected our women, even in war-time; but that was never the case with the Germans. Neither one's self, one's wife, nor one's children were safe under the Germans. The German soldiers treated us like dogs, every German did; and our young daughters, even those who had not yet grown to womanhood, were not safe from them. They are a very bad people. We have not a bit of respect for them. We never saw such white people. Our natives were shocked at what they saw the Germans do. As for thrashings and floggings by the police, I don t know where to begin when I talk about that. We saw no courts, and had no place to go to for justice. The German police governed us. They were the Government; we knew of no other Government. They could do as they pleased.

Speaking of the taking over of Okambahe and the Berg-Damaras by the Germans, the Chief Judas Goresib states on oath:–

> The Germans established a police post at Okambahe. They immediately began to flog our people and put them into gaol. Our liberty was curtailed in every way, and they interfered in such a way that Cornelius soon had no more control over his people and was only like an ordinary Berg-Damara. The German police sergeant was really the chief, and he did what he liked and treated all very badly. We remained neutral during the Herero rebellion, as we had all been disarmed and were afraid of war. The traders had also robbed us, but we had not nearly so much stock as the Hereros. The German traders were very dishonest, and we lost by trading with them. They used simply to come and take cattle and sheep for debts. Still, we always tried to obey the Germans and to avoid trouble, as we knew they were very strong. We hated the Germans. Never have we had the truth from them, and they never kept their promises. We could not trust them. Of course, I have met good Germans, but they are few. When my father Cornelius died in 1910 the Council and men of the tribe looked to me as the lawful Chief according to our ancient customs and usage. I proclaimed myself as Chief in succession to my father, but the German Governor refused to recognise me and said I was not to be Chief, as they had decided to do away with all Chiefs. They said they would govern the Berg-Damaras themselves with the aid of a Council of Five. They said I could be a member of the Council. I said I was the heir of the Chief, and declined to be member of any Council. I said that if I were not Chief I was nothing at all. They then ignored me. They appointed as a Council the following: Joshua, Hosea. Kaleb, Alpheus and Titus. This Council was merely to give advice. The German police were the masters. The large majority, I may say the whole nation, was upset and annoyed at this. They had never heard of five councillors without a Chief. The five men who accepted positions on the Council were severely criticised, and the Berg-Damaras did not respect or recognise them. Even now they are thought nothing of ...

It was only after the British conquest of South-West Africa in 1915 that the Chief Judas Goresib was recognised and tranquillity and satisfaction restored.

The persons who have made the above statements are all of the Omene or settled class of Berg-Damara.

The wild Chau-Damaras' views are also of interest. The writer succeeded in finding a comparatively tame and intelligent member of this class, Jacob Dikasip, living at Ghaub, between Grootfontein and Tsumeb under the so-called Bushman Chief, Johannes Kruger. Johannes is a Bastard who in early days had hunted with Erickson, Green and others. Eventually he settled down near Grootfontein, and in 1896 was formally appointed by Governor Leutwein as Chief of the Bushman Berg-Damaras and other natives in the Grootfontein area. Jacob Dikasip said:–

> I have been under German masters and have been brutally treated. I show you the scars on my back from the floggings I have received (he was marked like a zebra)... I look old and worn, but it is from the bad treatment... See! all my teeth in front are knocked out. A German policeman Grossmann did that. I had been pulled down for a flogging, and it hurt so much that I tried to get away, whereupon I was hit on the mouth and lost my teeth. I don t wish to see Germans ruling this land again, they have been too unjust. They came into the country, and ever since they came natives have been killed and flogged and beaten nearly to death. We never got justice or fair treatment... We cannot agree with the Germans, we hate them. A German has no respect for our women. They have been known to come into the pontoks and chase married men out of their beds in order that they might sleep there. We protested, but what could we do? ... I have seen this sort of thing with my own eyes.

Innumerable statements of this nature can be produced, but once again the details are too indecent and revolting for publication.

The Berg-Damaras never at any the rebelled or gave any trouble to their German masters, yet it availed them nothing. The treatment meted out to them seems to have been exactly the same as that received by the other tribes.

CHAPTER TWENTY-TWO

THE POLICY OF GERMANY AFTER THE GREAT RISING OF THE NATIVES UP TO THE BRITISH CONQUEST OF SOUTH-WEST AFRICA IN 1915.

It will be convenient at this stage, while the recorded experiences of Hereros, Hottentots and Berg-Damaras are fresh in the memory, to deal with German native policy after these people had become conquered races, i.e., after 1906.

The large and powerful Ovambo peoples, the Bastards of Rehoboth. and the nomadic wild Bushmen did not actually come under German Government in the same sense as the other three races did. The Ovambos were too powerful and too suspicious of German agreements, particularly after what had happened at Hornkranz, to agree or to be forced to agree to the overtures of the Kaiser's plenipotentiaries.

The Bastard "Republic of Rehoboth" was recognised, and up to 1914 these people were left in comparative peace; while the Bushmen were placed more in the category of wild animals than of human beings, and were treated accordingly.

It is proposed to deal with the Ovambos, Bastards and Bushmen in subsequent. chapters.

The statue book is naturally the first source of information to which it is necessary to turn with a view to obtaining some idea of the native policy of any Colonial Government. It is necessary in doing so, however, to keep in mind this fact, that, under a system of Crown Government like that which obtained under the German regime in South-West Africa, the statutes and ordinances are not to be accepted strictly on their face value. They are, in relation to the natives, merely what the responsible administrative officials make them. Their use, abuse or interpretation are dependent solely on the whims and ideas of the persons administering them. It is characteristic of all these German laws that their elasticity seems unlimited, and that their interpretation and practical application seems to have depended more on local senthent and personal and official prejudice than on the strict tennets of legal procedure and the administration of justice.

In other words, therefore, these laws were not based on any intention to do justice and to secure right and equity for the native races. The fundamental principle underlying them was abnegation of right and a denial of the very elements of freedom. They were imposed by a superior power on weaker and subject races, not with a desire to strengthen and uplift, but. with the express intention of further weakening, subjecting or degrading.

A brief reference to these laws and to their essential provisions will bear out what is alleged. By 1914 (*i.e.*, from 1890) the following laws having special references to the native races had been promulgated.[172]

> (1) The law relating to jurisdiction for the purposes of punishments and disciplinary control, dated 23rd April 1896.

Up to July 1903 this was the only law dealing with natives except the one immediately following, which does not affect local administration of justice or control. enacted during the first 13 years of German rule.

> (2) The law prohibiting the taking of natives out of the Protectorate for exhibitions and other purposes, and forbidding natives from traveling over the borders without prior permission of the Governor. This law was promulgated on 30th November 1901.
> (3) The Ordinance of the Imperial Chancellor regulating legal procedure and jurisdiction in cases between Europeans and natives, dated 3rd July 1903.

This law, prescribing claims against natives by traders and others after the lapse of 12 months, is generally known as the Credit Ordinance. It is also the law by which the first civil courts, to which natives might have recourse, were constituted. Its "application" by the purely military men who, at the the, were District Magistrates, was one of the primary causes of the great Herero rising early in 1904.

After the Herero and Hottentot rising had been finally crushed and two-thirds of the total native population exterminated, the following laws were enacted in regard to the now landless and pauperised people, who were entirely at the mercy of their masters.

> (4) The Ordinance of the Imperial Governor concerning the obligation on all natives to bear passes, dated 18th August 1907.[173] This applied to all natives except children under seven years of age and the Bastards of Rehoboth.
> (5) The Ordinance dated 18th August 1907, entitled "Measures for control of the Natives." In terms of this no native could acquire land or an interest therein, nor could he own "riding animals" or cattle without the Governor's consent. Natives wandering about "without visible means of subsistence" were punishable as vagrants.

---

[172] For a more detailed discussion of the impact of this legislation see Harry Schwirck 'Violence, Race and the Law in German South West Africa, 1884-1914' (PhD Thesis, Cornell University, 1998).

[173] On the German pass laws see Krüger, Gesine 'A pass token in the archives. Traces of the history of every day life after the German Herero War', Paper presented at the Symposium 'Writing History, Identity and Society in Namibia, University of Hannover, May 1994.

(6) The Ordinance dated 18th August 1907, relating to work and labour contracts with natives, whereby all contracts with natives who were over 14 years of age were only of force after due registration with the local police.

The conditions of labour and reasons entitling the master or servant to terminate the contract before expiration of the fixed period are also set forth.

Then follow in 1911 two laws relating to recruiting of native labour in general and recruiting of Ovambos. they do not require any special notice.

(7) A law regulating the admission of sick natives to Government Hospitals and the collection of fees for treatment. The charge per diem was fixed at 1*s*. 6*d*. (inclusive). This was to be paid in the first instance by the native and, if he had nothing by his master, who was entitled subsequently to deduct.

(8) Ordinance dated 23rd May 1912, relating to the "mixed population" and providing rules for the reporting of births of children the father of which is not a native.

The aforegoing represent, in brief, what was done from 1890 to 1914, *i.e.*, during a period of just on a quarter of a century, by legal enactment with a view to "uplifting the native," providing for his "moral and material advancement" and preserving him from "slavery."

The conditions arising out of the application of these laws will be best understood when one allows the natives to describe, in their own language, the experiences and treatment they underwent.

Before doing so however it is necessary to understand the significance and underlying principles of a policy which brought these laws into being.

First it was intended, as Professor Bonn has put it, to create a "new Germany" in South-West Africa.

Secondly, and in order to help to achieve this object, the remaining sources of native labour supply essential for the development of farming and other enterprises had to be drawn on and tapped to their fullest possible extent. The now conquered and thoroughly subjected native had to "be made serviceable in the enjoyment by the white man of his former possessions" (Rohrbach).

It was this objective which obsessed the Berlin Government in 1907 when, on 8th August, authority was given to the Imperial Governor of South-West Africa to promulgate the three laws (4, 5 and 6) dealing with "native passes", "measures for control" and "work and labour contracts."

To all intents and purposes these laws had one main object, and they might easily have been consolidated into one enactment entitled "a law regulating the permanent and forced slavery of the natives of South-West Africa, with a view to ensuring their perpetual degradation into a class of pauperised labourers."

A brief reference to these laws will make this contention clear.

In the first place, the Pass Law provided that all natives over the age of seven years of age (except the Bastards of Rehoboth) should carry passes. This pass was a numbered metal badge which each native had to display prominently on his person. It was not intended that any native might merely by getting a permit, say, to travel or move about or reside in a certain area, thereby be exempted from labour. The intention was that every native, male and female, over the age of seven years was liable for and compellable to work. The law was designed to ensure control and by regulation to make certain that no single native evaded his or her obligations. It was prohibited to give a passless native any work, support or assistance, and the law gave to "every white person" the right summarily to arrest such native and hand him or her over at the nearest police station.

Measures for Control

After the rebellion was over (1906), the Hereros and Hottentots possessed nothing. A native who tried to evade work could only succeed by avoiding registration and remaining "passless." Yet he had to live. For fear that the possession of stock or animals might give him that independence which obviated the necessity for labour, the law prohibited him from owning cattle or horses without the consent of the Governor. The prohibition was intended really to cover future cases. At the time (August 1907) no native possessed anything, and the idea underlying the enactment was, by controlling future acquisition, to keep the native always under the necessity of working for his living. The inhumanity of this measure, apart from its injustice, is emphasised when one recollects what a blow such a prohibition must have been to the cattle-loving Hereros. What inducement was there to work? A native might slave for years and years, but the prospect of having in his old age a few cows and calves of his own, on which to subsist when labour was no longer possible, did not exist. His present was slavery and misery, his past was, to most, no doubt, a horrible nightmare of death and bloodshed, and his future he had no future.

Having ensured that no native would be able to acquire possessions from which to exist, the law goes on to state that natives wandering about "without visible means of subsistence" are punishable as "vagrants."

The third enactment. providing for the form and conditions of labour contracts. does not need special attention. Were this law based on principles of voluntary labour and not on slavery, it would probably be the one law for natives which calls for some commendation, but the underlying principle is a false and unjust one, and it taints and negatives what might otherwise have been a useful measure.

In regard to the punishment of the native, this was laid down and provided for in the 1896 law "relating to jurisdiction for the purposes of punishment and disciplinary control."

The most iniquitous aspect of this law is the fact that it was, to an almost incredible extent, administered not by courts of law or responsible Magistrates, but by the police themselves.

The law provided for the following punishments:–

(a) Corporal punishment.
(b) Fines.
(c) Imprisonment with hard labour.
(d) Imprisonment in chains.
(e) Death.

The powers under the law were vested in the Governor and by him delegated to the District Officials, who, in their turn, were authorised to sub-delegate to their subordinate officials (*unterstelten beamten*), *i.e*.. the police. Sentence of death and to imprisonment over six months were subject to confirmation by the Governor. Corporal punishment might be inflicted all at once or in two instalments. On no occasion were more than 25 lashes to be inflicted, and the second application of lashes could only take place after a lapse of at least two weeks. This would indicate that the maximum authorised was 50 lashes, but the law does not say so.

When power was delegated to the police by District Officials, the maximum of lashes was generally fixed at 15, but there is no definite ruling or provision, and no one (except the native) seemed to have run any risks owing to a miscount.

The vast majority of recorded punishments under this law are for such offences as "laziness," "negligence," "vagrancy," "insolence" and "disobedience," and the average punishment was 15 lashes, awarded *ex parte*, merely on complaint of the master, and inflicted under the police sergeant s supervision. The native was never tried, he was not called upon to plead, he was simply flogged and ordered to return to his master.

The procedure was something after this fashion:–

A letter was written by the employer to the local police or the nearest police post, to the effect that *the bearer* –

(a) was cheeky to me to-day, or
(b) refused to obey my orders, or
(c) is lazy and does not work well, or
(d) has lost one of my cows through negligence.

The unfortunate culprit takes the letter and delivers it. After reading it the Police sergeant orders the native to be stripped, and according to the sergeant s taste or his sense of the fitness of things 10, 12, 15, and even more lashes are inflicted with a heavy sjambok. The sergeant makes a note of the complaint and his sentence, and returns the native to his employer with a note, 15 lashes given, endorsed on the foot of the letter of complaint.

More serious cases such, *e.g.*, as the theft of a pair of boots, would come before the District Head. A case in point, *i.e.*, theft of an officer s boots, was actually according to the records punished with 12 months imprisonment and twice 25 lashes

Naturally, when a policeman could go up to 15 lashes, a Magistrate could not well impose less than 25 or double 25 (*i.e.*, 25 administered twice with an interval between)

Evidence of natives relative to their treatment after 1906 and up to 1914

Gerard Kamaheke (Headman of the Hereros at Windhuk) states on oath:–

> When the troubles were all over I was sent to work ... at Heusis After the rebellion, the Germans forced all natives to work, men, women and children over several years of age, and prohibited us from owning or acquiring any cattle or stock. No regard was given to family ties and relationship. Husbands, wives and their children were separated and sent to work in places far apart from one another. They never saw one another again, and I know of cases where husband and wife after many years of separation have again met one another for the first the after the British troops occupied our territory in 1915. My wife and I were separated for a year only, but mine was an exceptional case, I was more fortunate than most people. The treatment of our young people was very bad. The boys and younger men were often flogged, and our women and young girls were immorally assaulted and made to act as concubines of the Germans. Windhuk location is full of the bastard children of Germans by Herero women. I think that in my location at Windhuk the number of bastards exceeds that of the pure-bred Hereros.

Hosea Mungunda (Assistant Headman of Hereros at Windhuk and cousin of the Chief Kamaherero) states on oath:–

> When the railways and the harbour works were completed, we were sent out to towns and to farms to work. We were distributed and allocated to farmers whether we liked them or not. The farmers could do as they liked; many thrashed and ill-treated us and fed us badly. If we ran away the police gave 25 lashes or even 30, and then sent us back to the farmer. The courts gave us no protection, the evidence of a native was never accepted as against that of a white man. No regard was had for family relationship. Often a man was sent to one place to work, his wife to quite another district or farm, and the children elsewhere. All children over seven years had to work. And were taken by force from the parents and sent away to work. Many men never saw their wives again, many wives lost their husbands, and the children often disappeared for ever. This state of affairs continued right up to the time of the British occupation of this country in 1915. It is only since the British are here that many families have been reunited after long years of separation. I know of men who only recently have met their wives for the first the in six or seven years. We were prohibited from acquiring cattle. No man could select his own master, no man got help or protection from the German police, all we could expect was to be called liars and to receive lashes.

Richard Kainazo (Herero, of Omaruru) states on oath:–

In 1905 the Germans made me chief police-boy at Omarurn to do the floggings. That was the sole work of the chief police-boy. Alfred Katsimune[174] was appointed my assistant. The custom was for the sergeant-in-charge of the police to decide on all complaints made by or against natives. If the charge was made by a German master and it was a very serious charge, such as theft, the sergeant would send the natives accused to the District Chief (*Bezirksamtmann*) for trial. Petty cases were dealt with summarily by the sergeant merely on verbal information by the white master. For instance, if a German brought his native servant to the sergeant and said the native had been idle or negligent or cheeky, the sergeant would immediately order me to take the native and prepare him for flogging. I and my assistant had then to take the native to the kraal near the police-station, strip him and make him lie over a tub or a box. We generally used a tub. The sergeant would then come along and in his presence and that of the German master I was ordered to give the native 15, 20, or 25 lashes with a heavy sjambok. The sergeant counted and generally told me when to stop beating. We nearly always kept on beating until the blood began to flow. I often had to beat men whom I knew well; I used to feel sorry for them and tried to hit as lightly as possible. When the sergeant noticed this he would swear at me and promise me 25 lashes for myself if I did not do my duty. Therefore I had to hit hard. These German police sergeants were nearly all ex-soldiers who had helped General von Trotha to exterminate our nation, and they had no mercy for us. They hated the Hereros. I remained in service as a police-boy only because it gave me some sort of protection. I was not treated like the rest of our natives as I had to help the German police.

Very often innocent people were badly flogged in this way merely to satisfy the spite of their masters. When a complaint was made by a white man the native was not allowed to speak or to give any evidence. We natives were always told that we did not know what was meant by truth, and that a white man could never lie. All cases which the police sergeant sent to the District Chief, the serious cases such as theft or assault, were punished with greater severity than these which came before the sergeant. But even before the District Chief the native was not allowed to give evidence or bring his friends to give evidence which might contradict what the white man said. A white man was always believed, and the native told that he had no defence. The District Chief generally gave 25 lashes as a minimum, plus terms of imprisonment. In many cases, however, 30 lashes and even 75 lashes were imposed, and in such cases I had to give them in instalments of 25 at certain intervals of not less than 14 days. Many prisoners were also kept in heavy chains fastened to the walls of their cells. Most prisoners were placed in chains. Although a white man was always believed, a native s complaint was never accepted by the police. I have seen dozens of natives who had been badly flogged by their own masters, and who came to complain of their treatment, kicked away and ordered to go back at once and resume work. In fact, some of the complainants were flogged over again by the police for the offence of leaving their master s farm (which they had to do to complain) without his permission. This was done after the Herero rebellion. and it grew worse and worse. After a while masters did not bring their native servants in to the police for flogging; they were allowed by the German authorities to flog their natives as they wished, and a complaint from a native was laughed at, and then my chief work was to flog those natives who had come in to report that their masters had flogged them. The

---

[174] Became a teacher and was reported, in 1957, to be aged 68 and one of the six members of the Board responsible for Otjohorongo Reserve (Köhler 1959c: 79)

result of all this was that our people lost heart and daily grew more despondent. The Herero loves cattle. Our forefathers possessed great herds of cattle; even when I was a boy I remember herds so great that we could not say how many there were. The Germans took all our cattle after the rebellion, and prohibited us from owning or purchasing cattle. So we had nothing to work for except our food, and nothing to look forward to except more ill-treatment.

Alfred Katsimune (Herero, of Omarurn) states on oath:–

When the Herero rebellion was over I was appointed a police-boy under the Germans. My chief work was to flog natives under orders from the German police. Afterwards Jacob Barnabus took my place, and he was succeeded by Heinrich Tjaherani and then Richard Kainazo. I was made assistant. The Germans gave as their reason the fact that neither Jacob nor I were strong enough in the arms, and that we could therefore not hit hard enough. We were stationed at Omarurn. The amount of flogging that went on was terrible. Hardly a day passed without flogging taking place of local natives or natives sent in from the farms. The number of lashes given varied from 15 to 25 at a the. Some natives got two or even three instalments of 25 each, given at intervals of two to three weeks. We used a heavy giraffe-hide sjambok, which sometimes drew blood at the first stroke; generally speaking, however, it took four to five strokes to draw blood. One day I was ordered to flog a middle-aged Berg-Damara, whose master complained to the police that he had been impertinent. I was ordered to give him 25 lashes. In the course of the thrashing the sjambok curled round his thigh and injured his private parts. No medical treatment was given to him. He went back to his hut and died a few days afterwards. There was no inquiry made after his death. The body was simply buried and nothing more said about it. His name was Narivatjub. On another occasion in Omarurn a native named Markus (a Herero) was convicted of having stolen a goat. He was sentenced to a term of imprisonment in chains and ordered, in addition, to receive 25 lashes. The sjambok cut his body very badly, and he bled a good deal. After punishment the customary sack garment was placed on him and he was put into chains. The next day he was set to work with a convict gang in the Government garden at Omaruru. Markus was sore, and his body was so cut that he was hardly able to move, let alone work. Police sergeant Reinhard, of the German police, was superintending the work. I was present. Reinhard told Markus to work more diligently and to hurry. He could not do so, and the police sergeant went up to him and cuffed and kicked him. He fell down to the ground and screamed with pain. We went and looked at him and found that his private parts had been badly hurt, and that there was, a strong emission of blood. The other convicts were ordered to carry him back to the cells. No doctor was sent for, and the injured native received no aid or attention. That afternoon and all night his screams could be heard even at the location, which is several hundred yards away. The next morning he died, and was buried by the convicts. No inquiry was made, and the police sergeant was not punished.

Jacob Barnabus Katjakundu (Herero, of Omaruru) states on oath:–

Shortly after the rebellion I was made a warder and put in charge of the native convicts in Omaruru gaol. Heinrich Tjaherani was in charge of the flogging work, and his assistant was Alfred Katsimune, Richard Kainazo succeeded Heinrich. We were all under a German police sergeant. After a native convict had received his flogging he was sent to the gaol, where it was my duty to put his chains on. No convicted native prisoner (male) was ever without chains. The women were not chained as a rule, though in a few cases this was done. I remember we had one chained by the neck for about two weeks once, but she made such an ado about it that we eventually took the chains off.

In addition to the ordinary handcuffed and wristlets. there were three other kinds of chains used in the gaol. I will try to describe them.

No 1. – *Ankle and neck chains.* Iron bands or rings were fastened round the ankles. The bands or rings were joined by a short chain about 18 inches long, and attached to the middle of this chain was another chain which joined on to an iron collar round the prisoner's neck. All convicts wore these chains, and had to work in them. The cross chain between the legs made it necessary for the wearer to straddle rather than walk. He also had to regulate his stride carefully. If he stepped out too far the rings hurt his bare ankles, and if he merely shuffled he ran the risk of tripping himself over the chain. As it was, the iron rungs used to cut and chafe the bare skin, and what with flies and dirt the cut parts used to become festering sores. Many convicts got so bad that they were eventually quite unable to walk. They used to pick up dirty pieces of rag and sacking and thrust them between their legs and the rings. Such prisoners were never medically treated by tine Germans, and if they got too bad we took off the chains until they were well enough to wear them again. Often when working with a gang out in the veld getting wood or stones, I used, out of pity, if I had the keys, to unlock the chains.

No. 2.- *The neck chain.* These chains were made up of neck rings to which were attached chains about 5 to 6 feet long. They were put on two or more prisoners at a the, and in that way linked together by the neck collars; the larger gangs were sent out to work generally inn batches of front four to six. These chains were worn in addition to those I have already described, and were only for outside work. They were taken off when the day s work was over, before locking the convicts up. They were also used by the police on the outside posts for the purpose of securing two or more prisoners on a journey to town by road or train. In addition, handcuffs were also used in such cases. If a single prisoner were brought in by the police he was handcuffed and made to trot in front of the horses. Often he would be tied to the saddle by a rope fixed round his neck. If he got tired he was urged on with a sjambok.

No. 3. The third kind of chain used was the rigid arm bar and the leg bar. They were never used at the same the, and were only put on prisoners or convicts who had attempted to escape from custody or who had been guilty of stock theft or some offence more serious than disobedience, laziness, or impertinence. This chain consisted of a heavy iron bar about 18 inches long with rings at each end. In the case of the arm bar, it was placed across the wrists and the rings locked; two heavy anklets were fixed on the legs. And from each anklet a heavy chain was fastened on the middle of the bar. When wearing this chain, in addition to the discomfort to his legs, the prisoner, owing to the weight of the iron cross-bar, was compelled to let his arms hang down as far as possible, and he could not possibly use his hands so as to touch his face, as the lower chains were too short for that. When lying down he was compelled to remain on his back. He could not lie either on his sides or his stomach. A similar chain was the leg bar chain, only in this case the bar was fixed on the ankles instead of the wrists and the connecting chain fastened to a ring in the cell wall. While wearing this the prisoner could not walk at all or move about. He had either to remain seated with his face to the wall, or, if he wished to rest, to he prone on his back. He could also turn over on his stomach, but could not lie on his side or cross his legs. If after a severe flogging, a convict were put in these chains, it was agony and torture to him, as he would be compelled always to lie on his stomach until his back healed. It was only in exceptional cases though that this was done.

In their bare cells, which were filthy and full of vermin of all sorts, the prisoners were herded together. They got no blankets, and had to sleep in their sack uniform on the cold stone floors even throughout the winter. No clothing was given to them. A convict was stripped naked on admission, and an empty sack (a grain bag) in which a slit had been made for his head to pass through and two holes cut for the arms was all he was allowed to wear. Otherwise he was quite naked. These sacks are rough and coarse and used to chafe and hurt many prisoners very much.

I may say that if a convict had a private blanket with him when he was convicted he was allowed to keep it and sleep in it in gaol, but the German Government never gave convicts any such luxuries. Many persons died in gaol of sickness and exposure to cold. When the war began in 1914, the former ration of meal which prisoners had received was stopped, and the convicts in the gaols were in a state of starvation. They got very thin, and several died I think because they had no nourishing food. All that the prisoners got were wild roots, which the German Government made them collect in the veld, or which were collected in Waterberg or elsewhere and sent to the Government. This wild root is something like a sweet potato and is called by us *Ovipeva*, and the prisoners did not get too much of that either. At one time I used to do the flogging of natives, but the Germans said I was not strong enough in the arms and could not hit hard enough. So they made me a warder, and Heinrich was made to do the flogging, as he is very big and strong. The flogging was done with a giraffe hide sjambok about 4 feet long. The average punishment was from 15 to 25 lashes. At one time 30 lashes were given, but it was found to be too much, and the number was reduced to 23. I have seen many prisoners get twice 25 and even three times 25. In such a case the lashes would be given in instalments of 25 once every two or three weeks, as soon as the old wounds healed. After about four or five blows the sjambok would cut the skin and blood would flow. I have seen a good hard sjambok cut the skin to ribbons, and often at the first blow blood would be drawn if the blow were well directed. The prisoner was generally held down over a barrel and beaten on the buttocks and hips. The large majority of the natives who were thus flogged were accused by their masters of disobedience, laziness, or impertinence. In such cases the boy would be sent into the police station with a note from the master saying that "Bearer has been cheeky," or "is lazy," or "has not done what I told him to do." On receipt of the note the police would at once order the native to be stripped and flogged. He was never asked for an explanation or his version. If he dared to open his mouth he was told to be silent, and if he denied his guilt be was told that his master could not lie, and often if a boy protested his innocence too much, the police gave him some extra lashes for being impertinent.

This sort of thing did not happen once or twice, but was the custom. It happened every day, and from week to week and month to month. It was bad before the Herero rebellion and twice as bad afterwards, and it gradually grew worse until 1914-1915, when the British troops made war. During the war things were very bad until the British entered the country and conquered it.

Willem Christian (son of the last Hottentot Chief of the Bondelswartz) states on oath:–

When the war broke out in 1914 the Germans did not trust us. They thought we would rise and help the English. So they collected our tribe and sent us to Tsumeb, in the extreme north of this country. We lost all our small stock, and when the

British troops released us at Tsumeb we had again been reduced to poverty. The British sent us back to our place at Warmbad and had to feed us to keep us alive. The British Government collected some stock for us and distributed it, but we have not yet recovered half of what we originally possessed in 1914. We cannot say what the Germans did with our stock. They must have died of exposure and disease, and some were slaughtered by the invading troops. The German Government was very severe and harsh. We got no protection from the law. We were forced to work for harsh masters who ill-treated us, and for whom we would not willingly work. We were not allowed to select our own masters. We were simply ordered to go and work for a man. If we did not go or tried to get permission to work for a more humane master, the only reply was a kicking or flogging. Our masters had the right to flog us; the police could flog us if our masters complained. Cases like this never came to court. The police dealt with such matters summarily. If our masters did not pay us for our work, or if they underfed us or ill-treated us and we complained, we got no consideration. We were not believed, and any excuse or explanation was accepted from a white man. If we left our masters farms to complain to the authorities, the result was that we were either flogged and sent back to the master or we were imprisoned for desertion. Many people died in prison.

The Berg-Damara Chief Councillor, *Gottlieb Goresib* (brother of the Chief Cornelius and uncle of the present Chief) states on oath:–

Up to the time the British came here in 1915 we had a hard life under the Germans. We had no protection for our lives and property. We had no courts to which to go for redress, we were not allowed to speak; the only people we saw were police sergeants, who thrashed and ill-treated our people all the time, just as if there was a war between us. It never looked like peace. They were always like savage roaring lions. We trembled in their presence, and they spoke to us as if we were lower than dogs. We were too afraid to open our mouths. That was the way the police treated us. We never came into contact with the other officials except when Major Leutwein or a big man occasionally visited our place.

Daniel Esma Dixon states on oath:–

German masters practically had power of life and death over their native servants. They could thrash and ill-use them as they pleased. If the native complained to the police he got another thrashing and was sent back to his master. No native was allowed to leave a master s service unless and until the master consented to release him. If he ran away the police went after him, thrashed him, and returned him to his master, where he generally received another thrashing. I will give one instance as an example.(one of many that I know of). It occurred at Usakos in 1909. I was then living for a while in the house of a German named Trautemann. On a certain Monday morning the native boy did not come to his work. After breakfast, Trautemann took a sjambok and went to the native s hut. The native was lying down and said he felt very ill and that was why he had not come to work. Trautemann said that he was only shamming sick and that he was a liar. The native persisted. He looked ill and I was inclined to believe him. Trautemann however refused to do so and ordered the native to come out of the hut. As he did so Trautemann set on him and gave him a severe flogging with the sjambok. The boy made no resistance and did not attempt to run away. Trautemann then ordered the boy to follow him to the police station. He did so. I accompanied them, as I was curious to see what would happen next. *Feld-webel* Laueras was the man in charge of the police. Trantemann complained that the native boy was lazy and shamming sick. The boy was asked no questions, but was promptly stripped and laid on his stomach over a cement cask and given 25 lashes with a heavy sjambok by order of Laueras. He was in a state of collapse, but was ordered to start work at once and promised another 25 if there was the slightest indication of laziness. The boy staggered away and tried to work, but I could see that he was very ill. He gradually got worse and shortly afterwards collapsed altogether and was sent to the hospital. That was the last we saw of him. This is the way the natives were treated all along.

The aforegoing statements, made on oath in the course of the past four months, will give some faint idea of the reign of terror which existed amongst the natives of South-West Africa. Instances of cruelty, injustice, and barbarism might be multiplied almost indefinitely. Instances of gross and bestial conduct, which for sheer depravity and immorality are well-night unbelievable, are also contained in the files of affidavits, but they are hardly fit for publication. The extracts reproduced have been selected almost at random from the affidavits of natives of all races throughout the country.

This state of affairs continued right, up to the occupation of South-West Africa by the British troops under General Botha, and the records of the Special Criminal Court appointed under the British regime will indicate that the German settlers, not quite appreciating that the old order had changed, took some time to grasp the fact that under British rule wholesale shootings and floggings of natives and inhuman brutality towards their defenceless servants would not for one moment be tolerated.[175]

The available German records indicate that the complaints of the native population as to merciless flogging for trivial offences are quite correct.

From the Returns of Crimes and Offences Committed and Punishments and Penalties inflicted during the period 1st January 1913 to 31st March 1914, filed at Windhuk (German Records, F.V.K.1, 3-18), details may be gleaned which throw a lurid light on the system of justice practised by the Germans.[176] Further details will appear in the chapter dealing with the native as an accused person (Chapter 1, Part II.). For present purposes it is sufficient to state

---

[175] A selection of these cases were published as 'Papers relating to Certain Trials in German South West Africa', HMSO, London, 1916, cd. 8371.

[176] An English summary of German records (FVK I, 3-18) of 'Crimes & Punishment & Penalties' for the period 1st January, 1913 to 31st March, 1914 can be found in the National Archives of Namibia (A41). It contains lists of individual crime and punishment for each district in the Police Zone. These have clearly been used to produce the statistics listed here. For example four typical entries from the records for Bethany District show that on 1st September, 1913 Friederika, K.K.F. was given '14 days in chains' for 'Disobedience and refusal to work'. On the 4th September three punishments were given. Adam, K.K. was sentenced to two years in chains and fifty lashes for 'Bodily harm', Hakeio, H.M was to serve six months in prison with hard labour and have 15 strokes with the cane (the cane was used on 'juveniles') and Rebecka, Ho. F was to spend two weeks in chains for also having been 'disobedient and refusing to work'.

That the total number of native convictions in the whole Protectorate front 1st January 1913 to 31st March 1914 was 4,356. Of these, 4,039 were males and 317 females.[177] The punishments include –

(a) 841 sentences of imprisonment with hard labour, with or without lashes.
(b) 507 sentences of imprisonment in chains, with or without lashes.
(c) 2,787 sentences to lashes (including also, in some cases, either (a) or (b) above), whereby 46,719 lashes were inflicted. This is equivalent to an average of about 17 lashes per punishment.
(d) 257 sentences to strokes with a cane, whereby 3,408 strokes were inflicted, averaging 13 strokes per punishment.

Lashes were invariably inflicted for such crimes as desertion, negligence, vagrancy, disobedience, and insolence. Strokes with a cane were inflicted on Juvenile offenders.

It is interesting to see how the bulk of the total of 4,356 convictions is made up. There were

894 for desertion.
826 for negligence.
429 for vagrancy.
414 for disobedience.
256 for insolence.
198 for contravening Pass laws.
150 for laziness.
―――――
3,167

These offences therefore constitute nearly three-fourths of the total. Under the compulsory labour system it is only natural that men who were forced to work for masters whom they did not like, and who treated them with harshness and brutality, were tempted at times to desert or to be disobedient. Often such offences arose solely out of the inability of the natives to understand the orders of their German-speaking masters. In regard to desertion, which, as will be observed, heads the list of crimes, the report of the officer in control of native affairs, the Imperial German Native Commissioner at Windhuk, filed with the records, is significant.

―――――
[177] In the period from its first session on 28th September, 1915 up to January, 1918 (when the Blue Book was compiled) the Special Criminal Court that was established by the Union of South Africa following the surrender of German forces in Namibia on 9th July, 1915, heard 158 cases. Of these 61 cases are referred to directly in Part 2 of the Blue Book and eighty-five of those directly accused in these cases are referred to. Details of the relevant cases can be found in Storage Units SCC1-10. National Archives of Namibia, Finding Aid, Special Criminal Court. Administrator 'Report of the Administrator of SWA, 9 July 1915-31 March 1916. A 272. Bk. 1.

Dealing with the period already referred to, he says:–

> Where desertion is an everyday occurrence, such has to be ascribed chiefly to ill-treatment, the result of too little or bad food, the payment of wages in goods instead of cash, the deduction of part of the wages, and too long working hours. A further reason for desertion by women and children is to be ascribed to failure to treat them with proper care.

But it did not avail the unfortunate native charged with desertion to advance such pleas. He was dealt with in 99 cases out of a hundred "by summary procedure."

The police sergeants gave him his lashes, and he was hurried back to work for the master whose ill-treatment had made service unbearable.

When considering this list of floggings amid punishments it must be borne in mind that it represents probably only a fraction of the thrashings actually meted out. Under the German system there grew up the custom of *Väterliche Züchtigung*, or paternal chastisement.[178] The German master was regarded as being *in loco parentis*[179] to the childlike native, and could thrash him whenever he wished and for any reason whatsoever without risk of punishment for assault. It was only when the native died or was sent to hospital as a result of such paternal chastisement that questions might be asked; even then no serious notice was taken as a rule. As Leutwein put it:–

> Beating to death was not regarded as murder; but the natives were unable to understand such legal subtleties.

If, after what he considered was an unmerited paternal chastisement, the angry native dragged his aching bones to the nearest police station to report, he generally got lashes at once for "desertion" and more paternal chastisement on his return to his master's farm.

The records given are those compiled shortly before the outbreak of war in 1914. So that up to that time the German system had in no way been altered or modified.

It is clear too, from a perusal of the Government files, that the German authorities, from 1910 onwards, were in a constant state of nervous apprehension. They were always expecting another native rising.

---

[178] The 'right' rested on a Supreme Court Judgement which stated "... from a mental and moral point of view the native on the average are not to be ranked higher than children at home who require to be educated. It is not feasible for the master forthwith to apply to the State punitive authorities in every case of shortcoming, insubordination, and disobedience, quite apart from the fact that the great distances often make it quite impossible. When admonition and reprimand, as is often the case, fail, then it must be permissible to resort to the energetic educative means of chastisement. A powerful box in the ears or a good whack across the back or buttocks often has a better effect than much talk." 'Judgement in Supreme Court, Windhoek, 26th January, 1911 re. the rights of Masters to inflict Corporal Punishment upon Native Servants' translated from Süd-West Bote, No. 24 & 25, 1911

[179] 'In place of a parent'

On 31st May 1912, Governor Seitz addressed the following secret circular to his Magistrates:–

The Imperial Governor of G.S.W.A. Windhuk,   31st May 1912

To all Magistrates
Secret and Personal.

Within recent weeks I have received information from various quarters to the effect that a desperate feeling is becoming prevalent of late amongst the natives in certain areas of the country.

The reason which is unanimously given for this fact is that brutal excesses of Europeans against natives are alarmingly on the increase it is much to be regretted in this connection that even police officials have become guilty of such offences in a few cases and that such offences do not find the punishment before the courts of law which they ought to receive according to the sense of justice of the natives.

In consequence thereof the natives are supposed to despair of the impartiality of our jurisdiction and to be driven into a blind hatred of every timing that is white. And as a final result would resort to self-help, that is another native rising.

It is quite evident that such feelings of hatred amongst the natives, if amelioration of their lot is not energetically provided for, must. lead within a short space of the to a renewed and desperate native rising, and consequently to the economic ruin of the country.

It is therefore in the interests of the whole European population that persons who rage in mad brutality against the natives, and who consider their white skin a charter of indemnity from punishment for the most brutal crimes, be rendered innocuous by all possible means.

Because a people, who make a claim to be regarded as a dominant, race. must first of all keep clean their own ranks.

If the crimes committed by Europeans against natives do not find punishment at all, or no sufficient punishment, it will become impossible in future to act with that severity in the cases of crimes committed by natives against Europeans, which is imperative in the general interest.

I have no influence on the jurisdiction as far as Europeans are concerned. but I shall, as far as that is possible, take care by administrative measures that the doubtlessly existing critical conditions are counteracted.

Above all things I intend to order, as such cases arise, that such Europeans who persist in ill-treating their native servants in a brutal manner shall no longer be supplied with native labour.

However. an effectual alteration will only be possible if the white population itself who, as far as I feel. condemns such brutalities of rough elements to the utmost, does not leave such individuals, who are a danger to the common weal, in any doubt about its attitude on the question, and actively co-operates to prevent such crimes or to bring them to justice in cases where they have occurred.

And as I am convinced that it will be possible for the District Councils to influence their co-citizens in this respect, I request that you will inform the District Councils in the strictest confidence of the contents of this communication at their next meeting.

I trust that with the assistance of the European population it will be possible to create conditions which will reinstate in the natives a confidence that they will find protection from the Europeans against the brutal excesses of a few individuals. You are requested to confirm the receipt of this communication.

    Seitz

This letter provides a striking commentary on the partiality and injustice of the German courts, And on the feebleness and futility of German native policy.

All the responsible Governor of the Protectorate could apparently do was to record the fact that he will punish "Europeans who continually commit brutal offences against natives" ... by taking care that they "are no longer supplied with natives as labourers."

Obnoxious and unjust laws are not amended; new and very necessary laws are not introduced; the native is thrashed and harshly ill-treated, and all that his brutal task-master receives as punishment is the threat that if he continues to do so he will be allowed no more native labourers from the State.

CHAPTER TWENTY-THREE

THE BASTARDS OF REHOBOTH

Since 1870 there has lived in the territory of Rehoboth a tribe of coloured people, persons of mixed blood (the result mainly of early intermingling at the Cape between the Dutch settlers and their Hottentot servants) who call themselves the "Bastard Nation." A large number of them are like Europeans in physical appearance except for a darker shade of colour, while others indicate unmistakably the presence of a strong Hottentot strain. A very small percentage is practically White, and outside of Rehoboth would probably be taken for pure-bred Europeans.

The language of these people is "Afrikaans," the colloquial Dutch of the Cape; they are all Christians, and their sole occupation appears to be pastoral farming.

Rehoboth is, taken all round, the finest and most suitable area in the whole of the South-West Protectorate for farming in large and small stock, and many Bastards have become very wealthy, while there are very few families who are entirely without stock of some kind.

When in 1882 Willem Jordaan and his party of Cape and Transvaal farmers moved into the country through Grootfontein, their intention was to travel down southwards to Rehoboth and to establish their new republic there. Jordaan went so far as to approach the Swartbooi Chief at Otjitambi within a view to obtaining a cession from him of the former tribal land of the Swartboois at Rehoboth.[180] Jordaan was too late, however, as the Bastards had already, over 12 years previously, purchased the area from Abraham Swartbooi. The purchase price was 100 horses at 25*l*. each and 5 wagons at 50*l*. each.

Notwithstanding this, Jordaan intended to move through Damaraland and, if necessary, oust the Bastards by force of arms. He and his party remained in the vicinity of Otjitambi and Outjo for nearly two years. waiting for a favourable opportunity. But this did not present itself. The Bastards had heard of his intentions and made representations to the Germans and to Kamaharero, in which they warned the Herero Chief of the grave danger of a Boer Republic in his immediate neighbourhood. Kamaharero thereupon notified Jordaan that he would under no circumstances allow a trek southwards through Damaraland. Seeing that further waiting was only a waste of the, Jordaan, in 1884, moved back to Grootfontein, purchased that area from the Ovambo Chief, and

---

[180] Otjitambi was the site where the Swartbooi community settled for a while in the second half of the nineteenth century

established there his Republic of Upingtonia.[181] As has already been related, the murder of Jordaan in 1886 brought about the collapse of the Republic and the dispersal of the burghers. After Jordaan had decided to return north, the Bastards experienced no further trouble. and they were allowed to settle down and live quietly in their territory. It was only in 1915 that they first tasted an impression of German power. To this reference will be made further on. There appears to have been a bitter antagonism in the Cape, in the early days, between the Dutch frontier farmers and these coloured people, who, bearing Dutch names, speaking the Dutch language, and having in their veins varying proportions of Dutch blood, were regarded by the white farmers as "Basters" (Bastards), and as such legally and socially on the same level and political plane as the aboriginal native.

Adversity and ostracism gradually drew the Bastard families together into little groups, the groups eventually joined up, and after a time, under the guidance of public-spirited and intelligent leaders, the foundations of a sort of tribal cohesion and control were laid. They moved away as far as possible to the outlying borders of the Cape Colony and settled down in villages at De Tuin, Pella, and other places on Crown lands on the frontier, and endeavoured to work out their own destiny.

Their ideals were frustrated in 1865 by the passing of the Land Beacons Act, an enactment of the Cape Parliament, whereby the occupiers of land were compelled to prove their title to land on which they lived, and Crown lands were thrown open for sale or lease to farmers.

In terms of this law the Bastards of De Tuin applied to the Government to purchase a large farm for themselves. In terms of the law, the application was gazetted and all persons having objection were called upon to lodge objections at the office of the Civil Commissioner of Calvinia before a certain date. On the day fixed the applicants would be heard, in reply to any objections raised.

News of the application was received with open and, one must say, somewhat ungenerous and narrow-minded hostility by the European farmers. At the appointed meeting the protesting farmers were present in a body, and before the Bastards could say a word the spokesman of the opposition made a bitter and unfounded attack on the applicants and concluded by saying that if the farm were sold to the Bastards they would become a curse to the country.

The Bastards left the meeting in a body and returned to their homes without waiting for a decision.

Later on they sent a deputation to Cape Town, but the Government, overawed by the agitations and political power of their opponents, was apparently not able to give any redress, and the deputation returned in disappointment.

It was then decided to migrate from the Cape and to seek fresh fields and pastures new.

This decision was precipitated by the depredations of bands of Korannas and marauding Bushmen, who at that time were a great source of annoyance

---

[181] For more on Upingtonia see: Gordon, *Bushman Myth*, pp. 40 - 42.

and danger and from whom the Bastards, living as it were on the outer edge of civilisation, had protection either from the Cape Government or from their inimically disposed neighbours.

In 1868 two leaders, Hermanus van Wyk and Giel Diergaardt, were sent over Orange River to spy out the land in the north. As a result of their investigations a general exodus from the Cape began in 1869. The main body, under Hermanus van Wyk, found its way to Rehoboth, which was acquired by purchase from the Hottentot Chief of the Swartboois. Another small party settled at Gabis, north of Warmbad, while a third and smaller band under the leadership of Klaas Swartz (or Swart) settled at Grootfontein South in the Protectorate. Another settlement of the so-called Vilander Bastards was formed at Rietfontein in the Kalihari, which is, however, in British territory, and needs no attention in this report.

In 1868, during a temporary halt of the trekkers near Warmbad, a provisional constitution was framed and approved of. It was merely a makeshift, and once the tribe (or "Nation," as they love to call themselves) had settled at Rehoboth. a new and permanent constitution was drawn up and approved of by the burghers.

The system of government created in this constitution was democratic and on republican lines. The head of the tribe, known as the Chief or Captain ("Kaptein"), was elected by all who held full burgher rights, and he retained the office for life. Administrative power was vested in the Chief and his elected Council, while all legislative functions vested in the "Volksraad" or elected Parliament. All Bastards and all persons who had married into Bastard families might become burghers. The franchise was enjoyed by burghers who paid taxes. A stranger was only admitted to citizenship after six months of probationary residence and circulation of notice of his application, in order that any objections might be lodged. After acceptance he was installed as a burgher in the presence of the Chief s Council and the Chairman of the Volksraad. The Chief and executive officials did not take an oath of office, but by a "stroke of the hand" (hand-slag) promised to do their utmost for the State and to suppress personal interests which might be detrimental to the general welfare.

By 1874 a complete code of laws and regulations had been framed. This code, a written one, gives very little cause for criticism and indicates that the framers were actuated by worthy ideals, by a desire to promote the general morality and welfare of their people and a determination to administer justice impartially.

The majority of the laws are, as may be supposed, modelled on the Roman-Dutch and Statute law principles of the Cape. There are others which are, however, quite original and not unworthy of notice by more enlightened and advanced communities. Space does not allow an exhaustive reference to these laws, but one may be quoted as an example:–

> D. Marriage and Divorce: (1) If a husband leaves his wife without reason, his goods shall be confiscated and given to his wife, and *vice versa*.

Courts of law were also regulated on the European basis, and provision was made for civil and criminal appeals.

Every male citizen of military age was liable and compellable to perform military duty when commandeered by the Chief, who was *ex officio* Commander of the Forces. Under the Chief the principal military officer was the War-Commandant, who took charge of operations in the field, and who likewise was elected by the burghers.

When Palgrave visited South-West Africa in 1876 he estimated the total Bastard population at 1,500. Today it is probably between 3,000 and 4,000. This latter figure was fixed by Leutwein as an estimate for 1892, but it was probably too high.

Allowance has been made by the writer for those Bastards who were exterminated or scattered by the Germans at Grootfontein South in 1901.

On 19th October 1876 the British Commissioner, Mr. Palgrave, received a long letter from the Bastard Chief and his Councillors, from which the following is an extract:–

> The circumstances of the country thus compel all those who are here seeking to obtain a livelihood and competence in security and peace, to wish for another and good Government to come into the country and protect it. We shall gladly see, aye, we long for the day when the Cape Government will undertake to rule the country and secure protection to us. Should the Government require our assistance in any way, we shall feel forced to give it with all our power and might.

As has already been explained in another chapter, the Cape Government was not allowed to extend British influence north of the Orange River, and eventually the Bastards, in common with their neighbours the Hottentots and the Hereros, came under German control.

On 15th September 1885 a Treaty of Protection and Amity was made between the German Empire and the Bastards of Rehoboth.

It reads as follows:–

TREATY OF PROTECTION AND AMITY between the GERMAN EMPIRE
and the BASTARDS OF REHOBOTH

His Majesty the German Emperor, King of Prussia, Wilhelm I., in the name of the German Empire on the one part, and the independent Chief of the Bastards of Rehoboth, Captain Hermanus van Wyk for himself and his heirs and successors, on the other part, are desirous to enter into a treaty of protection and amity.
For this purpose, the plenipotentiary of the German Emperor, Rev. C. G. Buettner, and the Captain Hermanus van Wyk. together with his councillors. have agreed on the following terms

I

Captain Hermanus van Wyk requests His Majesty the German Emperor to take over the protection of his country and people. His Majesty complies with this request and assures the Captain of his all-highest protection. As an outward sign of this protection the German flag is to be hoisted.

II

His Majesty the German Emperor acknowledges the rights and liberties which have been acquired by the Bastards of Rehoboth. And bids himself to maintain such treaties and agreements which have been entered into by them with other nations and the subjects thereof. and also undertakes not to hinder the Captain in the collection of the revenue to which he is entitled in accordance with the laws and customs of his country.

III

The Captain of the Bastards of Rehoboth binds himself not to dispose of his country or any portion thereof to any other nation or the subjects thereof, or to enter into agreements or treaties with any other Government without the consent of the German Emperor.

IV

The Captain promises to protect the life and property of all German subjects and friends. He confers on them the right and liberty to travel, reside, work, buy and sell within the boundaries of his territory. But the inhabitants of the District of Rehoboth reserve to themselves the right to stipulate the conditions in each case under which the foreigners may remain in their country.

On the other hand, the German subjects and friends shall respect the laws and customs of the country, commit no offence against the laws of their country, and pay such taxes and dues to the Captain, which have been customary hitherto or which may be agreed upon in future between the Captain and the German Empire. The Captain on the other hand binds himself not to concede greater rights and privileges to any other nation than to German subjects.

V

Within regard to the civil and criminal jurisdiction within the territory of Rehoboth, it is herewith decided that all disputes of the citizens of Rehoboth amongst themselves shall be adjudicated by their own judges. In the case of disputes between citizens of Rehoboth and such persons who are not citizens, a mixed tribunal shall have jurisdiction, to which judges shall be empowered by His Majesty the German Emperor and the Captain of Rehoboth. All disputes between persons who are not citizens of Rehoboth or who are not members of their families shall be adjudicated by that person who has been empowered by His Majesty the German Emperor to do so. This also applies to criminal cases.

In all disputes, including those of the citizens of Rehoboth, appeals may be lodged within the Court of His Majesty the German Emperor, by whom the final decision shall be given.

VI

The Captain binds himself to maintain as much as possible and assist in the maintenance of peace in Great Namaqualand and the neighbouring countries. And in case he should have any dispute with the other Chiefs in Great Namaqualand or of the neighbouring countries, he will first ask for the opinion of the German Government and request that the dispute be settled by the intervention of the German Government.

VII

In case there exist any other points which require settlement between the German Empire and the Captain of the Bastards of Rehoboth, these shall be settled by a future special agreement between the two Governments.

Rehoboth, 15th September 1885

Signed C. G. Buettner,

Plenipotentiary of His Majesty the German Emperor

Signed H. van Wyk
(x) Jacobus Moutton
Wilhem Koopman
Johannes Diergard
(x) Dierk van Wyk
(x) Jacobus Moutton
Willem van Wyk

As witness F. Heidmann, Missionary

In terms of this agreement the Bastards remained the loyal allies of the Germans until the outbreak of the present war in 1914. They rendered valuable assistance in the field against the Hereros and Hottentots, and lost many of their best men fighting for the German cause.

Soon after Leutwein arrived he made an arrangement by which the younger might undergo a period of military training under German supervision every year.[182]

Writing of these people, Governor Leutwein states:–

> They have rendered us very valuable services both in peace and in war. We must therefore attach them to us more and more and, in terms of their own expressed wishes, we should place them as near as possible to the whites.
>
> The fact that they had succeeded so far in gaining the approbation of the German Governor speaks well for the skill and state craft of their Chief and Councillors. A time came, however, when their past good services and loyal assistance were entirely forgotten. That was when, in 1915, the Bastards refused to assist Germany against the oncoming British troops. The story of what happened, told in their own words, is stated below.
>
> It is necessary to add that while the Bastards of Rehoboth happily preserved themselves from serious harm, the same cannot be said of the smaller community under Klaas Swart, which had settled in 1869 at Grootfontein South. In 1901, owing to a dispute about a census of horses, hostilities opened. The Chief Klaas Swart and several of his people were killed in action, and the community scattered, their hand and property confiscated. The Germans allege that the Bastards were the aggressors. The Bastards of Rehoboth deny this. However that may be, the happy settlement at Grootfontein South was broken up after having existed there over thirty years, and the few survivors became absorbed into the Rehoboth tribe.

---

[182] Leutwein became Governor in 1894, German military training in Rehoboth started in 1896. By 1903 it was reported that 130 men had received training Bayer, Maximilian *The Rehoboth Baster Nation of Namibia*, (trans. Peter Carstens), Balser Afrika Bibliographien, Basel, 1984: 28, 30.

CHAPTER TWENTY-THREE

The following extracts from sworn statements taken by Lieut.-Col. D. De Waal[183] in June 1915, and made by the Bastard Chief and other eye witnesses, detail what followed their refusal to render military assistance to Germany against the British troops.

EVIDENCE

(1) *Cornelius van Wijk*, duly sworn, states:–

I am Chief under the constitution of the Bastard people. During all the troubles which the Germans had during the years 1903 to 1907 with the Hottentots and Hereros, we always stood on the side of the Government. Also during the disturbances with Witbooi in 1892-1893. In 1892 the Government asked us for fifty men to fight against Witbooi. This we did. Seven of our people were killed.[184] Besides the seven, the Witbooi Hottentots also murdered and shot dead on transport wagons twenty-three of our people. I myself was wounded. The same attitude was taken up by us during the rebellion of 1903 to 1907. We always stood on the side of the white man against the aboriginal or native. During those years we supplied the Government with 130 soldiers besides a large number of transport-riders, leaders, oxen, horses, and wagons. The relations between ourselves and the Government continued to be of a friendly nature.

At the outbreak of the war in August 1914, there were none of our people under arms as soldiers who could be compelled by the Germans to fight for them.

Shortly after the beginning of August, however. we received instructions from *Bezirksamtmann* Von Hiller that we had to supply 150 men to protect the *Bezirk* Rehoboth against native and Hottentot raids, but not to fight against the Union troops. For this purpose we supplied 176 men. For the 176 we received forty rifles from the Government. The remaining 136 were armed with our own rifles. All the 176 men were clothed in German uniforms. The question of the wearing of uniforms was one which caused great dissatisfaction. We did not wish to have uniforms, but were forced. We could not see why it was necessary for the purpose for which the 176 men had to be employed that they should be clothed in uniform. It was distinctly understood that we would, under no circumstances, be employed against the Union troops. We did not wish to fight against the Union troops for various reasons, the most important of which was that we originate from what is now Union territory. It soon, however, appeared that the Government was not keeping faith with us. Our people were taken out of the District Rehoboth as far even as Ururas on the Walvis Bay boundary. I even sent Samuel Beukes and Albert Mouton as far as Kraaipoort and Onanes to speak to Dr. von Kleist and *Hauptmann* Von Hiller, and to protest against their action. Beukes and Mouton went as representatives of the Council. When it appeared that our people would not remain any longer with the German troops they were sent back, but they were then compelled to guard the Union prisoners of war. One hundred and forty of the Zandfontein Union prisoners were sent, from Windhuk to chop wood for the

---

[183] De Waal included statements from 21 witnesses in his report. Extracts from six of these statements are reproduced in this Chapter. The complete statements can be found in South Africa, Union of. *Report on the inquiry in regard to the German-Bastard question held at Rehoboth and other places in the Military Protectorate in June 1915*, Pretoria, 1915 [De Waal Report]

[184] There is a German colonial monument in Zoo Park in the centre of Windhoek that commemorates the German attacks on Hendrik Witbooi. The monument also mentions the names of Basters who died fighting alongside German colonial forces

trains at kilo. 120, and forty-six of our people were employed to guard the prisoners. These forty-six men stood under *Ober-Leut*. Hummnel and certain other non-commissioned officers. The Council was greatly dissatisfied with this, as it was contrary to the arrangement that we were not to be employed against the Union troops.

In March I went to Swakopmund to explain the whole position to General Botha, and to tell him that it was not in accordance with our wishes that our burghers were employed to stand guard over Union troops, but that our burghers were compelled to do so; and also to tell him that should he meet any of my people in the field with arms, he should feel assured that they were there by compulsion and not as voluntary soldiers. The German Government was not aware of my going there. I returned to my farm Garies on 26th April, after our people had already been fired upon.. Garies is situated 87 kilos, south-west of Rehoboth. I arrived on my farm and learned that the German troops had fired on our people. On the 4th May the Germans came to Garies, about 300 men. As I knew that the Germans had fired on our people, I sent my wife and five children into the mountain in order that, should the Germans come to Garies, they should not find my wife and children. Frederick van Wijk, his wife and three children, and also the wife of Stoffel van Wijk and one child, went along with my wife and children. I and Gert van Wijk, Frederick van Wijk, and two Hottentots remained behind on the farm, armed. On the 4th May the Germans came. When I saw the Germans approach we rushed to our horses to ride to the women, as we saw that the Germans were going in the direction of the women. When we reached the horses we were fired upon from all sides. I mounted my horse to try and escape. I succeeded in this. I could not, however, reach the women, as the Germans already had the women in their possession. The Germans remained there for two days, so that I could not reach the women for two days. After the second day the Germans left. When I came to the women's camp my wife was away with two children; also the other two women with their children. In the meantime I was informed that some had been killed. I then looked for dead bodies, and found those of two of my children, namely, Johannes, twelve years of age. and Anna, twenty-three years of age. The people told me that my wife had left with only two children. I then looked for the body of my other son. I did this during seventeen days. The Germans took my wife and two children with them as far as Leutwein. Leutwein is situated about 150 kilos. to the north of Garies, my farm. At Leutwein the Germans left my wife and two children behind. My wife, my two children, and the other two women within their children then went on foot to Garies. I met my wife at Kobus, three and a half hours on horseback from Garies. This was on the 19th May; up till then I had not found the body of my son. My wife explained to me where it was the Germans had taken our son away from her. I then went to the place indicated by her, where I found the body of my other son, Hermanus, eighteen years old. The body lay unburied. There was still a handkerchief tied over his eyes. The body lay on its back with the head slightly lower. He had two bullet holes through the back and two through the head, all from behind. The blood had flowed on his clothes from above to below, that is, from the head to the feet. From the position in which the body was lying, that is, with the head lower. I come to the conclusion that he was shot whilst in a standing position and when held by the hands. This son of mine was unarmed. Besides my wife and children, the wife and children of Frederick van Wijk, and the wife and child of Stoffel van Wijk, there were also others of our people on the mountain when the Germans attacked them.

In all the fights, including the people murdered by the Germans, there were, as far as I know, twenty-eight of our people who met their death. Besides, the

Germans dragged with them to the north twelve Bastard soldiers, two councillors, one elder, and also several others, including women and children. Up till now no word has been received from them.

Samuel Beukes, duly sworn, states:–

I was present when Cornelius van Wijk gave his evidence. I am now fifty-three years of age, and a magistrate under our constitution since 1906. My position as magistrate is also acknowledged by the Germans. I draw no salary from the German Government.

I was born in northern Cape Colony, and entered this country with my father in 1870.

The relations between the Germans and our people were always of a friendly nature. Civilisation is what we have always aimed at, and we have therefore always sided with the German Government against rebellion on the part of natives. This is the reason that we stood on the side of the Government in 1892-93, and again in 1903-07; moreover, we entered into a treaty of protection and friendship within the Germans in 1885, and have adhered to it.

These friendly relations the Germans began to encroach upon from the beginning of 1913. It then began to appear as if the German Government did not wish to acknowledge our independence any longer. Yet the main reason why they and we came to a collision was their dissatisfaction regarding our attitude in regard to the war. We refused from the commencement to take any part in a war against the Union forces. We refused to fight against the Union because we all originate from the Cape Colony. When the war broke out, the Government told us that they did not wish that the coloured people should interfere in the war, but that we should give 150 men to ward off native attacks on our Bezirk. For this purpose we agreed to give 150 men. The number was, however, later 176. The most of these were armed with our rifles. All were clothed in uniforms. With this we were dissatisfied. By clothing our burghers as soldiers the Government made soldiers of our men, and we were afraid that they would also be employed later on as soldiers. When it appeared later, namely, in November 1914, that the Government had even sent our people to Walvis Bay, I and Albert Mouton were deputed by the Council to go to Kraaipoort, where the Rehoboth *Bezirksamtmann* was then stationed, to confer with him, Von Hiller, regarding the breach of faith. We met You Hiller and Dr. Von Kleist at Kraaipoort. We drew their attention to their promise not to take our men outside the Bezirk of Rehoboth. They promised to confer with the Government at Windhuk. Von Hiller then went with the Bastard corps as far as Jakhalswater, and from there this corps was later on sent to Windhuk. From Windhuk they were sent partly to kilo. 120 to guard the English prisoners, partly left behind at Kraaipoort, and partly posted to police stations throughout the Bezirk Rehoboth. The employment of our people as a guard over the English prisoners caused dissatisfaction to our entire community, including the soldiers. The Chief, Cornelius van Wijk. then went to Swakopmund with our knowledge and consent.

On the 13th April 1915 we were notified by Von Hiller, Bezirksman, that the whole of the 176 Bastards who were under arms had to go to Otjiwarongo to guard the prisoners of war and other political prisoners. This we refused to allow. We pointed out that it had been the understanding all along that we should remain neutral and only do duty in our *Bezirk*. Von Hiller then said that we should meet Francke (*Oberst Leutnant*) the following morning, 14th April, at Rehoboth Station, 12 kilos. from here, and there submit to him our objections. This we did. We met Francke at Rehoboth Station. Francke again proposed that we should allow our soldiers to go to the north to guard prisoners. We refused. Francke then said that if we refused to allow our people to go to the north we should surrender our arms. There were at the station besides myself, Pieter Mouton, Martinus Swart, Daniel Cloete, and Carolus Swart (Carolus Swart was afterwards sent away by the Germans to the north). What Francke said was this: "Well, if you will not allow your people to go north you must surrender all your arms, for if the English or Boers find one man here with a rifle, such a man will be strung up on the nearest tree." He further said: "I will give you three days' time, and then I expect either your rifles or that your soldiers will go to the north." Francke spoke in Dutch. He can speak Dutch well. Francke further said in German to Von Hiller, who was also at the station: "If they refuse I will shoot them dead in one heap." Francke then proceeded to the south. On the second day Francke wired to Von Hiller asking for our reply. Von Hiller told us of this. Our reply was always the same: that we would not allow our burghers to go north, and that we would not surrender our own arms. We had agreed that the rifles with which the Germans had armed some of our 176 men should be surrendered. Von Hiller then further proposed that if we were unwilling to deliver our rifles we should hand in the locks thereof. This we also declined to do. Von Hiller warned us that it would be better for our "community" if we allowed our burghers to go north. We replied that we could not allow this. He replied: "This is the last warning." We then separated.

The following day we were again requested to meet Francke at the station. We went to see him about half-past five in the afternoon. Albert Mouton, Mathaeus Gertze, and Carolus Swart went. I did not go. What took place there they can tell. I cannot say whether Francke knew that Cornelius van Wijk had gone to Swakopmund. It appeared, however, later that the missionary knew this. The name of the missionary is Blecher.

I must mention that Von Hiller and the Secretary Widmann went with Mouton, Gertze and Swart from here to see Francke at the station.

At 8 o'clock that night the deputation returned and told us what had taken place with Francke. We took everything quietly and calmly, and went to bed. That night, about 2 o clock, a shot was fired towards the north in the village, about 300 yards from where we are now sitting in this school building. After a while, Missionary Blecher with two councillors, Albert Mouton and Carolus Swart, came to me. I was in bed. Blecher asked me whether I had heard the shot. I replied, "Yes." Blecher said: "This is the result of your soldiers deserting at kilo. 120 (about 25 kilos. from here), where they had to guard the English prisoners." I said: "But have they deserted?" Blecher replied: "Yes; they left about 1 o'clock tonight. We were informed of this by wire." I then asked: "But what has the desertion of our soldiers at kilo. 120 got to do with the shot being fired here in the village?" Blecher replied: "One of your soldiers escaped here in the village, and he was fired upon." (I must here explain that, in accordance with our agreement within the Germans, there were here in the village about thirty of our soldiers performing duty. Amongst other things they looked after German horses. Over them were placed one officer and five non-commissioned officers.) Blecher asked me to go to Hauptmann Von Hiller. I refused, as it was night, and I did not see why I should go. Blecher then left. The following morning, Sunday, Blecher and *Hauptmann* Muller, who also happened to be here, came to me. This was just at sunrise. Blecher asked me: "What does this trekking' mean that I see going on here?" (I must here state that, owing to the shot fired the preceding night and the previous threats of Francke, our people had become afraid, and some had commenced to trek from the direction of the station towards the mountain.) I replied: "Sir, it is the shot which was fired during the night. Gertze, who was also present, said:"Yes. sir, and also the company of soldiers which came in early this morning." Gertze knew that a company of German soldiers had entered the village early that morning, but I was until then not aware of this. I asked Blecher: "What is now really the meaning of the company here?" Muller replied: "They are here to protect the helpless people, women and children." (By "helpless people" he meant German women and children, of whom there was quite a number here.) I replied: "Yes, but we have protected them so long, I beg you take away the company; they are the cause of all the alarm and consternation amongst our people. I give you my hand and my word that not a single shot will be fired here." Blecher said: "You had better let the company come in, Beukes; the Government is bound to protect the white people. I said to Blecher: "I understand I am looked upon as the cause of all this disturbance, but my conscience is clear before God; I know I shall get the rope round my neck, but I will face death. My conscience is clear; there is a just Ruler who will judge. I once more give you my hand, on my side no shot will be fired in Rehoboth. I beg you once more to take the company away, if only as far as the railway station." The reply was: "A telegram has just, been received that the company had to march into the village at 9 o'clock. You had better let them come in." Blecher then asked me: "Shall I have the bell rung for church service?" I replied: "This is impossible." I was afraid of treachery, especially as there were all sorts of stories of treachery in circulation. I then went away to my house. When I came there a report had come in that our soldiers at Zandputz, where, about 40 kilos. from here, they had been stationed, had first been disarmed and then fired upon, and that one of them had been shot dead. I then went out on horseback to urge our soldiers not to come into conflict with the company when it entered the town. Our people were then terribly excited. They had then already heard of the Zandputz incident, of the running away of our soldiers from kilo. 120, of the firing of the shot in the night, and of the flight of women and children to the mountain. Shortly thereafter Hans van Wijk arrived here. He was one of the ten whom the Germans the previous night at Zandputz had first disarmed and then fired upon. Hans came running here on foot. At that moment Sergeant Maiwalt of the police happened to be there, and Hans van Wijk called out: "Yes, uncle, he (Maiwalt) is the man who last night at Zandputz started the firing upon us." Maiwalt was still at Rehoboth the afternoon before, but went to Zandputz that night and was back early again at Rehoboth. I then said to Maiwalt: "Yes, I hear you shot three of our people at Zandputz." Maiwalt replied: "No, this is not so. We only fired at three, but only in the air, when the three refused to surrender their arms." It was clear that, Maiwalt was greatly afraid. I then asked Maiwalt: "But why do shoot them?" He said: "Our orders were to arrest those people, and if they escape then to fire." I then said: "But why should the soldiers then be arrested?" He said: "Such were my orders." It was then about 8 o'clock in the morning. During all that time our people were continually trekking out. My wife also had then just gone. These people fled in a south-westerly direction as far as the Kobus mountains.

On Monday, Secretary Widmann came out to my laager to say that I, Dirk van Wijk and he (Widmann) should also go to Windhuk to speak within the Governor. I again refused; I even refused to go to the village Rehoboth. On Tuesdays morning our people who had been to Windhuk came to us. They told us what had taken place at Windhuk in their interview with the Governor, namely, that the Governor wished that the arms which were in our possession and which belonged to the Government should be surrender. We had ten such, and these were immediately handled over by us. I then sent a request to *Hauptmann* Muller that the arms belonging to our people and which had been taken from our burghers should be returned to us. Their reply was that they would not for the present return these arms, and requested total disarmament. The position then was this: The Governor requested the return of only those rifles which belonged to the Government, whilst Von Hiller and Muller demanded total disarmament. Wednesday afternoon a letter was sent by *Hauptmann* Muller requesting me whether he could send a patrol past my laager to repair the telegraph line to Tsumis. I consented. A patrol came that night. I sent out scouts to see what the patrol was doing. As the patrol did not however go along the line, but to the rear of my laager, it was clear to me that, the patrol was sent out to reconnoitre my laager from behind and that the Germans were up to treachery. The result was that I moved my laager that night. On Thursday morning Gertze came to my laager with a report that at night the Bastards who remained at Rehoboth had been arrested. Gertze, however, with his family, escaped in time. I then withdrew my laager as far as Zwartmodder, where there was water for our horses. I then went about 20 kilos. to the rear to commander our people who were living there. In this way I got twenty more men. Before my return to Zwartmodder the Germans fired on one of our outposts. When I went away from Zwartmodder I left Piet Beukes and Albert Mouton in command.

The twenty men whom I commandeered I sent in advance to my laager. I received information that there was a fight going on and first wished to remove the women and children to Kobus. I remained at Kobus until my laager arrived there a few days later. All that the Dirk van Wijk was still at Vetkop. He later on joined us at Kobus. When he joined us our total strength was about 300 men. In these are included the forty-six men who had fled from kilo. 120. The Germans continually drove us back as far as Kobus. The 300 men were stationed at Kobus around the Kobus mountains and our women and children within this circle. Before our commandos concentrated at Kobus there were small fights on the 27th, 28th, and 29th April; during these small fights none of our people were killed, but three were wounded. It is difficult to say what the German losses were, but we know that on the 27th, Leut. Von Melkom and a *Wachtmeister* and one soldier was killed. On the 3rd May there was again a small fight; on that day also the Germans lost one or two men. About the 8th May the German force was estimated at from 300 to 400 men. They then also had two cannon and three Maxims. On the 8th May the German force attacked us about dawn.[185] The fight lasted until dark that night. The guns and Maxims all took part in the fight. Our losses that day were nine dead and twenty-four wounded. It is difficult to say what the Germans losses were. I, however, saw two buck wagons going off with dead and wounded. Two of our girls and one child were wounded inside our laager by gunfire. That evening the Germans withdrew to where their guns were standing, and there they remained until the following morning. That morning they fired a few more shells at us. While this was going on they buried some of their dead. They then drew off in the direction of Rehoboth. This was the last we saw of them. We, that is to say our laager[186], remained at Kobus for eight days longer, and then we began gradually to trek back to Rehoboth.

We are not responsible for the bloodshed. The Germans are to blame for this. Between the 23rd April and 8th May we captured several German soldiers and also women and children. We treated them all well and sent them back unharmed to Rehoboth, supplying them with food and water for their journey. I can honestly and truly state that during all the days of the disturbances no German, German woman, or child was assaulted, robbed, or harmed by us.

---

[185] There is an annual commemmoration held on the 8th of May at Sam-Kubis to commemorate the battle at which Baster forces fought and held at bay German forces sent to defeat them. For accounts of the events described here see Britz et al., A Concise History: 22-27; Ivan Gaseb 'Remembering Rehoboth', *The Namibian Weekender*, 28th April, 2000.

[186] Afrikaans term for a camp usually associated with ox-wagons

Klaas Draghoender, duly sworn, states:–

I am fifty-five years of age. I was born in the District of Kenhardt, and came here with the first Bastards.

On Sunday, the 18th April, I went with the others to Windhuk to see the Governor. The following morning at 9 o'clock we met the Governor. Francke, Von Hiller, and Bethe were also present. Blecher acted as interpreter. The Governor however said more than what was stated by Gertze. Gertze is slightly deaf. Seitz also said this: "The Boers and English are now coming in with an overwhelming force, and for the time it appears that things go against us. Germany's position is, however, favourable. Three months hence the Union troops will have to return again; the country will have to be restored by them, and then you Bastards will have to account for your foolish acts which you are now committing. Go back and tell your people that they must deliver the arms which I gave them in service."

On Monday night we returned to Rehoboth. That night Major Bethe, who had come within us from Windhuk to Rehoboth. sent me on horseback to the laagers of Samuel Beukes and Dirk van Wijk to call in the councillors to meet him, Bethe. Peter Beukes and Albert Mouton came in, the others refused. Bethe demanded that we should deliver the Government rifles and that we could then retain ours. This we did. We delivered up the Government rifles, but found that our rifles had secretly been taken away.

Friday morning, the 22nd April, I was present at Heuras when the German troops fired on us for the first time. That morning early, while we were trekking with six wagons on the way to Kobus, the Germans charged past us, dismounted in front of us, and commenced firing on us. There was also a number of women and children with the wagons. When the Germans began to fire there was great confusion, and we, the women and children took to the mountains in all directions. One of us, Frederick Keikop, was shot dead, also a girl eighteen years of age, the daughter of Christian Vrij; two of us also were wounded, namely, Jan Witbooi and Willem Keikop. The oxen in the wagons were all shot dead and the wagons burnt. In addition, the Germans also killed at least 3,000 cattle and small stock. Of Daniel Cloete alone forty-eight head of cattle were shot dead. This attack upon us took place about 10 kilos. behind our commando. Our commando did not, however, know of this attack until it was over. The Germans must have moved that night round the rear of our commando for the purpose of attacking our convoy. This was the first time that the Germans attacked us, except that they fired the previous night on our outposts.

That afternoon the Germans returned to Rehoboth by another direction.

After their return I visited the battlefield. It was a terrible sight. There were hundreds and hundreds of dead cattle, goats. and sheep lying about, and also many which were not quite dead yet. A few German were killed there. I know of two who were shot by me.

The Germans on their return took with them ten women and twenty-four children and two men. All these were captured by them that day at Heuras.

Klaas Draghoender,
His X mark

Frederick Bok, duly sworn, states:–

I am forty years of age. I was born at Omaruru. Here at Rehoboth I am since 1904.
I was not one of the German soldiers.

On the 22nd April 1915 the party of which I was one began its trek from Bloemputz, 20 kilos. to the east of Rehoboth. The trek was making for Kobus, and we had to cross the railway line to the south of Rehoboth. The trek consisted of 32 armed and some unarmed burghers. We had under our protection 42 ox-wagons with from 16 to 20 oxen before each wagon, upwards of 50 families, consisting of women and children, and eight Cape carts. We had besides a very large number of loose stock, large and small; I myself had 95 head of cattle and 447 small stock. There were at least 1,000 head of cattle besides the cattle inspanned in the wagons and 3,000 small stock. Horses we had but few. Of all my stock I recovered 47 cattle and 100 sheep and goats.

No leader of ours was with the trek. Each was his own leader. Everyone was inspired by the one desire to flee across the railway line before the Germans could attack us. There was not the least intention on our part to attack the Germans. Our main object was to avoid falling into their hands.

In the afternoon at 6 o clock and while we were crossing the railway line at kilo. 108 or 109, the Germans attacked us. The Germans came upon us from the south by train. I cannot say how many there were, but there were three open railway trucks packed with soldiers. The tram first passed us, and then came to a standstill about 300 yards from where I stood. They jumped down and immediately began to fire upon us. They continued firing for two hours. They chased us as far as they could. Fortunately, it is thickly wooded and bushy at that place, and it was therefore difficult for them to shoot our people. Our loss was one Kaffir woman shot dead. The people fled into the bush and left behind six wagons and one cart. We also fired, but it is difficult to say with what result. There was a tremendous amount of dust, much shouting and hopeless confusion. The Germans also captured two women and took them with them. We escaped with the other wagons and carts. We however lost most of our loose cattle there.

We trekked that night in a westerly direction as fast as we could. Our object was to reach Kobus. That night, at 12 o clock, while we were trekking we were attacked by German troops coming from Heuras. These were the same troops who had that morning attacked the trek of Draghoender and Cloete. We did not, however, know anything about that attack. I and Klaas, Sarel, and Abraham van Wijk were behind the wagons as a rearguard. We were a few kilos. behind when we heard the firing upon our wagons. It was bright moonlight and quiet. We rode forward to the wagons as fast as we could. When we came to the wagons our people had all fled; only the wagons were still there, and these were all in the possession of the German troops. The Germans were not aware of the presence of the three of us that night. The three of us remained a few hundred yards from the wagons in the thick bush. The following morning about sunrise the Germans set the wagons alight, also the carts. There are now lying there thirty-six wagons and also some carts – I think six. Before they set the wagons alight they shot dead all the oxen which were still yoked to the wagons. The carcasses of the oxen can still be seen lying there today, most of them still in the yokes. It was a terrible sight to see the oxen being shot dead. After the wagons had been set alight, the three of us fled. The German then saw us and fired upon us. We also then fired a few shots at them.

Our women and children all escaped, also the men.

We began to come across these people at noon. They were terribly scattered. I had my wife and eight children in the trek. I saw my wife and three children eight days later for the first time at Kobus, and it was only after the fight at Kobus that I, on the 8th or 9th May, had my wife and all my children together.

Of the whole of our trek, consisting of wagons, carts, draught cattle, loose cattle, cows, and small stock, not one reached Kobus.

The wagons and carts were burnt, and the stock large and small was either shot dead or looted by the Germans.

CHAPTER TWENTY-THREE

Katrina Fredrika Sara van Wijk, duly sworn, states:–

I was born in 1861, in the District Amandelboom Cape Colony. I am daughter of Jan van Wijk, and wife of Cornelis van Wijk, the first witness,

My husband went in March 1915 to Swakopmund. He returned towards the end of April to his farm, Garies. On the return of my husband, there were reports that things were going wrong, and that the Germans were hostile towards our people. After we heard what had taken place at Heuras, my husband sent us away from our home into the mountains. The mountains run almost up to our house. I took my five children with me. The names of the children are

(1) Anna, 23 years old.
(2) Cornelia, 20 years old.
(3) Hermanus, 18 years old.
(4) Christina, 15 years old.
(5) Johannes, 12 years old.

With us also went the wife of Frederick van Wijk and the wife of Stoffel van Wijk with their children. We went with two wagons and camped some little distance from our house. On the 4th May the Germans came upon us. My husband was not then with us; he was at the house. Someone must have told the Germans of our whereabouts in the mountains, otherwise they could not have known of us there. It was still early in the morning when they came. We had no able-bodied man with us, neither a rifle. A few days earlier we had a shotgun with which we shot partridges, but this had been taken back to our house.

The Germans were evidently in the mountains to look for us. When we first became aware of them, two armed soldiers were standing in front of us. We were all lying under a krantz.[187] One of the soldiers then said to us "I will shoot every one of you dead this morning." On saying this he pointed his rifle at the wife of Stoffel van Wijk. She called out "Oh! please I am an old woman!" Immediately thereupon he, however, shot her through the breast. She died immediately. She is old and must have been about seventy years. The same soldier thereafter fired on the little boy of Frederick van Wijk, four years and a few months old. This child had part of his skull shot away and also died immediately. The others of us begged for mercy. The same soldier then fired upon the little son of Stoffel van Wijk. He is eleven years old and was wounded in the head. He is well again to-day. The soldiers then ordered us to get up. We got up, and the same soldier then fired two shots at my son Hermanus, but missed him. He then shot dead my other son Johannes. Thereafter they drove us in front of them to the farm. The dead were left unburied there. My daughter Anna then attempted to escape, and then one of another batch of four Germans, who came from another direction, fired at her and killed her. They jeered at us and said: "Where are your English now, that they don't come and help you?" We were kept there at the trees for several hours. The soldiers wished to know where my husband was. They were determined to capture him. I said: "My husband remained behind at the house, but has probably now fled after all this firing." That afternoon they again drove us on in front of them. When we came near the water, *Ober Polizei Wachtmeister* Dietrichs of Rehoboth, and Sergeant Kuhn, formerly of the police at Bulspoort, *Bezirk* Rehoboth, came up to us and kept my son Hermanus behind. He only was kept behind. All the others were driven forward. These two soldiers then took my son round a krantz, and a few minutes later I heard what appeared to be a very loud rifle shot. When I heard the shot I knew that it was fired at my son. They did not

---
[187] A natural wall of rock.

tell me that they had shot him, and I never saw him alive again. That night they put us on a wagon and took us away. Two days later I asked Dietriechs: "What did you do with my son the day before yesterday? How is it that I do not see him any longer?" His reply was: 'I have ordered him to drive on cattle." They took us with them as far as Leutwein Station, not far from Windhuk, where they released us on the 13th May. After they had released us we returned on foot to Garies. On the 19th May I met my husband at Kubis. I told my husband about Hermanus and that I thought that he had been shot. I also told him where the spot was. My daughter Cornelia and I then went with my husband to the place mentioned by me. There we found the unburied body of my son Hermanus. He was lying exactly where I had heard the loud shot fired. A handkerchief was still tied over his eyes. Four cartridge cases were lying close to him. He lay on his back with his head slanting downward. I did not wish to go any nearer and cannot therefore give further details. That same day he was buried.

I do not know the soldier who murdered the wife of Stoffel van Wijk and the others on the mountain. The *Wachtmeister* Dietrichs and the Sergeant Kuhn I, however, know well.

Sara van Wijk

Cornelia van Wijk, duly sworn, states:–

I am twenty years of age daughter of Cornelius van Wijk, Chief of the Bastard people, and Katrina van Wijk, the previous witness.

I was present this morning when my mother gave evidence. I confirm her evidence on all points, and I swear that it is correct in all details.

I was present when the two armed German soldiers murdered our people on the mountain near my father's farm. The soldier who shot my brother Johannes had a sandy beard. He was a fairly tall and fairly stout man. I am certain I will recognise him when I see him again.

Wachtmeister Dietrichs is a police sergeant. I know him well. I often saw him at Rehoboth and also at Garies. I also know the policeman Kuhn well. That day at Garies no shot was fired by anyone on our side as far as I know. Where my father was. who was with him and whether he or the people with him had fired on the Germans, I do not know. The shooting of the people mentioned by my mother in her evidence was nothing less than a cold-blooded murder.

Cornelia van Wijk

Before me:
D. DE WAAL. Lieut.-Col.,
Commissioner

CHAPTER TWENTY-FOUR

THE OVAMBOS OF SOUTH-WEST AFRICA

The arbitrary fixing of the northern boundary of the Protectorate, which is formed by part of the course of the Kunene and Okavango rivers and a line drawn from west to east between them, had as a result the cutting up of some of the land of the Ovambos, so that, after annexation by Germany, an unsatisfactory state of affairs was brought about. A certain proportion of these Ovambos then lived in German territory, while others were, by virtue of residence, under control of the Portuguese authorities in Angola.

It is probable that not only the Ovambos, but also the Portuguese have reason to feel grateful that German influence was never actually established north of the Etosha pan, and that the Ovambo Chiefs were, wise enough to take precautionary measures in good time and thereby to dissuade enterprising Germans from risking trouble by attempts to propagate their protection doctrines.

Had Germany succeeded in getting a foothold in Ovamboland, there is not the slightest doubt that another repetition of the Herero massacre would, sooner or later. have taken place, and Portugal would probably have been drawn into the business to her disadvantage.

About 1890 the Ovambos, according to Leutwein, were divided into the following subdivisions tribal groups[188]:–

---

[188] In the initial absence of a standardised othography, the spelling of names relating to the various Ovambo communities and kingdoms changed continually throughout the twentieth century. Researchers working on colonial Namibian documents are well advised to search amongst all possible spelling permutations of the name of the community being searched. The names commonly used in Namibia today for the kingdoms listed are given in brackets.

(a) Uukualuitsis (Uukwaluudhi)
(b) Ongandjeras (Ongandjera)
(c) Omabarantus (Ombalantu)
(d) Uukuambia under chief Negumbe (Uukwambi)
(e) Ondongas under two chiefs Kambonde and Nechale (Ondonga)
(f) Uukuanjamas under Nande (Uukwanyama)
(g) Ovakoimas (unidentified)
(h) Ovambuela (Mbwela – in Angola)

Harri Siiskonen, *Trade and Socioeconomic Change in Ovamboland, 1850 - 1906*, Helsinki 1990; Frieda-Nela Williams, *Precolonial Communities of Southwest Africa: A History of Ovambo Kingdoms 1600 - 1920*, Windhoek 1991; Patricia Hayes, *A History of the Ovambo of Namibia, c. 1880 - 1935*, D.Phil University of Cambridge, 1992. Carlos Estermann *The Enthography of Southwestern Angola Vol. 1*, Africana Publishing Co., New York/London, 1976.

(1) The Uukualuitsis, whose tribal strength and form of government were unknown. (Majority on Portuguese side.)
(2) The Ongandjeras. (Majority on Portuguese side).
(3) The Ombarantus (called by the Portuguese Ovambandje); their territory is cut through by the boundary line. Total strength estimated at 60 to 80,000.
(4) The Uukuambis under Chief Negumbe, population about 50 to 60,000.
(5) The Ondongas, divided into two sub-tribes under the Chiefs Kambonde and Nekale. The strength of each subdivision was estimated at 20,000 souls.
(6) The Uukuanjamas under a Paramount Chief and Under-Chiefs. Formerly Uejulu was (Chief; he was succeeded by Nande. The total strength of this tribe was estimated at 70 to 80,000 souls, but here again the arbitrary boundary line had placed the majority under Portuguese jurisdiction.

(The last-mentioned four tribes live in the area north of the Etosha pan, along the Kunene and in the gap between the courses of the Kunene and Okavango which is traversed by the settled boundary line.)

To the eastward of these tribes along the Okavango

(7) The Ovakoimas, a small tribe of 5 to 6,000. under a Chief.
(8) The Ovambuela and other tribes which lived more in Portuguese territory than to the south of the Okavango.

Of the above-mentioned tribes the only ones which need be regarded as of importance therefore are the Uukuambis, Uukuanjamas, and especially the two Ondonga subdivisions. The total minimum estimate of the population is about 150,000.

This number is now appreciably less owing to the ravages of the great famine in 1915-1916.

The South-West African explorer, Charles Andersson, who travelled extensively through Ovamboland and discovered the Okavango River, gave an interesting description of the Ovambo people of Ondonga. Full details appear in the book "Notes of Travel in South Africa," published in 1875, some eight years after Anderson's death.[189] He died in Ovamboland and lies buried near the Ondonga headquarters. A few extracts from his notes will be of interest, as the Ovambo people have not changed much since he lived and died amongst them:–

---

[189] See also: Andersson, C.J. Lake Ngami, London, 1856, Andersson, C.J. The Okavango River, London, 1861, Andersson, C.J. *Matchless Copper & Trade and Politics*, National Archives, Windhoek, 1987.

CHAPTER TWENTY-FOUR

There are neither towns nor villages in Ondonga. if we except perhaps the Chief's werft. which, from its great extent, might almost come under one or other of these categories. Each family, often consisting of father, grandfather, children, and servants, resides by itself in a very patriarchal sort of way. Their houses or huts are circular in form; the lower part consisting of slender poles about 2 feet 6 inches high. firmly driven into the ground, and further secured by withers, or other bands, the whole being plastered over with clay. The roof, composed of rushes, is in shape not unlike a beehive. The height of the hut, from the ground to the apex of the roof, does not much exceed 4 feet, and its circumference outwardly is about 16. The reason for their thus entombing themselves, as it were, is probably partly as a protection against the cold and partly on account of the great distance the wood has to be conveyed from the forest.

Besides the hut in which they themselves dwell, the homestead consists of various other erections, viz., the "palaver-house," or that wherein councils are held; several beehive-topped baskets in which the grain is stored away; pens for the cattle and goats, &c., the whole being surrounded by a high and strong palisade and, it may be, a thorn fence in addition, The pathways, or walks, leading to the several buildings enumerated, which are also lined on both sides with rows of poles, are exceedingly tortuous and to a stranger perfectly bewildering.

The residences of the great differ but little in design from the home-steads of the commonalty; but they are on a much more extensive scale that of Chykongo, the paramount chief, for instance, being something like half a mile in circuit. The defences, moreover, are very much stronger, the outer palisading, as well as that on either side of the pathways leading to the several buildings, consisting of two or more rows of poles or planks instead of single ones, and these so closely placed together as almost to exclude the light, and consequently impervious to ordinary fire-arms. Indeed, it would require canon to knock them down; and I have no doubt it is intended they should prove impregnable, if not to ordnance, at least to such weapons as are at the command of the natives.

Without fear of being thought to exaggerate, I will venture to affirm that at least one or two hundred thousand stout poles, together with a great many planks or rather slabs, for saw-mills have not as yet found their way into Ondonga were made use of in the construction of the werft in question; and as all the homesteads in the surrounding country, though on a very much smaller scale, are similarly constructed, it may readily be conceived what millions upon millions of young trees must annually be felled for their construction and needful repair.

In the erection of the residence of the Paramount Chief of Ondonga, be he who he may. I should add the whole population is compelled to assist, each man contributing his quota of materials and labour, and that without remuneration of any kind; but on these occasions a great quantity of beer is consumed, and, as I imagine, at the Chief s expense.

Besides grain, they cultivate small quantities of beans, of which there are also two sorts – one brown and the other white; both are very palatable, the last quite a delicacy. But, strange to say, neither kind is much prized by the natives themselves, who prefer corn. Tobacco is likewise extensively planted, but their way of preparing it quite destroys any flavour it may possess. If is mashed together in a hollow piece of wood, by means of a heavy pole, into little round balls of the size of an orange, which when dry are broken into smaller pieces. Calabashes are, besides, largely produced, but only to be converted into vessels for holding food, beer, &c. Pumpkins are rarely seen.

The cultivation of corn is associated with much toil and labour. Indeed, from the first preparation of the soil until the grain is cut, housed and cleaned, it is one continuous course of hard work. When the first heavy showers have fallen they begin operations. The seed, however, is not sown broadcast as with us, but little holes are made at regular intervals, into which a few grains are deposited. As soon as the plants are sufficiently grown these, with the exception of one or two that are left, are pulled up and transplanted elsewhere. This is going on almost incessantly, and it is amusing to observe how the area on which the corn was first sown grows under the process. Thus a field of grain that in the first instance was only half an acre in extent is eventually converted into one of many acres. As a matter of course, a large field of corn rarely ripens at one and the same time; but this is of no consequence, as only the ears are severed from the stalk. The ground, I should add, is carefully weeded by a small one-handed hoe, the only farming implement in use amongst these people. From the first dawn of day to dusk the women, and at times the men also, are employed about the cornfields.

Notwithstanding the care and labour thus bestowed on the cultivation of the soil, and the uncommonly large yield, still times of great scarcity occasionally occur. The soil consists, as I have said, of fine loose sand on a clay bottom; consequently evaporation is always great, and as there is little or no shade the ground is rapidly exhausted of its moisture, and unless replenished at regular intervals by copious tropical rains it becomes incapable of yielding the usual produce. In former times, when the Ovampo possessed many cattle, an occasional failure of the crop, though always more or less calamitous, was of less consequence, since they could fall back on a meat and milk diet until the return of more favourable seasons; but such is not the case at present, their enemies having of late years despoiled them of a large portion of their herds. However, as all the tribes bordering on Ovampoland are more or less corn producers, and as the rains are not everywhere equally uncertain, it follows that a supply may in general be obtained from one or other of their neighbours, sufficient at least "to keep the wolf from the door."

A word now in regard to the inhabitants of Ovampoland, who as a race are fine-looking people, and have nothing of the real negro type in their features. The men are tall and well-formed, and their upright, manly figures are set off to great advantage by a broad, stiff leather girdle. This, with a slip of dressed skin (more frequently the inside of an ox's stomach) in front, and the apology of a piece of hide behind, is the only covering they indulge in. Though they have now been for nearly twenty years in communication with Europeans, and eagerly buy guns, ammunition, &c., they strictly eschew anything approaching to clothing. They do not even make use of the skins of wild or domestic animals as coverings during the night. One can only account for this apparent perverseness of their taste by the fact that they look on their own lubricious and next-to-naked persons as a far prettier and more respectable sight than the most dandified Brummel,[190] costume; but let the cause be what it may, their going thus denuded of dress must ill agree with their constitutions, for during the rainy seasons they evidently suffer much from the cold. With the exception of ear-rings, composed of beads or shells, the men display but few ornaments.

Their arms consist of the bow and arrow, a dagger-shaped knife, and the "knob-keerie," a short straight stick, or rather club, with a heavy knob at the end: a most formidable weapon in experienced hands, as a single well-directed blow is sufficient to fell the strongest man to the ground. The natives of Africa, moreover, throw it with very great dexterity, seldom failing to hit the object aimed at. Harris, indeed, when speaking of the Matibili, goes so far as to say: "They rarely miss a partridge or a guinea fowl when on the wing."

---

[190] 'Beau Brummell' was a fashion setter and close friend of King George IV of England in the early nineteenth century

The features of the women, though coarse, are not unpleasing, and in early life many of them are very good-looking. As a rule they are exceedingly plump and well-fed; and. curiously enough. I have never seen amongst them any of those thin and scraggy females who are so common in Europe. And though they retain their roundness even in old age, it. is seldom they become corpulent. As with the men, they lubricate their persons with grease and red ochre, and are as innocent of clothing as their lords and masters, wearing only, like them, a belt about the waist and a slip of skin before and behind. Their persons, however, are profusely ornamented, or rather loaded, with various coloured beads and strings of round pieces of ostrich eggs, the latter resting gracefully in front.

But the Ovampo ladies have their fashions as well as those of more civilised countries. On my first visit to Ondonga they, for instance, wore the hair (the artificial portion of it, at least) straight down the back, each elf-like lock being fastened to a sort of comb, as depicted in "Lake N'gami."

Now all this is changed, and the hair is worn en neglig. Thus a few locks descend behind, whilst others are thrown coquettishly over the head and part of the face. Then again, at the period I speak of, it was customary for the fair sex to wear as ornaments heavy copper rings about the ankles. Now this fashion is altogether dispensed with, and the rings in question are used for a very different purpose, viz., to prevent servants and slaves, if suspected of the intention of running away, from carrying out their purpose for when several of the rings are attached to the legs, which renders the process of walking somewhat difficult, it is next to impossible for them to effect their escape. Both men and women, when grown up, I should add.chip the middle tooth of the under jaw.

The Ovampo are a light-hearted people, and, amongst other amusements, delight in music and the dance. Almost every evening, indeed, when the labours of the day are over, there are balls, which, in their way, are remarkable performances, and in which both sexes take part. The women stand in a ring, singing, clapping their hands, and keeping time with their feet, whilst the men join in a kind of chorus.

Their musical instruments are of a very simple kind, consisting of the well-known African "tom-tom" and a sort of guitar.

The staple food of the Ovampo may be said to consist of a kind of stir-about and milk, and, though partial to meat, it is seldom they slaughter their own cattle; chiefly for the reason, I believe, that as man's wealth and influence are judged of by the number of his herd, he is loth to make inroads on the latter but on very special occasions. With the exception of the hyena, and for a reason hereafter mentioned, they eschew not the flesh of any other animal, whether tame or wild. That of the dog would appear to be especially welcome to them. What is more than strange, however, is that both flesh and fish, even when in a high state of putrefaction, are eaten by them with great gusto; and, singularly enough, no evil consequences would appear to follow the banquet. What would doctors and inspectors of meat say if assured that not only putrid but diseased meat was perfectly healthy; but it must not be forgotten that those who partake of such dainties with impunity live and breathe in the purest of atmospheres during the greater part of the year. Beer is the favourite beverage of the Ovampo, and, if they can afford it, they drink it in large quantities.

These people, so far as I am aware, worship nothing either in heaven above or on earth beneath, whence one is led to conclude their religion, should they really possess one, must go in a very small compass. Still, they would appear to have a dim idea of a future state, as may be inferred from the awe and reverence evinced by them when the subject of death is mentioned. But, after all, may we not entertain incorrect notions in this matter as regards the Ovampo, attributable, not improbably, to our insufficient knowledge of their language and habits, and to shyness on their part to reveal such subjects as those in question to strangers. Certain it is, however, they are very superstitious, and the "Rain-maker" as well as other diviners of coming events are, as a consequence, held by them in high honour and repute.

The Ovampo are an industrious race, and the men, contrary to the custom of most other African tribes and nations, work fully as hard as the women. Besides taking part with the latter in the cultivation of the soil, they tend the cattle when pastured in the distant forest, furnish wood for the huts and enclosures, dig wells and perform various other laborious occupations. When, moreover, they have time to spare from their several duties, it is often employed in trading with their neighbours, for which purpose they not unfrequently make journeys of several hundred miles in extent; on these occasions they exchange iron and copper rings and beads, hoes, spear-heads (assegais), and a few other simple articles of their own manufacture (there being artisans, so to say, amongst them) for iron, copper, &c., &c. The women are never idle. as the men are. Independently of household duties, nursing their children, milking the cows and goats, they assist their husbands and brothers in field labours, reaping the grain, storing it away, &c.; but let them be engaged in what manner they may, they always seem a merry, happy set, laughing and chatting together and making sport, as it were, of labour.

THE OVAMBOS AND GERMANY

Beyond an occasional exchange of letters with their Chiefs, Major Leutwein, during the whole of his term of eleven years as Governor from 1894 to 1905 was unable to make any impression on the Chiefs and people of Ovamboland.[191]

True, indeed, German mission stations were established amongst them, but the preliminary political spade work of the missionaries bore no fruit, and all attempts to remove an instinctive suspicion and mistrust of Germany failed. The massacre at Hornkranz and the subsequent subjection of Hendrik Witbooi were known to the Ovambo Chiefs, who determined to resist all encroachments and by force of arms, if necessary, to defend themselves from German protection.

The first attempt to secure German influence was made early in 1895, and is referred to by Leutwein in the following terms (page 172):–

> ... Reports of the conquest of Hendrik Witbooi had penetrated to the Ovambo Chiefs and created a feeling of nervousness, which was intensified by the further news of the northward march of a strong detachment of German troops. Dr. Hartmann, the manager of the South-West Africa Company, who was in regular communication with the Ovambo Chiefs, brought it to my notice that they were preparing for war. In order that it might not be suspected of my troops that they had abandoned a contemplated visit to Ovamboland owing to fear, I wrote to the nearest Chief, the peacefully disposed Kambonde, to the effect that I, to my great

---

[191] Regarding German-Ovambo relations, with particular reference to the Ondonga Kingdom see, Martti Eirola, *The Ovambogefahr: The Ovamboland Reservation in the Making: Political responses of the kingdom of Ondonga to the German colonial power, 1884-1910*, Rovaniemi, Punjois-Suomen Historiallinen Yhdistys,1992.

CHAPTER TWENTY-FOUR

regret, had been unable, owing to pressure of work, to arrange for the possibility of a visit to him this time; but that he was to be assured of my friendly disposition towards him.

Some months later, through the medium of the Finnish missionary, Mr. Rautanen, Leutwein received a reply from Kambonde; but, as with his own letter, and contrary to his usual custom, the Governor does not give this reply verbatim. Leutwein says it was to the effect that:–

> All that I had written in my letter was very nice, but that, as far as concerned him, Kambonde did not wish to see me as long as he lived. Because the Germans came with friendly words, but once they were there they wished to rule, and that he (the Chief) could alone rule in his country.

This rebuff convinced Leutwein that until German authority had been thoroughly established in Hereroland and Namaqualand it would be a mistake to attempt to deal with the Ovambos in the same way as he had already dealt with Nikodemus, Kahimema. Hendrik Witbooi, and the other far less powerful Chiefs in the south.

The giving of the usual impression of German power to the Ovambos was therefore postponed indefinitely.

Over five years then elapsed before Germany renewed her attentions. Early in 1900 Captain Franke. who was then District Chief of Outjo. visited the Chiefs Kambonde and Uejulu and travelled as far as the Portuguese frontier fort at Humbe. This step annoyed and irritated the Portuguese authorities and, as the result of diplomatic representations made through Lisbon and Berlin, an order was issued prohibiting the crossing of the boundaries by German soldiers in uniform. Later other German officers travelled through the area, but their work was confined apparently merely to spying out the land.

About this time two German traders were robbed in the territory of the Chief Negumbo and only saved their lives by speedy flight. When the news reached Governor Leutwein, he happened to be at Outjo accompanied by his, at that the, inseparable companion, Samuel Maherero, the so-called "Chief-Captain" of the Hereros. It seems inconceivable, if he wished to gain any prestige with the Ovambos, that Leutwein should allow of any interference from Samuel Maherero. Yet what do we find? The Herero Chief is allowed to send a kind of ultimatum in his own name to Negumbo. A literal translation of this document is as follows:

> My friend Negumbo   Outjo, 15th November 1900
>
> I write these words to you. I and my friend the Governor Leutwein have heard bad things about your people and your tribe.
> And now I say to you, do what we demand of you. Pay the 60 oxen for what has happened, 50 for the traders and 10 for the children of the killed. If not we will come and shoot you, but we wish to remain friends. Enough.
>
>   Many Greetings.
>   I am, Samuel Maharero,
>   The Lord of the Hereros

This letter was sent through the Missionary Rautanen *viâ* the Chief Kambonde, who received a present for his assistance.

In the following January a message was received from Negumbo to Leutwein that it was not necessary to come and see him, as he intended to compensate the traders.

By June 1901 Negumbo had, however, not complied with Samuel Maherero's demands, and the then District Chief of Outjo, Captain Kliefoth, decided to visit the Chief in person. He was foolish enough to take with him a piece of artillery and twenty-five soldiers. On arrival at the Chief s village, Omukuju, Kliefoth found he had stirred a hornet s nest.

> The inhabitants rushed to and fro like a colony of ants, and received the troops with growling threats and shouts. All Kliefoth s attempts to obtain a hearing failed. As it appeared fruitless to go to any further trouble, he retired during the night as he rightly believed that he could not take upon himself the responsibility for an Ovambo war. (Leutwein.)

The matter of paying compensation by Negumbo to the traders was thereupon allowed to drop.

The next visit to Ovamboland was that made, towards the end of 1901, by Dr. Hartmann, who travelled to Port Alexandre and Mossamedes, accompanied by Lieut. von Winkler. The object of this tour was to report on the possibility of building a railway from one of these ports to the Tsumeb Copper Mine. They visited Chief Nechale, Kambonde, and Nejulu. but gave Negumbo a very wide berth. Again they were able to observe the ominous distrust and unrest (*Mistrauen und Unruhe*) of the Ovambos.

German plans and designs on Ovamboland, and possibly Southern Angola, were however now beginning to crystallise, and in the end of 1902 another mission composed of Dr. Gerber and the Architect Laubschat, both officials of the Administration, accompanied by Under-Officer Gass, as a civilian visited Nechale, Kambonde, and Uejulu. At first they were coldly received and before long with open hostility. It was thought that, being in plain clothes, they would arouse less suspicion than men in uniform. The Chief Uejulu accused them of being Government "spies," and their attempts to obtain anything like friendly treatment failed.

For this attitude of the Ovambo Chiefs the Germans were not slow to impute intrigue and unwarranted interference to their Portuguese neighbours over the border.

Feeling however that he had to do something, Dr. Gerber moved eastward and met Himarua, the most powerful of the Chiefs (living on the north bank of the Okavango). With this Chief, Dr. Gerber concluded a "most advantageous agreement" for the establishment of a German Catholic Mission. Other attempts were made to propitiate, during the period 1902 to 1903, the Ovambos living in the valley of the Okavango; but with no success.[192]

---

[192] For a detailed description of the efforts to establish the Catholic Church in northern Namibia see Adrianus Beris 'From Mission to Local Church: One Hundred Years of Mission by the Catholic Church in Namibia' (D.Theol., UNISA, 1996): pp. 79-87.

In March 1903 the missionaries who were to open up their labours at Himarua's village in terms of his agreement with Dr. Gerber, left for the north. On arrival at their destination, a post on the southern bank of the Okavango, the missionaries met Himarua, who professed to know nothing about any agreement with Dr. Gerber, and requested the missionaries to return home. In the course of discussion one of the missionaries was foolish enough to inform Himarua that he was not in his own territory, but that he was standing on German soil (*auf deutschmem Boden*), and they, as Germans, could not be interfered with. This, as Leutwein puts it, "knocked the bottom out of the cask" and the good missionaries found it very expedient to retire without delay.

It was then decided by the German authorities to punish Himarua so far as this could be done "without breach of the Portuguese boundaries." In July 1903, Lieut. Volkmann with a small party of men and maxims drew up on the south bank of the Okavango and treated Himarua s village on the north bank (in Portuguese territory) to an exhibition of volleys and quick firing which lasted for a day. The Ovambos returned the fire, but while their losses were reported to have been numerous (*zahlreich*), there were no German casualties. The German troops then withdrew, and arrangements were made at Windhuk for another punitive expedition on a large scale to move against the Ovambos early in 1904, as soon as the rainy season had passed.

The outbreak of the Herero rising in January 1904 and the subsequent general rising of the Hottentots in the south distracted attention so effectually that the Ovambos were left in peace and in the enjoyment of tribal freedom.

After the restoration of peace in Hereroland and Great Namaqualand in 1907, those areas, seeing that practically two-thirds of the population had been exterminated, were unable to supply a sufficiency of native labour for farming, mercantile and other pursuits. This compelled Germany to institute the system of forced labour, bordering on slavery, by which all natives, male and female, over the age of seven years were (with the one exception of the Rehoboth Bastards) impressed into service as labourers. The discovery of the diamond fields near Luderitzbucht a few years later placed the colonial authorities face to face with a problem which had been created by the inhumanity and shortsightedness of German soldiers and administrators. There was no labour available for the exploitation of these newly-found sources of wealth. Then it was that attention again turned to Ovamboland, and by means of much coaxing and the offering of tempting inducements such as good pay, good food and fair treatment, and the disbursement of much money, the Ovambo Chiefs were at length prevailed upon to allow their men to be engaged as labourers. The result was that the Ovambos became, and are now, the indispensable labour asset on which the whole of the mineral development and a great deal of other constructive work in the Protectorate depends. The Germans gradually growing wiser, now that financial interests were at stake, took every care and pains to cultivate the Ovambos and to propitiate the Chiefs in every respect. The Chiefs viewed the matter without sentiment and also purely from the point of view of the financial and material advantage such employment brought to them and to their people. Apart from supplying labour, their official and national bearing towards Germany and the Germans was one of studied suspicion and aloofness. They still felt towards the German official what Kambonde had stated in his letter to Leutwein. For fear of losing labour which could not be obtainable elsewhere in South-West Africa, Germany had to adopt an attitude of humble acquiescence which must have been galling in the extreme.

So recently as the beginning of 1915, when Colonel Franke led a punitive expedition against the Portuguese at Naulila, on the northern frontier, he wished to take a shorter route which would necessitate crossing through the territory of the Uukuambi tribe. Before making the attempt he sent messengers conveying a request with presents to the Chief Ipumbu. The Chief refused to accept the presents, and returned them to the German commander with a reply to the effect that if the Germans wished to take that route, it would only be possible for them to do so after having defeated the Uukuambis in battle. The German commander thereupon decided to make a wide d tour.

OVAMBOS ATTITUDE TOWARDS THE BRITISH

In strong contrast with the hatred and suspicion of the Ovambos towards the Germans may be mentioned the spontaneous outbursts of friendship and confidence with which they greeted the arrival of the British troops in their country.

A few months after the conquest of South-West Africa in July 1915, Major Pritchard, a Native Affairs Officer, and a party of British officers visited all the reigning Chiefs, and were everywhere received with demonstrations of friendship and cordial welcome.

In his report[193] on the results of his mission, Major Pritchard mentions the following conversation with the Paramount Chief, Martin, of Ondonga:–

> He frankly stated that the Ovandonga had no love for the Germans, whose wars with the natives they had heard of, that he and his people had always wished that the English would come into their country ... He added, with emphasis, that no German officer had ever entered his house, that I and these officers accompanying me were the first who had ever entered or camped near it.

Before Major Pritchard left Ondonga on his return journey. Martin, who is now the most powerful ruler in Ovamboland, sent the following message through him to the British Government:–

> I send my greetings to the great men who rule your country. I had always been afraid of the Germans, and have never had the opportunity, as I had wished, to invite the English to my country. I was pleased when I heard that the English were masters of the country; the words that have been spoken to me by you have given me such confidence that I feel as strong as a rock.

---

[193] South Africa, Union of *Report by the Officer in Charge of Native Affairs on his Tour of Ovamboland*, Cape Town, Government Printer, 1915: pp. 21-22.

CHAPTER TWENTY-FOUR 233

At the commencement of this chapter the writer gave the divisions of tribes, population, and Chiefs as estimated by the Germans at the time of annexation in 1890. It will be of interest to state the present allocation and position of the various tribes. The changes in numbers and name are due to the obtaining of clearer and more definite information, while inter-tribal wars have, during the past twenty-seven years, brought about changes in the position of the various Chiefs. The details which follow are taken from Annexure 13 to Major Pritchard's report.

TRIBAL DISTRIBUTION AND POPULATION

Summary of population

(1) Ovandonga	60,000
(2) Ovakuanyama	50,000
(3) Ovakuambi	20,000
(4) Ovangandjera	15,000
(5) Ovakualudsi	8,000
Others	3,000
About	156,000

(1) Tribe: Ovandonga.
Locality: Ondonga.
Area: Approximately 5,000 square miles – North to South, 40; South to West, 128.
Chief: Martin, a Christian, about 23 years of age; has one wife and a son (one year). Resides at Onotumba.
Population: Estimated by Rev. Martin Rautanen at 60,000. He states that until recently this portion of the country has not suffered so much as have some others from sickness and starvation, that the country is well ruled, with the result that its population has been increased from time to time by refugees from other tribes who, in order to escape the consequences of the practice of witchcraft or on account of famine, have taken up their abode in it.

(2) Tribe: Ovakuanyama.
Locality: Cuanyanma.
Area: Approximately 3.600 North to South, 30: East to West, 120. (In Protectorate
Chief: Mandume[194], a heathen, age about 21 years, unmarried.
Population: Estimated to be about 50,000.
The wholesale practice of witchcraft, coupled with the barbarous methods of government followed by this Chief, has had the effect of causing the deaths, by killing, of immense numbers of the people each year.

---

[194] (Page 142 in original) *Since deceased*. The Blue Book footnotes the fact that the Kwanyama leader Mandume ya Ndemufayo was 'since deceased'. It does not mention that he had died during an attack by a South African expeditionary force on 10th February, 1917. The 'warm welcome' allegedly provided to representatives of the Union of South Africa in 1915 had therefore, apparently, been of short duration. The Blue Book is certainly being 'economical with the truth' here. Silvester, *My heart tells me I have done nothing wrong: The Fall of Mandume*, National Archives of Namibia, Windhoek p. 32

(3) Tribe: Ovakuambi.
Locality: Ukuambi.
Area: Approximately 300 square miles North to South, 17: East to West. 17
Chief: Ipumbu, a heathen, age about 23 years, unmarried. Resides at Onulo.
Population: Estimated to be 20,000.
Witchcraft is reported to be extensively practised among the Ovakuambi.

(4) Tribe: Ovangandjera.
Locality: Ongandjera.
Area: Approximately 100 square milles North to South, 10; East to West, 10.
Chief Shanika, a heathen, age about 70 years.
Population: Estimated by Rev. Rautanen to be about 15,000; other missionaries place it at not more than 10,000.

(5) Tribe: Ovakualudsi.
Locality: Okualudsi.
Area: Approximately 25 square miles – North-east to South-west, 2?; South-east to North-west, 10.
Chief: Maula, a heathen, age about 50 years.
Population: Estimated to be about 8,000.

For the first time in the history of the Ovambos of South-West Africa, a European official, a British officer, was in 1915 stationed at the head village of Ondonga, where he now carries out the duties of Resident British Commissioner and adviser to the various Chiefs.

This appointment has been fruitful of very good results, and the Chief Martin has, throughout, proved himself to possess the fullest confidence and friendliness towards the new regime. The supply of Ovambo labour is steadily on the increase, and before many years are over the Ovambos will begin to show the beneficial results of contact with a humane and just system of government.

A return of this country to the Germans spells for the Ovambos only one thing, and it is that the fate of the Hereros will, sooner or later, inevitably overtake them, and they themselves know it only too well.

CHAPTER TWENTY-FIVE

THE BUSHMEN[195] OF SOUTH-WEST AFRICA

It. is generally accepted that the primitive Bushmen were the aborigines of South and South-East Africa. It is also quite probable that they have for long centuries inhabited South-West Africa.

These yellow and dark-brown-skinned pigmies are still to be found in considerable numbers all along the eastern border of the Protectorate in the Kalihari sandveld and in the Grootfontein and Kaokoveld areas. Scattered bands also roam along the Namib desert belt on the western side near the Naauwkloof and Tiras Mountains, and in the south-western corner where the Huib Hochebene Mountains and the rugged gorges of the Konkip and Great Fish rivers give that insolation and shelter which they need.

They live solely on the proceeds of the chase and the wild roots, berries and fruits of the veld.

Armed with very well-made bows and arrows, and possessing a knowledge of veldcraft and of the haunts and habits of antelopes and other game, in which they are unsurpassed, the nomad Bushmen are constantly on the move, following their quarry from one grazing ground to the other.

Probably the smallest people in the world, they are nevertheless wiry and firmly built. The hands and feet of the Bushmen are very small and delicately made, and in general appearance he is not unlike the Hottentot, though much shorter of stature. Very few pure bred Bushmen reach a height of 5 feet, the average being about 4 feet 10 inches, while the women are even smaller, but as delicately formed. Unlike the Hottentot women, they do not show with increasing years any signs of that very extraordinary and abnormal posterior development which is a characteristic, graceless and enigmatic feature in the Hottentot female.

---

[195] In the course of the twentieth century a small battle has been raging within academic circles regarding the correct terms to be used and applied to people. In southern Africa this debate has raged particularly stridently around the issue of what to call the earliest inhabitants of southern Africa. For an introduction to the terms used see, Emil Boonzaier et al., *The Cape Herders: A History of the Khoikhoi of Southern Africa*, (Cape Town 1996) pp. 1 - 3. A recent report identified sixteen different dialect groups amongst those classified today as San within Namibia and these names are generally used for self-identification. Robert Gordon has argued for the retention of the term in academic discourse within a historical context and that the term 'San' is itself derived from a word for 'bandit'. He argues that "To feel compelled to change the label is to submit to the effectiveness of colonial socialiszation. In order to confront this restrictive socialization we need to confront the same terms and infuse them with new meaning." Suzman, James *An Assessment of the Status of the San in* Namibia, Legal Assistance Centre, Windhoek, 2001: 3. Robert Gordon, *The Bushman Myth: The making of a Namibian underclass*, Westview, Boulder CO, 1992: pp. 5-8.

The very nature of their mode of life has always militated against a communal or tribal manner of living. They live scattered here and there in single families or in groups of one, two, or more families, but rarely in excess of thirty to forty souls in each group. Such "banding together" (which was in German times a crime and was punished by long periods of imprisonment in chains) would also be purely of a temporary nature, induced by the presence in their locality of plenty of water and sufficiency of game, and as water got scarce and game began to scatter, so also would the Bushmen separate in order thereby to be able the better to feed themselves.

The manner of life of the wild Bushmen may be described as being hardly on a higher plane than that of the lion and the leopard – his rivals in the chase. He is occupied from birth until death in one long war with nature and in the one unending task the preservation of himself and his family from death by hunger and thirst.

It will therefore be understood that among this primitive people, who build no huts and possess no domesticated animals except a dog or two, whose territory is to them bounded only by the horizon, who know few laws and few restraints, and have but the most vague ideas of property or ownership, a settled government under hereditary or nominated Chiefs has never existed, nor has there ever been any tribal organisation.

A knowledge of the same language conveying the idea of community of origin is all that binds the families together, and that promotes the rare and very occasional assembling of groups of families for feasts and festivities.

The control is therefore purely patriarchal. An ancient grandfather may live in a family group of two or three sons and a few daughters with their wives, husbands, and offspring, numbering perhaps fifteen or twenty persons. On being visited by a curious European and being asked to indicate the head or Chief, they naturally point to the old man. In other cases, where the elders have grown too feeble for the hunt, a younger man, generally the most daring and skilful hunter, may by common consent be acknowledged as the leader of the party; but this gives no ground for the erroneous ideas often published that Bushmen have tribal chiefs. They have no chiefs in the tribal or government sense at all.

In his Report on the Rietfontein Area of the Kalihari, published in 1908 (Cd. 4323), Major J. F. Herbst gave some most interesting and valuable details concerning the Bushmen and an extract from his account will indicate what manner of people they were.

He writes (page 10):–

> The *lares et penates*[196] of a Bushman consist of a few lean and hungry dogs, a short but heavy knobkerrie, a long bone *tsamma*[197] knife, a bow and arrows, the

---

[196] 'the valued possessions of a household'

[197] The Tsamma or 'Wild Watermelon' (*Citrillus lanatus*) and provided an important source of water and subsistence in arid areas. Van Wyk, Ben-Erik & Nigel Gericke, *People's Plants: A Guide to Useful Plants of Southern Africa*, Briza, Pretoria, 2000: 38.

dried body of the *gnubo* snake as an antidote against snake bite, a skin bag or two as a receptacle for these articles, and a tin for use as a kettle. Every *werf* has a large number of dogs which accompany their masters on the hunt, and it is really wonderful with what courage these lean mongrels will tackle a leopard a courage no doubt begotten of hunger and an absolute confidence in their masters who, with their knobkerries, are never far behind so soon as the dog has gripped his prey. The chief offensive weapon of the Bushman is the bow and poisoned arrow. The poison is obtained from snakes, insects, and the euphorbia, and mixed with the juice of the *melkbosch* (not that of the Colony) which grows in the Karasberg mountains in German South-West Africa. The milky juice is boiled, and when cool is quite black and sticky. It is applied to the barbed arrow-head made from old hoops, knives, &c., and fixed in a bone tied to a reed obtained from the distant river beds.[198] The *gnubo* snake is very rarely found, spending most of its the underground. It is small, of a brown colour, and said to be very poisonous. There are two kinds, one with two small, short fore feet. The dried body is carried by all natives and most of the Europeans in this country and German South-West Africa, and the dried flesh, ground to a powder and rubbed into the incised wound, is said by all to be an absolutely safe antidote to the most virulent snake poison. It is said to draw the poison "out in a stream." If I remember rightly, some *gnubo* was analysed in Cape Town some years ago. but no properties were found that could account for this action.

The Bushmen are the keenest hunters and the finest trackers in the world. Being dependent for their sustenance upon the products of the desert and in daily contact with its fauna, it is not surprising that their powers of vision and their perceptive faculties should be developed beyond those of ordinary man; and to one unversed in the ways of the desert their capabilities in these respects are little short of marvellous. As we look to our morning paper for a record of the events of the previous day, so the Bushmen will interpret the doings of the animal world during the previous night (when alone history is made by them) by the imprints left on the sand. Every footprint is familiar to him and he will announce to you what visitors his area has had, their number, time of visit during the night, and whether they were at ease or startled. In the loose sand, game spoors, old and new, in many hundreds, go in every direction; it would appear hopeless for us to follow a particular spoor; to them the problem presents no difficulty. Shoot at a buck in a herd that flees, he will follow their spoor for a short distance and return to tell you whether you have wounded your buck or not. The merest clot of blood on the spoor will give him his clue, and he could lead you on that spoor for miles and miles and never lose it. Fleet of foot, their powers of endurance are wonderful, and if one could only induce a specimen to compete at the Olympic games in Europe, methinks a world s record in long-distance running could be secured. The fleetest steenbok or duiker are run down by them during the hottest part of the day. The procedure is simple. By day these animals lie in the shade. Then the Bushman, club in hand, sallies forth, clad only in his *veldschoens*[199], and, with much shouting, drives up whatever game comes in his way. Then the stern chase commences. The buck will outstrip his pursuer and lie down again, but the Bushman on the spoor at a fast trot soon drives him up, and so the relentless pursuit goes on for about three or four hours in the hot burning sun. By that time the hot sand will have burnt the hoofs of the unfortunate animal to such an extent

---

[198] For a more detailed discussion of poisons see Shaw, E.M. 'Bushman Arrow Poisons', *Cimbebasia*, Vol. 7 (1963); also Watt, J.M. and Breyer-Brandwyk, *Medical and Poisonous Plants of Southern and Eastern Africa*, E.S. Livingstone, Edinburgh, 1962

[199] 'Veld shoes' made from animal skin.

that he falls an easy prey to the club of the Bushman. A duiker and steenbok cannot run far in wet sand, and after rain they are chased by Bushmen, who soon catch up to them; the wet sand gets between the cloven hoofs of the animals and chafes them so severely that they cannot run far. Where bush is scarce steenbok frequently spend the day in the numerous antbear holes. Finding a morning spoor leading to these holes, the Bushman, silently as a cat, creeps up to the hole and plants himself before it, leaving a small open space under the left arm for which the buck charges, when he is pinned and dealt a stunning blow over the head with the Kerrie in the right hand. In these ways numbers of these animals are killed, and one can see with what difficulties they must rear their young.

The strength of a Bushman is remarkable. I have seen an insignificant-looking fellow carry, one on each shoulder, the two complete legs of a full-grown male ostrich up a steep sand dune.

It is the most interesting experience imaginable to watch the ingenuity displayed by this savage when on the spoor of game. Possessed of a perfect knowledge of the habits of all game he is able to forestall them at every point. Employed as a guide, they will always precede the horsemen by a few yards, first throwing a handful of sand in the air to test the direction of the wind, which, of course, determines the route for the day. Not a word is spoken, for one s vision is limited by the sand dunes, and sound travels far. As he walks along he will indicate to you, by figures made on his fingers denoting the horns of the animal, what spoors he is meeting with and whether fresh or old, &c. Before mounting a dune he will creep on his stomach, and with eyes and ears on the alert, peer cautiously over the crest from behind the friendly cover of a tuft of grass, lying motionless the while, till he has examined every nook and corner of the area exposed to view. If there is game, his keen eye will take in the topographical features of the whole scene, and he will take you, after much creeping and climbing on all fours, to the nearest point affording cover, and there is no prouder moment in his life than when the crack of your rifle lays at his feet the much-prized meat. A particularly good shot is greeted with shouts of laughter and a salute of *Gai koms* (lit., big stomach) which in the native is synonymous with "big man."

The greatest ambition of a young Bushman is to catch his first steenbok, for no girl will have him to wed until he has shown his competency to provide the family with food. The capture of a buck is indicative of manhood. No ceremony takes place when a Bushman weds. It is a "taking" pure and simple. Their only method of giving expression to any exuberance of feeling is by dancing, which is indulged in by the men alone, the women circling round and wailing a weird chant in praise of either the gemsbok, ostrich, lion, &c. While these are sung, with clapping of hands, the men with horns on their heads and strings of hairworm shells fastened round their legs, making a peculiar noise, imitate the antics of the respective animals in their sportive moods.

Notwithstanding the fact that the Bushmen were regarded as outlaws and wild animals by the Germans, and despite the wholesale killing off which has taken place, there are today perhaps ten to fifteen thousand of these people left in South-West Africa. The majority live in the Grootfontein area, and in the Kaokoveld and the sandveld north of Gobabis, along the edges of the Kalahari desert.

In a most illuminating report made in January 1912 to the German Governor, the District Chief of Grootfontein (Herr von Zastrow), says:–

> I do not think I am making a false estimate when I fix the number of Bushmen in the Grootfontein District alone at from 7 to 8,000.

He goes on to add that the estimate of Professor Dr. Passarge (*Die Buschleute*) of a total population of the Bushmen in the northern areas at not more than 10,000 is much too low.

The Bushman language is merely a succession of clicks and gutturals, and there are reported to be several dialects, due in some measure to Hottentot influence.

Although there are subdivisions based mainly on differences of dialect and locality, there are two main groups or families into which the main body of Bushmen of South-West Africa may be divided, namely, the *Kung* and the *Heikom*.

The *Kung* are pure bred yellow-skinned pigmies, and are in every respect typical wild bushmen of the most primitive type known. They are easily distinguishable from the Heikom, who are taller and darker. These people live in parts of the Grootfontein District, in the northern and eastern sandveld, and along the Omuramba Omatako. They are timid and shy of the white man and keep out of his way. Should he happen to come on a party unexpectedly and they find flight inconvenient or undesirable, a dangerous situation is likely to result, as they never hesitate to use the deadly bow and arrows. For this state of affairs the entire blame must not be placed on the Kung Bushman.

The *Heikom* Bushman evidences in his physical appearance and in his language further proof of the ancient migration through this area of the Hottentot tribes. He is as tall as the average Hottentot and dark yellow of skin, while his language is Nama, like that of the Hottentot and the Berg-Damara.

This race is undoubtedly the result of intermixture between the Hottentots and some now extinct Bushman tribe. Some members of the race are dark and also bear unmistakable evidence of intermixture with the Berg-Damaras.

Their habitat is the Grootfontein District proper, the Etosha pan area, and the North-western part of the sandveld of the Kalahari border.

The Heikom Bushman is, as may be expected, less wild than his Kung neighbour and more amenable to control and civilisation. At one the, a year or two before the war, there were no fewer than 1,500 Bushmen farm workers in the Grootfontein area, the majority of them being Heikom Bushmen; but for reasons which will be referred to presently the majority of these people eventually decided that their free natural barbarism was more preferable than service with the Germans.

The extermination of the bulk of the natives in the south has now made it necessary to look to the northern areas for supplements to the insufficient sources of labour supply to carry on mining work and agricultural and other undertakings. There is no doubt about it that should South-West Africa receive an influx of white settlers after the War, the problem of native labour will become acute. The gradual taming and utilisation of the Bushman for farm work and herding of stock is therefore a subject which cannot be waived aside without serious consideration. It is unfair to urge that these wild people are irredeemable and that they are incorrigible thieves and dangerous neighbours. The Bushman will never steal cattle except as a revenge, or unless he is driven to do so by the desperation of an empty stomach, and in nearly every case it is the action of the white people, in shooting off all the wild game, or in proclaiming game reserves and stringent game protection laws, which has driven the Bushman to resort to theft as a means of existence.

Major Herbst in the already quoted report, says (page 13):–

> The strict enforcement of the game laws has made the country unsafe for them. They profess to be unable to understand by what right Government protects the game, and invariably ask to be shown the Government brand on the animals.

At other times it has been a means of revenge on the German settlers, whose ideas of the property of the Bushman in his wife were about as nebulous as the Bushman's idea of the rights of the settler to the land and his cattle, the majority of the German settlers had acquired their cattle by the doubtful means already outlined; they decided, very many of them, to appropriate the wives of their Bushmen in like manner, namely, by forcible acquisition.[200] The Bushmen retaliated by driving off the stock and sometimes by shooting the German.

This does not indicate or prove, however, that the Bushman is useless and that he constitutes a problem, the solution of which is only possible with a rifle and unlimited cartridges.

Herr von Zastrow says that extermination is out of the question. Referring to the estimated population of 7 to 8,000 Bushmen in his district, he writes:–

> Taking this number in conjunction with the fact that so many men are already working on the farms, and bearing in mind also the small number of natives now in the whole Protectorate, one cannot afford to pass over these people without consideration. More than half of the farmers would not be able to carry on their business were the available Bushman labour to vanish.
>
> The opinion so generally expressed that the Bushman cannot be utilised as a labourer, because he will not remain on a farm and is too weak, is not actually correct. Surely it must be clear that such people who have during their whole lifetime wandered about the veld and have never done any hard manual labour, cannot in a moment lose their habits and become efficient and energetic labourers... The present generation cannot entirely change its nature.
>
> It is remarkable to observe how the Bushmen serve the purpose of farm labourers. They learn to plough, to cultivate tobacco, to control oxen transport, and whatever else a farm labourer must do. Many remain for long years on the farms and become so serviceable as assistants that they are indispensable to the farmer.

---

[200] Robert Gordon quotes from one of the earliest reports of the South African Military Magistrate, Lt. Hull, who took control of Grootfontein District after the German surrender in 1915 and complained that "... their [Bushman] women were being constantly interfered with by both farmers and police" Gordon, *Bushman Myth*, p83

Dealing with stock thefts, the District Chief goes on to state very definitely that as a rule the wild Bushmen do not appear to be the thieves; but that the thefts are committed by fugitive Bushmen who have previously been farm labourers. He gives the following example, which is extremely significant:–

> In the case of the stock thefts on the Omuramba Ovambo, the perpetrators had suffered under the false and bad treatment of a farmer and were therefore driven to commit these crimes out of motives of revenge. Probably, though I cannot prove this, the same is the case in regard to the stock thefts at Jumkaub and Begus ...

In regard to remedial measures of control, von Zastrow considers that large areas should be left free as reserves for the wild Bushmen, and that by fair treatment it may be possible in the gradually to entice them to give up their wild nomadic life and to settle down as useful people. He is definite on the point that the putting of the terror of death into them will not influence them to abandon their old habits:–

> Other suggestions, such as extermination or the deportation of whole tribes, are so absurd as to merit no consideration.

It is refreshing to find in the ranks of German officialdom a man who is broadminded and far-sighted enough to express such views.

The writer, while at Grootfontein, had a short discussion concerning the Bushmen with Herr von Zastrow, wherein he confirmed the views expressed by him in the report quoted from, and he went so far as to declare that, in his opinion the Bushmen would in the future prove a valuable labour asset to the farming community.

The German temperament is not calculated, however, to make any native a valuable labour asset. Von Zastrow is most unpopular with his own people because he condemned and, it is feared unsuccessfully, tried to suppress and prevent indiscriminate flogging. He was prepared to deal with the native as fairly as the laws and the regulations would allow him to, and the majority of the white settlers hate him for his pains.

Extracts from two statements by intelligent representatives of the two chief Bushmen tribes will indicate how their compatriots were treated.

Jacob Haibib (a Kung Bushman of the Kalihari), says:–

> I was employed as a tracker to help round-up gangs of marauding Bushmen. We used to have fights with them, and often killed Bushmen. Those we captured were brought into Grootfontein. If they had committed murder they were hanged. If they had stolen stock they were transported to Swakopmund and Windhuk to work there. That was before 1912.[201] In 1912, however, a German sergeant named

---

[201] A concentrated German campaign took place in the years 1911-1912 with over 400 patrols sent out to police and capture Bushmen. Robert Gordon has described Swakopmund as 'a major Bushman holding center' with high mortality rates. For example, he quotes German files showing that amongst one group of 32 brought to Swakopmund as prisoners, 15 had died within a year and reproduces a disturbing photograph of a group of sixteen prisoners in Swakopmund in 1911. Gordon, *Bushman Myth*, pp. 69-71.

Heldfrich was murdered by a Bushman near Narugas, about 80 kilos. away. We then got a lot stricter, and Bushmen who killed stock were shot on the spot if they attempted to evade capture. Occasionally farmers took the law into their own hands and shot Bushmen: but they were forbidden to do so by the German magistrate von Zastrow, who said that thefts should be reported to the police in the first instance.

The Kung tribe is wild, and they do not work for anyone. They are also dangerous and readily use their bows and arrows. The Haikoms are less wild and come in some of them to work on farms. There were many working on farms in this district (they are good sheep and cattle herds, and work well); but the Germans treated them badly while the country was under German rule, and many used to run away back to the veld. They were badly fed, flogged, and very often got no money. In fact, they hardly ever got money for their work. They could not count their money, and got nothing, as they did not know the value of money. I know of my own experience that Bushmen, as well as Hereros, Damaras, and Hottentots, all that were natives (red or black), were brutally treated by the Germans. When they came into town to report their masters for brutality or cruelty, the only result was a severe flogging from the German police with a sjambok, and orders to return at once to their masters.

Hendrik Kasubie (a Heikom Bushman), says:–

I am a Heikom Bushman. I was born at Tsintsabis, north of Grootfontein. We never really had a captain, but each head of a family was a kind of leader. We generally lived in groups of relations. In the early days so many as a hundred would live together near water-holes in the wilds. That was before the Germans came into the land, and while we felt safe. After the Germans came into the land the people scattered and lived in small groups in the remote places. Many Heikom people went to work for the old Boer settlers, and the old Bushmen told me they were well treated and lived contentedly. When the German farmers came, the Heikom again went to work for them, but the treatment they received was far different to that they received from the Boer settlers. The Germans took their wives away from them and made them their concubines. A Bushman refused to see his wife used in this way by a white man, and they got very angry, but the Germans disregarded them and trouble arose. They gradually got tired of this and ran away back to the veld, taking the Germans stock with them. Then the Germans would hunt them and try to capture them. If they refused to stand, they were shot down like wild animals.

Those whom they captured were sent to gaol and compelled to work after punishment for the same farmer who had taken his wife and who had ill-treated him. If a Bushman dared to protest to his master, saving. "You cannot have my wife, she is mine," he would get a brutal thrashing. He had no rights and no redress. It was this which caused them to murder Germans, and under German rule here there was never peace. The Germans, moreover, made the Bushmen work only for a little food; they never got wages. They were getting wilder and wilder under German law, and more and more scattered through the veld. They were like hunted wild animals, too afraid even to come down to a water-hole in the daytime to drink, for fear a German might see and shoot them. They came down to water at night, like the wild animals. The Germans have shot very many of them. They were never left unmolested.

It was the grossly inconsiderate and immoral attitude of the German farmers in the north towards the wives of their Bushmen labourers that precipitated all the troubles between them and resulted eventually in reprisals by the Bushmen and their shooting by the farmers.

In Major Herbst's report, the capture of his first steenbok by the young Bushman is given as proof of his competency to provide the family with food and encouraged him to take unto himself a wife. The Bushman was no believer in polygamy; he found that it took him all his time to provide for one wife and her offspring. That wife was, however, his cherished companion, and with her and her children the husband shared every morsel of their rough and oft-times scanty diet. The killing of his first steenbok did not, however, imply that he would at once get married. It entitled him to a kind of provisional first claim on his lady-love; but her father saw to it that the prospective son-in-law, during months and often years of servitude (calling to mind the Biblical story of Jacob, Laban and Rachel) worked and hunted for the whole family, and proved beyond any doubt his efficiency as a hunter and a provider of food.

A prize so dearly won was not uncherished, and the one person he could look upon as a mate and a life s companion was not readily to be parted with.

Yet what do we find. The writer has it on the verbal evidence of missionaries and German officials, and on the statements of the natives themselves, that the chief cause of all the trouble between Germans and Bushmen was that the Germans would persist in taking the Bushwomen from their husbands and using them as concubines. The result was that the Bushmen revenged themselves by driving off cattle and, in some cases, by shooting their brutal masters.

Johannes Kruger, an intelligent Cape Bastard, who in 1895 was appointed by Governor Leutwein as "Chief" of the natives of Grootfontein, states under oath:–

> The first German I met was Von François, who passed through Grootfontein with troops towards N'gami. Some years later Major Leutwein came to Ghaub with Dr. Hartmann, the manager of the S.W.A. Company. He stayed there only a day and drew up an agreement for me to sign, wherein I was appointed Captain of the natives and had to recognise German sovereignty and control. Leutwein said I was Captain of the Bushmen and Damaras and of all people who lived at Ghaub. The agreement was signed on 31.8.1895. I identify the original agreement and my signature now shown to me. (Original agreement read over to deponent.) I signed the agreement most unwillingly. I at first refused to sign it, but they (Leutwein and Hartmann) insisted, so I eventually agreed.
>
> I knew the Bushmen had no real Chiefs, and that every head of a family was practically his own Chief and master. I told Leutwein that Bushmen would not readily submit to a Chief, especially as I was not a Bushman. The reply was that as I know the language and the people I might have influence over them. The Berg-Damaras, I felt, I could control, and also the Hottentots, though the Hottentots in particular strongly objected to the agreement being made. They said they did not want to be German subjects and preferred the English. The Berg-Damaras said nothing, and the few Bushmen were also silent, as they understood nothing of the matter. After the agreement was signed, Hartmann gave me 5*l*. a month. I had to provide labourers for the Company. I then tried to collect people

to live in Ghaub which, under the agreement, was given to us. I collected in time 212 Heikom Bushmen (men, women, and children) also 110 Berg-Damaras, and these, with the 35 Hottentots all lived on my werft at Ghaub. They all agreed very well, but the Bushmen only remained a short time, as there was not enough *veld kost* (wild fruits, roots, herbs, &c.) for them to live on. They had no stock. So they scattered and returned to the bush. Later on the Bushmen began to offer their services as labourers on the farms of the German settlers. The majority of the Heikom (several hundred families) left the bush and came in to the farm. Then the trouble started. The German farmers refused to pay them their wages, they said food and tobacco were enough for them. They did not want money. The food was poor and the Bushmen complained to me. I spoke to Lieut. Volkmann, the German Magistrate, and said the Bushmen were a wild people, but if they were properly treated and fed and got a little money, just a little they would get tame and become useful. He made promises, but nothing came of them. We got no redress. As a rule a Bushman only has one wife. If she is barren he may take another, but never has more than two. The majority of the Bushmen have only one wife. They are extremely fond of their women, whom they treat well. The Germans started to take their wives away from the Bushmen and made concubines of them The whole district is full of these German-Bushwomen crossbreeds. This conduct of the Germans annoyed and irritated the Bushmen more than anything else. They deeply resented it; I received numerous complaints from them. I made representations to the German Magistrate, Volkmann, but the trouble continued. This resulted in the Bushmen refusing to work on farms unless compelled by hunger to do so. Then they began, for the first time, to steal the cattle of the Germans and rush them away to the bush. One Bushman whose wife had been taken in this way, murdered the German farmer who had despoiled him. Bushmen were shot on sight by police and German farmers, and no mercy was shown to them. Those who were shot were men who, too afraid to stand, ran away on being seen by a German patrol or a farmer. They were in a state of terror. Often the Germans surprised and captured families of Bushmen in the veld. These people were then transported, with women and children, to Swakopmund or Luderitzbucht to work. Many died down there. I only saw two who had escaped and returned to the bush there. They said all their people perished there of cold and exposure. The Bushmen are human beings after all, and resent their wives being taken away, and object to ill-treatment. They are too terrified now and don t trust white men; but in time I think the Heikom will settle down and become useful labourers if well treated. The Kung or Kalahari Bushmen are more fierce than the Heikom, and will not readily settle down. I have always got on well with them though, and never was molested by any of them. The white men, especially the Germans, treated them as if they were wild animals, and therefore they retaliated and are naturally wild and timid. The Germans treated all natives with harsh brutality and gave them no justice. They all hate the Germans. The majority of the natives here have from time to time been badly flogged and thrashed for all sorts of small offences, such as petty thefts or vagrancy or laziness or impertinence. They were spoiled and driven to desperation by suppression, and many offences they committed and impertinence and lack of respect arose out of the Germans' intimate and immoral relations with their wives and daughters. If a native objected and was cheeky he got flogged for insubordination and impertinence. This was in peace time. In war time a German showed no mercy to man, woman, or child.

We were very unhappy under German rule, and I often deeply regretted their having come here. But what could we do – we were too weak.

I know the natives of Grootfontein. They are all much happier now than they were under German rule. They talk all day long about the new Government, and say they hope and pray that England will keep this country and govern us. They are in terror at the very idea of a German Government. coming back. They say they will all be killed, and will flee away to another country rather than stay. I say the same. The Germans hate me because I tried to protect my Bushmen and Damaras. I reported their cruelty, and they blamed me when the natives deserted their service. I won't stay here if the land is given back to Germany. I don t believe any of us will remain.

The present Magistrate of Grootfontein (Major Frank Brownlee) informed the writer that during a period of over two years service in that large area he has had little or no trouble with the Bushmen. They are no longer scared to death at the sight of a military man, but come down to the water holes and get tobacco and scraps of food from the travellers. They are only too willing to act as messengers and guides and to indicate water holes along routes to be followed. Even the wild Kung Bushmen will come in, very cautiously, one by one, and squat down round the white man's camp fire.

A message to a Bushman leader or head of a family will invariably, if it reaches him, result in his coming in to see the British Magistrate.

This fact alone has caused German officials to gape with astonishment, and Herr von Zastrow one day remarked to Major Brownlee: "How have you British managed within so short a period to gain the friendship and confidence of these wild Bushmen? Why. under my *régime*. I could send out fifty messages and they would be taken not the slightest notice of.

The dictates of personal courtesy prevented the British official from satisfying the curiosity of his German interrogator on this point; but the answer is contained in this Report.

PART TWO

NATIVES AND THE CRIMINAL LAW

CHAPTER ONE

THE NATIVE AS AN ACCUSED PERSON

In the remaining chapters of this report it is proposed to deal with some aspects of the criminal law of the Protectorate applied as against natives before the Occupation, some illuminating features of the administration of the law as against Europeans during the same period when the aggrieved parties were natives, and, finally, with the position between Europeans and natives in these respects as it has been forced on our notice since the Occupation from the point of view purely of the criminal law.

On the first subject what follows in this chapter will be sufficiently instructive. On the second it is felt that the surface merely has been touched, and that deeper investigations would lead to even more serious conclusions than are to be deduced from such cases as that of Ludwig Cramer, referred to in the next chapter. On the third, the bare facts are left to speak for themselves; but cases like those of Venuleth on the one hand, and Becker and Schmidt on the other, throw an unmerciful light on the estimation in which native life has been held within the borders of the Protectorate under German rule.

From the whole only one conclusion is to be drawn, viz., that if a native was killed or seriously injured as a result of a collision with a German it was a matter of small moment, to be disregarded if the authorities were not forced to take notice of it, and if otherwise even then to be minimised to the greatest possible extent. On the other hand, had a German the slightest of grievances against a native, the latter was made to suffer severely under the lash.

The Imperial German Criminal Code constitutes a comprehensive system of criminal law. It carefully defines all offences and provides the punishment for each, even going so far in the latter respect as to lay down maximum penalties for those misdemeanours which must of necessity under modern methods of Government be established by local or police regulation. In outstanding contradistinction to the codes with which we are familiar, it provides precise limits of penalization which leave to the Court, once the exact offence has been determined, but little discretion as regards the sentence to be imposed. It further endeavours to provide for those conditions of mind and circumstance which are usually regarded as reducing in gravity or nullifying entirely an act which is, on the face of it, a breach of the law. Its rigidity cannot be regarded with favour by any one who is familiar with the admirable elasticity of the Roman, Dutch or English systems of criminal jurisprudence, but none the less it affords a body of legal prohibition almost wholly complete in extent and of a nature which doubtless is thoroughly suitable to the meticulous German mind.

This code contemplates the following different forms of punishment:–

Death (by decapitation), severe imprisonment (*zuchthaus*), detention in a fortress *(festungshaft)*, lighter imprisonment *(gefägnis)*, simple imprisonment (haft), and fine.

Corporal punishment is excluded, and the death sentence is only applicable to murder and the most serious form of high treason. Murder is much more narrowly defined than in our law, and many acts which would in the Union of South Africa or Great Britain be regarded as such do not come within its limits under the German code. Consequently, the capital sentence can rarely be imposed. The pollution of a corpse, which we would regard as a grave moral crime, is, in itself, no offence, because, in the words of Mittermaier[202], it is no danger to public health or decency. These are merely individual points of the code which give one some idea of the spirit in which it is framed, and it is plain, after a study of the whole, that it was intended to comprise an up-to-date humane system of criminal law which, while satisfactorily punishing all transgressions, at the same time took into account and made the requisite allowance for all human weaknesses. Consequently it is remarkable to find that the lawgivers of a nation which could dive so deeply into the innermost recesses of the human mind, and fix an exact penalty for every separate evincement of its criminal evolutions, should be content when they came to provide for the similar vicissitudes of native mentality with the following law, promulgated in 1896.[203]

NATIVES – CRIMINAL JURISDICTION

Translation

CRIMINAL JURISDICTION WITH REGARD TO NATIVES: GERMAN SOUTH-WEST AFRICA

Decree of the Imperial Chancellor with regard to the exercise of Criminal Jurisdiction and Powers of Punishment over Natives in the German Protectorates of East Africa, Kamerun and Togo, dated 22nd April 1896 (Col. Gaz., p. 241) applied to the Protectorate of German South-West Africa by Decree of the Governor, dated 8th November 1896 (G. Col. Legisl. II., p. 294).

By virtue of the Imperial Ordinance of the 25th February 1896, the following is laid down with regard to the exercise of Criminal.Jurisdiction and Powers of Discipline over Natives in German South-West Africa in connection with the Decree of the 27th of the same month

---

[202] Carl Joseph Anton Mittermaier (1787-1867) wrote an extensive (686 page) account of standard criminal procedure, as applied in Germany after unification in 1870. *Die Gesetzgebung und Rechtsübung über Strafverfahren: nach ihrer neuesten Fortbildung*, Erlangen, F. Enke, 1856.

[203] A translation of this law is contained in a 'Memorandum on the status of natives in German South West Africa', Consul Müller, Luderitizbucht to Sir Edward Grey, 12th April, 1911: 13-14. Pretoria Archives, GG 276.

I. COMPETENCE

(1) Criminal Jurisdiction and Procedure in the case of the coloured population are exercised by the Governor. In the various Districts the *Bezirksamtmann* or independent Chief of the District (both these officials are included in the term "District Officer" used later) takes the place of the Governor. The *Bezirksamtmann* or independent Chief of the District is entitled to delegate his powers, on his own responsibility, to his subordinate officials for their areas, but is bound to inform the Governor to what extent he has made use of his powers of delegation. The right to inflict punishment shall not be given to a non-commissioned officer, even if in charge of a station. The officer in charge at Cape Cross, who retains his former powers, is exempted from the operation of this provision.

II. PUNISHMENTS

(2) The following punishments may be inflicted: Corporal punishment (flogging and caning), fine, imprisonment with hard labour, imprisonment in irons, death.

(3) Corporal punishment cannot be employed for the punishment of natives of better standing.

(4) No female of any age whatsoever shall be liable to be flogged or caned.

(5) The only punishment in the case of males under 16 years shall be caning.

(6) Flogging shall be carried out with an instrument specified by the Governor, caning with a light cane or rod. A sentence of flogging or caning may be carried out in one or two instalments. Where flogging is inflicted the number of strokes shall not at any one time exceed twenty-five, and where caning is inflicted the number of strokes shall not at any one time exceed twenty. The second instalment cannot be inflicted before the expiry of a fortnight from the first.

(7) The execution of a sentence of flogging or caning must always take place in the presence of a European appointed for this purpose by the official empowered to exercise criminal jurisdiction (paragraph 1), a medical man, for instance, where one is available.

(8) Before the infliction of punishment is begun the person convicted shall be examined in order to ascertain his physical condition.

(9) The medical man called in, or in his absence the European present at the flogging, has the right to stop or suspend the infliction of the flogging or caning if the state of health of the person convicted appears to make such a proceeding necessary.

(10) Sentences of imprisonment for more than six months require the sanction of the Governor, to whom the passing of the sentence must be immediately reported. The execution of the sentence shall be postponed until such sanction is received, unless the delay involved is likely to make the execution of the punishment impossible.

(11) The final decision in the case of a death sentence is the sole prerogative of the Governor. In cases where a District Officer has imposed such a penalty the fact shall be reported forthwith to the Governor, to whom the records in the case should be forwarded.

(12) A record of all criminal cases is to be kept in a book on the following lines

No.	Name.	Crime.	Sentence.	Date of Sentence.	Remarks.
		Theft	20 strokes with cane	26th June 1896	
		Murder	Death	1st August 1896	

Confirmed by the Governor. 12th November 1896.

(13) The Captain (Headman or Chief) or his substitute shall be present during the criminal proceedings. In the case of serious crimes the District Officer shall call in several reputable natives to assist him, though the sole responsibility shall rest with the District Officer. Minutes of the proceedings must be taken, and the verdict must be given in writing.

(14) In the case of outlying stations and official expeditions into the interior of the country the provisions contained in sections 1 to 13 of this Ordinance apply save that with regard to the exercise of criminal jurisdiction the officer in charge of the station or the chief of the expedition is substituted for the District Officer.

(15) In case the procedure laid down in Section II. cannot be adhered to in the case of outlying stations or expeditions into the interior (Section 14) in case of mutiny, hostile attack, or any pressing emergency owing to urgent reasons, but on the contrary the immediate execution of the death sentence upon a native seems required by the circumstances, then the officer in charge of the station or expedition shall institute summary proceedings against the accused after, if possible, calling upon at least two assessors to assist him, and shall thereafter forward the minutes of the proceedings with the sentence passed and reasons therefor together with a report of the circumstances to the Imperial Governor. If it should have proved impossible to call upon assessors as prescribed, the reason which made this impossible should be entered in the minutes.

(16) If Martial Law is declared in any portion or locality of the Protectorate by the Imperial Governor, his substitute or, in the event of urgent danger, by an independent Government official or Military Commander, then the summary proceedings laid down in Section 15 of this Ordinance immediately come into force as against natives who render themselves liable to punishment.

III. DISCIPLINARY POWERS OF DISTRICT OFFICERS AND OFFICERS IN CHARGE OF OUTLYING STATIONS

(17) Natives who are employed as servants or under a contract to work may, on the application of their masters or employers, be sentenced as a disciplinary measure by any officer entrusted with the exercise of criminal jurisdiction (Sections 1, 14) to the following punishments, viz., corporal punishment, together with imprisonment in irons or imprisonment in irons alone, for a period not to exceed 14 days, for the following offences Continued neglect of duty and idleness, insubordination or unwarranted desertion from their places of service or employment, as well as any other serious breach of the condition of service or employment. The provisions of Sections 2 to 9 and 12 with regard to judicial punishments are applicable to disciplinary punishments.

IV. CONCLUDING PROVISIONS

(18) District Officers and officers in charge of stations or, as the case may be, leaders of expeditions or their substitutes in case of their absence, are required to furnish a quarterly return of all punishments carried into effect to the Governor. These reports are to be submitted to the Imperial Colonial Office.

(19) This Ordinance comes into force on the day of its publication in the various Districts and Stations. Contrary regulations are simultaneously repealed.

(20) This Ordinance, as far as the administration of the judicial proceedings is concerned, is only applicable to disputes among the natives belonging to the same Captain, as far as is compatible with the terms of the Protectorate Treaties.

This law is deserving of study. In the first place and properly so, the supreme administration of justice is in the hands of the Governor. If magistrates, juries, judges all have erred, with the Crown remains the power to put matters right, and with it also rests the divine prerogative of mercy. Subject to this authority, the Ordinance is exercised, not by the ordinary Courts, but by the *Bezirksamtmann* or *Distrikt Chef*. These officers were Chiefs of Police of their Districts, and the undesirability of vesting the power of punishing crime in the same official who is responsible for its detection and investigation needs no emphasis.

Punishments are laid down under Section 2, but there is nothing whatever to indicate how they are to be applied. This was left entirely to the whim of the individual official, and there was in law nothing to prevent him except in regard to the offences against an employer set out in Section 17. from inflicting any punishment from a fine of 1s. to death for any offence. Examples of how this was carried out in practice appear later.

There is no reference whatever to the very material subject of evidence, but it is laid down that minutes (protocol) must be kept and the decision recorded in writing. In the case of Venuleth (see Chapter 3, Part II.) it was urged that the trial held by him was conducted under the authority contained in Sections 15 and 16 of this Ordinance. The entire record of the case charge, evidence, verdict and judgment is contained in the following document[204]:–

PROTOCOL

Okonjati,
9th June 1915

Proceedings of Court Martial, held at Okonjati on 9th June 1915, upon two Bushmen, names unknown.

Members of Court were: Lieutenant Venuleth, President.
Corporal Schulze.
Corporal Rapecki.

Statement of Facts:
The two Bushmen were discovered by Lieutenant Venuleth in the middle of October on the farm Schonbrunn busy slaughtering two wethers near a small cattle post. When the stock were counted it appeared that 367 had been stolen. Moreover, all over the neighbourhood a considerable quantity of stock had been stolen (Okaturua). On the 9th June, Lieutenant Venuleth searched the bush and found about twelve natives in it, but only succeeded in capturing the two in question.

The unanimous decision was that the crime of stock theft had been proved, and that they should be shot.

This sentence was carried out on the 9th June by Corporal Rapecki and Lance-Corporal Hitter, under the orders of Lieutenant Venuleth.

(Signed) Venuleth, Oberleutnant.
Okonjati,
9th June 1915

---

[204] For further discussion of the case involving Lt. Venuleth see Gordon, *Bushman Myth*, p79-81

This is the entire record of a case in which the supreme penalty was imposed, and immediately carried out, upon evidence every word of which would have been rejected by a British Court. One of the victims was a woman.

The Ordinance also contains no reference to the equally material subject of defence. In fact, the whole question of procedure is left in the air, and apparently the presiding officer could do as he liked. Although these omissions are apparent in the law, they would not perhaps obtrude themselves on the notice of any one familiar with all the safeguards established in Union and British law in favour of the accused were they not forced upon it by the examples of complete disregard of those safeguards displayed by persons exercising its provisions in this territory.

According to official records, on the 18th September 1914, a Court similar to that constituted by Venuleth, sitting at Waterberg, tried a native named Alfred for the offence of stock theft. The only evidence given was that of a farmer, Schneider[205], who stated that he had lost some 50 head of small stock, and that a Herero, by name Simon, had also lost one head; that this native had gone to look for his animal and had come across the accused in possession of some blankets which Simon claimed as his own. Schneider stated further that Simon had also found the head of his missing goat, and that lying about Alfred s camping-ground were the bones of a number of other small stock. This evidence was read over to the accused, who made the following statement "I have been loafing about the bush, have lived on veld food and caught guinea fowl, but I have not stolen cattle, but my two associates have stolen stock. I have always made them give me some their meat." Apparently a Herero named Sepp gave evidence similar to that of but only this bare fact appears on record. Upon these statements the accused Alfred was sentenced to death by hanging for repeated stock thefts, the Court giving the following reasons for its decision

"Though the accused denies all guilt, yet the Court has come to the conclusion that the accused himself assisted in the stealing of stock and that he has even been the leader of the gang. As a lot of small stock has disappeared in this locality lately, and according to the investigation of the police and troops the offences had been committed by natives, the court is of opinion that they must impose the death penalty in order to deter the natives and to protect the neighbouring farmers and small settlers against. further serious losses."

The judgement was promulgated forthwith and executed immediately.

Upon this case being brought to his notice, Governor Seitz telegraphed at once to the President of the Court, Lieutenant von Weiher, forbidding him to execute any more such sentences without His Excellency's consent. He also drew the attention of the Officer Commanding Troops to the case, pointing out

---

[205] Today the Schneider-Waterberg family has a farm at Klein Waterberg with a small private museum that mainly contains memorabilia from the decisive battle between the German and Herero forces which took place nearby at Ohamakari on 11th August, 1904. Tötemeyer, Andree-Jeanne, *The state of museums in Namibia and the need for training for museum services*, University of Namibia, Windhoek, 1999. p. 142

that as the native was not in the service of the Army a field court martial had no jurisdiction in the matter; that it is not proper to summarily punish stock theft with the death penalty; that it was doubtful whether the members of the Court had not rendered themselves liable to prosecution on account of unlawful proceedings, and that there could be no doubt that the case would have serious consequences upon the cessation of hostilities. The *Bezirksamtmann* at Omaruru, on his own initiative, also brought this case to the notice of Governor Seitz; but no one apparently took any notice of the point that, beyond the accused s admission of having had some of the meat, there was practically no evidence whatever as we regard it that he had committed any offence at all.

The forms of punishment provided by this Ordinance differ materially from those prescribed in the criminal code.

The place of honour is occupied by corporal punishment; then follows fine, which was rarely imposed, and rightly so since the natives as a rule were not in a position to pay; the next variety is imprisonment with forced labour, which is more severe than any of the forms of imprisonment mentioned in the criminal code. *Kettenhaft*, or imprisonment in chains, does not necessarily imply anything very serious. Its full value can only be appreciated when the chains themselves are examined (see Appendix 1).[206] It should be noted, moreover, that this punishment was applicable to women. While the death sentence was carried out on Europeans by decapitation, in the case of natives hanging was employed. No proper gallows appears ever to have been used, and in many instances the arrangements were of such a primitive character that slow strangulation was the result. (See frontispiece.)

Section 3 is a reasonable provision, but leaves a loophole through which abuse might creep in, since it remains to the official to decide the meaning of the words of better standing. Previous chapters show that this loophole was made use of in the cases of Chiefs of high standing, who were compelled to suffer lashes.

Sections 4 and 5 are in accordance with humane ideas of penal correction.

In regard to Section 6 it is clear from the German official records that the number of strokes imposed frequently exceeded 23. (Statistics on this point appear later in this chapter.) Further, the infliction of corporal punishment in two instalments has rightly or wrongly long ago been rejected by us as abhorrent.

Exception cannot be taken to Sections 7 to 13, nor is the principle of Sections 14 to 16 objectionable, though obviously it requires strict care in its application. In practice Section 13 was completely ignored.

---

[206] It had been reported in 1916 that the German prisons were "most primitive and, in some cases, totally unfit for human occupation. Prisoners wre prevented from escaping by neck chains, handcuffs, chains fastened to rings in the cell floors, and other barbarous methods of a byegone age". It is interesting to note that 'all chains' were removed and some were sent to 'the Departmental Museum in the Union'. Administrator 'Report of the Administrator of SWA, 9 July 1915-31 March 1916, p. 20. A 272. Bk. 1.

The most dangerous provision in the whole enactment is contained in Section 17, which provides for the infliction as a disciplinary measure of corporal punishment combined with imprisonment in chains, or the latter alone for breaches of a contract of service.

A damnable feature of this prescription is that apparently the only punishment for a refractory female servant was imprisonment in chains, but the worst aspect of all is that no trial was required. Punishment was inflicted "upon application of the master." Doubtless it is this section which is responsible for many of the abuses to which natives have been subjected here. That an executive official should be empowered to lash a native servant. with, be it remembered, so severe an instrument as a rhinoceros-hide sjambok, merely as an administrative measure, is repugnant to all our ideas of humanity, which would require a most exhaustive and scrupulous trial before such a penalty could be imposed for the most serious offence.

This short Section 17 contains the whole of the provisions of the German law corresponding to the punitive portions of what are known in the Cape as the Masters and Servants Acts (which it may be interesting to observe were once brought to the notice of the local authorities through the instrumentality of the British Government with a view to their adoption in the Protectorate, but were summarily rejected). In the whole body of the law of Great Britain there is but one offence of this nature, viz., feeding fodder to one animal which was intended for another against the master s orders, and the maximum penalty for such wrongdoing is a fine of 5*l*. (26 and 27 Victoria. c. 103). In the Cape the offences of this character which it was found necessary to establish in order to ensure satisfactory control of the native population have all been carefully defined; for example, desertion is "without lawful cause departing front the master s service with intent not to return thereto." The penalties are carefully restricted, the maximum for a first offence being two months hard labour and for a subsequent offence three months, while the option of a fine may be given in all cases. The utmost punishment for a woman is 2*l*., or in default of payment one month s imprisonment without hard labour. This measure (Cape Act 18/1873) has stood the test of time, and has been found entirely satisfactory in the interests both of the master and the servant; yet in this Protectorate, the immediate neighbour of the Cape Province, it has been found necessary to call in chains and the lash for acts which in countries whose population is solely European are not offences at all, but merely matters to be taken to a civil Court.

The German law, while containing provisions to which British people familiar with native races would take grave exception, has several safeguards of high value; and if these had always been carefully observed there could not, apart from the disgraceful Section 17, have been much room for abuse or criticism. There is, however, grave reason to fear, as the reader will have gathered from previous chapters, that this was not the case. It is, moreover, clear that extreme severity was the rule in the administration of the Ordinance, and that this was not officially discouraged. A casual glance at the official German returns made under Section 18 confirm this view. The following particulars are given from a return from the small district of Bethany, taken at random from a large number of such.

This return covers the period 1.1.13 – 31.3.14, and shows 103 punishments recorded. 38 of these were awarded by the District Court after trial; the other 65 were summarily administered, *i.e.*, by the police, without trial. The district in question is very sparsely populated, its native population – men, women andchildren – in 1913 being officially stated as about 1,400.

(1) For "negligence" Jan Thomas, a Hottentot, received 25 lashes; for "repeated negligence" a compatriot named David Klaas received 25 lashes, while Ahasmab received 25 plus 14 days in chains for "continual negligence." For "gross negligence and drunkenness" one Lukas was awarded 50 lashes and 14 days in chains.

(2) For "telling a lie" Herero Charlie was summarily punished with 25 lashes.

(3) For "desertion," Abraham, Jan, Hans and others received 25 lashes each, while Johannes received 14 days in chains in addition to his lashes.

(4) For "disobedience," Christian Jacob and others received 25 lashes each.

(5) For "vagrancy" Hendrik received 25 lashes and two weeks in chains; Jacob, a Cape boy, received the same punishment, as did several others; and a few youths were punished with 10 to 15 cuts with a cane for the same offence.

(6) The Hottentot woman Rebecca, for "disobedience and refusal to work," received 14 days in chains; Sarah. eight days in chains for desertion: while Elsa, Liesbeth and Katharina for vagrancy received 14 days in chains.

Of the total of 103 cases, 30 convictions were for desertion, 20 for negligence, 9 for vagrancy, 7 for insolence, and 18 for disobedience.

A similar return from the Gibeon District, also a very sparsely populated area, affords the following information.

During the period under review, 148 convictions are recorded. Of these, 37 are for negligence, 17 for desertion, 12 for laziness, 13 for vagrancy, and 21 for disobedience.

(1) Tstuchub. a Bushman, for the crime of serious theft in four cases, being a band leader and threatening, was sentenced to death and duly executed. A similar penalty was imposed on the Bushman Kunchab for "attempted murder, sedition and. banding."

(2) For the crime of congregating or "banding," the Bushman Lamzib received six years in chains, while his compatriots Eirub, Olip and

Keichaub each received three years in chains. Their women who, merely owing to being with them, were also guilty of "banding together" named Uibeneis, Kokus. Ubineis, Hamis, Hurus, Uibis, Batus, Hosas and Goakanus, received each four mouths' imprisonment with hard labour.

(3) Hans, a Hottentot, received:–
  (a) Two months in chains and 40 lashes for ill-treating an animal, and
  (b) Four months imprisonment with hard labour and 30 lashes for vagrancy.

(4) The Berg-Damara Junip received 50 lashes and six months hard labour for vagrancy, while a companion named Nunip was awarded four months' hard labour plus 40 lashes for the same offence. For the crime of "milking strange goats" the Berg-Damaras Otto and April each received six lashes.

At Gobabis

(1) The Hottentot Lucas for "repeated serious housebreaking" was sentenced to death, but the Governor commuted this sentence to 10 years us in chains.

(2) The Herero Lucas received 15 lashes for "creating a nuisance," and Matthias the same sentence for making a wrong accusation.

From these returns it appears that, during the 15 months ending 31st March 1914, 4,356 natives of both sexes were convicted, 4,039 males and 317 females. Out of the 4,039 males, 3,044 suffered corporal punishment, 2,787 being flogged and 257 caned, and of those caned some were boys under 16, and practically the whole of the remainder were labourers of mixed race from the Cape. No doubt they owed to their white blood the adoption of the milder form of punishment. The maximum number of strokes with the cane imposed was 40, and this was administered in four cases; in one, in two instalments of 20 each, while three persons underwent 20 strokes and the same number 30 in two instalments. For flogging a sjambok was used, generally made of rhinoceros-hide. This was a severe instrument one metre long and one centimetre thick at the thin end. The following table shows the number of persons on whom more than nine lashes were inflicted during the period:–

No. of Lashes	No. of Persons
10	609
12	13
15	1,141
20	77
25	435

30	9
15 twice	22
40	37
20 twice	16
50	59
25 twice	68
	2,486

The average number of lashes imposed was nearly 17 per individual. The total number of strokes. cane and sjambok, was 50,127. These figures indicate that the lash as an instrument of justice was indulged in to an appalling extent.

In the Union of South Africa the following whippings were inflicted on adult natives in the year 1913:–

6 strokes and under	345
7 – 12	1.110
13 – 24	488
Over 24 – 16	16
	1,959

The total number of male adult natives punished in that year was 296,965 that is to say, that in only one out of 150 cases was the rod called upon as against three out of four in this territory. Moreover, corporal punishment is rarely imposed in the Union save for sexual offences or repeated serious offences. Here it could be, and constantly was, imposed on a servant merely because he did not do his work. It must, moreover, be borne in mind in making these comparisons that, from the point of view of severity, there could be no question of equality between a rhinoceros sjambok of the official dimensions already mentioned and the rod employed in Union prisons.

On the 26th February 1907 the head of the Colonial Section of the German Foreign Office wrote to the Governor at Windhuk stating that objections had been raised in Togo and the Cameroons to the sjambok on account of the injuries it caused, and asking for his views on the subject in the light of the longer experience obtained in the Protectorate. The District Officers were consulted and, with one exception, were in favour of its retention. The Chief Government Medical Officer reported that in his opinion the sjambok ought to be condemned. The Governor's reply to Germany was that all District Officers save one were in favour of the instrument, and he proposed to retain it in use. He omitted to give the Medical Officer's view.

In. the year 1900 the Berlin Government pointed out that the number of natives punishment in this country was out of all proportion to the population, and that corporal punishment was awarded in an exceedingly large number of cases, and that it was feared that public opinion in Germany would draw very unfavourable conclusions as to the success of Germany methods of civilisation. It was accordingly directed that such punishment should only be, inflicted in very serious cases and where experience has proved other means for the moral improvement of natives to be ineffectual. The ability of officials was to be judged in future by their success in their chief duty, the education of natives, without too frequent recourse to punishment. Governor Leutwein called for reports from the District Officers, missionaries and others.[207] All, with one accord, deprecated any change in the matter, and the officers said that they knew of no case in which the sjambok had done harm. Captain Fourie, of the South African Medical Corps, who has in the course of his duties as officer in charge of the Native Hospital at Windhuk examined large numbers of male natives, has reported that a large proportion bear permanent injuries due to the sjambok.

It is probably due to this official reproof from Berlin that the exercise of the so-called fatherly right of correction (*Väterliche Zuchtigungsrecht*) became so frequent. By this means natives were punished by their masters without the necessity for any official record being kept or, in fact, any official receiving notice of it. In consequence, even the summary procedure laid down by Section 17 of the above-quoted Ordinance was constantly disregarded, and the administration of corporal punishment freely took place without being forced on the official notice of the authorities to their embarrassment.

The death sentence would appear in our eyes to have been abused, though not to the same extent as the lash. The returns referred to above disclose its imposition and execution, for attempted murder coupled with assault and theft, and for serious theft. Such a sentence was also passed in one instance for house-breaking, but was commuted by the Governor to ten years imprisonment in chains.

It is convenient here to remark on a further important point in which discrimination in the method of punishment as between European and native took place. Under the theory known as real-concurrence, if any one person committed several offences the penalty was assessed separately for each, the total amount was then usually reduced to a certain extent and this reduced total was the actual sentence put in force. The authority for this is Section 74 of the German Criminal Code. Cramer, whose case is dealt with in the next chapter, got the benefit of it. In the lower Court the sentences imposed on him totalled 27 months and they were reduced in this way to 21. On appeal the original sentences were altered to a total of five months, which was similarly converted into an actual sentence of four months. Compare this with the case referred to above of the native sentenced to death for repeated housebreaking, the maximum punishment for a single instance of which under the Code is 10 years' hard labour.

---

[207] English translations of Leutwein's order and twenty-eight responses form District Magistrates, District Advisory Councils and missionaries can be found in NAN A 41 're. Infliction of corporal Punishment on Natives'.

The foregoing shows how severely the law was administered when it was observed. Yet it is the firm conviction of British officials now in the country, forced on them by numerous instances which have come to their notice during their 2½ years of occupation, that the law was mainly honoured in the breach and that it was the general practice to disregard it on account of the rules whose observation it required. The ordinary police-post was in charge of a sergeant, who could not exercise the law of April 1896; yet evidence is constantly cropping up that these sergeants as a matter of practice assumed that. they had the necessary power and regularly thrashed natives for trifling offences. Beyond this it is abundantly clear that masters rarely went to the extent of troubling the sergeants until they had themselves gone to a grave limit in the direction of corporal punishment of their servants.

Attention must also be drawn to the fact that these police sergeants were ex-soldiers. with no training worthy of the name as policemen, and whose only qualification was that they had served in the von Trotha campaign and undergone its brutalising and degrading influences.

The pernicious theory of the parental right of correction already referred to which was allowed to grow up and encouraged by officials, was doubtless in the main responsible for the state of affairs that existed. Every German employer of native labour, except – to their credit be it stated – a few with feelings of humanity, claimed that he stood *in loco parentis* to his native servants, whether they were 15 or 50 years old, married or single, male or female, and as such asserted his right to administer "parental correction" to them. It appears that German law gives a master the right to administer such correction to his apprentices and, in some German States; to domestic servants. This defence was raised in practically every case (the number was not large) in which master or mistress was charged here with ill-treatment of a servant, and the local Courts appear to have laid it down that, although not expressly provided by law, nevertheless such right did exist, but that the correction must not exceed the limits of ordinary restraint not be such as to do serious injury. It must, in fact, be such reasonable punishment as a father would give to his unruly child. This view is perhaps not without its logical support; but a perusal of the case of Cramer dealt with later on, in which this defence was the only serious answer to the main facts, will show how far such a theory may carry an individual beyond the limits of self-restraint to the utmost excesses.

A question which has led to many of the disasters which have attended German administration of the criminal law in its application to natives is that of the oath. This is a matter of considerable difficulty, and some sympathy may be felt with the German side of it, however opposed to our ideas it may be. To a German Court – but not, unhappily, to every German individual – the oath was sacred. Its administration was a solemn function attended by divers ceremonies and, once taken, the witness's words received credence almost without reservation as against other evidence not on oath, no matter how powerful. The Germans have not progressed to the stage which we have reached of examining even sworn statements solely in relation to all the other proved circumstances of a case and testing their reliability accordingly, but gave a fictitious value to such statements. With them the sanctity of the oath is based on the theory of Divine punishment, and consequently natives who are usually heathen – and, even if Christian, mere babies in Christianity – cannot be permitted to take it since it has no such binding force on them as on a European, who may be described from this point of view as having reached his majority in Christianity.

Yet anyone who has read the statements in Part I. of this Report regarding the customs of the local natives will have gathered that they were thoroughly familiar with the oath, of which they had their own forms, and breach of which was a grave dishonour visited with heavy punishment. For centuries the most sacred oaths had a prominent part in their tribal life. and were universally respected. No doubt upon this is founded the experience of British officials that, in most instances, the statements of a native in a Court of law may, after making due allowance for his lower grade of intelligence, ignorance of the, and so on, be accepted quite as readily as those of his European fellow-inhabitants. Where a native has departed from the truth it has generally been found that he has done so through fear of his German master. Generally speaking, local natives in Court show a remarkably high regard for the truth. comparing very favourably in this respect with Europeans and remarkably so with the natives of the Union.

The writer of this part of this Report has had many years' experience in the Union of the behaviour under oath of Europeans, natives, coloured people, Indians, Malays and other races, and is probably better qualified than any other British official in the Protectorate to form an opinion in regard to local natives when in the same situation. It is sufficient to say here, without going into the grounds upon which the foregoing conclusion is based, that it is his deliberately-formed opinion in the light of such experience.

Only as proof, therefore, either of utter blindness or of deliberately fostered misconception as to the high standard of the natives in this respect can the following be regarded. In 1909 Herr Dernburg put forward proposals for certain reforms in judicial procedure in the German Colonies directed among other things towards improving the standing of natives. Among them was the following:–

> It is intended to introduce the administration of the oath to natives as a measure for their moral improvement.

The Swakopmund newspaper, *Deutsch Südwestafrikanische Zeitung*, in its issue of the 4th December 1909, commented upon this proposition in the following terms:–

> So, after all, the accursed administration of the oath to natives! We are much afraid that the Reichstag will not stand firm enough against the efforts of Dernburg, born of absolute ignorance of the nigger; and we are of the opinion that only the determined opposition of the peoples of the Protectorates and of our Protectorate Councils – if it does not come too late – can prevent such a calamity.

In giving evidence, therefore, natives could not take the oath and, owing to the fictitious value placed upon it, were consequently not so readily believed as Europeans who did. This, originally a possibly well-intentioned attitude of the Courts, led in the outcome to the dreadful situation that not even the most incontrovertible evidence, and oceans of it, was permitted to weigh against the bare statement of a single European witness. That this is no wild statement is proved by the following extracts from the deliberate judgement in Cramer's case:–

> In the determination of these facts the Court, contrary to custom, accepted the statements of the natives Heiweib and Grunas inasmuch as they adhered to their former statements which agreed with the former evidence of the accused and certain white witnesses. while the accused and the said witnesses today depart entirely from their former evidence…The Court could not accept this as established by the "evidence of the natives alone in view of the denial of the accused."…

That is to say, reduced to its logical conclusion, that if accused and his witnesses had lied consistently throughout there would have been no question of giving credence to the statements of the natives.

The following extracts (for original text see Appendix 3) from the German records at Windhuk (W. III., r. 2) also go far in support of this view:–

Letters from the Imperial Magistrate at Luderitzbucht to the Governor.

1

Imperial Magistrate
Luderitzbucht,
J. No. 295
31st January 1908
The Imperial Government,
Windhuk

ILL-TREATMENT OF NATIVES *in re*.

No cases have become known to me in which German farmers have ill-treated their natives or not provided them with sufficient food.

However, a whole number of cases have been reported in which employees of the railway have ill-treated Herero prisoners of war who have been working under their supervision.

In most of these cases I have laid a charge against the offenders with the Imperial District Court. However, these charges have very rarely resulted in a conviction, as in most cases only natives could be called as witnesses. whose statements were not considered sufficient and satisfactory by the Court.

(Signed) Boehmer

2

Imperial Magistrate
Luderitzbucht,
J. No. 5150
14th June 1911
The Imperial Government,
Windhuk

In consequence of the opinions prevalent in this country, every official whose duty it is to oppose the ill-treatment of natives on the diamond-fields and who has to prosecute such offences by laying corresponding charges in the Courts is only too readily suspected of negrophilism.

The opinion is very frequently held in this country that the Ovambo is "no human being" at all, and that the native does not possess the right of self-defence even in case of the most severe ill-treatment by Europeans, but that he has only the right to lodge a complaint with the Magistrate.

(Signed) Heilingbrunner,
Acting Magistrate

3

Imperial Magistrate
Luderitzbucht,
The Imperial Government,
21st April 1913
Windhuk

ILL-TREATMENT OF NATIVES *in re*.

Complaints regarding the ill-treatment of natives are once more on the increase, although for a short time an agreeable improvement had taken place in that respect.

How much times have changed is best proved by the remark passed by one of the heads of the largest diamond companies, who could find no other answer to the complaint of the Native Commissioner to the effect that one of his diamond sorters was continually striking the natives than: "I have complaints about the natives also." The change in opinion is apparently the result of the companies now having sufficient native labourers and consequently thinking that it is no longer necessary to look after them so well as formerly.

The Law Courts are utterly useless (*Die Gerichte versagen vollkommen*). One may occasionally obtain a conviction and a monetary fine in the first instance. An appeal is promptly lodged. The case is heard by a Chief Judge, who does not know the conditions on the diamond fields, nay, has perhaps never seen one. The native witnesses have left for home during the long period elapsing between the first and second hearings, and the reading of the scanty record of their statements made at the first hearing of the case makes no impression. The accused has learnt sufficiently from the first case how to conduct his defence; the natives are not believed, while the most doubtful statements of Europeans are given full credence as long as they are made under oath. Naturally the matter is settled by a brilliant judgement of "Not Guilty." There is no more thankless task than to act as prosecutor in such cases.

It is useless to deal with the Chamber of Mines. This institution hardly does anything else than dispute the actual facts, and very seldom gets beyond banalities.

Furthermore, the Chamber has not by any means the influence over its members which would be expected by the outsider.

(Signed) Boehmer

These are the opinions of a highly-placed official, not once expressed but at intervals over a number of years.

In German South-West Africa, therefore, the native was oppressed by a criminal law of mediaeval severity administered, not in the calm judicial atmosphere of a Court, but in the heat and turmoil of everyday administration by executive officials; and, if he came before a judicial tribunal, laboured under most serious disabilities.

CHAPTER TWO

THE POSITION OF A NATIVE WHEN COMPLAINANT

Coming here full of British ideas of the administration of justice, with echoes of German vaunts of superior civilisation in our ears despite hints from Belgium and not suspecting that that civilisation carried with it views of the exercise of the law in regard to natives utterly different from those with which it was carried out in regard to Europeans, for some the it did not occur to anyone to make serious investigation into the manner in which the German Government had fulfilled its obligations in this respect towards its coloured subjects.

From the to the, however, references to ugly occurrences cropped up, and recently a definite attempt to ascertain the truth was made. In the course of the inquiries the case of Ludwig Cramer, of which the full judgement follows later, came to notice. A glance showed its importance, and the papers were then fully examined.[208] The scantiness of the documents gives much room for conjecture, but the facts are sufficiently fully stated in the judgement to enable an unbiased person to form a conclusion as to the way justice was meted out to the unfortunate natives (all but one women) concerned in the matter, and the inhuman brute into whose hands it was their misfortune to fall.

Cramer was first of all tried by the District Judge at Windhuk. The charge brought against him was "dangerous assault," and there were 10 separate counts. On two of these, in which it was alleged that he had on separate occasions kept natives chained up in his "farm-prison" for many hours in such a position that they were unable to move, he was acquitted, the Court not being satisfied that they were fastened up immovably. The mere chaining up of a native for 24 hours was not worth taking notice of. On the remaining eight counts he was sentenced as follows:–

> For the assaults on Grunas, Auma, and Maria. five months' imprisonment in each case.
> For the assaults on Konturu and July, three months' imprisonment in each case.

---

[208] The German response to the Blue Book criticised the emphasis that it gives to the Cramer case, but condemned his actions, rather than the leniency of the judicial response – "The German Administration ... can only express the most intense regret that such persons should make their way to the colonies and injure the German name through their actions." German Colonial Office, *The Treatment of Native and other Populations in the Colonial Possessions of Germany and England ...*, Hans Robert Engelmann, Berlin, 1919: 135-141.

For the assaults on Alwine, Amalia, and Magdalena, two months' imprisonment each.
Or 27 months in all.

According to the rules of real-concurrence, as it is called by German jurists, which relate to repeated offences, this sentence was reduced to a combined penalty of 21 months' imprisonment. When the facts of these assaults, which appear later, are considered. the extraordinary leniency of this sentence is almost unbelievable; yet on appeal by accused it was actually reduced to four months' imprisonment and a fine of 135*l*.

As has been stated, the record is scanty, and the facts can only be gathered from the written judgement; but there is one piece of evidence with the papers which is more illuminating than any mere verbal description can be. The injured natives were attended to in Gobabis hospital by Dr. Hollander, who put in photographs of the backs of the two women Maria and Auma. These photographs were taken about 14 days after the assaults, and are reproduced in this chapter. The horrible condition to which these poor women s bodies were reduced through accused's brutality is clearly shown.

As throwing some light on the attitude of the officials toward the matter, the case of Auma may be referred to. She was an old, feeble woman of 55 or 60; she had been most severely beaten. as the medical evidence and photograph show; she was in danger of losing her life when admitted to hospital; she could not be cured except by skin-transference, which she was too old to undergo, and she died after 14 days hospital treatment. It is incredible that accused was not charged with murder in her case.

As to Maria a woman about 30, her life was in danger when admitted to hospital. She was released from hospital uncured and permanently incapacitated, and died six months later. In her case a charge of assault resulting in permanent injury, at least, for which the minimum punishment is one year. should have been laid.

The woman Konturu was in her first month of pregnancy, and had a miscarriage shortly after the assault upon her. Grunas was far advanced in pregnancy, and her condition must have been obvious to accused. She was thrashed two days running, and on the second or the following day gave birth to a dead child. Yet the only charge brought against accused in these cases was dangerous assault.

The minimum punishment for this offence is two months' imprisonment, the maximum five years. The Appeal Court in Auma's case found it committed without extenuating circumstances, and awarded three months. If mitigating circumstances are present the punishment is imprisonment of from one day to three years, or a fine not exceeding 1,000 marks. In all instances except that of Auma this was found to be the case; but in regard to Maria and Grunas the Court hardened its heart, refused the option of a fine, and awarded one month's imprisonment.

In the cases of July and Magdalena a fine of 40*l.* was imposed, and the same in the case of Konturu, although in addition to the beatings accused s conduct in regard to her was grossly indecent in one particular respect.

For thrashing Amalia and Alwine he escaped with 10*l.* and 5*l.* respectively.

It appeared front the proceedings in tile lower Court that the sjambok used by the accused was a heavy rhinoceros-hide instrument, such as has already been referred to in the preceding chapter.

In order to fully understand what follows, it is necessary to reproduce here certain provisions of the German Criminal Code[209]:–

> *Section* 211 – Anyone who intentionally and with deliberation kills a person shall be guilty of murder and shall suffer death therefor.
>
> *Section* 212. – Anyone who intentionally but without deliberation kills a person shall be guilty of intentional homicide and liable to penal internment of not less than five years.
>
> *Section* 220. – Anyone who intentionally procures the miscarriage or death of the child of a pregnant woman without her knowledge or consent shall be liable to penal internment of not less than two years. If the death of the woman results therefrom the punishment is penal internment for life or for not less than ten years.
>
> *Section* 222. – Anyone who by negligence causes the death of a person is liable to confinement not exceeding three years.
>
> If the offender is specially required by virtue of his office, calling, or trade to exercise caution and neglects to do so, the penalty may be increased to confinement not exceeding five years.
>
> *Section* 223. – Anyone who intentionally does injury to the body or health of another shall be guilty of assault and liable to confinement not exceeding three years or to a fine not exceeding one thousand marks.
>
> *Section* 223 (a). – If the assault is committed by means of a weapon, and in particular a knife or other dangerous instrument, or by means of a sudden treacherous attack, or by several persons jointly, or by treatment dangerous to life, the punishment is confinement for not less than two months.
>
> *Section* 224. – If the assault results in the loss of an important organ of the body, the sight of an eye, the power of hearing, speech or procreation, or in permanent serious deformity, protracted illness, paralysis or mental disorder, sentence of penal internment not exceeding five years or confinement of not less than one year shall be passed.
>
> *Section* 225. – If any of the aforementioned consequences is caused intentionally, sentence of penal internment of from two to ten years shall be passed.

---

[209] Waters was already extremely familiar with these laws. See Gage, R.H and A.J. Water *Imperial German Criminal Code Translated into English*, W.E. Hortor & Co, Johannesburg, 1917

Section 226. – If the assault results in death, sentence of penal internment or confinement of not less than three years shall be passed.

Section 228. – If there are extenuating circumstances the punishment may be, in the case of Section 223 (a), confinement not exceeding three years or a fine not exceeding one thousand marks; in the cases of Sections 224 and ... confinement of not less than one month; and in the case of Section 226 confinement of not less than three months.

Section 230. – Anyone who by negligence causes bodily injury to another shall be liable to a fine not exceeding nine hundred marks or to confinement not exceeding two years.

If the offender is specially required by virtue of his office, calling, or trade to exercise caution and neglects to do so, the penalty may be increased to confinement not exceeding three years.

Section 240. – Anyone who by force or threatening the commission of a crime or misdeed unlawfully compels another to an act of commission, submission, or omission, shall be liable to confinement not exceeding one year or a fine not exceeding six hundred marks.

The attempt is punishable.

Section 73. If one and the same act is a contravention of several provisions of the law, only that which imposes the heaviest penalty, and in the case of dissimilar forms of punishment that which imposes the severest form, is applicable.

Section 74.[xvii] –Anyone who by several independent acts has committed several crimes or misdeeds, or the same crime or misdeed several times, and has thereby incurred several terms of incarceration other than for a life period, shall be sentenced to a combined punishment which consists in an increase of the heaviest punishment incurred.

In the case of a combination of dissimilar forms of punishment by incarceration, this increase is made in the punishment of the severest form.

The amount of the combined punishments may not exceed the combined amounts of the single punishments incurred, and may not be more than penal internment for fifteen years, confinement for ten years, or military detention for fifteen years.

For the difference between Sections 211 and 212, a matter which is not of much importance here, the reader is referred to the next chapter.

A translation of the judgement of the Appeal Court now follows. It has been carefully made and revised, and may be taken as entirely correct.

[xvii] (Page 164 in original) Offences under the German Code are divided into three classes according to their gravity. The words: Crime, Misdeed and Delinquency are used in the translation by Messrs. Gage and Waters, from which these sections are taken, to represent the three classes. Somewhat similarly, Penal Internment, Confinement, Military Detention and Detention represent different forms of incarceration known to the German Criminal Code.

IN THE NAME OF THE KAISER*

In the criminal case against the Farmer Ludwig Paul Cramer, born on the 16th December 1866 at Warburg, married, Protestant, previously convicted, residing on the farm Otjisororindi:
Charged with dangerous assault.

The Imperial Supreme Court sat at Windhuk from the 28th March to 4th April 1913 to hear the appeals by the accused and the Crown Prosecutor against the judgement of the Imperial District Judge at Windhuk of the 9th and 10th August 1912.

The Court consisted of:–

(1) District Judge Werner, in place of the Chief Justice, as President:
(2) Farmer Gathemann,
(3) Farmer and Merchant Kotting,
(4) Brewery Director Mahler,
(5) Post Director Thomas, as Assessors:
(6) Government Councillor Dr. Kohler, as deputy of the Crown Prosecutor; Police-Sergeant Kudell, as Registrar;

and declared the following to be true justice in the case:–

The appeal of the Crown Prosecutor against the judgement of the Imperial District Judge at Windhuk of the 9th – 10th August 1912, is dismissed with costs against the Treasury.

On the appeal of the accused the said judgement is altered, and accused is sentenced for misdeeds in contravention of Sections 223 and 223 (a) of the German Criminal Code on eight counts (in seven in conjunction with Section 240 of the German Criminal Code) as follows, the order as to costs being confirmed:–

In the case of Auma to three months' imprisonment.
In each of the cases of Grunas and Maria to one month's imprisonment.
In each of the cases of July, Konturu, and Magdalena to a fine of M800.
In the case of Amalia to a fine of M200.
In the case of Alwina to a fine of M100.

The sentences of imprisonment are converted into a combined punishment of four months' imprisonment. Should the fine, amounting in all to M2,700, not be paid, one day s imprisonment shall be substituted for each M15.

The costs of accused s appeal shall be borne half by the Treasury and half by the accused.

REASONS FOR JUDGEMENT

The accused was, by the judgement of the Imperial District Judge at Windhuk, on the 9th and 10th August 1912, acquitted on two counts and sentenced on eight counts of dangerous assault combined with Section 240 of the German Criminal Code to one year and nine months' imprisonment and to pay the costs of the proceedings.

Against this judgement he, in writing dated the 16th August 1912 received the same day, lodged a timely appeal in due form for the reversal of the proceedings of first instance and an acquittal. The Crown also, in writing dated the 19th August 1912, received the same day, lodged a timely appeal in due form against the amount of the punishment awarded in these cases.[xviii]

---

* Translation
[xviii] (Page 165 in original) Here follows argument on a question of jurisdiction, which is of little interest and is omitted.

Hieweib, a Kaffir, who had been an excellent servant of Europeans in Gobabis for 12 years, was stationed with his wife, the Bushman woman Grunas, in charge of a small-stock post of the accused. At the end of September 1912 (?) he reported to accused the death of a valuable sheep. Accused went with the witness Kisker to Hieweib's post. Having satisfied himself that there was suffusion of blood under the skin of the neck of the dead sheep, and having in consequence come to the conclusion that the animal had been violently killed either by Grunas or Hieweib, he ordered the witness Kisker to beat Grunas, who was far advanced in pregnancy and naked, with a riding sjambok. Kisker refused out of consideration for the condition of the woman. Accused thereupon thrashed Grunas with the riding sjambok so heavily that she collapsed and could take no nourishment that evening.

Next morning, two more small-stock having died, accused removed Hieweib and Grunas from their post and took them in his cart with him to his farm. Here Grunas underwent another severe thrashing with the sjambok, and was then sent to gather grass.

On this or the next day Grunas gave birth to a dead child. The medical experts were unable to say with certainty that the abortion was a result of the beating.

In the determination of these facts the Court, contrary to custom, accepted the statements of the natives Hieweib and Grunas, inasmuch as they adhered to their former statements, which agreed with the former evidence of the accused and certain white witnesses, while the accused and the said witnesses today depart entirely from their former evidence.

The ascertained facts contain all the essentials of Section 223 (a) of the German Criminal Code. Severely beating a woman, a short time before childbirth, with a riding sjambok is treatment dangerous to life, especially when the woman has been beaten on two consecutive days and on the first occasion so severely that she collapsed. Further, a light riding sjambok is a dangerous instrument, since it is liable, if mechanically handed, to deviation which might bring about a by no means unimportant bodily injury.

Accused relies on his paternal right of correction. As to this the Court, although such a right is not established by law, agrees with the reasons of the judgement of first instance. The extent of this "paternal right of correction" for the purpose of parental control is, however, determined by the strict meaning of the words. No father, in his senses, would severely beat with a riding sjambok his daughter when in a condition of advanced pregnancy. Such treatment is not in accordance with educational requirements, but is rather sheer brutality. On this exception the accused cannot rely. He is therefore punishable under Sections 223 and 223 (a.) of the German Criminal Code.

The Court cannot declare an ideal-concurring misdeed against Section 240 of the German Criminal Code, since no one deposed that any declaration whatever was intended to be forced from Grunas by the beating.

On the 12th January 1912 the wife of the accused asked him to take her and the children out for a drive. He put her off because he had so much to do in his mealie lands. When, however, the horses had been brought for the drive, he, in a state of excitement which he could not understand or account for, had them inspanned in the spider[210] and set out with his wife and children for the drive. The family went to the Otjikango Pan, seven kilos. distant. A short way from the Pan the accused got out and went on ahead alone with his gun, as he hoped he might come across a head or two of game grazing on the Pan. On the Pan he noticed two

---

[210] A spider phaeton was a light horse-drawn carriage that was high off the ground with tall thin wheels

natives who bent down at intervals and touched the surface of the Pan with their hands. At first he believed he recognised them as two of his people; then he thought they were Jan and Kewas, two natives who had previously absconded and whom he regarded as dangerous stock-thieves. When the natives saw him they bolted. He fired two shots (*Schreckschusse*) after them to frighten them.

Accused declared he thought he recognised Jan and Kewas. At the Appeal proceedings it was credibly deposed on oath by the farmer von Michaelis that about that time (after the Ohlsen case) be had sent two natives on the spoor of the small stock of the farmer Spiro Theologo in the direction of accused s farm. These natives had returned unsuccessful with the excuse that they had run away because accused had shot at them twice. The remarkable behaviour of the two natives observed on the Pan having thus been simply explained by the fact that they were spoor-trackers, accused then made a new statement that Jan at least he had recognised definitely. In view of his original statement the Court did not accept this one, especially as he had made his observations at a distance of 400 metres. One of the medical experts accepted the definite declaration of the accused regarding his recognition of the native Jan at a distance of 400 metres, in conjunction with the preceding impulsive ordering of the drive after first refusing as basis for inquiry into accused's state of mind.

Next morning accused went with his daughter Hildegard to the small-stock post of the Herero woman Alwine, under whom the child Doris was placed as assistant. Just as on the previous day, so on this day, the accused asserts he established the loss of certain head of small stock from the flock of Alwine. He then took Alwine by the hand, his daughter took Doris, and both brought the shepherdesses to the farm. According to the evidence of accused, Doris freely admitted that Alwine had at their request given some small stock to the Hereros Jan and Kewas, lurking in the bush, whom the accused believed he had seen on the Pan Otjikango the day before. Alwine declared that Doris was forced to this admission by beating. Even without a beating a native child is easily influenced. After Doris had made this admission, the accused examined Alwine and ordered her to declare the names of the stock-thieves. Alwine said she did not know. Accused then said to her:

"Tell me the names of the stock-thieves or I will sjambok you till you die." As Alwine insisted that she did not know, accused began to beat her over her bare shoulders with a heavy leather sjambok. After some 13 strokes Alwine cried out "Enough," and indicated Jan and Kewas as the stock-thieves. Today, as at the first trial, she declared she had, under pressure of the pain, said all that accused wished simply in order that he should cease thrashing her. She had never at any time seen Jan and Kewas, and did not even know where they were. Two weeks later Alwine still had 13 broad weals across her shoulders.

Next day accused counted over his other flock of small stock which was in charge of the Herero girl Sosina (Josephine), and found a loss of animals. He took the girl to the farm and declared to her that hamels[211] had been stolen and she must tell the names of the thieves. If she told the truth he would only give her a little sjambokking; but if she lied, a great deal. She then named to him Jan, Kewas, and other natives as the thieves. Questioned regarding earlier losses of animals, which had not been cleared up, she indicated other natives of the neighbouring Farmer Faber as the stock-thieves, and even gave information as to the supposed whereabouts of three oxen.

Sosina has also declared today, as at the first trial, that through apprehension of a thrashing from accused she had "spoken with his mouth," that is, lied and

---

[211] Male sheep, rams.

falsely stated whatever he wished. This appears to the Court to be credible, since we know how simple it is to extract from a native any desired statement, and how difficult to procure from them the truth. During the appeal proceedings the Court witnessed a minor instance of how natives were examined at Otjisororindi. The wife of the accused was at his request confronted with a native witness. Frau Cramer placed her hand on the shoulder of this witness, looked at her with extraordinarily wide-opened eyes, and began to speak to her imploringly. This example so enlightened the Court that it straightway put an end to the confrontation. Moreover the native witness throughout this attempt to influence her stuck to her answer, because she is now in the service of another and has nothing more to fear from accused's sjambok. According to the consistent testimony of the native witnesses, the sjambok and serious threats throughout played a great part in accused s inquiries. Sosina and Amalia, from whom he obtained the most important statements, both declared he said to them "If you do not say just what I tell you, I will beat you till you kick the bucket."

After the above-mentioned pleasure drive, the accused spent a sleepless night wondering what the two natives he saw on the pan could have been doing. It then struck him that his neighbour Linde, exactly a year before, had lost 18 head of big stock and 50 to 60 head of small stock. The accused, with Linde himself and other farmers, had come to the conclusion at the time that poisonous plants were the cause of death. Linde is still today of the opinion that the beasts died of plant-poisoning, since it was the time when the poison plants grow, the grass was not yet green, and the animals through lack of green grass readily took other green stuff. In the night suspicion came to the accused that the Veld-Hereros might have poisoned Linde's watering-place at that time for hunting purposes, and now had also strewn poison on the Otjikango Pan. He therefore forbade grazing in the direction of the Otjikango Pan.

Accused next sent for Police-Sergeant Phillips from Steinhausen, near by. Before him Alwine and Sosina repeated their statements, but, as they constantly and consistently declared in the Court proceedings against the accused, only under the constraint of accused s presence.

After the departure of the Sergeant, the accused renewed his investigations according to his own method. He wanted to know something of the supposed poisoning of the Otjikango Pan; that it was poisoning he had definitely decided in his meditations during the sleepless night. In the belief, as he himself declared, that the Hereros only admitted what they believed the Europeans already knew, he behaved as if he knew the Otjikango Pan was poisoned, and so obtained from Sosina the desired information, namely, that the Pan was poisoned by the Veld-Hereros in order to poison his stock. She further indicated Kadwakonda, accused's foreman, a former Under-Captain and distant relative of Maharero, as the instigator, and several others of accused s natives as accomplices. This aroused in accused s mind the strongest suspicion against Kadwakonda, and he asked Sosina if Kadwakonda had not perhaps also ordered the poisoning of him himself. She answered that both he and his wife had already on one occasion through the Herero girl Lupertine received poison through their tea, and that this took place shortly before Christmas and at the instigation of Kadwakonda. This she learned from Alwine. Alwine was called and corroborated Sosina's statement.

At the trial both witnesses, being removed from the intimidating influence of accused, withdrew their statements and declared they had, through fear of accused, said just what he wanted them to. Accused had put the statements to them in question form, and they had simply said "Yes" out of fright. As a matter of fact, shortly before Christmas, accused and his wife had suffered from some intestinal and other troubles, which they themselves at the time put down to drinking thick milk. At the time when the suspicion of poison was first aroused, they agreed that the tea was poisoned the evening before and that they two alone had drunk it, while the remaining whites on the farm had not drunk the tea and remained well. Subsequently, however, accused himself stated that only he and not his wife had drunk the tea. He is now of the firm opinion that the senna tea[212] which his wife drank was also poisoned. In support of this, however, there was at no time any native evidence, and the medical experts declared that senna tea not administered in the right quantity or not prepared with sufficient care might produce severe disorder such as the wife of the accused had experienced. All these circumstances point to the view that the aroused distrust of the accused led him to connect his past symptoms of illness with poisoning, and that he sought to force corroborative evidence from the natives with the sjambok and threats.

Upon the declaration of Sosina and Alwine, accused had Kadwakonda seized and took from him a piece of carved wood which he carried. Then he questioned Lupertine. She declared she knew nothing. He began to beat her with the sjambok until she admitted that it was just as she stated. She had poisoned the tea with Kadwakonda's piece of wood which was exhibited to her, because a woman must carry out a man's orders.

The piece of wood in question is not poisonous. It is a wooden crook, a kind of amulet, which descends from father to son and which Kadwakonda had received from his dying father. It was impossible to poison tea with it.

Accused then continued his violent methods of inquiry in the manner and way already described. He wished to clear up the death of two calves which he had not been able to fathom. He obtained from the milking woman Amalia'a statement, which she has since retracted as having been forced from her. that they were poisoned and that it was done by Maria, the wife of Fritz. at Kadwakonda's instigation. Amalia even produced in support two roots said to be poisonous. Accused himself today no longer finds poison in them. The expert declares that they have a poisonous effect in large doses, but thinks that they are a native medicine.

Accused next examined the Herero Jacob. He stated he knew nothing of the stock poisoning, but he spoke of another instance of poisoning.

Accused in 1909, in the hot season. after superintending the clearing of trees until after midday, collapsed on his way back to the farm, and only returned to his senses a considerable while after he had been carried into the farmhouse.

Jacob now asserted that accused was the victim of poisoning by the Kaffir July; this man had put fire-poison in the camp fire, just when accused was to leeward of it; the smoke arising therefrom had reached and poisoned him.

Jacob has likewise retracted this assertion; he had only said so because accused had overborne him with questions. The medical experts, including the Government doctor and the bacteriologist Dr. Sieber, who is the Protectorate expert on chemistry. were in agreement that poisoning by poison strewn in an open fire, in the open, according to the method described and within the subsequent symptoms described by accused was impossible. Excepting perhaps cyanic acid compounds, no chemical was known to them which could produce such acute poisonous results as were described by such a method. It could not be imagined that natives were in possession of more efficacious substances. The medical experts held that it was undoubtedly a sunstroke or a fainting fit brought about by excessive exercise and the heat or a heart failure. The accused and his wife had also so described it previously.

---

[212] A tea made from dried leaves of the yellow-flowered *Cassia Angustifolia* or *Cassia Alexandrian*. Senna tea was believed to act as a laxative and to help 'clean' the body of impurities.

Jacob, questioned over the alleged poisoning of tea by Lupertine, declared he knew nothing of it. Lupertine had, however, asked him for the powerful poison "Omukeikei," but he had not given her any. This statement Jacob also withdrew.

Upon the return to Otjisororindi of Police-Sergeants Phillips and Muller II. from their patrol after stock-thieves, the statements of Alwine, Sosina, and Jacob were placed on record. Lupertine refused to repeat her confession. With the concurrence of Sergeant Phillips she was therefore sjambokked by the accused. Phillips declares this was as a punishment for lying *before*. Lupertine under the blows screamed "Enough," and then repeated her confession. Kadwakonda and Maria denied everything. Accused inspanned four oxen and a cart the same day, and with the help of Police-Sergeant Muller II. chained together to the back of the cart Lupertine, Alwine, Maria (Fritz s wife), Kadwakonda, Langmann and Harutonge, a woman captured by the police in the bush, and rode with the sergeants and prisoners to Gobabis.

On the way the Herero Jacob, so the accused believed, made a further attempt to poison him and the Police-Sergeants. This, he alleged, Lupertine voluntarily betrayed to him on the occasion of a bath in the Black Nosob. Lupertine says today he so bullied her with threats that she uttered everything according to his wish as he explained it to her beforehand. Moreover, the other witnesses declare they were compelled by accused to make their false accusations against Jacob, which, however, contradicted each other to some extent. Arrived at Gobabis, accused gave Jacob some 50 strokes on the chest and back with a sjambok in a room at a hotel, and searched his goods. He found among them a cartridge case containing some powder. Accused at first took it that the powder had been exchanged in Okakaue, and that originally there was a powerful poison in the cartridge case. Today he declares that he believes the powder produced is actually the poison. Jacob and Lupertine say it is a medicine for various sicknesses. After investigation, the bacteriologist, Dr. Sieber, stated that in large quantities it has a poisonous effect; he is of opinion it is a native medicine, perhaps a stomach cure.

For the ill-treatment of Jacob, accused was on a recent trial sentenced to a fine of M600. Against this sentence he has lodged an appeal.

In Gobabis. at the inquiry of the District Chief, Graf Schwerin, the natives at first adhered to their statements. Lupertine, however, would not at first repeat her confession. The District Chief then assented to the request of accused that she be sjambokked. He adopted this otherwise inadmissible method as he explained, because he wished to obtain an idea of how the accused had conducted inquiries which had produced such remarkable results. Lupertine repeated her confession under the blows.

Jacob, as he tells us today, out of fear, and being still under the influence of the severe thrashing, received in the room at the hotel assented to every question put to him. To the explicit question of the District Chief, accused made the false reply that he had not thrashed Jacob. The consistent and credible evidence of the witnesses Graf Schwerin and *Wachtmeister* Nakonz prove this. At the inquiry Jacob disclosed another four years' old poisoning of accused's wife by the Kaffir July. July had stated in the pondok[213] that he always had fire-poison which he had received from Bushmen, and he had put it in the kitchen fire in order to poison Frau Cramer. The latter was ill for a long time thereafter.

This explained to the accused a severe illness his wife had had for several mouths, which he at first diagnosed as typhoid.

Accused tells us something new – that at the illness of his wife the cooking

---

[213] A word originally derived from Malay, but widely used during the colonial period in Africa to describe a locally made hut

was done in the open, while before the talk was always of a kitchen fire in the kitchen. The experts in this instance also are of opinion that there can be no question of poisoning by poisoned smoke in the open with a half-year's illness as the result. They agree that it was chronic malaria lasting for some the.

Before the District Chief, Sosina, Alwine and Lupertine withdrew their accusations of poisoning when they were confronted with Kadwakonda. Graf Schwerin was already by no means satisfied as to the accuracy of the evidence of the natives regarding the alleged poisoning. At the request of the accused he, however, sent a mounted messenger to Otjisororindi to warn Frau Cramer against the Kaffir, July. Graf Schwerin had arranged a large police campaign against the Hereros squatting in the bush in the neighbourhood of Otjisororindi, and arrived there on the evening of 26th January 1912. Accused, who had traveled fast with his ox cart, reached there on the morning of 27th, January 1912.

The District Chief Graf Schwerin, at Otjisororindi, examined the natives of the Farmer Linde. who were accused of poisoning cattle; also the Kaffir July, accused of attempted murder by poisoning and Sosina as a Crown witness. Sosina made a deposition that Lupertine had wanted to poison the tea of accused s family, but had never carried her intention into execution. Graf Schwerin would not allow her to sign the record as he did not believe her. After the accused arrived, the inquiry was repeated, and Sosina made the same statement regarding the poisoning of Linde s cattle as before.

After examining July and Sosina, and imprisoning July in the prisoners' cell on the farm. Graf Schwerin believed he had done all he could for the safety of accused s family. He accordingly rode off, after directing that July and Sosina should be transferred to Gobabis later, on his campaign against the Veld-Hereros. Before he rode away he consented to permit the accused once more to examine July and question him as to the whereabouts of the poison.

About three o'clock Graf Schwerin had ridden off. Accused then fetched July out of the cell and questioned him about the alleged attempt to poison Frau Cramer. As July declared he knew nothing of it, accused began to thrash him over the naked back with a sjambok. Between the blows he continued his questions about the matter. As July's only answers were taken by accused to be lies, accused continued beating him further till he felt himself becoming faint and begged for water. Accused gave him brandy. and continued the thrashing. According to the witness, the mason Röder, accused asked him to fetch a firebrand and place it near July, who had fallen to the ground, to frighten him. July declared that the firebrand was laid against him as he cowered down under the blows. He had, in consequence, called out "My master may beat me to death, but I won't let myself be burnt," and rolled on the other side.

No statement of importance could accused extract from July. This scene of beating lasted a long time. According to July he was thrashed the whole afternoon; the accused sweated a lot over it, and often rested. If the Court does not give this statement implicit belief, still accused's own statement and the deposition of Röder show that the beating lasted a long while, because during the beating Röder went into the room two or three times and each the found accused at his investigation by means of the sjambok. Accused himself admitted July was cruelly ill-treated. The Court deduces from the fact that he called Röder repeatedly as interpreter that accused, in this inquiry by means of such severe violence, behaved without scruple, he could not even properly understand the tortured July.

His frightful scars prove today, after $1\frac{1}{4}$ years, how cruelly July was treated on this afternoon. At the medical examination two weeks after the ill-treatment. he was still feverish. According to medical opinion his whole back was thrashed to bits, as follows:– On the back there was an absence of skin from 13 to 10 centimetres big on both sides of the spine in the neighbourhood of the lowest chest-vertebra. The edges of this ulcerated area were sharply defined. On the day of the examination it was covered with matter and numerous fly-maggots. On the right shoulder-blade an irregular bow-shaped wound, similar to the above, 10.2 centimetres big. On the right shoulder a deeply-ulcerated wound of the same character of the size of a hand. Left of the edge of the "Kappen" muscle to two fingers breadth below the collarbone a similar wound 5 centimetres wide.

"The deposition of the injured party that these injuries were due to a sjambokking was supported by the conditions found."

After accused had had July locked up again, when the fruitless inquiry was ended, he summoned July s wife Maria. She has given evidence that she had crept up round the house that afternoon and had heard the blows of the sjambok and the groans of her husband. In consequence she was in great fear, and had therefore agreed to all the accused had said to her. Indeed, accused had told her that July had already confessed, and that if she did not say the same she would be beaten like the others. Since the Court has been able to gather by different proofs the manner and way in which accused conducted his investigations into the objective facts, it has no cause to doubt the new depositions of Maria. She, in her enforced statements at the time, declared:–

(1) That July, Jacob, and Piet had poisoned Frau Cramer with fire-poison. In regard to this matter reference is made to what has been said above.
(2) That in 1908 the Kaffir Piet had shot accused in the wrist on the road to Windhuk with a poisoned arrow. In this the accused found the explanation of a serious sickness in Windhuk, which extended over a long time and ended in inflammation of the testicles. Previously accused attributed this illness to infection from Lung sickness-vaccine. According to medical experts, an affection of the testicles may result from chronic malaria. Accused did not consult a doctor while lying sick in Windhuk.
(3) That July, Piet, and Acherab in 1908 had poisoned accused's mason, Steffenfausweh, with poison which they had put into caf–au-lait. The said mason was undoubtedly seriously ill in 1908. The statements of the natives regarding his poisoning have been retracted. There stands now only the evidence of the witness Piet that he had told July, who was looked upon as a sort of native doctor, that he should give Steffenfausweh, who had been very good to them, some of his medicine to cure him. Maria has also made some statements regarding earlier cases of poisoning by July.

A principal witness of the accused s was Ernestine July's daughter, who was called after Maria. She also has withdrawn her previous statements. When accused saw the impression which the appearance of this child, who was to give evidence on events far past, produced on the Court he abandoned her evidence. The same thing happened with his witness Haika. On the very evening before her examination by the presiding Judge, she was beaten in Windhuk by the accused, and immediately after questioned as to the evidence she would give next morning. In consequence she also, under the influence of the beating and accused's presence, gave her evidence next morning as he wished it; later she retracted her statements.

Before the examination of Maria the accused had caused July's pondok to be searched. Ruder and Hieweib brought to light several suspicious roots, a box of ointment, and a small quiver filled with the little magic arrows of the Bushmen.

According to the opinion of the expert Dr. Siebert, these must be regarded as native medicine. The arrows are used by the Bushmen in witchcraft. and are not poisoned. as examination proved. Some of the miniature arrows are wrapped up like the big Bushmen arrows intended for the reception of poison. No single case in which they have been poisoned was established. It is possible that the wrapping up was merely in imitation of the big arrows. Police-Wachtmeister Ramm, who has long lived among Bushmen, and has made inquiries, has in his possession over 5,000 of the small arrows, none of which were poisoned. In his opinion. they are only used for witchcraft. If they are shot in the direction of an enemy, be he 100 kilos, or more away, witchcraft will bring about his death. Farmer Rudiger has seen, among the Bushmen of Ovamboland, highly artistic healing processes carried out by the witch-doctors with the arrows. They also serve as toys.

The discovery, of these arrows before the questioning of Maria, her statement that in 1908 accused was shot by such an arrow which was poisoned and thereby became ill, and her declaration that she only said this because accused had put it in her mouth, supported the conviction reached by the Court through the whole course of the Supreme Court proceedings, that once the accused had become suspicious of poisoning he thought to connect all past cases of sickness in his house with poisoning, to make everything fit in with this, and in consequence to bring out by questions the desired evidence from the natives by the application of the sharpest means of compulsion. That this last is possible no one who knows natives doubts. For this purpose the numerous and severe "cudgel-cures" which he himself acknowledges may not even have been necessary.

Accused had now the little arrows and the evidence of Maria that they had already been employed for poisoning. He wished, therefore, to get into his possession the poison which, according to his view, appertained to the arrows. Maria, July s wife, had also asserted that Jacob and Langmann had bought small Bushman arrows and poison from July. He accordingly had brought before him Amalia and Sosina, the wives of these two men, who themselves had been taken to Gobabis. showed them the quiver with the little arrows, said he knew their husband had such arrows, and asked the women what their men wanted to do with them. They said their husbands intended to shoot accused with them if he became angry.

This reply also was forced out of the witnesses, and later withdrawn after the influence of accused was removed from them.

To his question as to the whereabouts of the arrows they declared Konturu and Maria, Jacob's wife, had received them with an order from Kadwakonda to work with poison on the farm in his absence against the people and stock, just as opportunity came. Several head of cattle had already been stabbed.

Accused with his daughter Hildegard now fetched Konturu, bound her hands together with an ox riem, tore the clothes from her body, and took away three purses with money and pins and a little bag of sand which was secreted under her modesty-apron. Then he began, while continually questioning her about the poison, to lay it on to her naked back with a heavy sjambok, so that she fell to the ground. As she lay on the ground he kicked her on the buttocks, back and head, then pulled her up and further thrashed her. He himself says that he gave Konturu an "energetic sjambokking." His wife begged him not to beat her anymore, but nevertheless he did not stop. His daughter looked on. Throughout the night Konturu was locked up naked in the farm prison with only one blanket to cover her.

Next day Konturu was brought back into the same room and sjambokked in the same energetic fashion, while continually questioned about the poison, although she said: "I have no poison." "I am not lying." "You can beat me until I go to my grave, I will not lie."

On the third day Konturu was once more brought out. On this day, however, she was only subjected to a thorough examination of her person. Accused even sought for the poison in her private parts with his finger.

Konturu was terribly mauled by the " cudgel-cure." Her body showed, even fourteen days afterwards, the following marks, according to the medical report:–

> "The woman shows the following injuries or signs of such: On the nape of the neck an already dried-up abrasion of the skin the size of a 10 mark piece. Under the left shoulder-blade an absence of the skin as big as the palm of a hand, covered with dry scab. Above that six weals, making good progress. Similar weals over the left shoulder-blade. Below the shoulder-blades 8-10 older weals running obliquely. In front, on the breast, numerous absences of skin, the size of a 10 *pfennig* piece, drying well; also three length wise 1 centimetre broad and from 4 to 7 centimetres long. On both arms older weals."

Even today the back shows deep and severe scars.

Konturu was in the first months of pregnancy, and on the journey to Gobabis soon after her ill-treatment had a miscarriage. The medical experts could not declare with certainty that the miscarriage was a result of the ill-treatment. Had it been positive, as she asserted, that during the ill-treatment her body was trodden on, the experts would have attributed the miscarriage to it. The Court could not accept this as established by the evidence of the natives alone in view of the denial of accused, although treading on the body would very probably cause a miscarriage.

In precisely similar fashion to Konturu, accused summoned Maria, Jacob's wife. She also was caught by her hands by accused and his daughter Hildegard and brought into the "Court House," as she aptly designated the farm house. They bound her hands to her back, cut her clothes from her body, and then she was energetically sjambokked with the same sjambok till she, as she credibly declares, fell unconscious to the earth. She deposed that she was beaten the whole evening, and even by lamplight. She suffered a further "cudgel-cure" the following day. Until removed to Gobabis she was kept in the accused's prison-cell. She gave no information regarding the concealment of poison.

Maria was marked by the accused in unheard-of (*unerhör-ter Weise*) fashion. On her reception into hospital a week later she, a big woman, could scarcely stand on her feet and had fever badly. According to the medical report her body showed as follows:–

> From the lower edge of the shoulder-blades right to the loins an absence of skin 20 by 18 centimetres in size covered with putrefying skin except at the edges, which had granulated for a distance of one centimetre, Under the mortified skin exuded stinking matter, and some fly maggots were also visible. The edges were sharply defined.
>
> On the right shoulder-blade were four to five deep length wise furrows, to the extent of a palm's breadth. On the right shoulder an absence of skin in extent 12 by 8 centimetres, also covered with putrefying skin, malodorous matter exuding under it. On the left shoulder an injury the size of a 5 mark piece in the same condition. On the upper lip, forehead, in front diagonally across the breast, were older weals as if from blows from a stick.
>
> The statement of the injured person that she received the wounds through a sjambokking agrees with the conditions found.
>
> The woman is not yet out of danger.

Maria never recovered. The doctor could not bring about the closing of the surface wounds, because the tissues underlying the skin were so broken to pieces. An operation failed on this account. Maria hovered for a long the between life and death, and had to be released from the hospital uncured. She would never again recover her full physical capacity. After about six months she died. No doctor saw her body. It has therefore not been determined whether Maria died as the result of her ill-treatment by accused.

As accused could obtain no information regarding poison by his barbarous ill-treatment of Maria and Konturu. he "belaboured with the Sjambok" (*bearbeitet mit der Schambock*) Amalia as well, to force it out of her. The witness Röder held her fast by the arms for the purpose, and the Kaffir Hieweib by the legs. She was thrashed for a long while, and at intervals questioned about the concealment of the poison. Her back looked as if some one had burnt it with fire. Even today, 1¼ years later, she bears frightful scars (*furchtbare Narben*). At last she fetched certain bones and roots, which are believed to be employed as native medicines. Next day she was taken about to show the place of concealment of the poison. As she could only give unsatisfactory information "she allowed herself to be beaten a long time," as accused put it then she indicated a fresh hole in the ground in which the poison was supposed to have been formerly hidden, and finally she accused Auma[xix] of having the poison. The accused believed this. In this case the Court was convinced that the accused started his investigations in a scarcely comprehensible state of delusion, and that in the same violent fashion he obtained false conclusions regarding the circumstances of the poisonings. It did not occur to him to regard the statements of thrashed women as worthless. It did not strike him that a woman would ever put the guilty possession of poison on another woman in order to free herself from his blows with the sjambok, till at last the guilt remained fixed on Auma and Magdalena, who had only been on the farm some three days.

Auma was a feeble old woman of from 55 to 60 years of age, whom the accused had received with Magdalena and other natives from the District Chief as substitutes when he left his first prisoners in Gobabis. After three days residence on the farm, though Kadwakonda and his associates were in Gobabis and July in prison, they had to share in the alleged poisoning conspiracy. This view is incredible to the Court.

This decrepit woman was terribly cut about (*furchterlich verhauen*) by accused with the sjambok, because he asked her for the poison and she could only produce harmless things as alleged poison. The blows were inflicted on her bare back. The accused himself described the procedure as "a powerful cudgel-cure." Old Auma was so injured by it that her lacerated back could not be cured except by skin-transference, which was out of the question in an old and feeble woman. When she was fetched away from Otjisororindi, she could only walk with an effort. Farmer Grabow, on his neighbouring farm, saw her collapse three times in a short distance. A police-boy had to pick her up. Grabow saw the frightful wounds, and out of pity gave her milk and offered her his cart to carry her.

[xix] (Page 174 in original) i.e. *Ouma* equals Old Mother

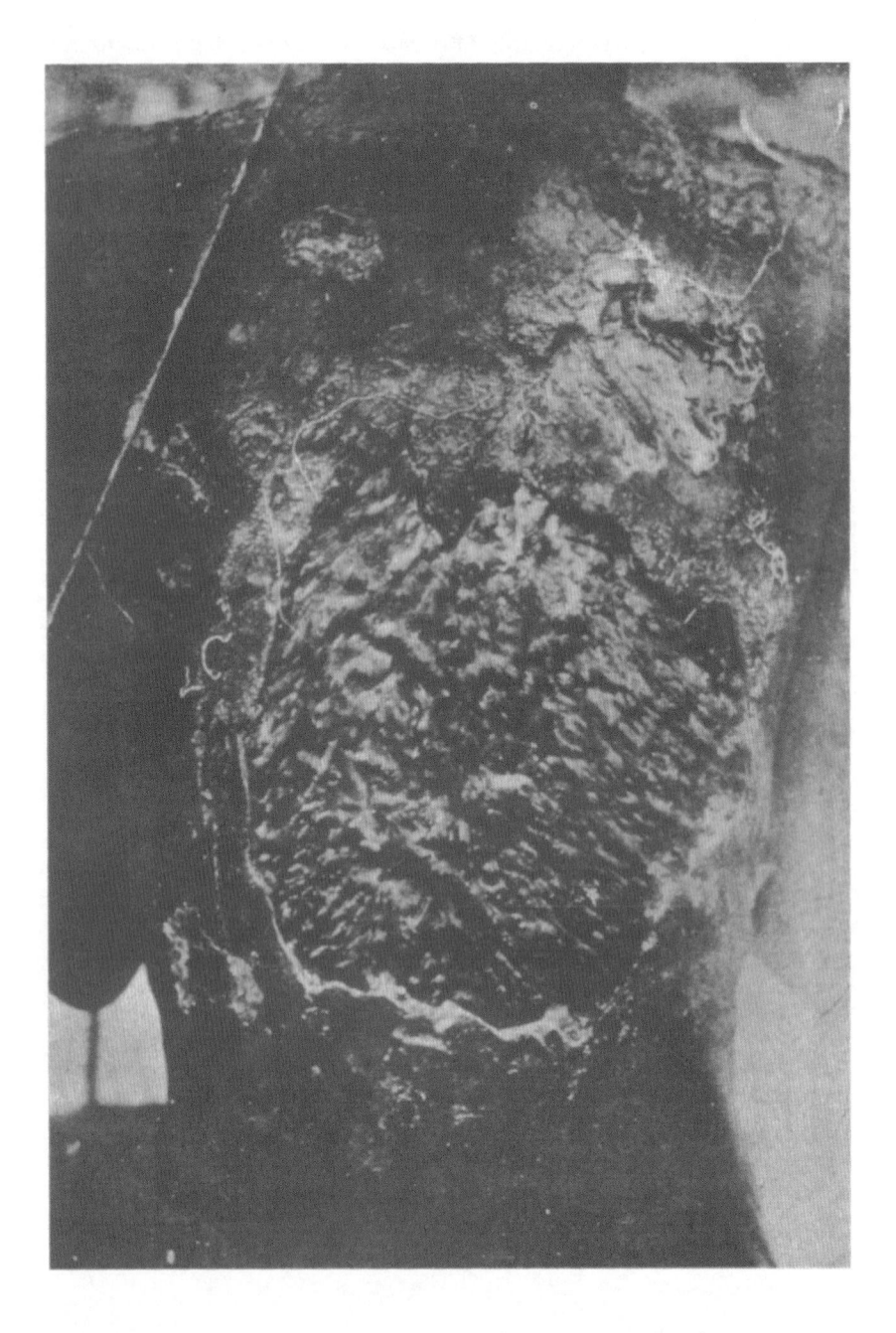

Plate 4: Photograph of the back of Maria taken in Gobabis hospital on the 15th february 1912.

Note: The original of this photograph was cracked across the top left-hand corner. This crack shows in the reproduction as a straight line.

CHAPTER TWO 283

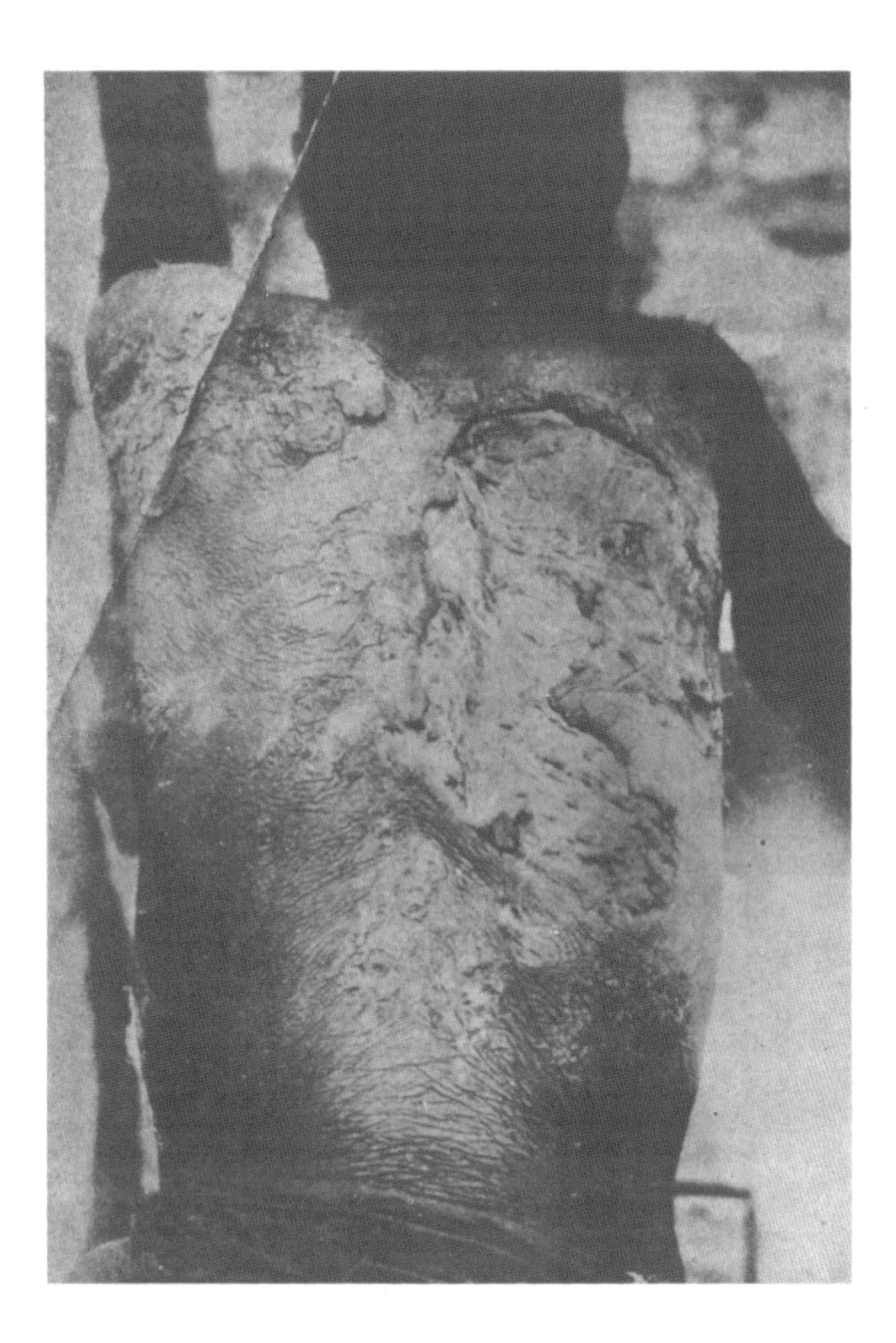

Plate 5: Photograph of the back of Auma taken in Gobabis hospital on the 15th february 1912.

Note: The original of this photograph was cracked across the top left-hand corner. This crack shows in the reproduction as a straight line.

Her medical condition at Gobabis was:–

"Feeble old woman from 55 to 60. Temperature 39.5.[xx] An irregularly-shaped absence of skin extending from over the right shoulder-blade as far as the region of the lowest rib, which, within the exception of the edges up to 1½ centimetres, was all covered with putrefying skin, size 20 by 18 centimetres. Under the putrefying scab exuded abundant stinking matter. There were also in the same place a great number of fly-maggots. Diagonally over the right shoulder-blade less deep abrasions of the skin, well advanced towards healing up.

On the left shoulder a smaller absence of skin 5 centimetres long. On the right shoulder older weals; on the right as well as the left breast an absence of skin the size of a *thaler*. The statement of the injured person that she received the wounds from blows from a sjambok agrees with the conditions found.

The woman is today still hovering between life and death."

After some two weeks hospital treatment, Auma died of dysentery. The establishment by the medical experts of a direct connection between the injuries and the death was impossible. The Court agrees within the medical experts that the injuries shook the old woman's power of resistance against the dysentery, so that they also contributed towards her death.

As accused obtained nothing from Auma, he administered a similar "cudgel-cure" to the Herero woman Magdalena, who likewise had only been at Otjisororindi three days. It was the same in her case.

The medical report on her injuries was:–

"Magdalena, about 40 years old, temperature continuously 39 0 to 39 6[xxi] Conditions: numerous abrasions of the skin covered within dried scab on the back, from the nape of the neck to the small of the back. On the right smoulder-blade deep furrows advancing in healing. The same on the right shoulder. On the left breast, which contained milk, on both sides of the nipple a swollen area the size of a *thaler*. Whether the high fever is connected within the injuries cannot be determined with certainty.

Under pressure of the ill-treatment, Amalia and Sosina had also accused Auma of stabbing a cow and three calves with a poisoned bodkin.[214] Police-*Wachtmeister* Franken examined the cow at an early stage, in company with Police-Sergeant Philipps. He at once satisfied himself that the poisoning of the cow by stabbing it with a poisoned bodkin was an invention. Both police officers agreed that the supposed bodkin marks on the calves were the punctures of the *Buschlaus*, a sort of tick. Police officers receive instruction regarding stock diseases, &c., and in the course of their duty generally acquire much practical experience of them. The alleged bodkin punctures looked exactly like places from which ticks had been pulled out.

When Police-*Wachtmeister* Franken took Amalia's statement his attention was attracted by her contracted shoulders and the evil smell of the matter. Nevertheless, she was still so under the influenced of the fearful cudgelling scenes that she only reluctantly gave information regarding her injuries. After Franken had discovered all the injured on the farm, he sent them to Gobabis for hospital

---

[xx] = 103°F
[xxi] 102°2 to 103°3 F

---

[214] A bodkin was a small dagger

treatment and set on foot a judicial inquiry. Accused said to him on this occasion that he had gone too far, and would put up with the consequences.

Exhaustive inquiry has resulted in establishing these as the material facts; for the most part they are supported by the assertions, or at any rate the earlier evidence, of the accused.

There can be no doubt that in the thrashings of Alwine, July, Maria, Konturu, Amalia, Auma and Magdalena, all the elements of the offence of contravening Sections 223 and 223 (a) of the Criminal Code were present. Even if it is doubtful whether the sjambok is a dangerous instrument, at any rate the grievous bodily harm which was inflicted within it is established. In the cases of July, Maria, Auma and Amalia, the Court agrees with the medical experts as to the presence of treatment dangerous to life.

As for the plea of paternal right of correction, it carries no weight in the said seven cases, since the accused in these cases did not punish but extorted statements about stock theft, poisoning and the place of concealment of poison. Moreover, these "cudgel-cures" are entirely beyond the limits of the paternal right of correction. All the said natives must be regarded as severely, even dangerously, injured. It is plainly not impossible that the wounds of the injured may have been aggravated by the journey of several days without treatment; nevertheless, upon the evidence and the corroborative opinions of the experts, the Court finds it proved that they were caused, in their *depth* and *danger*, by the sjambokkings inflicted by the accused.

The skin in its whole thickness and the underlying tissues were so beaten and crushed that the whole of the skin affected was bound to putrefy and mortify. There is no support for the argument that the natives intentionally aggravated their wounds to any extent worth mentioning. The fly maggots in the wounds are only an external condition of no importance as to the manner in which the wounds were caused; they were found in the mortifying parts and even without them the wounds would have been there.

The elements of the offence of contravening Section 240 of the Criminal Code are similarly present in the seven cases. He unlawfully compelled the natives by violence to acts, namely, answers about alleged stock theft and poisoning.

With the exception of the ideal-concurrence of Section 240 of the Criminal Code in the case of Grunas, the facts accepted as proved agree with those of the Court of first instance. In the six last-named cases accused claims exclusion of punishment on the grounds laid down in Sections 51, 53 and 54[xxii] of the Criminal Code. The Court disallows this plea.

The Court agrees within the medical experts that the accused carried out ill-treatment extending over several days in a normal state of mind and the exercise of his free will. Indeed, in his conduct of his inquires he acted throughout with a definite and logical consistency.

[xxii] Sections 51, 53 and 54 of the Code are as follows:-

51. If the offender at the time of the committal of an offence was in a state of unconsciousness or derangement of the intellect, due to illness, by which the free exercise of his will was prevented, the act is not punishable.

53. An act committed in self-defence is not punishable.

Self-defence is such a defence as is required to avert aim imminent illegal assault on oneself or another.

Exceeding the limits of self-defence is not punishable if the perpetrator has so acted through confusion, fear or panic.

54. An act committed in order to rescue the perpetrator or a relative from present danger to life or limb in an emergency other than self-defence, not caused through the fault of the former and not otherwise to be averted, is not punishable.

The presence of a person suspected of poison-murder – July – in the farm prison and the suspected existence of poison on the farm is a situation of danger (*zustand*), but self-defence presumes an imminent attack, some particular motion, an act, an active deed, and such is wanting. There was, furthermore, nothing present which accused could regard as an imminent attack. Admission of self-defence or putative self-defence is, therefore, out of the question. The assertion that the bringing of July out of prison, the thrashing of him into a state of unconsciousness and the frightening with firebrands, and further the unlimited thrashings of women for several days, were acts of self-defence by the accused, finds no support in law. At the very least self-defence was certainly exceeded, since such self-protection was no longer necessary after July was locked up. As regards exceeding self-defence the accused is criminally answerable, since the Court does not find that he was in the situation described in paragraph 3 of Section 53 of the Criminal Code, especially since he extended his ill-treatment over several days.

Nor does the Court find *Notstand* (emergency) as contemplated by Section 54 of the Criminal Code, since July was sitting in prison. At this the direct suspicion of poisoning pointed to him alone of all the natives at Otjisororindi, and he was harmless. Further, even if accused could have believed himself to be in an emergency, he could have avoided it in other ways. During these few days the accused could have locked up the rest of his natives and had the meals prepared by a member of his family; he could also have left the farm with his family. There was no occasion for this barbarous ill-treatment. Section 54 of the Criminal Code does not refer to danger to property.

Accordingly the punishment of accused for contraventions of Sections 223, 223 (a) of the Criminal Code in eight cases – in seven in conjunction with Section 240 of the Code – must, except in regard to the measure of punishment, be upheld.

As to the admission of mitigating circumstances and the extent of the punishment. the Court takes into account the following considerations.

It has not been proved that poisonings took place on accused s farm. If, from the result of accused s inquiries. the statements of the natives obtained by beatings and torture, which they withdrew on the cessation of their pain and fright, are deducted as is proper, there remain only matters of trifling importance carrying an innocent interpretation and nothing more. In particular the supposed poisons and little arrows obtained thereby were curative or witchcraft material of the natives. In this respect it is not generally denied that many natives know poisons and perhaps occasionally employ them. It is also possible that some of the accused s natives boasted in *pondok* gossip of his ability to kill people, or that the witchcraft of the little arrows was occasionally put to proof against the house of the detested master. The Court does not see that any real weight can be attached to the evidence regarding poisoning.

This, however, is not of any particular importance in regard to the question of guilt before the Court. Accused would be answerable for his unregulated conduct even if anyone had actually worked against him with poison on Otjisororindi.

Accused unites with a good intelligence an astounding want of capacity for objective thought. What he believed he knew to be the truth was for him the objective truth, and he believed himself entitled to torture his natives until they said what he considered to be the truth. He still takes his stand on this point today. It is utterly impossible for him to see that a statement extorted from a native is worthless. This want of objectivity arises from a boundless vanity, as he showed on many occasions in the Supreme Court proceedings. In everything he handled he very soon believed himself a master. He trusted nobody but himself. He arbitrarily conducted searches of other people's werfts. Although the police were kept so fully occupied by him, that in his opinion their tenfold increase was necessary if there was as much for them to do on all farms, he still held it proper to pursue his inquiries on his own account and lines, and occasionally to punish extremely severely. He had never made himself familiar on any other farm when he first came into the country with the handling of natives and how difficult it is, as is generally done, but he started farming and handling natives at ounce by himself. He quite forgot that he knew nothing of the treatment of natives. On this point the Court is fully satisfied. Full many a native came from the District Office, after a little complained of hard treatment and ran away. A marked case of wrong treatment is that of the Herero Christian. Farmer Linde had lent this man, his best servant, to accused. Being by accident present on Linde's farm, Christian had to help his master put out a grass fire, and in consequence his return to accused was delayed half a day. Accused did not attempt to prove the justice of Christian s excuse, but punished him with 25 strokes with a sjambok. When the affair was later on cleared up in Christian s favour by Linde the accused says he asked the native s pardon. In this instance not only the unwarranted punishment of Christian has weight, but also the circumstance that he beat another s servant. That was flagrantly improper according to the custom of the country.

When pursuing absconded natives, according to the statement of Farmer Grabow, accused fastened his two native spoor-trackers together at night with chains with a dog in between, and also during the day made them walk in chains. Even a native cannot endure such treatment for any length of time.

It is also a sign of self-conceit, almost amounting to infatuation, that accused regarded his daughter Hildegard, then just outgrowing childhood, who came to this country first in 1908, as a sufficient interpreter in Herero during his extensive inquiries into complicated matters. Everyone in the Protectorate knows the endless difficulties of interpretation of Herero. In the Supreme Court proceedings three of the best interpreters in the land were engaged together, and yet often could scarcely master the difficulty of a question or answer. And the accused today still points to this young girl, who has interpreted from the age of 14 to 18, as a satisfactory interpreter. Moreover, it has been actually proved that at Otjisororindi a native was beaten because Hildegard Cramer translated an expression wrongly. Herero Jacob is of opinion that she was quite unable to interpret. According to the statement of accused, she has since forgotten much of her knowledge of Herero, so that a test of her ability was useless.

As proof of the self-conceit of accused, the Court regards also the fact that he found fault with, and to some extent dealt roughly with, all witnesses the moment they said anything unfavourable to him: for instance, Graf Schwerin, whose sworn evidence the Court regarded as credible throughout on points material to the issue and provable thereby.

It was by reason of this self-conceit that accused believed himself justified in his unlawful conduct. This may have been increased by a certain distrust of everyone, especially officials, and a certain fear of the natives. The latter is frequently a symptom of improper treatment, and to white people living on a lonely farm this distrust is often all but a symptom of illness.

In this way, in the opinion of the Court, the accused reached his criminal methods of inquiry, which otherwise would appear incomprehensible in a man of good education and normal mental capacity.

Although the condition of limitless self-deception which he worked himself up to in a criminal manner does not, in the opinion of the doctors, fall within the terms of Section 51 of the Criminal Code, the Court still has to consider this condition in the fullest degree when dealing with the questions of mitigating circumstances and the amount of punishment. This the Court believes all the more must be done, since it is under the impression that accused has not found in his wife the usual pacifier, but even encouragement of his criminal conduct.

Although the behaviour of the accused in all eight cases is incomprehensible in a decent man, and is worse than the conduct of a slave owner of earlier days (*Sclimmer als das Gebaren eines Sklaven halters früherer Zeit*), the Court is nevertheless of the opinion, upon consideration, of all the facts, that in seven cases it must allow mitigating circumstances. Only the case of the deceased old woman Auma is found so serious that mitigating circumstances cannot be admitted. The cases of Maria and Grunas the Court finds further so bad that, while accepting mitigating circumstances, it considers imprisonment appropriate. In the remaining cases fines are considered sufficient.

The punishments of imprisonment in the three cases are moderately measured, although they approximate to the elements of the offences of Sections 224, 226 of the Criminal Code, which carry heavy penal internment, because the Court in this respect has again taken into account his self-deception as well as his blameless record and the circumstance that owing to his social standing accused will feel imprisonment sufficiently without it being of long duration. We have also given consideration to the fact that the accused ceased to defend himself in the arrogant and unregulated manner he adopted before the Court of first instance. On the same grounds, and in view of the inordinate amount of the costs of the cases, the fines are reduced to mild limits in spite of the seriousness of the matter.

Section 74 of the Criminal Code has been taken into consideration. It is on that account that sentences have been pronounced as they have been.

Sections 497 and 505 of the Criminal Procedure Ordinance govern the costs.

The first charge dealt with in this judgement is the assault upon Grunas, and the manner in which it is handled shows clearly how anxious everybody concerned in the matter was to favour the accused. It is plain that Kisker, accused, and natives all testified to the fact that this unhappy woman, far gone in pregnancy and naked, was thrashed till she collapsed and could not eat that night. The avowed object of this monstrous treatment was to extort from her a statement that either she or her husband had killed a sheep. Two more sheep died after the first thrashing. It is highly unlikely that Heiweib caused their death and impossible for Grunas to have done so. Probably, therefore, the first sheep died in some natural way. Heiweib is expressly given a good character. In spite of all this, he and Grunas are taken off to the farmhouse and there both are severely beaten, after which Grunas is sent to gather grass. This is the story told at the first trial by all parties, and at the second repeated by the natives but denied by accused and his witnesses. Yet the Court evidently accepted it with the greatest reluctance, and only because no other course was possible if it was to retain any reputation for justice at all.

At latest the day after the second assault Grunas gave birth to a dead child. It is safe to say that if she had been white the medical expert would have had no difficulty in ascribing this directly to the two thrashings she had received.

Accused was not even prosecuted for thrashing Heiweib. Apparently it was quite justifiable to administer to a native who had given Europeans in Gobabis good service for 12 years a severe beating on the flimsiest of pretexts. For the atrocious treatment of Grunas accused was awarded one month imprisonment.

The next charge relates to the woman Alwine. Without the slightest excuse, as the judgement plainly shows, he assumed that certain natives – Jan and Kewas had stolen some of his stock. By beating a child, Doris, he extorted from her a false statement that Alwine had given stock to these men. He then threatened to beat Alwine to death if she did not disclose their names, and when she said she did not know struck her 15 times over the naked shoulders within a heavy leather sjambok. A fortnight later she still bore 15 broad weals. For this line was fined 5*l*. Nothing was done regarding the beating of Doris.

The accused apparently would believe anything, and not merely believe it but go to the utmost lengths on the strength of it without further inquiry.

After beating Alwine he passed a sleepless night, not, as one might have hoped, over the fates of Grunas and Alwine, but because he was still puzzling over the perfectly innocent Jan and Kewas. This time he came to the conclusion, again on the absurdest evidence, that they had been using poison. By violence and threats he had obtained statements from Alwine as the result of which he thrashed a woman named Lupertine till she implicated a man, Kadwakonda. Lupertine, it should be noted, received two more thrashings, one in the presence of a police-sergeant and another before the investigating magistrate. No steps were taken in regard to the assaults on her, although false statements were extorted from her by them. After the second beating of Lupertine, she, Alwine, a woman Maria, Kadwakonda, a man Langmann and Harutonge, a woman captured in the bush, were all chained together to the back of an ox-cart and carried off to Gobabis prison, apparently on a charge of poisoning Cramer, unsupported by a scrap of real evidence. The distance from Otjisororindi to Gobabis is 72 miles as the crow flies.

On the way there he invented another flimsy charge of poisoning, this time against the native, Jacob. As a result he gave Jacob 50 strokes with a sjambok. in the hotel at Gobabis. This must have been very severe, as he was fined 30*l*. for it, yet no one at the hotel intervened.

On his return to his farm, after the officials had left, accused began again. By this time another native had been in the same way implicated in the supposed poisoning. He accordingly thrashed Juli till he became so faint he had to be revived with brandy in order that the thrashing might be continued. The medical statement shows how severe were the injuries. Yet he was let off with a fine of 40*l*.

Getting nothing out of Juli, he turned his attention to his wife Maria and bullied her into false accusations, which he put into her mouth, against Konturu and another Maria, wife of Jacob already mentioned.

With the aid of his daughter, a girl of 16 or 17, he shockingly ill-treated Konturu. All her clothes were torn off. she was severely beaten, and then locked up for the night naked in the farm prison (the very existence of which is highly significant) with one blanket only as covering. Next day this treatment was repeated, and she got another "energetic sjambokking," in accused s own words. Next day her person was closely and even indecently examined. The

Court described Konturu as "terribly mauled" (*bos zugerichtet*). and the medical certificate indicates serious injuries. She was in the first months of pregnancy, and shortly afterwards had a miscarriage. Apparently the natives asserted that accused trod on her body; if so, the miscarriage was at once accounted for, yet the Court refused to accept it as proved to be due to accused s conduct simply because he denied this. His statements were evidently obviously unreliable throughout, and it would seem that the Court would have been fully justified in rejecting this denial on that ground alone in view of the definite statements of the natives. Accused's punishment in this case was a fine of 40*l*.

His next victim was Maria. She was even worse treated, if it were possible, and her photograph shows the result. The worthy doctor, however, allowed her to leave hospital uncured; and when she died some six months later no medical man saw her body, and it was therefore impossible to connect the death with the assault. One thing is certain, and that is that she was permanently injured; but this point was lightly avoided by the Court. and the punishment imposed was one month s imprisonment.

Cramer now turned his attention to Amalia. When the Appeal Court heard the case 1¼ years later her back still looked as if it had been burned with fire. Each of these last three women got two severe thrashings on consecutive days (even the harsh German criminal law for natives demands an interval of 14 days between whippings), and each as a result passed on the blame for the mythical poisoning to someone whom she knew to be innocent, and who was in consequence severely handled in similar fashion. Amalia's case was considered so trifling that a fine of 10*l*. was enough. When examined by the doctor at Gobabis on the 10th February 1912, she showed numerous abrasions and one ulcerated sore 20 by 12 cm., i.e., about 8 in. by 4.8 in. in extent. She was a girl of 20, and recovered. Consider the position of the unfortunate girl Amalia. All the other natives on the farm had been dealt with except the two old women Auma and Magdalena, and in order to save them she heroically held out as long as she could, but at length even her fortitude gave way and to escape further punishment she reluctantly accused Auma. Probably she chose this old woman in the hope that her age and the impossibility of her having had anything to do with the poisoning would save her; but it was not to be.

This brings us to the worst case of all. When the accused took his first prisoners to Gobabis, the magistrate gave him other natives to take their place on the farm. Auma and Magdalena were two of them, and had only been on the farm three days when they were beaten. It was therefore, humanly speaking, impossible that they could have anything to do with the poisoning, but this consideration was of no moment to the accused. On the accusation – extorted from Amalia by two days' thrashing, so severe as to leave her marked by fearful scars for life – he meted out the same treatment to Auma.

This decrepit old woman of from 55 to 60 was terribly cut about in the course of what accused described as a "powerful cudgel-cure." She was practically in a state of collapse when taken away from the farm. Her injuries are described in the medical report and exhibited in the photograph, and there can be no reasonable doubt that her death (14 days after admission to hospital) was directly brought about by accused. Yet all German officialdom combined to procure his freedom from any such accusation. The doctor would not say accused caused her death, the State-prosecutor would not bring such a charge, and the Court refused to entertain it.

The ridiculous sentence of three months' imprisonment was passed.

Nothing was obtainable from Auma, so Cramer turned his attention to the sole remaining person, Magdalena, aged 40, who had also only been on the farm three days. She was also gravely injured, but a fine of 40*l*. was considered enough to meet the case.

It is when the Court comes to consider the question of mitigating circumstances that it reaches its most incomprehensible limit. It is pointed out that the allegations of poisoning were entirely without support; that accused was a man of good intelligence, but unable to draw the proper conclusions from obvious facts; that he constantly ill-treated his natives without cause; that his daughter, whom he used as an interpreter, was so poor a success that on one occasion a wrong translation by her procured a beating for an unfortunate native; that he abused the witnesses in Court; that he had his full mental powers but was given to self-deception; that his wife did not exercise the proper wifely pacifying influence over him; that his behaviour was worse than that of a slave-driver, and chiefly that he suffered from boundless self-conceit. It is doubtful whether anyone outside the five persons who sat on this case could be persuaded to discover in any of these arguments anything whatever in mitigation of accused s barbarism. On the contrary, most of them would be regarded by anyone of common sense as aggravations of his conduct.

Just before the appeal judgement, was delivered, Cramer's wife published in Germany a book, "*Weiss oder Schwartz*?" (White or Black?) which is one long protest against the injustice he had received at his first trial, and a plea for tightening up the administration of native affairs in the Protectorate.[215]

Cramer is no longer alive. A few months ago, while engaged with two natives preparing holes for planting trees in his orchard, for which purpose he was using dynamite, he was blown to pieces. The natives declared that this was due to accident, and in all probability were correct but if his death had been the result of design most people would admit that he merely received his just deserts.

That this was no isolated case is plainly shown by other records of the German Courts. As an instance, the case of Walter Boehmer may be referred to. This man was tried at Windhuk on the 1st May 1914. He was charged with a series of assaults committed on natives in his employ. The most serious case was that of Andreas. This man was suspected of theft, and accused had him

---

[215] Cramer, Ada, *Weiss oder Schwarz: Lehr und Leidensjahre eines Farmers in Südwest im Licht des Rasenhasses*, Deutscher Kolonial-Verlag, 1913.

stripped and tied up hand and foot with wire to some shelves in a storeroom. Accused then thrashed him with a *makoss*. described as a thong, 1 metre long and 2 cm.(⅘ in.) thick, with a wooden handle. After accused had beaten him, he ordered four of his natives to continue the thrashing, and one after another they did so. Andreas was then untied and sent into the veld with instructions to bring in the stolen articles. Upon his return without them he was again beaten with a donkey-whip and the *makoss*. Six natives gave evidence to this effect. Eight natives and a police-boy said that Andreas's body was as a result badly swollen, covered with blood and open wounds, and that he was exhausted. Two European witnesses who saw Andreas immediately after the beating testified to the swelling of his genitals and a large number of weals all over his back, some swollen to the thickness of a thumb and some burst. Andreas died some days after the assault. No medical man examined him either before or after death. The Court found Boehmer guilty of assault dangerous to life.

Another charge was that he had given a boy Wilhelm 30 strokes on his buttocks with a stick about 2 cm. thick. The boy s statement was corroborated by a police-sergeant who examined him the next day and found 22 distinct weals and eight open cuts. Wilhelm had deserted from his service, and accused claimed it was his right to beat him for so doing. The Court admitted this right, but decided that as actual injury had been caused it had been exceeded.

In giving judgement, the Court described Boehmer's conduct as absolutely inhuman and brutal, and pointed out that he was a well-educated man fully able to understand that such behaviour was contrary to the dictates of humanity. Mitigating circumstances were found in the facts that the accused had not been previously convicted, that he was excited on account of the theft and possibly also because his wife was in child-bed, and that Andreas was a very cunning native who had deserted about 14 times before. Accordingly accused was permitted to pay a fine of 50*l*. for the assault on Andreas and 7*l*. 10*s*. for beating Thomas.

Boehmer was further charged with having tied up a native, Hans, with wire hand-to-foot to an anvil and kept him so for a whole morning. The Court decided that on the evidence of several natives there was a strong suspicion that this was done as a punishment. Accused denied this, and said he had merely tied up Hans with a thong in order to take him to the police to be punished because he suspected him of having released one August, whom Boehmer had tied up for causing a grass fire. In view of his claim, admitted by the Court, that he had the right to punish his natives himself, this would appear to be a somewhat dubious theory, and it was uncorroborated, but the Court accepted it and acquitted him.

A further charge against Boehmer was that he had struck Hans twice with a drill and four thes with a hammer handle across the back. This was found to be proved, and the drill in Court was admitted to be a dangerous instrument; but on the ground that no actual physical injury had been caused, and Hans had merely suffered pain, it was found by the Court that the accused had acted with the limits of his right of correction and he was found not guilty. The same decision was arrived at in the case of Acherob, who had received 15 strokes with an ox-hide thong on the clothed buttocks, although accused could not give any reason for this beating.

A native, Automab, had also brought two charges against accused, and in the first his evidence had proved unsatisfactory. In considering the second charge the Court properly remarked that, in view of this, his testimony must be received with great caution. On the other hand, as appears above, the statements of accused were more than once disbelieved. yet his other evidence was fully accepted almost always when contradicted solely by natives.

These two cases show how anxious the Courts were to shield Europeans when accused of ill-treatment of natives. Every excuse was taken for rejecting native evidence, while that of a white witness was accepted without reserve. It was only when accused completely contradicted himself, or was faced with other white witnesses who disproved his statements, that the story of the natives was admitted, but even then it was discounted as much as possible.

It is now proposed to give details of what appears to be an instance in which two natives were thrashed to death by a white man or on his orders. and the whole thing was hushed up by the authorities. The Khan Copper Mine is a fairly prosperous concern situated in the desert some 60 kilos. from Swakopmund, and employed numbers of natives and others on its works. In 1911 it was under the management of a Dr. Sichtermann. The following extract is taken from a sworn affidavit recently made by one Dixon, who was employed in the mine as overseer in 1911 and 1912.

David Esma Dixon states:–

> As an example of how murders and brutal treatment were hushed up by the German authorities, I will mention the case of Dr. Sichtermann, who was at one time the Manager of the Khan Copper Mine near Swakopmund. This was after the Herero rebellion about 1912. I was working there at the time. One of the Ovambo mine labourers on the mine died suddenly. Two compatriots of the dead native had been reported to Dr. Sichtermann as suspects. It was alleged that they had poisoned the man. Dr. Sichtermann reported the matter to the police at Swakopmund, but before they arrived he decided to investigate the matter himself. He sent for the two Ovambos. I was the overseer who brought them to him. He then ordered thick ropes to be tied round their necks, and they were asked by him to say what they knew of the death of the other boy. They denied all knowledge and said they were innocent. Sichtermann then ordered them to be flogged. A German named Ahlefelder then beat them. The instrument used was a piece of 1½ in. India-rubber hosepipe. After a severe flogging they still pleaded that they were innocent, and after a while they were flogged and flogged again. Ahlefelder alternated the flogging by striking them with his fists. When they fell he kicked them with his booted feet until they rose again. They were both quite naked, and were held fast by the ropes round their necks. I had to hold one rope, and a native named David held the other. I protested, but Sichtermann said I had to obey his orders like everyone else. He said the boys were not going to get the better of him, and he would flog them until they admitted their guilt, of which he appeared to be convinced, though there was no evidence at all against the natives.

This treatment went on at intervals nearly the whole forenoon, until the boys' bodies were swollen terribly and cut and bruised all over. They cried out for water, but Sichtermann ordered that they were to receive neither food nor drink. They kept on protesting their innocence. Sichtermann then ordered their ankles to be bound together. They were then made to sit down with their knees drawn up to their chins, and their hands were then drawn round their knees and fastened together, while a stick was placed through under the knees and over the bent arms near the elbows. This meant that they could not stir and had to remain in this trussed position. It would be painful to do this even when one is well, but after the thrashings they had received it was barbarism to do that. However, Sichtermann would listen to no interference. I told him he was killing them, but he took no notice. He ordered them to be carried away and locked up in separate rooms. One boy we placed in the room where the oils were stored. I secretly gave him some water to drink, but I could see he was terribly hurt and I was anxious. After dinner I went and looked again and found he was quite dead. I rushed off and told Dr. Sichtermann, and he at once ordered the other boy to be unbound and washed, and told us to wash the dead boy and stretch him out carefully. Sichtermann had just heard that a doctor and police-detective were arriving from Swakopmund.

Shortly afterwards the German District Surgeon, Dr. Brenner, arrived; he was accompanied by the detective named Friederich. We all went into the room where the body was. Brenner looked at it, and although it was terribly cut and swollen he asked no questions. He then performed a post-mortem. When he had finished, he said "The organs appear to be quite normal; I trace no disease." This caused me to glance at Dr. Sichtermann, as I thought the statement would frighten him. At that moment I saw him wink very significantly at Dr. Brenner: the latter hesitated a moment and then opened up the boy s heart, which he carefully examined. He then said: "Ah, here it is – heart disease: I am prepared to certify."

The body was then taken away and buried.

The other Ovambo was taken by the detective to Swakopmund by rail, but he died on the train. I remained on the mine with Dr. Sichtermann for a year after that incident, and I can swear that no steps were ever taken against him by the German authorities although the incident was fairly well known and talked about.

Dixon is not certain of the date, but from official German records it appears that on the 26th October 1911 an Ovambo, Karuwappa, died suddenly at the mine and that the Ovambos, David and Chicongo, were suspected of poisoning him. Police-Sergeant-Major Springhorn held an enquiry at the mine, and took statements to the effect that Karuwappa had been ill for a week and complained of severe pains in his chest and stomach, and shortly before his death had accused Chicongo of having given him meat poisoned by David on the instructions of the latter. Certain Ovambo witnesses stated that David had poisoned other people in Ovamboland, and that they were quite certain that he and Chicongo were guilty of poisoning Karuwappa. It was also stated that after arrest both accused at first asserted their innocence, but subsequently admitted their guilt. Dr. Brenner held a post-mortem on Karuwappa, and found alcoholic kidney and liver, haemorrhage and swelling of the mucous membranes of the intestines and stomach "which probably caused death by poisoning." There was nothing else to support the theory of poisoning. It is stated on the papers that Chicongo "escaped on the morning of the 26th December, and died soon after his capture." He was not examined by Springhorn. Dr. Brenner dissected the body and certified:–

> On the 26th October this year at the Khan Mine I dissected Ovambo Chicongo, who died about an hour before and whom the assistant suspected of having been poisoned. The dissection disclosed heart failure as the cause of death. There were no external or internal injuries.

Springhorn endorsed on the papers on 26th October: "David will be removed to the gaol at Swakopmund." On the 31st October he made a further endorsement The instigator, David, died in the night of 29 - 30th October 1911. He was not examined as he was incapable of making statements. Dr. Brenner's report, dated 20.11.11, on the post-mortem on David is:–

> On the 30th October 1911 the Ovambo David (suspected at the time of poisoning) died in the gaol. He was already in a very miserable condition on the journey from Khan. The dissection disclosed as the cause of death a severe degeneration of the muscles of the heart, chronic inflammation on several sections of the lung, pleurisy on the right side, chronic inflammation of the kidneys. Further numerous injuries to the skin and muscles caused by blows with a hard instrument.

In a certificate to the Police Superintendent dated 30.10.11, Dr. Brenner gave the cause of death as: natural causes, degeneration of the muscles of the heart, chronic inflammation of the lungs and pleurisy, injuries to the skin and muscles, and inflammation of the kidneys.

This completed the record, and nothing further was ever done.

From the medical reports it is clear that Dixon's statement that David was severely beaten is true. The doctor found numerous injuries, and the internal condition he observed night well have been caused by a bad thrashing by a heavy instrument. There seems, therefore, no reason to doubt Dixon's assertion that Chicongo was also beaten, and that his account of what took place at the post mortem is correct. Dr. Brenner's certificate is extremely meagre and simply gives the cause of death as heart failure, thus corroborating Dixon's statement. The alleged escape and recapture of Chicongo probably never took place; but if a prisoner escaped it was perfectly legitimate to thrash him, and this may therefore have been invented to explain the external appearance of Chicongo's body to the doctor, who would then be inclined to overlook it. After David had once reached Swakopmund gaol it was impossible to conceal his state, as it must have been known to many different persons. The doctor was therefore bound to mention the injuries in his case, but does not emphasise in any way the fact that they might have contributed to the death. The final responsibility for shelving this matter rests with the *Bezirksamtmann* of Swakopmund, to whom Springhorn submitted all the papers. He did nothing; but most ordinary people will be of opinion that Dr. Brenner's report on David was alone sufficient to indicate that the matter was one calling for searching investigation. This would have disclosed, if Dixon's statements are true, a strong case against Sichtermann, and should have ended in his trial for murder;

but he was a well-known man, the manager of an influential company, and that was the end of it.

With such occurrences taking place, is it to be wondered at that the Governor found it necessary to issue his secret circular of the 31st May 1912 (see Chapter 22, Part I) to his District Officers?

CHAPTER THREE

THE RELATIONS BETWEEN GERMANS AND NATIVES AS EVINCED IN CRIMINAL PROCEEDINGS AFTER OUR OCCUPATION

Shortly after the surrender of the Protectorate to the Union Military Forces Military Courts were erected for the trial of criminal offences committed by the inhabitants in place of the German Courts, which it was not deemed politic to revive. Minor misdemeanours are dealt with by Courts of Military Magistrates stationed at various places in the country; serious crime comes before what is known as the Special Criminal Court, which sits twice a year at such points as may be convenient and has jurisdiction to try any offence whatever.[216] All these Courts are compelled by the dictates of International Law as accepted by us to follow the provisions of the German law when Germans are before them. Numerous cases have come before this last-mentioned Court which throw a violent light upon the relations between German inhabitants and the aborigines.

In this chapter it is proposed to give some account of these, taken direct from the original records of the trials.

The principal deduction to be drawn from the series of cases of which details will be given is that the relationship between Germans and natives has always been on an unhappy footing. Mutual confidence has been absent and mutual fear has taken its place.

The manner in which natives were dealt with under the previous *régime*, when suspected of criminal charges, has been discussed in a previous chapter. We have endeavoured to follow the wellfounded traditions of the Union, and have done our best in all such matters to follow the basic principle of law obtaining in all British countries that Justice is blind to any distinction of race or colour.

One grave source of trouble between the white and black inhabitants of this country has been theft of stock. In the case of Bushmen in particular a German farmer apparently believed himself justified, if he had the merest suspicion that they had stolen his stock, in shooting them out of hand. We have made it clear that we do not accept this view, and that such thieves may only be punished through the intervention of the Courts.

---

[216] In the period from its establishment 28th September 1915 up to January, 1918 (when the Blue Book was submitted) the Special Criminal Court that was established by the Union of South Africa following the surrender of German forces in Namibia on 9th July, 1915, heard 158 cases. Of these 61 cases are referred to directly in Part 2 of the Blue Book and a eighty-five of those directly accused in these cases are referred to. Details of the relevant cases can be found in Storage Units SCC1-10. National Archives of Namibia, Finding Aid, 'Special Criminal Court'. 'Report of the Administrator of South West Africa', 9th July, 1915 – 31st March, 1916', Windhoek, 1st April, 1916.

For the very reason that it is regarded as essential for the good government of the country to press home this attitude, the Courts have always taken a serious view of such thefts, as the following cases tried by the Special Criminal Court show

Rex versus Katai and seven others – Tried 6th April 1916. The accused, all Bushmen, were charged with the theft of four head of cattle, the property of one Baumgarten, a German farmer of the District of Grootfontein. They all pleaded guilty, and were sentenced to four years' imprisonment with hard labour.

Rex versus Sarrup – Tried 6th April 1916. Sarrup, a Bushman, pleaded guilty to stealing five head of cattle belonging to a farmer of Gobabis, named Hans von Hatten. On the outbreak of hostilities complainant was called upon to join the German forces, and it was whilst he was on active service that the Bushman helped himself to the stock. The skins were identified at accused's hut, and two accomplices, also Bushmen, turned King's evidence. Sentence of two years' hard labour and six lashes was imposed.

Rex versus Jacob Casob – Tried 10th April 1916. Accused was sentenced to three years' hard labour andl ten lashes for theft of a cow from a farmer named Duval of the Outjo District.

Rex versus Isaac Thithis – Tried 20th April 1916. Accused stole 37 head of small stock from a German named Bleichmer, and was awarded two years' hard labour and six lashes.

Rex versus Simon Ncaib – Tried 27th April 1916. Ncaib received two years' hard labour and ten lashes for stealing 43 sheep from a farmer named Jasperson.

Rex versus (1) *Jacob*; (2) *Titup* – Tried 9th October 1916. These men, formerly farm servants, had taken to the veld and committed a series of depredations, some small, some of more consequence, including thefts of goats, produce, &c. They were each sentenced to three years' hard labour and ten lashes.

Rex versus (1) *Ouxason*; (2) *David* – Tried on 18th November 1916. For the theft of five head of cattle from a farmer named Schweikhardt accused were each sentenced to three years' hard labour and twelve lashes.

Rex versus (1) *Aramib*; (2) *Hendrik* – Tried on 18th November 1916. These men received a similar sentence for the theft of two head of cattle from Joseph Stroka, a farmer.

Rex versus William Christian – Tried 8th May 1917. Accused stole 30 head of small stock from two farmers of Aroab District, and had to undergo 18 months' imprisonment in consequence.

Rex versus (1) *August*; (2) *Kukub* – Tried 29th May 1917. The accused were vagrant Bushmen who had caught in the veld, killed and eaten five cows belonging to a farmer named Voswinckel of Otjamibambo. Grootfontein District. in October 1916. They admitted their guilt and were each sentenced to 18 months' hard labour and seven lashes.

Rex versus (1) *Massinab*; (2) *August*; (3) *Andries*; (4) *Kukub* – Tried 29th May 1917. The two accused in the preceding case with two other members of their party had pleaded guilty to a similar theft of five sheep from a farmer named Wujack of the same neighbourhood. They each received sentence of 12 months' hard labour.

Rex versus (1) *Katjirora*; (2) *Kaitanagora*; (3) *Kapapie* – Tried 10th December, 1917. For stealing two cows from Farmer Schlettwein at Cauas Okawa, Outjo District, accused were sentenced to three years' hard labour each, with, in the case of Nos. 1 and 3, seven lashes as well.

Rex versus (1) *Kateminikwa*; (2) *Kambenjene*; (3) *Kanako* – Tried 10th December 1917. for stealing two bulls from the same owner at Otjitambi, Outjo District, these men received three years hard labour each, with seven lashes in addition in the cases of Nos. 1 and 2.

Rex versus Nampira – Tried 10th December 1917. Accused, a shepherd, ate five sheep belonging to his employer at Canas, Outjo District. He was sentenced to 18 months' hard labour and seven lashes.

In none of the foregoing cases was profit the object of the theft. They were all due to the overpowering desire for a good meal of meat which now and again attacks a native.

Although these sentences differ somewhat for various reasons which need not be gone into here, none of them can be regarded as lenient, and Germans who have sought personally to avenge similar acts cannot assert as an excuse that they are not sufficiently punished by the Courts. Corporal punishment, which is regarded by the local inhabitants as the only proper penalty for a native, was imposed in practically all cases where the physical condition of the offender did not preclude it.

In order to assist the reader to a more clear understanding of the cases now to be dealt with, a few words on the law of homicide, as laid down in the German Criminal Code, are necessary.

The capital offence, known as *Mord*, consists in the killing of a fellow-creature with intention and deliberation. What is meant by intention need not be enlarged upon now, but deliberation requires some explanation. since it is regarded by German jurists as an entirely distinct issue. Roughly, it may be defined as any sort of calm exercise of the intellect directed towards the choice of the means of execution, the rejection of unsuitable means, the prevention of the victim's escape, the procurement of immunity from prosecution or punishment or any other factor vital to the whole affair. In the most recent case on the point (*Rex versus Sokolicz*), in which there was very little evidence of a preconceived plan, but it was proved that accused had so arranged his victim's body as to give it all the appearances of that of a suicide, it was held that this fact was proof of deliberation.

The next variety of homicide is that known as *Totschlag*. This consists in the killing of another with intention but without deliberation. This in our law is, generally speaking, also murder and punishable with the capital sentence; but under the German Code the penalty is imprisonment with hard labour for a period of from five to fifteen years, unless there has been provocation in the shape of violence or gross insult, in which case a less rigorous form of detention for not less than six months may be imposed. To this distinction between *Mord* and *Totschlag* is attributable the fact, remarkable to British people, that in several of the cases referred to later on the death sentence was not inflicted.

Various special forms of *Totschlag*, such as killing a relation or killing while engaged in another offence, are specially punishable. but need not be considered here.

An assault which results in death but is not an intentional killing is punishable with imprisonment for from three to fifteen years.

Causing death by negligence, a form of what is known to us as culpable homicide, is punishable with three years hard labour at most.

If a bodily injury is caused by negligence, the maximum penalty is a fine of 900 marks or two years' imprisonment.

If there are mitigating circumstances in any case except that of *Mord* a more lenient punishment is applicable.

The following trials are concerned with instances in which grave violence was used by Germans towards natives, followed usually either directly or indirectly by the death of the victim.

Rex versus Heinrich Pieter Kreft – Tried 30th September 1915. It was alleged that accused in July 1915, and at Otjibonde, Omaruru District, murdered Gondjore, a native labourer in his employ. Accused reprimanded deceased for laziness, and while doing so endeavoured to take from him a light kerrie[xxiii] which he was holding in his left hand behind his back. Native witnesses denied that beyond changing the kerrie to his right hand Gondjore did anything of a threatening nature, and said that thereupon accused struck him two blows with a heavy piece of wood. The first brought him to his knees and the second, delivered while the boy was still in that position, fractured his skull. For the defence accused called a number of witnesses to show that deceased was of a truculent disposition, one of them basing this statement on the fact that Gondjore had once resisted an assault upon him by the witness. Accused said further that Gondjore actually hit him on the arm with his stick before he himself struck one blow. He admitted that Gondjore was brought to his knees by the first blow and used no further violence, and he admitted killing him with the second blow.

He was sentenced to one year s imprisonment with hard labour for assault resulting in death in mitigating circumstances.

[xxiii] (Page 186 in original) A knobbed stick used for hunting or protection. A heavy one is a dangerous weapon, a light one is not.

Rex versus Walter Barth. Tried 4th October 1915. On the 4th July 1915, at Guchab, near Otavi, accused, a mine manager, was alleged to have murdered Wilfred, a male adult native labourer on the mine. On the 3rd July 1915 our troops arrived at Guchab. Accused said it was reported to him that at this the deceased and others had attempted to break open the mine provision store, and that he found him near it and ordered him away. Wilfred denied knowledge of the matter, explaining his presence there by saying he had been holding the horses of the troops. The next day Barth came to the huts and again accused Wilfred of trying to break open the store. Wilfred denied this, and after a few words accused struck him with a sjambok. Thereupon, according to accused, deceased picked up a kerrie and threatened him. This was denied by native witnesses, who said that on the contrary Wilfred started to run away. However that may be, accused next fired four shots from a Browning pistol at Wilfred and killed him.

Accused s reason for using the sjambok in the first instance is instructive. He said: "I hit him because of the expression of his face. He looked impertinent. I also hit him because he lied to me, I thought I was justified in hitting him, because in German South-West Africa the High Court gave a decision that a manager had the so-called *Zuchtigungsrecht*, the right to apply a light punishment.

This *Zuchtigungsrecht* (right of correction) is dealt with elsewhere in this volume.

Accused was found guilty of *Totschlag* and sent to prison for three years.

Rex versus Hermann Albert Rudolph Eisentraut – Tried on the 6th October 1915. The charge was that on the 2nd August 1915, and at Niederungsfeld, Omaruru, accused murdered Joseph, a native in his employ. Accused lived in concubinage with a native girl. When our troops came into the neighbourhood all his servants, including the girl, ran away. He followed them, taking a Browning pistol with him, came upon them in the bush and immediately opened fire, killing Joseph with his first shot. He stated that he acted in self-defence as his life was in danger, giving as his reasons that the natives were all armed with bows and arrows or kerries. He did not say that any attack upon him was actually made or attempted. After killing Joseph he fired several more shots without effect and then drove the woman back to the farm, telling the men to follow, which some of them did.

He was found guilty of intentional homicide (*Totschlag*) and sentenced to three years' imprisonment with hard labour.

Rex versus Heinrich Petrus Witbooi – Tried on the 7th October 1915. It was alleged that accused, a native, shot a Bushman, Gaidip, near Hebron, Otavi, during July 1915. Accused had made a statement to the effect that, being out in the veld with his master, Kremer, they came upon three Bushmen; that Kremer at once opened fire, wounding deceased and killing another man, and that accused, on Kremer's instructions, fired at the wounded man with fatal results.

This statement was not admitted by the Court. The only other evidence was that of the third Bushman, who did not see his assailants and consequently was not of much value. Accused was acquitted.

Rex versus Henrich Christian Kremer – Tried on 8th October 1915. This was the man mentioned in the previous case, and he was charged with the murder of the two Bushmen therein mentioned. The principal witness against him was Witbooi, and in the absence of satisfactory corroboration he was acquitted.

Rex versus Frederick – Tried 8th October 1915. It was alleged that the accused on the 26th August 1915, at Gamrarab, Outjo, shot dead a Bushman named Gaidap. The principal evidence against him was his own statement that cattle of his master, Buntebardt, having been stolen, he and Buntebardt had followed the spoor and came to a Bushman werft, where fresh meat was hanging up.

They concealed themselves outside the hut until dawn broke. Just before this, Buntebardt handed accused a shot gun and cartridges, and ordered him to shoot any Bushmen he saw. He approached the hut, saw deceased in the doorway and immediately fired, killing him. He went on to say that thereupon a woman ran out of the hut and he fired at her and purposely missed her, whereupon his master told him that if he did so again he would shoot him and himself fired and killed the woman. Accused concluded his statement by saying that he shot Gaidap because he was ordered to do so, and that even if it had been his wife he was ordered to kill he would have obeyed, because it was his master who gave the order.

There was no other evidence of any value, and accused was acquitted.

Rex versus Fritz Buntebardt – Tried 1 9th October 1915. Accused was charged with the murder of Tanesis. the woman referred to above. The only witness against him was Frederick, and in the absence of corroboration he was acquitted.

Rex versus Walter Böhmer – Tried 11th October 1915. Böhmer is a farmer in the Protectorate. During hostilities he held some military position at Seeis, but on the approach of our forces, according to his own statement, he was told to lay aside his uniform and return to his own farm. His only other instruction being that he was to protect the neighbouring farmers against natives. He did not retain his rifle. On the 21st May 1915 four native servants of a neighbour of accused deserted from their service, after some form of dispute with their master, and set out for Windhuk. Accused was told of this by telephone. These natives had to pass accused's farm, and when they approached his homestead he got ready his weapons, a combination gun and a double-barrelled shot-gun, and summoned his own natives to his assistance. He then called to the four men to approach, and they did so. The accused says that when they were ten paces away he ordered them to stop and sit down, that they refused and continued to approach slowly, that one at least had a kerrie in his hand and that he fired because he was afraid that this would be thrown at him. He did not go so far as to say definitely that this man made any actual motion as if to throw the kerrie. He fired in all four or five shots, and the first two from the shotgun each killed one of the natives. The other two natives ran away, both being wounded in their flight. The medical evidence to the effect that one of the deceased was shot in the right breast and the other in the right side, both at from ten to fifteen paces distance, does not corroborate accused s story that the natives were advancing upon him when he fired.

During all this accused s own natives were standing by. The evidence given by them and the two who escaped is to the effect that the four natives halted in a line when accused told them to but refused to sit down when he ordered, saying they were going to Windhuk, and that accused shot them on account of this refusal.

The Court declined to accept accused s version of the affair and found him guilty of intentional killing without deliberation, and sentenced him to five years' imprisonment.

In 1912 accused was convicted by a German Protectorate Court of beating to death with a *makoss*[xxiv] a native who was in a weak condition and consumptive. He tied his victim hand and foot and beat him until he himself was tired and then called on his native servants to continue the thrashing. For this offence he was fined 50*l*. or 100 days' imprisonment, and the Court commented severely on the inhumanity of his conduct, but found mitigating circumstances in the facts that his wife was at the the lying in child-bed and the native was of bad character. Full particulars of this case have been given in the previous chapter.

Rex versus Karl Wilhelm Becker – Tried 25th October 1915. It was alleged that on the 24th August 1915, and at Tsumanas. Outjo District, accused attempted to murder a native, Kasinda, by shooting at him and wounding him.

Kasinda and another native went on to accused s farm to look for lost goats They were met by accused, who was armed with a rifle, which he said he never was without when he was away from the house; and he took them to his house. The parties were unable to understand one another. The boys said that after a time they became frightened and ran away, and that accused fired at them, slightly wounding Kasinda. Accused said that, seeing strange natives on his farm and having recently lost a lot of cattle, he took them to his house and questioned them, and understood that they were not in employment. He accordingly determined to take them to the police, and when they heard him say this they ran away. He shouted to them three times to stop and as they did not do so he fired two shots, that he did not aim at them, that when he fired the

---

[xxiv] (Page 188 in original) A short, very heavy sjambok, used to control the wheeler oxen of a wagon.

second shot they were out of sight in a hollow, that he did not know either shot had taken effect until two days later when a neighbour told him, and that the wound must have been due to a ricochet. The evidence of the medical man who attended Kasinda was not available.

Accused was convicted of causing bodily injury through negligence and hued 45l. or one year's imprisonment.

Rex versus Siegfried Alexander Wilhelm von Seydlitz – Tried 26th October 1915. It was alleged that on the 22nd September 1915, and at Schonfeld Omaruru, accused had attempted to murder a native named Simon in his service, by shooting at and wounding him.

Simon was late for his work, and accused remonstrated with him and then struck him, and there was a struggle between them. After it was over. Simon went to his hut. Another German then went up to him and struck him because he had hit accused. There was a further struggle between Simon on the one hand and accused and the second German on the other. After this Simon was ordered off the farm by accused, and his goats remained behind. Accused and his companion followed him to see him off, accused taking a rifle with him. When they got near Simon sprang towards them, and accused shot and wounded him. Accused said he fired because he thought he was being attacked. Simon said he was afraid accused was going to shoot him and sprang forward to get the gun away.

The Court accepted the view that accused acted in self-defence and found him guilty of attempted homicide in mitigating circumstances, and fined him 10l. or three months' imprisonment.

Rex versus Emil Kurz – Tried 16th November 1915. The charge was that in May 1915, at Omajette. Omaruru, accused shot dead a native woman named Kauchave.

An ox had been stolen from accused, who followed on the spoor with two native servants. They came to a spot where meat was hanging and, seeing figures moving through the bush, accused fired. He admitted that he wounded the woman but denied causing her death.

The evidence of native companions of deceased was that she was killed outright. No medical testimony was available.

Accused was found guilty of dangerous assault and sentenced to twelve months' imprisonment with hard labour.

Rex versus Julius Folkmann – Tried 18th November 1915. The charge was that on the 7th October 1915, and at Otjihua, Windhuk District, accused murdered a native named August, in his employ, by shooting him with a Browning pistol.

Some of accused s calves had been lost, and there was a quarrel at night between him and deceased over this, which ended in a struggle in which accused's wife also took part. She sent a small native to bring the pistol, and accused shot deceased with it. He maintained that deceased tried to take it from him, and that it went off in the struggle.

The case resulted in a verdict of intentional homicide in mitigating circumstances, and accused was fined 45*l*. or one year's imprisonment.

Rex versus Hermann Holtz – Tried 7th April 1916. Holtz, a German farmer of Sturmfeld, Gobabis, killed Fritz, a native whom he charged with deserting from his service. Accused was on trek when he came upon a German named Voss, for whom Fritz was acting as servant. Voss gave the native up through fear of Holtz, who was in an excited state, and accused and deceased left in company for the former s farm. On arrival at the farm two other native servants saw Holtz strike the servant Fritz on the head with a very heavy knife, and afterwards saw deceased going along a road in front of accused, who at this stage was carrying a gun. Accused came back some time afterwards without deceased, inspanned a wagon, took the same road, and on his return shortly afterwards brought back the body of Fritz. Native servants witnessed all this, and on examining the dead body found bullet wounds in the back and stomach. Accused had gone to another man on the farm, Frederick Sauer, and asked him to drive out to the veld where a native, Fritz, was lying. The accused told this man that he had wounded Fritz. Saner found Fritz in a dying condition. Holtz then told Saner that the boy had threatened to strike him in the morning and that he (Holtz) tried to get a piece of wood to defend himself, but that he could only reach a knife, with which he struck Fritz on the head. Holtz said that in the afternoon, on the veld, Fritz attacked him with a stick, whereupon accused shot him. Accused told another farmer that he was attacked by the boy in the veld whilst he (accused) was relieving himself, and that he shot the native in self-defence. The defence was that Fritz had lost one of accused s cows through neglect and that Holtz scolded him, to which he replied with insolence. Holtz was going to give deceased a blow with his hand, whereupon deceased picked up a stick. Accused stated that he tried to get a piece of wood but, failing in this, picked up a knife and used it on deceased, striking, however, with the broad side of the blade. Later accused and deceased started out in search of the missing cow, and it was then that accused shot Fritz, who was making an attack on him. According to Holtz the deceased, after being shot, admitted he was himself to blame for his injuries. Holtz left his water-bottle with deceased and went for assistance. Accused was found guilty of intentional homicide under mitigating circumstances and sentenced to two years' imprisonment.

Rex versus Carl Georg Schroeder – Tried 8th to 10th April 1916. Accused, a German farmer, residing at Kampe, in the District of Maltahohe, On Christmas Day, 1915, killed Johannes Xatjindu, a native servant employed by him. On the afternoon of that day Schroeder went to the huts of the servants and instructed deceased to attend to the lambs, which was deceased s usual duty. Deceased refused to carry out the order, and some words passed between him and accused. At the place where the altercation took place there were a number of other native servants. Accused had complained to deceased about the loss of small stock and charged him with negligence. Schroeder approached deceased with a sjambok and a revolver. He first struck him with the sjambok and afterwards fired three shots from the revolver, as the result of which deceased died in hospital about six weeks later. Schroeder declared that as he approached deceased the latter picked up a stone with the intention of attacking him, and that he (Schroeder) acted in self-defence. None of the native witnesses saw deceased threaten accused. Schroeder was found guilty of intentional homicide under mitigating circumstances and sentenced to two years imprisonment.

Rex versus Hendrik Stoetzer – Tried l4th-l5th April 1916. Stoetzer, a German farmer of Gobabis, was charged with the murder of Hans, a native herd in his employ, in August 1915. Accused pleaded not guilty. The Crown witnesses were natives, fellow-servants of deceased, and deposed that Stoetzer had words with Hans regarding his work, during which time, holding deceased by the arm, he led him away from the house. After the two had gone a few yards shots were heard, and Hans was seen to fall. The native witnesses stated that Hans went along without struggling, and that he never in any way threatened accused. It was established that when Stoetzer caught hold of deceased s arm the latter had a jackal-trap in his hand. Stoetzer said that he acted in self-defence, as deceased threatened him with this trap. Asked to account for the possession of the revolver at that particular time, he stated that he was carrying it for his protection. Stoetzer, however, fired not one but three shots, all of which took effect and any one of which was sufficient to disable the deceased according to medical testimony. Accused pleaded that as a result of ill-health and accidents which had befallen him he had become exceedingly nervous, so much so that when the native threatened him he drew the revolver and remembered very little of what followed. Stoetzer buried the body of the deceased immediately, but made no effort to bring the death to the notice of the police. It was only after several weeks had elapsed that the matter came to the ears of the authorities, and then through the instrumentality of a native servant from accused's farm. The Court found accused guilty of intentional homicide and passed sentence of five years imprisonment with hard labour.

Rex versus Carry Venuleth – Tried l7th-20th April 1916. This was a case of extreme interest from many different points of view.[xxv]

Rex versus Antonius Setecki – Tried 25th April 1916. Accused, a German farmer of Omaruru District ... (see p. 48 of [Cd.8371]) ... Accused refrained from giving evidence himself, and was fined 100*l*. or nine months hard labour.

[xxv] (Page 190 in original) The judgement, which is printed in full at pp. 42 44 of [Cd. 8371], is not reprinted here.

Rex versus Marie von Weiher – Tried 25th - 27th April 1916. Accused, a German woman residing in the Omaruru District, was on the outbreak of war left on the farm of her husband[xxvi] ... (see p. 48 of [Cd. 8371]) ... The Court found accused guilty of intentional homicide under mitigating circumstances, and sentenced her to pay a fine of 300*l*. or, in default of payment, to undergo eighteen months' imprisonment.

Rex versus Ludwig Dohling – Accused, a German farmer, of the Waterberg District.. (see p. 50 of [Cd. 8371]) ... The defence took the form of self-defence but was not accepted, and accused was found guilty of the charge of attempted murder and sentenced to eighteen months' imprisonment with hard labour.

Rex versus Johann Binkowski – Tried 2nd - 5th May 1916. Binkowski, a Police-Sergeant during the German regime ... (see p. 50 of [Cd. 8371])

The magistrate took no action against accused, but in Court admitted that he might have done so had he seen fit. When British troops occupied this part of the country, Petrus's body was discovered lying unburied, and the British police received reports which led to accused s arrest. It was established that Petrus was not one of the murderers of Luther, though evidence was forthcoming that Binkowski had been told that he was. The German magistrate sought to impress the Court with his power in the matter, but the fact that proceedings were not taken by him against the police-sergeant did not absolve the latter from the consequence of his action. The Court found accused guilty of intentional homicide and sentenced him to eighteen months' imprisonment with hard labour.

Rex versus Frank Juzek – Tried 6th May 1916. Accused, who like Binkowski was a German police officer, was charged with the murder of a native, named Fritz, at Okambahe, in January 1915....(see p. 51 of [Cd. 8371]) and accused was found guilty, in the absence of proof of the cause of death, of dangerous assault and sentenced to two years hard labour.

Rex versus Georg Frederick Nauhas and Theodor Jakubowski – Tried 18th May 1916. Nauhaus and Jakubowski, German farmers of Gobabis, were charged with the murder of Thabagab, an adult Bushman, on the farm Nabatzaub, in the District of Gobabis. the previous January ... (see p. 51 of [Cd. 8371])

The flogging was systematic with a view to induce confession or betrayal, but failed to secure its object. No medical evidence of the cause of death could be procured, and accused were convicted of dangerous assault and sentenced, No. 1 to eighteen months' and No. 2 to twelve months' imprisonment with hard labour.

[xxvi] (Page 191 in original) The Lt. v. Weiher referred to in Chap. I, of this part.

Rex versus Max Willy Frenzel – Tried 10th and 11th October 1916. Accused is a young German farmer, residing in the Maltahohe District., and it was alleged that he had committed rape upon a young Hottentot girl of about seven on the 2nd April 1916.

On that date in the morning the girl left the farm Grootfontein for Nieuwerust, where her mother worked, with a message. The same morning the accused, who had spent the night at Nieuwerust, left on horseback for Grootfontein. The girl's story, clearly told for so young a witness, was that they met on the road at a lonely spot, and accused got off his horse and committed the act charged.

On her arrival at Nieuwerust it was at once noticed that she was bleeding, and on examination it was seen that her injuries were such as to indicate penetration and were severe. In consequence of what she said, a European, named van der Merwe living at Nieuwerust, followed up accused's spoor. There had been a certain amount of rain, and the accused s and the girl s were the only tracks visible. He came to a spot where the accused had dismounted and tied up his horse, and here the girl s spoor diverged slightly from the road to a point a yard or so from it, where blood was seen. Accused had walked to this spot from the horse. This satisfied him that the girl's story was true, and he did not follow the spoors further. No one else had passed Nieuwerust in the direction of Grootfontein that morning, and accused was the first person to reach Grootfontein that morning. So far as could be ascertained he was the only person who had passed the girl on the road. Before going into the house at Grootfontein accused rode on a short distance to a water hole near by, but out of sight, remained there half an hour or so and then returned and entered the house.

Medical evidence that penetration had been effected was conclusive.

Immediately after his arrest accused shaved off most of his moustache and made other changes in his appearance. When asked to point him out soon after this the girl was unable to do so, but at the trial she was confident of his identity.

Accused denied that he had washed his clothes at the waterhole, and said he went there to get letters he had accidentally left there the previous day. He admitted meeting the girl on the road and seeing no one else on it. He stated that when he met her she was already injured.

On the ground that as van der Merwe had not followed the girl s tracks the whole way to Grootfontein there was nothing to disprove this, accused was acquitted.

The remark made by one witness in this case, that a small matter of this sort was not worth troubling about, is significant of the attitude of local farmers to cases of this character.

Rex versus Otto Rapmund – Tried 30th and 31st October 1916. The accused is a German farmer residing in the Okahandja District. He had been in the habit of forcing the wives of his native labourers to work for him under threat of turning them all off the farm if they refused. This system had been in vogue for about five years, and was commonly adopted on the farms of the Protectorate.

On the 26th April 1916 one of his men, Lucas Karoreke, refused to allow his wife to work any longer. The other natives took up the same attitude, and were all told by accused they must leave the farm.

On the following day they were ordered out by the foreman to work as usual. Lucas refused to go, stating that he was under notice to leave and that he wished to see his master, Rapmund, to obtain a pass from him. He was taken to his master, who assaulted him, first with his fists and then by firing three revolver shots at him, one of which entered the groin. He made a good recovery.

Native evidence was to the effect that Lucas did nothing to provoke this. Accused stated that when he went up to Lucas the latter looked at him impertinently and, in consequence, had his ears boxed; that, he then expected Lucas to return to work, but instead he sprang at him; and that, after his foreman had broken a stick over Lucas s head, he (accused) fired in self-defence. He also said that the pistol had gone off by accident.

He was convicted of dangerous assault and sentenced to a fine of 100*l.* or twelve months' imprisonment with hard labour.

Rex versus Walter Lichterfeld – Tried 17th October 1916. The accused, who is the manager of the farm Otjisongati in the Okahandja District, was charged with having assaulted a native labourer in such a manner as to cause death. The native, Jacob, had been employed as a herd by accused and, having lost a sheep, returned late with the cattle one evening. Lichterfeld informed him he must pay for the sheep and smacked his face several thes and, as he turned to run, kicked him. The kick caused a rupture of the urethra, and eventually resulted in death.

Lichterfeld's plea was guilty of assault resulting in death. The plea was accepted, and he was sentenced to a fine of 25*l.* or three months' imprisonment with hard labour.

Rex versus Ernst Fahrig – Tried 7th and 8th November 1916. Accused; a German police-sergeant, was charged with the murder at Okazongura, Omaruru District, in June 1915, of a native named Kamohombo. In May or June 1915, when our forces were approaching that part of the country, a farmer named Luther was killed by a native, who was subsequently convicted of intentional homicide by the Special Criminal Court. A German police patrol went out (unsuccessfully) in search of Luther's assailants. They found several natives and grossly ill-treated them with a view to extracting information.

Among other acts they seriously thrashed a native woman, and wished to mete out the same treatment to another who was *enceinte*, but their own natives interfered in her favour. One member of the patrol, Johann Binkowski,[217] is already undergoing sentence for causing the death of one of the natives whom they caught (see above).

---

[217] 'Pregnant'.

The Crown case was that Kamohombo was severely beaten on three occasions and eventually, when he became exhausted and was unable to proceed further, was shot by accused. One witness gave evidence to this effect, and a second, named Johannes Hausib, was called, who said that he had, under orders, administered the thrashings, and also testified to the shooting by the accused. This man, it transpired, had a very bad record, having several times been convicted of admitted offences under the German regime. The medical evidence was negative.

The defence was that the deceased was shot while trying to escape, which was permitted under German law.

The Court by a majority found the accused not guilty.

Rex versus Max Ahrens – Tried 8th November 1916. It was alleged that on the 9th June 1916 accused had attempted to murder his native servant, Appollis, at Aris, Outjo District, by shooting him with a rifle. Accused pleaded guilty of shooting without any intention of seriously injuring the boy. The evidence showed that, after a quarrel with Appollis, accused sent another boy to bring him the rifle and shot him through the thigh. Appollis had made a complete recovery from his injuries.

The Court found the accused guilty of dangerous assault and sentenced him to 18 months' hard labour.

Rex versus Karl Schilg and Wilhelm Lehmpuhl – The charge was murder of one Matthys, a Bushman male adult, at Obarura in Otjiwarongo District, on the 1st October 1916. The forefathers of Matthys had resided on this farm for many years. Their descendants were eventually dispossessed of it by the German authorities, and it came into the hands of Schilg. Lehmpuhl assisted him as a foreman on the farm.

For a time Matthys worked for Schilg, and about Christmas 1915 was sent away. At the end of September 1916 he returned, and when again ordered off by Schilg refused to go, saying that the Germans no longer owned the country and that the farm was his. Schilg went away and returned with Lehmpuhl with the intention (denied by them) of putting him off the place. Some sort of struggle took place between the two white men and Matthys and a native, Elias, which ended in Schilg drawing a Browning pistol and shooting Matthys through the right breast, lung, and spine, causing his immediate death. Both the natives were unarmed. Accused stated that he fired in self-defence, but the Court did not accept that view and found him guilty of assault resulting in death and fined him 100*l.* or 18 months' hard labour.

At the preliminary enquiry evidence was led that Lehmpuhl held Matthys while Schilg shot him. This was not substantiated at the trial, and he was acquitted.

Rex versus Georg Hounschild – Tried 16th, 17th and 18th November, 1916- There were three charges of murder against accused, alleged to have been committed at Okahabara, Outjo District, in April 1916

(1) Murder of an unknown adult male Bushman, thrashing him to death.
(2) A similar offence committed by shooting.
(3) Murder of an Ovambo named Salmon by thrashing him to death.

Some of the witnesses in Counts 1 and 2 were not forthcoming. As often happens in these cases, being Bushmen, they had run away through fear and have not yet been traced.

Count 3 alone was proceeded with.

Accused was employed by one von Rudno, a farmer, as also was Salmon, and they went with wagons to a salt pan to get salt.

On the way back an altercation took place between accused and deceased, and several native witnesses testified that accused severely thrashed Salmon, who was in consequence severely injured and died two days later after great suffering. Von Rudno, called for the defence, admitted that Salmon had been beaten by the accused, but denied the severity and stated that they were for three days before and two days after the assault without food and water, and that Salmon died of starvation, the swollen state of his body being due to dropsy caused thereby. He also admitted that the natives were frequently thrashed by accused and himself.

The medical evidence was negative, owing to the interval between the offence and the examination.

Accused did not give evidence, and was fined 50l. or eight months' hard labour for dangerous assault.

Rex versus Franz Ernst Becker – Tried 9th and 10th November, 1916. Accused is a farmer, and in 1915 was engaged in this occupation at Gransab. in the Tsumeb District.

A few days before Christmas 1915, Hendrik, a "wild" Bushman, drove off two of his oxen to a water hole 8½ miles from his farm. There he was joined by the rest of his family, and the animals were killed and eaten. The party consisted of two grown men, Hendrik and Kangob, two adult women, Ibis and Kaaigoos; two youths, Fritz and Tedrip, and two girl children, Ongaris and Arowas, aged about 12 and 6 respectively.

Accused, accompanied by a Bushman servant, Max, next morning followed on the track of the oxen and came upon the party still torpid from their meal. He at once opened fire with his sporting Mauser magazine rifle at close range. The second shot killed Hendrik and the third Kangob. Meanwhile the rest of the party scattered. Fritz and Tedrip got into a thickly-foliaged tree, and the women and children hid under a dense bush. Fortunately for them, the two youths escaped notice; but the track of the others was followed, they were detected, and both women and children were shot dead by Becker. In his defence Becker stated that he was attacked with arrows. This was entirely contrary to the evidence of his servant Max, Fritz and Tedrip. who were all agreed. that the party of Bushmen was completely taken by surprise, and in any case did not justify the shooting of the women and children after the men were killed.

Becker was sentenced to death. The sentence was commuted to imprisonment for life.

Rex versus Hans von Hatten – Tried 11th to 18th May 1917. Hans von Hatten, a German farmer, 32 years of age, residing at Oas in the District of Gobabis, was charged with attempting to murder Michael, an aged Klip Kaffir who had been in his employ, on the 21st December last, at Oas.

It appeared that von Hatten was for some reason dissatisfied with Michael, and about the 18th December took him to the police at Gobabis. According to Michael, he was made to perform the journey on foot, tied to accused s horse by a thong fastened round his neck. The distance was some thirty odd miles. Accused admitted this treatment, but only over a portion of the journey some four miles in extent. On arrival at Gobabis the police refused to charge Michael, and told him to return to Oas and remove his family and goods and thereafter seek another employer. On the evening of the 21st December Michael reached his huts and told his wives to prepare to leave. Later in the night accused rode up to the huts, accompanied by a Bushman named Sab. There was some conflict of evidence as to what happened thereafter. Accused s story was that having lost cattle he wished to search the huts for meat and ordered the natives to come out, that upon their refusal he threatened to set fire to the huts, and that thereupon Michael seized hold of him and tried to throw him down, and Michael s son, Hodebeb, also assumed a threatening attitude, and that he fired the Browning pistol he was carrying first at Hodebeb and them at Michael.

There was no evidence that Hodebeb bore any injury. Michael had received wounds from three bullets, one on the left side of the head, the entrance being behind the ear and the exit in the neck, another through the left side of the neck from back to front, and a third inwards and downwards through the covering of the right side of the stomach. All the wounds were slight and no serious injury was caused.

The Court was apparently not satisfied that accused intended to kill Michael, but found him guilty of dangerous assault. The punishment awarded was a fine of 50*l*. or six months hard labour.

Rex versus A. F. J. Bohme – Tried 28th May 1917. Accused, a German and a painter (out of work), aged 63, was charged with an offence upon a young native girl at Usakos on the 21st March 1917. It appeared that the police had some reason to suspect him of improper conduct with native children. On the day in question he was seen going in the direction of thick bush with two young girls and was followed by Constable v.d. Post, who found him lying down with one of them inside a bush which was so thick that he could not see plainly what was taking place. The girl ran away when she saw the constable, as did the other girl who was in the vicinity. Accused stood up, and van der Post saw that his clothing was disarranged. The girl was an unwilling witness, but admitted that accused had taken her to the bush for the purpose of having connection with her and failed in his purpose. He had given her 1s, and she was a consenting party. Medical examination showed that she had been tampered with, and accused admitted a certain degree of improper conduct.

There was some difficulty about the age of the girl. In appearance she was under 14, and the medical witness estimated that she was between 12 and 13. She had not yet menstruated. Accused produced a certificate that she was baptised in 1909, which stated that she was born in 1903. Her mother was unable to give the Court any satisfactory assistance on the point, as is usual with natives of this territory, who are as a rule extremely vague on the question of age.

The Court found the accused guilty of indecent conduct with a girl under 14 and sentenced him to six months hard labour.

Rex versus Carl Alfred Feuerstein – Tried 23rd May, 28th May-2nd June 1917. Feuerstein is a German ex-Postmaster, aged 33, who had taken up his residence on the farm Sus in the Grootfontein District. He was charged with the murder on the farm, on the 27th October 1916, of a Bushman named Hans.

At the time of his death Hans was the leader of a gang of Bushmen vagrants, and Hans himself was a renowned stock thief. He was also suspected of more than one murder. The facts of these as known to us indicated that he may have had considerable provocation; but it is undoubtedly the case that they were officially regarded, after some investigation by authority, in the light of murder. It may therefore be accepted that among the German population he was looked upon as a dangerous man.

For some few days before the 27th October Hans s presence in the vicinity of Sus was known to the residents. On the 26th they received information that he was in the immediate neighbourhood, and determined to try to effect his capture. Possibly they intended to kill him, but there was no direct evidence on this point.

There were on the farm accused and two other white men, who possessed between them two rifles and a Browning pistol, and a number of natives all said to be ill-disposed towards Hans.

On the 27th October, accused, accompanied by a Bushman, Guntsas, and followed at a short interval by another named Qabub, set out on horseback after Hans. He carried his rifle, as was his custom, and, in addition and contrary to his ordinary habit, took with him the Browning pistol, which was not his property.

It is to be presumed that if he had merely intended to capture Hans he would have taken with him some other natives and at least one of the other white men.

Hans was accompanied by the remainder of his band, composed of at least four other men, two women and two children. They had with them, as was probably known to accused, one rifle besides bows and arrows. In their possession was some stolen meat, but beyond that their purposes for the moment at any rate were peaceful. The accused had no interest in the stolen meat.

Accused overtook the band, charged into it, singled out Hans and fired at least three shots at him with the pistol. Only the last took effect, but it was fatal. He alleged that Hans first fired the gun at him without result, but stated that he threw it away before the fatal shot was fired.

It was said by one of the natives who accompanied Feuerstein that before setting out he had declared his intention of killing Hans. The Court did not say whether it accepted this as a fact and the declaration as seriously intended.

The Court found as facts proved: that Hans did not have the gun in his possession and did not fire it; that no one else fired it.; that Hans offered no resistance, and that he was lame on account of a poisoned foot and unable to get away from the accused, but made some attempt to do so; also that accused fired at him at comparatively and increasingly close range, and that the fatal shot was fired when Hans s back was turned. The wound was almost midway between and slightly below the shoulder-blades.

There was some evidence that Hans had attempted to escape into thick bush before the fatal shot was fired, but was prevented by accused.

A verdict of murder was returned, and accused was sentenced to death.

On the ground that there was no proof of deliberation, and that therefore the offence was *Totschlag* merely, the sentence was commuted to ten years' hard labour.

Rex versus Jacobus Markus – Tried 15th May and 2nd 3rd July 1917.
Rex versus John Annis – Tried 15th May and 2nd 3rd July 1917.
Rex versus Albert Schmidt – Tried 15th May and 4th 5th July 1917.

Although the accused in these cases were indicted and tried separately, it will be convenient to report on them together. Schmidt is a German farmer at Chamis South, Bethany District. Annis is the son of a Portuguese and a Bastard woman. He occupies a neighbouring farm and lives in a house on Schmidt s property. Markus is a coloured inhabitant of this country who was in the employ of Schmidt as a shepherd.

Annis had in his service a Hottentot named Lindip. Schmidt had in his possession a rifle and ammunition, and was anxious to conceal this fact from our officials, presumably to prevent them being taken away. Lindip became aware of this, and to prevent him disclosing his information to the authorities Schmidt determined to make away with him. He accordingly, on the 6th October 1916. arranged with Annis and Markus that Lindip should be sent out into the veld and the three of them would follow and shoot him. On the morning of the 7th October, Lindip was sent out by Annis. He took with him two dogs. Soon after his departure Markus received the rifle and two cartridges from Schmidt, concealed in sacking, and with Annis went after Lindip. As arranged. they waited at the foot of the mountain for Schmidt, but as he did not come went on to the top. There they found Lindip. and all three sat down. After Lindip and Markus had smoked a pipe, Markus, at the instigation of Annis, and after having expressed some hesitation. shot Lindip dead in cold blood. He fired two shots, the first through the body and the second through the head.

Having disposed of the body by placing it in a hole under a ledge of rock and walling it in with stones. they returned to Schmidt s house and told what they had done. They took the two dogs back with them. A report was made to the police that Lindip had absconded.

Some time after this Markus was given a bottle of paraffin by Schmidt and sent out by him to burn the corpse. He took the paraffin to the spot and left it there, and has explained that he was afraid to do anything further.

About the 12th January 1917 Schmidt and Annis proceeded to the spot and made a fire with bushes and the paraffin and destroyed the body, nothing being left but some calcined bones and certain metal articles. which Lindip was proved to have had in his possession on the 7th October.

Other natives on the farm had become uneasy and suspicious at Lindip's absence. One, Hans Lucas, received orders to go into the veld the day after Schmidt and Annis had gone out. He seized the opportunity to follow their spoors, and eventually found the fire and recognised the metal articles. He took another native to the spot and showed him what he had found, but they disturbed nothing.

On their return to the farm Lucas went to Chamis Police Station, which was not far away, and reported the matter.

Constable Enslin went to Chamis South and verified the facts. The next day Markus, who had apparently learned of his visit, arrived at the Police Station and said his conscience was troubling him and he wished to make a full disclosure of what had occurred. He then made a short statement to the above effect. Enslin, who was alone, sent him into Bethany, which he reached the next day but one. There he made a full confession to Sergt. Coetzee, which was reduced to writing. Subsequently he confirmed this confession before the magistrate. Annis also made a statement to the police on arrest which exonerated himself but implicated Schmidt and Markus.

The three accused were indicted and tried separately. The trial of Markus took place first. He now told a different story, obviously false, to the effect that Lindip had been shot by accident. He was convicted and sentenced to death.

Annis was next dealt with, and Markus was called as a witness against him. He reverted to his original story of the affair, explaining that on the way to Windhuk the other two accused had persuaded him to give a false account. The Court did not accept Annis s version, and he was also convicted.

Thereafter Schmidt was placed on his trial, and both Markus and Annis were called against him. Markus repeated his first story, and Annis, under examination by a member of the Court, seriously implicated Schmidt, who in his turn was sentenced to death.

The sentences were commuted to imprisonment for life.

Rex versus Wilhelm Halberstadt – Tried 6th December 1917. Accused, a German farmer at Wilhelmsruhe, Grootfontein District, had in his service a Bushman cow-herd named Kaan.

In May 1917 Kaan took to his bed, and sent a message to accused that he was sick. Accused said he must go on with his work. Kaan went out accordingly with the stock that day, and on his return in the evening accused struck him and threw him to the ground. Blood came from his nose and mouth. Next day Kaan again went out with the stock, but when he returned was weak. He again told his master he could not work, and was again thrown down with the same result as before. Next day he went out with the stock, and on his return some of the animals strayed as he was not able to run after them. On this account he was again ill-treated in the same way. He went out as usual next day, but the stock came back without him. Another native went to look for him and found him staggering along through the veld and falling down every now and then. He reached the kraal with difficulty. Then accused ordered him to do some work and, as he failed, threw a lump of sandstone at him which hit him and knocked him down. Accused then kicked him. That night Kaan disappeared from the farm, and two or three months later his dead body was found in the veld. The cause of death could not be determined.

Halberstadt was charged with murder, but was fined 50*l*. or six months' hard labour for common assault.

Rex versus Paul Arno Becker – Tried 11th December 1917. This man a German farmer at Chairos, Outjo District, had a Bushman boy, Hongrib. aged 15, in his service. He gave him a beating for an alleged theft, and the boy ran away. He was recovered, was again charged with stealing, and again absconded. Hongrib's mother, Dikpens, also lived on the farm. She had two other children, one about 5 years old and the other still at the breast. In order to get Hongrib back, Becker sent her out to look for him, first locking up the children in a room at the farmhouse. He told her not to return without Hongrib. She was away three days and three nights, and returned without him. Meanwhile the children had been kept locked up in the room with no covering, and had only received as food a little milk. On Dikpens s return Becker sent her out again at once to look for Hongrib. She went to the nearest police-station, and a patrol was sent out and the children were released and restored to their mother.

For his ill-treatment of the little children he was fined 50*l*. or three months hard labour.

Upon Hongrib s return subsequently Becker thrashed him, for which he was fined 5*l*. or 14 days hard labour. Thereafter Hongrib was taken out into the veld by another German and very severely beaten and left tied up in the hot sun all day. He became unconscious, and was found a day or so later by a native constable in the last stages of exhaustion. This matter is still *sub judice*.

At the present moment the following cases are pending:–

Rex versus Fritz Orthey – It is alleged that in January 1917, at Choiganaub, Grootfontein District, accused captured a Bushman stock-thief and took him into the veld and shot him. Native witnesses, who have since disappeared, stated that the Bushman was chained up. Accused's version is that he was taking him to the police-station; and that on the way his horse gave out, whereupon he set out on foot through the veld for the nearest farm with his prisoner. In the veld he was attacked by the prisoner, and shot him in self-defence.

Rex versus Georg Vosswinckel – There are two charges of murdering natives and concealing their bodies in ant-bear holes pending against this man.

Rex versus Rudolph Tommaschewski – There are two charges against this man of murdering a native man and woman and, in the case of the woman, destroying the body by fire.

Rex versus H. Ehmke – After a dispute with a farm servant over his duties accused is alleged to have picked up a large stone and struck the boy two or three blows over the head, giving him dangerous injuries which necessitated his detention in hospital for 14 days.

We now turn to the converse case of violence offered by natives to Germans. Only two have come before the Special Criminal Court, and particulars are as follows

Rex versus (1) *Fritz*; (2) *Massinab*; (3) *Langman* – Tried 27th April 1916. Accused were Bushmen, living in the Grootfontein District. Fritz was for a period in the employ of Europeans, but for some years had apparently lived as one of a predatory band of Bushmen who at that time infested the bush in this as in other parts of the Protectorate. He was charged with the murder of two German farmers, Olhroggen and Korting, on the 15th September 1915, On the farm Goroab West, in the District of Tsumeb, by shooting then with a rifle. Some Bushmen, servants of a farmer named Eckstein. the owner of Goroab West, had run away. He with other natives, Ovambos, went to a water-hole and found one of them, whom he took back to the farm. He also took five or six Bushmen women, his object being, as he stated, to induce their husbands to follow them, when he hoped to obtain their services as labourers. The chief of the party living at this water-hole was one Max, who was away at the time but returned later in the day. All the accused were said to be members of his band.

The party possessed two rifles and a few cartridges. Max ordered accused (Fritz) to take some of the other men, armed with the guns and bows and arrows, and go next day to recover the women.

When they reached the farm, Fritz carrying a Mauser rifle, Eckstein was away in the lands and a German named Angebauer was near the house. The latter was shot at and wounded, but no evidence was forthcoming as to who fired the shot except Fritz s admission that he did it. Eckstein them fled to the next farm and returned with two other men, Ohlroggen and Korting. They were unarmed. In the meantime the Bushmen had disappeared into the bush near the road. Eckstein left his companions and went to his natives in the lands to find out what had happened during his absence. Ohlroggen and Korting continued on the road. A shot was fired from the bush where the Bushmen had hidden, and Ohlroggen fell. Korting ran away, but was killed at once by another shot from the same spot.

There was no direct evidence as to who fired the fatal shot, but it was proved that Fritz was in the party and carried a Mauser. There was some evidence that Massinab and Langman were also with the party, but armed only with bows and arrows. No one could see any of the Bushmen when the shots were fired, although they were last seen shortly before in the immediate vicinity of the spot from which the shots came.

Fritz on three separate occasions admitted his guilt. He gave as his reasons:–

(1) That he acted under the orders of Max.
(2) That Max told him to kill Eckstein because the women had been carried off, and that he was not near enough to Eckstein to kill him, so he shot Ohlroggen and Korting instead.
(3) That the Germans have often killed Bushmen, and Bushmen were entitled to retaliate.

The statement made by Fritz at the Preparatory Examination is worth reproduction in full. It was as follows:–

Johannes Fritz, duly cautioned, states:–

I am a Bushman. About two years ago I was employed by a Mr. Bucherin in the Grootfontein District. I was not treated well by Mr. Bucherin, so I left his service and. lived in the bush. One day a Bushman named Max, who is headman of a Bushman family, came to me and told me that he had shot a white man named Ludwig on the farm Guntsas; he then gave me a rifle (Martini pattern) and told me to come with him, as I was a good shot and the Germans would soon be chasing him, and that I could help him shoot the Germans.

From that time I followed Max, and he was my captain and I had to do everything that Max ordered me to do. About the rains came last year Max instructed me to accompany him, together with five other Bushmen, named Noib, Acherob, a son of Noib, and Jakob, to the farm of a German named Fribohn, where he intended killing the Europeans because he (Max) had no tobacco left; so he said we must kill the white man and take his tobacco. When we reached the farmhouse the white man was not there, so we helped ourselves to his tobacco and clothing and also money. As we were standing outside the house Max went over to the dwelling of the farm servants and was captured by three natives (a Bushman, Herero, and a Kaffir). When I perceived that Max had been caught, I immediately went to his assistance and shot all three of the natives, who died. I know the names of two of these natives: the Kaffir's name was Koisib, the name of the Bushman was Kaikabas, and I do not know the name of the Herero. This occurred in the Grootfontein District. After that we were chased by the German police, so came and lived at the water-hole named Herab, in the Tsumeb District. On the 14th September 1915, Mr. Eckstein, of Goroab, came to Herab and took some of Max's Bushwomen away from his farm. Max then instructed me to proceed to Eckstein's farm. accompanied by Noib, Massinab, David and Acherob, and told me to kill Eckstein and bring his (Max's) people back. We arrived at Eckstein's farm in the morning, and waited in the bushes at the back of the house. I saw Mr. Angebauer and shot at him; I cannot say whether I hit him. I then saw Andries in the mealie lands and went down to him and told him he must not accompany white men when they went into the bush and stole Bushwomen who were doing no harm. I then intended to go to Goroab East in pursuit of Eckstein, who had gone away, and it was then I perceived three white men and two Ovambos conning from the direction along the road. I then went into the bush near the road and waited for them. Before they reached me Eckstein left the other two white men and went towards Andries in the mealie field, and the other two white men came past me. I shot the big man (Ohlroggen) first, and the small man (Korting) turned round and ran back, and I shot him also. I then fired at Eckstein once, and Eckstein fired three times at me. When I shot these two white men I was accompanied by Acherob; the others were some distance away in the bushes. I did not follow Eckstein after this, but took my people whom Eckstein had stolen and returned to Herab. Max did not accompany us, as he was suffering from sore eyes. All the crimes I have committed were done on the instructions of Max; he is my captain, and I cannot refuse to do anything he tells me to do. The Bushmen who accompanied me did not fire at the white men; I did all the shooting. Noib fired once at the house, just after I had shot at Angebauer, but did not shoot anyone. Acherob murdered a Kaffir named Fritz by striking him on the head with a log of wood at New Desenberg, in the Grootfontein District, about the time the rains came last year. Max has a Martini-Henri pattern rifle, but has no ammunition for it. The others have bows and arrows.

Johannes Fritz, his x mark

The Court acquitted Massinab and Langman, as there was no evidence to directly implicate them, but sentenced Fritz to death.

Rex versus Langmann and Jonas – Tried 2nd May 1916. The first accused was a Herero, the second accused a Berg-Damara. They were charged with the murder of Paul Luther, a German farmer in his lifetime residing at Omaroho, District of Omaruru, where the crime was committed. Deceased, accompanied by native servants, went in search of small stock which he had lost. This party reached the werft of accused, where they found some girls, who took alarm and ran to the men. Deceased, with the object of frightening these girls, fired a shot in the air. He and his native servants followed the girls and came upon accused. Deceased approached these men holding his rifle at the hip. Langmann jumped underneath the rifle and caught hold of it. Luther called to his servants for help, but before they could release him Jonas, the second accused, came up and struck deceased with a bar of iron on the base of the skull. He fell dead, and his body was further mutilated after death. The second accused admitted that he killed Luther, was convicted of intentional homicide, and sentenced to two years imprisonment with hard labour. The first accused was acquitted.

In both these cases it will be seen that there was something to be said on behalf of the natives. In the first, several women had been carried off and detained by the Germans; and, whatever the motive of this, it was not to be wondered at that their husbands endeavoured to rescue them. In the second, deceased had already fired one shot and approached with his rifle in a position to fire another, so that the accused had some reason for supposing that he meditated an attack on them.

On the other hand, in most of the cases of violent conduct towards natives on the part of Germans, which are quoted above, there was no evidence of any adequate motive.

It will be observed, and perhaps wondered at in view of what has been stated in Part I of this work, that sexual offences against native women are only represented in this chapter by one case, in which conviction followed. There is, however, good reason to think that the true facts as to the position in this respect have not been disclosed through the medium of the Courts. The native races have been so subjugated by their white overlords that their women have for years been defenceless and at the mercy of any European male who cared to make use of them. Complaint to the police in German time would have been worse than useless. They have, in consequence, become accustomed to submit more or less tamely to the advances of white men and to offer but little resistance, however distasteful such overtures may be to them, and least of all to make complaint to authority. This was but one more misery added to all the other miseries of life. After years of docile submission it is obvious that time must elapse before they can realise that matters have changed. that they can look to us for protection, and that attacks upon their virtue may now be resisted, and resisted with impunity.

It has not been the purpose of the writer to offer extensive comment on the foregoing. His object has been to give concisely the bare facts of each case as found proved by the highest tribunal in the land – whose members are a barrister of high standing in the Union with large experience of criminal matters, and two stipendiary magistrates of similar experience – and leave the reader to form his own conclusions. He should meet with no difficulty.

APPENDICES

APPENDICES

I   Medical report on German methods of punishment of natives (with photographs):

        A. – Chains
        B. – Corporal punishment
        C. – Hanging

II   Original German text of secret letter addressed by His Excellency the German Governor to his District Officers on the subject of the treatment of natives (see Chapter XXII).

III   Original German text of three letters addressed by the District Officer at Lüderitzbucht to the Government at Windhuk Protesting against the ill-treatment of natives and the attitude Of the German Courts (see Chapter II. of Part two).

APPENDIX I

DESCRIPTION OF HANDCUFFS, LEG AND NECK CHAINS, USED
BY THE GERMANS IN THE TREATMENT OF PRISONERS

These may be divided into four classes, viz:–

(1) Gang Chains (Plate A)
(2) Combined Leg-Irons and Handcuffs (Plate B)
(3) Handcuffs (Plate C, *Figs*. 1, 2, 3, 4, 5, 6 and 7).
(4) Leg-Irons

A
(1) GANG CHAINS:
Plate A. (*See also* Plates A1 and A2.)

Fig. No. 1 shows a chain, 8 feet long, connecting two iron neck-collars. The collars are made of flat iron bands, 1¼ inches wide and [three-sixteenths] inch thick, have a hinge and lock attachment, and do not have a leather or other

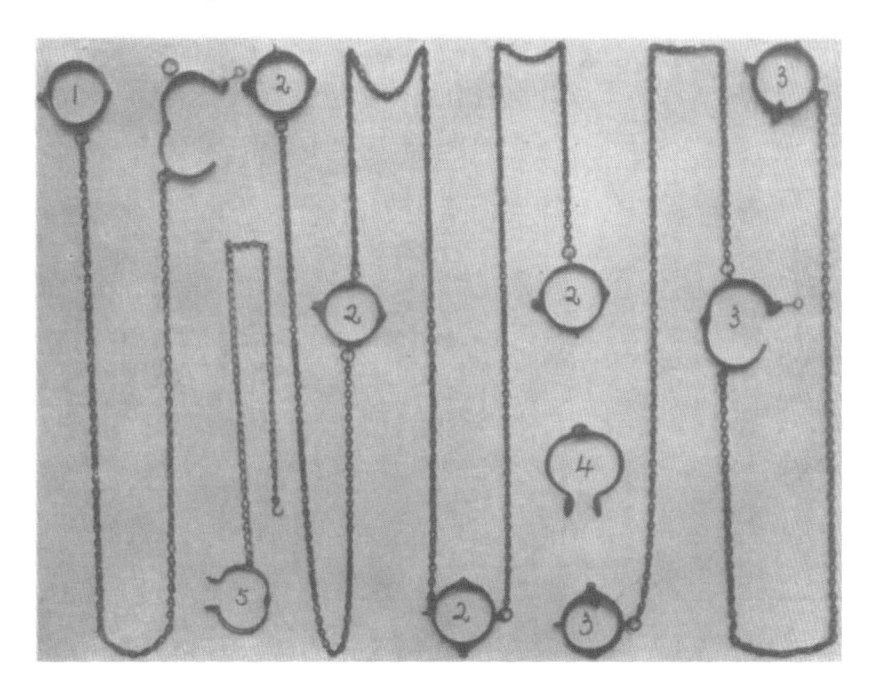

Plate A

326 APPENDICES

Plate A1

Plate A2

covering for the protection of the skin. The combination weighs 7 lbs. 3 oz., viz., chain 3lbs. 7 oz., and each collar 1 lb. 14 oz. The defect in the open collar close to the link from which it is suspended was caused by the passage of a bullet, showing that in all probability a prisoner was shot through the neck, while actually in chains. (*See also* Plate A2.)

Figs. 2 and 3 show gang chains for four and three prisoners respectively, similar in construction to No. 1 but of lighter material. The collars are covered with leather and the chains are 6½ feet long. No. 2. weighs 14 lbs. 10 oz., and No. 3, 10 lbs. 3 oz., while the weight of each collar is 1 lb. 5 oz., and of the connecting chain 3 lbs. 2 oz.

Gang chains were applied as shown in Plate A1. Working gangs were sent out and had to perform their work in these chains, and instances are recorded where prisoners were marched long distances, *e.g.,* from Warmbad to Keetmanshoop, a distance of 140 miles, chained together in large groups. When the weights of these appliances are teaken into consideration, it will be found that each prisoner, with the exception of those at the extremities of the gang, had to support from 4½ to 5¼ lbs. from the neck. Their continued use is bound to lead to local injury, and the constant and inevitable interference with the circulation and respiration to serious impediment of the health of the prisoner.

Fig. 4 represents a rough neck-collar, made from round iron, half an inch thick. It is not provided with a lock, but the ends are furnished with eyes, through which a chain can be run to connect up the prisoners. Its weight is 1¾ lbs. It has not been possible to determine whether this type was actually made use of.

Fig. 5 is a rough collar made out of a horse-shoe and furnished with a chain for locking a prisoner to the saddle. It weighs 2½ lbs., and demonstrates one of the ways in which prisoners were led from one station to another by mounted escorts. In addition to the neck chain, the prisoner was invariably handcuffed.

COMBINED LEG-IRONS AND HANDCUFFS:
(Plate B). (*See also* Plates C1 and C2.)

Fig. 1. – This combination consists of a heavy hand-bar connected by means of a chain to the leg-irons. The hand-bar is 15 inches long, weighs 5¼ lbs., and is provided with sockets for the wrists at each end. The leg-irons are 2 inces wide and from a quarter to half an inch thick. These weigh 3½ lbs. each, and are connected by a chain 28 inces long, from the centre of which another connects them with the hand-bar. The handcuffs and leg-irons are not provided with a covering for the protection of the parts, and even if they were covered, serious injury to the arms and legs is bound to result owing to their weight and the crude manner in which they are made. During progression the chain drags along the ground, and to relieve the ankles the prisoner has to flex the arms. As soon as this is done, a weight of 8 lbs. is thrown on the latter. When the arms are exhausted and allowed to drop, the hand bar becomes tilted antero-posteriorly owing to the peculiar attachment of the chain, and painful pressure is immediately exerted by the sharp edges of the sockets, while simultaneously an increased burden falls on the ankles. The result is that constant and inevitable pain and torture are produced by this vicious circle of events. Even in the recumbent position the effects are similar. As a means of inflicting

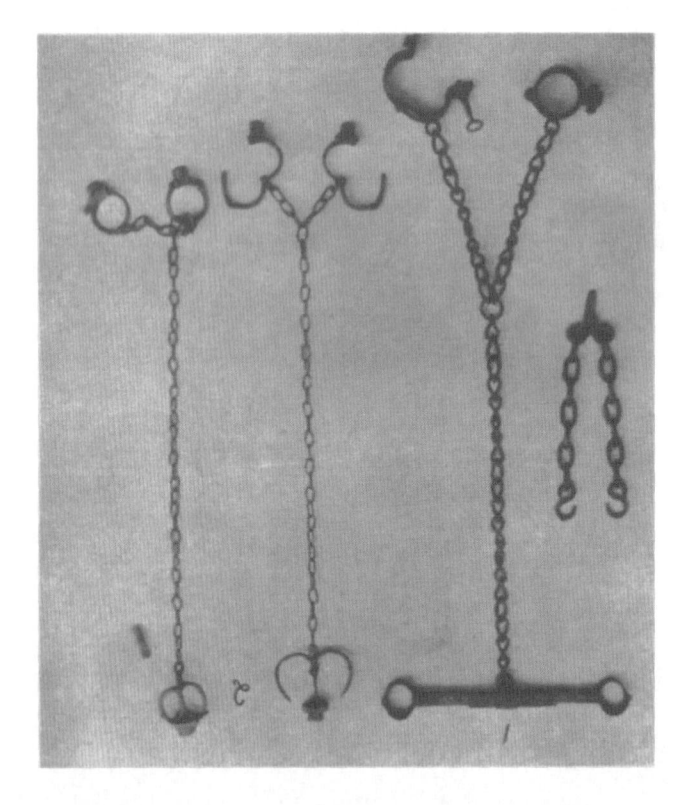

Plate B

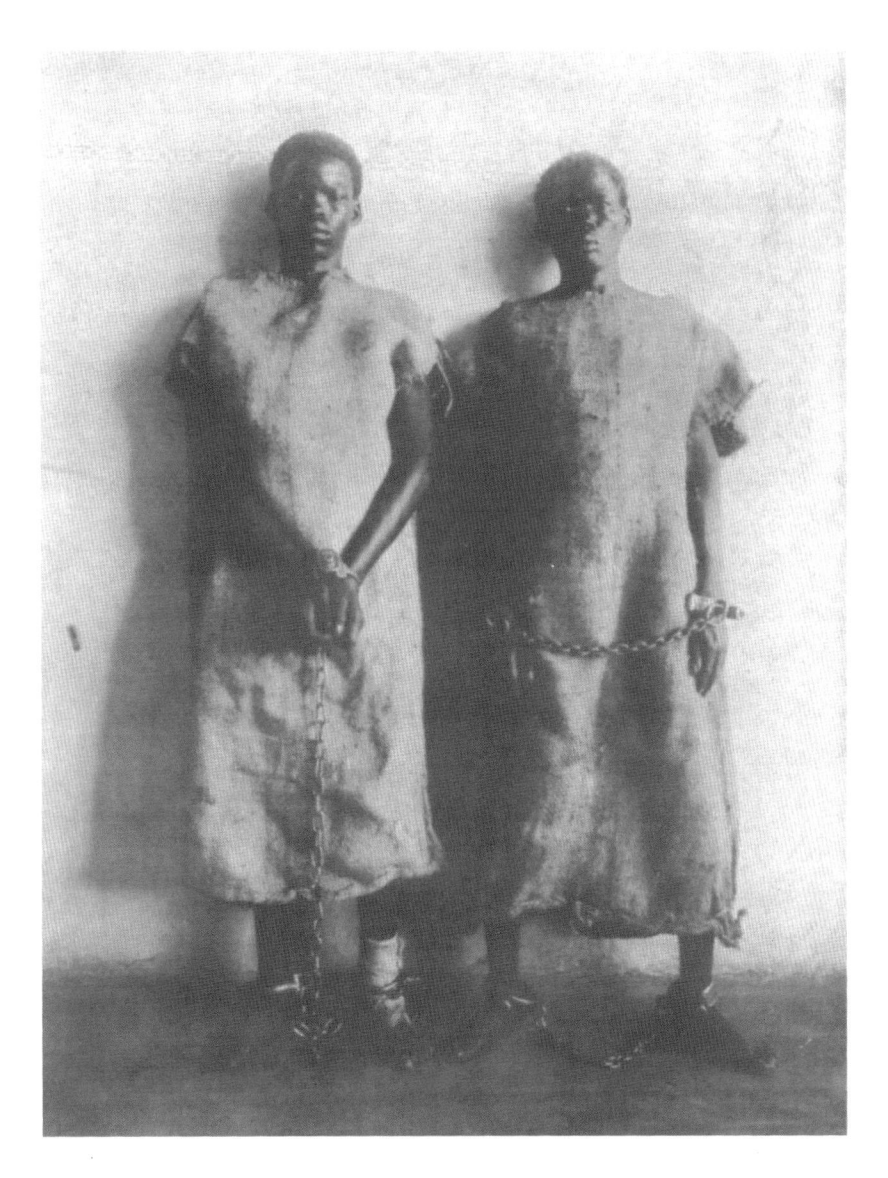

Plate C1

barbarous cruelty on prisoners this diabolical instrument is unrivalled. (See also Plate C2.)

Fig. 2 represents a light combination of leg-irons and handcuffs, which seriously impedes progression and causes very great discomfort. The hands are in very close opposition and in a most uncomfortable attitude. It offers a severe means of punishment and as a method of restraint is unnecessarily cruel (See also Plates C and C2).

330   APPENDICES

Plate C2

HANDCUFFS:
Plate C, *Figs.* 1,2 3, 4, 5, 6 and 7. (See also Plates C1 and C2)

Fig. 1 shows a bar handcuff, 2 feet long, made of flat iron, 2 inches wide and ³/₈ of an inch thick. It weighs 12 lbs.

In the upright position it produces painful pressure in whatever attitude the arms are placed. The same also applies to the sitting and recumbent postures, when every change of position causes pain and torture. Its use cannot be justified under any circumstances, not even as a temporary measure for restraint. If worn for any length of time very serious injury will result to the arms and also to the general health of the prisoner. (See also Plate C2).

Figs 2 and 3 – This type of handcuff varies in weight from 1½ lbs. to 2 lbs. No objection could be raised against them as a temporary means of restraint, provided that the correct size is fitted. Their use for long periods or in conjunction with leg-irons (*Figs.* 9 and 10, Plate C) especially in the cae of women, cannot be too strongly condemned.

Figs. 4 and 5 represent the ordinary types of handcuffs, and require no description or comment.

Figs. 6 and 7. – These handcuffs are used for transferring prisoners by mounted escort from one station to another, sometimes over long distances. The prisoner, attached to the saddle by the chain, had to regulate his pace according to that of his escort. The hands were, more often than not, handcuffed behind the back. This method of conveying prisoners may be perfectly humane, but lends itself to gross abuse by an inconsiderate escort.

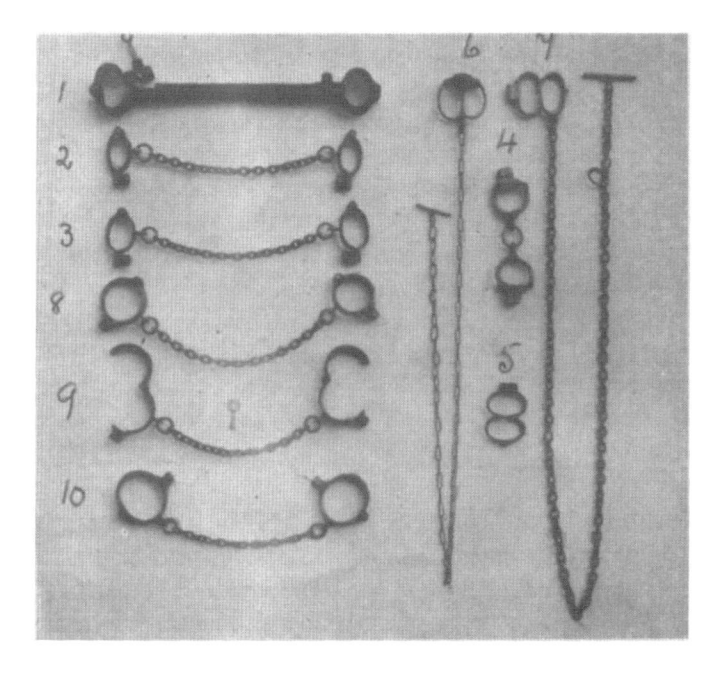

Plate C

The hands are in too close opposition to be comfortable, and when the distance is great considerable suffering will result.

Figs. 8, 9 and 10 are leg-irons, which were generally used in conjunction with Nos. 2 and 3, as described above. They vary in weight from 2½ to 3½ lbs. The cell floors were provided with ring bolts to which prisoners were frequently secured by means of these chains. While the actual use of them as a temporary means of restraint, in the case of dangerous criminals, cannot be considered inhumane, there is, unfortunately, abundant evidence to show that they were designed and actually used as means of punishment, and their use for the chaining of women for such offences as laziness, impertinence or vagrancy could not possibly be justified. During progression they are a constant source of discomfort, and when worn for any lengthy period, destruction of the skin and underlying parts takes place, with very painful and even serious consequences to the prisoner. (See also Plates C1 and C2).

No more cruel system of slow and deliberate torture could be devised than this chain system. In addition to the torture inflicted by these chains, prisoners were made to do as much work as if they were unfettered. Further, being clad in sacks only, their sufferings were aggravated in winter by the cold in the dark and badly ventilated cells. (The original chains and fetters appearing in these plates are all in my possession.)

B
(1) OBSERVATIONS ON CORPORAL PUNISHMENT AS PRACTISED IN THE UNION OF SOUTH AFRICA

Corporal punishment is inflicted only in the most serious offences, such as robbery with violence, rape, certain contraventions of the Immorality Laws, and habitual stock theft, the object being to cause temporary pain but not prolonged suffering. Experience has shown that the rattan cane is the most suitable instrument for this purpose, as it meets the requirements of justice at a minimum cost to the health of the prisoner. The prescribed cane is ½ inch in diameter and 4 feet long (*vide* Plate D). It is light, elastic and under perfect control, allowing of an even distribution of the strokes across the buttocks. It does not cut the skin, but merely produces superficial abrasions, which heal readily. Punishment is always carried out under the supervision of a medical officer, who has the pwer of stopping it shuld signs of serious shock or collapse appear. After punishment the prisoner is given some light duty, such as cleaning, for two or three days, when he is usually well enough to return to hard labour. The number of strokes rarely exceeds 12, and only in the case of very serious offences are more inflicted. Any number in excess of this leads to superimposition of the lashes, resulting in greater local injury and intense shock, which might seriously cripple and even endanger the life of the prisoner, while, at the same time, such a degree of loss of sensation in the parts is produced as to render the vicitim insensitive to pain, thus frustrating the main

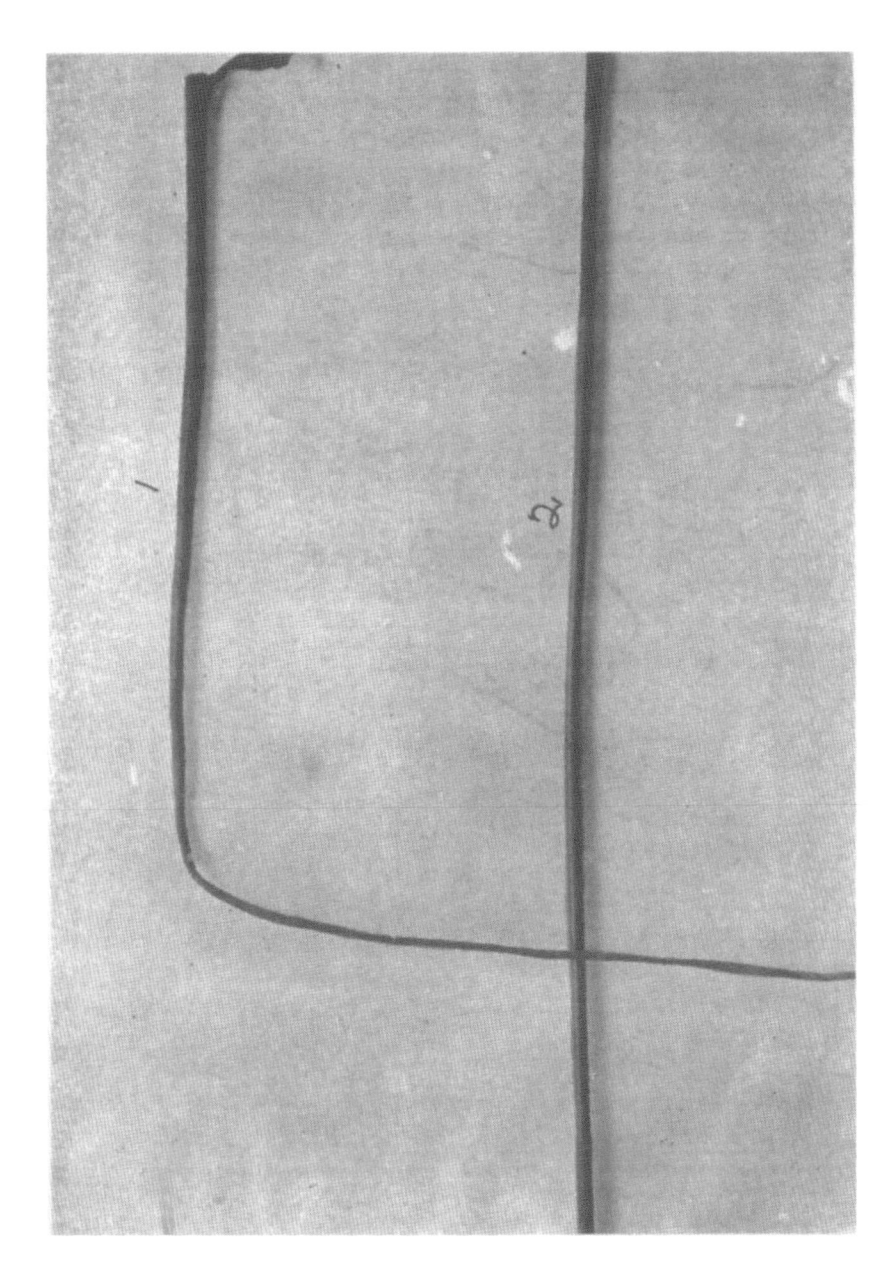

Plate D

object of justice. The cane is soaked and disinfected as far as possible before use, and the strokes are horizontal and not vertical. Great care is exercised to protect adjacent vulnerable parts by means of pads, and to confine the strokes to the buttocks, by immobilizing the prisoner on a tripod. By these precautions

E1. Natives hanged by Germans

E2. Closer view of two of these

injury to such organs as the genitals, and cutting of the skin over bony prominences, are prevented. Before the administration of the strokes the prisoner is examined by a medical officer, who advises as to his fitness, or otherwise, to undergo punishment.

(2) IN S.W. AFRICA UNDER THE GERMAN RÉGIME

The sjambok was the prescribed instrument for inflicting lashes in S.W. Africa during the German *régime*. It may be described as a short handwhip, varying in length from 3 to 4 feet, and composed entirely of the raw hide of such animals as the giraffe, rhinoceros, or hippopotamus. The handle is rigid, and the lash gradually tapers towards the point, which is very supple and consequently not under control (*vide* Plate D). It is generally used for driving cattle, and will, if sufficient force is applied cut clean through the skin of even these animals. The lashes were administered by a native policeman, who was selected on account of his strength. The prisoner, after being stripped, was placed prone over a barrel, box, log of wood, or other convenient object, and held securely by the hands and feet by two or more assistants. This position allows of the delivery of downward and more focible strokes with the sjambok, and greater laceration of the tissues necessarily results. Further, as the prisoner was able to wriggle about while being flogged, it was impossible to place the lashes accureately, and very often the point of the sjambok reached round the abdomen or other parts. Of the antives who have passed through the Native Hospital at Windhuk since our occupation, a very large percentage bore unmistakeable evidence of having been brutally flogged. For instance: A boy who received nearly 10 years ago, 60 lashes, in instalments of 15 at fortnightly intervals, was laid up in the prone position in hospital for two months after the flogging. The buttocks show extensive scarring, due to the complete destruction of the skin and a distribution of scars over the upper and outer part of thigh and abdomen, caused by clean cuts of the sjambok. Another native, who received, about 10 years ago, 37 lashes for desertion from service of a brutal master, in two instalments of 24 and 13 respectively, shows similar scarring, which extends beyond the buttocks. This boy required a month's hospital treatment after the flogging. Similar instances could be multiplied indefinitely.

C
OBSERVATIONS ON CAPITAL PUNISHMENT AS PRACTISED BY THE GERMANS IN SOUTH AFRICA

Executions were carried out in a very crude and cruel manner. The condemned prisoner was conducted to te nearest tre and placed on an ammunition, biscuit, soap, or other box or convenient object, and the rope, after being run round his neck and through a fork of the tree, was fixed to the trunk. The box was then removed and death resulted from asphyxiation. There was no privacy about the proceedings, nor, except in towns or in their immediate vicinity, was the body taken down and buried.

The majority of the victims shown in the photographs of executions bear evidence to the cruelty and torture of the chain system. Note the rags covering the wounds produced by the chains above the ankles.

Where a number of executions had to take place, a rough gallows was put up and the hanging carried out in the manner described above. (See frontispiece).

In other instances the condemned prisoner was strangled by merely hoisting him off his feet by utilizing the fork or branch of a tree.

When rope was not available, telegraph or telephone wire or other convenient material was used.

Very rarely could death have resulted instantaneously.

19th January 1918
L. Fourie, Captain, S.A.M.C
District Surgeon, Windhuk

APPENDIX 2

KAISERLICHER GOUVERNEUR VON DEUTSCH-SÜDWESTAFRIKA,
J. NO. 14200

Geheim! Windhuk, den 31. Mai 1912

An den Herrn Kaiserlichen Bezirksamtmann, Distriktschef pers*önlich!*

In den letzten Wochen sind mir von verschiedenen Seiten Nachrichten zugegangen, wonach unter den Eingeborenen in einzelnen Gegenden des Landes in der letzten Zeit eine verzweifelte Stimmung um sich greifen soll. Als Grund wird mir übereinstimmend die Tatsache bezeichnet, dass sich rohe Ausschreitungen Weisser gegen Eingeborene – es haben sich leider in einzelnen. Fällen auch Polizeibeamte derartiger Vergehungen schuldig gemacht – bedenklich mehren und oft nicht die dem Rectsgefühl der Eingeborenen entsprechende Sühne vor Gericht finden. Die Eingeborenen, die an der Unparteilichkeit unserer Rechtsprechung verzweifelten, würden dadurch in einen blinden Hass gegen alles, was weiss ist, und im Endresultat zur Selbsthilfe, d.h. zum Aufstand getrieben. Dass derartige Gefühle des Hasses unter den Eingeborenen, wenn nicht energisch Abhilfe geschaffen wird, über kurz oder lang zu einem erneuten verzweifelten Eingeborenen-Aufstande und damit zum wirtschaftlichen Ruin des Landes führen müssen, liegt auf der Hand. Es ist also im Interesse der gesamten weissen Bevölkerung, dass Elemente, die in wahnsinniger Roheit gegen die Eingeborenen wüten und ihre weisse Haut als Freibrief für brutale Verbrechen betrachten, auf jede Weise unschädlich gemacht warden. Den nein Volk, das ANspruch darauf macht, als herrenvolk betrachtet zu warden, muss vor allen Dingen seine eigenen Reihen reinhalten. Wenn die Verbrechen Weisser gegen Eingeborene keine oder keine genügende Sühne finden, ist es auf die Dauer nicht möglich, bei Verbrechen von Eingeborenen gegen Weiss emit derjenigen Strenge vorzugehen, die im allgemeinen Interesse geboten ist.

Es steht mir kein Einfluss auf die Rechtsprechung über Weisse zu, ich werde aber im Wege der Verwaltung, soweit, es mir möglich ist, dafür sorgen, dass den zweifellos vorhandenen Missständen entgegengewirkt wird. Vor allen Dingen werde ich von Fall zu Fall anordnen, dass solchen Weissen, die sich fortgesetzter Brutalitäten gegen ihre Eingeborene schuldig machen, keine Eingeborenen mehr als Arbeiter überwiesen warden dürfen.

Eine wirksame Abhilfe aber wird nur dann möglich sein, wenn die weisse Bevölkerung selbst, die, wie ich weiss, derartige Brutalitäten roher Elemente auf das Schärfste verdammt, über ihre Stellungnahme solch gemeingefährlichen Individuen gegenüber keinen Zweifel lässt und tätig mitwirkt, um derartigen Verbrechen vorzubeugen und dieselben, falls sie geschehen sind, zur Bestrafung zu bringen. Da ich überzeugt bin, dass es den Bezirksrä möglich ist, in diesem Sinne auf ihre Mitbürger einzuwirken, ersuche ich Euer Hochwohlegeboren, dem Bezirksrat in der nächsten Sitzung den Inhalt dieses Schreibens streng *vertraulich* mitzuteilen. Ich hoffe, dass es möglich sein wird unter Mitwirkung der weissen Bevölkerung Zustände su schaffen, die den Eingeborenen das Vertrauen zurückgeben, dass auch sie bei den Weissen Abhilfe gegen brutale Ausschreitungen Einzelner finden.

Den Empfang dieses Erlasses bitte ich, mir zu bestätigen.

(*gez.*) Seitz

APPENDIX 3

Kaiserlichen bezirksamt,
J. No. 295   Lüderitzbucht, *den* 31. *Januar* 1903

An das Kaiserliche Gouvernement, Windhuk.
Betr.: *misshandlungen gegen eingeborene.*
Auf die Verfügung vom 2. d. Mts. J. Nr. 153: – Fälle, in denen Ansiedler sich Mishandlungen gegen ihre Eingeborenen haben zu schulden kommen lassen oder ihnen keine ausreichende Verpflegung verabfolgt haben, sind hier nicht bekannt geworden. Jedoch ist eine ganze Reihe von Fällen, in denen Behnangestellte die ihnen unterstellten oder zur Beaufsichtigung zugewiesenen Herero-Kriefsgefangenen misshandelt haben, zur Anzeige gelangt.

Ich habe in den moisten Fällen gegen die Betreffenden Straffantrag be idem Kaiserlichen Bezirksgericht hier gestellt, das jedoch nur selten zu einer Bestrafung gelangt ist, da in den weitaus moisten Fällen nur eingeborene als Zeugen in Betracht kamen, deren Aussagen von Seiten des Gerichtes nicht für genügend gehalten wurden ...

                                                  Die Kaiserliche Bezirksamtmann,
                                                          (*gez.*) Boehmer

Kaiserliches bezirksamt,
J. Nr. 5150.   Lüderitzbucht, 14. *Juni* 1911

Dem Kaiserlichen Gouvernement, *Windhuk.*

In den Verdacht der Negrophilität great derjenige Beamte, der berufsmässig den auf den Diamant-Feldern grassierenden Eingeborenenmisshandlungen entgegen zu treten und sie durch Anzeige beim Bezirksgericht zu verfolgen hat, bei den hier teilweise herrschenden anschauungen nur allzuleicht. Die Anschauung, das der Ovambo "kein Mensch" sei und dass dem Eingeborenen selbst bei schweren Misshandlungen durch Weisse kein Recht der Notwehr, sondern nur das Recht der Beschwerde an das Bezirksamt zustehe, wird häufig genug vertreten ...

                                                         (*gez.*) Heilingbrunner

Kaiserliches bezirksamt,
J. Nr. 3269.   Lüderitzbucht, *den* 21. *April* 1913

An das Kaiserlich Gouvernement, *Windhuk*

Betrifft: eingeborenen-misshandlungen.
Im Anschluss an den Bericht von 15. Mai 1912, J.Nr. 4304, und den Erlass vom 13 Juni 1912, J.Nr. 13126: – (1) In neuester Zeit mehren sich wieder die Klagen über Eingeborenenmisshandlungen, nachdem eine Zeitlang eine erfreuliche Besserung eingetreten war.

Wie sich die Zeiten geändert haben, zeigt am besten die Bemerkung eines der Leiter einer der grössten Diamantgesellschaften, der auf die Beschwerden des Herrn Eingeborenenkommissärs, dass ein Sortierer die Eingeborenen dauernd prügele, keine andere ANtword fand, als: "Ich habe hier auch Beschwerden über die Eingeborenen."

Derselbe Herr hatte im Mai 1912 noch eine lange Verfügung an sämtliche Betriebe erlassen, worin er "jede Züchtigung von Eingeborenen" bei Strafe sofortiger Entlassung verbot. Anscheinend kommt der Umschwung der Meinungen daher, dass man jetzt, wo genügend Arbeiter da sind, ihnen nicht mehr soviel Aufmerksamkeit schenken zu müssen glaubt.

Die Gerichte versagen vollkommen. Wenn das Beweismaterial geradezu erdrückend ist, gelingt es vielleicht in dem einen oder anderen Falle in der I. Instanz eine Verurteilung zu einer Geldstrafe herbeizuführen. Dann wird Berufung eingelegt. Ein Oberrichter, der mit den Zuständen auf den Feldern nicht vertraut ist, ja zuweilen noch nie ein Diamantfeld gesehen hat, verhandelt. Die eingeborenen Zeugen sind in der langen Zeit zwischen der 1. und der 2. Verhandlung in die Heimat abgereist, die Verlesung der mangelhaften Protokolle der ersten Verhandlung über ihre Aussagen macht keinen Eindruck. Der Angeklagte hat aus dem ersten Urteil gelernt, wohin er seine Verteidigung zu lenken hat, den Eingeborenen wird nicht geglaubt, noch so zweifelhafte unter Eid geleistete Aussagen Weisser finden Glauben. So endet die Sache mit einem glänzenden Freispruch. Es gibt nichts undankbareres, als in solchen Sachen die Staatsanwalschaft zu vertreten.

Mit der Minenkammer zu verhandeln, ist wertlos. Sie kommt über ein Bestreiten der Tatsachen, günstigenfalls über allgemeine Redensarten nicht hinaus. Zudem hat sie auf ihre Mitglieder nicht entfernt den Einfluss, den ein Fernstehender anzunehmen geneigt ist ...

(gez.) Boehmer

ADDITIONAL APPENDIX

ARTICLES AND CORRESPONDENCE FROM THE CAPE ARGUS, 25TH-30TH SEPTEMBER, 1905 (SELECTED BY THE EDITORS)*

1. 'The German Operations: British Subjects as Combatants: Further Evidence: Women and Children Hanged and Shot: Sensational Allegations, 25th September, 1905 *Cape Argus*.

In the course of interviews on Friday with various men who have returned from German South-West Africa where they have been engaged in assisting in the operations against the rebels, various statements were made by them that confirmed the allegations made in these columns as to the employment of British subjects as combatants.

In some cases our informants desired that their names should not be published, in others they had no objection, and in all cases it was made by us a condition of publication that we should be free to disclose their names and addresses to the Colonial Government and that if the German authorities approached the Colonial Government on the subject the latter should be free to disclose these particulars to them.

It will be seen that the information supplied by these men does more than confirm the allegations as the employment of British subjects as combatants. They told of shocking treatment of native women and children.

Our informants, some six or seven in number, are all men of a distinctly respectable type.

They all complained that, apart from the fact that while engaged as non-combatants they were compelled to fight, their contracts were not properly carried out by the German authorities.

Young Dutchman's Story

F. Wepener, a young Transvaal Dutchman, said he had been engaged on September 13 1904 in Johannesburg, with 42 other men, mostly Dutchmen for transport riding for the Germans, at $3 and all found in the way of food and clothing.

"But", he added, "we never got any boots or clothing. When we came down to Cape Town our contracts were signed before the German Consul. When we arrived at Lokahandja [sic] we were served out with rifles and 20 rounds of

---

* i.e. J.B.G. and J.S.

ammunition each, and further on with 71 rounds. None of us wanted to fight. We had gone there to make a living by transport-riding. Near Okanjiso we came in contact with the natives, and we were compelled by the Germans to go into the fighting line and take our share of the fight. One of our men, De Wet, was wounded in the leg. That night we had all to take our share of picket duty. We refused at first to fight or to do picket duty, but we were told that we were now under German martial law, and must obey orders. On that road we were in action four times, and on each occasion we were made to fight, and during the whole time I was with the forces we had at least a dozen fights, in which we had all to join. We were also put to digging roads, and those of us who refused were fined $5 each. There was a good deal of flogging. An Afrikander named Weeks was flogged for refusing to drive cattle on foot."

Our informant, when asked for the names of some of those who enlisted with him and went through the same experience, mentioned among others, J. Prinsloo of Bloemfontein, Van Wk of Clanwilliam, J. Opperman of Johannesburg, a miner on the Ferreira Deep, Van Sthavee of Bloemfontein. These and others whose names he could recall if desired, would confirm all he said.

Horrible Allegations

"At Okanjiso about February 12, I saw a number of women and children executed. There were eight women and six children. They were all strung up to trees by the neck and then shot."

"But why were they killed?"

"The Germans said they were spies, but they ere captured with the natives with whom we had been fighting and some of the children could not have been older than five. A lieutenant gave the orders. Five soldiers would take each woman or child in turn, put a rope round their neck, string them up over a branch and then shoot them. No, the women did not shriek for mercy. They never said a word. They were glad to be released from their suffering, for they had been very cruelly treated. The children were quiet, too, as a rule. Like the women they had had an inch of bayonet into them time after time, a s well as being badly treated in other ways.

"All the women and children we captured while I was on the march were treated in the same way. I have seen at least twenty-five of them with my own eyes hanged and shot."

It may be remarked here that some of the most striking statements came out in the course of conversation, being casually elicited.

Women Driven to Death

Another man who was present then referred to the treatment of the women captives, who are made to work at Angra Pequena. The statements that followed were given or corroborated by practically all the party.

The women who are captured and not executed are set to work for the military as prisoners. They saw umbers of them at Angra Pequena put to the hardest work, and so starved that they were nothing but skin and bones.

"You will see them," said one, "carrying very heavy loads on their heads along the shore in connection with the harbour works, and they are made to work until they fall down. While I was there, there were five or six deaths every day. The other women have to bury them. They are made to work till they die. All they have on is a blanket. If one falls down of sheer exhaustion as they constantly do, they are sjambokked."

Another man said he had seen the same sort of thing in Windhoek.

Another, confirming the state of things at Angra Pequena, remarked that he had often seen those women dropping down of exhaustion, under a heavy load and trying in vein to raise herself under a shower of blows and failing.

She Kissed His Feet

As a rule they seem to suffer with the dumbness of anguish that marks the beast of burden.

"They are given hardly anything to eat, and I have very often seen them pick up bits of refuse food thrown away by the transport riders. If they are caught doing so, they are sjambokked.

"Yes" added Mr C. Vos, a very intelligent young Dutchman of 2, Pineroad, Woodstock, who has recently returned. "I have often seen all this. And I remember that on one occasion when I gave a two pfennig piece to one of them she knelt down and kissed my feet".

Mr Vos had a fine record of service during the late Boer war in the Imperial Yeomanry Scouts with Colonel Pilcher's column as head conductor, also as scout with General Rundle's [?] eighth division. He had previously been for some years in the Bechuanaland Border Police and served in the Matabele campaign of 1899 and he strikes one as an admirable type of the quiet self-reliant Afrikander that border life had bred in this land.

He was engaged for transport conducting in German South West Africa on November 26, with some fifty other men. He was next in command under the chief conductor and was engaged at $20 per month. He states that the rank and file who were paid between $3 and $7 10s were obliged to spend most of their pay on food, owing to the poor quality of the rations served out.

The Wounded would be Shot

When he arrived at Angra Pequena with some twenty-five of this lot, they had to enter into another contract, which provided again for transport riding. There was no sign of transport riding, and they were all served out with a rifle apiece and fifty rounds of ammunition and a few days rations. They left for Kubub where the party was split up into two portions. Mr Vos's going on to Bethany. On arrival there they were made to relieve the garrison there by taking over their duties. Two months had now elapsed "and still", as Mr. Vos put it, "we had not even seen transport".

"On Christmas Day, Lieut Von Trotha, a nephew of the General, arrived at Bethany with the rest of our party. We left there an hour later, at ten o'clock in the morning, on a 20 day patrol. Lieut. Von Trotha sent us word that as there was no doctor and no arrangements for dealing with the wounded, any man who was badly wounded would be shot so as to save him from falling into the hands of the natives. Still no signs of transport. Some days later we got into action and six or seven natives were killed. Two natives, a man and a woman were found wounded after the fight.

Please, Baas, Don't Shoot Me

The officer gave orders for them to be shot. The men whom he ordered were named Van Dyk, of the Transvaal, Caldwell, who used to be a tram-guard in Cape Town, and Botha, who comes from the Transvaal – did the shooting. The woman was only some ten or twelve yards away from me, on the other side of some rocks. I heard her implore him in Dutch, 'Please, baas, don't shoot me!' And I heard the two shots. When she implored him, he replied 'I must do it, these are my orders'.

"A little later Cornelius found the two corpses and he sent a message to say he would deal with us later on for murdering those two."

"You say that Lieutenant Von Trotha said that any badly wounded of his men would be shot to prevent them falling into the hands of the enemy. Was it because he had no medical assistance to give those two natives that he shot them?"

"How could it be? Their own people would come to them and look after them as soon as we left. After this Von Trotha wanted us to go on to Gibeon, but most of the men refused, as they had had no food for two or three days..

"Then we were told to go back and we would be put on transport. We complained all along that we had been engaged to do transport riding and not fighting. This was about the end of January. On our way back to Bethany we escorted some German families to safety."

Some of the statements above are, of course, of a very serious nature, and were it not for the fact that we have no reason whatever for doubting the bona fides of our informants, who are prepared, if called upon, to make affidavits in support of all their allegations, and who must, f they are not adhering to the truth be engaged in a conspiracy with no particular object, we would prefer not to publish them.

2. 'In German S.W. Africa: Further Startling Allegations: Horrible Cruelty: British Subjects as Combatants, *Cape Argus*, 28th September, 1905.

Further statements of a startling character have been obtained from various men, all of them British subjects, who have returned recently from German South-West Africa.

The information given by most of them concerns three main points, namely, the forcing of British subjects to fight against the natives, although recruited for transport riding (every man engaged for transport riding, they state, was armed either on arrival at the coast port or on going in and, whatever may be the case, since the matter had been taken up in the Press), the cruelty of the manner in which the natives are dealt with, and the manner in which the men's contracts are broken in such matters as the supply of clothing, boots and so forth.

Compared with the first two the latter point is not of great importance as far as public interest is concerned, and for the most part only those portions of these statements that deal with the first two will be published.

Four men interviewed yesterday endorsed what has already been published as to the treatment of the native prisoners, mostly women and children, at Angra Pequena or Swakopmund, although for some reason or other the case would seem to be worse in this respects at the first mentioned place. On the other hand, this difference may be due simply to the difference in the amount of observation taken by our informants from the two places.

Sjamboked for being hungry

One man, whose name and address are at he disposal of the Colonial Government, as are those in the case f all those whose statements are published in these columns, stated: "I have seen women and children with my own eyes at Angra Pequena, dying of starvation and overwork, nothing but skin and bone, getting flogged every time they fell under their heavy loads. I have seen them picking up bits of bread and refuse food thrown away outside our tents. And I have seen them flogged for it when they were caught doing so".

Most of our informants referred to the bad feeling existing between the Germans and the Dutch. The former thought at first that they would be personae gratae with the Germans, but before long the same ill-feeling sprang up between the two as exists between the German soldiers and the British who engage for service there.

Assaults by overwhelming numbers of German soldiers on both British and Dutch are said to be very common. There may be plenty of faults on both sides in this matter an there is no need to go into full details of some of the occurrences.

D. McLeod, an Australian, confirmed the statements as to the employment of British subjects as combatants. Engaged for transport riding he left Angra

Pequena on May 15 with a number of others, going to Keetmanshoop with wagons.

Armed with Rifles

There they were armed and provided with ammunition. Then they went to a plae which he spells phonetically "Hau-ais". There they were told to be prepared for action at any moment, as the Hottentots were all around, and Cornelias was expected to attack. "They returned alone from that place without any escort of German soldiers. When at Spitzkop two or three of them were out shooting when they saw three Hottentots. The conductor went to the helio station and reported it, with the result that four German soldiers came down form the camp with another fifteen rounds of ammunition for each man and told our informant and other transport riders to go out and look for the Hottentots.

They did so, but failed to find them. Later, while at a place named Chanas, the Hottentots shot a German soldier dead outside the place, and Mr. McLeod with others of the transport were asked to go out and help to bring in the body, bringing their rifles with them. But they refused, as they had not been engaged to fight or to run such risks.

Our informant gave details of the manner in which he and some of his companions had been assaulted by German soldiers at Angra Pequena at night time, being knocked senseless with yoke-skeis, one of his companions being stabbed in the thigh with a bayonet. They heard the day they arrived that this party had been saying in the daytime: "Some more Englishmen have landed" and threatening what they would do. They came in the night with a lantern, while the Britishers were asleep.

Children starved and sjamboked

The next one interviewed was Mr.Percival Griffith, a young man, an accountant of profession, who owing to hard times, took on transport work at Swakopmund for some two months, and then worked at Angra Pequena for seven months discharging cargo. He said that most of the prisoners, who compose the working gangs at Angra Pequena, are sent up form Swakopmund. There are hundreds of them, mostly women and children and a few old men. There are many small children among them and not a few babies. Children as young as five or so years of age are made to work and are ill treated like their unfortunate elders. The work in which [unclear] whom he had the best opportunity of observing, were engaged, was in connection with the improvements to the jetty. Heavy loads of sand and cement have to be carried by the women and children, who are nothing but skin and bone.

"The loads", he said, "are out of all proportion to their strength. I have often seen women and children dropping down, especially when engaged on this work, and also when carrying very heavy bags of grain, weighing from 100 to

160lbs. For the stores to the wagons, a distance sometimes of some 300 or 400 yards, through very heavy sand.

"When they fall they are sjamboked by the soldier in charge of the gang, with his full force, until they get up. Across the face was the favourite place for the sjamboking and I have often seen the blood flowing down the faces of the women and children and from their bodies, from the cuts of the weapon. I have never seen one actually die under this treatment but I have seen one woman who in spite of all the soldier's sjamboking could not get to her feet, being at last carried away, and I feel sure, although I cannot say so positively that she must have been dying. Their funerals took place daily. They averaged while I was there from 9 to a dozen daily, with many children and babies among them.

The Mothers' Double Load

The women had to carry the corpses and dig the hole into which they were placed. They had no burial ceremony of any kind. If they wanted to, they would not dare to ask. The corpse would be wrapped in a blanket and carried on a rough stretcher. They seemed bereft of all power of emotion of or showing it, and I have never heard one cry, even when their flesh was being cut to pieces with the sjambok. All feeling seemed to have gone out of them. They never cried out, they never complained.

"And what about the babies?"

"There were a good number of them. The mothers have to work like the others, carrying them on their backs, and get treated and beaten in exactly the same way. The babies, like the others, all look like skeletons. The babies and small children are dying off at a terribly fast rate because they can not stand the ill-treatment and starvation as well as their elders. The youngest children I have seen working, boys and girls, would be about four or a little over.

"Where a woman or child falls, the rest of the gang goes on, while the soldier remains behind to shower blows with the sjambok on her or it. If the others halt for a moment to look he beats them also. Each gang consists o from 30 to 40, and there is one soldier in charge of each. I cannot say how many gangs there are as they work in different parts of the town. A lot of them work on the island, where we were not allowed to go."

But the Baby Cried

"On one occasion I saw a woman carrying a child of under a year old slung at her back, and with a heavy sack of grain on her had. The sand was very steep and the sun was baking. She fell down forward on her face, and the heavy sack fell partly across her and partly o the baby. The corporal sjamboked her for certainly more than four minutes and sjamboked the baby as well."

"Are you ready to swear that you saw a white man sjamboking a baby, as well as its mother?"

"I am; I am ready to make an affidavit if it is required. I saw it with my own eyes. The woman, when the sjamboking had gone of for over five minutes, struggled slowly to her feet, and went on with her load. She did not utter a sound the whole time, but the baby cried very hard."

"Did many people see this? Did no one interfere?"

"It was no use for we few Britishers to attempt to interfere. The woman would have got more of it. The Germans do not seem t see anything out of the way in this kind of thing. I did speak to this corporal on another occasion, but I speak very little German, and he could not speak English. He seemed to look on it all as very amusing, and so far as I could understand him, he said he was ordered to treat the prisoners like this."

It may be mentioned that several of our informants have stated that when they spoke to soldiers who were guilty of this conduct, the reply was: "The Kaiser has ordered us to do this".

No rational being of course can believe otherwise than that if the German Emperor knew of what is being done in his name he would put a stop to it immediately.

How a Chief was Tortured

"All this", went on Mr. Griffiths, "is of daily occurrence. It was in full swing when I arrived in Angra Pequena some eight months ago, and it was going on when I left about a month ago. I have seen other forms of torture inflicted. There was a petty chief whose name I do not know who ad been captured. He was originally a British subject, but had settled down in this territory some considerable time, I understand, before the war broke out. He had been captured and was made to work in one of the gangs, and had fallen exhausted while carrying heavy stores for building purposes. The soldier in charge did the usual sjamboking, and at last the man got up and lifted his hand as if to strike the soldier. He was put under arrest and tried. I did not actually see what occurred before he trial, but the whole thing was common talk, and I spoke about it after the trial with several soldiers who spoke a little English, and what they told me is what I have told you.

"What happened after the trial I myself saw. The man was a smallish man with no particular strength, and apparently his action of lifting his hand was the instinctive one that would come to most men who are being cruelly beaten under such circumstances."

Struck Him as They Passed

"Anyhow, he was tried by court-martial, the court being presided over by an officer, and this was the punishment he got. He was tied up t a wagon wheel in such a position that he was practically hanging by his wrists, the tips of his toes just touching the ground. The strain must have been the same as if he had been crucified, I should imagine," added our informant without, of course, meaning the least irreverence.

"This was done early in the morning after the trial, and he was kept there for three days and three nights. During the whole of that time he was kept without food, and worse still, without water, and so that he should suffer as much as possible, from the burning sun, they kept turning the wagon during the day so as to keep him exposed to the full strength of the sun. They never allowed the shade from the wagon to fall on him. They did not sjambok him, but every soldier who passed him, he was quite close to where I was working at the time, and I saw everything that happened after the trial – kicked hm or struck him with their rifles most brutally"

"Did he ever complain or cry out?"

"Never, from the start to the finish he kept silence. At the end, when they untied him to take him t be hanged, he was not dead and they made him totter for a mile to the hill where he was to be hanged. There is a big iron beacon there, on which they had made a platform. They put a rope over the beacon, he climbed up, put the noose round his neck himself and jumped off. He struggled after that, but not for very long. Practically the whole town turned out to see his execution. You could see it from a long way off, as it took place on the hill. A lot of people went out into the bay in boats to see it. And that was the ed of him. This is only a sample of what is going on at Angra Pequena.

A Garrison of Transport Riders

A.J. Hammond, a young South African, whose family reside in Fordsburg, Johannesburg, states that he was engaged in Johannesburg as transport-rider at $5 per month and all found, with some 31 others at the beginning of last March, by a Mr. Kosck, who acts as recruiting agent there for the German authorities.

They arrived at Swakopmund bout March 12, and after two months in the transport camp there they were sent on to Windhoek. When they got there, the head conductor, a German, ordered them to go on to an outstation about 20 miles from Windhoek. They refused at first to go, as the rebels were all around, and they did not want to fight the natives, having been engaged to act as transport-riders.

They were told that if they did not do so they would be dealt with for disobeying orders and that they would have to keep themselves, and not be paid any wages. The head conductor promised them an extra pound per month if they went, and they did so, but they state they were unable to obtain the promised bonus. They had been armed.

Fight with the Natives

"There was only one German soldier – an under-officer at this station, and we formed the garrison, numbering twenty-one or so, all of whom had been engaged for transport-riding, and objected to fighting. We were there for fifteen days, and during that time the natives attacked for about four or five hours, getting within two or three hundred yard of the station. None of us were wounded. Next morning the under officer told us to go out after the natives. We caught two and killed one. This was about the end of May or the beginning of June. The usual practice so far as I saw, when a native is captured is to tie him up and give him fifty lashes. I have not seen any shot or hanged, but it is common knowledge that of lot of this is done. It depends I suppose, on the sort of man the officer in charge is. After that we went out on patrol, night and day, on many occasions. This went on till my time was up on the first of this month. We protested at Windhoek at the start that we did not want to fight but we were compelled to, being threatened as to the consequences if we disobeyed orders. We never got a quid of the extra money they promised us. It was the head conductor who promised it to us. He admitted that we had only signed on for transport.

Extract from letter – " … it is only quite recently that clothing has been issued in Cape Town – and such clothes, a shoddy corduroy that barely survived the first trek. Prior to the issue in Cape Town, the clothes given out to the transport riders for over a year were the soldiers cast-off garments, ragged, and indifferently washed, or soused in cold water by the prisoners. The boots were in the last stages of decrepitude, and let in the sane which blistered the feed and crippled the wearers. The shirts and underpants, one of each expected to last six months without change were ragged and infested with vermin. The food is so 'good', especially upon trek, that the men of necessity have to mortgage their pay in advance to obtain edible nourishment, and they have to expend a considerable portion of the remainder of their 'good' pay monthly for clothing … In conclusion, we [transport riders from GSWA] may state that we have seen the same cruelties perpetrated, and some unmentionably worse then any published in the article that 'Vindex' weakly attempts to belies. We append our signatures and you have our addresses to give to the Colonial Government if desired. We are, etc. C. Hughes, T. Petzer, A.J. Hammond, F.H. Windle, M.J. Pretorius, Percival Griffith, F.H. Smith, F.S. Cooke, O. McLeod.

3. 'German S.W. Africa: Alleged Atrocities, the other side', *Cape Argus*, 30th September, 1905

Sir, – If one follows the venomous outbursts of anti-German feeling so persistently ventilated in the columns of the Cape Argus, it necessarily becomes apparent that there is either a total absence of sensational news at hand or the editor has decided to erase the German Empire from the map of the world. The constant unfounded and unwarranted accusations against the German Army in general and the select troops operating in German South West Africa are becoming somewhat monotonous to the reading public, which is saturated already with the tales of cruelty perpetrated y German soldiers on the bodies of innocent women and children of the harmless Hereros and Witboois. And all this in the face of the solemn declarations to the contrary officially made by the Consul-General, Dr Von Jacobs. Has it ever struck the overzealous editor of The Argus that he at any time can test the veracity of the statements made to him by either unreliable of foul-purposed individuals, by calling at the Consulate, where he is sure to get all the information, in order to set his troubled mind at rest? Is he not aware of the fact that Dr. Von Jacobs is always ready to disprove lying allegations of any king? Dos The Argus editor really believe all the stories told to him? Does his moral duty towards his readers coincide with his actions as a conscientious journalist? Or is it within the precincts of his purpose to enrich his paper by publishing falsehoods, which he knew could easily have been disproved by facts?

The last weekly edition of The Argus carried Home some illustrated incidents at the war, which meant for novelty, will highly amuse the good people in Europe, all the more so when they happen to look in ain for the date of the occurrences. There is one picture representing the remnants of a German corps after a defeat all huddled together in merriment as if they enjoyed the stroke of ill luck recently experienced. Now, where, except in the phantastic brain of the Parliamentary editor is an army to be found anxious to face the camera after a heavy defeat, in order to immortalise the fact of their partial annihilation? And what can be the object of reproducing an imaginary event of so little interest to anyone? The only answer is a faint endeavour to ridicule a set of men who are bent upon restoring order in real earnest to a disturbed area. The editor wisely omitted to mention the date, for he very good reason that this event never took place.

Another illustration to be mentioned is the engagement between Karibib and Okahandya [sic]. On the top of a rock is pointed as outlook a sailor from the man-of-war Halrichte. The novelty of this event dating back more than a year ago, and it is now dished up as if it had happened last week. The sensation is naturally tame, but is serves to freshen up the public mind to past history.

One of the most serious accusations is the cue arising from the arming of white men – Boere – every man is evidently a Boer in the mind of the editor. He could easily have ascertained the bogus charge on enquiring at the proper quarter. There he would have been told, in accordance with the strict truth, that arms have been given to the transport riders and men attached in that service for the sole purpose of self-defence and protection of the trains in case any of the loitering bands should venture to attack them or their valuables. In this sense only the wording 'arming' may be used, not as The Argus is in the habit of putting the term 'recruiting'.

I would strongly advise the editor of The Argus to leave the Germans to themselves in adjusting their affairs, which they are quite capable of doing, and rather concentrate his unlimited abilities upon the concerns of the country of which he shines as a prominent representative. I am, etc. A German with 43 years of cape colonial experience.

Sir, – I have read with surprise and indignation the statements made by men returned from service in German South West Africa, and I though it at first better not to take any notice of the accusations made because most of your readers will sum them up pretty quickly, but especially because I cannot absolutely contradict them, I can, however, relate my personal experience in the country itself.

I have not been in Damaraland, but I have been lately off and on for a considerable time in German Great Namaqualand, and particularly on the Dach Country stations. I have talked to a great many officers, men and South African transport-riders, and I have never heard of any cruelties committed towards natives. I have seen one batch of native women prisoners arrive with a convoy; they all sat on wagons, wrapped up in blankets, and after they arrived at the station, they were sent out into the veld to fetch fire wood on two ox wagons; they simply collected the wood, put it on the wagons and brought it into camp. They received their daily rations (the same as the loyal natives), that is a panniking of meal, some rice and twice a week they received meat. Of course, this was at a station where the military had enough food. When soldiers had to starve, I can barely imagine that the prisoners fared better. If anybody suffered it was the officers and men in the Karas Mountains, when it rained for days, the officers and soldiers clothes were torn, their boots were worn through and the only food they had was trek-ox and nothing else. A native might even stand this, but for a white man, such living is a great hardship. It is astounding how the troops stood the cold and privations, but these particular transport-riders, who were with that column shared their lot bravely with the soldiers.

I have made inquiries and find that some 3,000 men were engaged by the German Government for transport services in the Cape Colony and Natal and naturally there were strictly drawn from the unfortunate unemployed. Many of the men were very glad indeed to be able to earn a living, but some, I am afraid, are men who want work when they have just not any, but as soon as they obtain something to do, they consider themselves entitled to wages, etc, without any work.

As regard the rations supplied to transport riders I can only say, that they get exactly the sae as the German soldiers and he does not fare badly, except on extraordinary occasions. Most men, who are engaged as transport riders, manage to save a good deal of their wages and I myself have forwarded remittances for transport riders to their respective wives.

Lieutenant Von Trotha who was so severely attacked, fell some time ago to the Fish River Mountains, so he is unable to defend himself.

It is true that I am myself one of the barbarous race, the Germans, but I have always been and am still a good friend of many a Britisher. Of course, my name is at the disposal of the local authorities. I am, etc. Barbarian.

Sir, – I have noticed with great regret the articles you have published in your issue of the 28th inst. Concerning the alleged cruelties to natives in German South West Africa and the forcing of British subjects to fight the natives. It is all the more regrettable that you start this campaign of calamny again, as it is a positive fact that former statements concerning the same subject in your and other Cape papers have been repudiated by responsible persons, who have a good insight in affairs in GSW Africa. I very much regret that I cannot repudiate the statements made by your correspondents, as I have not been in Swakopmund and Angra Pequena, but trust this will be done by persons who have been up in these parts. However, if such a state of affairs exists in that part of GSW Africa it would only be right to argue that similar things would happen in other parts of that country. For the last five [?] months I have resided in Warmbad and R'drift and have had every opportunity to watch the treatment of natives and transport-riders in that [six words unclear]. I have come to the conclusion that the former have been altogether too well treated – in fact spoiled – by the Germans, while the latter were perfectly happy with their lot, being well paid, well fed and treated with all the respect due to white men, irrespective of nationality. The transport riders were certainly never armed by the Germans in that part. I remember the time – some three months ago – when Warmbad and R'drift, which were only garrisoned by a handful of soldiers, were both in continual danger of being attacked by the Hottentots who were in the neighbourhood in considerable numbers. At that time some ten transport riders were at R'drift, and although they applied to the Commandant for arms of their own free will, he refused to give them, and they were told to camp at the bank of the Orange River, where a boat was in readiness to take them over to British territory should the place be attacked. I have spoke to many of these men, and they expressed themselves as being perfectly content, but I must at the same time state that they were men of a superior stamp, and sensible enough to understand that in wartime things will sometimes go wrong and that they had not been engaged for soft jobs. I am afraid, Mr Editor, that in many cases, you are being imposed upon by men whose characters will by no means allow a close investigation, and before publishing such very serious allegations, it would be wise to have a close scrutiny into the matter. Our German soldier has his faults, just as your Tommy Atkins, but downright cruelty, such as your correspondent's picture it in such a drastic manner is not one of his faults. This is, at least, as far as my experience goes.

A few remarks as the treatment of natives. As I mentioned before, I consider they are well treated – in many cases too well, as to be utterly spoiled for good work. In Warmbad some five months ago there was a considerable number of persons (all Hottentots) in gaol. They were well fed, s I have seen myself, and were released from gaol after a few weeks on the condition that they were to remain in Warmbad and work for the Government a a fair rate of pay and rations. They did so for a few more weeks, and one night they joined their commandos again, and are now fighting against a foe who had treated them generously, and whose leniency they misused. I could go on telling you of many similar instances, but would it be of any use?

In conclusion, I can only one more entreat you, Mr Editor, to be more careful in publishing all these startling stories before you know who the men are that make them and what their reason is for making them ... I am, etc. W. Rathmore.

Sir, – You have published lately long accounts of transport-riders and others reporting the most horrible atrocities having been committed by German soldiers. I am not in a position actually to deny that such occurrences have taken place, not having been present for instance, when you informant was content to watch women and children being flogged without interference, cost what it may. I have travelled in the German colony for the last two months to every place approachable by rail, and during that time I have never seen or heard of prisoners being ill-treated. In Angra Pequena, I have only seen a few women at work, most of the prisoners being kept on an island in the bay, connected with the shore by a bridge. This island is reserved for the prisoners and as no construction works are carried on there, nor are there any sheds or stacks of goods, the poor blacks can hardly be made to work too hard – if they work at all. In Swakopmund a goodly number of women can be seen working near the landing stage, and in the goods yards. They have to load and unload trucks and push them along for little distances, but although this may look as if they were working hard, this is not the case. Each bag or case requires a whole swarm to lift it up, and their movements are slow to a degree. Further, up-country I have seen women working on the railway carrying baskets of coal to the engines and children oiling the wheels or turning [?] the brakes, and doing such light work. I have also seen them employed to bring in materials for building houses. But never once have I had reason to believe that they were made to work more than they are capable of. As to their treatment they are ordered about as the German 'Unter O[unclear]' order their soldiers, and no doubt [unclear] way of speaking to ladies was not agreeable to the cultivated senses of your informants. Their daily food consists of one cup of Boer meal – nearly the size of of [sic] 2lbs tin of jam – and half a cup of rice with occasionally a handful of yellow sugar thrown in. Meat they get a couple of times a week. I am not sure how often. They are also supplied with coffee, but as they do not drink this as a rule, the merchants buy the coffee beans and supply them with other goods in exchange – at least this is the case in the more northern districts. The appearance of men and women is perfectly healthy; and in Swakopmund I was particularly struck that the Herero women had such tall and strong figures, the flesh on their limbs showing that they had no lack of nourishment. In this port they are also all provided with clothing, as the climate is rather cold owing to frequent fogs. The death rate is large owing to this fact, but this is not any fault of the Government, as they cannot keep all prisoners up-country, when they are even now unable to send up sufficient supplies. In Windhoek and other places I have sometimes seen men and women terribly thin and with legs like sticks, but on inquiry I have always found that they were prisoners only just taken, or people who had come to subject themselves forced to do so by hunger.

Another point raised by your correspondents is that women captured with rebellious Herero have been shot. I believe that this had actually happened, but if it was known that it is the custom of the Herero women to cut from the wounded but still living soldiers and particularly officers pieces of their flesh – without going into details – and to give them roasted to their husbands, thinking to instil them with the courage of the fallen, then one will hardly wonder that the soldiers can sometimes not be constrained from killing such bestial creatures.

The third allegation made, which you consider the most serious, viz. the arming of British subjects to take par in actual fighting, is so unfounded that even a man who has never seen the country there could find enough reasons to contradict such an indictment. Surely nobody engaged here by the German authorities expected to go to a peaceful country where his life was watched over always by a policeman. They were no bound to do any actual fighting but on the other side is it unreasonable to expect that each wagon or convoy should have such a strong escort, that it was impossible for any enemy to attack it. This would naturally happen now and then, and Boers I have met up there have told me that they were only too glad to obtain in the form of a rifle the means to help the soldiers to defend their own lives; in fat, I have heard numerous complaints that the military did not supply them with enough ammunition.

There is, however, another class of Boer or Englishman – as the case may be – the sweepings of South Africa, those who had planned to organised themselves as a band of robbers to attack Windhoek and then escape over the border with all they could lay hands on. Form these all arms have been taken away and they are shunted again as quickly as possible out of the German colony. They are the men who do not want to go back again. As to the story that clothing and boots etc. were not supplied as agreed, to which you rightly attribute only minor importance all the men engaged here, or at least their foremen, have their written contracts, and if these were not carried out the proper place to lodge their complaint would be the Imperial German Consulate here, where

I am told some such claims have been willingly met. Of course, it could not be helped that in the field transport-riders should have to put up with the same privitations as the soldiers.

In conclusion, I repeat that I cannot actually deny the statements made by your correspondents, but I leave everyone to judge from the relation of my experiences whether or not all these terrible stories have been painted in their true colours. Anyway [unclear – twelve words] ... have happened at all, can only be allegations.

By the bye, how is it possible to tie up a man on a wagon wheel so that he hangs by his wrists and only the tips of his toes just touch the ground? This particular man must have been something of a dwarf.

From inquiries made by telegram in Paaarl I find that the height of the largest wheel of transport wagons is 51 [half] inches, I am, etc. Karl Brehmer.

[Our correspondents have confused the conduct of the editorial columns of a newspaper, and the publication of statements for which, true or false, the authority was given. We are equally ready to publish the above letters and there we leave the matter for the present – Ed, CA]

BIBLIOGRAPHY

Alexander, J.E. *Expedition of Discovery into the Interior of Africa* (2 vols.), London, 1838.
Andersson, C.J. *Notes of Travel in South Africa* (ed. L. Lloyd), London, 1875.
Amery, L.S. *The German Colonial Claim*, London, 1939.
Bayer, Maximilian *The Rehoboth Baster Nation of Namibia*, (trans. Peter Carstens), Balser Afrika Bibliographien, Basel, 1984
Bley, Helmut, *South-West Africa under German Rule, 1894-1914*, Heinemann/Evanston, London, 1971
Boonzaier, Emile, Candy Malherbe, Penny Berens and Andy Smith, *The Cape Herders: A History of the Khoikhoi of Southern Africa*, David Phillip/Ohio University Press, Cape Town & Johannesburg, Athens, 1996
Bridgman, Jon *The Revolt of the Hereros*, University of California Press, London, 1981.
Britz, Rudolf Hartmut Lang and Cornelia Limpricht, *A Concise History of the Rehoboth Basters until 1990*, Klaus Hess Publishers/Verlag, Windhoek/Göttingen (1999).
Brockmann, Clara 'Deutsche Frauen in Südwestafrika' in *Kolonie und Heimat*, vol. 22, 1909.
Bryce, James and Arnold Toynbee, *The Treatment of Armenians in the Ottoman Empire, 1915-1916* (Uncensored edition), Reprint, Gomidas Institute, Princeton, 2000 (original HMSO, London, 1916).
Cramer, Ada, *Weiss oder Schwarts: Lehr und Leidensjahre eines Farmers in Südwest im Licht des Rasenhasses*, Deutscher Kolonial-Verlag, 1913.
Dedering, Tilman 'Southern Namibia c. 1780-c.1840: Khoikhoi, missionaries and the advancing frontier'. PhD, University of Cape Town, 1989
——, 'The German-Herero War of 1904: Revisionism of Genocide or Imaginary Historiography?', *Journal of Southern African Studies*, Vol. 1, no. 1 (1993).
——, '"A Certain Rigorous Treatment of all Parts of the Nation": The Annihilation of the Herero in German South West Africa, 1904' Ch. 10 in Levine, Mark and Penny Roberts (eds), *The Massacre in History*, Berghahn Books, New York/Oxford, 1999.
De Vries, Joris, *Manasse Tjiseseta: Chief of Omaruru 1884-1898, Namibia*, Rüdiger Köppe Verlag, Köln, 1999.
De Vylder, Gustaf, *The Journal of Gustaf de Vylder*, reprint edited and annotated by Ione and Jalmar Rudner, Van Riebeeck Society, Cape Town, 1998.
Dove, *Karl Deutsch-Südwestafrika*, Wilhelm Süsserott, Berlin, 1913.
Drechsler, *Let Us Die Fighting*, Akademie-Verlag: Berlin 1966
Dreyer, Ronald, *The Mind of Official Imperialism: British and Cape Government Perceptions of German Rule in Namibia from the Heligoland-Zanzibar Treaty to the Kruger Telegram (1890-1896)*, Reimar Hobbing Verlag, Essen, 1987.
Eirola, Martti, *The Ovambogefahr: The Ovamboland Reservation in the Making*, Historical Association of Northern Finland, Jyväskylä, 1992
Epstein, Klaus 'Erzberger and the Colonial Scandals', *English Historical Review*, Vol. 74 (1959)
Erichsen, Casper 'A Legacy of Neglect', *The Namibian Weekender*, 11th December, 1998.
Fetter, Bruce editor, *Colonial Rule in Africa: Readings from Primary Sources*, (University of Wisconsin, Madison 1979)
Frenssen, Gustav *Peter Moor's fahrt nach Südwest: ein Feldzugsbericht*, G. Grote'sche, Verlagsbuchhandlung, 1906
——, *Peter Moor's Journey to Southwest Africa* (trans. Margaret Ward), Archibald Constable & Co., London, 1908
Gage, Capt. R.H. and A.J. Waters *Imperial German Criminal Code: Translated into English*, W.E. Hortor & Co. Ltd., Johannesburg, 1917.
Gann, L.H. and Peter Duignan *The Rulers of German Africa, 1884-1914*, Stanford UP, Stanford, 1977.
Gaseb, Ivan 'A historical hangover':The absence of Damara from accounts of the 1904-08 war', paper presented at the 'Public History: Forgotten History' Conference, University of Namibia, August, 2000.

German Colonial Office, *The Treatment of Native and other Populations in the Colonial Possessions of Germany and England*, Engelman, Berlin, 1919
Gewald, Jan-Bart 'The Great General of the Kaiser' in: *Botswana Notes and Records*, Vol. 26 1994
——, *Herero Heroes* (James Currey: Oxford 1999)
Gifford, Prosser & Roger Louis, *Britain and Germany in Africa: Imperial Rivalry and Colonial Rule*, Yale University Press, New Haven/London, 1967
Gordon, Robert *The Bushman Myth: The Making of a Namibian Underclass*, (Westview Press: Boulder 1992)
Great Britain *Treatment of Natives in the German Colonies* Foreign Office Handbook, 1919.
Haarhoff, Dorian, 'A Soldier in Namibia: Gustav Frenssen's Peter Moor's Journey to Southwest Africa', *Logos*, Vol. 8 (2), 1988
Hardinge, Rex *South African Cinderella: A Trek through Ex-German West Africa*, Herbert Jenkins Limited, London, 1937.
Henderson, W.O. *The German Colonial Empire, 1884-1919*, Frank Cass, London, 1993.
Henrichsen, Dag 'Herrschaft und Identifikation im vorkolonialen Zentralnamibia: Das Herero- und Damaraland im 19. Jahrhundert', PhD thesis University of Hamburg 1997
Herbst, J.F. *Report on the Rietfontein area*, Cape Town, 1908
Heywood, Annemarie and Ebeb Maasdorp (trans), *The Hendrik Witbooi Papers*, Archeia 13, Windhoek, 1989
Heywood, Annemarie, Brigitte Lau and Raimund Ohly *Warriors, Leaders, Sages and Outcasts in the Namibian Past*, MSORP, Windhoek, 1992.
Hintrager, Oskar *Südwestafrika in der Deutschen Zeit*, Kommissionverlag R. Oldenbourg, München, 1955.
Hoernlé, Winifred, *The Social Organization of the Nama and other Essays*, edited by Peter Carstens, Witwatersrand University Press, Johannesburg, 1985
Irle, Jakob, *Die Herero. Ein Beitrag zur Landes-, Volks- und Missionskunds*, Bertelsmann, Gütersloh, 1906
Köhler, O. *A Study of Gobabis District* (Government Printer, Pretoria, 1959a).
——, *A Study of Grootfontein District* (Government Printer, Pretoria, 1959b).
——, O. *A Study of Omaruru District* (Government Printer, Pretoria, 1959c).
Knoll, Arthur 'Decision-making for the German Colonies' Ch. 8 in Knoll, Arthur and Lewis Gann, *Germans in the Tropics: Essays in German Colonial History*, Greenwood Press, New York/Westport/London, 1987.
L'Ange, Gerald *Urgent Imperial Service: South African Forces in German South West Africa: 1914 - 1915*, (Ashanti Publishing: Rivonia 1991)
Lau, Brigitte *Namibia in Jonker Afrikaner's Time*, Archea 8, Windhoek 1987
——, 'Uncertain Certainties: The German-Herero War of 1904', *Mibagus*, 2 (1989)
——, '"Thank God the Germans Came": Vedder and Namibian Historiography' in Brigitte Lau, *History and Historiography* (Discourse/MSORP, Windhoek, 1995
——, 'Uncertain Certainties: The Herero-German War of 1904' in Brigitte Lau, *History and Historiography*, Discoures/MSORP, Windhoek, 1995
Leutwein, Theodor *Elf Jahre Gouverneur in Deutsch-Südwestafrika*, E.S. Mittler und Sohn, Berlin, 1908.
——, *Elf Jahre Gouverneur in Duetsch-Südwestafrika*, (Reprint), Namibia Scientific Society, Windhoek, 1997
Levine, Mark 'Introduction' in Levine, Mark and Penny Roberts (eds), *The Massacre in History*, Berghahn Books, New York/Oxford, 1999.
Lewin, Evans, *The Germans and Africa*, London, 1939.
Lewis, Gavin 'The Bondelswarts rebellion of 1922', MA Thesis, Rhodes University, Grahamstown, 1977.
Louis, W.M. Roger 'Great Britain & German Expansion in Africa, 1884-1919' in Gifford, Prosser & Roger Louis, *Britain and Germany in Africa: Imperial Rivalry and Colonial Rule*, Yale University Press, New Haven/London, 1967.
Meinhof, Carl *Die Sprachen der Hamiten*, Friederischen & Co, Hamburg, 1912.
Meyer, Felix 'Wirtschaft und recht der Herero: Auf Grund eines in der' *Internationalen Vereinigung für vergleichende Rechtswissenschaft und volkswirtschaftslehre am 30 Januar 1905 gehalten Vortrages*, Springer, Berlin, 1905.

Miers, Suzanne 'The Brussels Conference of 1889-1890: The Place of the Slave Trade in the Policies of Great Britain and Germany', Ch. 3 in *Gifford, Prosser & Roger Louis, Britain and Germany in Africa: Imperial Rivalry and Colonial Rule*, Yale University Press, New Haven/London, 1967.

Noyes, John *Colonial Space: Spatiality in the Discourse of German South West Africa, 1884-1915*, Harwood Academic Publishers, Chur, 1992.

——, 'National Identity, Nomadism, and Narration in Gustav Frenssen's *Peter Moor's Journey to Southwest Africa*' in Sara Friedrichsmeyer, Sara Lennox, and Susanne Zantop, *The Imperialist Imagination*, Ann Arbor, University of Michigan Press, 1998

O'Connor, J.K. *The Hun in our Hinterland or The Menace of G.S.W.A*, Maskew Miller, Cape Town, 1914 (?)

Oermann, Nils Ole *Mission, Church and State Relations in South West Africa under German Rule (1884-1915)*, Franz Steiner Verlag, Stuttgart, 1999.

Palgrave, William Coates *Report of W. Coates Palgrave Esq., Special Commissioner to the tribes north of the Orange River, of his mission to Damaraland and Great Namaqualand in 1876*, Solomon, Cape Town, 1877.

Passage, Siegfried 'Die Buschmänner der Kalahari' in *Mitteilungen aus den deutschen Schutzgebieten*, Vol. 18, 1905.

Poewe, Karla *The Namibian Herero. A History of their Psychosocial Disintegration and Survival*, Edwin Mellen Press, Lewiston/Queenston N.Y., 1985.

Pool, Gerhard *Die Herero-Opstand, 1904-1907*, Hollandsch Afrikaansche Uitgevers Maatschappij, Pretoria, 1979

——, *Samuel Maharero*, Gamsberg Macmillan, Windhoek, 1990

Rohrbach, Paul, *Deutsche Kolonialwirtschaft*, Buchverlag der 'Hilfe', Berlin-Schöneberg, 1907

Schildknect, Jörg, *Südwestafrika und die Kongokonferenz: Die völkerrectlichen Grundlagen der effektiven Okkupation und ihre nebenpflichten am Beispiel des Erwerbs der ersten deutschen Kolonie*, Lit. Verlag, Hamburg, 1999.

Schinz, Hans *Deutsch-Südwest-Afrika: Forschungsreisen durch die deutschen Schutzgebiete Gross-Nama-und Hereroland, nach dem Kunene, dem Ngami-See und der Kalaharis, 1884-1887*, Oldenburg &c, 1891.

Schmokel, Wolfe *Dream of Empire: German Colonialism, 1919-1945*, Yale UP, New Haven/London, 1964.

Schwabe, K. *'Mit Schwert und Pflug in Deutsch-Südwestafrika. Vier Kriegs- und Wanderjahre* Mittler und Sohn, Berlin, 1904' (2nd ed), 1904

Silvester, Jeremy and Casper Erichsen 'Luderitz's Forgotten Concentration Camp', *The Namibian Weekender*, 16th February, 2001.

Silvester, Jeremy, Werner Hillebrecht and Casper Erichsen 'The Herero Holocaust? The Disputed History of the 1904 Genocide', *The Namibian Weekender*, 10th August, 2001.

Smith, Woodrow D. 'Anthropology and German Colonialism', Ch. 3 in Knoll, Arthur and Lewis Gann, *Germans in the Tropics: Essays in German Colonial History*, Greenwood Press, New York/Westport/London, 1987.

South Africa, Union of *Report by the Officer in Charge of Native Affairs on his Tour of Ovamboland*, Cape Town, Government Printer, 1915

——, *Report on the inquiry in regard to the German-Bastard question held at Rehoboth and other places in the Military Protectorate in June 1915*, Pretoria, 1915 [De Waal Report]

Stals, E.L. P. *The Commissions of W.C. Palgrave, Special Emissary to South West Africa, 1876-1885*, Van Riebeeck Society, Cape Town, 1990

Steenkamp, W.P. *Is the South-West African Herero Committing Race Suicide?*, 1944.

Steer, G. L. *Judgment on German Africa*, Hodder & Stoughton, London, 1939.

Stow, G.W. *The Native Races of South Africa: A History of the Intrusion of the Hottentots and the Bantu into the hunting grounds of the Bushmen*, Macmillan, London/New York, 1905

Swanson, Maynard 'South West Africa in Trust, 1915-1939', Ch. 21 in Gifford, Prosser & Roger Louis, *Britain and Germany in Africa: Imperial Rivalry and Colonial Rule*, Yale University Press, New Haven/London, 1967

Tabler, E. *Pioneers of South West Africa and Ngamiland*, Cape Town, 1973.

Taylor, M 'Archives of the Secretary for South West Africa, 1920-1959' (Finding Aid, National Archives of Namibia, Windhoek, 1985).

United Nations Institute for Namibia, *Independent Nambia: Succession to Treaty Rights and Obligations: Incorporating Namibian Treaty Calendar*, (Lusaka 1989)

Vedder, Heinrich *South West Africa in Early Times*, OUP, London, 1938.
Von François, Curt *Deutsch-Südwest-Afrika, Geschichte der Kolonisation bis zum Ausbruch den Krieges mit Witbooi, 1893*, Berlin, 1899.
Williams, Frieda-Nela *Precolonial Communities of Southwestern Africa: A History of Owambo Kingdoms, 1600-1920*, National Archives of Namibia, Windhoek, 1991.
Williams, Henry *The Historians History of the World: A comprehensive narrative of the rise and development of natives from the earliest times as recorded by over two thousand of the great writers of all ages*, The Times, London, 1907.
Wilmsen, Edwin (ed) *The Kalahari Ethnographies (1896-1898) of Siegfried Passarge: Translations from the German*, Rüdiger Köppe Verlag, Köln, 1997.
Zimmerer, Jürgen "Der totale Überwachungsstaat? Recht und Verwaltung in Deutsch-Südwestafrika", in Rüdiger Voigt und Peter Sach (Hrsg), *Kolonialiesierung de Rechts. Zur Kolonialer Rechts und Verwaltungsordnung*, (Schriften zur Rechtspolitologie, Bd 11) Nomos, Baden Baden 2001, s. 183-205.
——, "Kriegsgefangene im Kolonialkrieg: Der Krieg gegen die Herero und Nama in Deutsch-Südwestafrika (1904-1907)", in *Inde der Hand des Feindes: Kriegsgefangenschaft von der Antike bis zum Zweiten Weltkrieg*, Rüdiger Overmans (Hrsg), Boehlau Verlag Köln 1999, s. 277-294.
——, *Deutsche Herrschaft Über Afrikaner: Staatlicher Machtsanspruch und Wirklichkeit im kolonialen Namibia*, Lit Verlag Hamburg 2001.

INDEX

All spellings – as given in Blue Book! Where relevant spellings of leaders that are used in Namibia today have been given in brackets. Where insufficient information was provided in the text to identify individuals they have been omitted from the index.

Afrikaner, Christian 23, 127
Afrikaner, Jan Jonker 23, 24
Afrikaner, Jonker 21, 23
Afrikaner, Samuel 127
Afrikaners 126, 127, 139, 157
Ahlefelder 293
Ahrends, Max 310
Alexander, Capt, J.E. 71, 72
Aman (Aman) 27, 128, 139
Amiraal, Chief 141
Andersson, Charles 224
Angebauer 318, 319
Angra Pequena – see Lüdertizbucht xxiv, 27, 29, 33, 342, 343, 345-346, 348, 349, 353, 354
Annis, John – son of Portuguese and Baster parents. Neighbour to Albert Schmidt 314
Aris 79, 310
Aus xxxv, 172, 173, 174
Barkly, Sir Henry 25, 142
Barth, Walter 301
Bartlet, Leslie, Cruikshank 179
Bastard (Basters) 25, 34, 38, 40, 44, 49, 51, 53, 60, 61, 77, 100, 102, 115, 116, 117, 119, 120, 123, 126, 127, 139, 156, 163, 164, 166, 167, 172, 190, 191, 192, 194, 196, 207, 208, 209, 210, 211, 212, 213, 215, 218, 219, 222, 231, 243, 314, 359
Baumgarten 298
Bechuanaland (Botswana) xxix, 36, 41, 106, 147, 148, 343
Becker, Franz, Ernst 311
Becker, Karl, Wilhelm 303
Becker, Paul, Arno 316
Berg Damaras (Damara) 62
Berseba 54, 124, 128, 129, 131, 142, 145, 148, 167
Bethany (Bethanie) 21, 27, 53, 128, 139, 167, 169, 170, 172, 173, 202, 257, 314, 315, 344
Beukes, David 144
Beukes, Samuel 213, 215, 219
Bezirksamtmann 13, 14, 197, 213, 215, 251, 253, 255, 295, 337, 339
Binkowski, Johann 307, 309
Blecher, Miss 216, 217, 219
Bleichmer 298

Bloemputz 219
Boehm, J. 28
Boehmer, Walter 13, 14, 15, 263, 265, 291, 292, 339, 340
Bohme, A.F.J. 312
Böhmer, Walter 302
Bondelswartz (Gami Nûn) 3, 54, 57, 97, 127, 128, 137, 140, 141, 157, 159, 161, 162, 163, 164, 167, 169, 200
Bonn, Moritz Prof. 180, 186, 193
Booyse, Jonathan 155
Brandt, Piet 72
Brenner, Dr. 294, 295
Bucherin 318
Buettner, C.G. Miss 210, 212
Buntebardt, Fritz 302
Burger, Benjamin 171
Bushmen (San) xxxiv, 3, 14, 29, 34, 51, 53, 60, 61, 65, 117, 123, 124, 125-126, 181, 184, 185, 191, 208, 235, 236, 237, 238, 239, 240, 241, 242, 243, 244, 245, 253, 276, 278, 279, 297, 298, 301, 302, 311, 312, 313, 317, 318, 319
Büttner, Carl 28
Cameroons 166, 167, 173, 259
Campbell, Hendrik 117, 119, 172
Casob, Jacob 298
Cauas-Okawa 299
Chains xi, xviii, 94, 156, 160, 195, 197, 198, 199, 202, 203, 236, 255, 256, 257, 258, 260, 287, 323, 325, 327, 332, 336
Chairos 316
Chamis South 314, 315
Choiganaub 317
Christian, Jan, Abraham 161
Christian, Willem 39, 54, 97, 128, 129, 132, 137, 140, 160, 170, 200
Cloete, Daniel 216, 219
Cloete, Jan 116, 156
Cloete, Willem 156
Coetzee, Jacob xvi, 71, 72, 315
Conrad 90
Cooper, Simon (Simon Kooper) 81
Cramer, Hildegard 274, 276, 277, 278, 287
Cramer, Ludwig, Paul xvi, 249, 260, 261, 263, 267, 271, 289, 290, 291
Credit Ordinance 90, 159, 192
D'Almeida, Francisco 125

De Waal, Lt.-Col. D. 213, 222
Deutsche Südwestafrikanische Zeitung 262
Diamond Mining 11
Diehl. G. Missionary 54
Diergaard, Petrus 119, 172
Diergard, Johannes 212
Dikasip, Jacob 190
Dixon, Daniel, Esma 119, 156, 201, 293, 294, 295
Dohling, Ludwig 307
Dove, Prof. Dr. Karl 77, 87, 93
Duval 298
Eanda 67, 68, 69, 72, 85, 186
Eckstein 317, 318, 319
Ehmke, H. 317
Eisentraut, Hermann, Albert, Rudolph – Farmer (?) at 'Niederungsfeld' in Omaruru District 301
Enslin 315
Etosha 65, 223, 224, 239
Extermination order (Vernichtungs Befehl) 106, 108, 109, 121, 165, 166, 175, 185
Faber 273
Fahrig, Ernst 309
Feuerstein, Carl, Alfred 313, 314
Fledermuis, Jonathan 144
Flogging xi, xvii, xviii, xxv, xxvii, xxxiii, 84, 93, 94, 134, 135, 159, 160, 161, 174, 189, 190, 197, 198, 199, 200, 201, 202, 204, 241, 242, 251, 258, 293, 307, 335, 342
Folkmann, Julius 304
Fourie, Louis Capt. xix, 67, 260, 336
Francke, Ober-Lt. 215, 216, 219
Franken 284
Franzfontein 128, 152, 153, 154, 155, 156
Fraser, Hendrik 120, 174
Fredericks, Cornelius 27, 169, 172
Fredericks, Edward 172
Fredericks, Joseph 27, 53, 172
Fredericks, Paul 27, 139
Friederich 294
Gabis 209
Gamrarab 302
Garies 214, 221, 222
Gathemann 271
Gautheta, Leonard 86
German Colonial Company 28, 41
German law xvi, 32, 56, 191, 242, 256, 261, 297, 310
Gertze, Mathaeus 216, 217, 218, 219
Ghaub 117, 190, 243, 244
Ghoudab, Jacobus 144, 146
Gibeon 27, 36, 43, 48, 71, 128, 137, 146, 149, 163, 164, 165, 166, 171, 172, 257, 344
Gilers 91

Gobabis 50, 51, 54, 65, 77, 78, 80, 83, 105, 106, 107, 120, 128, 141, 142, 144, 145, 146, 185, 238, 258, 268, 272, 276, 277, 279, 280, 281, 282, 283, 284, 288, 289, 290, 298, 305, 306, 307, 312
Gochas 128, 146
Goering, Dr. jnr. Heinrich Ernst 28, 29, 30, 31, 35, 36, 37, 38, 39, 40, 42, 53, 54, 55, 56, 70, 139, 141
Goldammer 28
Goliath, Christian 124, 131, 165
Gorambuka, Elias 86
Goresib, Chief Judas 182, 185, 189, 190
Goresib, Gottlieb 185, 187, 201
Goroab West 317
Grabow 281, 287
Gransab 311
Graves xxxv, 70, 92, 160, 174, 175
Green, Frederick 23, 24, 75, 127, 190
Griqua 17, 117
Grootberg 153, 154, 155
Grootfontein 12, 14, 29, 65, 117, 124, 152, 154, 163, 167, 185, 190, 207, 235, 238, 239, 240, 241, 242, 243, 244, 245, 298, 308, 313, 316, 317, 318, 319
Grootfontein South 209, 210, 212
Gross Barmen 119
Grossmann 190
Grundoorns 160
Guchab 301
Guntsas 313, 318
Habicht 119
Hahn, Dr. Theophilus 131, 134, 135, 137
Hahn, Rev. Hugo 24, 33, 70, 124, 181, 182
Halberstadt, Wilhelm 316
Halbich 23, 138
Hamakari xiii, xxi, 115, 116, 117
Hanging xi, xvii, 12, 118, 120, 254, 255, 302, 304, 323, 336, 348
Hartmann, Dr. 152, 228, 230, 243
Hausib, Johannes 310
Haybittel 23
Hebron 301
Heibib, Piet 53, 128, 136, 139
Heidmann, M. 212
Heikom 239, 242, 244
Heilingbrunner 264, 339
Heldt 91
Hendrick 40
Hendricks, Jan 54, 128
Herbst, J.F. Major xvii, 147, 236, 240, 243
Heuras 219, 220, 221
Himarua 230, 231
Hite, Thomas, Alfred 173
Hoachanas 50, 53, 77, 128, 167
Hollander 268
Holtz, Hermann 305
Holy cattle 66, 71, 77, 85, 86, 91
Holy fire 64, 66, 68

Holzapfel 165
Honk, Johannes 156
Hornkranz xxv, 36, 37, 38, 41, 42, 43, 45, 46, 48, 49, 50, 53, 128, 132, 141, 143, 146, 148, 149, 163, 191, 228
Hosea 86, 114, 189
Hounschild, Geog 311
Hummnel, Ober-Lt. 214
Isaac, Fritz 173
Isaac, Samuel 47, 173, 180
Izaak, Jantje 161
Jacob, Christian 257
Jaeger, Josephat 154
Jakhalswater 215
Jakubowski, Theodor 307
James, Christopher 70
Jasperson 298
Joel (Herero leader) 106, 107
Jonas, Councillor 187, 319, 320
Jordaan, Willem 29, 53, 207, 208
Joshua, Councillor 187, 189
Juzek, Frank 307
Kadwakonda 274, 275, 276, 277, 279, 281, 289
Kaffir 63, 173, 181, 186, 220, 272, 275, 276, 277, 278, 281, 312, 319
Kageneck, Count 81
Kahimena (Kahimemua) 51
Kaikabas 319
Kain, Willie (Cain) 94
Kainazo, Richard 197, 198
Kaitanagora 299
Kalahari xiii, 65, 101, 105, 114, 115, 148, 162, 238, 239, 244
Kaleb, Councillor 189
Kamaheke, Gerard 106, 196
Kamaherero (Maharero) 28, 29, 30, 31, 32, 35, 36, 38, 51, 52, 66, 75, 76, 85, 86, 92, 139, 183, 185, 196
Kamana, Louisa 95
Kambazembi 51, 72, 75, 99, 179
Kambonde (Kambonde KaMpingana) 48, 51, 114, 223, 224, 228, 229, 230, 232
Kamerun – see Cameroons 250
Kampe 305
Kanapirura, Traugott 54
Karas Mountains 164, 352
Karibib 96, 120, 128, 155, 172, 175, 187, 351
Kariko, Daniel xviii, 84, 95, 100, 113, 114, 175
Karoreke, Lukas 309
Kasambouwe 95
Katjakundu, Jakob, Barnabas 198
Katsimune, Alfred 197, 198
Katsimune, Christof 86
Kavingava 72
Kayata 90
Kayser, Dr. 77

Keetmanshoop xxxi, 54, 72, 120, 128, 137, 141, 148, 157, 160, 163, 164, 165, 167, 178, 179, 327, 346
Khan Copper Mine 293
Khauas (Amraal, Gei /Khauan) 50, 54, 77, 78, 80, 83, 128, 129, 131, 141, 142, 143, 144, 145, 146, 155, 167, 188
Khoi-khoi (Khoekhoe) 123, 126, 182, 183
Klaas, David 257
Kobus 214, 217, 218, 219, 220
Kohler, Dr – Government Councillor 271
Kooper, Simon 56, 128, 129, 132, 141, 146, 147, 148, 162, 167, 168, 169
Koopman, Wilhelm 212
Korob 172
Korting 317, 318, 319
Koses 171
Kotting 271
Kraaipoort 213, 215
Kreft, Heinrich, Pieter 300
Kremer, Heinrich, Christian 301, 302
Kruger, Johannes 117, 190, 243
Kubas, Jan xiii, 117
Kubub 174, 343
Kudell 271
Kurz, Emil 304
Kutako, Samuel 70, 86, 91, 177
Lambert, Andreas 80, 128, 141, 142, 143, 144, 145, 147, 148
Lambert, Eduard 145, 146
Lambert, Franz 173
Lambert, Manasse 145
Lehmpuhl, Wilhelm 310
Lehututu 147, 148, 168
Leutwein, Theodor xvii, xx, xxix, 3, 16, 26, 29, 31, 45, 46, 48, 49, 50, 55, 56, 57, 59, 61, 75, 76, 77, 78, 79, 80, 85, 87, 89, 90, 93, 94, 96, 99, 100, 101, 102, 105, 117, 121, 141, 142, 143, 144, 145, 146, 147, 148, 149, 150, 151, 152, 153, 154, 155, 157, 159, 161, 162, 163, 164, 165, 166, 167, 168, 179, 184, 187, 188, 190, 201, 204, 210, 212, 214, 222, 223, 228, 229, 230, 231, 232, 243, 260
Lewis, Robert 25, 30, 31, 35, 168
Lichterfeld 309
Linde 274, 277, 287
Losche, Pechual 70
Lucas (farm) 315
Lucas, Councillor 187
Lucas, Hans 315
Luderitz, Adolf 25
Lüderitzbucht (Luderitz) xxiv, 33, 323, 339
Ludwig 318
Luther, Paul 319
M'Buanjo 72, 75, 85
Maherero Tjamuaha 36
Maherero, Samuel 106, 229, 230
Mahler 271

Manasse Tysiseta (Tjiseseta) 54
Markus, Jakobus 198, 314, 315, 316
Mbaratjo 90
Meinhof, Pastor 64
Meyer 64, 70, 75, 76, 77, 80, 92
Morris, Abraham 159, 164, 168, 170
Mouton, Pieter 216
Moutton, Albert 213, 215, 216, 218, 219
Moutton, Jacobus 212
Muambo 90
Mueller, Major 79, 153
Muller 216, 217, 218
Mumpurua, Elephas 107
Mungunda, Hosea 85, 92, 94, 114, 177, 196
Munqunda, Johannes 107
Mutate. See Mutati 54
Mutati 114
Naauwkloof (Naukluft) 48, 141, 148, 163, 235
Nabatzaub 307
Nachtigal. Dr. 53
Nakob 157
Nakonz 276
Nauhas, Georg, Frederick 307
Ncaib, Simon 298
Nechale 29, 51, 223, 230
Negumbo (Negumbo lya Kandenge) 51, 114, 229, 230
Nels, Louis 28, 54
Niederungsfeld 301
Nieuwerust 308
Nikodemus (Nikodemus Elias Kavikunua) 51, 75, 76, 77, 78, 79, 80, 81, 83, 86, 91, 146, 229
Noreseb, Manasse 128, 139
Norop River 172
Nossanabis 142, 143, 144
O'Reilly, Maj. T.L. xvii, xviii, xix, xx, 18, 66, 177
Oas 312
Oasib 44, 139
Obarura 310
Okahabara 311
Okahandja 21, 28, 29, 30, 31, 32, 36, 38, 51, 52, 53, 54, 66, 69, 70, 72, 75, 77, 78, 79, 80, 81, 86, 91, 92, 95, 96, 99, 107, 115, 117, 119, 120, 156, 173, 308, 309
Okahua 91
Okakaue 276
Okamaraere 91
Okambahe (Okombahe) 177, 182, 183, 184, 185, 186, 187, 188, 189, 307
Okatumba 90
Okawayo 172
Okazongura 309
Okokadi 120
Okonjati 253
Olhroggen 317
Omajette 304

Omaroho 319
Omaruru xvii, xviii, xix, 18, 32, 51, 52, 54, 66, 72, 75, 84, 85, 86, 95, 96, 100, 103, 113, 114, 115, 116, 119, 120, 152, 156, 179, 183, 188, 198, 219, 255, 300, 301, 304, 306, 307, 309, 319
Ombakaha xxx, 106, 107, 117
Ombarantus (Mbalantu) 224
Omborombonga (Omumborombonga) 66
Ombuyonungondo 106
Omitara 91
Omuramba Omatako 239
Ondongas (Ndonga) 223, 224
Ongandjeras (Ngandjera) 223, 224
Orange River xxx, 21, 27, 71, 125, 126, 128, 140, 157, 164, 181, 209, 210, 353
Orthey, Fritz 317
Orumbo 90, 91
Oruzo 68, 69, 76, 77
Otjamibambo 298
Otjibonde 300
Otjihaenena 106, 180
Otjihua 304
Otjikango Pan 272, 274
Otjimbende 117
Otjimbingwe 22, 23, 24, 30, 32, 51, 86, 94, 95, 103, 127
Otjipaue 91
Otjisaesu 91
Otjisongati 309
Otjisororindi 271, 274, 276, 277, 281, 284, 286, 287, 289
Otjitambi 128, 148, 152, 153, 154, 156, 207, 299
Otjivero 91
Otjonga 107
Ouparakane 119
Outjo 12, 65, 128, 148, 152, 153, 155, 207, 229, 230, 298, 299, 302, 303, 310, 311, 316
Ovakoimas 223, 224
Ovambo labour 234
Ovamboland 12, 13, 29, 51, 60, 127, 157, 223, 224, 228, 230, 231, 232, 279, 294
Ovambuela 223, 224
Ovampoland (Ovamboland) 226
Ovampuvu 66
Ovatjimba 65
Pakriver 172
Palgrave, William Coates 25, 30, 31, 51, 60, 61, 65, 72, 129, 142, 184, 186, 210
Phillips 274, 276
Pienaar, Adam (aka. Adam Christian) 160, 170
Poison 123, 237, 274, 275, 276, 277, 278, 279, 280, 281, 285, 286, 289
Population statistics 3, 59
Protection Treaties xvi, 51
Purainen, Andreas 54

Railway xxvi, xxxv, 73, 171, 173, 177, 178, 179, 180, 196, 217, 220, 230, 263, 354
Rapmund, Otto 308, 309
Red Nation 53, 128, 139, 152
Rehoboth 3, 25, 39, 40, 43, 45, 49, 53, 56, 71, 116, 117, 123, 127, 139, 163, 172, 191, 192, 194, 207, 209, 210, 211, 212, 213, 214, 215, 217, 218, 219, 220, 221, 222, 231
Reichmann 152, 153, 154, 156
Reichstag xiv, 105, 262
Reiter, Cornelius 144
Rhenish Mission Society 21, 23, 24, 43, 91
Rhodes, Cecil 30
Riarua, Asa (Assa) 77, 79
Richardt, Hauptmann 116
Richter, Sarah 156
Richter, Timotheus 156
Rietfontein 147, 168, 209, 236
Rietkuil 171
Röder, Mason 277, 281
Rohrbach, Dr. Paul 8, 23, 28, 29, 31, 34, 62, 78, 83, 90, 91, 99, 107, 108, 121, 145, 169, 193
Sauer, Frederick 305
Saul, Chief 106, 107, 117
Schayer, Joseph 159, 170
Schilg, Karl 310
Schinz, Dr. Hans 65, 182
Schlettwein xxix, 299
Schmerenbeck (of Ommandjereke) 90
Schmerenbeck (of Otjipaue) 91
Schmidt, Albert 314
Schonfeld 304
Schroeder, Carl, Georg 305, 306
Schultze, Dr. Leonard 13, 14, 34, 124
Schwabe, Kurt xx, 46, 47, 61, 81, 84, 143, 150
Schwerin, Graf 276, 277, 287
Seeis River 80
Setecki, Antonius 306
Shark Island xxi, xxvi, xxxv, 171, 172, 173, 180
Sichtermann, Dr. 293, 294, 295
Sieber (or Siebert), Dr. 275, 276, 278
Solomon, Councillor 187
Sosina, Josephine 273, 274, 275, 276, 277, 279, 284
Springhorn 294, 295
Steffenfausweh 278
Stoetzer, Hendrik 306
Stopke 90
Stow 125
Stroka, Joseph 298
Sturmfeld 305
Surmon, Capt. 147
Sus 313

Swakopmund xx, xxi, xxiv, xxxv, 14, 65, 78, 102, 119, 171, 172, 174, 175, 177, 180, 187, 214, 215, 216, 221, 241, 244, 262, 293, 294, 295, 345, 346, 349, 353, 354, 355
Swart, Carolus 216
Swart, Martinus 216
Swartbooi, Abraham 128, 154, 207
Swartbooi, David 117, 148, 152, 153, 154, 155
Swartbooi, Lazarus 152, 153, 154, 156
Swartbooi, Samuel 153, 154
Swartbooi, Sem 154
Swartbooi, Willem 155
Swartboois (//Khau /gôan) 127, 128, 152, 153, 156, 207, 209
Tamm 23, 138
Theologo, Spiro 273
Thithis, Isaac 298
Thomas 271, 292
Thomas, Jan 257
Timbu, Manuel 115
Titus, Councillor 189
Tjaherani, Heinrich 103, 198
Tjaherani, Michael 96
Tjaherani, Willem 103
Tjetjoo (of Okandjose) 51, 72, 75, 78, 86, 99, 114
Tjetjoo, Hugo 86
Tjienda, Traugott 178
Togo 152, 166, 250, 259
Tommaschewski, Rudolph 317
Topnaar (≠Aunin) 27, 28, 128, 129, 139
Traugott, Under-Chief 107, 114
Tseib 54, 128, 141
Tses 152, 167
Tsobasib, Simon 183, 189
Tsumanas 303
Tsumeb 12, 29, 178, 190, 200, 201, 230, 311, 317, 319
Uejulu 51, 114, 224, 229, 230
Ugab River 128, 187
Ukamas 160, 168, 169, 170
Usakos 201, 312
Uukuambis (Kwambi) 224, 232
Uukuanjamas (Kwanyama) 223, 224
van der Merwe 308
van der Post 313
van Renen, Willem 72
van Wijk, Cornelius 213, 215, 216, 222
van Wijk, Frederick 214, 221
van Wijk, Gert 214
van Wijk, Stoffel 214, 221, 222
van Wyk, Dierk 212
van Wyk, Hendrik 117
van Wyk, Hermanus 209, 210, 212
van Wyk, Willem 212
Väterliche Zuchtigungsrecht ('fatherly correction') 260

Vernichtungs Befehl – see extermination order 108
Vilander Bastards 209
Voigts 52, 70, 91
Volkman, Ober-Lt. 119, 231, 244
von Caprivi, Count 42
von Estorff, Capt. xxi, 81, 145, 153, 155
von Falkenhausen 91
von François 31, 32, 35, 38, 39, 40, 41, 42, 45, 46, 47, 48, 49, 59, 70, 72, 75, 77, 141, 143, 148, 149, 243
von Hatten, Hans 298, 312
von Hiller, Bezirksamtmann 213, 215, 216, 218, 219
von Kleist, Dr 213, 215
von Lindequist xxix, 13, 89, 107, 138, 152, 170, 175, 177, 178, 179
von Michaelis 273
von Rudno 311
von Schmelen, Missionary 21
von Seydlitz, Siegfried, Alexander, Wilhelm 304
von Trotha, Gen. Lothar xxi, 8, 70, 103, 105, 106, 107, 108, 109, 111, 113, 114, 115, 116, 117, 119, 121, 122, 152, 164, 165, 166, 167, 168, 169, 170, 171, 172, 173, 174, 175, 177, 179, 185, 197, 261, 344, 353
von Weiher, Marie 254, 307
von Ziethen, Lt 81
von Zulow, Capt. 177
Vosswinckel, Georg 317
Walfish Bay (Walvis Bay) 14, 24, 25, 27, 28, 30, 47, 139, 141, 155
Wandres, Missionary 165, 166
Warmbad 54, 97, 128, 137, 141, 157, 159, 160, 161, 163, 164, 166, 167, 201, 209, 327, 353, 354
Waterberg xxxv, 51, 70, 72, 105, 114, 115, 116, 117, 119, 120, 166, 179, 183, 185, 200, 254, 307
Waters, A.J. xvi, xvii, xix, 18, 269, 270
Werner, District Judge 271
Westphal 90
White Nosob River 78, 90, 146
Widmann 216, 217
Wilhelmsruhe 316
Windhuk (Windhoek) 13, 21, 42, 44, 46, 47, 48, 50, 65, 77, 78, 79, 80, 85, 87, 89, 90, 91, 96, 99, 102, 106, 114, 129, 134, 142, 143, 144, 146, 148, 149, 150, 152, 153, 154, 155, 156, 165, 166, 177, 181, 183, 187, 188, 189, 196, 202, 203, 205, 213, 215, 217, 219, 222, 231, 241, 259, 260, 263, 264, 267, 271, 278, 291, 302, 303, 304, 315, 323, 335, 336, 337, 339
Wint, Jan 117
Witbooi, Heinrich, Petrus 301

Witbooi, Hendrik xiv, xxvi, xxvii, 24, 35, 36, 37, 38, 39, 40, 41, 42, 43, 44, 45, 46, 47, 48, 50, 53, 56, 81, 89, 102, 127, 128, 129, 132, 133, 137, 138, 139, 141, 146, 147, 148, 150, 163, 164, 165, 166, 167, 168, 171, 172, 173, 180, 213, 228, 229
Witbooi, Hendrik (Young) – deported to the Cameroons 47, 48, 173
Witboois (Khowesin) 43, 45, 46, 47, 48, 128, 139, 141, 143, 150, 164, 166, 170, 171, 173, 186, 351
Wolff, Under-Officer 119, 120
Women, abuse of 177
Wosillo 91
Wujack 299
Xatjindu, Johannes 305
Zacharias 51, 75, 78, 94, 95, 96, 103
Zandfontein (Sandfontein) 213
Zelow, Ober-Lt. 119
Zerua, Bermenias 86, 95, 103
Zwartmodder 218
Zweinicke, Ober-Lt. 172

SOURCES FOR AFRICAN HISTORY

1. J. SILVESTER and J.-B. GEWALD. *Words Cannot be Found*. German Colonial Rule in Namibia: An Annotated Reprint of the 1918 Blue Book. 2003.
ISBN 90 04 12981 2